THE ICSA COMPANY SECRETARY'S HANDBOOK

THE ICSA
COMPANY SECRETARY'S HANDBOOK

EIGHTH EDITION

Douglas Armour FCIS

Published by ICSA Information & Training Ltd
16 Park Crescent
London W1B 1AH

Typeset in 9½ on 12½ pt Kuenstler by Hands Fotoset, Mapperley, Nottingham
Printed in Great Britain by Hobbs the Printers Ltd, Totton, Hampshire

British Library Cataloguing in Publication Data
A catalogue record for this book is available from the British Library

ISBN 978-1-86072-419-0

Acknowledgements

The author would like to thank the following people for their invaluable assistance during the work on this new edition of the *Company Secretary's Handbook*:

Han Nee Ang
JJ Baikie
Melissa Bourgeois
Sara Hollowell
Kelly Millar
Chloe Kerr Peterson
Finbar Stevens

Contents

CD contents

Preface

The object of writing this book is to provide a practical guide to company secretarial procedures undertaken by company secretaries, solicitors and accountants. The book will also help students preparing for the corporate secretaryship examination of the Institute of Chartered Secretaries and Administrators (ICSA).

In compiling this book, I have drawn considerably on my and my colleagues experience as chartered secretaries in public practice. The book covers all of the core tasks generally associated with the work of the company secretary. The commentary is illustrated by Precedents for all key transactions and additional reference material is presented in the Appendices section. The book has a detailed contents list and index, and the text is fully cross-referenced. Key terms are highlighted in bold on first use, and defined in an end of book Glossary. The *Handbook* is also accompanied by a free CD-ROM, which includes the text of all Precedents, sample documents and guidance, useful links and tables.

The eighth edition is published following the final implementation stage of the Companies Act 2006. It reflects the law as at 1 October 2009. Chapters referring to the Listing Rules, Prospectus Rules and Disclosure and Transparency Rules refer to release 74 of those rules in February 2008. Articles of Association references throughout the book are to the new model articles introduced by the Companies Act 2006 and reproduced in full on the CD. However, where appropriate, references to previous versions are noted, and it should be stressed that, in relation to companies incorporated prior to 1 October 2009, their Articles of Association are unchanged by the implementation of the Companies Act 2006. The most recent version of Table A prior to 1 October 2009 is also reproduced at Appendix 2 and is available on the CD resource bank. Whenever you are contemplating any course of action it is always extremely important to check the provisions of the Articles of Association as these vary from company to company.

In common with previous editions, this book is intended to be a practical guide to the legislation governing companies and company secretarial procedure. Where a more detailed analysis of the legislation is required, or an obscure procedural matter is being considered, readers should refer to the ICSA's more detailed information service, *Company Secretarial Practice* (CSP) (see Directory). As with all legislation, the provisions of the Companies Acts and related legislation are open to interpretation and must be assessed in the context of the circumstances at hand, the Memorandum and Articles of Association of the company in question and any relevant shareholders' agreement or other ancillary agreements.

This eighth edition could not have been updated without significant contributions from my colleagues within David Venus & Company, to whom I am extremely grateful; I am also grateful for the continued support and patience of the team at ICSA Publishing

Whilst every effort has been made to ensure the accuracy of the content of this book, neither the author nor the publisher can accept responsibility for any loss arising to anyone relying solely on the information contained herein.

DOUGLAS ARMOUR
January 2010

Introduction

Although this *Handbook* is aimed primarily at readers who already have a working knowledge of companies and company law, there will be some who are less familiar with the concept of the company as established in the United Kingdom.

For UK businesses, there are a number of different forms of entity available through which that business can trade. These include:

- sole traders;
- partnerships;
- limited liability partnerships;
- limited partnerships;
- friendly and provident companies;
- European Economic Interest Groupings;
- companies incorporated under the Companies Acts.

This book is written for managers and administrators, and their advisers, of incorporated companies. The vast majority of trading entities established in the UK are companies of one type or another, incorporated under the Companies Acts, as amended. Unless stated otherwise, a reference to a 'company' will mean to a company incorporated under the Companies Act 2006 and not to any other trading entity, whether known as a 'company' or not.

Although there are three different types of company – companies limited by shares, limited by guarantee and unlimited companies – they all have certain basic characteristics. The majority of companies are limited by shares.

Guarantee companies are best suited for use with charitable enterprises and sporting or social associations particularly where the membership is to be subject to an annual subscription. Unlimited companies will normally be utilised in the case of a professional company where limited liability is not permitted or where, for reasons of secrecy, the owners do not wish to publicise their accounting information.

Corporate persona

A company is a legal entity in its own right, separate from that of its owners (members/shareholders) or managers (directors). Accordingly, a company can enter into contracts and own assets in its own name, unlike a sole trader or a partnership, which does not have a legal identity separate from the owner in whose name(s) all contracts and assets are made/held.

Like a natural person, a company has a 'home' address where legal documents and notices may be served. This address is known as its registered office and, among other things, determines the company's VAT and corporation tax office and the tax office dealing with any PAYE. This is the official address for serving of official notices, including notice of Court action against the company to recover monies owed.

When a company is formed, there is an obligation to register information with the Registrar of Companies, and subsequently to register changes to this information. This will include the names and addresses of the persons forming the company and the company's registered office.

Ownership

All companies are owned by their members. In companies limited by shares this will be the shareholders; companies limited by guarantee will be owned by their guarantors; and unlimited companies can have shareholders or some other method of determining the proportion in which the company is owned. The majority of companies are limited by shares, either as private limited companies, usually referred to as 'limited companies', or public limited companies, more usually referred to as 'public' or 'Plc' companies.

Liability

The phrase 'limited' refers to the liability of the owners (the members/shareholders) for the debts of the company. Members of limited companies, whether limited by shares or guarantee, have limited liability for the debts of the company. The amount of their liability is limited to the amount agreed to be paid for the shares on their issue by the company. Accordingly, once shares are fully paid, members have no further liability. The majority of shares are issued as fully paid shares and accordingly there is no liability on the part of the owners for any trading or other debt of the company.

The liability of a guarantor of a company limited by guarantee is limited to the amount of their guarantee and is usually some nominal amount such as £10.

Members of unlimited companies, as the name implies, have no limit on their liability to meet the debts of the company should it fail.

Management

The management of all companies, regardless of type, is undertaken on behalf of the members by the directors. Directors need not be members, although in the majority of private companies the members and the directors will be the same group of individuals.

Even where they are members, the directors have a duty to manage the affairs of the company for the benefit of the membership as a whole and not just some part of the membership.

Although certain individuals, including bankrupts and disqualified directors, cannot be appointed as directors of companies, there are no qualifications required to act as a director of a company and no need to show any previous management experience.

Failure to act properly as a director may lead to serious consequences, including disqualification from acting as a director. The Companies Act 2006 has for the first time set out core duties of the directors (see Chapter 2).

Company secretary

All public companies are required to have a company secretary. Private companies may appoint a company secretary but are not required to have a company secretary. Other than the company secretaries of public companies, the company secretary need have no qualifications or previous experience. Company secretaries of public companies are required to be a member of one of a group of professional bodies or to have appropriate experience.

Articles of Association

The Articles of Association detail the provisions relating to the regulation of the company in terms of the rights of its members and the authority of the directors.

The CA2006 provides model sets of Articles suitable for private, public and guarantee companies. Although there are regulations in the model articles setting out the rights of members and their relationship to the company, there are very few details concerning the rights of directors and their relationship with the company. Accordingly, whilst there are strict timescales for giving notice to shareholders to convene shareholders' meetings, directors' meetings are convened on reasonable notice, which can vary not only from company to company but also on the matter to be considered.

Under previous Companies Acts the model articles were contained in Tables A to F. As the model set for a private Company was in Table A the model articles were often referred to as Table A. In this book references to Table A are to the model articles for companies incorporated prior to 1 October 2009 and Model Articles refers to the model articles for companies incorporated on or after 1 October 2009.

Share dealing, mergers and acquisitions

A company raises capital by issuing shares in the company to investors in return for money. These shares may subsequently be sold by the shareholders. Shares in public limited companies may be quoted on the London Stock Exchange or PLUS Listed markets, where they are freely traded.

A company may wish to expand its business or avoid competition by merging with or acquiring another company.

Accounts and auditors

Incorporation as a limited company brings with it responsibilities to prepare and publish annual accounts, and for larger companies to have the accounts approved by an auditor. The prime reason for publishing accounts is so that potential trading partners can assess the risks of doing business since if the business fails the owners have no liability to meet the debts.

Dissolving the company

A company may have a limited life span and may eventually be wound up. This is the process of closing the company's affairs, selling any property and equipment, settling any liabilities and distributing any surplus funds to the owners. If the company is unable to pay its debts while it is trading it may go into liquidation, administration or receivership. In these cases an outside party is appointed to oversee the winding up so as to secure as much funds as possible to meet the debts of the company. In most cases there will be no surplus funds remaining for distribution to the owners.

A note on the Companies Act 2006

After a long gestation period lasting eight years, the Companies Act 2006 (the CA2006) finally received Royal Assent on 8 November 2006.

During its passage through the House of Commons further amendments were made and all the company law provisions of the Companies Act 1985 being retained were restated in the CA2006. The only provisions of previous Companies Acts remaining in force are those contained in Part 14 of the Companies Act 1985 (CA1985) relating to investigations and Part 2 of the Companies (Audit Investigations and Community Enterprise) Act 2004 (C(AICE)2004).

The other non-company law provisions of previous Companies Acts will remain in force and are:

- Part 18 CA1985 – floating charges and receivers (Scotland);
- Part 3 Companies Act 1989 (CA1989) – powers to require information and documents to assist overseas regulatory authorities);
- ss.112–116 CA1989 – Scottish incorporated charities;
- Part 7 CA1989 – provisions about financial markets and insolvency;
- Sch.18 CA1989 – amendments and savings consequential upon changes in law made by CA1989;
- ss.14 and 15 C(AICE)2004 – supervision of accounts and reports;
- ss.16 and 17 C(AICE)2004 – bodies concerned with accounting standards etc.

Structure of the CA2006

The CA2006 is an extremely lengthy piece of legislation comprising 1,300 sections arranged in 47 Parts together with 16 Schedules. The primary legislation is also supported by a number of statutory instruments as well as transitional arrangements for companies incorporated under earlier Acts.

The 47 Parts are grouped into ten areas as follows:

Part	Summary
1–7	Fundamentals of what a company is, formations and company names
8–12	Shareholders and directors
13–14	How companies may take decisions
15–16	Directors' accountability to shareholders
17–25	Share capital, capital maintenance, annual returns and company charges
26–28	Company reconstructions, mergers and takeovers
29–39	Regulatory framework, application to companies not formed under the Companies Acts and other company law provisions
40–42	Disqualification of overseas directors, business names and statutory auditors
43	Transparency obligations
44–47	Miscellaneous and general

Territorial extent

Unlike previous companies legislation the CA2006 applies to all UK companies.

Northern Ireland

Company law remains a transferred matter from Northern Ireland and accordingly the CA2006 could be separately amended or repealed. References in the CA2006 to any provisions restating or replacing provisions originally contained in CA1985, CA1989 or C(AICE)2004 should be read as references to the corresponding provisions in the Companies (Northern Ireland) Order 1986, the Companies (Northern Ireland) Order 1990 or the Companies (Audit, Investigations and Community Enterprise) Order 2005.

Scotland

Company law is a reserved matter and consequently applies equally to Scottish companies. However the CA2006 also contains non-company law provisions some of which are devolved matters. These devolved matters were given legislative consent by the Scottish Parliament on 16 March 2006.

The devolved matters are:

- Changes to the regulation of business names in Part 41 reflecting the changes contained in Part 5 which are a reserved matter.
- Statutory guidance issued by the Lord Advocate in Scotland to prosecutors and enforcement agencies in relation to the new offence of knowingly or recklessly causing an audit report to be misleading, false or deceptive (s.509).
- Audit exemption requirements for Scottish charities (s.1175).
- Giving the Auditor General for Scotland power to specify public bodies for his audit. (s.483).

Wales

Company law is not a matter transferred to the Welsh assembly and so there are no devolved matters.

Crown dependencies

To reflect the existing jurisdiction of the Takeover Panel Part 28 of the CA2006 contains provisions enabling it to be extended by Order in Council to the Isle of Man or any of the Channel Islands.

Table of Abbreviations

AIM	Alternative Investment Market
BACS	Bankers' Automated Clearing System
BIS	Department for Business, Innovation & Skills
BNA1985	Business Names Act 1985
CA1985	Companies Act 1985
CA1989	Companies Act 1989
CA2006	Companies Act 2006
C(AICE)2004	Companies (Audit, Investigations and Community Enterprises) Act 2004
CCSS	CREST courier and sorting service
CDDA1986	Company Directors Disqualification Act 1986
CIC	Community Interest Company
CIS	Community Interest Statement
CJA1993	Criminal Justice Act 1993
CLRA2002	Commonhold and Leasehold Reform Act 2002
CPA1985	Companies Consolidation (Consequential Provisions) Act 1985
CSP	Company Secretarial Practice, the official ICSA information service
DGFT	Director General of Fair Trading
EA2002	Enterprise Act 2002
ECD	Excluded Company Declaration
EDC	Electronic data capture
EPA1985	Enduring Powers of Attorney Act 1985
EPA1990	Environmental Protection Act 1990
FA1986	Finance Act 1986
FSA	Financial Services Authority
FSMA2000	Financial Services and Markets Act 2000
FTA1973	Fair Trading Act 1973
IA1986	Insolvency Act 1986
ICSA/The Institute	The Institute of Chartered Secretaries and Administrators
ICTA1988	Income and Corporation Taxes Act 1988
IR1986	Insolvency Rules 1986
NED	Non-Executive Director
OFR	Operating and Financial Review
OFT	The Office of Fair Trading
RIE	Recognised Investment Exchange
SRO	Self-regulatory Organisation
UKLA	UK Listing Authority

1 Company registration

Introduction

In most cases, **company registration** (**incorporation** or **formation**) is a relatively straightforward process and can be undertaken without any legal training, although the majority of companies are formed by specialist registration **agents** (also referred to as formation or incorporation agents).

This chapter looks at the most common forms of incorporation and the differences between them, the process of registration, including the issue of company and business names, and the documentation that must be filed with the **Registrar of Companies** in order for the company to begin trading. It also covers the procedures necessary for re-registering existing companies under different corporate structures.

Although falling outside the scope of this book, there are alternatives to incorporation. Anyone setting up in business may wish to consider trading as a sole trader, as an unregistered unlimited **partnership** or as a registered **limited liability partnership**. The choice between incorporating or trading without limited liability will depend on the desire to keep the financial status of the business secret and/or the different taxation regimes applying to companies and unincorporated entities.

Forms of incorporation

There are four types of companies that may be incorporated: **private companies** limited by shares, private companies limited by guarantee, private unlimited companies and **public companies** limited by shares. The majority of companies are formed as private companies limited by **shares**. Companies limited by guarantee and **unlimited companies** can only be registered as private companies (CA2006 ss.4 and 5). Until 1980 it was possible to incorporate a public company limited by guarantee with shares, and there are a few of these companies still in existence. The differences between private and public companies are discussed on pp. 3–4.

The **company secretary** should also be aware of other forms of incorporation available for private companies.

Community Interest Company

Community Interest Companies (CICs) are private companies limited by shares or by guarantee that have lodged a Community Interest Statement at the time of incorporation or subsequently. CICs are also required to have an asset lock provision under which the assets and profits must be permanently retained within the CIC and used solely for the benefit of the community. The assets and profits may be transferred but only to another organisation which has an asset lock. A CIC cannot obtain charitable status.

Right to Manage Company (England and Wales only)

Right to Manage (RTM) Companies are private companies limited by guarantee. RTM companies were introduced under the Commonhold and Leasehold Reform Act 2002 (CLRA2002). This enables leaseholders to transfer the landlord's management functions to an RTM company that they register. The Articles of Association of an RTM company must comply with the requirements of the CLRA2002.

An RTM company name must end with the words 'RTM Company Limited' or 'Right to Manage Company Limited' or the Welsh equivalent.

Commonhold Association (England and Wales only)

Commonhold Associations (CA) are private companies limited by guarantee. Like RTMs, CA companies were introduced under the CLRA2002. A CA combines freehold ownership of a single property (a unit) in a larger development with membership of a limited company that owns and manages the common parts of the development, for example a block of flats where each flat is a unit and all the other parts, such as the hallway, are commonhold. The Articles of Association must comply with the Commonhold Regulations 2004 (SI 2004/1829).

A CA company name must end with the words 'Commonhold Association Limited' or the Welsh equivalent.

Companies limited by guarantee

This is a form of incorporation mainly used by charitable or non-profit-making organisations. For a company to be registered as a charity, it must be formed as a company limited by guarantee. Registered charities can convert their company to a CIC but will lose their charitable status.

Unlimited companies

Mainly used by professional practices and some special types of trading organisations where corporate status with perpetual succession is required. The advantage of perpetual succession is that the company carries on notwithstanding the changes in the membership of the company that will inevitably occur from time to time. This form of company can also be used to keep financial information secret at the 'price' of losing limited liability for the owners, since unlimited companies are not required to file accounts with the Registrar of Companies.

Limited liability partnerships

Created in April 2001 (and outside the scope of this book), this form of corporate body combines the organisational flexibility and taxation regime of a partnership with the financial disclosure and creditor protection regime of a limited company.

Differences between companies limited by shares and those limited by guarantee

The main differences between companies limited by shares and companies limited by guarantee are that in the case of a company limited by guarantee, the following conditions apply:

1. Although members do not buy shares in the company, if the company is wound up they guarantee to pay an amount to the company in order that it may meet some or all of its liabilities. The amount of the guarantee is usually a nominal amount and is frequently as little as £1.
2. Companies limited by guarantee may only be formed without **share capital** and all guarantee companies incorporated since 1 July 1985 are private companies. Before 22 December 1980, a **guarantee** company could be formed with or without share capital, and before July 1985, guarantee companies with a share capital could also be public companies if they met the appropriate conditions.
3. The Memorandum of the company must be in the relevant form set out in Schs.1 and 2 of the Companies (Registration) Regulations 2008 (SI 2008/3014). Schedule 1 is for companies with a share capital and Sch.2 is for companies without.
4. Different sets of model articles are prescribed under CA2006 for private companies limited by shares and companies limited by guarantee.
5. The members of the company are the original subscribers to the Memorandum of Association and any other persons whom the directors may approve for membership and who agree to be members.
6. If the company is non-profit-making it may be permitted to omit the word 'limited' from its name (CA2006 s.60). An application for exemption can be made as part of the incorporation process using the relevant part of Form IN01.
7. Notwithstanding the exemption from including the word 'limited' in its name, the company is required to disclose on business letters and order forms that it is a **limited company** (CA2006 s.82).
8. By CA2006 s.64 the Secretary of State may withdraw the exemptions and require the company to include the word 'limited' in its name if he considers that the company no longer complies with the provisions of CA2006 s.60.

Differences between companies limited by shares and unlimited companies

The main differences between companies limited by shares and unlimited companies are that in the case of an unlimited company, the following conditions apply:

1 Members of unlimited companies are liable for the company's liabilities without limit.
2 Unlimited companies must always be private companies.
3 Any transfers of shares must be on the old 'common' form of transfer, which is signed by both **transferor** and **transferee**, and not the form prescribed under the Stock Transfer Act 1963, which requires only the signature of the transferor. (The transferor is the person who wishes to sell/pass on his shares to another person; the transferee is the person who is acquiring those shares, thereby becoming a member of the company.)
4 Unlimited companies are exempt from filing accounts with the Registrar of Companies unless they are a **holding company** of a limited company or a subsidiary of a limited company (CA2006 s.448).

Public companies and private companies

The definitions of public and private companies set out in CA2006 s.4 are as follows:

1 A public company is limited by shares (or limited by guarantee with a share capital provided it was incorporated prior to 22 December 1980), complying with the following conditions:
   - the certificate of incorporation states that the company is a public company;
   - the company must have been registered or re-registered as a public company on or after 22 December 1980.
2 A private company is a company that is not a public company.

Additional requirements for public companies

The following is a summary of the main requirements on public companies that do not apply to private companies. Although this list is not exhaustive, it is clear that the legislative burden on public companies is greater than that for private companies.

1 The name of a public company must end with the words 'public limited company', 'plc' (or 'Public Limited Company' or 'PLC'), or the Welsh equivalent.
2 A public company must have an issued share capital with a nominal value of not less than the authorised minimum, which is currently £50,000 or the prescribed euro equivalent (CA2006 ss.761 and 763) before it can commence business or borrow (see 3 below).

3 The issued shares must be paid up to not less than 25 per cent of their nominal value, together with the whole of any premium (CA2006 s.761(3)). The **share premium** is the excess amount, if any, paid for a share over its nominal value.
4 Only public companies may offer their shares or debentures to the public (CA2006 s.755).
5 Strict rules are imposed on public companies to ensure that full value is given for any shares allotted (CA2006 ss.584–609).
6 A public company must file its accounts with the Registrar of Companies within six months of the end of its **financial year** (CA2006 ss.441 and 442(2)(b)).
7 A public company must have at least two directors, one of whom may also be the company secretary (CA2006 s.154). The company secretary of a public company must be suitably qualified (CA2006 s.273).
8 A public company must hold **annual general meetings**, annually laying accounts before its shareholders and annually reappointing its auditors.
9 A public company may not approve **resolutions** by **written resolutions** of its members (CA2006 s.288) unless this is authorised by its Articles of Association.
10 There are strict regulations on a public company's ability to purchase its own shares or provide financial assistance for the purchase of its own shares. In particular, a public company may not fund the purchase of its own shares out of **capital**.
11 Although private companies need not have restrictions on the transfer of their shares, many do in order to retain ownership with the existing shareholders. Such provisions also provide protection from a disgruntled shareholder who might wish to sell shares to an 'outsider' or competitor. A public company whose shares are traded on a market (i.e. listed, AIM or **PLUS**) cannot, with one exception, place restrictions on the transferability of its fully paid shares. Public companies whose shares are not traded can adopt similar provisions to private companies. The exception relates to companies whose articles contain a provision requiring a specified percentage of their shares to be held by UK residents.
12 The election of directors in a **general meeting** must be dealt with by separate rather than composite resolutions (CA2006 s.160(1)).
13 Public companies do not qualify as small or medium-sized companies and thus cannot take advantage of the provisions enabling such companies to file **abbreviated accounts**.
14 Listed, AIM and PLUS public companies may purchase their own shares and hold these in the form of Treasury shares.
15 Listed public companies must propose a resolution at their annual general meeting to approve the company's remuneration report (CA2006 s.439).
16 The directors of public companies and private companies with more than one class of share may only be given authority to issue additional shares pursuant to CA2006 s.551 for a maximum of five years.

17 The Articles of Association of a public company may not exclude the **pre-emption rights** on the issue of new shares set out in CA2006 s.561.

18 Whilst quoted companies are no longer required to produce an operating and financial review, many choose to do so voluntarily. The legal requirement for companies to produce a business review in their directors' report applies to all companies except 'small' companies.

19 Public listed companies are required to draw up their financial results using International Accounting Standards.

20 For a company whose shares are admitted to a regulated market a member who holds shares on behalf of another person may nominate them to enjoy information rights in respect of those shares as set out in CA2006 ss.146–153.

21 The articles of a public company must contain specific authority before the directors can authorise a transaction or arrangement where a director has a conflict of interest (CA2006 s.175(5)).

Matters to consider when incorporating a company

Table 1.1 summarises the various types of trading entities available and the range of factors to consider when incorporating a company.

Table 1.1: Types of trading entity

Factors to consider	*Plc*	*Ltd*	*Unltd*	*Guarantee*	*LLP*	*Unincorporated*
Profit	✓	✓	✓		✓	✓
Not for profit				✓		
Liability of members limited	✓	✓		✓	✓	
Liability of members unlimited			✓			✓
Financial information confidential			✓			✓
Financial information public	✓	✓		✓	✓	
Profits to be assessed for tax on owners					✓	✓
Profits to be assessed for tax on trading vehicle	✓	✓	✓	✓		
Shares to be offered to the public >100 persons	✓					
Shares to be offered to a defined restricted membership		✓	✓	✓	✓	✓

Registration

Registration is the process by which a company is incorporated and becomes a legal entity separate from its owner(s) (i.e. the shareholders). This process is commonly referred to as registration, incorporation or formation. This is the case even with a private company, which may have only one shareholder. This principle is stated in CA2006 s.7(1):

> 'A company is formed under this Act by one or more persons –
> (a) subscribing their names to a memorandum of association; and
> (b) complying with the requirements of this Act as to registration.'

Registration is effected by delivering the relevant documentation to the Registrar of Companies. Guidance on incorporating a company is available from the Registrar by post or from the Companies House website (see Directory). Registration of companies can be effected electronically, although only via an approved software package developed by a company supplying statutory record software or electronic forms software (see below). The monthly workload statistics published by Companies House consistently show this to be the preferred method of forming a company. For example, the workload statistics for June 2009 showed that 92.1 per cent of incorporations were processed electronically. The process and requirements for registration are set out below.

Registration of private limited companies

These are the most commonly formed companies.

The first step is to find a suitable name. An index of company names is kept by the Registrar of Companies and must be checked to make sure that the proposed name will not be the same as or too similar to the name of any existing company.

The name should not be one to which the Registrar or other persons are likely to take exception. When a name has been selected, the documents listed below, completed and executed, must be sent to Companies House (New Companies Section, Cardiff for English/Welsh companies and Edinburgh for Scottish companies – see Directory).

If registration is required for a specific date, this can be accomplished by submitting the registration documents together with a covering letter to that effect. As a standard incorporation is usually processed in five days or fewer, it is suggested that the paper be submitted at least ten days before the required date. Alternatively, registration can be effected on a same-day basis (see p. 10).

1 *Memorandum of Association*. There must be at least one **subscriber** to the Memorandum, who must agree to take at least one share in the company. The number of shares which each subscriber has agreed to take is shown against his name in the Memorandum. One witness must sign against the name of each subscriber. A subscriber to the Memorandum need not necessarily be an individual; it may be a corporate body, in which case the

Memorandum is signed by someone duly authorised on its behalf. The Memorandum for a private company limited by shares must be in the form contained in Sch.1 of the Companies (Registration) Regulations 2008 (SI 2008/3014).

2 *Articles of Association*. All companies must register Articles of Association and a section concerning Articles of Association is provided on Form IN01 which is used when making an application to register a company. This provides three options: (i) to adopt the relevant set of model articles in their entirety; (ii) to adopt the relevant set of model articles with modification; or (iii) to adopt an entirely bespoke set of articles.
3 *Form IN01*. Details of the proposed company must be submitted on Form IN01 'Application to register a company'. Details to be provided include the proposed name, situation of registered office, details of the proposed secretary (if any) and directors, together with their service address.
4 *Name approval*. Formal approval of the name of the company (if required) (see p. 11).
5 *Registration fee*. A cheque payable to Companies House for the registration fee of £20.

If all is in order, the Registrar of Companies will issue a **certificate of incorporation** bearing the date of incorporation, the company's registered number and stating that the company is a private company. The certificate should be kept safely, but duplicate certificates of incorporation can be obtained from the Registrar of Companies for a fee (currently £15). A private company may commence business as soon as it is incorporated.

Registration of public companies

The documents to be sent to the Registrar of Companies for the formation of a public company are essentially the same as those for a private company.

A public company must have at least two directors (CA2006 s.154). The Registrar's certificate of incorporation states that the company is a public company. Unlike a private company, a public company cannot immediately commence business on the issue of the certificate of incorporation or exercise any of its borrowing powers. Before this can happen the company must deliver the 'Application for a trading certificate for a public company (Form SH50), following which the Registrar will issue the trading certificate, confirming that the company complies with s.761 of CA2006 concerning the capital requirements of public companies. This application includes confirmation that the nominal value of the authorised minimum share capital has been subscribed, giving details regarding the payment for the shares and certain other matters. The Registrar is entitled to rely on the statement of compliance as sufficient evidence of the matters stated in it (CA2006 s.762(3)). The issue of the trading certificate by the Registrar of Companies means that the company can commence its business and exercise any of its borrowing powers. If it does so before the issue of the certificate, the company and any **officer** in default may be liable to criminal penalties, although the transactions are not affected. In such an event, the Secretary of State may call upon the company to comply with the provisions of CA2006 s.761 within 21 days. If the company fails to do so, any party to the transaction who has sustained loss or damage may claim against the directors, who are jointly and severally liable to indemnify that party.

Registration of a Community Interest Company

The legislation under which CICs may be registered is contained in the Companies (Audit, Investigations and Community Enterprises) Act 2004 (C(AICE)2004) and the Community Interest Company Regulations 2005, SI 2005/1788. In addition to the usual forms and documents required to incorporate a company there are additional requirements for the incorporation of a CIC as follows.

The Memorandum and Articles must comply with the provisions of Part 3 of the Community Interest Regulations 2005. These requirements set out details of the asset lock and other features of a CIC.

The name of the CIC must, if it is not a public company, end with the words 'Community Interest Company' or 'CIC'. If the registered office is situated in Wales the Welsh equivalent may be used instead 'cwmni buddiant cymunedol' or 'CBC'. If the CIC is a public company the name must end with 'community interest public limited company' or 'community interest plc' or their Welsh equivalent 'cwmni buddiant cymunedol cyhoeddus cyfyngedig' or 'cwmni buddiant cymunedol ccc'.

A CIC must clearly demonstrate how it will meet the community interest test. One way it can do this is to closely define its objects rather than using the general commercial objects clause.

Form CIC36 is the community interest statement (CIS), (C(AICE)2004 s.27). The CIS is to confirm that the company will benefit the community and sets out the intended activities of the CIC and demonstrates how these will benefit the community. The Regulator will rely on the CIS in determining whether the proposed company is eligible for CIC status.

The final document is the Excluded Company Declaration (ECD) in the form approved by the Regulator. The purpose of the ECD is to confirm that the company is not excluded from being eligible from being a CIC. Excluded activities include involvement in political activities, lobbying for changes in legislation, and activities for the benefit of a restricted segment of the community.

Additional supporting information may also be provided in an accompanying letter.

The incorporation documents are all filed at Companies House. There is an additional £15 fee in respect of the Regulator's fees. These may, however, be included in the normal incorporation fee payable to Companies House.

As the Regulator must confirm that the proposed company meets the eligibility criteria for a CIC, same day incorporations are not possible.

Same-day registration

The registration of private or public companies is usually effected within five days of receipt of the registration documents. Registration can also be effected on the date of document receipt if they are sent to Companies House (Cardiff) or the London office, addressed to the *New Incorporation Section – same day incorporations*. The fee for a same-day registration is £50 for paper filings and £30 for electronic filings. In practice, the documents need to be received by midday for the company to be registered on the same day. Alternatively, where appropriate software is used and the incorporation documents lodged electronically, incorporation can usually be effected in between one and three hours. There is a reduced fee for this of £15 although an account does need to be opened with Companies House.

Memorandum of Association

The Memorandum of Association must be in the relevant statutory form, as set out in Schs.1 and 2 to the Companies (Registration) Regulations 2008 (SI 2008/3014) for companies with and without a share capital respectively.

The Memorandum of Association of a company incorporated under CA2006 is a brief statement of the intention of the subscribers to be incorporated. The document merely states the subscribers' names and that they agree to become members of the company. Unlike the position under CA1985, the memorandum is not a document of continuing importance. Rather it shows limited information about the company at the time of incorporation and cannot be amended.

Company name

The company's name is no longer required to be stated in either the Memorandum of Association or the Articles of Association. Previously the name was stated in the Memorandum of Association. If it is a private company, the name must end with the word 'Limited', 'Unlimited' or the relevant abbreviation, unless advantage has been taken of CA2006 s.60 to omit the word Limited or Ltd. The name of a public company must end with the words 'public limited company' or 'plc' or, if preferred, 'Public Limited Company' or 'PLC' (CA2006 s.58). A company limited by guarantee may apply to omit the word 'Limited' or its abbreviation from its name (CA2006 s.60). The names of private or public companies may end with the appropriate Welsh equivalent, provided the company's registered office is situated in Wales.

The company's name must be displayed outside every office or place of business and engraved on the company's **common seal** (if it has one). Place of business includes a share **transfer** or share registration office. In addition, it must appear on all business letters and other specified documents, as stipulated in the Companies (Trading Disclosures) Regulations 2008 (SI 2008/495). Additional requirements apply in the case of companies incorporated outside Great Britain which have a place of business (including a share registration office) in Great Britain (CA1985 s.693). The Secretary of State may require an overseas company to use a different name in Great Britain (CA1985 s. 694) if its name is the same as or similar to an existing company registered in Great Britain.

Control of company names

It is the responsibility of the persons forming the company to check the Company Registration Office's index of names. In particular it should be noted that:

1. A company will not be registered by the Registrar of Companies if the name is 'the same as' an existing name on the index of names or where it does not bear the appropriate status, i.e. 'Limited' in the case of a private company or 'public limited company' (or an abbreviation) in the case of a public company. A name will not be registered if it is offensive or if its use constitutes a criminal offence (CA2006 s.53).
2. A name will not be approved if it gives the impression that the company is connected with central or local government or contains an expression which may only be used with the approval of the Secretary of State (CA2006 ss.54 and 55) unless written approval has been obtained from the appropriate authority.
3. Where a company has been registered with a name which is 'the same as' or 'too like' a name shown on the Company Registration Office's index, within 12 months of the registration the company may be directed by the Secretary of State to change its name within such period as he may specify (CA2006 ss.67 and 68). This period is extended to five years of registration where the company has provided, for the purpose of registration, information which is misleading or which has not fulfilled assurances given at the time of registration (CA2006 s.75). At any time after registration the Secretary of State may direct a company to change its name within six weeks, or such longer period as he may allow, where the company's name is so misleading in regard to the nature of its activities as to be likely to cause harm to the public (CA2006 s.76). From 6 April 2008 new provisions were introduced by CA2006 ss.68–74. Under these provisions any person may object to the company names adjudicator that a name is the same as or similar to a name they are associated with or have goodwill in. The adjudicator must announce their decision within 90 days and can order a company to change its name.
4. There are detailed guidance notes on the provisions regarding company names which may be obtained from the Registrar of Companies on request or downloaded from the Companies House website (see Directory).

Change of company name

A company may change its name by **special resolution** or by other means as provided in the company's articles of association (CA2006 s.77). The change of name takes effect on the issue of a certificate of incorporation or certificate of change of name by the Registrar of Companies.

The detailed procedure for the change of name of a public company by special resolution is as follows (some of these steps are not relevant for private companies and in particular it is likely that the shareholder consent would be obtained by written resolution rather than at a general meeting):

1 The proposed new name is checked against the Company Registration Office's index of names and approval of the name obtained if required.
2 The directors resolve to convene a general meeting to consider the special resolution to change the name. [***See precedents 2, 4, 5 and 6.***] Alternatively, for a public company, the resolution to change the name can be done as special business at an annual general meeting.
3 The directors approve a circular explaining to all members and persons nominated by members under CA2006 ss.145 or 146 to receive notices the reason for the proposed change of name and, if a general meeting is to be convened, a notice is sent to the members. If the change of name is to be approved at an annual general meeting, the explanation can be included in the **directors' report**.
4 (*Listed, AIM and PLUS companies only*) A form of three-way proxy must be sent out with the notice of meeting (*LR 9.3.6*). [***See precedent** 7.*]
5 (*Listed, AIM and PLUS companies only*) It is no longer necessary in most instances for proof copies of notices, resolutions, proxy forms or circulars to be vetted and approved by the UK Listing Authority prior to issue, provided the documents comply with the requirements laid down by the *Listing Rules* and are certified by the company's sponsor as so doing. However, two copies of the circular, notice and proxy form must be submitted to the UK Listing Authority, together with any required letter(s) of compliance, no later than the date of issue to shareholders (*LR 9.2.14, 9.6.1*).
6 A certified copy of the special resolution [***see precedent** 8*] and the relevant Notice of Change of Name (Forms NM01 to NM05) should be prepared for filing with the Registrar of Companies immediately following the meeting, certified by signature of the chairman, together with the fee payable for a change of name (currently £10). If the change of name is urgent, it can be processed by Companies House on a same-day basis on payment of an increased filing fee of £50. In practical terms, the resolution needs to be with Companies House by midday in order for the change to be effective on the same day. It is desirable that the resolution for change of name be sent to the Registrar separately from any other resolutions that may need to be registered in order to avoid delay.

7 *(Listed, AIM and PLUS companies only)* Two prints of the special resolution must also be sent to the UK Listing Authority at the same time as it is sent to the Registrar of Companies (*LR 9.6.2*).
8 A certificate of incorporation on change of name is issued by the Registrar. The change of name has legal effect from the date of the certificate and not the date of the resolution (CA2006 s.81(1)).
9 *(Listed, AIM and PLUS companies only)* Once the change of name is effective, the company must make an announcement via a regulatory information service and forward a copy of the change of name certificate to the UKLA (*LR 9.6.19*).
10 The new name must be displayed outside the registered office and other places of business and elsewhere, such as on the company vehicles or on the packaging of its products.
11 The company's stationery must also be reprinted, or at least overprinted, with the new name where this is feasible. If the new stationery is to be prepared in advance, it is wise to avoid substantial expenditure in case the Registrar raises any objections to the new name. The company's website (if it has one) and e-mail must be updated with the new name (the Companies (Trading Disclosures) Regulations 2008 (SI 2008/495) reg.6(2)).
12 If the company has a common seal, a new seal must be adopted by the directors at a board meeting, as well as a new securities seal, if appropriate. [***See precedent 9.***]
13 Banks and other organisations with which the company has dealings may require production of the certificate of incorporation on change of name certified by the company secretary. If an official copy of the certificate is required, this can be obtained from the Registrar.
14 The **special resolution** must be attached to all copies of the Articles held in stock.
15 It is not necessary in this case to file a new copy of the Articles with the Registrar of Companies. However, all persons known to be in possession of a copy of the company's Articles, e.g. the directors and the company's auditors and solicitors, should be sent a print of the special resolution to be attached to their copies.
16 If the change of name was directed by the Secretary of State, the same procedure applies but no change of name fee is payable.

Business names

If a company carries on business under a name which is not its corporate name, it must comply with the provisions of Part 41 of CA2006. These are as follows:

1 Although the controls on 'same' or 'too like' names do not apply in relation to business names, names implying connection with central or local government or containing certain words and expressions may be used only with the written

approval of the Secretary of State (CA2006 ss.1193 and 1194). If the business name is used on business letters, written orders for goods, invoices, etc., the full name of the company must also be stated and an address within the United Kingdom at which service of any document relating to the business will be effective must be given (CA2006 ss.1201 and 1202).

2 The full name of the company must be displayed in all premises where the business is carried on under the business name so that customers or suppliers may refer to it. The name must also be given immediately in writing to any person doing business with the company who may request it (CA2006 ss.1204 and 1202(2))

Failure to comply with any of the above provisions renders any officer of the company responsible liable to criminal penalties. In addition, if the provisions have not been complied with, the company may not be able to enforce contracts made under the business name (CA2006 ss.1205 and 1206).

Although the restrictions on 'same' or 'too like' company names do not apply to business names, care must be taken not to infringe any trade marks or to use an existing name of a company operating in the same or similar industry. Use of an existing name might lead to an action for 'passing off'. 'Passing off' is where one company is seen to be benefiting from the reputation of another established business by using the same or a very similar name and 'passing itself off' as that other business.

Care must also be taken not to infringe any existing trade mark registrations which might take precedence over a registered or business name.

Registered office

1 When forming a company, the application for registration, Form IN01, must state the country within the United Kingdom in which the registered office is to be situated, with special provisions applying where the registered office is in Wales. The application for registration must also state the address of the initial registered office. Notice of a change in address of the registered office must be given to the Registrar on Form AD01. The change in address is effective once registered by the Registrar (CA2006 s.87(2)). However, the registered office of a company must be situated within the country specified in the application for registration, so that, for example, a company registered in England and Wales may not alter the Memorandum to provide for the registered office to be situated in Scotland.

2 It is possible to serve a document on a company registered in Scotland which carries on business in England and which may, therefore, become subject to Court proceedings in England, by serving it at the company's principal place of business in England provided that a copy of the document is sent to the company's registered office in Scotland by post.

3 The situation of the registered office is determined by the directors and any change is made by resolution of the directors. [***See precedent 10.***]
4 If the address of the registered office changes, the company's headed stationery, any signage outside its registered office, its website (if it has one) and email must be amended within 14 days of the change (CA2006 s.87(3).
5 Service of any document may still be made at the old registered office for a period of 14 days following registration of the change by the Registrar of Companies.
6 Details of the change of registered office must be notified to the company's corporation and income tax offices and its VAT office, if appropriate. Notification should also be given to the company's professional advisers.
7 To facilitate service of documents by post or hand, the address must be the full postal address and not a PO Box or DX address.

Objects clauses

Under CA1985 every company was required to state its objects in its memorandum. However, there is no longer provision for new companies to have an objects clause in the Memorandum under CA2006 and a company's objects will be unrestricted unless restrictions are specified in the Articles of Association (CA2006 s.31). For a company incorporated prior to 1 October 2009, the objects specified in its Memorandum will be deemed to be part of the Articles, and if the company wishes its objects to be unrestricted, it must amend its Articles accordingly. By CA2006 s.31(2), where a company amends it Articles to add, remove or alter a statement concerning the objects of the company, notice must be given to the Registrar and the change only takes effect once the entry has been made on the Register. When forming a company, consideration will need to be given as to whether it is necessary to include restrictions in the company's articles. This is of particular importance to charitable companies, which will certainly need to include restrictions.

Companies with registered office in Wales

If the Memorandum of Association (for companies incorporated before 1 October 2009) or the Form IN01 (for companies incorporated after 1 October 2009) states that the registered office of the company is to be situated in Wales, the company may, if it wishes, have the Welsh equivalents of 'Limited', 'Unlimited' or 'public limited company' in its name ('cyfyngedig', 'anghyfyngedig' and 'cwmni cyfyngedig cyhoeddus', respectively). However, if the Welsh alternative is used, the fact that the company is limited must be stated in English on its stationery, bill heads and other official documents and it must also be included in a notice displayed at every place of business of the company.

The company's Memorandum and Articles of Association delivered to the Registrar of Companies prior to incorporation may be in the Welsh language, but must be accompanied by an English translation. This must be certified as being a correct translation by a notary public or solicitor.

Articles of Association

The Articles of Association are the rules and regulations by which the internal affairs of the company are governed. They must be printed and numbered in consecutive paragraphs (CA2006 s.18(3)) and, in the case of the Articles registered at the time of the incorporation of the company signed by the subscribers. Three sets of model Articles are provided under CA2006 for private companies limited by shares, private companies limited by guarantee and public companies, as set out in the Companies (Model Articles) Regulations 2008 (SI 2008/3229) [see Appendix 1]. These model Articles can be adopted in their entirety on incorporation, adopted with modification or excluded entirely, as was the case with the various versions of Table A. Public companies in particular will usually wish to adopt an entirely bespoke set of Articles and it is envisaged that the model articles for public companies will be used primarily as a drafting resource.

Certain types of company adopt specialised forms of Articles which depart further from the model Articles. These include **subsidiaries**, residents' management companies, and charitable and non-profit-making organisations. CIC companies are required to modify their Articles to comply with provisions of Part 3 of the Community Interest Company Regulations 2005. RTMs and CAs are required to amend their articles to comply with CLRA2002.

Companies may also wish to adopt Articles relating to the rights of shareholders so as to create different classes of shares with different rights attaching to each class. Broadly speaking, these rights can be split into voting rights, **dividend** rights, rights of the return of capital and rights relating to the issue of new shares and the transfer of shares. These are considered in more detail in Chapter 4.

Companies limited by guarantee usually adopt bye-laws in addition to the Articles. These are essential where the company operates a membership separate from its shareholders or guarantors. Often there will be different types of membership and differing levels of annual subscriptions. The Articles would not be an appropriate document in which to set out rules and regulations relating to the membership and internal regulations of the organisation and, accordingly, these are set out in a separate document.

For companies formed prior to 1 October 2009, the introduction of the model Articles has no effect, as the version of Table A that was in force at the time of incorporation (or when new Articles was adopted) continues to apply. For the vast majority of companies incorporated before 1 October 2009 the applicable version of Table A will be the Companies (Tables A to F) Regulations 1985, SI 1985/805 (as amended by the Companies Act 1985 (Electronic Communications) Order

2000 SI 2000/3373), although this was further amended by the Companies (Tables A to F) (Amendment) Regulations 2007 (SI 2007/2541) and, for companies registered between 1 October 2007 and 30 September 2009, the Companies (Tables A to F) (Amendment) (No. 2) Regulations 2007 (SI 2007/2826).

Alteration of Articles

The Articles may be altered by amending the wording of one or more of the Articles, deleting or adding Articles or by adopting a completely new set of Articles to take the place of the original ones. In order to do this, a special resolution must be passed as follows:

1 The directors in a board meeting resolve to convene a general meeting to consider the special resolution, to approve a circular to members explaining the reasons for the alterations and, in the case of a listed company, to approve a three-way proxy form (*LR* 9.3.6). [***See precedents 2, 4, 5 and 11.***]
2 All amendments in wording may be included in the resolution. However, if it is intended to adopt new Articles, the circular will usually summarise the main provisions and state that a copy of the proposed Articles is available for inspection either at the company's registered office or at the office of the company's solicitors from the time the notice is sent to members to the date of the meeting.
3 If a significant proportion of the shares are held by financial institutions, e.g. insurance companies and pension funds, it may be appropriate to obtain confirmation that the proposed new Articles are acceptable. This may be particularly relevant where changes are proposed to require greater involvement of shareholders, in line with the company's corporate governance strategy.
4 A certified copy of the resolution must be sent to the Registrar within 15 days of the meeting. This must be accompanied by a printed copy of the Articles as amended or a certified copy of the new Articles, as appropriate (CA2006 s.26(1)). [***See precedent 8.***]
5 (*Listed, AIM and PLUS companies only*) Two prints of the resolution and of the new or amended Articles must be sent to the UK Listing Authority (*LR* 9.6.2).
6 A reprint of the Memorandum and revised Articles incorporating a copy of the special resolution should be prepared or, alternatively, copies in stock should be suitably amended. Copies of the reprinted Memorandum and Articles or amended copies should be sent to directors of the company, its auditors, solicitors and others known to use copies of the Memorandum and Articles.
7 Copies of the amended Articles must be sent to any members on request (CA2006 s.32).
8 Where a number of amendments dealing with separate matters are proposed it may be appropriate to deal with those by different resolutions rather than bundled together. In this way shareholders can consider each matter separately and vote on each amendment as appropriate.

Companies' registered numbers

On incorporation, every company is allocated a registered number; this consists of one or more sequences of figures or letters. The Registrar has power to change a company's registered number but, for a period of three years following notification of a new registered number, the company may use either the old number or the new one on business letters and order forms (CA2006 s.1066).

Company letterheads

The company's full name must be shown on all business letters, website and email and other documents, as specified in the Companies (Trading Disclosures) Regulations 2008 (SI 2008/495), including publications, cheques, orders for goods and services on behalf of the company, invoices and receipts. The place of registration and the registered number of the company as shown on the certificate of incorporation must also be shown on business letters, website and email and order forms, together with the address of the registered office. In addition if a company has a website, they must disclose their VAT number if they are registered for VAT, regardless of whether the website is used to sell goods or services or not.

It is not necessary to show the amount of the share capital on business letters, but if this is done the reference must be to the **paid-up share capital**.

The names of directors need not be shown on business letters, but if it is desired to do so, the names of all the directors must be stated and not just one. However, it would still be in order for a letter to be signed by a director with that title under his signature without showing the names of all the directors on the paper (the Companies (Trading Disclosures) Regulations 2008 (SI2008/495) reg.8).

If it is intended that directors of the company should have headed paper stating their office it is essential that care is taken not to breach the provisions. Although it is acceptable to show that the letter is from the 'Office of the Chairman' it would not be acceptable to state from the 'Office of Mr J. Smith, Director', unless the names of the other directors were also shown. It is not necessary for the names to appear with equal prominence, merely that they are all legible.

Where a company uses a trade name which is different from its registered name, this can be shown on the headed paper; however, the company's full name as registered must also be shown, usually in small print at the foot of the page.

Re-registration

Provided certain conditions are met, companies incorporated as private limited companies can re-register as public companies. There is a much easier process for a public company to re-register as a private limited company. Additionally limited companies can re-register as unlimited and vice versa unless the unlimited company was originally a limited company in which case it cannot revert back to limited status. Although an unlimited company cannot re-register as a public company it can re-register first as a limited company and subsequently re-register from a private limited company to a public limited company.

Re-registration of a private company as a public company

A private company meeting the necessary conditions can re-register as a public company (CA1985 ss.89–96). The re-registration must be approved by special resolution and application made to the Registrar.

To qualify for re-registration as a public company, the company must have:

- at least two directors (CA2006 s.154);
- issued at least £50,000 or euro equivalent (CA2006 s.763) of share capital, in nominal value, of which all of any premium and at least 25 per cent of the nominal value on each share must be paid (the authorised minimum) (CA2006 s.91).

A balance sheet must be prepared for a date not more than seven months prior to the date of the application together with an unqualified **audit** report, made up to a date not more than seven months prior to the date of application. If the company has previously taken advantage of CA2006 s.477 and has not prepared audited accounts, it must prepare audited accounts prior to its application for re-registration. If the auditor's report is qualified, the auditor must confirm that the qualification is not material for the purposes of establishing that the net assets are not less than the aggregate of the called-up share capital and undistributable reserves (CA2006 s.92(5)).

The auditor must report that the balance sheet shows that the net assets are not less than the aggregate of the share capital and any undistributable reserves (CA2006 s.92(1)(c)).

If between the date of the balance sheet and the date of application for re-registration the company has issued shares for non-cash consideration, a report confirming the value of the consideration in terms of CA2006 s.1150 must be prepared (CA2006 s.93).

Where the company has insufficient share capital in issue it is common practice to undertake a capitalisation issue at the same time as the special resolution to re-register the company is proposed. The procedure for re-registering a private company as a public company is as follows:

1 The directors, at a board meeting, resolve to convene a general meeting to approve a special resolution that the company be re-registered as a public company, to alter the Memorandum of the company to state that the company is to be a public company and to make other amendments necessary to make the Memorandum and Articles conform with the requirements for a public

company. [*See precedents 2, 4, 5 and 12.*] This includes changing the name of the company to end with the appropriate suffix, i.e. 'public limited company', a permitted abbreviation or the Welsh alternative.

2 When the special resolution has been passed, an application is submitted to the Registrar of Companies on Form RR 01 ('Application by a private company for re-registration as a public company'), signed by a director or the company secretary. The following documents must accompany the application:
   (a) a copy of the special resolution approving the re-registration
   (b) a printed copy of the Articles as altered by the special resolution;
   (c) a copy of the auditors' written statement in relation to s.92(1)(c) of CA2006.
   (d) a copy of the relevant balance sheet, together with a copy of an unqualified auditors' report on it ;
   (e) if shares have been allotted by the company between the relevant balance sheet date and the passing of the special resolution, other than for cash, a report with regard to the valuation of any asset in consideration for which the shares were allotted (CA2006 s.93(2)(a));
   (f) if there is no company secretary appointed, a statement of the company's proposed secretary in accordance with CA2006 s.95 needs to be completed on section 2 of the application; and
   (g) a cheque in respect of the re-registration fee payable of £20. If it is proposed to change the name as well as re-register the company the fee increases to £30. The fees for same-day re-registrations or re-registrations and change of name are £50 and £100 respectively.

3 If the application is approved, the Registrar of Companies will issue a certificate of incorporation stating that the company is a public company. When the certificate is issued any alterations to the Memorandum and Articles take effect.

4 See 'Change of company name' (pp. 12–13) for guidance on other matters to be dealt with.

Re-registration of a public company as a private company

As the provisions regulating public companies are more stringent than those for private companies, it is not necessary for the directors to ensure that the company meets any requirements prior to putting an appropriate resolution to the shareholders. The procedure to re-register a public company as a private company is as follows:

1 The directors, at a board meeting, resolve that a general meeting be convened to pass a special resolution that the company be re-registered as a private company, altering the Memorandum so that it no longer states that the company is a public company and making such other alterations to the Memorandum and Articles as are required. This includes a change of the

name of the company deleting the suffix 'public limited company' or any abbreviation and substituting the word 'Limited'. [***See precedents 2, 4, 5 and 13.***]

2 When the special resolution has been passed a copy must be sent to the Registrar of Companies within 15 days.

3 If holders of not less than 5 per cent of the issued share capital or a group of not less than 50 of the company members object to the change they may apply to the Court for cancellation of the special resolution within 28 days of its being passed (CA2006 s.98(1)–(3)). Shareholders who voted in favour of the resolution are barred from calling for the cancellation of the resolution. If such an application is made the Registrar of Companies must be informed immediately on Form RR03 (CA2006 s.99(1)). The Court will either cancel or confirm the resolution and a copy of the court order must be lodged with the Registrar within 15 days of the order being made, or such longer time as the Court may allow (CA2006 ss.98(3) and 99(3)).

4 Assuming that no application for cancellation is made or if the special resolution is confirmed by court order, application for re-registrations submitted to the Registrar of Companies on Form RR02 ('Application by a public company for re-registration as a private limited company') signed by a director or the company secretary. The form must be accompanied by the following documents:
   (a) a printed copy of the special resolution;
   (b) a printed copy of the Articles, as altered by the special resolution. If all the company's shareholders voted in favour of the resolution, the application may be made immediately following the meeting;
   (c) a cheque in respect of the re-registration fee payable of £20. If it proposed to change the name as well as re-register the company the fee increases to £30. The fee for same day re-registrations or re-registrations and change of name are £50 and £100 respectively.

5 If the Registrar of Companies is satisfied that the application is valid, he will issue a certificate of incorporation appropriate to a company that is not a public company. The alterations to the Articles take effect upon the issue of the certificate.

6 See 'Change of company name' (pp. 12–13) for guidance on other matters to be dealt with. The above procedure is for voluntary re-registration.

7 All public companies whether listed or not are subject to the City Code on Takeovers and Mergers (see Chapter 17). The Code provides protection to shareholders in the event of a takeover or merger.

Provided the company was not a listed company or offered any of its shares to the public in the previous ten years by re-registering as a private company, the company may no longer fall within the scope of the City Code. Although not a statutory or City Code requirement, unlisted public companies with external shareholders are recommended to contact the Takeover Panel if they are proposing to re-register as a private company. The Takeover Panel will be concerned to ensure that shareholders are made aware that in the event of re-registration they will lose the protection afforded by the City Code. For contact details, see the Directory.

Re-registration of other types of company as public companies

Unlimited companies may not be re-registered as public companies (CA2006 s.105(1)). They could, however, first re-register as a private company by virtue of CA2006 s.105 and subsequently re-register as a public company by virtue of CA2006 s.90.

Re-registration of private limited company as unlimited

A private limited company may re-register as an unlimited company (CA2006 s.102).

Re-registration of unlimited company as private limited company

An unlimited company may re-register as a limited company (CA2006 ss.105 and 106); however, a limited company which has previously re-registered as an unlimited company cannot later re-register as a limited company (CA2006 s.105(1) and (2)).

Dissolution

The Registrar of Companies is authorised by the Companies Act 2006 to remove from the Register companies he believes are defunct, for example, where a company has failed to file accounts and annual returns and no response is received to letters sent to the company's registered office.

Under CA2006 s.1003 a private company which is not trading may make a voluntary application to have the company's name struck off the Register. This procedure may not be used if, within three months of the proposed application, the company has changed its name, traded, disposed of property or rights for value, or engaged in any activity other than that required to effect the dissolution or where application for a scheme of arrangement or petition or order under the Insolvency Act has been made.

Dissolution may not be appropriate in circumstances where the company has any assets or liabilities even if there is no chance of payment being either made or sought.

Procedure

One of the most common causes for an application for dissolution to be stopped is on application of HM Revenue & Customs. HMRC will object in any circumstances where they believe there is or might be any tax due. Accordingly unless the company has been dormant for some years clearance from HMRC should be sought and any liability to tax settled.

Application is made on Form DS01, signed by the director(s) or a majority of directors, together with the filing fee (£10).

A copy of the application must be sent within seven days to any person who, at any time on or after the date of application but prior to dissolution, was an employee, a member, a **creditor**, a director or a manager or trustee of any pension fund established for the employees. On receipt of the application the Registrar will publish a notice in the ***Gazette*** inviting any objections as to why the company should not be struck off. If no objections are made within three months of publication, the Registrar will strike off the company and publish a further notice in the *Gazette* notifying that the company has been dissolved.

The directors may halt the dissolution process by submitting Form DS02 and are obliged to do so if any of the events set out in CA2006 s.1009 occurs.

Restoration

Under CA1985 a company could only be restored to the register by obtaining a court order. Under ss.1024 to 1028 of CA2006, however, an application may be made to the Registrar by a former director or member of the company to restore the company to the register under a new, simpler administrative restoration procedure. The procedure is only available in the circumstances prescribed by CA2006 s.1025, and it is envisaged that the procedure will be used primarily by companies that were dissolved for default in complying with filing requirements but which continued to trade at the time of being struck off.

A procedure for restoration to the register by way of court order is also provided under CA2006 ss.1029 to 1032. A wider range of people may apply to the court to restore a company to the register than may under the administrative procedure, including the Secretary of State, directors, members, employees, creditors or managers or trustees of any employee pension scheme. The procedure is available to companies struck off under CA1985 on or after 1 October 2007. For companies struck off between this date and before 1 October 2009, the application to the Court may be made before 1 October 2015 or within 20 years of the first notice being published in the *Gazette*, whichever is sooner. For companies dissolved under CA2006, there is a period of six years from the date of dissolution within which an application for restoration may be made (CA2006 s.1030(4)).

Procedure

The Court may order restoration if it is satisfied that:

- the person was not given a copy of the company's application;
- the company's application involved a breach of the conditions of the application; or
- for some other reason it is just to do so.

The Secretary of State may also apply to the Court for restoration if this is justified in the public interest.

Where a company is dissolved, the liquidator or any other interested party such as a creditor can apply to the Court for the dissolution to be declared void. In most cases an application must be made within two years of dissolution, but it can be made at any time if its purpose is to bring proceedings against a company for:

- damages for personal injuries; or
- damages under the Fatal Accidents Act 1976 or the Damages (Scotland) Act 1976.

Applications are made to the High Court. The Registrar of the Companies Court in London usually hears restoration cases in chambers once a week on Friday afternoons. Cases are also heard at the District Registries. For more detailed guidance on restoration, see *A Guide to Company Restoration*, available online from the Treasury Solicitor's Department (see Directory).

The Court will require an affidavit or a witness statement confirming that:

- the originating document was served; and
- the solicitor dealing with the *bona vacantia* assets has no objection to the restoration of the company.

The affidavit or witness statement should also cover, as appropriate to the application:

- details of the company's original incorporation and objects;
- members, directors and company secretary;
- its trading activities;
- an explanation of any failure to file accounts, annual returns or other documents at Companies House;
- details of the striking-off and dissolution;
- details concerning the company's solvency;
- the purpose for the application.

Before the order can be granted the company will need to file all documents required to bring the company's statutory filing up to date.

All costs of the restoration are met by the applicant including the Treasury Solicitor's costs, fees payable to the Registrar and any late filing penalties due in respect of accounts. The penalties are those that had already been imposed but not paid prior to dissolution or in respect of any accounts that were overdue for filing when the company was dissolved. The period when the company was dissolved is ignored for the purposes of calculating the amount of penalties due.

An office copy of the Court Order with the Court seal impressed must be delivered to the Registrar of Companies. The company is regarded as restored when the order is delivered.

2 Directors

Introduction

The definition of a director contained in CA2006 s.250 is very general. It states that a director is any person who occupies the position of director, by whatever name called.

A **shadow director** is a person who is effectively directing the affairs of the company but who is not called 'director' (CA2006 s.251).

The definition refers to any person rather than any individual and thus will include corporate bodies having a legal persona. In this way it is possible for one company to be appointed a director of another company. Incorporation agents frequently use an in-house company rather than an individual to act as the director of a new company for the purposes of incorporation. It should be noted, however, that from 1 October 2008 all companies are required to have at least one director who is a natural person (CA2006 s.155).

This chapter looks in detail at types of directors, how they are appointed, resign or are removed, and at their powers, duties, liabilities and disclosure requirements. It also examines meetings of directors (board meetings and committees), and the company secretary's role in convening and managing meetings and keeping records of meetings. Additional material on duties, responsibilities and accountability will be found in Chapters 14, 16 and 18.

Appointment

Eligibility

No qualification requirements are specified in the Companies Acts 1985–2006. A company's Articles of Association may, however, require the holding of a specified qualification. For example, a company carrying on business as a registered auditor may require that all directors are capable of being appointed as auditors in their own right.

Alternatively, the directors of a residents' management company will often be required to be property owners or tenants of the particular development. The Act does, however, set out a number of conditions which, if met, *prohibit* the appointment of that person as a director:

1 A bankrupt person may not be appointed as a director. If a director becomes bankrupt after appointment, he must immediately resign unless leave to continue is given by the courts (CDDA 1986 s.11).
2 A person who has had a disqualification order made against him may not act as a company director unless leave has been given by the courts (CDDA 1986, ss.2 and 5).
3 The auditor of a company cannot also be a director or company secretary of that company (CA2006 s.1214).
4 A director of an insolvent company cannot, without the leave of the Court, be appointed as a director of a company with a 'prohibited' name (IA 1986 s.216).

In addition, the Act and the company's Articles of Association may provide further instances where appointment may not be made or may cease, for example:

1 If a registered practitioner who is treating that person gives a written opinion stating that the person has become physically or mentally incapable of acting as a director and may remain so for three or more months (Model Articles, reg.18(d)).
2 If a composition is made with the person's creditors in general satisfaction of that person's debts (Model Articles, reg.18(c)).
3 Since 1 October 2008 all directors must be aged 16 or over (CA2006 s.157).
4 Failure to meet a share qualification or other qualifying criteria specified in the Articles (CA1985 s.291).
5 If the maximum number of directors permitted by the Articles has been reached.
6 The Articles of a company incorporated before January 2007 may require directors to retire annually upon reaching the age of 70. This reproduced the effect of CA1985 s.293 which has now been repealed.

Procedure for appointment

The first directors of a company are those whose names are entered on Form IN01 on the incorporation of a company. Subsequent appointments as directors are governed by the provisions of the company's Articles of Association. These usually provide that the board itself may fill any casual vacancies or appoint additional directors up to the maximum number permitted by the Articles. However, elections or re-elections of directors following **retirement by rotation** or removal of directors must be approved in general meeting (Table A, regs.73–80, reg.21 of the Model Articles for companies limited by shares). Also, at the company's first annual general meeting (if applicable), all the directors retire from office and have to be re-elected by the shareholders at the meeting (Table A, reg.73, reg.21 of the Model Articles for companies limited by shares). A casual vacancy is one arising from the death or resignation of a director. Once it has been established that the proposed replacement is willing to be appointed (consent is formally required by signature of the consent-to-act section of Form AP01 for individual directors and

AP02 for corporate directors), the procedure for appointing an individual director to fill a casual vacancy is as follows:

1 The board resolves to appoint the new director. [***See precedent 14.***]
2 The secretary writes to the newly appointed director confirming his appointment by the board and dealing with the following:
   (a) requesting personal particulars, including date of birth, which are required to complete Form AP01 and to make the necessary entry in the register of directors(CA2006 s.162). The date of birth is required for all directors (CA2006 s.163(1)(f));
   (b) asking the new director to sign the consent section on Form AP01; alternatively details of the new appointment may be made online either using an appropriate software package or online via the Companies House website. Pre-registration is required for both these services;
   (c) if the director will be signing cheques on the company's behalf, requesting a specimen signature to be sent to the company's bank;
   (d) informing the director of any share qualifications which must be acquired under the Articles and the time allowed in which to do this;
   (e) inviting the director to give a general notice of his interests in any proposed or existing contracts with the company (CA2006 ss.177 and 182) [***see precedent 15***];
   (f) giving dates of forthcoming board meetings;
   (g) enquiring how the director wishes his emoluments to be paid, e.g. sent to his home address or paid direct into his bank account, including information regarding his PAYE coding and National Insurance contributions (if he is already paying the maximum contributions in connection with another employment, he should obtain and submit to the company a certificate of exemption from contributions);
   (h) providing general information about the business of the company if the newly appointed director is not already involved in the company. Copies of the Memorandum and Articles, reports and accounts for recent years and interim reports and circulars should be made available if required;
   (i) (*Listed, AIM and PLUS companies only*) providing a copy of the company's rules for securities transactions based on the Model Code (*LR 9 Annex 1*) and asking him to acknowledge receipt.
3 (*Listed, AIM and PLUS companies only*) A Regulatory Information Service should be notified of the appointment by the end of the business day following the decision to appoint the director (*LR 9.6.11*). Details of the director's other business activities must be disclosed to a Regulatory Information Service within 14 days (*LR 9.6.13*). Details of any interests in shares of the company must also be disclosed within five days of their appointment (*LR 9.6.13*).
4 If appropriate, a press announcement should be sent to newspapers or through the company's press agents.

5 On receipt of the relevant information from the director, the necessary entries in the register of directors and secretaries and in the register of directors' share and debenture interests should be made. The completed Form AP01 whether on paper or electronic must be sent to the Registrar of Companies within 14 days of the date of appointment. There may also be other matters to be attended to, depending on the circumstances.
6 The Model Articles do not contain any provision requiring directors to obtain a share qualification and this is not usually required by modern forms of Articles. However, it is usual for a director to wish to have some share interest in the company of which he is a director and, in this event, a notice of his interests must be included in the company's report and accounts each year. Where a director is not required to have a share qualification it is usual for the Articles to provide that the director may receive notice of, and attend and speak at, general meetings of the company. As a non-shareholder, he would not otherwise have such power except if acting as chairman of the meeting.
7 If the company has an insurance policy covering directors and officers of the company against liabilities incurred in carrying out their duties, the insurance company should be notified of the appointment of the new director, either at the time of appointment or at renewal, depending upon the wording of the policy.

Directors' addresses

From 1 October 2009, an individual director will be able to take advantage of having a service address. This address can be their residential address, the company's registered office or any other address that they may choose (such as the address of their solicitors or accountants). It will be this service address that will appear on the public records, as opposed to their usual residential address, as it has been in the past.

A director will still need to provide their residential address when filing Form AP01 to record their appointment, but it will be held on a private register and will only be accessible to limited groups of people, i.e. specified bodies carrying out a public function or credit reference agencies.

A director can make an application under CA2006 s.243 and reg.5 of the Companies (Disclosure of Address) Regulations 2009 to prevent his/her residential address being disclosed to a credit reference agency. A pre-existing confidentiality order that was in force on 30 September 2009 will be valid evidence to prevent disclosure of the director's residential address to a credit reference agency, however when the confidentiality order runs out, the director will need to make an application under s.243.

In addition a person (such as a director, company secretary or shareholder) or a company can make an application under s.1088 and the Companies (Disclosure of Address) Regulations 2009 to have removed from the public file their residential addresses which have been placed there since 1 January 2003.

If there is any change in a director's residential or service address, they will need to inform Companies House on Form CH01. PO box numbers can only be used for the director's service address, and only then if a full address is also provided.

Alternate directors

There is no provision in the Act authorising a director to appoint an alternate to act on their behalf in their absence, so alternates may be appointed only if the Articles of Association of the company specifically provide for this.

Regulations 25–27 of the Model Articles for a Public Limited Company and regs.65–69 of Table A make provision for a director to appoint another director to be their alternate, or they may appoint any other person as their alternate subject to that person being approved by the board of directors. [***See precedent 16.***]

Alternate directors are included in the definition of 'director' in CA2006 s.250 and their particulars should be entered in the register of directors and filed with the Registrar of Companies on Form AP01 or AP02 (depending on whether they are an individual or a corporate director). These forms do not differentiate between the appointment of a person as a director or as an alternate director.

Accordingly, a search of the records at Companies House will reveal alternate directors' as well as directors' appointments without any distinction. They are subject to the same rules as directors with regard to disclosure of interests in shares and debentures of the company and transactions with the company. Their names must also be shown on letterheads if it is company practice to show the names of directors on such stationery. An alternate director may act only in the *absence* of the appointing director: it is not a complete assignment by the director.

Shadow directors

A person who either controls the management of a company or on whose instructions the directors act is a 'shadow director' of the company and is deemed to be a director of the company for all purposes (CA2006 s.251). The appointment of a shadow director should be notified on Form AP01, although a shadow director may be unwilling to sign the 'consent to act' declaration of the form. In such circumstances an existing officer should countersign the form and it should be submitted to Companies House with a covering note explaining the circumstances of the 'appointment'.

Although directors will usually act on the advice of their professional advisers, this would not normally imply that those advisers were shadow directors provided their advice is limited to a particular part of the business such as accounts or commercial property transactions and they do not provide advice on all matters.

Minimum number of directors

A public company must have at least two directors and a private company must have at least one director (CA2006 s.154). From 1 October 2008 all companies must now have at least one director who is a natural person (CA2006 s.155). The Articles may stipulate that there must be a higher minimum number of directors. If for any reason the number of directors falls below this number, the remaining directors have power to fill a casual vacancy or to convene an extraordinary general meeting only for the purpose of allowing the shareholders to appoint additional director(s). If, for any reason, it is not discovered that the number of directors has fallen below the minimum number once the number has been restored, it is recommended that the board ratify the decisions made whilst there were insufficient directors. Provided the acts being ratified were within the board's authority they can be ratified by the board. In such circumstances many companies will also seek ratification by the shareholders to ensure that the decisions are not queried in the future.

Defective appointment of directors

If the appointment of a director is found to be defective in any way, CA2006 s.161 provides that, for the protection of third parties, any earlier acts made by the person acting as a director remain valid. CA2006 s.239 provides that the members of the company may ratify prior acts of directors either individually or collectively for acts of negligence, default or breaches of duty or trust.

Managing directors and other executive directors

The appointment of directors as managing or executive directors is usually governed by provisions contained in the company's Articles, giving the directors power to appoint such directors, to determine the terms of their appointment and remuneration and to delegate to them such powers of the board as may be desired (Table A, reg.84). Under the Model Articles directors are deemed to have authority to exercise all the company's powers unless restricted by the Articles (reg.3 of the Model Articles). Since the office of managing director is normally a full-time executive appointment, it is good practice for this appointment to be governed by a formal service agreement, rather than just a note of the principal terms, so that the remuneration and other benefits associated with the appointment may be made clear. The agreement should also contain any provisions relating to confidentiality and some control over the director's activity in the event of their leaving the service of the company. The contracts of directors who also hold salaried executive positions with the company should specify whether the remuneration stated in the contract is exclusive or inclusive of directors' fees. For a smaller company, the terms of appointment could be set out in the minutes of the board appointing the director and a letter sent to the director containing a copy of the minute and asking for them to confirm acceptance of the proposed appointment in writing.

The Articles normally give the board of directors power to revoke any appointment of a managing director subject to the terms of any service agreement with the company. The appointment would also cease if the director ceased to be an employee of the company for any reason.

Non-executive directors

A non-executive director (NED) is a member of the board of directors without executive responsibilities in the company. The role of non-executives is to contribute skills and experience to board decision making which might not otherwise be available, and to provide a suitable balance of power in the boardroom. Most smaller companies will have no need to appoint non-executive directors, but the role of NEDs is seen as increasingly important for larger, listed companies, and the issue of the balance between executive and non-executive directors on boards has become a key tenet of good corporate governance practice (see Chapter 18). Where appointed, NEDs have the same powers, duties and liabilities as executive directors.

Special types of director

Some companies' Articles provide for the board to appoint persons to offices with the word 'director' as part of their title, e.g. divisional director, associate director. Such a person is not a director within the meaning of CA2006 s.250 and is not entitled to attend board meetings. Such a person is not subject to the statutory responsibilities and liabilities of a director, provided that they do not represent themselves as being a director, in terms of the Companies Act, in dealings with third parties. It can be misleading to appoint officials with the word 'director' in their job titles when they are not subject to the legal duties of a director. However, the practice is sometimes followed in order to give an added measure of status to senior executives to facilitate their dealings with customers and suppliers, especially if the company has substantial dealings in overseas territories.

Local boards are also sometimes formed by companies under provisions contained in their Articles. These persons are not full directors for the purposes of the Companies Act 2006.

Contracts of employment

A director's employment contract (often referred to as a service contract) that cannot be terminated other than for breach of contract within a period of two years must be approved by the shareholders in general meeting (CA2006 s.188).

Shareholders' approval may be given by an ordinary resolution passed at a general meeting [***see precedent 17***], provided that a written memorandum setting out the terms of the proposed agreement or a copy of the service contract is available for inspection by members of the company at the registered office for a period of not less than 15 days prior to the date of the meeting. Companies are required at all times to keep copies of directors' service contracts available for inspection by members at an address specified for that purpose by the company (CA2006 s.228).

In accordance with the **Combined Code**, listed, AIM and PLUS companies are encouraged to have service agreements with their directors with a notice period of not more than one year (see Chapter 18).

Powers of directors

The directors of a company are authorised by the Articles of Association to manage the business of the company and to exercise the company's powers (Table A reg.70, Model Articles, reg.3). This seemingly unlimited authority is usually balanced by the fact that this authority is subject to the provisions of the Companies Acts, the company's Articles of Association and by resolution of the shareholders.

The power of the directors is given to the board collectively and not individually. Directors are usually also given power to appoint one or more of their number to executive office and to delegate any or all of their power to one or more committees consisting of one or more directors (Model Articles regs.5–6, Table A, regs.84 and 72).

Directors have authority to exercise the powers of the company only as stipulated or restricted by the company's Articles of Association. For example, the Articles of Association of a company limited by guarantee will often prohibit the declaration of a dividend. In this situation, regardless of the level of retained profits, the directors would be unable to declare a **distribution** by way of dividend or indeed any other way to members.

Duties

A director's prime duty, which he holds together with his fellow directors, is to manage the company for the benefit of its members. The directors may delegate some or all of their powers to particular directors (perhaps constituting a committee of the board) and/or other senior officers in the company, but they cannot delegate their duties.

The Companies Act 2006 introduced four duties of directors on 1 October 2007 and a further three came into effect on 1 October 2008. These duties codified, with some amendments, existing case law.

1 To act within their powers (CA2006 s.171): Directors must act in accordance with the company's constitution and only exercise powers for the purposes for

which they are conferred. The company's Articles of Association should be consulted to ascertain the extent of a director's powers and any limitations placed upon them.

2 To promote the success of the company (CA2006 s.172): A director must 'act in the way he considers, in good faith, would be most likely to promote the success of the company for the benefit of its members as a whole', and in doing so have regard (amongst other matters) to:
   - the likely consequences of any decision in the long term;
   - the interests of the company's employees;
   - the need to foster the company's business relationships with suppliers, customers and others;
   - the impact of the company's operations on the community and the environment;
   - the desirability of the company maintaining a reputation for high standards of business conduct; and
   - the need to act fairly as between members of the company.

3 To exercise independent judgement (CA2006 s.173).

4 To exercise reasonable care, skill and diligence (CA2006 s.174): The duties imposed by CA2006 ss.173 and 174 require that a director owes a duty to exercise the same standard of care, skill and diligence that would be exercised by a reasonably diligent person with:
   - the general knowledge, skill and experience that may reasonably be expected of the person carrying out the same functions as a director in relation to that company (an objective test); and
   - the general knowledge, skill and experience that the director actually has (a subjective test).

   For example, a finance director would be expected to have a greater knowledge of finance issues than, say, the HR director (the objective test); but if the HR director is also a qualified accountant, then he would be expected to have a greater knowledge than would normally be expected of a HR director although not necessarily the same knowledge as the finance director (the subjective test).

5 To avoid conflicts of interest (CA2006 s.175): Directors must avoid situations in which they have or might have a direct or indirect interest that conflicts or might conflict with the interests of the company. Of particular importance are conflicts relating to property, information or opportunity regardless of whether the company could take advantage of such opportunities (CA2006 s.175(2)).

   The duty does not apply to conflicts arising out of transactions or arrangement between the company and the director.

   Where the company is a private company, authorisation may be given by resolution of the directors [***see precedent 18***] provided there is nothing in the company's Articles of Association which invalidated the authorisation.

   Where the company is a public company, authorisation may be given by resolution of the directors provided there is specific authority in the company's Articles of Association which permits directors to authorise such transactions.

Such authorisation, whether for a private or public company, is only valid if the necessary quorum for a meeting of the directors is present excluding the director with the conflict of interest and without that director voting (CA2006 s.175(6)).

6 Not to accept benefits from third parties (CA2006 s.176): Directors must not accept a benefit from a third party being given by virtue of their being a director or due to any action or inaction by the director.

Benefits received by a director from a person by whom his services are provided are not to be regarded as paid by a third party.

The duty is not infringed if the acceptance of the benefit cannot reasonably be regarded as likely to give rise to a conflict of interest.

7 To declare interests in any proposed transaction or arrangement (CA2006 s.177): A director must declare the full nature and extent of any direct or indirect interest in any proposed transaction or arrangement before that transaction or arrangement is entered into [***see precedent 15***]. The declaration may be given at a meeting of the directors or by notice in accordance with CA2006 ss.184 or 185.

Where a previous notification or interest becomes inaccurate or incomplete additional notification(s) must be made.

Notification is not required where the director is not aware of the interest or is not aware of the transaction or arrangement.

Notification is not required where the nature of the interest is such that it cannot reasonably be regarded as likely to give rise to a conflict of interest, to the extent that the other directors are already aware of the interest without requiring specific notification or where the transaction relates to the director's **service contract**.

Directors also have additional non-Companies Act duties and responsibilities and these are considered in Chapter 14.

Liabilities

Directors properly exercising the powers of the company and acting as agent for the company will not incur personal liability in the event of a breach of contract. However, directors may incur personal liability if they have given personal guarantees or if they have not made it clear that they are acting as agent of the company and not in a personal capacity.

There are also a number of circumstances under which a director may be personally liable to the company or third parties from a breach of duty or statutory offence including:

- acting as a director whilst disqualified (CDDA1986 s.15);

- a director of an insolvent company carrying on a business with a company with a prohibited name (IA1986 s.217);
- employing illegal immigrants (Asylum and Immigration Act 1996);
- evasion of VAT (FA1986 ss.13 and 14);
- failure to show company name on correspondence, cheques, etc. (CA1985 s.349);
- fraudulent preference (IA1986 ss.238–40);
- fraudulent trading (CA2006 s.993);
- irregular share allotment (CA1985 s.85(2));
- making false statement in a prospectus (CA1985 s.70);
- non-observance of pre-emption rights on allotment (CA1985 s.92);
- public company trading prior to issue of trading certificate (CA1985 s.117);
- trading with intent to defraud (IA1986 s.213);
- wrongful trading (IA1986 s.214).

Derivative action claims

CA2006 ss.260–269 introduce a derivative action procedure, making it easier for shareholders to sue directors or others for a broader range of acts or omissions than was possible under **common law**.

Due to the different legal systems in England, Wales, Northern Ireland and Scotland the legislation is split with ss.260–264 applicable to proceedings brought in England, Wales or Northern Ireland and ss.265–269 applicable to proceedings brought in Scotland. The provisions themselves are intended to have the same effect in all territories.

Grounds for bringing a derivative action

A derivative action claim may only be brought under the provisions of the CA2006 or under a court order and may be brought in respect of an actual or proposed act or omission involving negligence, default, breach of duty (including the codified duties described above) or breach of trust and may be brought by a member whether the cause of action arose before or after they first became a member (CA2006 ss.260 and 265).

Application for permission to continue derivative claim

A member who has brought proceedings must apply to the Court for permission to continue the claim.

If a company has brought a claim and that claim could be continued as a derivative action claim a member may apply to the Court to continue the claim as a derivative action claim on the grounds that:

- the manner in which the company brought or is continuing the claim is an abuse of a process of the Court; or

- the company has failed to prosecute the claim diligently; or
- it is appropriate for the member to continue the claim.

The Court must dismiss the claim if the evidence filed by the member does not disclose a *prima facie* case for giving permission. In dismissing a claim the Court may make any consequential order it considers appropriate, including a costs order.

If the evidence does disclose a *prima facie* case, then the Court may give directions as to the evidence to be provided by the company and may adjourn the proceedings to allow that evidence to be obtained (CA2006 ss.261, 262 and 266, 267).

Grounds for permission to continue

On hearing the permission application, the Court must refuse permission to continue the claim if a person seeking to promote the success of the company for the benefit of its members would not continue the claim or if the conduct complained of has been authorised or ratified by the company (i.e. the shareholders). On any resolution to ratify a director's negligence, default, breach of duty or breach of trust the votes of those members personally interested in the ratification must be disregarded.

In exercising its discretion to allow an action to be continued, the Court must consider:

1 whether the member is acting in good faith;
2 the importance a director promoting the success of the company would attach to continuing the claim;
3 whether the conduct would be likely to be authorised or ratified by the company;
4 whether the company has decided not to pursue the claim; and
5 whether the applicant should pursue a remedy in his own right instead of on the company's behalf.

The Court must have particular regard to the evidence of independent shareholders in deciding whether to grant permission (CA2006 ss.263 and 268).

Application to continue action brought by another member

Where a member has commenced a derivative action claim another member may apply to the Court to continue the claim on the grounds that:

1 the manner in which the first member brought or is continuing the claim is an abuse of a process of the Court; or
2 the first member has failed to prosecute the claim diligently; or
3 it is appropriate for the member to continue the claim.

The Court must dismiss the claim if the evidence filed by the member does not disclose a *prima facie* case for giving permission. In dismissing a claim the Court may make any consequential order it considers appropriate, including a costs order.

If the evidence does disclose a *prima facie* case, then the Court may give directions as to the evidence to be provided by the company and may adjourn the proceedings to allow that evidence to be obtained (CA2006 ss.264 and 269).

Vacation of office

The office of director is vacated on the death of the office holder or under a provision in the Articles of Association of the company. Such a provision might be that the directors are appointed for a fixed term and on expiry of that term their appointment automatically ceases.

Vacation of office may also arise under statute as follows:

1 If the director becomes bankrupt, unless the court permits the appointment to continue (CDDA1986 s.11).
2 If the director is disqualified from being a director by court order (CDDA1986 ss. 1–6, as amended by CA1989 Sch.10, Part II, para.35 and CDDA1986 Sch.1 as similarly amended and CDDA1986 ss.9a–e as inserted by Enterprise Act 2002 s.204). A register of such disqualification orders is maintained by the Secretary of State for inspection by the public (CDDA1986 s.18).
3 If on 1 October 2008 the director had not attained the age of 16 (CA2006 s.159).

Under the Articles further methods of vacating office may be specified as follows:

1 Where the Articles stipulate any qualifying criteria and that criteria has not been met the office of director would be vacated at the conclusion of the qualifying period.
2 In the case of a company where the director reaches the relevant age limit set out in its Articles, the office of director would be vacated at the conclusion of the next following annual general meeting.
3 *Resignation.* This will usually take effect from the date on which the letter of resignation is received by the company, unless this states some subsequent date on which the resignation is to become effective. To be effective the resignation does not need to be accepted by the board, unless the Articles provide otherwise.
4 *Absence.* If the director is absent from board meetings for some specified period (often six months) without leave of absence. In order to monitor the operation of any such Article, therefore, the secretary should arrange for the board to grant leave of absence where it is known that a director is likely to be absent for a period exceeding six months, e.g. because of overseas travel on the company's business or long illness.

5 If a receiving order is made against a director or the director compounds with their creditors generally.
6 If an order is made by the Court on grounds of mental disorder.
7 If the director is removed from office, e.g. by a notice signed by all co-directors or by any holding company.

Retirement by rotation (public companies only)

The Model Articles for Public Limited Companies provides for the retirement of one third of the total number of directors by rotation every year (Model Articles reg.21, Table A, reg.73). As private companies are no longer required to hold an annual general meeting, any provisions in their Articles requiring directors to retire by rotation at annual general meetings cease to have any effect if they have chosen to forgo the need to have an annual general meeting. There is no general requirement in the Act for directors to retire by rotation at annual general meetings. It is usual for the Articles to provide that a person appointed as a director by the board to fill a casual vacancy, or as an additional director, must be re-elected at the next following annual general meeting of the company.

For a listed company, the Articles will normally contain provision for directors appointed to fill casual vacancies or persons appointed as additional directors to hold office only until the next following annual general meeting, when they will be eligible for re-election. In the case of additional directors, any maximum number of directors specified in the Articles must not, of course, be exceeded.

The procedure to be followed for the retirement of directors by rotation depends on the wording of the Articles but, based on the Model Articles and Table A provisions, is as follows:

1 At the first annual general meeting of the company, all the directors must retire and be elected by the members. **[*See precedent 19.*]**
2 At subsequent annual general meetings, must retire from office. Directors who are retiring because they have been appointed since the last annual general meeting and directors who are excluded from the retirement by rotation provision, e.g. managing directors, are not taken into account for this purpose. Some companies' Articles differ from the model provisions by providing that the number of directors to retire by rotation shall be one-third of the directors or, if their number is not three or a multiple of three, then the number nearest to but not exceeding one-third shall retire. For example, in the case of a board of directors consisting of eight directors, under the model provisions, three directors would retire; under these alternative Articles, only two directors would retire.
3 The directors to retire at any annual general meeting should be those who have been longest in office since their last election. If two or more persons became directors on the same day, those to retire (unless they otherwise agree among themselves) shall be determined by lot.

4 Directors retiring by rotation are eligible to offer themselves for re-election by the members.
5 In the case of a public company, the resolutions at a general meeting for the appointment or reappointment of directors must be voted on individually unless the meeting first agrees unanimously that the appointments or reappointments may be made by a single resolution (CA2006 s.160).

Removal of directors

The shareholders may remove a director at any time by **ordinary resolution** [***see precedent 20***] regardless of anything to the contrary in the Articles or any agreement with the director (CA2006 s.168). Removal, however, does not deprive the director of any rights they may have to compensation or damages payable in respect of the termination of their appointment as a director.

Special notice must be given to the company of the intention to propose such a resolution. [***See precedent 21.***] A copy of the notice must be sent to the director concerned to give them the opportunity to make representations in writing to the company and to request that these be circulated to the members.

Where such special notice is received by the company, care must be taken to ensure that the requirements of CA2006 s.169 are strictly complied with. It may be advisable to obtain legal advice as to the precise procedure. In the case of a public company a resolution could be proposed at the next annual general meeting. In all other cases the removal will be dealt with at a general meeting and special notice must be given to the company of the intention to propose a resolution to remove a director not less that 28 days prior to the meeting as specified in CA2006 s.168(2).

Articles of Association may not exclude the provisions of CA2006 ss.168 or 169, but may make additional provisions for removal of directors such as by unanimous resolution of the other directors or by written notice of the holding company.

A private company may not use the written resolution procedure to remove a director, which must be by way of a resolution approved at a general meeting (CA2006 s.288).

No directors

Many private companies have only one director and, if this sole director were to resign or die, any shareholder may request the company secretary to convene a shareholders' meeting to appoint a new director.

This would also be the case if a company with more than one director found itself with no directors as a result of mass resignations or some accident resulting in their deaths. In this scenario it would be quite likely that all the shareholders would also have died as in many private companies all shareholders are also directors. In such circumstances it would be prudent to include a provision in the Articles of Association allowing the executors of a deceased shareholder to nominate new director(s) in the event of there being no directors. [***See precedent 22.***]

The Secretary of State has power under CA2006 s.156 to give a direction as to the procedure to follow to appoint a new director or directors.

Procedural issues

A number of administrative matters must be dealt with when a director ceases to hold office.

1 The board should formally minute the vacation of office. **[*See precedent* 23.]**
2 The date of ceasing to be a director must be recorded in the register of directors and secretaries.
3 A notice on Form TM01 or electronic equivalent should be sent to the Registrar of Companies within 14 days of the date of vacation of office.
4 Any fees for the period to the date of cessation of office should be paid to the director or, if deceased, to their personal representatives. HM Revenue & Customs should be informed of the cessation of fees.
5 If the name of the director is shown on company stationery, it should be removed.
6 *(Listed, AIM and PLUS companies only)* A Regulatory Information Service/ Newstrack must be notified as appropriate.
7 It may be appropriate to issue a press release.
8 If the director was authorised to sign cheques, the bank should be informed.

The director should be requested to return all documents and other company property to the company. If the director had use of a company car, arrangements should be made for its return to the company.

Disqualification

Directors may be disqualified under the CDDA1986 either automatically, resulting from a defined event, or where application has been made to the Court that a person is unfit to be a director.

A person who has been disqualified may not during the period of disqualification be a director, liquidator, **administrator**, receiver or manager of a company whether directly or indirectly without the consent of the Court.

Contravention of a disqualification order is a criminal offence punishable by up to two years' imprisonment or an unlimited fine. Application for disqualification is made under the appropriate provision of the CDDA1986 and disqualification may be automatic or discretionary.

Disqualification for unfitness

The court is obliged to disqualify a person who was or is a director of an insolvent company where their conduct makes them unfit to be involved in the management of a company.

A director can be found unfit to be a director as a result either of their actions or as a result of inaction.

Disqualification on conviction

The courts may make a disqualification order if a person has been convicted of an indictable offence in connection with the management, promotion, formation or **liquidation** of a company.

Disqualification for breach of statutory obligations

A disqualification order may be made for persistent failure to file accounts or annual returns or other documents required to be filed with Companies House or failing to keep statutory records.

Disqualification for fraudulent or wrongful trading

A disqualification order may be made against a person if, during the course of a winding up, it appears that he is guilty of an offence under CA2006 s.993 for fraudulent trading or has committed some other offence or breach of duty or where the director is required to make a contribution to the company's assets for insolvent trading.

Disqualification in the public interest

The Secretary of State has power to apply to the Courts for a disqualification order on the grounds of public interest. This would usually follow from an enquiry by the **Department for Business, Innovation & Skills** inspectors.

Disqualification undertaking

The Secretary of State may, where an individual would otherwise be subject to disqualification proceedings under CDDA1986 ss.7 and 8, accept a disqualification undertaking from that person. The maximum periods of such a disqualification undertaking is two years if in respect of a matter subject to CDDA1986 s.7, and 15 years if relating to offences under CDDA1986 s.8 (CDDA1986 s.1A).

Competition disqualification order

The Court must make a disqualification order (maximum 15 years) against a person if a company of which that person is a director commits a breach of competition law and the court considers the conduct of that person makes them unfit to be concerned in the management of a company (CDDA 1986 s.9A).

Competition undertaking

The Office of Fair Trading or the specified regulator may accept a disqualification undertaking from a person in circumstances where the OFT or the regulator believes a company of which that person is a director has committed a breach of competition law and that person's conduct makes them unfit to manage a company (CDDA 1986 s.9B).

Meetings of directors and committees

Unlike shareholders' meetings, which are strictly governed in terms of notice periods, who may attend and speak, rules concerning voting and the differing majorities required for certain resolutions, the Companies Act 2006 is silent on how directors should conduct their meetings.

There are detailed provisions obliging directors to disclose their interest in matters being discussed and preventing abuse of their positions by running the company for their own benefit (see below), but little else.

Listed company directors are also required to comply with the Model Code [see Appendix 5] and to comply with the provisions of the Combined Code or explain any departures from the Code (*LR 9.8.5 (5 and 6)*) (see Chapters 11 and 18).

In practice, public companies with external shareholders and large private companies will hold regular board meetings at which executive management strategy is determined. For the vast majority of private companies, formal board meetings are seldom held, and any formal resolutions are approved as written resolutions (see below). In this case, the management of the company is dealt with on a day-to-day basis by a series of informal discussions between the relevant directors with no formal written record.

Directors must ensure that they are fully aware of all decisions being reached in this informal manner as they are collectively responsible for the company's activities. Ignorance is no excuse and, as seen above, in extreme circumstances can lead to disqualification and personal liability.

Board meetings are general discussion meetings and, unlike the formal structured nature of shareholders' meetings, usually proceed on an informal basis. The chairman assesses whether the general view of the meeting should be incorporated into the minutes of the meeting as the decision of the board, either in narrative form or, where appropriate, as a formal resolution. If, however, the views of directors are fairly evenly balanced on the pros and cons of a particular course of action, it would be appropriate to put the matter to a formal vote.

Appointment of committees

Model Articles reg.6, and Table A reg.72 provide that directors may delegate their powers to committees, who must follow procedures based on the Articles that govern the taking of decisions by directors, or the directors themselves may set out the rules of procedure for the committees with such powers as the board may decide. [***See precedent 24.***] The proceedings of committees will follow those that apply to the board as a whole. Anything done at a meeting of directors is valid, notwithstanding that it may subsequently be discovered that there was a defect in the appointment of one or more of the directors. In certain circumstances, it may also be desirable that the action taken by a committee should be validated by the directors or by the company in general meeting.

Frequency and notice

Board meetings do not have to be held at fixed intervals and are usually convened from time to time, as the directors see fit. Large companies will also usually have an executive committee, composed of executive directors, which meets between board meetings.

If meetings are not held on fixed dates, the chairman will usually instruct the company secretary to convene a meeting. It is, however, open to any director, either acting independently or by instructing the company secretary, to convene a board meeting. No specific length of notice is required. For some companies reasonable or normal notice might be one week and for others much shorter. Even where meetings are held regularly in accordance with a fixed timetable, it is still appropriate to issue reminders, sending a copy of the agenda at the same time.

The notice of a directors' meeting will usually include the place, date and time for the meeting and an agenda of the general topics to be discussed. [***See precedent 25.***] The notice can be circulated in any manner appropriate to the company, e.g. verbally, by letter, fax, e-mail or by hand.

Agenda and minutes

The matters to be discussed at a board meeting will naturally depend on the nature of the company's business and the number of directors. According to the size of the company, board papers and reports will either be circulated with the agenda or tabled at the meeting. Where any complex matters are to be considered it is helpful to the directors, and in particular any non-executive directors, for board papers to be circulated in advance of the meeting.

It is advisable to number minutes and resolutions serially to facilitate reference to any particular minute, if necessary. This may arise when the board is approving authorised cheque signatories, where it may be desired in the future to refer to the minute by its number and refer to the deletion or addition of certain names.

Chairman

Model Articles reg.12, Table A reg.91, permit the directors to appoint one of their number to be chairman of the board; in addition, some Articles provide for the appointment of deputy chairmen and vice-chairmen. [***See precedent 26.***] A person appointed chairman of the board will also usually take the chair at general meetings of the company and will be regarded as chairman of the company, although there is no provision for such an appointment.

Where the Articles are silent, CA2006 s.319 provides that any member or a proxy (CA2006 s.328) may be elected to be chairman of a general meeting.

Regulation 13 of the Model Articles (Table A regs.50 and 88) grant the chairman of the directors' meetings a casting vote if there are equal votes for and against any resolution. This casting vote is in addition to any other votes that the chairman may have. It is normal practice for the chairman to use this casting vote to maintain the status quo on the grounds that there is no majority in favour of change. However, it is at the chairman's decision how to use the casting vote, if at all. Unlike Table A, the Model Articles do not provide for the chairman at a members' meeting to have a casting vote.

Quorum

The quorum for board meetings is fixed as two directors by Model Articles reg.11(2) (Table A reg.89), unless the directors otherwise decide. If the company had only two directors and one resigns or dies, Model Articles reg.11(3) (Table A, reg.90), provides that the sole continuing director may appoint another director. This should be done formally by signing a suitable document, which is inserted in the directors' minute book. [***See precedent** 27.*] Where the number of directors falls below the minimum required by the Articles of Association the remaining director(s) have no power other than to appoint another director or directors, or to call a general meeting of the company at which another director or directors could be appointed.

It is increasingly common, however, for private companies to incorporate in their Articles a provision vesting all the company's authority in the hands of a sole or surviving directors, even where their number has fallen below the minimum number stipulated elsewhere. [***See precedent 28.***]

Resolutions in writing

It is sometimes necessary for the directors to make a decision urgently and Model Articles reg.8 (Table A reg.93), provides that a resolution signed by all the directors entitled to attend a board meeting is as valid and effectual as if passed at a duly constituted board meeting. [***See precedent 29.***] If convenient, such a resolution could be a single document, which is signed by each director in turn. Alternatively, a separate copy of the resolution could be sent to each director for signature. The document or documents signed by the directors should be inserted in the directors' minute book.

It is now common practice for companies to adopt Articles allowing directors to conduct meetings by video or telephone, either by a conference facility or by the chairman ascertaining the views of the directors individually. In addition, resolutions agreed by facsimile or e-mail are being used, although it is desirable for any written resolution to be signed to provide a permanent record.

Maintenance of minute books

Companies are required by CA2006 s.248 to maintain minutes of all meetings of the directors and for these to be available for inspection by any director. There is no provision or right for the shareholders to have access to minutes of the meetings of the directors. (Shareholders can, however, request to see minutes of shareholders' meetings.) The taking of minutes, maintenance and safekeeping of minutes is one of the core duties of the company secretary (see below).

Certification of minutes

Where a third party, such as the company's bank or landlord, requests to see a copy of a particular board resolution, it is clearly not advisable to submit the entire minutes of that meeting or even a particular page of the minutes, as these may contain confidential information. In such circumstances it is normal for the resolution in question to be reproduced on a separate sheet and for the company secretary or a director to certify the extract as a true copy of the original minute. **[*See precedent 30.*]**

The role of the secretary

The company secretary usually plays a central role in the preparations for, and management of, board meetings, and is responsible for any administration arising from the meeting.

Preparation for a board meeting

Prior to the board meeting, the secretary should:

1. Send a notice to each director stating the time, date and place of meeting with a copy of the agenda and supporting papers.
2. If any of the company's managers are to attend the whole or part of the meeting, e.g. the company's accountant, they should also be advised of the meeting and sent a copy of the agenda and supporting papers. If they are to attend only part of the meeting, they should be sent the papers for the relevant items only.
3. It is sensible for the secretary to ensure that he has spare copies of the agenda and supporting papers to take to the meeting.
4. In preparing the agenda for the meeting, the secretary should consider those items that come up on a recurring basis, e.g. half-yearly staff report, and if necessary remind the appropriate department to have the report ready in time for circulation with the agenda. Matters on which no decision was reached at a previous meeting or which were deferred from a previous meeting should also be included in the agenda.
5. Sometimes the supporting papers will incorporate a formal resolution, which the board is to be asked to pass. This will save time when the minutes of the meeting are prepared.

6 Just before the meeting, arrangements should be made to ensure that everything necessary for the meeting is ready in the boardroom. It is also usual to have a copy of the company's Memorandum and Articles, the Companies Act 2006 and other relevant material in the boardroom in case it is necessary to refer to them during the meeting.
7 In the case of listed companies the opportunity is often taken to have schedules of transfers available for inspection by board members. For those companies with an active share register, these summaries will usually be restricted to the largest transfers, as otherwise the reports would be too lengthy to be of any use.

At the board meeting

1 For incorporation in the minutes, take a note of those directors present and report any apologies for absence. [***See precedent 1.***]
2 Ensure that a quorum is present. If any item in which a director has an interest is to be considered, ensure that there will still be an independent, disinterested quorum to deal with it.
3 Take notes during the course of the meeting on any action decided on by the board and of its decisions reached. The minutes should not be a verbatim record of what is said; if they were, this could cause complications.
4 It is usual to note in the minutes the arrival of any director after the proceedings have started or the departure of a director before the meeting has ended.
5 The chairman may ask the company secretary to advise on any point of procedure regarding the conduct of the business of the meeting, but it would be appropriate for the company secretary to intervene in the meeting (unless he is himself a director) only if the board were proposing to do something that was unlawful or contrary to the company's Articles.
6 If a manager is to be called in for discussion of a specific item, ensure that he is ready to be called when that item is reached on the agenda.
7 If any confidential papers are left behind on the board table by the directors, these should be collected by the company secretary before staff come in to clear the room.

After the board meeting

1 (*Listed, AIM and PLUS companies only*) If the company has made a decision with regard to the payment of a dividend on the company's **ordinary shares** or yearly or half-yearly accounts have been approved, a Regulatory Information Service should be advised immediately by telephone or fax (*LR 9.7.2*). If necessary, a Regulatory Information Service should also be advised of any decision to make an issue of shares or debentures or to postpone the payment of a preference dividend or of interest (*LR 9.6.4, 9.7.2.2*).

2 The company's managers should be notified of any action which the board require them to take, e.g. by sending a memorandum or letter to the managers concerned.
3 Make a note of any item that has been deferred for future consideration to ensure that it is not overlooked.
4 If the directors have asked for a report on a specific subject to be prepared for their next meeting, ensure that the manager responsible for preparing it is notified.
5 Prepare the minutes of the meeting, showing the names of the directors present, those whose apologies were noted, and the arrival and departure of any director who was not present at the beginning or end of the meeting.
6 The procedure to be followed after preparation of the minutes will vary from company to company. However, it is usual to send a copy of the draft minutes to every director present with a request that he returns any comments by a given date, following which the minutes can be prepared in their final form for distribution to all directors.
7 If a director makes a comment about the wording of a particular minute, the alteration should be agreed with the chairman, who will then mention the amendment at the subsequent board meeting before signing the minutes. Since the chairman has agreed the amendment, it is unlikely that any director present at the subsequent board meeting will object to the alteration. Other than obvious mistakes, alterations should be confined to what was said rather than what any particular director meant to say or, on reflection, would have preferred not to say.
8 It is not desirable in board minutes to include the individual expressions of opinion of any particular director, although it would be appropriate, at the request of a director, to record in the minutes that he had dissented from a decision taken by the board as a whole.

Interests in contracts

Where a director is directly or indirectly interested in a contract or a proposed contract with the company they must declare the nature of their interest at a meeting of the directors. Model Articles reg.14 (Table A reg.94), imposes restrictions on a director in voting on a matter in which they are personally interested. The type of interest relevant for this purpose is widely defined and includes contracts by the company with any other company of which the director is also a director. However, if the director's interest in a contract arises merely because they are a minor shareholder in another company which is a party to the contract, this would not constitute a declarable interest provided the shareholding was not material, e.g. less than 5 per cent of the voting capital.

A useful procedure for a director to give general notice of interests is given by CA2006 ss.182–185. [***See precedent 15.***]

Where notice of an interest is given in writing it must be given by the director to each other director in hard copy by post or by hand or by such other means as may be agreed between them. Written notice of an interest is deemed to form part of the proceedings of the next meeting of the directors (CA2006 s.184).

A director may give general notice, either at a directors' meeting or in writing, of an interest in or with another company, firm or person and that will constitute a declaration of an interest in any future transaction or arrangement with that company, firm or person.

Where the director required to give a notification is a sole director such notification must be in writing (CA2006 s.186).

Material transactions between the company and its directors must be disclosed in the company's accounts. The Companies Act 2006 imposes restrictions on substantial property transactions between companies and their directors, as discussed below.

In the case of listed companies it is usual to find that the Articles include a provision prohibiting the directors to vote on all but a few matters in which they have an interest. Such allowable interests include arrangements for approved pension schemes and directors and officers' insurance schemes. Non-disclosable transactions with companies, where the interest is in that company's share capital, are limited to holdings not exceeding one per cent.

Substantial property transactions

A director of a company or of its holding company may not enter into any arrangement to acquire from or transfer to the company a 'non-cash asset' without prior approval of the members by ordinary resolution passed in general meeting (CA2006 s.190). [***See precedent 31.***]

The restriction on substantial property transactions extends to persons connected with a director, to shadow directors and requires that, where a director or connected person is also a director of the holding company, additional approval in general meeting of the holding company be sought.

A 'substantial non-cash asset' is defined in CA2006 s.191 as any asset of the company if its value is greater than £5,000 and which is also in excess of 10 per cent of the company's net asset value or £100,000 (whichever is the lower). Transactions exceeding this limit require approval by the shareholders.

The net asset value is determined by reference to the most recent statutory accounts or, if there are none, to the company's aggregate called up share capital.

Transactions not requiring approval

Exemptions for transactions not requiring approval in general meeting include:

- a non-cash asset valued at less than £5,000;
- an arrangement between a wholly owned subsidiary and either the holding company or a fellow wholly owned subsidiary;

- an arrangement where the company is being wound up (except a members' voluntary winding up);
- in circumstances where the director is acquiring the asset in his capacity as a member of the company and not as a director, i.e. issue of shares pursuant to a rights issue.

Whilst such transactions do not require approval of the shareholders by ordinary resolution in general meeting, they must still be approved and formally recorded in the minutes of a meeting of the board of directors.

Disclosure requirements

A transaction approved pursuant to CA2006 s.190 is likely to be 'material' and will require disclosure in the company's audited accounts (CA1985 Sch.6).

The UK Listing Authority normally requires that, other than small transactions, transactions between directors and a listed company are the subject of a circular to shareholders and require prior approval of the shareholders in general meeting (*LR 11.1 and 11 Annex 1*).

Contravention of CA2006 s.190

Where requirements of CA2006 s.190 are contravened and a transaction does not receive the necessary approval, the director or connected person and any other directors who authorised such arrangements or transaction are liable to:

- account to the company for any direct or indirect gain made from the transaction; and
- jointly indemnify the company from any loss or damage resulting from the transaction.

However, where advance approval was not obtained the transaction can be affirmed by members in general meeting within a reasonable period thereafter (CA2006 s.196).

Loans to directors

Prohibitions on a company making loans or financial assistance to directors are imposed by CA2006 ss.197–214.

With specified exceptions, a company may not make loans to its directors or to directors of its holding company nor may it give guarantees or other securities for such loans or enter into credit transactions for the benefit of the director. Although a loan that is outstanding when a person is appointed a director is permitted to continue, any additional amounts of principal or rolled-up interest would come within the prohibitions.

Additional restrictions apply to public companies and companies that are members of a group containing a public company. **Quasi-loans** to directors and loans or quasi-loans to connected persons of directors of such companies are prohibited. A quasi-loan is a transaction under which one party pays a sum for someone else, or agrees to reimburse expenditure incurred by someone else, on the terms that that person will reimburse the person making the payment or where the circumstances give rise to a liability on that person to reimburse the payer.

A director's 'connected persons' are family members as defined in CA2006 s.253 including spouse, civil partner, parents, children or step children but excludes grandparents, grandchildren, siblings, aunts, uncles, nieces and nephews even if they live at the same address. A connected body corporate is defined in CA2006 s.254 as any company of which they have at least 20 per cent control or the trustees or any settlement for the benefit of such persons. The exceptions which apply to a company making loans or quasi-loans to directors or persons connected with them are strictly limited and are as follows:

1. An advance of up to £50,000 may be made to a director to enable them to meet expenditure incurred for the purpose of the company or to enable them to perform their duties properly (CA2006 s.204).
2. Approval is not required where the company meets the expenses in defending an action in connection with an alleged negligence, default or breach of duty or trust provided the amounts are repayable on conviction, judgment being given against the director or being refused relief (CA2006 s.205).
3. Approval is not required where the company meets the expenses in defending an action or investigation brought by a regulatory authority in connection with an alleged negligence, default or breach of duty or trust. The company may not fund the payment of any fines imposed on the director personally (CA2006 s.206).
4. A quasi-loan is permissible provided that the amount concerned does not exceed £10,000 (CA2006 s.207(1)).
5. A credit transaction for an amount not exceeding £15,000 is permitted (CA2006 s.207(2)).
6. A transaction entered into in the ordinary course of the company's business, provided that the value of the transaction and the terms on which it is made are not more favorable than those which would be offered to a person of similar financial status unconnected with the company (CA2006 s.207(3)).
7. Special exemptions apply for loans made by money-lending companies (including banks) in the ordinary course of their business provided the value of the loan and any terms are not different from those imposed on a person not connected with the company but otherwise under similar circumstances (CA2006 s.209).

The provisions prohibiting loans to directors contained in CA2006 are detailed and reference should always be made to the legislation in the Act and, if thought desirable, legal advice taken. In particular, care should be taken if reliance is placed on the exemption relating to advances to enable a director to properly carry out his duties as there is potential for this exemption to be abused.

Interests in shares and debentures

Those performing managerial roles for listed, AIM or PLUS companies are required to notify the company in writing within two business days (*DTR 3.1.2*). The following information must be given:

1. Particulars of the interests which subsisted on the date of their appointment as a director.
2. Details of subsequent acquisitions or disposals of shares specifying the price paid or received.
3. Details of the assignment of any right granted by the company to subscribe for shares or debentures, giving the consideration received. (This will include renunciation of rights for shares or debentures provisionally allotted on a renounceable allotment letter in a rights issue.)
4. Details of the grant by any other company within the group of a right to subscribe for its shares or debentures, the exercise of any such right or the assignment thereof, giving particulars of the consideration received in the case of an assignment.
5. A director is not required to give notice at the time of the original grant of a right to subscribe for shares or debentures or of its exercise since the company will be aware of the details and should enter them in the register of directors' share and debenture interests.
6. The company must inform a Regulatory Information Service or Newstrack of any notification received from its directors or those performing a managerial role. Notification is required to be given no later than the day following the date of notification by the director concerned. Disclosure is also required of interests of connected persons (*DTR 3.1.4*). In addition to notifying the information received by the company, the company must specify the date on which it received the notification.
7. The interests of the spouse of a director (assuming the spouse is not a director in his or her own right) are aggregated with the interests of the director, as are the interests of directors' children under the age of 18 if not themselves directors.

There are a number of exemptions from notification, including:

1. No disclosure is required of interests in shares or debentures of any person in their capacity as trustee or personal representative of any trust or estate of which the Public Trustee is also a trustee (other than as custodian trustee) or a personal representative.
2. No disclosure is required of an interest of a person in their capacity as trustee

or as a beneficiary under a trust relating exclusively to a retirement benefits scheme or similar scheme, provided it is an approved scheme or fund for the purposes of the income tax legislation.

3 Notification need not be made to a company that is the wholly owned subsidiary of a company incorporated outside Great Britain of interests in the shares or debentures of the foreign holding company.

4 Notification need not be made of an interest of a director of a wholly owned subsidiary, who is also a director of its holding company, in the shares and debentures of the holding company and any other group company (being a wholly owned subsidiary), provided that the holding company is itself required to keep a register of directors' share and debenture interests. This exemption simplifies the secretarial administration of groups of companies as directors of subsidiaries are often also directors of the holding company and have interests in the holding company's shares.

If a director has interests (including family interests) in shares or debentures in a variety of different capacities, he may merely disclose the total interest, provided that disclosure is made separately in the various classes of shares or debentures. Alternatively, he may disclose each interest separately, showing the nature and extent of the interest where applicable, and may require the company to record that information in the register of directors' share and debenture interests.

A director has a defence for non-disclosure of any interests of which they may be unaware, for example, if the director is separated from their spouse and is unaware of acquisitions or disposals of shares in the company where the husband or wife is a director.

The Model Code

Listing Rules (*LR 9.2.7*) requires a listed company to adopt rules governing dealings by directors in the listed securities of the company in terms which are not less exacting than those laid down in the UK Listing Authority Model Code which is contained in the *Listing Rules* as Annex 1 to Chapter 9 and reproduced in full in Appendix 5. The Model Code provides that directors must not deal in the securities of the company concerned on considerations of a short-term nature and, in particular, provides that directors may not generally deal in the securities of the company in the two-month period preceding the announcement of the annual results and half-year results. Further, such dealings may not take place prior to the announcement of matters of an exceptional nature which are likely to affect the share price in the stock market.

The Model Code also provides that directors should not deal in the securities of the company at any time without first notifying the chairman (or other director(s) appointed for the purpose) and receiving an acknowledgement. A chairman, wishing to deal, should first notify the board at a board meeting or other director(s) appointed for that purpose and receive acknowledgement.

As part of good company secretarial practice, therefore, the secretary should establish the necessary procedure for recording the receipt of such notifications and issue of acknowledgements.

Any dealings by directors of listed companies in the shares or debentures of the company must be notified immediately to the UK Listing Authority (*DTR 3.1.2*). In addition, the secretary should ensure that a list of any dealings by directors in the securities of the company since the date of the last list is tabled at a board meeting or, alternatively, ensure that the register of directors' share and debenture interests is available for inspection by directors at each board meeting.

Insider dealing

Dealing in shares on a regulated market whilst in possession of price-sensitive information ('**insider dealing**') is a criminal offence. The legislation is contained in Part V of the Criminal Justice Act 1993 (CJA1993).

Three offences were introduced by CJA1993 s.52:

1. Dealing in company securities whilst in the possession of inside information.
2. Encouraging another person to deal whilst in possession of inside information.
3. Disclosing information other than in the proper performance of an office, employment or profession.

The insider must either know that they possess inside information or knowingly acquire inside information from an inside source. It is no longer necessary for the insider to be connected with the particular company; a person can be an insider simply by having access to inside information. Accordingly, the husband or wife of a director could be convicted if using inside information passed on by their spouse, and any friends could also be guilty of an offence if they dealt in shares on the basis of inside information gained directly from the director or indirectly from the spouse or some other third party.

The definition of 'securities' has been expanded and now covers not only shares, debentures and debt securities, but also their derivatives (CJA1993 s.54 and Sch.2). Thus 'securities' includes any asset that can be traded and not just the contract itself.

Similarly, the definition of 'dealing' has been expanded. Although deals of a purely private nature even on the basis of inside information will not normally be covered by the legislation, any transactions on a regulated market (i.e. the Stock Exchange) and any deals undertaken via professional intermediaries whether or not through a regulated market will be covered (CJA1993 s.55).

The inside information must be specific, relate to the company whose securities have been dealt and must not be public knowledge. It must also be shown that if that information were to have been made public, it would have had a significant effect on the price of the securities concerned. There is, unfortunately, no definition or guidance as to the meaning of 'significant' in the legislation (CJA1993 s.56).

The defences against a charge of insider dealing are set out in s.53 of the CJA1993 and include:

1 that the person did not expect the dealing to result in a profit attributable to the information being price-sensitive;
2 that the person had reasonable grounds for believing that the other party to the deal was also in possession of the information;
3 that the person would have dealt irrespective of whether or not they had been in possession of the price-sensitive information. It should be emphasised that the provisions contained in the CJA1993 are lengthy and complex and many companies issue detailed notes of guidance for their directors and senior executives.

The Disclosure Rules

The Disclosure Rules came into force on 1 July 2005, replacing the old rules concerning the publication of price-sensitive information and related matters, and implementing the Market Abuse Directive (2003/6/EC). The Directive introduces a common EU approach for preventing and detecting market abuse and ensuring a proper flow of information to the market.

The primary obligation of listed companies under the Disclosure Rules is to publish 'inside information' that directly concerns them as soon as possible (*DTR 2.2.1*). There is guidance on how companies should identify inside information and apply the tests set out in the statutory definition. Disclosed information must be posted on the company's website by the close of the business day after the announcement is made, and must remain there for at least a year (*DTR 2.3*). A short delay of disclosing inside information will be permissible if an unexpected and significant event occurs and the company needs to clarify the situation.

The Disclosure Rules oblige companies to establish effective arrangements to restrict access to inside information within their own organisations. Companies will be further obliged to draw up a list of persons working for them with access to inside information. Insider lists must be kept for at least five years from the date on which they are drawn up or were last updated and must be delivered to the FSA as soon as possible if requested (*DTR 2.6, 2.8*).

Political donations

Companies may not make a political donation to a political party or other political organisation or incur any political expenditure unless that donation or expenditure has been approved in advance by its members or, in the case of a wholly owned subsidiary, by its holding company (CA2006 s.366) [***see precedent 32***].

Approval is not required where the aggregate amount of political donations and political expenditure does not exceed £5,000 for the 12-month period ending on the date the donation is made or expenditure incurred (CA2006 s.378).

The resolution must specify the maximum amount that may be donated or the maximum amount of expenditure that may be incurred (CA2006 s.367). Unless the resolution specifies an earlier date, the authority has effect for a maximum of four years commencing on the date the resolution is passed (CA2006 s.368).

The directors of the company at the time of any unauthorised donation or expenditure are liable to repay the amount of the unauthorised donation or expenditure and are also liable to compensate the company for any loss or damage incurred (CA2006 s.369).

Where a company has incurred any unauthorised donations or expenditure, members holding at least 5 per cent of the nominal value of the company's issued shares or 50 members may bring an action to enforce repayment of those amounts and any compensation. The costs of the action can be reclaimed by the members from the company only by way of a court order (CA2006 ss.370–372).

Donations and subscriptions to trade unions (other than donations to a trade union's political fund), trade associations, all-party parliamentary groups and groups specified by regulation are exempted as these groups are not political parties or political organisations (CA2006 ss.374–377).

From 1 October 2008 these provisions were extended to include donations and expenditure incurred in relation to independent election candidates.

3 Company secretary

Introduction

The role of the company secretary can encompass all areas of a company's activities, depending on the size and nature of the company and the qualifications and experience of the individual. These activities can be divided into three principal categories.

The board

The company secretary should ensure that proper board procedures are in place and are adhered to and that all relevant papers are circulated to board members in advance of meetings; provide practical support and guidance, particularly to non-executive directors; and monitor and guide the company's corporate governance policies.

The company

The company secretary should ensure the company's compliance with relevant legislation and codes of conduct specific to the company's business activities. The company secretary will often provide a central source of information to the board and senior executives.

The shareholders

The company secretary is often the primary point of contact for shareholders and institutions, particularly in matters related to corporate and environmental governance.

In brief, the company secretary is the person principally concerned with company administration. This chapter outlines the qualifications necessary for acting as a company secretary; how secretaries are appointed, removed or resign; and the range of functions they are generally called upon to fulfil – a list which forms the basis of the following chapters.

The office of company secretary

With effect from 6 April 2008 only public companies are required to appoint a company secretary (CA2006 s.271). Private companies will be able to retain a company secretary and the following provisions apply equally to both private and public companies (CA2006 s.270).

The duties of the company secretary are not specified in detail in the Companies Acts. However, in various sections of the Companies Acts the company secretary is named as one of the people who may sign prescribed forms on behalf of the company, make statutory declarations and sign the annual return. Additionally, the company secretary is recognised as a responsible officer by the Taxes Management Act 1970, the Trade Descriptions Act 1968, the Unsolicited Goods and Services Act 1971 and the Data Protection Act 1998.

The company secretary is an officer of the company as defined by CA2006 ss.1121 and 1173 and consequently may incur personal responsibility for not complying with requirements of the Act affecting the company. A corporate body may, subject to certain restrictions, be appointed company secretary. A partnership may be appointed company secretary in the name of the firm. In England and Wales this has effect as an appointment of all the partners as joint secretaries. In Scotland, where partnerships have corporate status, the firm may be appointed company secretary in its own right. It is also possible to appoint deputy or assistant company secretaries, who may act in the office of company secretary if that office is vacant or there is no company secretary capable of acting (CA2006 s.274).

Following the coming into force of the Limited Liability Partnerships Act 2000, a limited liability partnership (LLP), as a corporate body, whether registered in England and Wales or in Scotland, can be appointed as company secretary.

As well as the statutory requirements, a company's Articles of Association frequently contain provisions with regard to the appointment of the company secretary, as in Table A, reg.99. For those companies incorporated on or after 1 October 2009 who wish to adopt the Model Articles, there are no provisions in relation to the appointment of the company secretary in the Model Articles. However those companies may include specific provisions in relation to the appointment of company secretary in their Articles if they wish to.

Qualification

The company secretary of a private company need have no professional or other qualification, or have any previous experience. In the case of a public company, CA2006 s.273 provides that the directors must take all reasonable steps to ensure that the company secretary is a person who appears to have the knowledge and experience necessary to discharge the functions of company secretary of the company and who also meets other requirements laid down in CA2006 s.273.

Other persons qualified to be company secretary of a public company under these provisions include:

1 a barrister, advocate or solicitor, called or admitted in any part of the UK;

2 a member of various professional bodies, including the ICSA, and members of various accountancy bodies in England and Wales, Scotland and Ireland;
3 a person who is a member of any other professional body who appears to the directors to be capable of discharging the functions of the company secretary;
4 a person who, for at least three of the five years immediately preceding his appointment as company secretary, held the office of company secretary of another public company.

Prohibited appointees

The auditor of a company and any employee of the auditor may not be appointed as company secretary (CA2006 s.1214).

The sole director of a company is no longer prohibited from being appointed as its company secretary. However there is little to be gained in practice from doing so as any documents requiring signature by a sole director and the company secretary cannot be signed by the same person acting in both capacities.(CA2006 s.280). Accordingly, while it is now possible for a private company to have one person as sole director and shareholder, it is still necessary for another person to be appointed either as company secretary or as an authorised signatory to execute certain documents.

Appointment

On incorporation of a new company, the person named as company secretary on Form IN01 is deemed to have been appointed as the first company secretary of the company (CA2006 ss.12 and 16). Form IN01 is delivered to the Registrar of Companies for registration, together with the Memorandum and Articles of Association of the company. Subsequent appointments are made by the directors in accordance with the provisions of the Articles of Association. [***See precedent 33.***] The following action should be taken:

1 At a meeting of the directors or by written resolution the directors must resolve to appoint a new company secretary. Where the new appointment is to replace an incumbent company secretary rather than to fill a vacancy, the resolution will also include the replacement of the previous company secretary be it by way of resignation, retirement, removal or another cause.
2 The particulars relating to the new company secretary must be entered in the company's register of directors and secretaries and notified to the Registrar of Companies on Form AP03 (Appointment of Secretary) or Form AP04 (Appointment of Corporate Secretary) within 14 days of the appointment (CA2006 s.276). The form can be filed either in paper form or electronically. See Chapter 14.
3 If the company secretary is an authorised signatory of the company's bank account, notification of the change of company secretary and a copy of his

signature should be sent to the bank, together with any additional verification of identity documents required by the bank.

4 If thought appropriate, announcement of the new appointment should be made to the company's staff, suppliers and customers.
5 A formal service contract should be drawn up for signature by the company and by the company secretary.
6 If the company has an insurance policy covering officers of the company against the liabilities that they may incur in carrying out their duties, the insurance company should be notified, usually at renewal, of the appointment of the new company secretary.
7 In the case of a traded company, the company secretary should be supplied with the company's rules governing transactions in its securities, which should comply with the terms of the Model Code (*LR annex 1 to chapter 9*), or AIM Rule 21 as appropriate.

Assistant and joint company secretaries

The directors may appoint an assistant or deputy company secretary (CA2006 s.274). This person may be appointed and removed by resolution of the directors subject to any provisions contained in the company's Articles of Association. There is no requirement for the appointment to be notified to the Registrar of Companies.

Rather than an assistant or deputy company secretary, some companies may wish to appoint one or more joint company secretaries. Details of any joint company secretaries must be notified to the Registrar of Companies (CA2006 s.276). Appointment or removal of a joint company secretary is carried out in the same way as for a sole company secretary and will be by resolution of the directors. [***See precedent* 33.**]

Resignation and removal

Subject to any service contract in force, the company secretary may resign by notice in writing to the board. [***See precedent* 34.**] The board may remove the company secretary and replace that person by simple majority. [***See precedent* 35.**] Any termination will be subject to the terms of any service contract and removal of an individual from the office of company secretary need not necessarily also require termination of employment.

Whether the company secretary has resigned or been removed from office the following procedures should be followed:

1 In the case of a removal, the directors must approve a resolution to remove the company secretary, either at a meeting or by written resolution.
2 The fact of the resignation or removal of the company secretary must be entered in the company's register of directors and secretaries and notified to

the Registrar of Companies on Form TM02 within 14 days of the resignation or removal. The form can be filed either in paper form or electronically. See Chapter 14.

3 If the company secretary is an authorised signatory on the company's bank account, notification of the change in company secretary should be given to the bank.
4 A new company secretary must be appointed as soon as practical and the procedure on appointment outlined above should be followed.

Changes of particulars

Under CA2006, the register of directors and secretaries kept by a company will be treated as two separate registers, in accordance with s.162 and s.275 respectively. The company has a duty to notify the Registrar of any changes in the particulars that take place on or after 1 October 2009 under CA2006 s.276; the provisions under CA1985 continue to apply in relation to a change occurring before that date.

For an existing company, the relevant existing address of a company secretary is deemed to be a service address after 1 October 2009. Any entry in the register of secretaries after that date must comply with the requirement in CA2006 s.277(1)(b) to state a service address. Any notification of the change of relevant existing address occurring before 1 October 2009 but received by the company on or after that date is treated as being notification of a change of service address under s.276 of the CA2006.

Company secretarial duties

None of the Companies Acts, Table A nor most Articles of Association specifically define the powers of a company secretary. As a consequence, the position has been considered by the courts at various times. In the nineteenth century the company secretary was considered as a servant or clerk exercising little authority, but in 1971 the Court of Appeal decided that the company secretary is the chief administrative officer of the company and, with regard to matters affecting the administration of the company, has ostensible authority to make contracts on behalf of the company (*Panorama Developments (Guildford) v Fidelis Furnishing Fabrics* [1971] 2 QB 711, CA). Although matters falling within this administrative function are not explicitly set out or defined, this authority will often extend to the employment of staff, the company's premises, data processing and other office machinery, printing and stationery requirements, and the acquisition, maintenance and sale of company vehicles. If the company secretary is responsible for data processing, their responsibilities will be governed by the Data Protection Act 1998, especially if they are the person appointed Data Protection Coordinator for the company. However, without express authority, the company secretary's responsibilities will not extend to negotiating trading contracts, e.g. sale or purchase of goods and materials or production machinery, which are matters affecting the company's business operations and will, in most cases, be the responsibility of other managers. In many companies the company secretary may be the appropriate person and be authorised to sign contracts relating to such matters on behalf of the company.

If a company secretary acts beyond his authority, whether express or ostensible, the company will be bound by such acts, but the company secretary may be held liable by the company for any loss incurred as a result.

Core duties

The Company Secretaries Group of the ICSA considered the duties of the company secretary and has published a guide distinguishing between the core duties which all company secretaries should perform and those additional duties they may be called upon to undertake, as set out below.

Board meetings

Coordinating the operation of the company's formal decision-making and reporting machinery; formulating meeting agendas with the chairman and/or chief executive; attending and minuting meetings; maintaining minute books; certifying copies of minutes; and ensuring that correct procedures are followed. (***See Chapter 2.***)

General meetings

Originating and obtaining internal and external agreement to all documentation for circulation to shareholders; coordinating the administration and minuting of meetings; and ensuring that correct procedures are followed. (***See Chapter 9.***)

Articles of Association

Ensuring that the company complies with its Articles of Association; drafting and incorporating amendments in accordance with correct procedures. (***See Chapter 1.***)

General compliance

Monitoring and ensuring compliance with relevant legal requirements, particularly under the Companies Acts. (***See Chapter 14.***)

UKLA, AIM and PLUS requirements

Monitoring and ensuring compliance with the *Listing Rules* and *Disclosure and Transparency Rules, AIM Rules* and *PLUS Rules*; managing relations with the UK Listing Authority, Stock Exchange or PLUS Market through the company's advisers; releasing information to the market; ensuring the security of unreleased, price-sensitive information; and making applications for listing and admission of additional issues of securities. (***See Chapters 15, 16 and 18.***)

Statutory registers

Maintaining the following statutory registers:

- members (see also Share Registration below) – s.114;
- company charges – ss.877 and 892;
- directors – s.162;
- secretaries – s.265;
- debenture holders (if applicable) – s.743; etc.

(See Chapter 12.)

Statutory returns

Filing information with the Registrar of Companies to report certain changes regarding the company or to comply with requirements for periodic filing. Of particular importance in this regard are:

- annual returns;
- report and accounts;
- amended Articles of Association;
- returns of allotments;
- notices of appointment, removal and resignation of directors and the secretary;
- notices of removal or resignation of the auditors;
- change of registered office.

(See Chapter 14.)

Report and accounts

Coordinating the publication and distribution of the company's annual report and accounts and interim statements in consultation with the company's internal and external advisers and, in particular, preparing the directors' report. (***See Chapters 10 and 11.***)

Share registration

Maintaining the company's register of members; dealing with transfers and other matters affecting shareholdings; and dealing with queries and requests from shareholders. (***See Chapter 8.***)

Shareholder communications

Communicating with the shareholders (e.g. through circulars); payment of dividends and interest; issuing documentation regarding rights issues and capitalisation issues; general shareholder relations; and relations with institutional shareholders and their investment protection committees. (***See Chapter 16.***)

Shareholder monitoring

Monitoring movements on the register of members to identify any apparent 'stake building' in the company's shares by potential takeover bidders; and making inquiries of members as to beneficial ownership of holdings.

Share and capital issues and restructuring

Implementing changes in the structure of the company's share and loan capital and devising, implementing and administering directors' and employees' share participation schemes. (***See Chapter 4.***)

Acquisitions and disposals

Participating as a key member of the company team established to implement corporate acquisitions and disposals; protecting the company's interests by ensuring the effectiveness of all documentation and that due diligence disclosures enable proper commercial evaluation prior to completion of a transaction. (***See Chapter 17.***)

Corporate governance

Reviewing developments in corporate governance and advising and assisting the directors with respect to their duties and responsibilities in order to ensure compliance with their personal obligations under company law and, if applicable, stock exchange requirements. (***See Chapter 18.***)

Non-executive directors

Acting as a channel of communication and information for non-executive directors. (***See Chapter 2.***)

Company seal

If the company has a company seal, ensuring its safe custody and proper use.

Registered office

Establishment and administration of the registered office; receipt, coordination and distribution of official correspondence received by the company at its registered office; and ensuring the provision of facilities for the public inspection of documents.

Subsidiary companies

The administration of subsidiary companies; implementing changes to, and maintaining a record of, the group's structure.

4

Share capital, debentures and loan stock

Introduction

A company is owned by its shareholders. Companies without a share capital will have some other method of determining ownership, but the overwhelming majority of companies have a share capital consisting of one or more classes of shares.

Authorised capital

The Companies Act 2006 abolished the requirement for new companies to have an authorised share capital with effect from 1 October 2009. On application for registration of a new company which has a share capital, a statement of capital and initial shareholdings must be submitted to the Registrar of Companies. The information which must be contained in the statement of capital includes: the total number of shares to be taken on incorporation by the subscribers to the memorandum; the aggregate nominal value of those shares; for each class of shares, the rights attached to those shares, the total number of shares in that class and the aggregate nominal value of the shares of that class; and the amount to be paid up and the amount to be unpaid on each share.

For existing companies, authorised share capital will continue to act as a ceiling on the number of shares that can be allotted and will be considered as a restriction in the articles of association of the company. If the company wishes to allot shares beyond this ceiling the shareholders will be able to remove the deemed restriction by ordinary resolution, rather than by special resolution which would normally be required to amend the articles of association. [***See precedent 36.***]

Issued capital

Issued capital is the total capital which has been issued and taken up by the members of the company, after it has been issued for cash or for a consideration other than cash, and is expressed by reference to the aggregate nominal value of the shares issued. Accordingly, a company which issues 250 shares of £1.00 each has an issued share capital of £250. Provided there are no restrictions in the

Articles of Association, a company can increase its issued share capital by allotting new shares.

Paid-up capital

Paid-up capital refers to the nominal amounts that have been paid up on the company's issued capital. For example, if a company has 500 shares of 50p each in issue, then the issued capital is £250. If they are fully paid, the paid-up share capital will be £250. However if the shares are issued only partly paid, for example 25p paid up on each share, with the balance due at some point in the future, the paid-up capital will be £125.

Changes to capital

Chapter 8 of Part 17 of CA2006 sets out the provisions relating to the alteration of share capital. Section 617 provides that a limited company with a share capital may not alter its share capital except as provided in Parts 17 and 18 of CA2006. Companies may still, however, make the same types of alterations to share capital as under CA1985, although significant changes to procedures have been made.

Under Parts 17 and 18 of CA2006 a company may:

- increase its share capital by allotting new shares;
- subdivide or consolidate all or any of its share capital;
- reconvert stock into shares;
- redeem shares;
- purchase its own shares;
- redenominate its share capital;
- cancel its shares (duty to cancel shares held by or for a public company);
- reduce its share capital.

No other alterations are permitted.

One alteration that may be requested by directors, but not permitted, is the conversion of non-redeemable shares into **redeemable shares**. There is no power under the Companies Act to convert non-redeemable shares into redeemable shares. Furthermore, CA2006 s.684 states that a company may issue shares that are, or are liable to be, redeemed. It can be seen that shares can only be issued as redeemable, and not converted to be redeemable after issue. This problem can usually be overcome by undertaking a purchase of own shares by the company and by the shareholder(s) making application for the issue of redeemable shares and using the consideration monies to effect the purchase. It is also worth noting that a private company need no longer be authorised by its articles to allot redeemable shares although the articles can restrict or exclude their issue. A public company wishing to allot redeemable shares will still need to be authorised to do so by its Articles of Association.

The 2006 Act removes the requirement for prior authorisation in the company's articles in relation to the following alterations of capital:

- reduction of share capital;
- subdivision and consolidation of share capital;
- redemption of shares;
- share buybacks;
- reconversion of stock into shares.

A company will be authorised to pass resolutions to effect the above alterations to its share capital unless it is specifically restricted by its Articles of Association.

Authorised capital

As stated above, CA2006 abolishes the requirement for new companies to have an authorised share capital with effect from 1 October 2009. Under CA2006 s.617(2)(a) a company may increase its share capital by allotting new shares. Shareholders wishing to restrict the number of shares that can be issued in the company will need to amend the Articles of Association by special resolution to include suitable provisions, if the Articles do not already contain such restrictions. [***See precedents 11 and 37.***]

For companies existing before 1 October 2009, authorised share capital will continue to operate as a restriction in the company's Articles of Association. Any company wishing to allot shares beyond this ceiling will need shareholder approval to remove the restriction from the company's Articles, although this can be done by ordinary resolution rather than special resolution.

Consolidation of shares

The Companies Act 2006 removes the requirement for a company's Articles of Association to permit the consolidation of shares, but the Articles may restrict or exclude the exercise of such power under CA2006 s.618. Consolidation means that the shares of the company will be divided into shares of a larger nominal value, e.g. five shares of 10p each would be consolidated into one share of 50p.

Consolidation does not often arise, but if a company has issued a large number of ordinary shares which are below the normal denominations of 25p, 50p or £1, it might be convenient to consolidate the shares. However, there are many companies with shares having a nominal value of 5p or 10p. Subject to the company's Articles of Association the share capital may be consolidated by ordinary resolution using the following procedure:

1 The directors, at a board meeting, resolve to recommend the proposed consolidation of share capital, authorise the issue of a notice convening a general meeting to pass the resolution required and to approve a circular for issue to members explaining the reasons for the consolidation [***see precedents 2, 4, 5 and 38***]. Instead of convening a separate general meeting, it may be possible

for a public company to include the resolution as special business at the company's next annual general meeting, if the timing is convenient.

In addition to the normal requirements for listed, AIM and PLUS companies to submit copies of notices, proxy forms and circulars to the UK Listing Authority, in the case of a listed company (*LR 9.6.1, 9.6.2*), the London Stock Exchange for AIM companies (AIM rule 20) and PLUS in the case of PLUS companies (PLUS rule 30) no later than their issue to shareholders, when changes to the listed company's share capital are proposed, a Regulatory Information Service must be notified without delay (*LR 9.6.4*).

2 When the resolution to consolidate the specified shares has been passed by the members, the company must within one month give notice to the Registrar, specifying the shares affected. It is not necessary to file a copy of the resolution if it is an ordinary resolution.

3 The notice must be accompanied by a statement of capital which must state, with respect to the company's share capital immediately following the passing of the resolution:
(a) the total number of shares of the company;
(b) the aggregate nominal value of those shares;
(c) for each class of shares –
– prescribed particulars of the rights attached to the shares;
– the total number of shares of that class; and
– the aggregate nominal value of shares of that class; and
– the amount paid up and the amount (if any) unpaid on each share (whether on account of the nominal value of the share or by way of premium).

In the case of a listed company, two copies of the resolution should be sent to the UK Listing Authority (*LR 9.6.2*).

4 The register of members will need to be updated to show the holdings of each member in the new nominal value. Some holdings of members will not consolidate into an exact number of new shares, and those members will 'lose' that fraction of their holding. In a listed company, the directors will aggregate and sell all these fractional shares on the market and distribute the proceeds to the appropriate member(s), subject to a minimum amount of, say, £3. Any proceeds amounting to less than this would be retained by the company.

In the case of listed companies, it is necessary to apply to the UK Listing Authority for the listing to be amended, whilst AIM and PLUS companies will need to amend their admission particulars with the London Stock Exchange or PLUS, as appropriate. In each case it will also be necessary to coordinate the change with Euroclear UK and Ireland Ltd relating to the maintenance of the electronic sub-register (CREST).

Share certificates may be called in for amendment, but it is more usual to send members a notice that the consolidation has taken place, and enclosing a new share certificate, all existing certificates being cancelled.

Subdivision of shares

The Companies Act 2006 removes the requirement for a company's Articles of Association to permit the subdivision of shares, but the Articles may restrict or exclude the exercise of such power under CA2006 s.618. Subject to provision in the Articles, an ordinary resolution of the company in general meeting may be passed subdividing the company's shares into shares of a smaller nominal amount to make them more marketable. This process is also referred to as splitting shares. For example, if the company has £1 shares quoted on the market at £10 each, these could be subdivided into four shares of 25p each, which would then carry a market value of just 250p each. If the shares are partly paid, the proportion between the amount paid and unpaid would remain as before.

The procedure for subdividing shares is similar to that for the consolidation described above, except that fractions of shares cannot arise. [***See precedents 2, 4, 5 and 39.***] Notice must be sent to the Registrar of Companies within one month of the passing of the resolution, along with a statement of capital.

Following a subdivision, the register of members will have to be rewritten to show the number of shares held in the new nominal value by each member.

In the case of listed companies, it is necessary to apply to the UK Listing Authority for the listing to be amended, whilst AIM and PLUS companies will need to amend their admission particulars with the London Stock Exchange or PLUS as appropriate. In each case it will also be necessary to co-ordinate the change with Euroclear UK and Ireland Ltd (EUI) relating to the maintenance of the electronic sub-register (CREST).

Share certificates may be called in for amendment, but it is more usual to send members a notice that the consolidation has taken place and enclosing a new share certificate, all existing certificates being cancelled.

Conversion of shares into stock

The Companies Act 2006 abolishes the power to convert shares into stock.

Reconversion of stock into shares

The Companies Act 2006 allows the reconversion of existing stock back into paid-up shares of any nominal value by means of ordinary resolution (CA2006 s.620) [***see precedent 40***]. The 2006 Act omits the requirement that the company's Articles of Association must permit the reconversion.

If a company exercises its powers to reconvert stock into shares, it must give notice to the registrar within one month, specifying the stock affected. The notice must be accompanied by a statement of capital (see **Consolidation of shares** for details of what this should include).

Duty to cancel shares (public companies only)

Section 662 of the Companies Act 2006 applies in the case of a public company:

(a) where shares in the company are forfeited, or surrendered to the company in lieu of forfeiture, in pursuance of the articles, for failure to pay any sum payable in respect of the shares;
(b) where any shares in the company are surrendered to the company in pursuance of s.102C(1)(b) of the Building Societies Act 1986;
(c) where shares in the in the company are acquired by it and the company has a beneficial interest in the shares;
(d) where a nominee of the company acquires shares in the company from a third party without financial assistance being given directly or indirectly by the company and the company has a beneficial interest in the shares; or
(e) where a person acquires shares in the company, with financial assistance given to him, directly or indirectly, by a company for the purpose of or in connection with the acquisition, and the company has a beneficial interest in the shares.

Unless the shares or any interest of the company in them are previously disposed of, the company must cancel the shares and reduce the amount of the company's issued share capital by the nominal value of the shares cancelled [***see precedent 41***]. Where the nominal value of the company's allotted share capital is brought below the authorised minimum, it must apply for re-registration as a private company, stating the effect of the cancellation. The company must cancel the shares and apply for re-registration (if applicable) no later than three years from the date of forfeiture, or surrender in relation to points (a) and (b), no later than three years from the date of acquisition in respect of points (c) and (d) and no later than one year from the date of acquisition in relation to point (e).

The company must, within one month of cancellation, give notice to the Registrar, specifying the shares cancelled. The notice must be accompanied by a statement of capital (see **Consolidation of shares** for details of what this should include).

Reduction of share capital

Under CA2006 s.641, a limited company having a share capital may reduce its capital:

- in the case of a private company, by special resolution supported by a solvency statement (CA2006 ss.642 to 644);
- in any case, by a special resolution confirmed by the Court (CA2006 ss.645 to 651).

A specific authorisation in a company's Articles of Association to reduce its share capital is not required. A company will be permitted to reduce its capital unless there is a specific prohibition or restriction in the Articles. The following examples of undertaking a reduction are given in CA2006 s.641(4):

1 Extinguish or reduce the liability on any of its shares in respect of share capital not paid up.
2 Either with or without extinguishing or reducing liability on any of its shares:
   (a) cancel any paid-up share capital which is lost or unrepresented by available assets, or
   (b) repay any paid-up share capital in excess of the company's wants.

The secretarial procedures are similar to those used in a consolidation of shares with an appropriately worded resolution [***see precedent 42***]. The company secretary will be required to give an affidavit confirming that the necessary procedures have been followed. Accordingly, the date of issue of the notice, date and timing of meeting should be carefully recorded. Careful attention should be paid to procedural matters at the meeting to ensure that the proceedings cannot be challenged later. If the reduction is being undertaken for the reasons stated in 2(a) above and the company's share capital is divided into different classes, great care must be taken when deciding which class, if not all, should bear the reduction. Whilst it may appear reasonable for **preference shares** with a limited right to participate in future profit to bear the reduction, leaving ordinary shares untouched, this is not necessarily the case. In a liquidation it is the ordinary shares that rank last rather than the preference shares. It may therefore be 'reasonable' for any loss in value of assets to be borne by the ordinary shares as if in a liquidation.

Where a public company, or a private company not following the solvency statement route, has approved a resolution reducing its share capital, application to the Court must be made for an order confirming the reduction (CA2006 s.645).

If the proposed reduction includes the diminution of any liability on unpaid share capital or the payment to a shareholder of any paid-up share capital or if directed by the Court, any creditor of the company with an admissible claim in winding-up proceedings may object to the proposed reduction. The Court will settle a list of creditors entitled to object. This list, depending on the particular circumstances, may be published. After publication, any other creditor may apply to be added to or removed from the list. Normally, the company will discharge or make provision for the **debt**. If, however, the debt in whole or in part is disrupted or the company is unwilling to make a provision, the Court has power to appropriate such funds as it thinks fit to meet such claims as if the company were being wound up by the Court.

When the Court is satisfied with the arrangements to protect the interests of the creditors and, if relevant, the members, the Court will make an order confirming the reduction either as proposed or with any modifications deemed fit.

Where the Court confirms the reduction, it may order the company to publish the reasons for the reduction of capital or it may require the company to add the words 'and reduced' after its name for a specified period (CA2006 ss.648(3) and

(4)). The Registrar, on production of an order of court confirming the reduction of capital and the delivery of a copy of the order and a statement of capital (approved by the Court) will register the order and the statement. The statement of capital must state with respect to the company's share capital as altered by the order:

1 the total number of shares of the company;
2 the aggregate nominal value of those shares;
3 for each class of shares:
   (a) prescribed particulars of the rights attached to the shares;
   (b) the total number of shares of that class; and
   (c) the aggregate nominal value of shares of that class; and
   (d) the amount paid up and the amount (if any) unpaid on each share (whether on account of the nominal value of the share or by way of premium).

The resolution for reducing share capital, as confirmed by the court order, takes effect:

(a) in the case of a reduction that forms part of a compromise or arrangement sanctioned by the Court:
   - on delivery of the order and statement of capital to the registrar; or
   - if the Court so orders, on the registration of the order and statement of capital;
(b) in any other case, on the registration of the order and statement of capital.

When the reduction takes place the Registrar issues a certificate of registration in respect of the order and statement of capital. The certificate is conclusive evidence that the provisions of the Companies Act 2006 have been complied with and that the company's share capital is as stated in the statement of capital.

Where a public company proposes a reduction of share capital that will cause its issued share capital to fall below the authorised minimum (£50,000), the Registrar will not register the order unless directed to do so by the Court or unless the company re-registers as a private company (see pp. 20–22). The Court may authorise the company to be re-registered as a private company without a special resolution of the members having to be passed. If it does the Court must specify in the order the changes to the company's name and Articles to be made in connection with its re-registration. The company can then be re-registered as a private company if an application to that effect is delivered to the registrar along with a copy of the Court's order, notice of the company's name and a copy of the Articles of Association as altered by the court order. A re-registration fee is also payable (currently £20, or same-day fee £50).

Private company reducing share capital under CA2006

A new procedure has been introduced by the Companies Act 2006 under which private companies can reduce their share capital without the requirement to obtain a court order.

CA2006 s.642 provides for private companies to reduce their share capital by special resolution of the members provided the resolution is supported by a solvency statement.

The solvency statement must be declared by the directors not more than 15 days prior to the date of the resolution and this must be registered at Companies House within 15 days together with a statement of revised capital and the special resolution of the members (CA2006 s.644).

The solvency statement requires each director to confirm that in their opinion there are no grounds at the date of the statement that the company could not meets its debts and that during the period of 12 months following the statement the company will be able to pay its debts as they fall due.

Effect of alterations of capital on voting rights

At the time an alteration of capital is made, the effect that it might have on the existing voting rights of shareholders should be taken into account, so that, if appropriate, suitable action may be taken to keep the voting rights between the different classes of shares in the same proportion that applied prior to the alteration. It may be necessary to hold meetings to obtain the consent of each class of shareholder [***see precedent 43***]. If the voting or other rights of different classes are being changed, it will be necessary to hold separate class meetings of the affected classes in addition to the general meeting. This is so even if any particular class has no vote at general meetings. **Class rights** cannot be changed without approval of the class members whose rights are being changed.

Serious loss of capital

There is one other provision to be noted in connection with the capital of a public company. If the net assets of a public company become equal to one half or less of its called-up share capital, the directors must convene a general meeting of the company (CA2006 s.656) [***see precedent 44***]. The notices must be issued within 28 days of the deficiency becoming known. The purpose of the meeting is to allow shareholders to consider what measures should be taken to deal with the situation. There is no requirement for a resolution to be put to the meeting, merely that the meeting be convened.

Because CA2006 s.656 stipulates that the directors must convene a general meeting it is not possible for the resolution to be added to the business of an annual general meeting. However, it would be possible to convene a general meeting to be held at the conclusion of the annual general meeting.

Shares and stock

References to shares should also be taken as including references to stock, unless inappropriate in the context. The Companies Act 2006 abolishes the power to convert shares into stock, but allows the re-conversion of existing stock back into paid-up shares of any nominal value by means of ordinary resolution (CA2006 s.620).

Share premiums

A share premium is the amount of the issue price of a share in excess of its nominal value, e.g. in the case of a 50p share issued for £1.60, 50p is the nominal value and £1.10 is the premium. In a statement of a company's share capital only the nominal amount of the shares is included. The amount of any share premium must be credited to a share premium account (CA2006 s.610). This is a special form of capital reserve which can be used only for paying up unissued shares to be offered to members as fully-paid shares and for certain other purposes stated in CA2006 s.610. However, the share premium account is treated as part of the company's paid-up share capital and provisions applicable to the reduction of capital apply to this account (CA2006 s.610).

It should be noted, however, that CA2006 ss.611 and 612 provide for a number of exemptions from the strict application of CA2006 s.610 following a merger or reconstruction where this is effected by an exchange of shares, and the company issuing its shares in exchange for shares in the other company issues its shares at a premium.

Where two companies merge and the acquiring company purchases the shares of the second company in consideration of the issue of fully paid shares, relief from CA2006 s.610 is given by CA2006 s.612, provided at least 90 per cent of the target company's shares are acquired. Relief from CA2006 s.610 applies also to the issue of consideration shares for non-equity shares of the target acquired at the same time as the equity shares, whether the consideration is effected by the issue of new shares in the acquiring company or by the cancellation of shares in the target company not held by the acquiring company. For the purposes of this section, the 90 per cent holding may include shares held before the transaction took place and shares held by the acquiring company's holding company or any subsidiary or any fellow subsidiary of its holding company.

Where a group reconstruction is being undertaken, relief from CA2006 s.610 is given by CA2006 s.611 when the issuing company is a wholly owned subsidiary and allots shares to its holding company or a fellow subsidiary in exchange for the transfer of non-cash assets, provided the transferor company is a member of the same group. For the purposes of this section, the group means the holding company and any wholly owned subsidiaries.

The value of the premium on which relief has been given by CA2006 ss.611 or 612 is disregarded for the purposes of valuing the consideration shares in the company's balance sheet (CA2006 s.615).

Classes of shares

The Articles of Association will set out the division of shares into different classes, with the respective rights of each of the classes being stated. The most common classes into which shares of a company may be divided are as follows:

1 *Ordinary shares* which rank after the preference shares as regards dividends and return of capital but carry voting rights not normally given to holders of preference shares unless their preferential dividend is in arrears. These shares constitute the company's 'risk capital', i.e. each year the directors declare a dividend to be paid on the ordinary shares out of the profits of the company. If the company does well, the dividends will be good and increase year by year; but if the company does badly, the dividends may be reduced or even, in a very bad year, omitted entirely. The word 'ordinary' is commonly omitted from the description of the shares in the Articles of Association where a company only has one class of shares in issue. In some companies the risk capital is called 'deferred shares' or 'deferred stock'.
2 *Ordinary shares which are non-voting shares*, usually distinguished from the voting shares by calling them 'A' shares. Some companies have classes of ordinary shares which have restricted voting rights. In both cases, however, the shares otherwise have similar rights to those of the other ordinary shares as in 1 above.
3 *Preference shares*, which carry a preferential right to a fixed rate of dividend and, on a winding up, to return of capital with or without a premium, together with arrears of dividend. They constitute part of the company's share capital and repayment of capital on preference shares would rank ahead of repayment of capital on the ordinary shares (or the deferred shares or deferred stock) in a liquidation. The fixed rate of dividend is expressed as a percentage. Holders of preference shares get the same rate of dividend year in and year out, unless in any year the profits of the company are insufficient to pay the preference dividends, which, of course, take priority over payment of dividends on the ordinary shares.
4 *Cumulative preference shares*, which provide that if in any year the profits of the company are insufficient to pay the dividend on the preference shares the dividends not paid will be paid in subsequent years, together with the previous year's (or years') dividend(s), when the company's fortunes improve. The payment of such arrears would rank ahead of payment of dividends on the ordinary shares.
5 *Redeemable preference shares* or *cumulative redeemable preference shares*, which will be redeemed by the company at their nominal or par value (i.e. the face value) at some stated date in the future. The amount of the repayment, however, is the actual nominal value of the shares, e.g. £1 preference shares would be redeemed at £1 per share notwithstanding that the market value of the shares might be higher or lower than this amount.

6 *Debentures and loan stocks*, which are in effect loans to the company by investors who receive a fixed rate of interest on the debenture or loan stock. They are mentioned here, although they are not a class of share, since they are frequently met with when considering a company's financial structure. Generally, debentures are secured loans on the assets of the company, whereas loan stocks are normally unsecured.

Payment of the interest on debentures and loan stocks ranks ahead of the payment of preference dividends and ordinary dividends. They would also rank ahead of preference and ordinary shares in repayment of capital in a liquidation. It should be noted, however, that debentures and loan stocks do not form part of the company's capital, although quite often they are colloquially referred to as 'loan capital'. The company's capital is confined to the company's share capital, which includes preference shares as well as ordinary shares.

Rights attaching to a class of shares

The rights attaching to all shares will be stated in the Articles of Association. The most common rights differentiating one class from another are as follows:

1 *Right to vote*: the right to attend and vote at meetings may be restricted or enhanced.
2 *Right to receive dividend*: the right can be to a preferential dividend, whether fixed or not, or can be that dividends may be declared on any individual class or all, at the directors' discretion, or that a particular class has no right to dividend.
3 *Right to capital on a winding-up or a return of capital*: the right to capital is often linked to the right to dividend. A class of shares with enhanced dividend rights may have restricted rights to any further benefit in an increase in asset value of the company. The right will vary from the right to the return of the amount paid up on each share to full participation in the retained profit.
4 *The right of pre-emption on transfer and allotment*: these rights will affect the shareholders' ability to realise their investment and their protection from dilution in the event of an issue of shares of the same class.
5 *Right of redemption*: normally given to shares carrying enhanced dividend rights but no right to capital, redemption rights allow investors to realise their investment at a predetermined date or following a stipulated formula.
6 *Right to conversion, normally to ordinary shares*: like redemption rights, rights to conversion are usually given to shares carrying enhanced dividend rights but no other rights, enabling realisation at some future time.

A company can create classes of shares with as many or few rights as it wishes. The rights will often depend on the investor where new capital is being invested to enable an existing business to expand. Although the majority of rights attaching to shares can be altered whether the shares have been issued or not, it is not possible to convert issued shares which were not redeemable into redeemable shares.

Variation of rights

The Companies Act 2006 provides that the rights attached to a class of shares or members shall be varied in accordance with the provisions of the company's Articles of Association, or if the company's Articles do not make provision for the variation of class rights, in accordance with the provisions of Chapter 9 of Part 17 of the Act. This allows a company to specify less demanding procedures for varying class rights in its Articles of Association.

Section 630 provides that class rights may only be varied by either the written consent of the holders of at least three-quarters in nominal value of the issued shares of the relevant class, or a special resolution passed by the holders of that class sanctions the variation [***see precedent 43***]. Where the company's Articles impose a higher threshold for consent to the variation of class rights, the company must comply with the more onerous regime. Section 631 provides that for companies without a share capital consent in writing from at least three-quarters of the members of that class or a special resolution passed at a separate general meeting of the members of that class sanctioning the variation will be required to vary class rights.

Holders of not less in the aggregate of 15 per cent of the issued shares of a class (or 15 per cent of the members of a class in the case of a company without a share capital) who did not consent to, or vote in favour of, the variation may apply to the Court for it to be cancelled within 21 days of the resolution consenting to the variation being passed. In this case the variation will not take effect until it is confirmed by the Court. The application may be made by one or more of these shareholders (or members) on behalf of those entitled to make the application. The Court will disallow the variation if it is satisfied that the variation would unfairly prejudice the holders (or members) concerned; otherwise, the Court will confirm the alteration (CA2006 ss.633 and 634). A copy of the court order must be filed with the Registrar within 15 days of it being made.

Companies creating new classes of shares or members, or varying the rights of existing classes of shares or members, are required to notify the Registrar of the particulars of the rights created or affected within one month of the date of variation (CA2006 ss.636 to 640).

Membership

The subscribers to the Memorandum of Association are deemed to have agreed to become members of the company and, on registration of the company, their names should be entered in the register of members. A person may subsequently become a member by applying for new shares or by the transfer or transmission to him of shares already in issue and the entry of his name in the register of members.

Two criteria must be met to become a member: first, the person must agree to be a member; and second, they must be entered as a member in the register of members (CA2006 s.112). Both requirements must be met before a person is regarded as a member of the company.

Single-member companies

A company need have only one shareholder. Public companies are required to issue at least £50,000 in nominal value of shares with each share at least 25 per cent paid up as to its nominal value and 100 per cent of any premium before commencing to trade and to maintain this minimum capital at all times. The Companies (Single Member Private Limited Companies) Regulations 1992, SI 1992/1699 reduced the minimum number of shareholders required for a private limited company from two to one. The Companies Act 2006 dropped the requirement for a public company to have at least two members with effect from 1 October 2007. Any company incorporated prior to the coming into effect of these provisions may need to amend their Articles of Association if they specifically state that the company must have two or more shareholders. Any rule of law requiring a private company to have two members has been modified by the statutory instrument.

Any sole shareholder may also be a sole director of a private company. Any company reducing its membership to one must, when updating the register of members, add a note stating that the company has only one member and the date on which the change occurred (CA2006 s.123). If a company with only one member increases its membership, a note should be added to the register of members stating this fact, together with the date on which the change occurred (CA2006 s.123).

CA2006 s.318 provides that for a single member company, notwithstanding any provision in a company's Articles, one member present by person or by proxy shall constitute a valid quorum. Additionally, as the discipline of duly convening meetings for a single-member company is cumbersome, it is in order for a single member to take decisions normally requiring a meeting, provided that any decisions are formally recorded in writing (CA2006 s.357). Any agreements made between a single member and a sole director who is also the member must be set out in a written memorandum or recorded in the minutes of the next meeting of the board of directors (CA2006 s.231). Although this provision applies only to contracts other than in the normal course of business, to prevent any innocent omission it is recommended that a written record be kept of all contracts between the company and a sole member/director. It may also be appropriate for the director to declare his interest in the matter pursuant to the Articles of Association.

As long as there is no provision to the contrary in the Articles, any legal person such as a company may hold shares in a company. The Articles of some companies, however, exclude certain categories of person from membership, e.g. persons who are not able to give a declaration of British nationality. At the same time, it is necessary to ensure that in the case of a registered company, for example, the company's Articles of Association do not preclude the holding of shares in other companies.

However, an unincorporated body like a partnership, club or association not registered under the Act should not be accepted as a member of the company because it does not possess legal personality. If such a body wishes to hold shares, the shares should be registered in the name of an individual or individuals, or a person having a legal personality such as a bank nominee or a trustee company.

Similarly, the holder of an office should not be accepted as a member in that capacity unless it is an office created by statute, such as the Treasury Solicitor or the Accountant General. Some public officers are legally deemed to be a corporation, e.g. the Public Trustee, and these may be registered as members of companies.

Shares should not be registered in the name of an English partnership. They should be held in the names of two or more partners and no reference should be made in the register of members to the partnership. Scottish partnerships, however, have legal personality and may, therefore, be registered in the firm name as members of the company. Shares held by a limited liability partnership can be registered in the name of the limited liability partnership as it is a corporate body with a legal persona. Shares in a company may be held by a number of persons in a joint account. However, some Articles of Association limit the number of persons who may be so registered.

In the case of a listed company, the maximum number of joint holders is not permitted to be fewer than four.

Unless a subsidiary company is acting only as personal representative or trustee without having any beneficial interest in the shares or acting as an authorised dealer in securities, a subsidiary company is not permitted to be a member of its holding company (CA2006 S136). Section 139 makes provisions to enable a company's subsidiary company to act as trustee for a group employee share scheme or pension scheme. There is, however, no prohibition on the holding of shares by a subsidiary in its holding company if it held shares in the company that acquired it (which thereby became its holding company) prior to its becoming a subsidiary of that company. However, in this case the subsidiary is not permitted to vote at meetings of the holding company (CA2006 s.137(4)). It would not be lawful for any further shares in the holding company to be allotted to such a subsidiary company, a situation which could arise if the holding company undertook a capitalisation issue.

Minors as members of a company

Since becoming a member of a company may involve the assumption of liabilities in respect of the shares held, it is not considered good practice to accept minors as members of a company in their own name as their responsibilities would be voidable during their minority (i.e. under the age of 18 in England, Wales and Northern Ireland; see below for details of the position in Scotland). This is especially important where the shares are partly paid, as this imposes an obligation to pay any calls that may be made by the directors.

The Articles of Association may give express power to reject allotments and transfers in the name of a minor, but if not, a right of rejection is conferred by general law. Accordingly, the company may repudiate the contract for the allotment of new shares and in the case of a transfer the transferor may be reinstated as the holder of the shares. It may come to light at some later stage that a minor is a member of the company and until any repudiation or rejection of their membership any minors can enjoy the full rights of membership. Rejection of a minor can take place only during that person's period of minority. The *Listing Rules* (*LR 2.2.4, AIM rule 32 and PLUS rule 3*) require that the Articles of Association of companies contain no restrictions on the transfer of fully paid shares, although the right of rejection is maintained under the general rule of law. From a practical point, especially for publicly traded companies, minors may well become members of the company without the company's knowledge.

Any member transferring shares to a minor, even in ignorance, is liable for any future calls on those shares whilst the minor is still the registered holder and a minor. Any person who procures the acquisition of shares and their registration in the name of a minor makes himself liable to indemnify any transferor in respect of any future calls.

In Scotland, persons are pupils until the age of 12 (girls) and 14 (boys), after which they become minors until the age of 18. Pupils have no capacity to contract, although their guardian (tutor) may contract on their behalf. Minors who live independently and hold themselves out as having reached the age of 18 have the capacity to contract. If a minor has a guardian (curator), contracts will normally be made only with that person's approval.

A pupil or minor who validly acquires shares is able to reduce (cancel) the contract not only whilst still a pupil or minor, but until the age of 22 (this additional age limit does not apply to business contracts). In order to reduce the contract, the pupil or minor only has to show that the contract was unreasonable.

Warrants

A warrant is a document rather like a share certificate which entitles the holder to subscribe for equity capital in the company at some future date or dates at a price which is determined at the time of issue of the warrant. It should not be confused with a share warrant to bearer, which is a document evidencing title to shares already issued. Warrants to subscribe may be listed and traded on the Stock Exchange or PLUS and the company would normally have a register of holders of the warrants; but the warrants do not form part of the company's capital and holders are not entitled to receive dividends or interest.

If warrants are to be issued, they must be permitted by the company's Articles of Association. They should not be confused with the rights to convert into ordinary shares attached to convertible loan stocks, which cannot be bought or sold separately. Warrants may, however, be bought and sold on the Stock Exchange or PLUS separately from other securities of the company. Warrants are often issued in connection with takeover offers in order to make the terms more attractive without immediate cost to the bidding company.

A register of holders is usually maintained in a form similar to that of the register of members. It will be necessary in the statement of the terms of issue to include the procedures regarding transfer of warrants, inspection of the register, requests for copies of the register and the dispatch of annual reports and accounts to warrant holders, although there are no statutory provisions covering these matters. Stamp duty is payable on transfers of warrants in the same way and at the same rate as transfers of shares.

Subscription rights

Sometimes the issue of a loan stock includes an associated right to subscribe for shares in the company concerned. This is not the same as the conversion rights under a convertible loan stock, where the loan stock is surrendered in exchange for shares. With subscription rights the loan stock remains in issue and holders subscribe additional money in order to exercise their subscription rights. An alternative method of giving subscription rights is by the issue of option certificates. The exercise of subscription rights does not affect the company's register of loan stock holders, as it does in the case of a convertible loan stock where a person's holding of convertible loan stock would be reduced by the amount of stock which he converted into equity capital.

Debentures and loan stocks

The legislation governing the registration of charges is contained in CA2006 ss.860 to 894.

The directors have implied power to borrow money on behalf of the company under their general powers to manage the business of the company, subject to the provisions of the Act and the Articles of the company (Table A, reg.70 and arts.3 and 4 of the Model Articles for both private and public companies).

However, the Articles of some companies are more specific and impose restrictions on the amounts that may be borrowed and it is necessary for the company in general meeting to alter the appropriate Article if it is considered desirable that the directors' borrowing powers should be amended. A common provision in the Articles is that the amount of monies borrowed or secured on the undertaking and property of the company (apart from temporary loans obtained by way of overdraft from the company's bankers) for the time being remaining undischarged, shall not, without the previous sanction of the company in general meeting, exceed the nominal amount of the share capital of the company for the time being issued.

If the company's Articles contain an article restricting the directors' borrowing powers, it must be carefully followed, since if they were to borrow in excess of the limit specified they might find themselves personally liable. The position of third parties acting in good faith would not, however, be affected by any restriction imposing a limit on the directors' powers to borrow on behalf of the company.

The ways in which the company borrows money may be in the form of debentures of various types, unsecured loan stocks and convertible loan stocks, apart from borrowing from the bank by way of overdraft for the company's day-to-day business.

Types of debenture

A debenture is defined in CA2006 s.738 as debenture stock, bonds and any other securities of the company, whether or not constituting a **charge** on the assets of the company. In effect, a debenture is a document that creates a debt or acknowledges a debt. It may, therefore, be an unsecured promise to pay or a promise to pay secured by a mortgage or charge over the property of the company.

Occasionally, debentures may be issued in bearer form similar to the share warrants to bearer, which may be issued in respect of shares. Arrangements for the payment of interest on bearer debentures are similar to those that apply in the case of the payment of dividends on **bearer shares**. In practice, issue of bearer debentures by companies is rare although euro currency securities may be in this form.

The more common method is to issue a series of debentures in registered form. The conditions relating to interest, redemption or security will be printed on the reverse of each debenture issued. Registered debentures may be transferable on **stock transfer forms** under the Stock Transfer Act 1963 and such transfers are exempt from stamp duty (with a few exceptions). When a debenture or one of a series of debentures is transferred, the name and address of the new holder are endorsed on the debenture itself by the company.

If the company keeps a register of debenture holders, the transfer should be recorded in the register. If it creates a charge over the undertaking or any property of the company, an entry should be made in the company's register of charges and the charge registered with the Registrar of Companies. The period allowed for registration of particulars of a series of debentures is 21 days beginning with the day after the day on which the deed is exercised, if there is a deed containing the charge; or if there is no such deed, 21 days beginning with the day after the day on which the first debenture of the series is executed (CA2006 s.870(3)). Registered debentures are normally issued only in the case of private companies, although a public company may issue such a debenture to its bank by way of security for a loan.

Public companies normally issue their debentures in the form of debenture stock secured on the company's assets and constituted by a trust deed between the company and a corporate trustee, e.g. an insurance company or a trust company. Where debenture stock is not secured by a charge over the undertaking or property of the company, it is described as 'unsecured loan stock'.

Secured debentures

The security for a mortgage debenture may be fixed or floating, or a combination of the two. **Fixed charges** are equivalent to mortgages and the company is restricted in dealing with the asset or assets charged without the prior consent of the debenture holder or of the trustee for the debenture stock. The difference in the case of a **floating charge** is that this extends over the whole of the undertaking of the company and is not restricted to particular assets. This enables the company to deal with its assets in the ordinary course of its business. It is possible for a fixed charge to be given over an asset that is already the subject of a floating charge. This would then take priority over the floating charge, although it would be usual to expect the terms of issue of a debenture creating a floating charge to prohibit the company from doing this.

A floating charge crystallises and becomes a fixed charge if an event should happen which allows the debenture holders or the trustee to take possession of the security or to appoint a receiver. The circumstances in which this may happen will be specified in the debenture or the trust deed. Usually, of course, one of these circumstances will be the non-payment of interest within a specified time from the due date or if a resolution should be passed to wind up the company. Subject to the rights of preferential creditors specified in s.614 the debenture holders have priority, to the extent of the security held, over the ordinary and other secured creditors on the crystallisation of a floating charge. In Scotland a floating charge only crystallises on the commencement of a winding up or the appointment of a receiver. Notice of the appointment of a receiver or manager of a company's property must also be notified to the Registrar within seven days of the appointment (CA2006 s.871).

Particulars of a charge to secure any issue of debentures in Great Britain must be registered with the Registrar of Companies on Form MG07. The period allowed for registration is 21 days beginning with the day after the day on which the deed is exercised, if there is a deed containing the charge or if there is no such deed, 21 days beginning with the day after the day on which the first debenture of the series is executed (CA2006 s.870(3)). If there is a deed this must be delivered along with the form. If there is no deed one of the debentures must be delivered with the form. Further, the company must deliver to the Registrar particulars of an issue of secured debentures in a series in the prescribed Form MG08.

Particulars of charges registered with the Registrar must be entered in the company's own register of charges.

It is not necessary to send the Registrar the original or a copy of the charge document with the particulars. The Registrar will not check the particulars, although he may reject particulars that he considers to be unregisterable. Copies of instruments creating or evidencing a charge over the company's property, brief particulars of which are included in the company's register of charges, must be kept at the company's registered office or a place specified under s.1136 (CA2006 s.877(2)) and be available for inspection by any creditor or member of the company without fee, or by any other person on payment of such fee as may be prescribed (CA2006 s.877(3)). It is important to the debenture holders that the particulars of a charge created by an issue of debentures is registered with the Registrar of Companies, since a charge is void unless particulars are filed with the Registrar within 21 days of its creation (CA2006 s.870(3)). It is usual, therefore, for the trustee for the debenture holders to attend to the registration under the authority contained in CA2006 s.860, which provides that registration of a charge may be effected on the application of any person interested in it.

Unsecured loan stock

Unsecured loan stock carries a higher risk for investors. To compensate for this it is usual for such stocks to bear a higher rate of interest than if it were a secured debenture stock. Sometimes it is also necessary to offer options in the form of a right to convert the stock into equity shares of the company at certain dates in the future (i.e. convertible loan stock; see below). The ratio is determined at the time of issue of the stock; alternatively, a right to subscribe for equity shares at a future date in a ratio and price determined at the time of issue is agreed. With regard to the latter, it should be noted that the loan stock continues in existence after the holder has exercised the subscription rights to which he is entitled. In the case of a convertible loan stock, the exercise of the holder of his right to convert into ordinary shares extinguishes his holding of the convertible loan stock to the extent that it is exercised.

The trust deed constituting unsecured loan stock will usually cover:

1 details of the terms of issue, payment of principal and interest and any conversion or subscription rights which may be attached to the stock;
2 restrictions on issuing further unsecured loan stock;
3 restrictions on further borrowing
4 restrictions on disposal of the business or specified assets;
5 a covenant by the company to maintain sufficient equity capital to satisfy any conversion or subscription rights, further issues of equity capital and in regard to the business generally;
6 events in which the whole of the stock becomes immediately payable (e.g. default in payment of interest or ceasing to carry on business);

7 the remuneration of the trustees;
8 schedules which will be attached to the trust deed containing the form of stock certificate, the detailed conditions for redemption by drawings or purchase and of any conversion or subscription rights;
9 regulations regarding the register of holders of the stock;
10 arrangements for transfer and transmission of the stock; and
11 regulations governing meetings of holders of the stock.

If the loan stock is listed, a summary of the conditions, instead of the full conditions, may be printed on the reverse of the certificate, provided that the trust deed does not prohibit this. The holder of the stock is entitled to be supplied with a copy of the trust deed at his request on payment of a fee (CA2006 s.749).

Convertible loan stock

Convertible loan stock is a form of loan stock, usually unsecured, which includes provision for the stock to be converted into equity shares at ratios determined at the time of issue of the stock. There is a requirement for the company to give the stockholders notice of their right to exercise the conversion rights in every year in which the right exists.

The company secretary or the company's registrar will be concerned with the proper procedure for dealing with applications from holders to exercise their conversion rights.

5

Share allotments

Introduction

The Companies Act 2006 has abolished the concept of authorised share capital, and accordingly a company has unrestricted authority to issue shares, except to the extent of any restrictions in the company's Articles of Association. As all companies incorporated prior to 1 October 2009 had a capital clause in their Memorandum of Association, which is now deemed to form part of their articles, this is deemed to be a cap on the total number of shares that may be issued.

When issuing new shares for a company incorporated prior to 1 October 2009, care must be taken to ensure that there are sufficient unissued shares in the authorised share capital to satisfy the issue. For all companies it is necessary to ensure that there is sufficient current authority in terms of CA2006 s.549 for the directors to approve the issue and that any rights of pre-emption, whether as set out in the CA2006 or in the company's own Articles, are observed or waived.

The terms 'share issue' and 'share allotment' refer to very slightly different aspects of the process of issuing shares, and for most purposes are intended to mean the same thing. When issuing shares these are first allotted by the directors between those applying for them, and then they are issued to those successful applicants.

Once a company has issued shares there are only limited circumstances under which they can be returned to the company. Failure to pay calls on partly paid shares can lead to them being forfeited (see pp. 98–100). Under strict conditions a company can purchase its own shares or redeem shares provided they were issued as redeemable (see pp. 102–103 and 106–111). Under CA2006 private companies can now undertake a reduction of share capital, which may include returning capital to members, without the need for court approval. As a result, reduction of capital for a private company is a feasible alternative to a company purchasing its own shares. (See pp. 69–71 for reduction of share capital.)

Whether shares are admitted to trade on a public exchange or not, most shares are transferable. Most private company Articles contain pre-emption rights on transfer designed to ensure that the pool of issued shares is retained within a relatively small number of owners who are usually directly involved in the management of the company.

Public companies with traded shares will be prohibited by the exchange/market operator from imposing any restriction on the transferability of the shares, with one exception allowed where certain companies, such as British Airways, are required to maintain a minimum percentage of UK residents holding shares.

Authority for allotment

Shares in a company may not be allotted unless the directors are authorised to do so by an ordinary resolution of the company or by the Articles of Association in terms of CA2006 s.549. The authority may be given in general terms or made subject to conditions, but must state the maximum amount of the relevant securities that may be issued and specify the date on which the authority will expire. In the case of a public company, authority may be given for a maximum of five years from the date of the resolution (CA2006 s.551). In the case of a private company with only one class of shares the directors have authority to exercise any powers of the company to allot shares and issue rights to subscribe for shares subject to any restrictions in the company's Articles of Association (CA2006 s.550). Companies with few shareholders will often adopt the longest period permissible and, to safeguard existing shareholders, will ensure that any shares allotted must be offered to them as discussed below. Companies with a large number of shareholders, and listed companies, will renew the authority in respect of all the then unissued shares. [***See precedent 45***.] The authority to allot relevant securities may be revoked, varied or renewed by ordinary resolution even if the authority was given by a special resolution or contained in the Articles of Association (CA2006 s.551(8)). A resolution renewing an earlier authority must state the amount of shares which may be allotted and an expiry date, within five years. Securities may be allotted after the expiry of the authority, provided that the allotment is in pursuance of an offer or agreement made prior to the expiry of the authority. A copy of a resolution giving authority to directors to allot relevant securities must be filed with the Registrar of Companies within 15 days after it is passed (CA2006 ss.30 and 551(9)).

Pre-emption rights

It is quite common for the Articles of private companies to provide that, where new shares are to be allotted, they must first be offered to existing shareholders in proportion to their existing holdings. In the case of a listed company, the UK Listing Authority requires that any new issues of shares for cash should first be offered to existing holders as in a rights issue (*LR 9.3.11*).

Pre-emption rights for existing shareholders in respect of the allotment of equity securities are provided by statute in CA2006 ss.561 to 576, even though there may be no special provisions in the Articles of Association. These provisions may be excluded by the Articles of a private company or by special resolution of the members. [***See precedent 48.***] Equity securities are defined in CA2006 s.560 as ordinary shares in the company and ordinary shares means shares of the company on which the rate of dividend varies according to the profits of the company and which carry no preferential right in the repayment of the capital in the event of winding up. Securities that can be converted into ordinary shares (i.e. convertible loan stocks) are also included, but shares, which as regards dividends and capital, carry right to participate only up to a specified amount in a distribution are excluded.

The pre-emption rights regime does not apply to the following share allotments:

- allotment of shares by way of a bonus issue; (s.564)
- allotment of shares which are to be partly or wholly paid up for non-cash consideration; and (s.565)
- allotment of shares to be held under an employees' share scheme (s.567).

The second exception effectively restricts pre-emption provisions to issues for cash. This is particularly useful where a company is looking to acquire another business or assets in exchange for the issue of its own shares, credited as fully paid.

Any pre-emption rights contained in a company's Articles of Association take precedence over the statutory pre-emption rights. The requirement of CA2006 is that no equity securities may be allotted unless they have first been offered to the holders of all the ordinary shares in the company in proportion to their existing shareholdings. Shares held in treasury by the company are disregarded. The detailed provisions with regard to the communication of the offer to the existing shareholders, who must be given a period of not less than 21 days in which to accept the offer, are laid down in CA2006 s.562. A record date to determine the holders entitled to receive the offer must be set in the period of 28 days immediately before the date of the offer (CA2006 s.574). In the case of share warrants to bearer, the offer must be made by advertisement in the *London Gazette* or *Edinburgh Gazette* stating how copies of the offer may be received. It is normal practice to place an advertisement in a national newspaper as well.

The company and every officer who knowingly permits an allotment of shares to be made in contravention of the statutory pre-emption provisions are jointly and severally liable to compensate any person who may suffer loss as a result. Claims must however be made within two years of the date of filing of the return of allotments or date of grant of a right to subscribe for shares (CA2006 s.563).

Disapplication of pre-emption rights

Private companies may exclude or amend the statutory provisions contained in ss.561 and 562 by provisions contained in their Articles (CA2006 s.567). These will prevail even if they are inconsistent with the statutory provisions. Where a company excludes s.561 and its articles include alternative pre-emption rights and procedures, the provisions of s.562 regarding communication of the pre-emption offer will apply to those alternative procedures unless s.562 is also excluded or amended by the company's Articles.

Private companies with only one class of shares can authorise their directors, either by provisions in their Articles or by special resolution, to allot shares as if s.561 did not apply, or with such modifications as the directors determine (CA2006 s.569).

It is also possible for both public and private companies to exclude the operation of the statutory pre-emption rights in CA2006 s.561 in circumstances where the directors already have general authority to allot shares under CA2006 s.551 if the directors obtain authority by a special resolution of the company passed at a general meeting [***see precedent 46***] or, alternatively, by a provision in the company's Articles (CA2006 ss.570, 571). If the company's Articles do not already contain a suitable provision, an alteration to the Articles would be necessary and require the approval of shareholders by special resolution in a general meeting.

In the case of a listed company, unless shareholders in general meeting otherwise permit, or the company has a general authority to disapply pre-emption rights under CA2006 s.570, a company must first offer equity securities, to be issued for cash, to its existing equity shareholders in proportion to their existing holdings (*LR 9.3.11*).

The authority to disapply pre-emption rights is contained in CA2006 s.570. It is also quite common for the special resolution required by CA2006 s.570, giving the directors power to disapply the CA2006 requirements concerning pre-emption rights in regard to the allotment of securities up to a limit specified in the resolution, to be proposed as part of the regular business at the annual general meeting of a listed company. In most cases, listed companies will seek the waiver of pre-emption rights of up to an additional 10 per cent of the issued share capital. [***See precedent 19.***]

The grant of the power to directors to disapply the pre-emption rights makes it possible for the company to make a rights issue of its shares and exclude or make such other arrangements for certain, usually overseas, shareholders. Otherwise it may be impossible to allot equity securities to all shareholders of the company in proportion to the respective numbers of shares held by them. This arises because in some countries (e.g. the United States) it would not be possible to offer the securities to residents of those countries without going through lengthy and costly procedures required by the local legislation. The rights of the persons concerned would, whenever practicable, be sold for their benefit. Circumstances may also arise where the company might wish to make small allotments of equity shares for cash to persons other than existing shareholders. The disapplication of the pre-emption rights would cease when the general authority of the directors to issue equity securities under CA2006 s.551 lapsed. However, an offer made before the expiry of the authority to disapply the pre-emption rights would remain valid notwithstanding the fact that the actual allotment did not take place until after that date.

Disapplication resolution

The special resolution to disapply pre-emption provisions must be recommended by the directors, who must make a written statement setting out their reasons for the recommendation, the amount to be paid for any shares to be allotted and a justification of that amount. Where approval is sought by written resolution, the directors' statement must be sent to each member at the same time as the resolution, and if approval is sought at a general meeting, the statement must be sent with the notice convening the meeting (CA2006 s.571).

Allotment procedure

The required steps are as follows:

1 It may be necessary for any restriction on the total number of shares that can be issued to be increased because the present limit is insufficient to cover the proposed allotment. [***See Chapter 4 and precedent 36.***] This is particularly relevant, as the authorised capital previously required for all companies incorporated prior to 1 October 2009 is deemed to be a restriction on the total number of shares that can be issued.

2 The person wishing to subscribe for shares completes a form of application and returns it with the required payment. [***See precedent 47.***]

3 The directors should pass a resolution to allot the shares to the persons applying for them and, if the company has a seal, authorise the sealing of the share certificates and their issue to the applicants. [***See precedent 48.***]

4 A share certificate is then prepared for each applicant on the company's printed share certificate forms. In the case of small companies, blank certificates for completion by hand may be obtained from law stationers. In many cases, a stock of such certificates is included in the combined statutory registers supplied upon incorporation by the registration agents (see pp. 150–152).

5 The share certificates after sealing (if appropriate) are sent to the applicant for safe keeping. All these steps should be taken as soon as possible since, until the applicant is notified that his application for shares has been accepted, he may, subject to the terms of application, be free to withdraw it. The company is required to issue share certificates within two months of allotment (CA2006 s.769).

6 The names of the persons allotted shares must be entered in the register of members of the company within two months of the allotment (s.554) and they thereupon become members of the company.

7 Return of allotments on Form SH01 must be filed with the Registrar within one month of the date of allotment.

Shares allotted for non-cash consideration

A public company is prohibited from allotting shares either fully or partly paid up for a non-cash consideration unless the consideration has been valued in the previous six months and a copy of the valuer's report has been sent to the proposed allottee (CA2006 s.593). There are, however, exemptions from this provision in the following cases:

1 allotments of shares made in a takeover by way of share exchange if the offer is open to all holders of the class of shares concerned (CA2006 s.594);
2 where the shares are allotted under a capitalisation issue by the capitalisation of reserves or sums standing to the credit of the profit and loss account (CA2006 s.593(2));
3 allotments of shares in connection with a company merger where shares are issued in exchange for the transfer of all of another company's assets and liabilities to that selling company's shareholders (CA2006 s.595).

The valuation report must be made by an independent person who would be qualified to be a statutory auditor of the company, unless he considers that it would be appropriate for some other person with the required knowledge and experience to make the report. That person should not be an officer or servant of the company.

The valuer's report must state the following:

1 the nominal value of the shares being allotted wholly or partly paid for a consideration other than cash;
2 the amount of any premium payable on the shares;
3 a description of the consideration which has been valued and the method used to value it;
4 the amount of the nominal value of the shares and any premium treated as paid up for a consideration other than cash.

If the person appointed to make the valuation has appointed someone else to make it, the valuer's report must mention this and state:

1 the name of the other person with details of his knowledge and experience;
2 a description of the consideration that was valued by the other person and the method used to value it. The report must include a statement that the value of the consideration, together with any cash payable, is not less than the aggregate of the nominal value and any premium of the shares to be issued, and that there has been no material change in its value since the date of the valuation (CA2006 s.596).

A copy of the report must be sent to the Registrar of Companies with the return of allotments form, SH01 (CA2006 s.597). The person making the report is entitled to call for such information from officers of the company as he may require and it is an offence for misleading or false information to be given (CA2006 s.1153).

It is also an offence to contravene the requirements for the allotment of shares for a non-cash consideration, including failure to send the allottee a copy of the report. The allottee and any subsequent holder of the shares will be liable to pay the company the amount equal to the nominal value and premium treated as paid up for a consideration other than cash on the shares allotted to him if he knew, or should have known, of the contravention. A subsequent holder of the shares, purchasing the shares for value without knowledge of the contravention, will not be liable and will also not be liable if the previous holder was not himself liable.

Procedure for the transfer of non-cash consideration

Usually, a formal contract is entered into for the transfer of the non-cash consideration to the company and for the allotment by it of shares in consideration for the assets transferred. This formal contract should be approved by the board of directors. The agreement must be sent to the Registrar of Companies with the return of allotments form, SH01. This should be accompanied by a certified copy of the agreement if the Registrar is to be requested to return the original agreement.

It will be seen that the issue of shares for a consideration other than cash involves certain formalities and expense and arrangements may be made for the transaction to be structured so as to constitute an allotment for cash.

Allotments by public companies

Special provisions apply in the case of issues of shares to the public by public companies. These are as follows.

An allotment cannot be made unless the amount stated in the prospectus, if any, as the minimum amount required to be raised has, in fact, been subscribed and the sum payable on application for the shares concerned has been received by the company.

There can be no allotment if the amount of capital offered for subscription is not fully subscribed, unless there is an express term in the offer that an allotment may be made notwithstanding that there has not been a full subscription. This applies in the case of offers of shares for cash and offers of shares for a consideration other than cash.

If these two requirements are not met within 40 days of the offer commencing, the cash subscribed or other consideration paid must be returned to the applicants (CA2006 s.578(2)).

Other procedural matters arising in connection with the allotment of shares pursuant to offers to the public are covered more fully in Chapters 15 and 16.

Nominee shareholding

These arise where the beneficial owner of shares does not wish to have them registered in his own name. The shares may be registered instead in the name of a person or group of people or a company (the nominee). Historically the beneficial owner of the shares had no contact with the company since the company was required to address all communications to the registered shareholder, in this case the nominee. Following implementation of CA2006 ss.145 and 146 this is no longer the case. Even though there must be no reference in the company's register of members to the identity of the beneficial owner, since by CA2006 s.126 a company is not permitted to recognise any trust affecting any of its shares, nominee shareholders of listed, AIM and PLUS companies may give notice that the beneficiary is to enjoy 'information rights'. For all other companies registered shareholders may nominate others to exercise specified rights as permitted by the company's Articles.

This rule prohibiting the recognition of trusts is not contravened if a company accepts a body corporate as a shareholder with the word 'nominees' or 'trustees' in its name. At the same time, notwithstanding CA2006 s.126, public companies are required by CA2006 s.808 to keep a register of responses to enquires made under CA2006 s.793. CA2006 s.126 does not apply in Scotland. This is dealt with in more detail in Chapter 12.

The need for a nominee shareholding can arise in the case of wholly owned subsidiary companies if the Articles require two or more shareholders. In practice, one or more of the shares in the subsidiary must be registered in the name of a nominee on behalf of the company. This requirement is often met by arranging for one share to be registered in the joint name of a director of the holding company as the first named holder and the holding company as the second named holder. The second shareholder, i.e. the holding company, would hold the balance of the shares in the subsidiary company.

The nominee should provide a dividend mandate requesting that all dividends be paid to the beneficial owner and should also execute a transfer of the shares, the name of the transferee and date being left blank. Thus, if the director were to leave the company, it would be possible for his nominee share to be transferred to another director who remained a director of the holding company. A short declaration of trust should also be executed by the nominee declaring that the share(s) he holds are held by him as a nominee for the beneficial owner and that he has no beneficial interest in them. [***See precedent 49.***] The declaration of trust will often include the following provisions:

1 The nominee will pay any dividends on the shares as the beneficial owner may direct.
2 The nominee will transfer or deal with the shares as the beneficial owner may direct.
3 The nominee will vote at general meetings or by written resolution as the beneficial owner shall direct or execute proxies as required, and, if any rights or options should be offered to him as holder of the nominee share, he will act in relation to the offer as directed by the beneficial owner.

If the declaration of trust is executed, there is no need for a blank transfer or dividend mandate. However, it may still be prudent to obtain a blank transfer signed by the nominee in case he is unwilling to cooperate in giving up the nominee shares.

When a subsidiary company's Articles are being changed, if it is a private company the opportunity should be taken to remove any provision requiring the membership of the company to be two or more.

Payment for shares

There are two ways in which shares may be paid for:

1 in money or money's worth, including goodwill and know-how;
2 by way of capitalisation of the company's existing reserves.

The following methods are prohibited:

1 Payment for shares or any premium on them by a person undertaking to do work or perform services for the company, being a public company, or any other person (CA2006 s.585).
2 The allotment of shares at a discount, i.e. at an issue price for a share below its nominal value (CA2006 s.580). However, a company may pay commission as consideration for a person subscribing or procuring the subscription for shares in the company since this is not treated as a discount (CA2006 s.553).
3 Shares may not be allotted by a public company (other than under an employees' share scheme) unless at least one-quarter of their nominal value and the whole of their premium is paid up (CA2006 s.586).
4 Public companies may not allot shares as fully or partly paid up (both as to their nominal value and any premium on the shares) if the consideration for the allotment includes an undertaking which is to be, or may be, performed more than five years after the date of the allotment (CA2006 s.587). If an allotment is made for a consideration which includes an undertaking to be performed within five years and the undertaking is not performed within that period, the allottee becomes liable to pay the company an amount equal to the agreed issue price plus interest.

Shares taken up by a subscriber to the Memorandum of Association of a public company must be paid for in cash, both as to nominal value and any premium (CA2006 s.584).

Subsequent holders of shares may incur liability if any of the above provisions relating to the payment for shares are contravened (CA2006 s.588).

Financial assistance by a company for the purchase of its own shares

Unless provided for in the Act, it is not lawful for a public company to provide financial assistance for the purchase of its own shares or the shares of its holding company whether at the same time as the acquisition of the shares or before

(CA2006 s.678(1)). Financial assistance is very widely defined as follows (CA2006 s.677):

1 financial assistance by way of gift;
2 financial assistance given by way of guarantee, security or indemnity, other than an indemnity in respect of the indemnifier's own neglect or default, or by way of waiver or release;
3 financial assistance by way of loan or other agreement under which any of the obligations of the person giving the assistance are to be fulfilled at a time when in accordance with the agreement any obligation of another party remains unfulfilled or by way of novation of or assignment of rights arising under such loan or agreement;
4 any other financial assistance given by a company the net assets of which are thereby reduced by a material extent or which has no net assets.

A limited relaxation of CA2006 s.678(1) is available where the principal purpose was not to give assistance for the purchase or acquisition of its shares or the giving of it was only an incidental part of some larger purpose of the company and the assistance was given in good faith in the interests of the company (CA2006 s.678(2),(4)).

Various transactions not subject to the general prohibition of CA2006 s.678(1), including distribution of assets by way of lawful dividend, distribution on a winding-up, allotment of bonus shares or the redemption or repurchase by a company of its own shares are set out in CA2006 s.681.

Financial assistance is not prohibited by CA2006 s.678(1) where:

1 the lending of money is part of the company's ordinary business and the loan is made in the ordinary course of business;
2 the loan is given in good faith for the purposes of an employee share scheme or where the loan is made to an employee, but not a director, in good faith for the purpose of acquiring shares in the company or its holding company.

The relaxation of CA2006 s.678(1) provided by CA2006 s.682 is only available to a public company to the extent that its net assets are not reduced or, if they are reduced, that the payment is made out of distributable profit.

Financial assistance by private companies

The restriction on private companies providing financial assistance for the purchase of their own shares was repealed from 1 October 2008.

Acquisition of non-cash assets from subscribers or from certain shareholders

Special requirements apply if a public company proposes to acquire non-cash assets from a subscriber to the Memorandum of a company formed as a public company (or from any person who was a member of the company at the date of the re-registration of the company as a public company) within the period of two years from the date on which the company became entitled to commence business (or the date of re-registration) (CA2006 s.598).

Unless the provisions of CA2006 ss.599 and 601 have been complied with, a public company may not accept the transfer of a non-cash asset to it during a period of two years from the date of issue of the certificate authorising the company to commence business, or if the company was formed as a private company from the date of its re-registration, if the transferor was a subscriber to the Memorandum and Articles of Association, or the value of the consideration represents 10 per cent or more of the nominal value of the company's issued share capital at the time of the transaction.

The conditions of CA2006 s. 599 are as follows:

1. The asset must be independently valued pursuant to CA2006 s.600.
2. A report of the valuer must be made to the company during the period of six months immediately preceding the date of the transaction.
3. The proposed transaction must be approved by the members of the company. [***See precedent 50.***]
4. A copy of the report and resolution must be circulated to the members and the person with whom the transaction is being made no later than the date of issue of the notice convening the shareholders' meeting to consider the transaction.
5. The transfer of assets carried out in the normal course of business or under the supervision of the court or an authorised officer of the court is exempted from the provision of CA2006 s.598(4) and (5).

Where an agreement is entered into in contravention of CA2006 s.598 and the person with whom the arrangement is made does not receive a copy of the report of the valuer, or is aware or should have been aware of any other contravention of CA2006 s.599 or 600, the company may recover from that person any consideration given under the agreement or an amount equal to the value of the consideration. In such a case, the agreement, or those parts of it not carried out, are void. If the agreement includes the allotment of shares the allotment will stand; however, the allottee is liable to pay to the company an amount equal to the aggregate nominal value of the shares and any premium (CA2006 s.604).

Exemption from liability

Where a person is liable to a company under CA2006 s.605 in relation to a payment for shares, that person may apply to the court for exemption from liability in whole or in part. The court may grant exemption only if it appears just and equitable to do so under the circumstances set out in CA2006 s.606.

Calls and instalments on shares

Calls on shares

Calls on shares arise when shares have been issued on a partly paid basis and a further payment of all or part of the balance becomes due. It should be noted that reg.21 of the Model Articles for private companies does not permit the issue of partly or nil paid shares, other than the subscriber shares.

Calls on partly paid shares are made by a resolution of the directors under provisions contained in the company's Articles (e.g. CA1985 Table A, regs.12–17). The resolution will specify the amount of the call, the due date for payment and where payment should be sent. Where shares are registered in two or more names the joint holders are jointly and severally liable for the calls. In the case of deceased shareholders the estate continues to be liable for outstanding calls unless the shares have been transferred into the personal names of the personal representatives, in which case the personal representatives are personally liable. The company's Articles will also make provision for action to be taken in the event of default of payment of a call (e.g. CA1985 Table A, regs.18–22).

A general point to note is that registration of transfers of shares on which a call is unpaid should not be accepted for registration. This is because liability for payment of the call remains with the holder of the shares who was registered on the date that the call was made unless the transferee assumes liability for the unpaid call.

It is necessary to draw a distinction between shares issued by companies as partly paid and the issue of new shares payable in instalments, as in some privatisation issues, where the procedure in the case of non-payment of the instalments as they fall due is different from the non-payment of calls made by the directors on partly paid shares.

The procedure for dealing with the payment of a call made by the directors on partly paid shares (i.e. other than the payment of predetermined instalments on shares) of a listed company is shown below. A similar procedure with suitable changes would be used by an unlisted public company or a private company.

Procedure

1 The directors pass the appropriate resolution making the call. [***See precedent 51.***]
2 *(Listed, AIM and PLUS companies only)* The UK Listing Authority must be sent a copy of the resolution and the proposed call letter.
3 Bulk printing of the call letters is arranged, if appropriate incorporating any amendments required by the UK Listing Authority.
4 The call letters are prepared by the company to be sent to the individual shareholders, specifying the number of shares and the total amount of the calls to be paid and the date and place of payment of the calls [***see precedent 52***]. Each

call letter is serially numbered and a note of the issue of the call letters made in the register of members.

5 The call letters are dispatched to the shareholders.

6 A receiving agent, usually the company's share registrar will usually have been appointed to receive the money for the calls.

7 After the final date for receipt of calls a reconciliation of the amounts received should be made and a list of unpaid calls agreed.

8 Reminder letters are sent out to the shareholders who have not paid the call stating that immediate payment must be made and that interest may be charged on the amount left outstanding. [***See precedent 52.***]

9 If payment is still not received within a reasonable period, such as seven days, a further letter should be sent to the shareholders concerned warning them that unless the call is paid promptly the directors will consider the possibility of forfeiting the shares under the company's Articles.

10 *(Listed, AIM and PLUS companies only)* The company's stockbrokers should be requested to arrange for the listing of the shares to be amended as regards the further amount called up.

11 The partly paid share certificate should be endorsed with the payment of the call and returned to the person lodging the certificate, i.e. the shareholder or an agent acting on behalf of the shareholder.

12 The accounts of the shareholders in the register of members should be noted with the payment of the call.

13 A note must be included in the company's balance sheet or annual return if there are any unpaid calls at the time when these documents are prepared.

Instalments on shares

Although partly paid shares are rare, payment for shares by instalments is frequently used in the case of an offer for sale of shares where the price is substantial, as in the case of some privatisation issues. It is usual in such cases for the shares, which may already be fully paid, to be held by a custodian bank, which in turn offers the shares to the public for payment by instalments. In these cases non-payment of an instalment may result in the loss of the shares and the forfeiture procedure described below does not have to be followed. The terms of issue will provide for the payment of a first instalment on application and for a second instalment (and perhaps a third instalment) to be paid at a subsequent date (or dates) which are determined in advance. Accordingly, there is no need for the call to be formally made by the directors since information regarding the amount(s) of the instalment(s) and the due date(s) for payment are mentioned in the letter of acceptance sent to the shareholder on receipt of his application payment.

The shares may be sold by the holder of a letter of acceptance before payment of the second instalment by signing the form of renunciation on the back of the letter of acceptance. After about two months after dispatch of the letters of acceptance, however, holders become registered and the shares may then only be transferred by completion of a transfer form. Holders wishing to sell their shares must return the completed transfer form to their stockbroker, accompanied by the letter of acceptance.

The usual arrangement for the payment of the second instalment is for reminder notices to be sent out by the custodian bank about four weeks before the instalment is due setting out the procedures for payment and transfer of shares. An interim certificate is sent with the reminder notice, which will be duly receipted and returned to the registered holder (or to his agent) by the receiving bank following payment. The procedure for the payment of a third instalment, if there is one, would be similar. After payment of the final instalment, a fully paid share certificate will be issued.

The letters of acceptance and interim certificates make it clear that, in the event of the non-payment of any instalment, the entitlement of the registered holder may be cancelled and the related shares sold. Instalments previously paid will be returned to the registered holder less expenses and any loss suffered by the custodian bank in disposing of the shares. It should be noted, therefore, that in such cases there is no need to go through the forfeiture procedure described below.

Forfeiture

It may become necessary to forfeit shares, if the Articles so permit, because of non-payment of calls made by the directors on shares offered by companies for subscription on a partly paid basis. In this situation it is important to ensure strict compliance with the requirements of the company's Articles since, if these are not followed, the forfeiture could be declared invalid. The power is rarely exercised in practice; and it is recommended that legal advice should be taken before setting up forfeiture arrangements. When the shares have been forfeited the person concerned ceases to be a member of the company and the forfeiture should be entered in the register of members.

Private companies incorporated after 1 October 2006 adopting the Model Articles will not require this process, as shares cannot be issued partly paid (reg.21).

Subject to the Articles, a forfeiture of shares may be cancelled if the call should subsequently be received (with or without interest), assuming that at that time the shares have not been sold by the directors under the powers given to the company in its Articles of Association (e.g. CA1985 Table A, reg.20).

To protect the company where forfeited shares are sold, a statutory declaration on the lines set out in CA1985 Table A, reg.22, should be sworn. It should be noted that forfeiture does not apply in the case of failure to pay instalments on shares (see above), since the shares would have been issued as fully paid to the custodian bank.

In the case of a public company, special requirements are imposed by CA2006 s.662 where shares are forfeited or surrendered to the company in lieu of forfeiture under the company's Articles of Association for failure to pay calls. Under these provisions the company must cancel the shares and diminish the amount of its share capital by the nominal value of the shares forfeited or surrendered if the shares are not disposed of within three years of the forfeiture or surrender. Voting rights may not be exercised in respect of the forfeited or surrendered shares during this three-year period.

If the cancellation reduces the company's nominal capital below the authorised minimum for a public company (£50,000), the company must apply for re-registration as a private company. In these circumstances the directors have power under CA2006 s.664 to take steps to reduce the company's capital without complying with the special provisions laid down by the Companies Act 2006, i.e. a special resolution under CA2006 s.641(1)(b) to reduce share capital and application to the Court for approval under CA2006 s.645. The company makes application to the Registrar of Companies to be re-registered as a private company on Form RR09 ('Application by a public company for re-registration as a private company following cancellation of shares'). This is accompanied by a copy of the altered Articles of Association.

It should be noted that a private company becoming re-registered as a public company, after forfeiting, surrendering or otherwise acquiring any of its shares as stated above, must also comply with the above requirements within three years from the date of re-registration as a public company (CA2006 s.668).

Procedure

The following is the company secretarial procedure to be followed in connection with the forfeiture of shares:

1. Send a reminder letter to the relevant shareholders within seven days of the due date for payment requesting that payment be made immediately and that interest may be charged from the due date for the payment. [***See precedent 52.***]
2. Send a second reminder if no payment is received after seven days.
3. If after a further period of seven days the amounts remain unpaid, send a final warning notice by recorded delivery requesting payment with interest not earlier than 14 days from the date of the notice and stating that in the event of non-payment by the specified date, the shares will be liable to be forfeited.
4. If the amounts continue to be unpaid, the directors pass a resolution without further notice which includes the names of the members and the numbers of shares held by each shareholder which are forfeited and giving authority to the directors to sell or reissue the forfeited shares. [***See precedent 41.***]
5. When the resolution has been passed, send a notification of the forfeiture by recorded delivery to the shareholders concerned requesting surrender of their share certificates or, if appropriate, allotment letters or letters of acceptance. [***See precedent 53.***]

6 Debit the accounts of each shareholder in the register of members whose shares have been forfeited and place the appropriate shares to the credit of a 'forfeited shares' account.
7 Sell or reissue the shares, debit the forfeited shares account and credit the account of the purchaser of the shares in the register of members with the number of shares purchased.
8 A note should be made in the company's balance sheet or annual return of any forfeited shares remaining unissued at the time of preparation of the balance sheet or annual return.
9 The Articles may allow the directors to accept surrender of shares. This power can be used only to avoid the formal forfeiture procedure and can be accepted only if the shares are liable to forfeiture. Surrender of shares may not be used to avoid an uncalled liability on partly paid shares.
10 Any member whose shares have been forfeited is still liable to pay the unpaid amount, although the directors may waive such liability in full or in part, or may seek to recover such sums and need not take into account the value of the shares on forfeiture or any proceeds from their sale.

Company's lien on its shares

As well as rights to forfeiture, the Articles of most companies (e.g. CA1985 Table A, regs.8–11 or the Model Articles for public companies, reg 52) give the company a lien on its shares and on dividends payable thereon for all money due in respect of the shares. The lien would be enforced by sale of the member's shares after he had been given due notice of the debt owing to the company which remained unpaid, the notice being given in a similar manner to that described above in the case of forfeiture. If the amount realised by the sale exceeds the amount of debt, the surplus must be paid to the shareholder upon the surrender of the share certificate. Additionally, the lien can be used only for amounts owed by a shareholder as a shareholder and not for debts incurred in another capacity, i.e. commercial debt.

It should be noted that a public company can create a charge on its own shares only in respect of amounts payable on partly paid shares unless it lends money or gives credit during the normal course of business. A private company that has re-registered as a public company may have a charge over fully paid shares provided the charge was registered prior to its re-registration.

Exercise of subscription rights and warrants

Occasionally companies will raise funding by way of an issue of loan notes or loan stock which contain subscriptions rights or warrants for new shares, usually at the prevailing share value for a period of time, such as 24 months. The company secretarial procedure for the exercise of the subscription rights and warrants is similar to that which applies in the case of convertible loan stock but additional matters require attention, as follows:

1 The cash received for shares subscribed is recorded and banked. The original loan stock certificates should be returned for cancellation.
2 New loan stock certificates without the subscription rights are prepared and sent out with the share certificates. In the case of a partial exercise there will be two loan note certificates to be returned.
3 The register of holders of the loan stock should be divided into two parts, one containing holders who still possess subscription rights exercisable at some future date and the other part the names of holders of loan stock to which subscription rights are no longer attached. If the loan stock is listed, there will be two prices on the Stock Exchange, one for the stock which still has subscription rights attached and the other for the stock on which the subscription rights have been exercised.
4 A return of allotments on Form SH01 must be prepared and sent to the Registrar of Companies.

In the case of the exercise of warrants to subscribe for shares, a similar procedure will be followed as in the case of the exercise of subscription rights attached to loan stock; but there is no need to issue new warrant certificates since, once the right under it has been exercised, it is cancelled. Balance certificates for warrants, however, may be required if the holder does not exercise the whole of his rights and some rights remain exerciseable at a future date.

Bonus issues

A capitalisation issue is often referred to as a **bonus issue**, and is referred to as such by CA2006. This is, however, misleading since the total value of a member's holding in shares of the company will not change because of the issue of 'bonus shares'. All that happens is that the member has more shares of a lower value. A capitalisation issue is often used to make shares with a high value easier to sell or to improve the ratio between retained profit and capital when securing loan finance. For a private company proposing to re-register as a public company it is an ideal way to ensure that the minimum capital requirement is met without requiring the shareholders to inject additional funds to the company. The following procedures should be followed by private and unlisted companies. There are additional requirements for listed companies set out in the *Listing Rules* considered on p. 270. The capitalisation issue may be made out of distributable profit, the share premium account or the revaluation account and requires approval of the members by ordinary resolution.

1 Ensure that the Articles permit the issue of bonus shares, that the directors have authority to allot additional shares in terms of CA2006 s.549 and that

there is sufficient headroom if there is a restriction on the total number of shares that can be issued. If any of these requirements is lacking, the appropriate resolutions will need to be added to the notice of the general meeting or written resolutions being issued to approve the bonus issue.

2 Convene a board meeting to recommend the bonus issue to the shareholders [***see precedent** 54*], to determine the basis of the issue and the method for dealing with fractions, if any. The directors must also decide whether the allotment will be renounceable by the existing members in favour of any third parties. For a private company, it is not normally desirable for the right to bonus shares to be renounceable other than to existing shareholders, except under strictly controlled conditions. It should be noted that the holding of any members not taking up their rights will be diluted and the aggregate value of their shares will fall. The directors will also convene a general meeting or approve the circulation of a written resolution to approve the necessary resolution(s).

3 Following the board meeting the secretary prepares, signs and issues a notice convening a general meeting enclosing proxy forms if wished or circulating a written resolution [***see precedents 4, 5 and** 7*]. The meeting will require 14 days' notice (CA2006 s.307) unless amendments to the Articles are required, in which case longer notice may be required as set out in the Articles of the company such as CA1985 Table A reg.38. A private company may authorise the resolutions using the written resolution procedure (see p. 191).

4 Once the members have approved the issue, letters of allotment or renounceable letters of allotment, as appropriate, are issued [***see precedent 55***]. In the case of renounceable allotments, it will be necessary to wait for registration of any renouncements, following which a directors' meeting must approve the final allotment of shares and approve the issue of share certificates evidencing the additional shares [***see precedent** 48*]. Form SH01 must be filed with the Registrar within one month of the date of issue of the shares. Where amendments to the Articles or an increase in the directors' authority to allot shares are also necessary, appropriate resolutions and forms should be filed within 15 days of the general meeting, together with a reprint of the Articles incorporating the changes .

Redeemable shares

Issue of redeemable shares

Redeemable shares, or shares which are liable to be redeemed at the option of the company or of the shareholder, may be issued by a company limited by shares or limited by guarantee and having a share capital. Under previous Companies Acts, companies could only exercise this power if specific authority was contained in their Articles. Under CA2006 private companies are deemed to have this power subject to any restrictions contained in their Articles. Public companies however require specific authority in their Articles (CA2006 s.684).

Redeemable shares may be issued by a company only if the following conditions are satisfied:

1. The Articles must be checked to ensure that in the case of a private company there is no prohibition or restriction on the issue of redeemable shares, and in the case of a public company that there is authority for the issue of redeemable shares.
2. At the time of issue of redeemable shares, the company must have other shares which are not redeemable.
3. Redeemable shares may not be redeemed unless they are fully paid.
4. The terms of redemption must provide for payment on redemption.
5. The redemption money must come only out of distributable profits or out of the proceeds of a fresh issue of shares made for the purpose. Private companies, however, subject to certain conditions, may make redemption out of capital.
6. Shares which have been redeemed must be cancelled on redemption, and the amount of the issued share capital is diminished by the nominal value of the shares redeemed. If a company is about to redeem any shares, it may issue shares up to the nominal amount of the shares to be redeemed as if those shares had never been issued. Where redemption takes place wholly or partly out of distributable profits, a transfer must be made to the company's capital redemption reserve.

Capital redemption reserve

Where redemption or purchase of shares is effected out of the company's distributable profits the nominal value of the shares so redeemed or purchased must be transferred to the company's capital redemption reserve. If part of the redemption or purchase money comes from the proceeds of a fresh issue of shares, the amount transferred to the capital redemption reserve is the aggregate value of the proceeds of the new issue less the nominal value of the shares redeemed or purchased (CA2006 s.733). The capital redemption reserve is treated as part of the capital of the company, but it may be used in connection with allotting fully paid shares to members under a capitalisation issue.

Premium on redemption of shares

Any premium over the nominal value payable on redemption of redeemable shares must normally be paid out of the company's distributable profits (CA2006 s.687(3)). If, however, the redeemable shares were issued at a premium, the premium payable on redemption may be paid from:

1 the proceeds of a fresh issue of shares made for the purpose of the redemption up to an amount equal to the aggregate of the premiums received by the company on the issue of the shares redeemed; or
2 the current amount of the company's share premium account (including any sum transferred to that account in respect of premiums on the new shares),

whichever is the less. In this case, the company's share premium account must be reduced by the amount of the premium paid on the redemption out of the proceeds of the fresh issue (CA2006 s.687(5)).

Drawings of redeemable shares

A company's Articles may require shares to be redeemed by a specified date and it is usual to establish a sinking fund for this purpose. The fund is normally operated by annual drawings of shares to be redeemed at the redemption price or by purchases on the market if they can be bought there at a lower price. If making market purchases, this should be done prior to the date on which the annual drawing would normally take place. It is much easier for the company to meet its target for annual redemptions by making market purchases. The arrangements for making drawings are complicated and more costly since, in order to ensure impartiality, it is usual to arrange for the drawing to be supervised by two or more professional persons such as a solicitor, a chartered accountant or a notary public. Of course, if the price of shares in the market to be redeemed is higher in the market than the redemption price, it is appropriate to effect the annual instalment of redemption by a drawing.

Where purchases are made on the market, the company's brokers are instructed to purchase the number of shares required for the annual instalment of redemption. However, if the price is favourable on the market, there is nothing to stop the company from continuing to make market purchases at prices lower than the redemption price to cover future annual instalments of redemption.

The following is a summary of the procedural points that arise where a drawing is to be undertaken:

1 A complete shareholder listing as at the record date is prepared. In practice a listed company will obtain this listing from its registrar.
2 Depending on the amount of shares to be repurchased, the holdings are broken down into parcels of (say) 5,000 shares, and each parcel allocated a unique reference number. Where a particular shareholder's holding is not an exact multiple of 5,000 the balance is consolidated into composite parcels. Accordingly, a holder with 15,000 shares would have three parcels and a holder with 12,500 will have two parcels and shares in a third.
3 A schedule showing the allocation of the parcels and composite parcels amongst the shareholders is prepared and reconciled.

4 Tickets are prepared for each parcel showing the reference number to allow the draw to take place.

5 The date and place of drawing are arranged. The requirements of the Articles must be observed in regard to the manner in which the drawing is to be made, e.g. in the presence of a notary public or solicitor.

6 (*Listed, AIM and PLUS companies only*) The UK Listing Authority should be advised of the date of drawing, the record date for the drawing, the number of shares to be drawn and the redemption price.

7 The following documents are prepared:

(a) a formal notice to be sent to shareholders whose shares have been drawn for redemption, stating that the necessary payment authority and discharge form will be sent in due course;

(b) a circular letter to be sent to shareholders whose shares have been drawn for redemption, giving details of the procedure for redemption and enclosing the form of payment authority and discharge form to be returned with the appropriate share certificate(s) [***see precedent** 56*]. The letter will explain that if the shares being redeemed are only part of the holding, and the shareholder cannot give certificate(s) covering the exact number, he should send certificate(s) to the nearest number over the number of shares drawn for redemption and that a balance certificate for the excess (i.e. the shares not redeemed) will be sent to him. It will also explain that no further dividends will be paid on the shares redeemed;

(c) payment advice with attached cheque.

8 It is desirable that the drawing should be made in the presence of at least three persons. One, e.g. an accountant or a solicitor, will draw the numbered tickets, the two others each has a list of the shareholders on which the numbers drawn are noted against the relative holding. The tickets drawn should be kept separate to enable the preparation of a master list of the holdings that have been drawn for redemption. The last ticket drawn will usually represent a fractional number of shares so as to complete the drawing to the exact sinking fund redemption instalment. If this ticket applies to a composite group, the Articles usually authorise the person in charge of the drawing to determine the holding to which it is to apply.

9 (*Listed, AIM and PLUS companies only*) After the drawing, the UK Listing Authority must be advised that it has taken place, noting the number of shares which are still in issue which will remain listed (*LR 9.6.4, 12.5.2*).

10 The formal notices prepared under 7 above are sent to the shareholders whose holdings have been drawn for redemption, informing them of the fact and that a further circular and letter of authority will be sent to them in due course informing them of the procedure to be followed in order to secure the proceeds of the redemption. This will normally take place some two or three months after the actual date of drawing.

11 It is no longer possible to transfer the shares which have been drawn for

redemption, and brokers instructed to sell shares in listed companies should ascertain from the list posted by the UK Listing Authority that they have not been drawn for redemption.

12 About three weeks before the date on which the payment of the redemption monies is due, the circular letter prepared under 7 above is sent to the shareholders concerned detailing the procedure and enclosing the forms of payment authority and discharge to be signed by them and returned to the company with the appropriate share certificate(s). All joint holders should sign the form of authority and corporate shareholders, if they have a seal, would execute the form of authority under seal. Cheques for the redemption payments are prepared to be available when the forms of authority are received back from the shareholders.
13 A redemption account is opened with the company's bankers and the necessary funds transferred to the account to cover the cheques to be issued.
14 When forms of authority are received from the shareholders they should be checked to ensure that they have been properly completed and, if the certificate(s) lodged is (are) for more than the number of shares being redeemed, balance certificates should be prepared for issue to the shareholder.
15 Before sending cheques, the payment advice prepared under 7 above should be checked against the official drawing list. The cheques should be sent out so as to arrive on the due redemption date.
16 Reminders should be sent to shareholders who have not returned their forms.
17 The shareholders' accounts in the register of members are debited with the number of shares redeemed.
18 The secretary formally reports to the board the completion of the redemption following the annual drawing for the sinking fund purpose.
19 Notice of the redemption must be sent to the Registrar of Companies on Form SH02 ('Notice of consolidation, division, sub-division, redemption or cancellation of shares, or conversion, re-conversion of stock into shares') within one month of the redemption.
20 If the shares redeemed are preference shares, they will remain entitled to any dividend for the half-year ending on the redemption date and warrants should be prepared for the payment of the preference dividend to be dispatched to the holders in the ordinary way. Payment of the preference dividend should be dealt with quite separately from the payment of the redemption money.
21 If the shares are redeemed at a premium over the nominal value, the amount paid on redemption which exceeds the original issue price will be treated as a taxable distribution. The company should therefore issue a tax voucher to cover the amount of such distribution.

Purchase of redeemable shares

The following summarises the procedure to be followed by listed companies where the necessary shares to cover the sinking fund redemption instalment have been purchased on the market:

1 The company checks the contract notes received from its brokers in respect of the shares purchased.
2 The UK Listing Authority must be advised of the number of shares purchased and the number remaining outstanding (*LR 9.6.4, 12.5.2*).
3 The company secretary arranges to pay the brokers for the shares purchased on the relevant settlement date against the contract notes.
4 Forms of discharge and certificates received from the brokers are checked.
5 If the shares have been purchased cum dividend, the holdings concerned must be withdrawn from the dividend list, since no dividend will be paid on them. If the shares have been purchased ex-dividend, no special action is necessary and the shareholders who have sold their shares will be entitled to the dividend in the usual way.
6 The entries of the relevant shareholders in the register of members are debited with the shares purchased. These are transferred to a redemption account and on the redemption date the shares will be utilised for the redemption instalment.

It should be noted that, whilst the above procedure is described as a 'purchase' of redeemable shares, the operation is, in fact, another form of redemption of shares.

Procedure for redemption of loan stock and debentures

The procedure for the redemption of loan stocks and debentures through the operation of a sinking fund is similar to that described above in respect of the drawings of redeemable shares and purchase of redeemable shares. Debentures and loan stocks may be redeemed by annual drawings or by purchases on the market in order to meet the sinking fund requirements.

Purchase of own shares

A company may purchase its own shares which were not issued as redeemable shares provided that the purchase is prohibited or restricted by the company's Articles of Association (CA2006 s.690) but must be authorised by the members. There are, however, certain procedural requirements to be followed. Generally, the procedures are similar to those applying when a company purchases its redeemable shares on the market. In particular, the consideration for the purchase must be paid on completion and cannot be deferred or left outstanding on a loan account (CA2006 s.691(2)).

It is advisable for a company contemplating purchasing its own shares to take legal advice at the outset. One of the points that arises is that if the amount paid by the company for the purchase of its shares exceeds the issue price of the shares, on general principle the excess is treated as a distribution by the company and is taxable as income in the hands of the vendor. A tax voucher should be issued in respect of the excess. If the company is not a listed company or the subsidiary of a listed company, s.219 of the Income and Corporation Taxes Act 1988 (ICTA 1988) contains a provision to the effect that the excess will not be treated as an income distribution, but will be treated as part of the capital proceeds of the sale of the shares.

Advance clearance that a proposed purchase will be treated in this way can be obtained from HM Customs & Revenue, but it is recommended that the company's taxation advisers are consulted before taking any action in this respect (ICTA 1988 s.225). A public company, whether listed or not, may only purchase its own shares out of distributable profit or the proceeds of a new issue of shares made for that purpose only. A private company that has no or insufficient distributable profit may make the purchase out of capital.

Procedure for off-market purchases

The requirements for purchases by a company of its own shares are contained in CA2006 ss.690 to 708. Purchases would be either:

1 purchases made other than on a recognised investment exchange called 'off market purchases'; or
2 purchases on a recognised investment exchange but where the shares are not subject to a marketing arrangement on that exchange, i.e. (a) the shares are not listed on that stock exchange; or (b) if the company may, without prior permission, effect individual transactions on that stock exchange without time limit as to the time during which those facilities are to be available (e.g. the Alternative Investment Market).

The following procedural steps must be complied with to effect an off-market purchase of shares by a company:

1 A special resolution of the company must authorise the terms of the proposed contract of purchase before the company enters into the contract. [***See precedent 57.***] The purchase may also be made under a contingent purchase whereby a company becomes entitled or obliged to purchase its own shares provided this has been authorised by special resolution. Authorities may be varied, revoked or renewed by a special resolution. If the Articles do not contain authority for the company to purchase its own shares, the Articles should be amended by special resolution of the members. However, in the case of a public company, the special resolution confirming or renewing authority for a company to purchase its own shares must specify a date for its expiry, which must be not later than 18 months from the date of passing the special resolution.
2 The special resolution will not be effective unless a copy of the proposed contract of purchase [***see precedent 58***] (or a written memorandum of its

terms if it is not in writing) is made available for inspection by members of the company at the company's registered office for not less than 15 days prior to the meeting and is available for inspection at the meeting. The memorandum must include the names of the members holding the shares to which the contract relates. If it is the contract itself that is available for inspection, it must have annexed to it a written memorandum specifying the names if they do not appear in the contract itself. Similar arrangements must be made in the case of the variation of an existing contract, which also has to be approved by a special resolution. A private company may authorise the purchase of its own shares by written resolution under CA2006 s.288. To be valid a copy of the proposed contract or a memorandum of its terms must be made available to each member no later than the date on which the written resolution is forwarded to them for approval and signature. In practice, it is normal to circulate a copy of the contract or the memorandum of its terms, together with the written resolution for signature and return.

3 The votes of any member whose shares are being repurchased should be disregarded for the purposes of establishing whether there is the necessary 75 per cent majority in favour of the resolution. The resolution will be ineffective if this provision is contravened.
4 The same provisions as those set out in 2 above apply to any resolution varying the terms of an existing agreement or the proposed release by the company of its rights to make a purchase under an existing agreement.

Procedure for market purchases by listed companies

The provisions of the Companies Act 2006 in respect of market purchases by a company of its own shares are less stringent than those that apply in the case of off-market purchases. It should be noted, however, that in the case of listed companies the requirements of chapter 12 of the *Listing Rules* will need to be complied with. It will also be necessary to adhere to the best practice guidelines issued by institutional shareholder bodies such as the ABI.

The following procedural points should be observed:

1 Other than where an existing authority is being renewed, a decision to seek authority for a market purchase must be notified to a Regulatory Information Service without delay (*LR 12.4.4*), together with notification of the result of the vote (*LR 12.4.5*). Although only an ordinary resolution is necessary, institutional shareholders have requested that the authority be sought by special resolution. The resolution must stipulate the maximum number of shares that may be purchased and the maximum and minimum purchase prices. [***See precedent 59.***]
2 The circular to shareholders must include, where appropriate, those details required by the *Listing Rules* (*LR 13.7.1*) in addition to the usual circular requirements (*LR 13.3*).

3 The circular will require approval by the FSA if the shares are to be acquired from a related party or is in respect of 25 per cent or more of the issued share capital (*LR13.2.3*) unless a tender is made to all holders or the purchase from a related party is without prior agreement and pursuant to a general authority.
4 The company should not purchase shares at any time when the directors would not be free to do so on their own account under the Model Code (*LR 15.1*).
5 Institutional shareholder bodies have issued guidance that they will support market purchases of up to 5 per cent, and that purchases of up to 10 per cent will be supported where circumstances make this appropriate. Proposals for the purchase of more than 10 per cent are likely to be resisted unless specific proposals are put to shareholders for approval.
6 Purchases of more than 15 per cent (excluding treasury shares) must be by way of a tender offer (*LR 12.4.2*). Purchases of less than 15 per cent may be by way of a general authority provided the price is not higher than 5 per cent above the average market value over the previous 5 business days.
7 Details of any purchases made must be notified to a Regulatory Information Service no later than 7.30 am on the business day following the purchase.

The ordinary resolution conferring, varying, revoking or renewing authority to make a market purchase of the company's own shares must be filed with the Registrar of Companies within 15 days of it being passed together with a statement of capital.

The possible need to send tax vouchers to the vendors of the shares purchased should not be overlooked as the purchase of shares will usually be treated as a taxable distribution with tax payable on any excess consideration over the original issue price. Specialist advice on the tax consequences of any share purchases should be taken.

Procedural requirements for both off- and on-market purchases

Form SH03 ('Return of purchase of own shares') must be filed with the Registrar of Companies, duly stamped, within 28 days of the delivery of the shares purchased by the company (CA2006 s.707). The return includes information on the number, class and nominal value of the shares purchased, the date of delivery to the company and, in the case of a public company, the aggregate amount paid by the company for the shares to which the return relates together with the maximum and minimum prices paid. Where the consideration exceeds £1,000, stamp duty is payable by the company on the consideration paid by it on the purchase of its shares at the usual rate (currently 0.5 per cent, rounded up to the nearest £5). A copy of a contract to purchase the company's shares (and a copy of any variation of it), or a memorandum of the terms if it is not in writing, must be kept at the registered office or its alternative inspection place of the company from the conclusion of the contract for a period of ten years commencing with the date on which the purchase of the shares was completed. This document must be kept open for inspection by any member without charge and, in the case of a public company, it may be inspected by any other person also without charge (CA2006 s.702(6)).

Details of any shares purchased must be included in the directors' report together, in the case of a listed company, with details of any existing authority to purchase shares (*LR 12.43(n)*). An amount equal to the nominal value of the shares purchased must be transferred to a capital redemption reserve and any premium paid in excess of the nominal value written off against distributable profits (CA2006 s.733).

Treasury shares

With effect from 1 December 2003 companies whose shares are listed, admitted to AIM or an equivalent regulated market in the EEA, this includes the PLUS quoted companies may acquire their own shares and hold these in treasury (CA2006 724) Unlike the existing provisions relating to purchase of own shares (see pp. 107–111) shares purchased under the treasury shares provisions are not cancelled on purchase but may be retained or sold (CA2006 s.724(3)).

The procedural steps for purchases into treasury are the same as for purchases of own shares with the following additional provisions:

1. A listed company wishing to purchase 15 per cent or more of its shares into treasury must do so by way of a tender offer (*LR 12.4.1*).
2. The company should not sell shares from treasury or transfer treasury shares to an employee share scheme at any time when the directors would not be free to do so on their own account under the Model Code (*LR 12.6*).
3. Details of any allotments by way of capitalisation issue or the sale or transfer to an employee share scheme, or cancellation of treasury shares must be notified to a regulatory information service as soon as possible and no later than 7.30 am on the first business day following the event (*LR 12.6.3 and 4*).
4. Once the company has purchased the shares to be held in treasury, a Return on SH03 must be submitted to the Registrar, stating the number of shares and the class of shares together with the nominal value of the shares and the date on which they were re-purchased (CA2006 s.707(1)). The re-purchase of shares to be held in treasury by a company is subject to stamp duty, the duty being payable on the consideration and not the nominal value at the rate of 0.5 per cent (rounded up to the nearest £5).
5. If the shares are subsequently cancelled, sold or transferred SH04 must be filed (CA2006 ss.728 and 730). If a company holding shares in treasury ceases to qualify to hold treasury shares, any shares held in treasury are cancelled (CA2006 s.729).
6. Shares held in treasury may be sold for cash, transferred to satisfy claims under employee share schemes or be cancelled (CA2006 s.727). Shares held in

treasury have no voting or dividend rights but may take up rights in respect of bonus issues and may be redeemed if the shares are redeemable (CA2006 s.726).

Redemption or purchases by private companies out of capital

Purchases by a public company of its own shares may be made only out of distributable profits or the proceeds of a fresh issue of shares (CA2006 s.693). In the case of private companies, however, CA2006 s.692 provides a procedure to effect purchases or redemptions of shares out of capital. Very stringent and complicated additional procedures have to be complied with. In practice for a private company it will most likely be easier to undertake the acquisition using the reduction of capital provisions (see pp. 69–71).

A private company may purchase its own shares out of capital (CA2006 s.709). Under the previous Companies Acts, companies required specific authority in their Articles to do so but under CA2006 companies are deemed to have this authority unless their Articles contain any prohibition or restriction. The amount of the payment that may be made out of capital is known as the 'permissible capital payment'. The amount of the permissible capital payment is the amount to be paid for the shares after deduction of all distributable profits and the amount of any funds raised by the issue of new shares.

Thus, no capital payment may be made until all available profit has been used. Capital is defined as any payment made other than out of distributable profit or the proceeds of a new issue. Accordingly, the use of funds raised by way of a loan will be treated as a capital payment (CA2006 s.713).

The additional procedural steps to be followed in the case of the purchase by a private company of its own shares out of capital are contained in CA2006 s.713, as follows:

1 A statement must be made by the directors which specifies the amount of the permissible capital payment for the shares. The form also incorporates a statement by the directors that, having made a full enquiry into the affairs of the company, they have formed the opinion that once the payment out of capital has been made, there are no grounds on which the company would then be unable to pay its debts and that, in the year following the payment, the company will be able to carry on its business as a going concern and pay its debts as they fall due [***see precedent 60***]. This statement must take into account any contingent or prospective liabilities of the company at the time the statement is made (CA2006 s.714).
2 An auditor's report must be attached to the statutory declaration confirming that:
   - the auditors have enquired into the company's state of affairs;

- the amount specified in the declaration as the permissible capital payment for the shares has been properly determined;
- the auditors do not consider that any opinion expressed by the directors in the declaration is unreasonable. A company which qualifies as small and has taken advantage of the exemption from appointing auditors will need to appoint auditors and have their accounts audited before this statement can be given (CA2006 s.714).

3 A special resolution of the company must be passed on or within one week of the directors' declaration, approving the proposed payment out of capital, and copies of the statutory declaration must be available for inspection by members of the company at the meeting at which the resolution is passed [***see precedent 61***]. A member whose shares are the subject of the special resolution may not vote on the resolution (CA2006 s.716).

4 Publicity must be given to the proposed payment out of capital in the following manner (CA2006 s.719):

- within one week of the passing of the special resolution, a public notice must be published in the *London Gazette* or *Edinburgh Gazette,* together with a notice in a national newspaper or a notice in writing to each of the creditors of the company stating that the company has approved a payment out of capital for the purpose of acquiring its own shares by redemption or purchase [***see precedent 62***];
- within one week of the passing of the special resolution, copies of the statutory declaration and auditor's report must be filed with the Registrar of Companies, to be received not later than the date on which the public notice is given.

5 From the date of the public notice to the end of the fifth week following the date on which the special resolution was passed, the directors' declaration and auditor's report must be kept at the company's registered office or alternative inspection location and be open for inspection by any member or creditor of the company without charge.

6 Payment out of capital must be made within the period commencing five weeks after the date of passing the special resolution and terminating seven weeks after the date of the special resolution.

7 Up to the end of the fifth week following the date of passing the special resolution, any member of the company (other than a member who voted in favour of the resolution) and any creditor may apply to the Court for the resolution to be cancelled (CA2006 s.721). If such an application is made, notice must be given to the Registrar of Companies immediately on Form SH16 ('Notice of application to the court for the cancellation of a resolution for the redemption or purchase of shares out of capital'). On the making of a court order a copy must be filed with the Registrar within 15 days of it being made or a longer period if the Court allows (CA2006 s.722). The Court has wide powers in considering any such application and may alter or extend the date or period specified in the resolution or in the Companies Act 2006. It may also direct any necessary alterations to be made to the company's Articles, which will then have the same effect as if passed by a special resolution of the company. If the Court makes alterations to the Articles the company must obtain the Court's permission before making further alterations which would be in breach of the Court's requirements (CA2006 s.721(7)).

Failure to redeem or purchase shares

A company failing to redeem or purchase its shares under an agreement will not be liable to pay damages if other remedies could be available to the shareholder concerned (CA2006 s.735). The position if at the commencement of the winding-up of the company any shares have not been redeemed or purchased pursuant to the special resolution is also covered in CA2006 s.735.

Issue of debenture stock

The issues in relation to public issues of shares (see Chapters 15 and 16) apply equally in the case of a public issue of debenture stock and, subject to the provisions of the trust deed, arrangements for the transfer, payment of interest, meetings of holders, etc., will also be similar. There are additional requirements contained in the Prospectus Rules to be met if the debenture stock is to be listed.

A trust deed to secure the issue of debenture stock will usually cover the following:

1. details of the stock, terms of issue, payment of principal and interest, any conversion rights and stock certificates;
2. the provisions constituting the charges of assets of the company in favour of the trustee, stipulating the events on which the security becomes enforceable;
3. the trustees' powers to concur with the company in dealings with the charged assets;
4. covenants by the company in relation to its business and to the charged assets;
5. the remuneration of the trustees;
6. where a floating charge is constituted, a prohibition on the issue of any other security ranking ahead of the stock without the consent of the holder;
7. schedules to the trust deed containing the form of stock certificate, the detailed conditions of redemption in whole or in part by drawings or purchase and of any conversion rights, regulations with regard to the register of holders, provisions governing the transfer and transmission of the stock, and regulations governing meetings of holders of the stock.

If the debenture stock is listed, the reverse of the certificate will have printed on it a summary of the conditions rather than the full conditions, unless this is prohibited by the trust deed. The holder of debenture stock is entitled to be supplied with a copy of the trust deed at his request on payment of a fee (CA2006 s.749).

The trust deed for listed companies that intend that the debt security will also be listed must contain the details set out in the *Prospectus Rules and Listing Rules (LR 17)*. These include:

- repayment dates;
- conversion rights;
- rights to attend and vote at meetings;
- rights of transfer;
- the fact that if the security is unsecured it must be designated as 'unsecured';
- appointment and powers of the trustees;
- power to forfeit unclaimed interest, not to be used until 12 years from the date of payment.

Conversion of loan stock

The company secretary or the company's registrar will be concerned with the proper procedure for dealing with applications from holders to exercise their conversion rights. The following is a summary of the procedure to be followed:

1. Send a letter prior to each conversion date in each year to those holders of the loan stock who have not yet converted, reminding them of the opportunity to convert into ordinary shares. Enclose a form of nomination and acceptance to convert or instruct them that if they wish to convert, they should complete the form printed on the reverse of the convertible loan stock certificate. [***See precedent 63.***]

   Where the company is a listed company, the circular reminding holders of the loan stock of their conversion rights should follow the format set out in the *Listing Rules* (*LR 13.8.16*). If this format is followed, approval from the UK Listing Authority is not required, although two copies of the circular must be submitted to the UK Listing Authority no later than their issue to the holders of the loan stock (*LR 9.6.1*). If the circular is not in the prescribed format, approval will be required and two draft copies of the circular together with the documents required by *LR 12.2.4* must be submitted to the UK Listing Authority at least ten days prior to the intended date of publication (*LR 13.2.5*). Once agreed, two copies of the final version must be submitted to the UK Listing Authority, as above.
2. Unless the board has delegated its powers, submit the documents to be approved by the board.
3. Order the final prints of the circular letter and form of nomination and acceptance, sending them to the holders of the loan stock who have not yet converted into ordinary shares.
4. On receipt of loan stock certificates from holders, check that the form of acceptance to convert, or the notice of conversion on the back, has been properly completed and is accompanied by a completed form of nomination and

acceptance if the holder has nominated another person to receive the allotment of shares.

5 Prepare a record sheet for each holder who has lodged a notice of conversion, showing:
   - name and address;
   - the amount of stock to be converted;
   - the number and date of the stock certificate lodged;
   - any balance of convertible loan stock remaining which is not being converted;
   - the name and address of any other person nominated to receive the ordinary shares arising from the conversion;
   - the name and address of any agent to whom the new share certificate and any balance certificate for unconverted loan stock is to be sent;
   - the number of shares to be allotted as a result of the conversion and whether there are any fractions of £1 of loan stock remaining to be redeemed at par.
6 Maintain a daily running total of stock lodged for conversion, showing the total number of shares to be allotted and the fractions (if any) of loan stock to be redeemed at par.
7 When the last day for the receipt of notice of conversion has passed, notify the UK Listing Authority (if the stock is listed) and the trustee for the holders of loan stock of the amount of stock converted and the number of ordinary shares to be allotted.
8 Prepare the new share certificates, together with any balance certificates for unconverted loan stock and cheques drawn for any amounts for fractions of £1 of loan stock to be redeemed at par. The serial numbers of the new share certificates and the balance certificates for unconverted loan stock are entered on the record sheet.
9 (*Listed, AIM and PLUS companies only*) Apply for the new shares to be listed and admitted to trading as appropriate.
10 The board or an allotment committee of the directors formally allot the shares to the holders of the loan stock who have converted, or to their nominees if they have nominated another person to receive the shares arising out of the conversion [***see precedent 48***]. The certificates relating to the loan stock converted are cancelled. If the company has a common seal or a securities seal the share certificates and balance certificates are sealed. The certificates are sent with any remittance for fractions of £1 of loan stock which have been redeemed.
11 Make the necessary entries in the register of members, recording the holdings of ordinary shares by those who have converted. Also make entries in the register of loan stock holders from the information contained on the record sheets.

12 Within one month of the allotment a return of allotments must be delivered to the Registrar of Companies on Form SH01.

Redemption of debentures

Although debentures may be reissued (CA2006 s.752), this is unusual. In practice debentures and debenture stock are redeemable not later than a fixed future date. The title of the stock will give the date of redemption, e.g. '10.5 per cent Mortgage Debenture Stock 2002/2012', in which case the whole of the stock outstanding is redeemable between specific dates in 2002 and 2012, usually at par but possibly with a small premium.

The company should give notice of its intention to redeem the stock to every holder. The money for the redemption may come from a new issue of securities, out of profits or out of a combination of the two. Where redemption is out of profits of the company the proceeds will usually have come from a sinking fund or similar arrangement. It is not unusual for the trust deed to provide for partial redemptions of the stock during the course of its life in advance of the final redemption date by making annual drawings or by making market purchases at prices not exceeding those laid down in the trust deed. In addition to funding any redemption out of distributable profit or the issue of new shares a private company may redeem debentures out of capital subject to the provisions of CA2006 s.709.

The procedure for the redemption of loan stocks and debentures redeemable through the operation of a sinking fund is similar to the procedure for the redemption of redeemable shares issued by the company under the provisions of CA2006 ss.690 to 723.

Where debentures or debenture stock, secured by a charge over the company's property, are redeemed or converted in whole or in part, a memorandum of satisfaction that the property ceases to be affected by the charge may be filed with the Registrar of Companies signed on behalf of the company (CA2006 s.872). Although this procedure is not obligatory, it is in the best interests of the company for charges to be deleted from the public register immediately they are satisfied in whole or in part to avoid misleading any banks or other creditors who would otherwise form an unduly adverse view of the company's credit. The appropriate entries in the company's own register of charges should also be made.

6

Share transfers and transmission

Transfer of shares

Companies whose shares have been admitted to CREST will be authorised to accept electronic instructions to effect the transfer of shares (see pp. 124–127). On the whole, only companies whose shares are listed and traded on either the main market of the London Stock Exchange or the PLUS traded market operated by PLUS Markets Group, or admitted to trading on either the AIM or PLUS quoted markets, will have their shares CREST enabled. Companies whose shares have been de-listed may still have their shares enabled within CREST.

In the case of a private transaction in the shares of both private and public companies, a member wishing to dispose of his holding (i.e. the transferor) will complete a stock transfer form in the form contained in Sch.1 to the Stock Transfer Act 1963. This is passed to the purchaser (i.e. the transferee) with a share certificate or certificates for at least the number of shares being transferred, in exchange for the agreed price. The transferee enters his name and address as transferee on the transfer form, dates it and has it stamped by HM Revenue & Customs where required (see pp. 121–122). The transfer and share certificate(s) are then lodged with the company for registration. The transferee does not have to sign the stock transfer form, provided the shares are fully paid (see point 3 below).

Procedure on receipt of transfer

On receipt of the transfer the following procedure should be followed:

1 Check that details of the transferor and shareholding transferred agree with the share certificate and with the appropriate entry in the register of members. See p. 120 on checking the validity of transfers.
2 If the company has several classes of shares in issue, check that the shares transferred are fully and correctly described. There should be a separate stock transfer form for each class of shares being transferred.
3 If the shares are only partly paid, the amount shown as paid up on each share on the share certificate must be correctly shown on the transfer. If the company has recently made a call on the shares, the transfer should not be accepted until the call has been paid. In the case of partly paid shares, the transfer form should be in the old common form of transfer in general use

prior to the Stock Transfer Act 1963, which must also be executed by the transferee.

4 The share certificate(s) accompanying the transfer must be the original or a duplicate. If an original certificate is lodged and a duplicate has also been issued, the duplicate must also be surrendered to the company prior to registration.

5 Check the execution of the transfer by the transferor (or by his attorney). Since the transfer has been lodged with the company by a private individual, it may be desirable to obtain confirmation of the authenticity of the signature of the transferor.

6 Check the company's registration records to make sure that there is no lien or restraint on a transfer of the shares.

7 Check that the transfer has been duly stamped by HM Revenue & Customs, if required, and that the duty is appropriate for the consideration shown. If not stamped, the transfer must be certified as exempt (CA2006 s.770).

8 If all the above matters are in order, cancel the share certificate(s) and prepare a new certificate in the name of the transferee. Where only part of the holding covered by a certificate is being transferred, prepare a balance certificate in the name of the transferor.

9 The transfer should be approved by the company's board and authority given for the new certificate to be sealed, if appropriate, after checking that the transfer does not contravene any pre-emption rights in the company's Articles [***see precedent 64***]. The directors of listed, AIM and PLUS companies are required to ensure that shares are freely transferable and a resolution authorising the company secretary or the registrars to process transfers as they are received will have been given (*LR 2.2.4, AIM rule 32, PLUS rule 3*).

10 Where the Articles of Association of a company contain pre-emption provisions on the transfer of shares these provisions must be strictly followed. The existing shareholders can waive their rights, whether in full or in part, either by letter or by the approval of a special resolution [***see precedent 65***]. If a transfer is registered and pre-emption provisions have not been followed, the transfer can be challenged by the existing shareholders. If the directors resolve to refuse registration for any reason, the transferee must be informed within two months of lodgement of the transfer.

11 Enter the name of the transferee in the register of members, crediting the number of shares transferred to him. Debit the transferor's account in the register with the number of shares transferred.

12 File the transfer and cancelled share certificate(s).

13 Send the new certificate to the transferee or to his agent, after it has been sealed, if appropriate. If there is a balance certificate this should be sent direct to the transferor or his agent. Certificates should be ready within two months from the date on which the transfer is lodged (CA2006 s.776).

For listed companies, the new certificate(s) should be dispatched by first class mail or equivalent to members resident within the EU and by airmail to members not resident in the EU.

Checking the validity of transfers

The details on the transfer form and the share certificates must be carefully checked to ensure that they relate to the same holding. The register should also be checked to ensure that the certificate(s) is still valid and has not previously been reported as lost. The following points should be noted when checking the validity of transfers:

1. If the shareholding is in joint names, the names of the transferors should be shown on the transfer in the same order as they appear on the certificate and in the register of members. This avoids confusion if there are other holdings on the register in the same names but in a different order.
2. If the shareholder's account is designated, it should be checked that the correct designation appears on the transfer. It is clearly important to avoid the wrong account being debited in the register.
3. The transfer should deal with only one holding in the register as far as it concerns the transferor and transferee. If the same persons are concerned with other holdings with names in different order or bearing different designations, separate transfers will be necessary.
4. A transferor should be described as an executor or administrator only if he remains on the company's register in that capacity.
5. A transfer should deal with only one class of share unless (which is unusual) the Articles of Association permit a single transfer to cover more than one class.
6. A transfer signed by the registered holder and lodged for registration after his death can be accepted for registration if otherwise in order, and if only a relatively short period has elapsed since the death, and provided that no grant of representation has been registered by the company.
7. A transfer signed by an attorney of a registered holder must not be accepted for registration if it is known that the shareholder has died (whether or not a grant of representation has been registered with the company). This is because the death of a principal automatically revokes any power of attorney unless the power is coupled with an interest of the donee.
8. If a transfer has been executed by mark because of infirmity or illiteracy, it should be attested to the effect that the transfer has been read and explained to the transferor and that it appeared to have been understood by him. The attestation should be made by two witnesses, one of whom should have medical, legal or religious qualification, or by some other person of public standing. If the transfers are executed in Scotland, the procedure for notarial execution should be observed.

9 Unless the Articles of Association provide otherwise, a transfer of shares may be registered up to the last moment before liquidation (regardless of the means or standing of the transferee) so long as the transfer is bona fide in the sense that the transferor retains no interest in the shares.
10 Transferees must be individuals or corporate bodies without qualification as to any representative or nominal or trustee capacity in which they may hold the shares. Unincorporated bodies such as partnerships (in England and Wales) or clubs are not acceptable.
11 Transfers to the holder of an office rather than to a named individual should be accepted only if the office is of an official and public nature.
12 If there are a number of transferees, the number should be checked to ensure that it does not exceed the limits specified in the Articles of Association. Listed companies are required to allow at least four joint holders of shares.
13 If the details of the transferee on the transfer have been altered (the alteration should in any event be initialled by the transferor) a 'no subsale' declaration should be obtained from the person lodging the transfer, unless it is clear that the alteration does not affect the identity of the transferee.

Stamp duty

Unless the transfer is exempt (see below), the stock transfer form should be stamped by HM Revenue & Customs prior to being lodged with the company for registration. Stamp duty is currently payable at the rate of 0.5 per cent of the consideration paid for the shares, rounded up to the nearest £5. Stamp duty is payable within 30 days of the date of the transaction. If transfers, or other documents, are submitted for stamping late, interest and/or penalties may be payable.

The person responsible for maintaining the company's register of members (e.g. the company secretary or the company's registrar) is legally responsible for ensuring that all transfers accepted for registration are properly stamped or correctly certified as exempt (CA2006 s.770). There is no need to ascertain if the consideration is in accordance with the market value. It is only necessary to ensure that the stamp duty corresponds to the consideration stated on the transfer. Adjudication should be requested in any case where the transfer appears not to have been properly stamped. There is an arrangement between the United Kingdom and Eire to accept each other's stamps on transfers signed in either country.

Transfers exempt from stamp duty

With effect from 13 March 2008, share transfers which would have incurred stamp duty of not more than £5.00, are exempt from stamp duty. The new threshold for liability to duty is for transactions where the consideration for the transfer exceeds £1,000. The £5.00 fixed charge on certain instruments are also now exempt from stamp duty apart from duplicate or counterpart documents of substitute bearer instruments both of which still need to be presented to HM Revenue & Customs for denoting of the relevant particulars. These changes do not affect electronic transfers of stock which remain liable to stamp duty reserve tax.

An instrument executed on or after 13 March 2008 where the amount or value of the consideration is £1,000 or less will need to be certified on the reverse to confirm that the transaction does not form part of a larger transaction or series of transactions with an aggregate value in excess of £1,000. The certificate is printed on the reverse of the transfer form and if completed the form may be sent direct to the company or its registrar for processing.

Transfers to market makers in the ordinary course of business are also exempt from stamp duty. These must carry the HM Revenue & Customs supplementary stamp denoting that they are not chargeable to duty under s.81 of the Finance Act 1986.

Where shares are being transferred under a reorganisation or on an acquisition, the transfers may be exempt from stamp duty. An appropriate application should be submitted to the stamp duty adjudication section claiming exemption from stamp duty. The most common exemptions from duty are given for transactions complying with the conditions of s.42 of the Finance Act 1930 or s.77 of the Finance Act 1986. Broadly speaking, these exemptions are available for transfers between companies within a group or, in the case of a share exchange, where the shareholders in the acquiring company after the transaction mirror the shareholders in the company being acquired prior to the transaction and they hold the shares in the same proportions.

Forged transfers

A forged transfer is a nullity and can pass no rights whatsoever to any transferee. On discovery of the forgery, the purported transferor is entitled to receive a similar number of identical shares to those transferred. It is the company's responsibility to provide these, together with any dividends or other entitlements that his wrongful removal from the register has prevented him from receiving.

If, before the forgery is discovered, the shares are transferred for valuable consideration to a third party acting in good faith and without knowledge of the forgery, the company is liable in damages to that person to compensate him for any loss he may have suffered. This is in addition to the liability to restore the name of the defrauded owner to the register of members in respect of the shares. Because the third party relied on a certificate issued by the company under seal, the company is prohibited from denying the validity of its certificates under seal or executed as deeds.

The company has a corresponding right of action against the person lodging the transfer for registration as by lodging the transfer he implies that it is genuine.

This does not, however, absolve a company and its officers from exercising care in connection with the registration of transfers and consequential actions. Despite all practicable precautions, however, it is not possible to be certain that a company will not at some time incur liability in respect of a forged transfer. Under the Forged Transfer Acts 1891 and 1892 any company has power to make compensation by cash payment out of its funds for any loss arising from a forged transfer. Companies usually effect a forged transfer insurance policy to cover this risk. These will generally include cover for documents lodged for registration, dividend warrants, transfer receipts, etc.

Rectification of transferee details

Amendments to the register should be made only under the sanction of a court order for rectification (CA2006 s.125). In practice, however, minor clerical errors are informally corrected on the register under the authority of a responsible officer (such as the company secretary or registrar), following receipt by the company or its registrar of a duly completed form of request for rectification of transferee details.

Where a major alteration is requested affecting the identity of the transferee (e.g. a completely different name is to be substituted), the legal position as to whether rectification without recourse to the Court is permitted is not entirely free from doubt.

Practical difficulties are, however, unlikely to arise if the following points are observed:

1. Particular care should be exercised if the circumstances suggest that some change of beneficial ownership or sub-sale has taken place or that there has been a change of mind on the part of the broker or the client as to the names in which the shares concerned should be registered. If there is any doubt, rectification without recourse to the Court should be permitted only if satisfactory assurances that the circumstances permit such rectification are obtained from the lodging agent.
2. If the original certificate was issued more than three months before the receipt of the request for rectification or if, in the meantime, a dividend has been paid or accepted, or there is other evidence that the transferee has accepted the shares concerned, rectification without recourse to the Court should not be permitted. In this event, rectification by the Court is required or a duly executed and stamped transfer from the present registered holder to the 'correct transferee' should be obtained.

Transmission of shares

'Transmission' of shares has been defined as dispositions by operation of law, compared with 'transfers' of shares, which are dispositions by voluntary act.

Transmissions are most commonly encountered upon death or upon bankruptcy or upon a member becoming of unsound mind and the subject of an order of the Court of Protection.

CREST: The electronic share settlement system

The Companies Act 1989 s.207 empowered the Secretary of State to make provision for a paperless system for recording title to and transfer of securities. In July 1996 this power was used to create CREST.

The Uncertificated Securities Regulations 2001 (SI 2001/3755) provide the basis and regulation of CREST. CREST is an electronic system whereby ownership of shares can be transferred by alterations in computer records, which serve as evidence of title. CREST is operated by Euroclear UK & Ireland Ltd (formerly CRESTCo).

Residual settlement

Although virtually all listed, AIM and PLUS listed or quoted companies market transactions are settled using CREST, transactions in shares which have not been admitted to CREST are usually settled through the residual settlement system established by Euroclear UK & Ireland Ltd, the CREST operator.

Stock in the form of share certificates and executed stock transfer form is delivered through the CREST courier and sorting service (CCSS) to the buying member firm. The consideration is then made by the buying member firm through the CREST system.

The completed stock transfer form or, in the case of multiple transferees, broker transfer forms and the share certificates will be sent to the company's registrar for processing either directly or via CCSS. The registrar will process the transfer(s) as set out on pp. 126–127. The certificates resulting from the transfer will be returned via CCSS if delivered that way or by post. Transfers effected this way settle on the basis of a rolling settlement period.

Overview

Where the company's shares have been admitted to settlement in CREST, the register of members is split in two with Euroclear UK & Ireland being responsible for the electronic sub-register enabling electronic transfer of title on settlement. An individual shareholder may have two accounts: one certificated and the other uncertificated. Movements between the uncertificated accounts are authorised by electronic messages from the system operator (without the use of paper transfers). Movements from uncertificated to certificated accounts (stock withdrawals) are also effected by electronic messages. A movement from a certificated account to an uncertificated account (stock deposit) is a paper-based transaction. The registrar may also initiate adjustments to the register, sending a registrar's adjustment message to the system operator, to correct errors or give effect to certain corporate actions involving the issue of further units of the security concerned.

At the end of each business day there is reconciliation between the operator and the registrar and by the operator with the other system members. The system members include institutional investors and nominees' brokers and banks. Corporate or private investors who are unable or unwilling to meet the requirements of full membership may become sponsored members, appointing a full member to act on their behalf.

Listed, AIM and PLUS companies are required to appoint CREST compliant registrars to facilitate electronic settlement of their securities (*LR 6.1.23, LR 9.2.4, AIM rule 36, PLUS rule 3*).

CREST preserves much of the 'name on register' aspects of the former system although it may become more difficult to identify shareholders if they move (because of CREST or shortening settlement times) to holding shares through nominees.

Where a nominee holds shares for a number of beneficial holders, the company can send just one aggregate dividend payment to the nominee, leaving the nominee to split the dividend between those entitled and to issue subsidiary tax vouchers. As regards reports and accounts, there is an obligation to supply only one copy to the nominee although companies will usually make bulk deliveries available on request.

Joining CREST

Where a company's shares are being listed (or admitted to AIM or PLUS) for the first time, as part of the arrangements for the listing the company will be required to apply for the shares to be admitted to CREST. The Articles of the company should make provision for the shares to be held and transferred through CREST. The company's registrars will liaise with Euroclear UK & Ireland to ensure that the CREST functionality for the shares is enabled at the appropriate time. There are two alternative methods of ensuring a company's shares are capable of CREST settlement:

1 If the Articles do not permit the company's securities to be transferred through CREST (as will usually be the case), they can be changed by special resolution to allow this form of transfer. [***See precedent 66.***]
2 Alternatively, in the case of shares, a board resolution may be used for this purpose. This route will override provisions of the Articles which are inconsistent with the holding or transfer of shares in uncertificated form. There may, however, be other inconsistencies not covered by the directors' resolution, in which case amendment of the Articles by special resolution will be necessary.

Notice of the directors' resolution is required to be given either before it is passed, or within 60 days of its being passed, to every member of the company. To save costs it is desirable to include the notice in a routine mailing to shareholders.

A combined course of action may be taken:

1 Pass the board resolution that title to the company's securities shall be transferred through CREST.
2 Explain the matter in the annual report and include in the annual general meeting notice a special resolution effectively ratifying the board's decision by changing the Articles as necessary. In this way, additional consequential changes may be made whilst enabling CREST settlement prior to the date of the annual general meeting. A copy of the directors' resolution must be filed at Companies House within 15 days of being passed. It must be included in or annexed to any copy of the Articles of Association issued after the resolution had been passed (reg.40(3)).

As well as making itself eligible for electronic settlement, as described above, a security application form must be submitted to Euroclear UK & Ireland 48 hours prior to the commencement of settlement, usually by the registrar, for each class of securities to commence CREST settlement. Such securities are known as being 'CREST enabled'.

CREST transaction procedure

Once a security is enabled in CREST, all market transactions are settled through the system whether or not they are uncertificated.

The procedures are as follows:

1 A member of CREST which wishes to move its certificated securities into its uncertificated CREST account does so by lodging the relevant certificates and a completed dematerialisation request form with the CCSS. Alternatively, if a CREST member acquires shares in certificated form and wishes them to be credited to their uncertificated account, the share certificate(s) are lodged with the CCSS, together with a signed stock deposit form. The CCSS passes these documents on to the company's registrar for action.
2 Prior to lodgement, the member sends an electronic data capture (EDC) message to the CREST operator. The CCSS forwards the member's EDC message to the registrar when it has accepted a stock deposit or dematerialisation request, which enables the registrar to check that the documentation is subsequently received. If, upon receipt of the documents, these are found to be in order, the securities concerned are transferred by the registrar from the certificated account of the client and credited to the uncertificated account of the CREST member. They will then be available for delivery through CREST under the usual settlement procedures. Such CREST transfers are exempt

from stamp duty although the underlying transaction may itself have attracted an SDRT charge, collected through the CREST system.

3 If a CREST member wishes securities held on its uncertificated account to be held in certificated form, the member sends a stock withdrawal request electronically to the registrar through the CREST system. This message includes full details of both parties to the transaction as well as the number of shares involved. The registrar moves the securities into the relevant (existing or new) account in the certificated part of the register and issues a certificate in the required name, which is forwarded to the CREST member via the CCSS. These stock movements are exempt from stamp duty and SDRT (though the settlement of the underlying purchase of the securities for the client may itself have attracted an SDRT charge, collected through the system).

Shareholder visibility

Due to the structure of CREST, there is a growing trend for private shareholders to hold through CREST member nominees. One way of preserving the direct link between the company and its shareholders is by means of designated accounts in the register. Under company law as it currently stands, however, this does not in itself give any membership rights to the underlying owner of the shares. The company must treat the nominee on the register as the legal owner of the shares (CA2006 s.126). The use of multiple designation of accounts involves extra costs for the CREST member concerned and would seem also to compromise much of the welcome simplicity of the CREST system. It is, however, increasingly being used by brokers with substantial private clients as it facilitates quicker dealing and settlement and significantly reduces the amount of paperwork.

Sponsored members

These obstacles to shareholder visibility are partially overcome by the adoption of the concept of sponsored membership.

CREST allows investors who are not connected electronically to the CREST system to become sponsored members. Their accounts are operated on their behalf by a full institutional member of CREST (a participating member). A sponsored member communicates with the CREST system via the relevant participating member. Clearly, for those investors who wish to take this route, this will resolve the questions of visibility and rights of shareholders as they will appear on the register in their own names. However, a sponsored member needs to have its own (debit capped) assured payment arrangement with a payment bank, although the arrangement will be operated by the relevant participating member. The investor must apply to be a member of CREST, a nominal subscription being payable.

Information rights

CA2006 s.146 permits registered members holding shares on behalf of another to nominate that person to exercise 'information rights' over those shares.

Information rights means:

1 the right to receive a copy of all communications that the company sends to its members generally or class meetings; and
2 the right to require copies of the accounts and reports and the right to require hard copy versions of documents provided in another form.

An election under CA2006 s.146 must relate to all communications, not just some of them.

In order to exercise their rights, the beneficial owner of the shares must notify the nominee that they wish to exercise their rights and provide an address for the receipt of the communications (CA2006 s.147).

The nominee must then inform the company that the nominated person wishes to receive hard copies of all communications and provide the company with the address provided by the beneficial owner of the shares. If the member holds shares on behalf of more than one other person when notifying the company of the details of any nominated persons the member must also notify the number of their shares to which each nomination relates.

In the absence of a notification to receive hard copies of the documents or where no address is supplied, the nominated person is deemed to have agreed to the receipt of documents in electronic form or via a website (CA2006 ss.152 and 153).

The arrangement may be terminated by either the nominee or the nominated person. The arrangement will also cease upon the death or bankruptcy of the nominated person, being a person, or if a body corporate by their dissolution or commencement of winding up (CA2006 s.148).

If a member nominates more persons than the number of shares they hold, the right to exercise information rights is terminated.

The company may enquire of a nominated person if they wish to retain the information rights they hold. If no reply is received with 28 days the information rights lapse. The company may not make such an enquiry more than once in any 12-month period (CA2006 s.148(7)).

Where a company sends a copy of a communication to a nominated person there must be included a statement that (CA2006 s.149):

1 the nominated person may be entitled to be appointed or have someone else appointed as proxy for the meeting; and
2 if there is no such right to be appointed as proxy they may have the right to give instructions as to the exercise of the voting instructions.

The right under CA2006 s.146 to nominate a person and the enjoyment of those rights by the nominated person are enforceable only by the member against the company, not by the nominated person (CA2006 s.150).

Corporate actions

For securities that have been admitted to CREST, the system has an impact on a number of possible corporate actions or stock events. Specialist advice will be required and consideration given to the use of CREST when a company contemplates the following:

- rights issues;
- takeover offers;
- issue of loan stocks;
- conversion or redemption of shares;
- new issues and placings;
- payment of dividends, etc.;
- consolidation or share splits.

Court orders and transmission of shares

The procedures outlined in pp. 154–169 cannot be applied to a CREST holding as most individuals will hold through a nominee and the issuer will not be concerned with the beneficial ownership. Where such matters are appropriate to the uncertificated holding of a CREST member the following procedural points will apply:

1. A member is required to notify Euroclear UK & Ireland immediately if the member is aware that a stop notice or other court order affecting a security held by it through CREST is to be granted or served or if application is being made for such an order. When Euroclear UK & Ireland becomes aware of any such order inhibiting the transfer of a member's holding through CREST it will immediately transfer the securities concerned to an escrow account under the control of Euroclear UK & Ireland.
2. A member is required to notify Euroclear UK & Ireland of any event by which it becomes incapacitated as regards transfer of securities held by it through CREST. In this situation, Euroclear UK & Ireland will suspend the member from CREST membership to prevent any further processing of transactions affecting the member. Euroclear UK & Ireland will then liaise with the relevant authorities regarding further action.
3. If a member who is an individual dies, on receipt of the death certificate Euroclear UK & Ireland will arrange for the relevant holdings to be re-certificated. The usual procedure detailed on pp. 155–160 can be followed.

7 Dividends

Introduction

Dividends represent a distribution of accumulated profit to shareholders in proportion to the number of shares they hold. The company can only pay a dividend to its shareholders if it has sufficient distributable profits under CA2006 s.830.

Dividends are declared by the directors. For listed, AIM and PLUS companies there is a timetable for the declaration and subsequent payment of dividends. This is to ensure the smooth operation of the market. Once the record date is reached the share price will be reduced to reflect that the purchaser of the shares will not be entitled to receive the dividend payment. This is known as the 'Ex date' as the shares are sold excluding the dividend.

Dividends

Responsibility for the arrangements for the payment of dividends on a company's shares or interest on its debentures and loan stocks lies with the company secretary's department or with its registrar. Before dealing with the procedures to be followed and the related documents used, consideration should be given to the statutory powers and restrictions imposed on companies by the Companies Acts in regard to making distributions, as defined in the Acts.

There is an implied power for trading companies to distribute their profits to the members subject to any limitations included in the Memorandum and Articles of Association and subject also to the provisions of the Companies Act 2006 (Part 23 – Distribution) and the general law. In the case of shares (both ordinary shares and preference shares) the distributions are made in the form of dividends which are expressed as a specified amount of money per share.

In the case of a company with different classes of shares, the Articles may provide for the priority of dividend payments, e.g. the fixed rate of dividend on the preference shares must be paid before any dividend is paid on the ordinary shares. Unless there are provisions to the contrary, the preference dividends are presumed to be cumulative. This means that if in any year the profits of the company are insufficient to pay the fixed preference dividends, the entitlement will be carried forward to the next year or following years when the company is able to make the payment. Some companies have participating preference shares, which may be cumulative or non-cumulative; these shares give entitlement to a specified share in the profits related to the level of dividends paid on the ordinary shares, in addition to the fixed annual preferential dividend.

Model Articles regs.30 (private) and 70 (public) set out the procedures for the declaration of dividends (Table A, regs.102 and 103). These provide that the company (members) may declare dividends by ordinary resolution. These dividends are usually referred to as final dividends and are considered as part of the business of the annual general meeting. Directors may also declare interim dividends without seeking authority from the members. An interim dividend is one decided solely and approved by the directors between general meetings. Final dividends are subject to member approvalfollowing a recommendation from the board of directors. Whether the dividend is a final dividend or an interim dividend, the ability of the company to pay dividends is governed by the provisions of the Act on the distribution of profit (CA2006 s.830).

Mandates

Form and completion

Shareholders can lodge mandates with the company authorising it to pay dividends on their shares direct to their individual bank accounts. The ICSA has prepared a standard form of dividend mandate known as 'Request for payment of interest or dividends' [***see precedent*** 67]. The dividend mandate is the authority from the shareholder to the company to pay dividends becoming due to a specified branch of a specified bank. It incorporates an authority to send dividends to a new branch of the bank if the company receives notice the shareholder's account has been transferred.

Dividend mandates must be signed by the shareholder. If there are joint holders, the dividend mandate should be signed by all the joint holders. In the case of a corporate body, the mandate may be signed by an official who should state his office. In the case of administrators, attorneys, executors, receivers, trustees in bankruptcy, etc., or any other person acting on behalf of the shareholder, the authority under which they sign the dividend mandate must be registered with the company.

Bank mandates

Companies should, ideally, not receive mandates direct from shareholders. Any mandate so received should be returned to the shareholder with a request that it is lodged with the company by the shareholder's bank. The submission of the mandate through the bank, authenticated by the stamp of the branch of the bank on the mandate form, ensures that the mandate contains the correct address and title of the branch, the branch's sorting code number and the account number to which the dividend is to be credited. Most banks and building societies accept full liability in respect of the customers' bank account numbers shown on the dividend mandate form and bearing their stamp, and for this reason mandates should ideally not be accepted direct from shareholders. Companies should also make sure that they receive mandates on the accepted standard form of mandate approved by the ICSA.

The sorting code and a customer's account number are used in connection with the payment of dividends through the Bankers' Automated Clearing System (BACS). Occasionally, it may be necessary to send individual warrants direct to other banks and in such cases the numbers should also be given on the warrants to ensure that the dividend reaches its correct destination.

Registration of mandates

It is not usual to send acknowledgements to shareholders when dividend mandates are received, especially in the case of the larger companies. The shareholder will be aware that his instructions have been received by the crediting of the next dividend to his bank account.

Dividend mandates must be recorded when received by the company. Although it may be convenient to record this information in the register of members, it should not be made available for inspection of the register by the public. Accordingly, mandate information should bc recorded separately in a manual system and where a computerised register is used this information must be suppressed where inspection is afforded to members of the public. When notification of marriage is received from a shareholder it is desirable to obtain confirmation of any existing mandate instruction in case the shareholder also has a new address and/or bank account. The lodgement of a power of attorney with the company does not affect the payment of dividends in accordance with any existing mandate unless the attorney has been given specific authority under the power to give a dividend mandate. In this situation the attorney may lodge a revised mandate form.

To encourage shareholders to agree to mandate their dividends to a bank, some companies include a form of mandate with the dividend warrants sent out direct to the shareholders whose dividends are not mandated.

Third party mandates

For personal reasons a shareholder may wish dividends to be paid to some other person instead of to a bank, e.g. a firm of solicitors or accountants, however, this is not common.

Revocation of mandates

A mandate may be revoked at any time by the shareholder giving notice in writing to the company. It also lapses automatically upon the death of the shareholder, when the company should withhold payment of further dividends until the appointment of executors or administrators has been registered. It would then be in order for the company to accept instructions from the personal representative for the payment of dividends.

If one of the holders in a joint account dies the dividend mandate continues to apply. There may, however, be a separate account in the name(s) of the survivor(s), in which case the accounts would normally be merged in the register of members. If it is desired to keep the two accounts separate it will be necessary to designate one of the accounts, since the accounts will both be in the same name. It should be noted that a bankruptcy or protection order (or their Scottish equivalent) does not terminate a dividend mandate, although the receiver, trustee, curator or factor may give their own instructions that supersede any existing mandate.

In the case of a small company with few shareholders the closing of an account in the register of members does not involve the lapse of the dividend mandate, which would be revived if the account were to be re-opened. However, it is impracticable to follow this procedure in large companies since the accounts in question will be moved to a closed section of the register, either by the removal of the account cards or appropriate computer instructions. Consequently, if a new account is opened, fresh dividend instructions will be required.

Change of branch notice

Banks may issue change of branch notices if a customer transfers his account to another branch of the same bank. A company will frequently receive change of branch notices shortly after the payment of a dividend since the payment of the dividend to the old branch will bring to light the need for a change.

The existing branch prepares and signs the notice, which is then passed on to the new branch, which inserts and verifies the details of its sorting code number and account number of the customer. The notice is then stamped by the bank in confirmation of this information and forwarded to the company to be recorded, as in the case of an original mandate form.

Like the ordinary dividend mandate, the change of branch notice applies to all shares and stocks of any class which are currently registered or may in future be registered in the name(s) of the shareholder(s) concerned. A change of branch notice limited to a particular holding or class of shares or stocks should not be accepted by a company, although the existing holding may be mentioned for reference and identification purposes.

It should be noted that a change of branch notice may not be used if the customer transfers his account to a different bank altogether, as this would be outside the authority given in the original mandate by the shareholder to the company. In this case, the shareholder should be given a new mandate for completion.

A change of branch notice should not be accepted if it is not possible to identify the notice with the original mandate given by the shareholder. The procedure for recording an acceptable bank change of branch notice on receipt by the company is the same as that which applies in the case of an original mandate.

BACS

The Bankers' Automated Clearing System (BACS) is the system used by many companies to pay dividends direct to banks and buildings societies.

Under this system, a computer file containing details of the shareholders, their bank account details and the amounts due must be submitted to BACS at least three working days before the due date.

BACS will verify the data and transmit instructions to the banks who then credit the shareholders' accounts with the amount of the dividend. The company will issue a separate tax voucher direct to the shareholders. Any errors in the BACS payment details in respect of incorrect account numbers or accounts that have been closed are notified to the company or registrar and the amounts unpaid credited to the dividend account. The reasons for the error can then be investigated and manual cheques issued.

BACS payments are often preferred by shareholders as they are simple and do not require any further action. The use of BACS also eliminates the possibility of cheques being lost in the postal system or being intercepted.

Where a company proposes to use BACS for the first time to distribute dividend payments, the Articles of Association should be checked to ensure that they do not provide that payment must be made by cheque or warrant, such as Table A, reg.106, in which case they will require amendment (see p. 17). Regulation 31 of the Model Articles for Private companies, and reg.72 of the Model Article for Public companies provide the flexibility that the payment can be made in any other means as agreed by the directors with the recipient either in writing or by such other means as the directors decide.

CREST

For those who hold their shares through CREST, it is possible for dividends to be paid via CREST. Tax vouchers can be sent electronically and can be transmitted through CREST. The company's Articles must be checked to see if the payment by CREST is permitted, otherwise it can be changed to include the provision to enable dividends to be paid through the CREST. CREST members may also make dividend elections through CREST by indicating to the issuer that the holder wishes to receive payment in a particular currency, or wishes to take up a scrip dividend or participate in a dividend reinvestment plan. Companies wishing to take advantage of dividend payment via CREST should liaise with their share registrar.

Dividend warrants

There is a standard form of dividend/interest warrant and related tax voucher which has been agreed by all parties concerned, including the ICSA, the banks and the London Stock Exchange [***see precedent 68***].

The UK Listing Authority (UKLA) requires that, in the case of limited securities, the full ISIN code of the company be printed in a box to be located as close as possible to the top right hand corner of the tax voucher. ISIN numbers are published against the names of companies in the UKLA Official List as well as companies admitted to AIM or PLUS. The UKLA has special requirements in the case of warrants and tax vouchers for convertible loan stocks or stocks carrying subscription rights.

Because of the large number of shareholders and the increase in the number of warrants to be issued it is now usual for warrants to bear printed facsimile signatures of the persons authorised by the company to sign them. In this case the banks require an indemnity from the company to protect them against the issue of unauthorised warrants. The banks also require the indemnity to cover the issue of warrants if the amount is shown in figures only instead of in both words and figures as fraudulent alteration of figures is potentially easier.

Tax vouchers

The tax voucher is a statement and explanation to the shareholder or stockholder and shows the number of shares (or the amount of stock) on which payment has been made, the tax deducted and the net amount payable. If the tax voucher is in respect of an interest payment the gross amount is also shown.

There is a form of wording for the tax voucher agreed between the ICSA Registrars' Group and HM Revenue & Customs [*see precedent 68*]. Regulations to enable companies to issue electronic tax vouchers came into force on 1 January 2004 (the Income and Corporation Taxes (Electronic Certificates of Deduction of Tax and Tax Credit) Regulations 2003 (SI 2003/3143)). The regulations adopt the same model as is used for elections to receive electronic versions of the annual report and AGM notices. Electronic delivery can be effected by sending an electronic version of the document or by making it available on the website and notifying the intended recipient of its availability together with an explanation of how it might be accessed. Under the regulations a statement under ss.234(1) or 234A(2) of the Income and Corporation Taxes Act 1988 by a company making a qualifying distribution may be delivered by means of electronic communications provided it satisfies certain conditions. The Income and Corporation Taxes (Electronic Certificates of Deduction of Tax and Tax Credit) (Amendment) Regulations 2009 (SI 2009/2050) which came into force on 1 September 2009 have added a reference to s.234A(3) of the Income and Corporation Taxes Act 1988 to apply these provisions where a payment of dividend or interest is made into a bank account or building society held by a person.

Some countries have double taxation agreements with the United Kingdom and residents of those countries who are holders of debentures or loan stocks of UK companies may receive their interest payments without deduction of income tax at the basic rate or under deduction of tax at a reduced rate. Non-resident holders of equity capital (i.e. ordinary shares) may in some cases also receive their dividend payments with the tax credit appropriate to a dividend subject to UK withholding tax instead of the normal UK tax credit. The authority for payment of interest and dividends to such non-resident shareholders or stockholders is issued by HM Revenue & Customs. Companies should therefore not make special arrangements (including the preparation of amended or special tax vouchers) until the authority is received from HM Revenue & Customs. This will identify the shareholder's/stockholder's account precisely and set out the reduced rate of tax to be applied or the rate of tax credit to be allowed.

Payment procedure

The payment of a dividend needs to be very carefully planned and it is of great assistance if, in advance of the payment of each dividend, a control sheet or timetable is prepared setting out all the various steps which have to take place so as to ensure that nothing is overlooked. Companies with securities listed on the main market (see rule 3.8 of the London Stock Exchange's Admission and Disclosure Standards) and AIM (see rules 24 and 25 of the AIM rules) must take account of the Dividend Procedure Timetable published each year by the London Stock Exchange (LSE).

1 (*Listed, AIM and PLUS companies only*) Immediately after the board meeting at which a dividend is declared or recommended, a Regulatory Information Service should be informed (*LR 9.7A.2*). The announcement of the dividend will usually be accompanied by the company's half yearly report or preliminary figures for the year, and this is sent to the UK Listing Authority at the same time.
2 Announcements of dividends should follow the Stock Exchange's recommended record dates, a list of which is published every year for the guidance of companies. Dividend timetables which fall outside these guidelines must be cleared in advance by the LSE. Adherence to these dates facilitates the Stock Exchange's dividends claims procedure, enabling the shares to be dealt with on the Stock Exchange in ex-dividend form at the earliest possible date after the announcement. This reduces the number of dividend claims which have to be made against the seller of shares who may have sold his shares xd (i.e. ex dividend), but whose shares are still registered in his name on the company's record date (see below) for the payment of the dividend. It is also helpful to include in the announcement the actual date of payment of the dividend.
3 (*Listed, AIM and PLUS companies only*) In the case of dividends on preference shares and interest payments on debentures and loan stocks which fall due for payment on fixed dates each year, the UK Listing Authority should be advised of the record date for each payment.
4 Model Articles, reg.31 (Private companies) or reg.71 (Public companies), (Table A, reg.106) and most companies' Articles, provide that in the case of

joint holders of shares the company is legally bound to pay the dividend to the first-named shareholder in the joint account.

5 If prior to the record date a shareholder has disposed of all or part of his holding and the transfer has not been registered by the record date, the company is bound to pay the dividend to the registered shareholder at the record date. It is the responsibility of the purchaser's stockbrokers to claim the dividend from the seller. The tax voucher for the dividend will have gone to the seller of the shares together with the dividend payment. When they receive the dividend, the purchaser's stockbrokers will provide the purchaser with their own form of certificate giving the tax credit deducted from the dividend or the amount of income tax deducted from an interest payment on debenture or loan stock. This is acceptable to HM Revenue & Customs. Claims arise only if the shareholder has purchased his shares cum dividend. No claim arises if the shareholder purchased his shares ex dividend, since the amount of the dividend would have been taken into account by adjustment of the share price on the Stock Exchange on the first day on which the shares were quoted ex dividend. In this case the dividend belongs to the seller, who may retain the dividend on receiving it although he has sold his shares. The schedule of dates, referred to above, should be adhered to in order to minimise claims.

6 If a transaction in shares is effected outside the Stock Exchange, the right to any current or pending dividend will have to be settled between the parties concerned. This is of no concern to the company, who will pay the dividend to the registered holder on the record date.

7 The draft of the dividend warrant and tax voucher should be prepared in good time to allow for any corrections necessary to the proof. The bulk order for printing can be given to the printers when the rate of dividend is known. At the time of the Budget it is necessary to bear in mind the possibility of a change in the basic rate of income tax. When part of the dividend will be paid through BACS a separate supply of tax vouchers should be ordered. It is usual for warrants to be serially numbered and also for each dividend payment to be given its own identifying number. This assists in reconciling different dividend accounts. If there are several classes of stock on which dividends are to be paid it is a good idea to use different coloured paper for each class of security.

8 Arrangements should be made to ensure that all transfers, transmission documents, probates, confirmations, letters of administration, marriage certificates, changes of address, dividend mandates, etc., received up to the close of business on the record date are duly processed so that the dividends or interest payments may be correctly dispatched. It should also be checked whether there are any stop notices or other restraints on dividends; if so, the relevant payments must be withheld.

9 The dividend sheets should be prepared. In the case of a computerised system the dividend record sheets and completed warrants will be produced simultaneously.

10 With a manual system each shareholder's holding has to be entered on the dividend sheets with the amount of dividend and tax credit alongside his name. The overall total of the number of shares on which the dividend is paid should agree with the company's issued capital and the columns relating to the tax credits and net dividends balanced to the total amount of the payment. It will, of course, be necessary to round off net payments resulting in odd fractions of a penny, but the total of the dividends to be paid should not exceed the total cost of the dividend when calculated by reference to the company's issued capital. In the case of a manual system, the warrants and vouchers will need to be fully addressed from plates or stencils for dispatch. The information on the warrants and vouchers should agree with that shown on the dividend sheets and, to make sure that they have been accurately completed, the warrants should be totalled and agreed with the totals on the dividend sheets.

11 If payments are being made through BACS the necessary computer file must be sent or transferred electronically to BACS at least three working days before the due date.

12 In the case of warrants sent direct to shareholders who have not mandated their dividends, each one should be signed. The signature may be applied either autographically (i.e. handwritten) or with a machine-affixed facsimile signature which involves passing each warrant through a machine for the signature to be applied. However, in the case of most large companies, the signatures will be pre-printed on the warrants, usually in facsimile form. If, following the record date, documents other than transfers and transmissions have been received appointing personal representatives of a deceased shareholder, change of name on marriage, etc., the shareholder's warrant should be withdrawn and endorsed appropriately prior to dispatch. It may also be possible to deal with some changes of address or the receipt of bank mandates before dispatch of the warrants.

Computer-based registers will automatically update the address details to be printed on the warrants. There may be other queries in relation to a holding, e.g. the advice of a death in respect of which the grant of probate has not yet been received by the company with the names and addresses of the executors or administrators. In these circumstances, the warrants concerned should be withdrawn and retained until lodgement of probate or letters of administration. If it is known that the shareholder's previous dividend warrant has remained uncashed a reminder letter about the uncashed warrant could be sent with the new dividend warrant although it may be necessary to request a shareholder to return the warrant to the company or to the registrar for re-dating. It may be found that a number of earlier warrants have remained unpaid, despite the reminder; in this case it would be advisable to withdraw and retain further warrants until the matter of the shareholder's whereabouts can be clarified. However, this may be prohibited by the provisions of the company's Articles of Association with regard to the dispatch of dividend warrants.

In the case of listed companies, it is usual to take power in their Articles to cease sending dividend warrants by post where warrants have been returned undelivered or left uncashed. This power may not be exercised until such warrants have been returned or left uncashed on two consecutive occasions or where after the first occasion enquiries have not established any new address.

13 Although some companies only maintain one dividend account it may be convenient to ask the bank to open a separate account for each dividend designated with the title and the identifying number of the dividend payment. The total amount of the dividend can be credited to this account on the payment date by transfer from the company's current or deposit account. Of course, the bank should already have had instructions informing it of the persons appointed by board resolution to open and operate banking accounts in the name of the company. If only one dividend account is maintained, i.e. in respect of the current dividend in course of payment, it will be necessary to open an unclaimed dividend account into which any amounts which remained unclaimed at the time of funding the dividend account are transferred to pay a new dividend. Even if more than one dividend account is maintained, it is undesirable to leave separate dividend accounts open indefinitely. Balances on earlier separate dividend accounts may be transferred to an unclaimed dividend account when the quantity of old warrants being presented for payment becomes reduced to a trickle.

14 Many companies arrange for their registrars to deal with the printing and dispatch of warrants. The envelopes should be dispatched in time to be received by shareholders on the payment date, the date of posting being dependent on whether first-class or second-class post is used.

15 Inevitably a number of envelopes containing warrants will be returned by the Post Office as undeliverable, usually because the shareholder has not notified the company of a change of address. Efforts should be made to trace the new address of these shareholders by making enquiries of the bank at which warrants for previous dividends were paid in or, if it is the first dividend sent to a new shareholder, through the stockbroker who acted for the purchaser.

16 Some warrants may be returned because the shareholder has died. These should be retained until probate or letters of administration are received, in the case of a sole shareholder, or the death certificate relating to a shareholder who was the first named in a joint account. These warrants may then be appropriately endorsed and, if necessary re-dated and reissued to the persons entitled to receive them.

17 After the payment date, statements will be received from the bank. The bank statements should be checked against the dividend lists so that eventually a list of outstanding uncashed warrants can be prepared, the total of such warrants agreeing with the bank balance. Now that the banks use electronic sorting equipment, it is possible for the warrants to be sorted into numerical order, providing details of the outstanding warrants and the balance of the dividend account.

Unclaimed dividends

When dividends are paid direct to shareholders, warrants may occasionally be lost in the post or they may be mislaid by the shareholder. Outstanding unpaid dividend warrants are a nuisance to the company and it is usual for them to indicate on the warrants that unless they are paid within six months (or sometimes 12), they will have to be returned to the company for re-dating or verification.

A reminder may be sent to shareholders who have not yet banked their warrants about a month before the expiration of the six-month period. If the warrants are banked, they may then be debited against the current dividend account before that account is closed and the balance transferred to the unclaimed dividend account.

If there is no response to the first reminder notice, it may be followed by a further reminder notice with the next dividend payment sent out to the shareholder, to the effect that the previous warrant is still unpaid and requesting that it be returned for re-dating if more than six months have elapsed.

If the shareholder indicates that the warrant has been lost, a duplicate can be issued against signature of a simple form of indemnity or, if the dividend is not of a large amount, by signature of an undertaking. The difference between the indemnity and an undertaking is that, in the case of an indemnity, the shareholder undertakes to indemnify the company against any losses which it may incur as a result of the issue of a duplicate warrant. In the case of the undertaking the shareholder merely agrees that if the original warrant is found it will be returned to the company for cancellation. Before the issue of a duplicate warrant, payment of the original warrant should be stopped at the bank and an appropriate note made on the dividend sheets.

If it is found that the shareholder has died, the usual procedure followed on receipt of notice of death of a shareholder should be followed, i.e. the dividend withheld until probate, letters of administration or confirmation is lodged.

It is in the company's interests to clear outstanding dividends as quickly as possible since the queries arising may result in a need to alter the register of members and it is desirable for this to be kept as up to date as possible. Similarly, prompt action should be taken in the event of the return as undeliverable of copies of the company's report and accounts sent to shareholders.

At least two dividend warrants should be sent to shareholders before action is taken to withhold the dispatch of further warrants. In the case of listed companies, the UKLA requires that dividend warrants should not be withheld unless two consecutive dividend payments have been returned as undeliverable or left uncashed.

However, if the company's Articles follow Model Article 31 (private), 72 (public) or Table A, reg.106, it could be argued that the company has no right to withhold the dispatch of dividend warrants to shareholders. Clearly, from the security point of view, it is unwise to continue to send out dividend warrants when it is known that they will not be received by the shareholder or, if received, will not be acted upon by him. Dividends become statute-barred (in England) under the Limitation Act 1980 after 12 years from the date of declaration, although some Courts have held that the period may be six years. In the case of Scotland, the Prescription and Limitation (Scotland) Act 1973 applies and the limitation period is five years after the date of declaration. However, most companies do not dispute dividend payments, since the publication in the company's accounts of the unclaimed dividends may be held to be an acknowledgement of the debt by the company. This means that the limitation periods start afresh each time an entry is made in the accounts. In order to deal with this matter, therefore, the UKLA allows listed companies to include the following powers in their Articles of Association:

1 to forfeit dividends which have not been claimed for 12 years or more after the date of declaration;
2 to sell shares of untraceable shareholders, the company retaining the net sale proceeds of the shares pending the possible receipt of claims from the shareholders concerned.

To meet the UK Listing Authority's requirements in this respect, however, the Articles must stipulate the following:

1 during a period of 12 years, at least three dividends in respect of the shares in question have become payable and no dividend during that period has been claimed;
2 on expiry of the 12 years the company gives notice by advertisement in two national newspapers of **its** intention to sell the shares and notifies the UK Listing Authority of that intention.

The new Model Articles 33 (private) and 75 (public) contain provisions whereby shareholders lose the right to claim a dividend 12 years after the date of declaration.

Duplicate tax vouchers

It has been noted that companies are required to issue with every dividend or interest warrant a voucher relating to the tax deducted applicable to the payment. Shareholders, or their tax advisers, may sometimes request duplicates from the company. Duplicate tax vouchers may be issued without an indemnity, but they should be clearly marked duplicate. A nominal charge may be made.

Scrip dividends

Some companies allow shareholders to elect whether to receive dividends in the form of shares instead of in cash. This is effected by the issue of fully paid shares to equity shareholders in lieu of cash dividends, but authority to do this must be contained in the company's Articles. The shareholder is thus able to build up his shareholding in the company without incurring brokerage expenses and stamp duty, and the money which would otherwise be distributed in cash as dividends is retained in the business for the benefit of the company. However, the value of the shares issued is still taxed as a distribution of income in the same way as a cash dividend, which means that the shareholder must be provided with a tax voucher. Many companies now follow the practice of offering scrip dividends. The Investment Committee of the Association of British Insurers (ABI) requires that any authority in the articles of listed companies should be subject to renewal by an ordinary resolution of the members at least once every five years.

The procedure for dealing with a scrip dividend is as follows:

1 Ensure that the company's Articles give power to the board to offer shareholders the right to elect to receive new ordinary shares in the company instead of receiving a dividend in cash. If not, the company's Articles will require changing by a special resolution [***see precedents** 2, 4, 5 **and** 11*].
2 At a general meeting of the company (usually the annual general meeting for a Plc), pass an ordinary resolution for the board to offer shareholders the right to elect to receive new ordinary shares instead of cash for all or any part of any interim and final dividends for the financial period of the company ending on the next accounting date [***see precedent** 69*].
3 When the board declares an interim dividend or recommends a final dividend on the company's shares, it should also resolve to make the offer of new shares to shareholders as an alternative to the cash dividend. This is subject, of course, in the case of the final dividend, to that dividend being approved by shareholders at the annual general meeting.
4 Entitlement to the alternative scrip dividend instead of a cash dividend will be to those shareholders on the company's register of members on the record date for the dividend.
5 In the case of a listed company, the price of the new shares will be determined by taking the average of the middle market quotations for the company's shares derived from the UKLA Official List for the five business days commencing on the date when the company's shares were first quoted ex dividend on the London Stock Exchange. For non-listed companies the price of the new shares would be calculated by the directors and may include reference to recent share issues or transfers and/or the net asset value disclosed in the latest accounts.
6 Prepare a circular letter to be sent to shareholders giving the price of the new shares and explaining the action they should take if they wish to receive new

shares instead of the whole or any part of the cash dividend to which they are entitled. Also state in the circular that shareholders who do not wish to elect to receive any new shares need not take any action and that their dividend will be paid in cash in the usual way on the payment date.

7 Prepare a form of election, which must be signed by the shareholder(s), to accompany the circular letter. This will be personalised with the following information:
   (a) number of shares held on the dividend record date;
   (b) maximum number of shares on which election may be made (this number will be an exact multiple of the number of shares required to be elected to receive one new share);
   (c) number of shares on which the dividend will be paid in cash if the maximum number of shares is elected as in (b) above (i.e. the balance of the shares being less than the multiple required for one new share);
   (d) the maximum number of new shares to be issued if the maximum number of shares is elected as in (b) above;
   (e) the number of shares which the shareholder wishes to elect for new shares if he wishes to elect fewer than the maximum in (b) above.

8 Special dividend warrants will be prepared with boxes to show the number of elected shares and the number of non-elected shares on which the normal full cash dividend will be paid. On these dividend warrants the pence per share, tax credit and amount payable boxes will be as usual.

9 Shares elected for the scrip dividend may receive a nominal dividend once in each year, paid on the occasion of either the interim or the final dividend, in order to preserve the wider range investment status of the company's shares under the Trustee Investments Act 1961. The company's Articles may, however, refer to shares issued under a scrip dividend as fulfilling the requirement for the dividend to be paid in which case the provisions of the Trustee Investments Act 1961 will have been adhered to although the restrictions of the 1961 Act have now been largely replaced, e.g. for charities, by the more general investment criteria in the Trustee Act 2000. Specific legal opinion on this matter should be sought if scrip dividends are to be made available on an ongoing basis.

10 New share certificates will be prepared for each shareholder for the number of shares issued in lieu of cash dividend. These certificates should have a counterfoil attached showing information on the number of shares on which a valid share election was made, number of new shares allotted, total cash equivalent of new shares allotted (i.e. the cash dividend multiplied by the number of shares elected) and the notional tax (i.e. what would have been the tax deducted if the dividend on the elected shares had been paid in cash). This information is to assist shareholders in preparing their income tax returns. The counterfoil should also state the number of shares on which the full cash dividend is being paid, for which a separate tax counterfoil with the dividend

warrant attached will be received. It is usual to attach an explanatory note explaining how the figures in the counterfoil have been determined.

11 A sum equal to the aggregate nominal amount of the new ordinary shares allotted pursuant to the elections for new shares made by shareholders will be capitalised out of any amount standing to the credit of any reserve or fund (including the profit and loss account), as determined by the directors.

12 (*Listed, AIM and PLUS companies only*) Application is made to the UK Listing Authority and the London Stock Exchange/Plus Markets Group for the new shares issued as scrip dividends to be listed and/or admitted to trading.

Enhanced scrip dividends, under which the value of the shares being offered exceeds the value of the cash payment, are becoming increasingly popular. They are used by companies to encourage shareholders to take up the scrip dividend alternative. If an enhanced scrip dividend is to be offered, prior approval from HM Revenue & Customs is required. If the company's shares are listed, the price of the shares must be calculated with reference to a period as close as practical to the first dealing day of the new shares.

It is usual for companies offering scrip dividends to notify shareholders on the occasion of each dividend payment of the terms on which scrip dividends may be elected for that particular dividend. This is because the terms depend upon the rate of dividend and the price of the company's shares at the time in question. This also gives shareholders the opportunity of deciding on each occasion whether or not they wish to receive that particular dividend in the form of shares rather than in cash. This does not arise, of course, in the case of those shareholders who have given the company continuing scrip dividend mandates (see below).

If the shareholder signs a scrip dividend mandate, all his future dividends will be in the form of shares, until he cancels the mandate. This will exclude any part of the dividend paid in cash in respect of any balance of his holding of shares which does not make up the multiple required for a new share. Alternatively, the company may carry forward to the next dividend payment any balance of the cash dividend on shares which are insufficient in number to make up the multiple required for a new share, to be added to the amount of the next dividend payment. The total is then used for the purpose of the scrip dividend on that occasion, any further balance of cash again being carried forward. The procedure described for the implementation of a scrip dividend scheme must be appropriately modified in the case of shareholders who have signed scrip dividend mandates.

If shareholders have signed ordinary dividend mandates for dividends to be paid into a bank, the payment made will comprise the cash dividend on the balance of their shareholding which did not add up to the multiple required for the allocation of a new share under the scrip dividend scheme. The bank mandates still operate for a dividend which is paid in cash irrespective of whether or not the shareholder has signed a scrip dividend mandate.

When prices on the Stock Exchange are volatile, companies may afford protection to their shareholders by providing that all share elections will be automatically withdrawn if, due to a price fall, the market value of the shares received is substantially less than the cash dividend forgone. Some companies may propose a specific amount for this purpose, e.g. a fall of 15 per cent or more in the company's share price. Most scrip dividend schemes give the director wider powers to suspend or terminate the offer at any time (where the price of the company's shares has fallen dramatically).

Dividend reinvestment schemes

Dividend reinvestment schemes should not be confused with scrip dividend schemes, described above. Under these schemes a shareholder signs a mandate to the effect that all dividends on his shares in future be paid to the company or its registrar to be used in the purchase of additional shares in the company on the stock market and added to his existing holding. The shares are purchased as a single transaction on the day the dividend is paid at the current market price, taking advantage of the lower dealing costs involved in a bulk purchase. The shareholder will be taxed as if he had received a cash dividend and in addition the shareholder will have to pay a minimum of £5.00 stamp duty on the transaction.

A few weeks after each purchase, particulars of the transaction are sent to the shareholder with a certificate for the additional shares purchased. These shares are added to his holding and a tax voucher for the dividend paid. Any balance of dividend that is insufficient to buy one new share is carried forward in the shareholder's dividend reinvestment account and added to the next dividend paid. This scheme is not often used by commercial companies but it is popular with investment trust companies in connection with regular savings schemes.

As the shares are not new shares there is no dilution of the company's share capital, but at the same time the cash saved on the dividends which are not paid in cash is not retained in the company for its benefit as in the case of a scrip dividend scheme.

Waivers of dividends

Shareholders with substantial holdings, particularly directors of small companies, may elect to waive future dividend payments by executing a form of waiver as a deed which, to be effective, must be received by the company prior to the declaration or payment of an interim dividend or the approval by shareholders of a recommended final dividend. If the waiver is dated after the declaration of the dividend the shareholder will still be liable to the income tax on the dividend that would have been paid. This is because, once declared, the dividend becomes a debt due by the company. As a matter of tax law, a dividend is taxed in the tax year in which it becomes payable, rather than the year in which it is declared.

In the case of listed companies, the UK Listing Authority requires that particulars of waivers be given in the company's annual report unless the amount(s) are minor (less than 1 per cent) and that some payment has been made on each share of the relevant class during the relevant calendar year (*LR 9.8.4(13) and LR 9.8.5*).

Disclosure of any waiver(s) of dividends must also be made in any prospectus or listing particulars where a UK listing is sought and must be reported upon by the auditors in their report accompanying such prospectus.

8

Share registration

Introduction

Most practitioners associate share registration with listed, AIM and PLUS companies. Whilst it is true that, on the whole, it is only public companies with large numbers of external shareholders that use the services of share registrars, all companies with a share capital must maintain a register of members.

The register

The register of members of a company may be kept in manual form, either as bound or loose-leaf books, or may be kept on computer, whether on a simple spreadsheet or database or using specialised share registration systems. Whatever form the register takes, it must include as a minimum the information set out in CA2006 s.113:

- the names and addresses of the members;
- the date on which each person was registered as a member;
- the date on which any person ceased to be a member;
- if the company has share capital, the number of shares of each class or classes held and the amounts paid or agreed to be paid on the shares.

The register of members must be kept available for inspection at:

- the registered office of the company; or
- at the alternative inspection location specified by the company.

If the register has not always been maintained at the company's registered office, notice of the location of the register must be given to Companies House on Form AD03.

Branch registers

Where a company has a substantial number of overseas shareholders, consideration should be given to establishing a branch register in terms of CA2006 s.129. It is not possible to establish a branch register in all countries and CA2006 s.129(2) contains details of those countries where a branch register may be established. When a branch register is established, notice of its location or any change in its location must be given to Companies House on Form AD06 within 14 days of the establishment of the branch register (CA2006 s.130). A duplicate branch register must be kept at the same place as the main register and is treated as part of the main register for all purposes.

A branch register enables dealings of shares in that overseas country to be registered locally. This has the added benefit that such transfers will not be subject to UK stamp duty, although any local equivalent tax will be payable.

The branch register may contain details only of those members whose addresses are within the country where the branch register is maintained.

Shares may be moved onto the branch register following receipt of an appropriate form of request, accompanied by the relative share certificate(s). A receipt is issued, which enables the member to apply direct to the keepers of the branch register for a new certificate evidencing the holding recorded on the branch register. A schedule of the requests is prepared and the transfers to the branch register are approved at a board or committee meeting (in a similar fashion to the approval of normal share transfers).

Copies of the schedules and requests should be notified to the holders of the branch register so that it can be brought up to date and requests for the issue of certificates checked. The share certificates issued by the branch register should clearly state that they are in respect of holdings recorded on the branch register and that documents transferring such shares should be forwarded to the branch registrar.

A similar procedure should be followed for transfers of shares from the branch register to the main register. If the company closes the branch register, notice must be given to Companies House within 14 days of the closure of the register on Form AD07 (CA2006 s.135).

Designated accounts

There is no obligation for a company to allow shareholder records to include account designations, unless required to do so by the company's Articles of Association. However, this is becoming increasingly common and companies rarely refuse to allow account designations. The designations will be in the form of an alphanumeric reference, but should not imply the existence of a trust over the shares. The use of designated accounts is increasing, particularly where shares are held in a CREST account on behalf of the beneficial owner. The designation of a CREST account may be up to eight characters and must not include punctuation or spaces.

A request for designation or a change of designation must be given by the shareholder on the standard form, which should indicate the number of shares to which the designation applies. The request should be submitted together with the appropriate share certificates for cancellation and the issue of new certificates bearing the designation(s). Alternatively, the designation details may be included on the transfer documents where a transfer of shares is taking place. If permitted by the Articles, a company may charge for the designation or re-designation of accounts in respect of the same shareholder. A charge is not normally made where the designation details are included in the transfer details where a new shareholder account is being established.

Joint accounts

The Articles of Association usually place a limit of four on the number of joint holders for any particular holding. The Listing Rules and the CREST rules also impose a maximum number of joint holders of four. The following are suggested courses of action regarding various matters that arise from time to time in relation to joint accounts. These are subject to the provisions of the Articles of Association of the company and cannot be said to be statements of uniform practice:

1. If a request is received to divide an existing account into more than one account with the names of the joint holders in different orders, this may be processed provided that the request has been signed by each joint holder and confirmation has been given that, in each case, there is no change in beneficial ownership.
2. Equally, the order of the names of the joint holders for an existing joint account may be changed provided that the request is signed by each holder and confirmation is given that there has been no change in beneficial ownership.
3. The full names of all the holders on a joint account should be entered in the register and on share certificates. All communications will be sent to the address of the first-named holder together with either the names or initials of the other joint holders. Although joint holders may request that correspondence should go to someone other than the first-named holder, companies will usually be reluctant to agree to this due to the administrative complexities. Instead, the company may suggest that the order of the names of the joint holders be amended as set out in 2 above.
4. Changes in address should, where possible, be recorded against all joint holders, not just the first named holder. Otherwise, in the event of the death of the first named holder, the address information for the surviving joint holder(s) may be out of date.

Inspection of the register

The register of members must be available for inspection during normal business hours free of charge to members and upon payment of the prescribed fee for non-members. Copies of the register must be supplied within five days of the receipt of the request on payment of the prescribed fee unless application to the Court is made on the grounds that the request is not for a proper purpose (CA2006 ss.116 and 117). The new rights to inspect copies of the register introduced under CA2006 only apply after the company has filed its first annual return dated on or after 1 October 2008.

Under CA2006 s.116 the fee is payable by both members and non-members according to the following scale:

- First 100 entries £1.00
- Next 90 entries £10.00
- Next 900 entries £20.00
- Next 900 entries £20.00
- Next 49,000 entries £40.00
- Remainder £40.00

The requirement to provide copies relates to a printed copy.

Accordingly, if a copy is requested in electronic form and if the company agrees, the cost of provision of the electronic copy is at the discretion of the company or service registrar.

The requirement to provide a copy of the register applies to the whole register or any part of it.

There is no requirement to provide the register details printed on labels in order to enable a mailing to the shareholders. All requests for a copy of the register in any form other than that laid down by the Companies Act 2006 should be considered by the company secretary or the board.

Former members

Companies are required to keep details of former members on the register of members for a minimum period of ten years commencing on the date the members ceased to hold shares (CA2006 s.121).

Share certificates

A sealed or executed share certificate is *prima facie* evidence of title to those shares (CA2006 s.768). The company is prohibited from denying the title of the person named in the certificate to the shares specified in it. Accordingly, it is essential that the details on the certificate are correct and that supplies of blank certificates are kept secure. However, if the certificate has been executed without the company's authority, this is void as a forgery and not binding on the company. The company is also prohibited from denying that shares are fully paid if they are so described in a share certificate. It is universal practice for public companies to effect an insurance policy against forged transfer. Liabilities in respect of the issue of certificates will usually be covered under the terms of the policy.

Small private companies commonly use certificate forms available from law stationers. Larger companies and/or listed companies use specially printed share certificates. A share certificate should contain at least the following basic information:

1. a unique certificate serial number;
2. the name and registered number of the company;
3. the name of the registered holder;
4. the number and description of the shares to which the certificate relates, including a statement as to the extent to which the shares are paid up; and
5. the date of the certificate.

Listed companies must also comply with the detailed requirements of the *Listing Rules* (*LR 9.5.16*). For security reasons, the number of shares should be shown twice on the certificates of listed companies. This may be once in figures and once in words, or once in figures and once in figures contained in boxes referring to millions, hundreds of thousands, tens of thousands, thousands, hundreds, tens and units. The full names (and titles) of the registered holder and of any joint holders must be given on certificates. There is no requirement to show decorations or professional qualifications. The full name of a corporate holder should be shown in the same form as on its certificate of incorporation.

If the address of the registered holder is shown on share certificates, the full address as recorded in the register of members should be shown. For joint holders, only the address of the first-named holder need be shown. However, it is not necessary to show addresses of shareholders on share certificates and this may be preferable since this information is rarely kept up to date. On the other hand, an address shown on a share certificate may help to resolve a query as to the identity of a shareholder.

The certificates of companies with only a few shareholders will usually be signed by two directors or by one director and the company secretary, either under seal or as a deed. For companies with a large number of shareholders or a large number of transfers, arranging for certificates to be manually signed is not practical. In such circumstances, the board of directors should adopt a security seal (CA2006 s.50), which may be affixed to share certificates and also, in accordance with the authority given in the Articles of Association, omit signatures attesting the seal on share certificates.

Issue of certificates

Companies are required to issue share certificates to shareholders within two months after an issue of shares or the date when the documents necessary to effect a transfer have been received by the company (CA2006 s.769).

Listed, AIM or PLUS companies are required to ensure that their shares are eligible for electronic settlement (*LR 6.1.23, LR 9.2.3, AIM rule 36, PLUS rule 3*).

Listed companies must ensure that share certificates are sent to addresses in the United Kingdom or elsewhere within the European Economic Area by first class post, or by an equivalent service that is no slower (*LR 9.3.4 and 5*).

Listed companies must ensure that share certificates are sent to addresses outside the European Economic Area by airmail or an equivalent service (*LR 9.29*). Where the company's securities have been admitted to CREST, certificates arising from withdrawals of stock from a dematerialised account will not be posted to the CREST members concerned, but will be sent via CCSS (the CREST courier and sorting service) to the firm that submitted the stock withdrawal request instructions, usually within three business days of the stock withdrawal being requested. Articles of Association generally provide that a company may replace a defaced or worn-out certificate on payment of a small fee. If a member requests the issue of more than one certificate for his total holding, if the Articles so permit several certificates may be issued, subject to payment of any fee determined by the directors.

Lost certificates

Where a shareholder has lost his share certificate(s) the following procedure should be followed:

1 Ask the shareholder to make a careful search for the certificate(s).
2 If the shareholder confirms that the certificate(s) still cannot be found or it is known that the certificates have been destroyed (i.e. in the event of a fire or flood), it is recommended that the shareholder should be asked to complete an indemnity in respect of the lost certificate(s) [***see precedent 70***]. This indemnity should be joined in by a bank, insurance or trust company. Some companies are prepared to dispense with a guarantee if the value of the shares comprised in the lost certificate is very small, although it should be borne in mind that the future value of the shares may rise significantly. If a certificate is lost in transit between an agent for the member and the member, it is usual to accept an indemnity from the agent, the indemnity to include the guarantee of a bank, insurance company or trust corporation unless the agent itself comes within any of these categories.
3 On receipt of the duly completed indemnity, a duplicate certificate, clearly marked as a duplicate, is prepared and issued on payment of any fee required under the Articles. The register is amended to note that the original certificate has been lost and a duplicate issued in its place.

Change of name of shareholder

Changes of name can arise in a number of ways:

1 A person may alter his name with or without formality. Provided there is no fraudulent intent, this is quite lawful. Before registering the change of name

the shareholder should be asked to provide a statutory declaration as to the change of name or a declaration of identity by some independent person of public standing.

2 By execution of a deed poll duly stamped, or a copy of the *London Gazette* or the *Edinburgh Gazette* containing the advertisement of the deed poll.
3 By marriage, in which case the marriage certificate provides the necessary evidence. The original should be requested, although companies may accept photocopies of certificates if certified as a true copy by a professional person such as a chartered secretary, accountant or solicitor, or a statutory declaration as to the shareholder's identity. In Scotland, however, a photocopy must be authenticated by signature of the District or Assistant Registrar. Clearly, a shareholder may not wish to submit the original marriage certificate and in this case a certified copy or a statutory declaration is an acceptable alternative.
4 Grant of an honour, such as the conferment of a knighthood, may involve a change of name. This may be proved by a copy of the *London Gazette* containing the grant of the honour.
5 For a corporate shareholder, the certificate of incorporation on change of name or certificate of re-registration (or a certified photocopy) should be produced for registration.

On receiving appropriate evidence of change of name for registration, the change should be recorded as follows:

1 Check that there is complete identity between the document (which should be accompanied by the share certificate(s)) and the registered shareholding.
2 Make appropriate entries, including date, in the register of members.
3 Endorse the share certificate(s) validated by the company's registration stamp and return it or them to the shareholder. Alternatively, issue a new share certificate showing the amended name details.
4 If a dividend mandate has previously been submitted it may be appropriate for a revised mandate to be completed by the shareholder.

Change of address of shareholder

Changes of address notified by a shareholder should be signed by the shareholder wherever possible. If the notification is on a printed card, this should, if necessary, be returned for signature. Some companies are prepared to accept notifications of change of address given on behalf of a shareholder by a bank, solicitor or stockbroker. A notification of change of address purported to be given by a member of the shareholder's family should never be accepted. Ideally, notifications of change of address should give both the old and the new addresses as this facilitates identification.

Upon receipt of an acceptable notification of change of address, the change should be noted in the register of members. It is not usually necessary for the share certificates to be amended. As discussed above, many companies no longer show address details on share certificates.

Although it is not necessary to issue acknowledgements of changes of address, this can prove useful to ensure that the new details been have been correctly entered and to help prevent fraud. If confirmation of the change is sent to the old addresses, the true shareholder will have the opportunity to query a fraudulent change. This is particularly relevant if notification of a lost certificate is made a few weeks after a change of address.

Registration of documents

Recording of documents

In this section, reference is made only to 'shares' and 'shareholdings', but the procedures indicated apply to any class of shares, stock, debentures, loan stocks or other securities of a company. Where reference is made to a document register this may be a loose-leaf register containing copies of original documents or a bound register in which the relevant information is extracted or summarised from the document being registered. Additionally, where the register is kept in electronic form, notes on the register would also be in electronic form.

General points regarding documents

The following general points should be noted:

1. Any person lodging a document with the company is deemed to represent to the company that the document is genuine.
2. Where only a small shareholding is involved, some relaxation of the strict requirements may be accepted if the person lodging the document is a professional person such as an accountant, solicitor, etc.
3. The particular shareholding must be clearly and precisely identified and include the full name and address of the shareholder as registered. In the case of joint holdings the names in the documents should be in the same order as they appear in the register of members. If there is any discrepancy between the names in the document and the names in the register a declaration of identity should be obtained before registration of the document.
4. A company registered in England and Wales may not note in the register any nominee or trustee capacity in which registered shareholders hold their shares (CA2006 s.126). However, this does not preclude the use of designations.
5. It may be necessary to make endorsements or alterations to existing share certificates. These should be signed and marked with an official stamp so as to prevent unauthorised alterations or endorsements being made.
6. If authorised by the Articles of Association, a fee may be charged for the registration of documents. Listed companies are not permitted to make such a charge.

Differences between English and Scottish practice

There are substantial differences between the law of England and the law of Scotland on matters of both property law and common law. For example a grant of probate or letters of administration in England generally establishes the right of the executor or administrator to deal with the whole of the estate. In the case of a Scottish confirmation, however, the executor is given power to deal only with such part of the estate to which he has been confirmed; other assets not included in the confirmation may be the subject of a further grant to the executor or of a grant to other persons.

The Administration of Estates Act 1971 permits a company registered in England and Wales or in Northern Ireland to register a confirmation issued in Scotland without further formality. Some documents issued by the English Courts are acceptable in Scotland, although in some cases validation by a Scottish Court is required. In all other cases, however, documents issued by English Courts are totally unacceptable in Scotland.

Apart from confirmations, some documents issued by Scottish Courts are acceptable in England. In some cases validation by an English Court may be required; while other Scottish documents are unacceptable in England. For example, in the case of shares, in Scotland a majority of the holders in a joint account may sign a transfer for the shares registered in their names when registered as trustees, whereas in England all the holders would be required to sign a transfer of the shares without reference to their trustee capacity.

Documents issued by other jurisdictions

Orders or documents issued by Courts outside England and Wales and Scotland are not acceptable for registration either by English or Scottish companies and consequently should not be accorded any recognition. It is possible for such orders to be validated for use here, but if there are no such equivalent procedures a fresh English or Scottish order must be obtained.

Common registration procedures

Death of a shareholder

Probates

Grants of probate are issued by the High Court in England to the person or persons named in a will of a deceased person as his executor(s). It is usual for probate to be granted to all the executors (or surviving executors named in the will), although one or more may renounce probate or reserve power to prove subsequently, in which case a further grant known as a double probate would be issued. Where a sole surviving executor dies before the estate is completely distributed and without himself having named an executor by will, application should be made to the Court by a person or persons interested in the original estate for the grant of letters of administration. However, where a deceased sole or surviving executor has named an executor in his own will, then upon such an executor obtaining a grant of probate to the estate of the deceased executor, he is entitled to continue executorship of the original estate. This is known as the 'chain of representation'.

A probate includes a copy of the will and is issued over an impressed seal of the High Court. In order to speed up the process of administration of the estate, executors or their advisers may obtain additional office copies of the grant of probate, bearing an impressed seal of the Court which does not include a copy of the will but does include the names of the persons authorised to deal with the estate. These 'office copies' are extremely useful where the deceased held shares in a number of companies and it is desired to avoid delay in registering the probate with those companies.

In the case of grants of probate issued overseas or in the Commonwealth, the Court will on application of the executor re-seal grants of probate. Companies should only accept such grants for registration which have been resealed.

Grants of probate issued in Northern Ireland and confirmations issued in Scotland do not require to be re-sealed in England. A separate English grant of probate must be obtained, however, in the case of the Isle of Man, Channel Islands and the Republic of Ireland, since probates issued in these countries cannot be re-sealed in England. The original grant of probate or an office copy should be submitted to the company for registration together with the share certificate(s) relating to the holding. Although the probate can be registered without production of the share certificates these should be endorsed with the details of the probate by the company.

The procedure for registering probates is as follows:

1 Check that there is complete identity between the deceased named in the probate and the registered shareholder. If there is any doubt, a declaration of identity should be obtained from the person lodging the document, who would usually be the solicitor acting for the estate, or from the bank at which the account of the deceased executor was held.
2 Record the names of the executors named in the probate in the document register.
3 Record in the register of members the date of death and the date of registration of the probate with the name and address of the executor(s) named in the probate and with the word 'deceased' added after the name of the deceased shareholder.
4 Endorse the share certificate(s) with the fact and date of death, the date of registration of probate and the name and address of the executor(s) and validate the endorsement by the company's registration stamp.

5 Impress the registration stamp on the back of the probate, which should then be returned to the person who lodged it with the company, together with the endorsed share certificate(s). If appropriate, include a new dividend mandate form for completion by the executors since the mandate lodged by the shareholder will have been revoked by his death.
6 It is also usual to send a form known as a letter of request with the returned documents. The executors can complete this form to register the shareholding in their names. This is helpful to the company as it is then no longer concerned with the 'chain of representation' if any of the named executors should die before the shares are sold or transferred to a beneficiary. A letter of request need not be sent if the person lodging the transfer indicated that the shareholding was to be disposed of by transfer.
7 Registering the shares in the name of the executor(s) also has the added benefit of removing the deceased shareholder from the mailing list. If this is not done, as the deceased shareholder's estate is still the legal owner of the shares until the shares are transferred, correspondence must still be addressed to that shareholder with the words 'deceased' after the shareholder's name. This can cause understandable distress to family members.
8 Registration of a double probate should be accepted only if the original executors are still registered in their representative capacity, i.e. if they have not been registered in their own names following submission of a letter of request.

Communications from the company would be sent to the first-named executor.

Letters of request

Letters of request are addressed to the company by executors or administrators of a deceased shareholder and request the company to enter their names in the register of members as the holders of the shares held by the deceased [***see precedent 71***]. The letter may only be registered by the company if a grant of representation in respect of the deceased shareholder has already been registered, appointing the persons who signed the letter of request as the executors or administrators of the deceased's estate. The letter must be signed by all the executors and administrators but their signatures need not be witnessed. The executor or administrator may be a body corporate, in which case a letter must be executed under its seal unless an officer of the company has authority to execute such documents. If so, the authority under which it is signed should be produced to the company.

When a letter of request is received, the procedure for registering it is similar to that which applies in the case of non-market transfers, considered earlier in this chapter.

Letters of administration

Letters of administration are granted by the High Court, appointing a person or persons to administer the estate of a person who died without having made a valid will.

Like probates, grants of administration bear the stamp of the High Court and sealed office copies may be obtained to facilitate registration with a number of companies.

As regards the Commonwealth, Isle of Man, Channel Islands, Republic of Ireland and foreign probates, the points made above regarding probates originating in those countries apply equally to grants of letters of administration.

The procedure for registering letters of administration is also similar to that set out in the case of probates, administrators taking the place of the executors.

There are a number of different forms of grant of letters of administration and entries in the register of members and endorsements on certificates should indicate the exact form of the grant. Usually a letter of request for the administrator(s) to be personally registered as holder(s) of shares is appropriate only in the case of a grant of letters of administration with the will annexed. This is issued by the High Court in cases where the deceased left a will but did not name any executor, where the executor may have predeceased the shareholder or where the executor has renounced probate.

Confirmation

Confirmation is the Scottish document issued by the Sheriff Court. It has similar effect to an English probate or letters of administration, and the procedure for registration by companies in England and Wales is the same as in the case of probates. It is granted to the executors named in the will, who are termed 'executors nominate'. If there are no surviving executors or if the deceased left no will the Court makes a grant to a person or persons to administer the estate who are termed 'executors dative' (called administrators in England).

The chief difference to note between English probates and letters of administration is that the Scottish confirmation has annexed to it an inventory of the deceased's property to which the executors have been confirmed. The executors may deal only with the property listed. Consequently, companies must check that the list includes the securities of the company. If not included, they can be added by the Court. Extracts are issued, to assist companies and others, under the seal of the Court and signed by the clerk. Reference should be made to the Institute's Manual (4.55) for guidance as to the procedure to be followed where a sole or surviving executor dies before the estate has been completely administered, as Scottish practice is quite different from that in England.

Death of a holder in joint account

If shares are registered in the names of two or more joint shareholders, upon the death of one of the holders the shares remain registered in the name(s) of the surviving holder or holders and no executors or administrators are involved. All that the company requires is the production of the certificate of death of the joint holder. This should be the original, although some companies will accept photocopies if they are lodged by a person of professional standing. This does not apply in Scotland where any photocopy must be authenticated by signature of the District or Assistant Registrar or, alternatively, the death may be proved by a decree of the Court of Session.

A grant of probate or grant of letters of administration or confirmation to the estate of the deceased joint holder may be submitted instead of a death certificate and this is equally acceptable as evidence of the death. Upon receipt of a death certificate or other evidence of death of a joint holder, the following procedure should be adopted:

1 Check that there is complete identity between the person named in the certificate and the registered shareholder, obtaining a declaration of identity in the event of doubt.
2 Record the particulars of the document (i.e. death certificate, probate or confirmation) in the document register.
3 Enter the fact and date of death and date of registration in the register of members, deleting the name and address of the deceased joint holder. If the deceased joint holder was the first named in the account, then the person who was second named in the account will become the first-named holder, involving transfer of the account to a different part of the register of members.
4 Endorse the share certificate, validated by the company's registration stamp, and return it to the surviving shareholder accompanied by the document submitted to prove death. If the latter was a probate or confirmation, it should be endorsed as registered as 'proof of death only'.
5 Continue to pay dividends on the holding in accordance with any existing mandate unless the surviving shareholder executes a new mandate.
6 If there is no dividend mandate in force, dividends are paid to the first-named survivor in the account, to whom all communications are also addressed.
7 Where the first-named holder has died, care must be taken to ensure that correct and up to date addresses for the surviving joint holder(s) are recorded on the register.

Bona vacantia

If a person dies domiciled in England and Wales without having made a will and no one has lawful rights of succession, the High Court will issue a grant of administration (known as *bona vacantia*) appointing the Treasury Solicitor or officers of the Duchy of Lancaster or the Duke of Cornwall to administer the estate. The procedure for registration is the same as in the case of a probate. In such cases, it would be usual for the shareholding to be disposed of forthwith and consequently no letter of request would be issued. The appropriate Scottish document is *ultimus haeres*; in this case the Queen's and Lord Treasurer's Remembrancer takes possession of the estate.

Small estates

There is no statutory definition of a small estate in relation to shareholdings in companies but many companies permit concessionary procedures where the total estate does not exceed £20,000 in value and the value of the shares does not exceed £5,000. Many companies are prepared to dispense with the formalities of obtaining a full probate or confirmation where the total value does not justify the expense of obtaining a grant of representation from the court. However, some risk is involved and some companies may specify a lower limit.

Applications to waive such formalities are normally considered individually. If it is decided that it would be appropriate in the circumstances to dispense with the formalities the personal representative or beneficiary should be required to submit the following:

1. the death certificate;
2. a statutory declaration as to the identity of the person claiming to deal with the shareholding and of his entitlement to deal with it;
3. a letter from the Capital Taxes Office confirming that on the information supplied to it, no liability to inheritance tax arises in connection with the holding;
4. the share certificate(s);
5. a letter of indemnity under which the applicant undertakes to indemnify the company if any liability on the company should arise by permitting the concessionary procedure and also undertaking to obtain and produce a formal grant of probate, confirmation or letters of administration should the company require this at any time.

Occasionally it may be appropriate to dispense with the production of a letter from the Capital Taxes Office where the applicant is an elderly widow or widower because of difficulties the applicant would experience in providing the necessary information to obtain the letter. If this concession is granted a paragraph concerning the absence of liability to inheritance tax should be included in the indemnity referred to above. Care is needed, because the reason why the estate is small may be that the deceased made substantial gifts in his lifetime to try to avoid inheritance tax.

Powers of attorney

A power of attorney is an appointment by an individual or body corporate of a person or persons to act on his or its behalf to the extent and for the time specified in the power. Such appointments are usually made when the person granting the power is going to be absent abroad for a considerable period or is facing a long illness or just because he wishes to free himself from dealing with matters of routine.

The Powers of Attorney Act 1971, Sch.1 sets out a short form of general power of attorney. This may conveniently be used to confer wide powers on the attorney. This form is most suitable for use by individuals as it is short and simple.

Powers of attorney granted by bodies corporate would generally be in more extended form, setting out in detail the precise extent of the powers granted. This would also apply in Scotland, as the short form of general power of attorney under the 1971 Act is not available for powers created in Scotland.

It is advisable for the power of attorney to be executed under seal since the attorney himself may have to execute documents under seal on behalf of the principal, i.e. the 'donor' of the power. Since 26 March 1985 it has not been necessary for powers of attorney to be stamped by HM Revenue & Customs. Powers executed before this date should be stamped with 50p duty. The signature of the principal on the power of attorney should be witnessed; one witness is needed in the case of powers executed in England and Wales and two if executed in Scotland. A power of attorney given by a company should be under its common seal or executed as a deed. When completed abroad, powers of attorney require notarial attestation or consular legalisation.

The person granting a power of attorney may be unable to execute it because of physical infirmity. In this case the power may be signed and sealed by some other person in the presence of two other persons as witnesses, who must also sign the document. Companies may register copies of powers of attorney instead of the original if they are copies certified by the principal or by a solicitor or stockbroker. The certificate should certify that the copy is a true and complete copy of the original. Power of attorney is sometimes expressed to be irrevocable for a period of one year, after which it may be revoked by the donor of the power. The power is automatically revoked on the donor's death. The Powers of Attorney Act 1971 gives some protection to companies which have registered powers of attorney in relation to a shareholder. It provides that where a power has been revoked and a person without knowledge of revocation deals with the donee of the power, the transaction is as valid as if the power had continued in existence. This applies only in England and Wales. Where the power of attorney is not in the general simple form provided by the Powers of Attorney Act 1971 the company should read it carefully before acting in order to ensure that the action to be taken is within the powers set out. Companies will be particularly concerned with the provisions in the power regarding the purchase and sale of investments, receipt of dividends, interest or capital monies, attendance and voting at meetings and completion of such documents as may be issued in connection with the shareholding. An attorney may not delegate his powers or appoint a substitute unless the power granted to him specifically provides for this. It is emphasised that the law governing powers of attorney is wide and complex and in cases of doubt reference should be made to the more detailed information given in the Institute's Manual (4.54).

Procedure

The following procedure should be followed when a power of attorney is received for registration:

1 The document must be either the original power, bearing 50p impressed stamp if it was executed before 26 March 1985, or an authenticated copy.
2 Check that there is complete identity between the donor of the power and either a registered shareholder or a person in the course of acquiring shares for registration, evidenced by a stock transfer form, a CREST stock withdrawal, a renounced allotment letter or a renounced certificate lodged for registration.
3 Photocopy the complete power for the company's records.
4 Carefully scrutinise the execution, continued validity, scope and the general interpretation of the power.
5 Note whether the power appoints more than one person as the attorneys; if so, check whether the appointment is joint, in which case all the attorneys must act together, or whether it is joint and several, when any of the attorneys may act individually.
6 Check whether the power affects the registered address of the shareholding or manner of payment of dividends. If not, the registered address remains as before, as do any instructions for payment of dividends.
7 Affix the company's registration stamp to the power and return it to the sender.
8 It is not usual practice to send a protective notice to the donor of the power informing him that the power of attorney has been received and that it will be assumed to be in order and registered unless he notifies the company otherwise. Such a notice should, however, be sent where the person executing the power by the direction of the donor because of physical infirmity is himself the attorney appointed by the power.
9 Every time a document executed by the attorney is lodged with the company, the validity of the particular transaction should be verified by reference to the copy of the power of attorney held by the company.

If the power of attorney is revoked or lapses the company's copy should be marked accordingly and moved to a separate file for lapsed powers of attorney.

No entry need be made in the register of members regarding the registration of a power of attorney nor should any alteration be made in the heading of the relevant account in the register of members.

The Mental Capacity Act 2005

The Mental Capacity Act 2005 (MCA2005) came into force on 1 October 2007 and applies to England and Wales only. Enduring powers of attorney made prior to 1 October 2007 that have not been revoked remain valid provided that in the case of a donor who has become mentally incapable the eduring power has been registered under MCA2005 with the Public Guardian.

Under the MCA2005, individuals may give a lasting power of attorney in the form prescribed in the appropriate regulations which will continue in force even if the donor should become mentally incapable, subject to the power being registered with the Public Guardian. If the power is in the prescribed form, the following further points arise:

1 The company may act on the power even though not registered by the Court of Protection if it is unaware that the donor has become mentally incapable. This protection derives from the Powers of Attorney Act 1971 s.5(2).
2 The company may not act on the power if it is aware that the donor has become mentally incapable but no application has been made to the Public Guardian for registration of the power.
3 The company may act on the power if it is aware that the donor has become mentally incapable and has evidence produced to it that an application for registration has been made to the Court of Protection, even though the registration has not been completed. The EPA1985 gives certain powers of maintenance and for the prevention of loss to the estate of the donor of the power. It also gives statutory protection to a company acting under a power governed by the EPA1985 provided that it is not aware of any irregularity in the exercise of the powers by the attorney.
4 The company may act on the power if it has documentary evidence of the registration of the power with the Public Guardian. The documentary evidence which the company should require to see are office copies of the fact of registration by the Public Guardian. The company is protected in this instance if there should be any irregularity concerning the power or if it should have been revoked by the Court provided that the company is unaware of the irregularity or the revocation. Companies or their registrars may consider it prudent to obtain legal advice before dealing with powers created under the MCA2005 if they have not had previous experience of these provisions. It has already been ruled by the Court that the appointment by a person (i.e. the donor of the power) already suffering from a degree of mental illness and, therefore, unable to manage his affairs, is valid if the person making the appointment was aware of what he was doing.

Other documents

Court of Protection orders

A receiver may be appointed by order of the Court of Protection to manage the income of a person described as 'the patient' if based on medical evidence the Court is satisfied that the patient is incapable, by reason of mental disorder, of administering their own property and affairs. These orders authorise the receiver to receive all income of the patient. The order will contain such other directions as are appropriate in the circumstances. Accordingly the effect of orders varies and care must be taken to ensure that all acts by the receiver are within his powers as set out in the order. All orders bear the seal of the Court. The equivalent Scottish document is known as an appointment of judicial factor, guardian or *curator bonis*.

Procedure

If a protection order is received the following procedure should be adopted:

1 There must be complete identity between the documents submitted and a registered shareholding in the company. In the case of doubt a declaration of identity should be obtained from the person lodging the document (usually a solicitor); alternatively a declaration may be given by the receiver.
2 The details should be recorded and a copy of the order retained for future reference.
3 Future communications to the shareholder are addressed to the receiver, who should be described as 'receiver for . . .'. The issuing of a Court of Protection order does not change the beneficial ownership of the shares.
4 The order should be endorsed on the reverse with the company's registration stamp.
5 The shareholder's share certificates need not be endorsed and they need not be submitted to the company.
6 It may be appropriate for a revised dividend mandate to be completed by the receiver.
7 The order will continue in force until either it is revoked or the death of the shareholder. On the death of the shareholder the order automatically lapses and the powers of the receiver terminate, whereupon the company may then take the usual action in relation to a deceased shareholder (see pp. 155–160).

Directions in addition to or varying existing directions may be issued under the seal of the Court from time to time. If further directions are received the same steps as noted above should be followed.

Notice of lien

A notice of lien is not an official document or court order but is written advice given usually by a bank to the effect that certificates representing a shareholding have been deposited with the person giving the notice by way of security for a loan or advance. If the notice is given by a bank or other corporate body, it will be signed on its behalf by an authorised official.

Such notices should not be acknowledged as acceptance would be contrary to CA2006 s.126. Rather than taking possession of the physical share certificates, banks will often require that the shares are registered in the name of their own nominee on behalf of the shareholder. There is no equivalent Scottish document.

Stop notice

A stop notice is an official notice given under rules of Court, which is usually submitted to the company by a solicitor, restraining the transfer of (and in some cases the payment of dividends on) a specified shareholding because of the interest of a third party in the shares. The original documents evidencing the debt due will have been previously filed with the Court. The notice will identify the shareholding and must be signed by the person who gave the affidavit. There is no equivalent Scottish document.

Procedure

If a stop notice is received for registration, the following procedure should be adopted:

1. There must be complete identity between the holding specified in the notice and a shareholding in the company. Service of the notice should be acknowledged to the sender, unless the shareholding cannot be identified, in which case it should be returned to the sender. The office copy will be retained by the company for future reference.
2. Details of the stop notice should be entered in the register of members.
3. The details should also be entered on the 'stop list'.
4. If any transfer (or redemption) of the shareholding or part of it is lodged for registration, 'warning-off' letters should be sent both to the person who lodged the notice and to the person on whose behalf it was lodged, who then have 14 days in which to obtain an injunction restraining the transfer.
5. If no injunction is served within the 14-day period, the stop notice lapses in respect of the shares being transferred and the transfer or redemption notice may be processed.
6. The details in the register of members and the 'stop list' should then be amended as appropriate. The notice should be endorsed with the details of the transfer (or redemption) if there is any balance of the holding to which the stop notice still applies.
7. A stop notice may be withdrawn in which case the register of members, stop list and copy of the stop notice would be amended or noted appropriately.
8. If a stop notice is received for registration relative to a holding in uncertificated form within the CREST system, the notice should immediately be transmitted to the operator of the CREST system, Euroclear UK & Ireland Limited so that it may initiate the necessary changes to the register (this will result in the holding being moved into a CREST escrow account).

Charging order

This is a court order securing a shareholding for the benefit of a judgment creditor. The order is made in two parts. First, an order nisi, which acts as a stop notice (see above). If the settlement of the debt is made, the order will be discharged. If settlement is not made the order may be made absolute. If made absolute, the judgment creditor is empowered to realise the shareholding to settle the debt. The duly sealed order or an office copy will identify the relevant shareholding. The equivalent Scottish document is a letter of arrestment, which cannot be registered by English companies.

Procedure

If a charging order is received the following procedure should be adopted:

1 There must be complete identity between the holding specified in the order and a shareholding in the company. Service of the order should be acknowledged to the sender unless the holding cannot be identified in which case the order should be returned to the sender.
2 The order or office copy submitted to the company is retained by the company.
3 An appropriate entry in the register of members should be made to indicate the existence of the order.
4 Details of the order should be entered on a 'stop list'.
5 If any transfers of the relevant shareholding are lodged for registration, a 'warning-off' letter must be sent to the judgment creditor detailed in the order, who may then perfect his security by obtaining a further order of the Court making the charging order absolute. The terms of the order must be strictly followed.
6 If an order absolute is made, these details should be entered in the register of members, the 'stop list' should be amended and the order absolute retained with the original order.
7 An order absolute usually authorises the sale of the shares with payment of the proceeds into the Court.
8 If debt due to the judgment creditor is settled, the charging order nisi must be withdrawn. The advice of withdrawal must be made personally by the judgment creditor before a practising solicitor. The discharge of the order nisi should be acknowledged, the details recorded in the register of members and the 'stop list' amended. The notice of discharge should be retained with the original order.

Garnishee order

A garnishee order is a court order attaching all debts for the benefit of a judgment creditor. The debts will be amounts due from the company to a shareholder and the judgment creditor will be a person owed money by that shareholder and who has obtained judgment from the Court to that effect. The terms of the order usually include rights to income (dividends) as well as capital. The order does not restrict the transfer of securities. As with a charging order, the order is made in two parts. An *order nisi* is made requiring the company to attend (through a representative) a court hearing. If before that time the judgment debt has been satisfied, the order is discharged. If the debt is not satisfied, the order is made absolute. If the order is made absolute, the company is under an obligation to pay the judgment creditor the amount of any debts due by the company to the shareholder concerned. The judgment creditor will be empowered to give to the company a discharge of its debt to the shareholder. The sealed court order or duly authorised office copy will identify the shareholder concerned and the amount of the debt. There is no equivalent Scottish document.

Procedure

The procedure for registration of a garnishee order is the same as that for registering a charging order. As the order attaches to income and not just capital any dividends must be paid to the creditor until such time as the debt is settled and the order is discharged.

Bankruptcy order

A company may be required to register a court order adjudicating a shareholder bankrupt. The effect of a bankruptcy order is to transfer the shares to a trustee for the benefit of the shareholder's creditors generally. Trustees are usually appointed following the issue of the adjudication order and this is evidenced by a certificate of the Department for Business, Innovation & Skills naming the trustee and confirming details of the appointment. Either the original order bearing the seal of the Court or a duly authenticated office copy of the order or a copy of the *London Gazette* notifying the order with the relevant certificate from the Department for Business, Innovation & Skills should be submitted to the company together with the shareholders share certificate(s).

The equivalent Scottish document is an act and warrant appointing a trustee in sequestration.

Procedure

The following procedure should be adopted:

1. There must be complete identity between the person named in the order or *Gazette* advertisement and a registered shareholding.
2. Relevant details of the documents submitted should be recorded and a copy retained for future reference.
3. The heading of the account should be changed to 'the trustee of the estate of ..., a bankrupt' adding the name and address of the trustee by way of note.

The shares of the bankrupt vest in this case in the trustee by operation of law without the need for any instrument of transfer (IA1986 s.306).

4 The share certificate(s) should be endorsed with the details of the order and the certificates and the order or *Gazette* advertisement validated with the company's registration stamp.
5 All further communications should be addressed to the trustee in his representative capacity or as directed by the trustee.
6 It may be appropriate for a dividend mandate to be completed by the trustee.

Order for rectification of register

An order may be made by a Court under CA2006 s.125 for the rectification of the register of members. The rectification can take any form including removals or additions to the register or the substitution of one person for another whether in respect of the entire holding or only part of it. Original orders will bear the seal of the Court or an office copy may be presented for registration. The order will identify the shareholding to which it relates which should be submitted together with the share certificates where appropriate.

An order for rectification of the register made only be made by a Court in the country of registration of the company concerned. Accordingly an order made by a Scottish Court may not be registered by English companies and an order made by an English Court may not be registered by a Scottish company.

Procedure

On receipt of such an order, the following procedure should be adopted:

1 There must be complete identity between the holding referred to in the order and a shareholding in the company.
2 The amendment authorised in the order should be made in the register of members, and the date of the order and its registration should be entered as the authority for such amendment and there may be consequential changes to other company records. A copy of the order should be retained for future reference.
3 Although the share certificate(s) could be endorsed, preferably a new certificate should be issued.
4 The order should be endorsed with the company's registration stamp and returned to the sender with the new share certificate.
5 It may be appropriate for a dividend mandate to be completed.

Appointment of receiver

The company may receive notice of the appointment of a receiver, or a receiver and manager in relation to a shareholder which is a body corporate. The appointee may act only within the terms of the relevant court order, debenture or trust deed under which they were appointed.

The equivalent Scottish document is the appointment of a receiver.

Procedure

The following procedure should be adopted:

1 There must be complete identity between the body corporate in respect of which a receiver is being appointed and a shareholding in the company.
2 Service of the order or notice should be acknowledged to the sender unless the holding cannot be identified in which case the order should be returned to the sender.
3 The details of the appointment, name and address of the receiver and date of registration should be entered in the register of members. The account in the register should be amended to the name and address of the receiver, described as 'receiver of . . . Limited/plc'.
4 Where a notice is received, this should be retained. If the appointment is made by court order this should be endorsed and returned. A copy of the order should be kept for future reference.
5 Share certificates do not need to be endorsed.
6 All future communications should be addressed to the receiver or as directed by the receiver.
7 It may be appropriate for a dividend mandate to be completed.
8 The receivership may be brought to an end following which the entries in the register of members should be amended accordingly. Any dividend mandate in favour of the receiver should be terminated. The notice or order ending the appointment should be retained with the original notice or copy order.

Appointment of liquidator

The company may receive notice of the appointment of a liquidator in relation to a shareholder which is a body corporate. The person appointed liquidator assumes the functions of the board of directors of that body corporate to facilitate the realising of its assets, collection of debts and distribution of any surplus to creditors and, if the surplus is sufficient, to shareholders.

The company may receive notice in the form of a copy of the resolution appointing the liquidator in the case of a voluntary liquidation or in the form of an original court order or an office copy in the case of a compulsory liquidation. In either instance a copy of the *London Gazette* containing notification of the appointment may also be accepted.

If the company receives notice of appointment of a liquidator the procedure is the same as that for the appointment of a receiver. In the case of the appointment of a liquidator, the company will also receive a stock transfer form when the liquidator realises the shareholder company's assets.

9 General meetings

Introduction

The requirement for companies to hold general meetings of shareholders is laid down in the Companies Act 2006, and reinforced by the company's Articles. The provisions of the Act cannot be overruled by a company's Articles where the effect would be to deprive the shareholders of any rights provided by statute. However, in instances where the procedure stipulated by the Articles is merely different from the statutory position, the Articles may still prevail. Care needs to be taken therefore to establish that the correct requirements have been observed. Many companies' Articles will still be based on Table A, and therefore reference is made to Table A as well as the Model Articles under the Act.

The Act's requirements cover the convening of general meetings, notice of general meetings, proceedings to be followed at general meetings and the votes of members, including provisions for proxies for members unable or unwilling to attend.

There are three main types of general meetings:

- annual general meeting;
- general meetings;
- class meeting of the holders of a particular class of the company's capital.

Notice of general meetings

The minimum periods of notice required for general meetings is specified in CA2006 s.307. These periods cannot be reduced by the company's Articles, although the minimum periods can be extended.

Listed companies are required where possible to comply with the Combined Code, which contains a best practice requirement for notice of annual general meetings to be 20 working days in all cases. The minimum notice periods specified in CA2006 s.307 are:

General meeting of a private company	14 days
Annual general meeting of a public company	21 days

For traded companies, the notice periods are set out in CA2006 s.307A, as follows:

General meetings where specified conditions met	14 days
All other general meetings	21 days

In order for a general meeting of a traded company to be held on 14 days' notice, the circumstances specified in CA2006 s.307A must be met. This section was inserted into the Act by the Companies (Shareholders' Rights) Regulations 2009 (SI 2009/1632) with effect from 3 August 2009. These circumstances are as follows:

1 the meeting is not an annual general meeting;
2 members are offered an electronic voting facility; and
3 a special resolution has been passed to reduce the notice period to 14 days. This must have happened at either the immediately preceding annual general meeting or at a general meeting held since the last annual general meeting.

If all three conditions are met, the notice period will be 14 days. In all other cases 21 days' notice will be required.

Resolutions requiring special notice (CA2006 s.312)

Notice to company of intention to put resolution	28 days
Notice to members at same time as notice given to members of meeting	28 days if practicable; otherwise not less than 14 days

However, great care needs to be taken as, whilst the Model Articles do not contain any provisions regarding notice periods, reg.38 Table A has different notice periods which may have been adopted, varied or excluded by any particular company:

General meeting of a private or public company to consider special resolutions or the appointment of a director	21 days
Annual general meeting of a public company	21 days
All other general meetings of private or public company	14 days

In all cases, the period of notice is expressed as clear days' notice. This means that the day on which the notice is given and the day on which the meeting is to be held are excluded (CA2006 s.360). The date on which the notice is deemed to be served varies with different companies' Articles. Table A, reg.115, provides that clear days excludes the date the notice is served or deemed served and also the date of the meeting and that a notice sent either by post or electronically is deemed to be served 48 hours after posting or sending, respectively.

For example, if a private company wishes to hold a general meeting on 17 May, the latest date for posting the notice of meeting would be 1 May. The notice would be deemed to be served on 3 May and the 14 days counted from 4 May would expire on 17 May.

Entitlement to notice of general meetings

Table A and most companies' Articles provide that notice is to be given to every member who is entitled to attend and vote at the meeting, with the exception of those whose registered addresses are outside the UK (Table A, reg.112). In this case, notice need be given only when the member has notified the company of an address in the United Kingdom for the service of notices.

Listed companies are required to send notice to overseas members by airmail (*LR 9.3.4.5*).

In addition, Table A, reg.116 provides that executors or administrators of a deceased member or the trustee of a bankrupt member must be given notice, even though they may not have the right to vote at the meeting.

The auditors have a statutory right to receive notice of general meetings (CA2006 s.486), as do directors under Table A, reg.38. Listed companies should ensure that two copies of any notices are sent to the UK Listing Authority no later than the day the notice is issued to shareholders (*LR 9.6.1*).

Surprisingly, the company secretary has no formal right to receive a copy of the notice or to attend general meetings. Holders of preference shares or non-voting shares will not be entitled to receive notice of general meetings unless, because of a particular event, they are entitled to vote at them. In practice, however, and especially in the case of listed companies, notices will usually be sent to every holder of shares or debentures whether or not the registered address of the holder is in the United Kingdom and irrespective of whether the securities held entitle that member to vote at the annual general meeting. This is because, under CA2006 ss.431 and 432, every member and holder of debentures must be sent a copy of the report and accounts, and the notice of meeting is usually incorporated in this document. It is, however, usual practice to include an explanatory note stating that the notice is sent for information only to debenture holders, who are not entitled to attend and vote at the annual general meeting.

For a class meeting, only the holders of the shares of that class are entitled to notice. There is provision in most companies' Articles (e.g. Table A, reg.39) affording protection to the company in the case of accidental omission to give notice to any person entitled to receive it.

The Model Articles do not contain any provisions concerning entitlement to notice.

Uncertificated Securities Regulations

Regulation 34 of the Uncertificated Securities Regulations 1995, SI 1995/3272 (USR1995) provides for a time to be specified in the notice of meetings for establishing the entitlement of members who hold shares in uncertificated form to attend and vote at general meetings. This cannot be more than 48 hours prior to the meeting. This takes account of the CREST settlement system, which operates on a real-time basis, with transactions being registered up to and indeed during the meeting. The specified cut-off time allows the entitlement to attend and vote, including by proxy, to be fixed. Current practice is to stipulate the close of business two days prior to the meeting. This results in a weekend cut-off date for meetings held on Mondays or Tuesdays, but as there are no settlements at weekends it has no adverse effect.

USR2001, reg.41, paras.(3) and (4) provide for the company to stipulate a date not more than 21 days prior to the date of issue of the notice as the record date for the purposes of establishing the right to receive notice of the meeting.

Content of notices

The notice must state the time, place and date of the meeting and the general nature of the business to be transacted (CA2006 s.311). [***See precedent 5.***] Where a special resolution is to be proposed, the notice must contain the text of the resolution and must state that the resolution is to be proposed as a special resolution (CA2006 s.283(6)). Since the directors normally instruct the company secretary to convene the general meeting, the notice is usually signed by the company secretary on behalf of the board (sometimes referred to as 'by order of the board').

Listed companies must follow the provisions of the *Listing Rules* (*LR 9.3.6, 7*) in regard to proxies, i.e. every member must be given the opportunity to vote for or against every resolution included in the notice (the so-called 'three-way proxy': see below). In order to facilitate this, resolutions in the notice of meeting should be numbered so that the numbers can be included on the proxy form, with boxes for the member to tick either for or against the resolution.

Every notice must include a prominent statement which makes clear that the member entitled to attend and vote may appoint one or more proxies to attend, speak and vote on his behalf (CA2006 s.325). A proxy need not be a member of the company. Any provision in the company's Articles requiring proxies to be lodged more than 48 hours (excluding any day that is not a working day) before the meeting is invalid (CA2006 s.327). [***See precedent 19.***]

The notice of an annual general meeting of a public company must state that the meeting is to be the annual general meeting (CA2006 s.337).

Agreement to short notice of meeting

There is a useful concession under CA2006 s.307(5) in circumstances where it is not possible (or desirable) to give the minimum period of notice required by subsections (1) and (2) of that section or by the Articles under which a general meeting may be held on short notice.

Advantage of the concession, however, can usually be taken only by companies with a small number of members. It is a good practice for the agreement to short notice to be in writing so that there is no doubt that the meeting was validly called. It should be noted that the provision does not allow the complete dispensation of giving notice. [***See precedent** 72.*]

The number of members required to give valid consent to short notice is defined in CA2006 ss.307(5) and (6), which provides that for a private company the requisite majority to agree to short notice is a majority in number of the members having a right to attend and vote at the meeting, and together holding not less than 90 per cent of the share capital of the company. This 90 per cent limit may be increased by the company's Articles to not more than 95 per cent. Thus, if in the case of a company with 100 shares, one member held 97 shares and three other members held one share each, the one member with more than 95 per cent of the share capital could not hold the meeting at short notice because they would not constitute a majority of the members. This provision protects minority members holding less than 10 per cent of the shares.

For a public company the percentage required for a general meeting is 95 per cent.

In the case of an annual general meeting, consent must be given by all the members entitled to attend and vote (CA2006 s.337(2)). Thus the concession is useful only to small public companies. The form of consent to short notice for an annual general meeting should include agreement to accept the company's report and accounts (if necessary), even though they were not sent to members not less than 21 days before the date of the meeting, as required by CA2006 s.424.

Although not legally required, it may be advisable to obtain a letter of non-objection to the short notice from the company's auditors. Notice of all general meetings must be sent to the auditors under CA2006 s.486, which gives them the right to attend such meetings.

Types of resolutions which may be passed at general meetings

The following types of resolution may be passed at a general meeting:

1 an ordinary resolution which may, in certain circumstances, require special notice to have been given (see below);
2 a special resolution.

Ordinary resolutions

A simple majority of those present and voting is all that is required to pass an ordinary resolution. The practical effect of this should be considered. If there are 12 members entitled to vote present at a meeting, the resolution would be passed if seven voted in favour and five against. The resolution would also be passed if nine of the 12 members abstained from voting, and of the three who did vote, two voted in favour of the resolution and one against.

Examples of this other type of resolution include:

- alterations to the share capital under CA2006 ss.617 and 618;
- a capitalisation of profits (Table A, reg.110);
- the grant of authority for the allotment of securities (CA2006 ss.550 and 551);
- subject to provision in the Articles, a resolution authorising the directors to offer shareholders the right to elect to receive new ordinary shares for the whole or part of a cash dividend.

Special resolutions

The majority required to pass a special resolution is one of not less than 75 per cent of those voting. It is essential that the notice of the meeting states that it is intended to propose a resolution as a special resolution. Under CA1985, at least 21 clear days' notice had to be given and this is reflected in Table A reg.38. However, by CA2006 s.307 only 14 days' notice needs to be given of a general meeting at which a special resolution is to be passed. This does not apply to general meetings of traded companies, where 21 days' notice will still be required unless a resolution reducing the notice period to 14 days has been passed.

The type of business that must be dealt with by a special resolution is specified in the Act and/or the company's Articles. It includes alteration of the Articles (CA2006 s.21); change of name (CA2006 s.77); disapplication of pre-emption rights (CA2006 s.571); and reduction of capital (CA2006 s.641).

The notice convening the meeting at which a special resolution is to be considered must include the full text of the resolution. With the exception of obvious typographical errors, the meeting cannot amend the wording of a special resolution (CA2006 s.283(6)).

Special notice

This must not be confused with special resolutions. Special notice of certain ordinary resolutions must be given to the company (CA2006 s.312), as follows:

Under CA2006 s.489, resolutions:

1. to appoint an auditor other than a retiring auditor [***see precedent*** 73];
2. to fill a casual vacancy in the office of auditor [***see precedent*** 73];
3. to reappoint as auditor a retiring auditor appointed by the directors to fill a casual vacancy [***see precedent*** 73];
4. to remove an auditor before the expiration of his term of office [***see precedent*** *73*].

Under CA2006 s.168, resolutions:

1. to remove a director before the expiration of his period of office [***see precedent*** *20*];

2 to appoint somebody in place of the director removed at the meeting at which he is removed [*see precedent* 74].

The company is required to give notice of the resolutions to all members in the notice of meeting or, if not practicable, by advertisement in a newspaper not less than 14 days before the meeting (CA2006 s.312(3)).

Where the special notice relates to a resolution proposed by the directors, such as the appointment of an auditor other than the retiring auditor, it is common practice for the special notice to be given by a director.

Registration of resolutions with the Registrar of Companies

The resolutions that must be filed with the Registrar of Companies are specified in CA2006 s.29. These include all special resolutions, as well as the following:

- to authorise the allotment of securities (CA2006 s.551(9));
- to authorise a market purchase of the company's own shares (CA2006 s.701(8)).

Circulation of members' statements or resolutions

Companies have a duty to circulate resolutions or statements of not more than 1,000 words with respect to that or any other business of the meeting if requested to do so by members (CA2006 s.314).

The request for circulation may be given by:

1 members holding not less than 5 per cent of the voting rights at the meeting concerned; or
2 no fewer than 100 members holding shares with an average paid-up value of not less than £100.

The request to circulate a statement must identify the statement to be circulated or the text of the resolution, must be authenticated by the persons making it and must be received by the company at least one week prior to the meeting.

The cost of circulating the statement need not be met by those requesting it if it relates to an annual general meeting and sufficient requests to require circulation are received prior to the end of the financial year. In all other cases those seeking the circulation of the statement must meet the costs unless the company resolves otherwise. Unless the company has previously resolved to meet any costs an amount reasonably sufficient to cover the costs must be deposited with the company not less than one week prior to the meeting failing which the company need not circulate the statement (CA2006 s.316).

The company may apply to the Courts for leave not to comply with the request if the company or an aggrieved person believes the request is of a defamatory nature or the rights under CA2006 s.314 are being abused (CA2006 s.317).

Shareholders' right to propose directors

Regulation 76 of Table A states that no one other than directors retiring by rotation may be appointed or reappointed as a director at a general meeting unless:

1 they have been recommended by the directors; or
2 not less than 14 days and not more than 35 days before the date of the meeting, notice has been received from any member entitled to vote at the meeting of his or her intention to propose the appointment or reappointment of that person as a director, together with a notice executed by the proposee of his or her willingness to be appointed or reappointed.

The new Model Articles have no such provision, and any person willing to be appointed, and not prohibited by law, may be appointed as a director by ordinary resolution of the members or by resolution of the directors. (Model Articles regs.17 (private) 20 (public).)

Where such a notice is received, notice must be given to all shareholders not less than seven or more than 28 days prior to the meeting of the names of any persons recommended by the directors or to be proposed by a shareholder for appointment or reappointment as a director. The notice to the company must include the information about that person that is required to be entered in the register of directors, if appointed. It will be seen that in order to invoke reg.76, all that is required is the holding of one voting share. Accordingly, most companies with external shareholders will either increase the shareholding qualifications to, say, 5 per cent or remove the provision entirely.

Annual general meetings

Annual general meetings of private companies

Under the Companies Act 2006, private companies are no longer required to hold an annual general meeting. The requirements of the 1985 Companies Act for companies to hold an AGM, lay their accounts at an AGM and to reappoint auditors annually were repealed on 1 October 2007.

Any private company required by its Articles to hold an AGM will need to comply with the general provisions on meetings in Part 13 of the CA2006, together with any more onerous requirements in its Articles.

Members of private companies no longer have the statutory right to demand that the company holds an AGM, except by amending the Articles to require this. However, members of private companies holding 10 per cent of the voting rights can requisition a general meeting (CA2006 ss.303–305) and members holding 5 per cent of voting rights have a new right to requisition a written resolution (CA2006, ss.292–295).

Public companies: convening an annual general meeting

Every public company must hold an annual general meeting within the period of six months commencing on its accounting reference date (CA2006 s.336).

In most cases, the directors convene the annual general meeting (Table A, regs.36 and 37). Under CA2006 s.306, the Court has power to order an annual general meeting and may direct the manner in which it should be held and conducted. If the Articles do not contain provisions with regard to the convening of the annual general meeting, under CA2006 s.303, members holding not less than 10 per cent of the issued share capital may call a general meeting. It is likely that a meeting convened under the direction of the Court will be a general meeting rather than the annual general meeting.

Circulation of members' resolutions

Companies have a duty to circulate resolutions if requested to do so by members (CA2006 s.338).

The request for circulation may be given by:

1 members holding not less than 5 per cent of the voting rights at the meeting concerned; or
2 no fewer than 100 members holding shares with an average paid-up value of not less than £100.

The request to circulate a resolution must specify the text of the resolution, must be authenticated by the persons making it and must be received by the company at least six weeks prior to the meeting or if later the time at which notice is given.

The company need not comply with the request if the effect of the resolution is ineffective, is defamatory, frivolous or vexatious.

The cost of circulating the statement need not be met by those requesting it if sufficient requests to require circulation are received prior to the end of the financial year. In all other cases those seeking the circulation of the statement must meet the costs unless the company resolves otherwise. Unless the company has previously resolved to meet any costs an amount reasonably sufficient to cover the costs must be deposited with the company not less than six weeks prior to the meeting or if later the time that notice is given failing which the company need not circulate the statement (CA2006 s.316).

Business at annual general meetings

The following is the routine business of an annual general meeting [***see precedent 19***]:

1 Receiving the report and accounts laid before the meeting, as required by CA2006 ss.437–438.

2 The declaration of a dividend.
3 The election of directors. (This will include both the election of directors who have been appointed since the last annual general meeting and the re-election of directors who have retired by rotation as required by the company's Articles.)
4 The reappointment and remuneration of the auditors.

Apart from routine business, any other business may also be undertaken at the annual general meeting, for example:

1 Ordinary resolutions to increase the company's capital.
2 Special resolutions for any required alterations to the company's Articles.
3 Authority to the directors to issue capital as required by CA2006 s.551.
4 Authority for the directors to disapply pre-emption rights (CA2006 s.571).
5 Where it is company practice, and there is provision in the company's Articles, to authorise the directors to offer shareholders the right to receive new ordinary shares instead of cash for all or part of any dividend.

'Other' business used to be described as 'special' business, but Table A no longer makes a distinction between the two; hence, the suggested use of the terms routine business and other business.

Receiving report and accounts

It is not appropriate for the minutes of an annual general meeting (including a general meeting of a private company) to state that: 'The report and accounts for the year ended 20XX were received and approved/adopted'. The relevant provision of the Companies Act 2006 makes no provision for the report and accounts to be *approved/adopted* by the meeting (CA2006, ss.437–438). All that is legally required is that the accounts be laid before the meeting. Although there is no legal obligation to have any resolution at all, best practice is for shareholders to resolve to receive the accounts and to have the opportunity to question directors about them. The appropriate minute would be more correct if it stated:

> 'The report of the directors and audited accounts for the year ended 20XX were laid before the meeting' (or 'were received by the meeting').

There is a common misconception that shareholders approve the accounts and, by implication, can refuse to approve them. The accounts are the accounts of the directors; shareholders merely receive them. Shareholders have no right to reject accounts or request their amendment.

For a listed company any vote against receipt of the accounts would be taken as a vote of no confidence in the board.

Declaration of dividend

A declaration of a final dividend is usually included in the resolution to receive the directors' report and accounts. The Articles of the company will normally follow reg.102 in Table A, which provides that the company may, by ordinary resolution, declare dividends in accordance with the rights of the members, but that no dividend shall exceed the amount recommended by the directors. This is also the stance taken in the Model Articles (art.30 for private companies limited by shares and art.70 for public companies). Thus, although the accounts may show an amount of the proposed dividend, this could be reduced or even rejected by the members, whether the accounts are accepted or not.

The Model Articles and Table A, reg.103 authorise directors to pay interim dividends on their own authority.

'Other' general meetings

Convening general meetings

Subject to the Articles, general meetings may be convened at any time in order to transact business that needs to be dealt with. The directors may convene a general meeting under authority contained CA2006 s.302. Alternatively, under CA2006 s.303, the directors may be required to call the meeting by a requisition of the members. The Court also has authority under CA2006 s.306 to convene a general meeting.

Quorum at general meetings

The quorum for meetings is stipulated in CA2006 s.318 and provides that for a company with a sole shareholder the quorum is one and that in all other cases, subject to any provisions in the company's Articles of Association, two members present in person or by proxy may constitute a quorum. A company's Articles usually make provision for a procedure to be adopted in the event of a quorum not being present.

Table A, reg.41 requires that if a quorum is not present within half an hour, or if a quorum ceases to be present after the commencement of the meeting, the meeting is adjourned to the same day, time and place in the following week or to such time and place (but not day) as the directors may decide. This regulation is frequently amended so that at the adjourned meeting those shareholders present shall constitute a quorum even if below the 'normal' quorum.

Similar provisions for adjournment feature in the Model Articles (art.41 for private companies and art.33 for public companies), with the difference that there is no default adjournment to the same day, time and place in the following week. Rather, the chairman must either specify the time and place for the adjourned meeting, or state that the meeting will continue at such time and place as the directors may decide.

Chairman at general meetings

If the company's Articles follow Table A, regs.42 and 43 or the Model Articles, art.31 for private companies and art.39 for public companies, the chairman of the board will also be chairman for general meetings. If the chairman is not present, then another director (e.g. a deputy chairman or vice-chairman) takes the chair. In the absence of any director, one of the members present takes the chair.

CA2006 s.319 states that subject to any provisions in the company's Articles any member may be elected by the meeting to be chairman of that meeting. CA2006 s.328 permits a proxy holder to be elected chairman of the meeting subject to any provisions in the Articles.

The role of the chairman at a shareholders' meeting is to ensure that the meeting is properly and fairly conducted, allowing all opinions to be expressed. Table A also gives the chairman specific powers relating to the conduct of meetings:

1. To demand that a poll be taken (reg.46).
2. To declare the result of a vote taken by a show of hands (reg.47 also in CA2006 s.320).
3. To insist that a demand for a poll be withdrawn (reg.48).
4. To direct the manner, time and place when a poll will be undertaken (reg.49).
5. To have a casting vote in the event of equality of votes for and against a resolution (reg.50).
6. To rule on any question of the validity of votes cast at the meeting (reg.58).

The role of the company secretary

Preparation for an annual general meeting of a public company

As well as the routine business of annual general meetings outlined above, it is common practice to include the following business:

1. To pass an ordinary resolution to give the board authority under CA2006 s.551 to allot securities up to a maximum nominal amount during the period from the passing of the resolution until the conclusion of the company's next annual general meeting.
2. To pass a special resolution under CA2006 s.571 to allot equity securities up to a certain aggregate nominal amount, to expire at the conclusion of the company's next annual general meeting after the passing of the resolution, as if s.571 requiring such securities to be allotted to shareholders on a pre-emptive basis did not apply to the company. Alternatively, the authorities mentioned above can be provided for in the company's Articles but, if so, any changes in the amounts of capital covered by the authorities will have to be made by the more cumbersome procedure of altering the company's Articles.

It is also routine business for companies with the appropriate provision in their Articles to pass an ordinary resolution giving authority to the directors to offer shareholders the option to receive the whole or any part of their dividends in new ordinary shares rather than in cash.

Other items of non-routine business (e.g. alteration of Articles) should be described in a separate circular to members dispatched with the notice of the meeting.

The venue for the meeting will probably have been fixed several months in advance, and the date of the annual general meeting included in the programme of board meetings for the year and previously approved by the directors.

Following approval of the audited accounts, the following matters should be undertaken by the company secretary:

1 It is quite common for the report and accounts to incorporate the notice of the meeting as well as the chairman's statement. Three proof copies of the booklet containing the notice of meeting and the accounts will be required and all three copies will require signature for each of the reports.
2 Send another copy of the report and accounts with the names of the signatories and dates printed in to the company's printers for a final proof prior to running off the bulk supply for dispatch to shareholders.
3 Advise the company's registrar (either the company's own in-house registrar or a firm of service registrars) of the amount of the recommended dividend, if any, in order that they may prepare the dividend warrants for dispatch to shareholders following approval at the annual general meeting.
4 If a dividend is to be paid the company should also arrange with its bankers for a dividend account to be opened in which the money required to pay the dividend will be placed.
5 Prepare proxy forms for dispatch with the report and accounts to shareholders. These can be either separate cards inserted in the booklet or a tear-out page in the booklet.
6 The report and accounts will normally be sent directly to shareholders by the company's printers. They should be instructed as to the date on which posting should take place and whether the document is to be sent by first or second class post. The names of the signatories on the bulk printed supply should be printed in exactly the same way as the original signatures on the three signed copies, e.g. 'Albert Smith' and not 'A. Smith'.
7 One of the three signed copies of the report and accounts booklet will be placed in the company's directors' board minute book, one copy will be retained by the company's auditors and the third copy is sent to the Registrar of Companies. (This is in accordance with CA2006 s.444(7) which requires the auditor's report sent to the Registrar to state the names of the auditors and to be signed by them.) The signed copy of the report and accounts for the Registrar of Companies could be sent either at the same time that these are dispatched to members or at a later date within the time allowed by CA2006 s.442.
8 It is usual to invite the company's solicitor to attend the meeting. The company's auditors are entitled to attend under CA2006 s.502(2).
9 The forms of proxy returned by shareholders should be checked against the

register of members. A report on the result of the proxy count should be made available for the board after the expiry of the deadline for receipt of proxies (usually 48 hours before the time of the meeting).

10 Consider the preparation of ballot papers in case a poll is demanded (for more detail, see below). It might be prudent to do this if many proxy cards have been returned with votes against any particular resolution(s).
11 If the chairman is going to make remarks at the meeting, additional to those contained in his statement in the report and accounts, prepare copies to give to the company's press agents at the meeting and, for listed, AIM or PLUS companies, to be sent simultaneously to the regulatory information service (see *LR 9.3.1, DR 2.2.1*).
12 A copy of the register of members should be available at the annual general meeting. This is required in case it is necessary for persons attending the meeting to be identified, to ensure only those entitled to attend are present.
13 Provide attendance sheets for shareholders, the press, proxies and representatives of corporate shareholders who are attending the meeting under authority of CA2006 s.323.
14 Make available for inspection copies of the directors' service contracts.
15 Prepare an order of proceedings, setting out the various resolutions to be passed at the meeting. There is no requirement for resolutions to be seconded and it is perfectly in order for the chairman of the meeting to propose all resolutions with no seconder.
16 From the outset, always bear in mind practical considerations, such as making room bookings in good time, checking catering arrangements and whether a photographer or video-conferencing facility is needed.

At the annual general meeting

The company secretary should first check that a quorum is present and then be ready to read the notice of meeting. If the meeting consents (and it usually does), this may be taken as read, since it will have been included in the report and accounts sent to all members. The auditor's report must cover the accounts laid before the meeting and state the name of the auditor. This will, of course, have been included in the booklet containing the report and accounts. Further, the copy of the auditor's report delivered to the Registrar of Companies must also state the name of the auditors and be signed by the auditor (CA2006 s.444(7)).

The company secretary will assist the chairman in counting the votes (if necessary) on a show of hands. This is not normally necessary, except in the case of a special resolution, where there might be some doubt about whether the necessary three-quarters majority of those attending and voting was achieved.

All proxies are entitled to speak at the meeting including demanding or joining in the demand for a poll vote on any resolution (CA2006 ss.324 and 329).

The company secretary is involved if a poll is demanded on any resolution, to be taken either at the meeting or after the meeting (see pp. 184–185 and 188–189).

After the meeting

The minutes of the meeting should be prepared. It is not always necessary for these to be sent out in draft to the directors for comments since the minutes will cover only routine business or such other business as may have been specified in the notice convening the meeting.

If any special resolution has been passed at the meeting, a copy signed by the chairman of the meeting must be sent to the Registrar of Companies within 15 days of the meeting.

Assuming that the dividend is duly approved at the meeting, the necessary arrangements may be put in hand for its payment. The actual payment date will usually be some weeks after the meeting. If the company prefers to pay the dividend as soon as it is approved, the cheques and tax vouchers for the mandated dividends must be sent to the head offices of banks some days in advance so that the banks are authorised to pay the dividend immediately after the meeting.

Voting at general meetings

Initially, resolutions are put to the meeting for members to vote on a show of hands. If a resolution is defeated on a show of hands and the chairman is aware that he has a substantial proxy vote in favour of the resolution, he will demand a poll. On a show of hands, every member present in person or by proxy and entitled to vote has one vote only irrespective of the number of shares held or the number of proxies that an individual holds. (CA2006 s.285(1)). A person appointed as a proxy by more than one member may however cast one vote for and one vote against each resolution on the show of hands (CA2006 s.285(2)). On a poll, however, the number of shares held determines the number of votes the member may cast either in person or by proxy. In the event of an equality of votes, most Articles (including Table A, reg.50) give the chairman a casting vote.

On the declaration by the chairman of whether the resolution has been carried or lost and an entry made in the minute book to that effect, the validity of the resolution cannot be questioned (CA2006 s.320) and it is unnecessary to insert in the minute book the number of members voting for or against the resolution. However, before declaring that a special resolution has been passed, it is necessary to ensure that the requisite majority was present to pass such a resolution.

Abstaining

The increasing role of corporate governance and the need for shareholders, particularly institutional shareholders, to express their opposition to various aspects of a company corporate governance performance has seen an increasing use of abstentions on proxy forms. In law an abstention is not a vote. Although not a vote, abstentions can affect the outcome of a vote. If the majority is to be calculated by reference to the votes cast, as in Table A, then abstentions would not be counted. But if the majority is by reference to the total votes returned, then abstentions are counted and might very well prevent resolutions from being approved as less than half the votes returned were in favour. If this were the case, abstentions would in effect be votes against a resolution. CA2006 ss.282(4) and 283(5), however, states that the majority on a poll is to be calculated by reference to the voting rights of the members who vote; accordingly abstentions have no effect. The ICSA has issued a guidance note, which recommends that companies allow members to instruct their proxy to vote for or against a resolution, as at present, but also to allow them to indicate that the proxy has discretion on how to vote or that they should abstain from voting. In order to avoid confusion, it is suggested that abstentions should be rephrased as 'vote withheld'.

Corporate shareholders

A shareholder which is a corporate body may be represented at a company meeting by a person appointed as its representative by a resolution of the corporate body's directors under CA2006 s.323. Following the changes to proxy rights introduced by the Companies Act 2006 the only practical difference between a corporate representative and a proxy is that details of a proxy must be lodged in advance whereas a corporate representative can bring their letter of appointment to the meeting.

Proxies

Under CA2006 s.324 an individual or corporate member of a company may appoint one or more proxies to attend, speak and vote both on a show of hands or a poll (CA2006 s.284) at one particular meeting only, but proxies have no other right. A proxy need not be a member of the company [***see precedent*** 7].

The notice of meeting of a public company should also state clearly the right of the shareholder to appoint one or more proxies (CA2006 s.325) [***see precedent 19***].

For unlisted public companies and private companies, it is not obligatory to send proxy forms with notices of meetings. In general, this is done only if controversy is anticipated.

Where proxy forms are used, they must be issued to all members of the company and not just to those who favour the board (CA2006 s.326). The company may accept proxy forms lodged at the last minute provided they are in an appropriate form. It is unlawful for a company to require proxies to be lodged with the company *more* than 48 hours prior to the time of the meeting (CA2006 s.327), excluding any days that are not working days. Proxies may be submitted in electronic form, but only to an address supplied by the company for that purpose (CA2006 s.333). Accordingly, sending a form of proxy by e-mail to the company secretary's normal e-mail address would not constitute a valid proxy.

At the meeting

Shareholders who appoint a proxy may still attend the meeting and vote in person; attendance and voting at the meeting effectively revokes the proxy appointment. The right of a person appointing a proxy to attend and vote at a meeting is conditional upon this not being prohibited by the Articles, but such a provision would be exceptional.

Three-way proxies

Listed companies must issue three-way proxy forms (*LR 9.3.6*). A three-way proxy includes provision for members to indicate which way they wish the proxy to cast their votes in the event of a poll being demanded. It must cover all the resolutions on the notice of meeting. The form must also state that, if it is returned without any indication as to how the proxy shall vote on any resolution, the proxy may exercise his discretion.

The proxy form cannot restrict the shareholder to appointing the chairman or another director as his proxy; it must include provision for the shareholder to appoint a proxy of his own choice. Corporate shareholders will usually be satisfied with the appointment of a proxy, and will usually send a representative only if they wish the representative to comment at the meeting and vote on a show of hands.

Form and dispatch of proxy forms

The pattern of voting indicated on returned forms of proxy will show whether or not there is likely to be any disagreement on the business. The chairman will thus know in advance whether he should demand a poll in the event of a motion being defeated on a show of hands since he will know whether the majority of proxies lodged with the company are in favour of the resolution.

It is usual for proxy forms to be in the form of pre-paid postcards. If there is to be a number of meetings following the annual general meeting, e.g. an extraordinary general meeting or a meeting of any particular class of the shareholders, the proxy cards for those meetings are usually of a different colour to facilitate sorting. Table A, reg.62 and most companies' Articles require that proxies must be lodged at the company's office not less than 48 hours before a meeting. Articles may provide for a shorter period, but not a longer period (CA2006 s.327). It is also usual for Articles to permit proxies to be lodged between an original meeting and an adjourned meeting. However, this can be done only if specifically provided for in the Articles.

The address to which proxies are to be returned may be the company's office, which in most companies' Articles and in Table A is defined as the registered office of the company, or to some other place specified in the notice convening the meeting. For example, if the share registration work of the company is carried out by a service registrar at a place other than the registered office, the proxies may be sent to the address of the registrar. It is worth noting that the Model Articles for public companies do not assume the company's office will be the registered office address, referring instead to a 'proxy notification address', which is the return address specified in the notice.

Notwithstanding anything contained in a company's Articles, or in Table A or the Model Articles as adopted by the company, proxies may be submitted by an electronic communication to an address notified by the company for that purpose (CA2006 s.333A).

In addition to providing numbered boxes for each resolution, so that the shareholder can indicate with a tick whether he votes for or against a resolution, it is useful for the proxy form to include a phrase to the effect that, on any other business arising at the meeting (including any motion to amend a resolution or to adjourn the meeting), the proxy will act at his discretion. The absence of such a sentence may be taken to preclude the proxy from voting on an amended resolution or on a resolution whether or not to adjourn the meeting. It also gives a proxy power to vote on any matter which may arise in connection with the procedure of the meeting. **[*See precedent* 7.]**

Evaluation of proxies

The proxy cards should be sorted and scrutinised as they are received by the company or its registrar, to check that they have been properly completed. A running total should be kept of the votes for and against each resolution as well as open votes. If the chairman of the company is appointed as the proxy, he will usually vote in favour of the resolutions. It should be noted that shareholders may limit their proxies to only part of their holdings and that, except in the case of private companies, they can appoint more than one proxy, each proxy appointed covering separate parts of their shareholding. Sorting proxy cards will be determined in the light of experience. The awkward ones are those where the proxy is to vote in favour of some resolutions and against others.

The proxy card should be signed personally by individual shareholders. Corporate shareholders must complete the proxy card in accordance with their own Articles of Association. This may be, for example, under seal if the company has a seal, or by a named individual appointed by board resolution to sign the proxy card on the company's behalf. In this case, the authority under which it is signed should be lodged with the proxy card if not already registered with the company. For joint holdings, CA2006 s.286 and most Articles, including Table A, reg.55, provide for the voting rights to be exercised by the first-named holder in the account (the 'senior') and they would normally sign the proxy form on behalf of all the joint holders. Unless stipulated by the Articles, it is not necessary for signatures on proxy forms to be witnessed.

Incorrectly completed proxy forms must be rejected, but if there is time and if the shareholding is substantial, they should be returned for amendment. A proxy may be revoked by the lodgement of a subsequent appointment, provided that the appointment is received by the company in time prior to the meeting. A proxy lapses if the person who gave it dies prior to the meeting, provided that notice of the death is received by the deadline for receipt of proxies (i.e. usually 48 hours prior to the meeting).

Demand for a poll

The rules governing the demanding of a poll are laid down in the company's Articles. The provisions of CA2006 ss.321 and 329 must also be taken into account, as they may render void certain provisions.

Regulation 46 of Table A provides that a poll may be demanded by:

1 the chairman;
2 at least five members with the right to vote at the meeting;
3 a member or members representing not less than one-tenth of the total voting rights of all the members with the right to vote at the meeting;
4 a member or members holding shares conferring a right to vote at the meeting, being shares on which an aggregate sum has been paid up equal to not less than one-tenth of the total sum paid up on all the shares conferring that right.

Regulation 36 of the Model Articles for public companies also provides for a poll to be demanded by the directors, or two or more persons having the right to vote on the resolution.

Proxies are entitled to demand or join in the demand for a poll to be conducted.

For a demand for a poll to be valid, it must be called before or immediately on the declaration by the chairman of the result of the vote on a show of hands.

When a poll is demanded

When a poll is demanded, if appropriate the chairman may suggest that, since he holds proxies overwhelmingly in favour of the resolution, the person or persons requesting the poll should consider withdrawing their demand.

If the demand is not withdrawn, the validity of the demand should be checked by confirming that those who have demanded it are, in fact, shareholders or, for example, if the member demanding it is a single member, that he holds not less than one-tenth of the total voting rights. This is a task for the scrutineers.

If the scrutineers advise that the poll has not been properly demanded, the chairman makes a statement to this effect and the meeting proceeds to its next business, or to a show of hands if the poll was requested before a vote by a show of hands has taken place. If the demand for the poll is valid and is not withdrawn, the chairman advises the meeting to this effect. If he has not already advised the meeting as to the proxy position when the poll was first demanded, he should now do so. Assuming the poll is still not withdrawn, the chairman announces the time for holding of the poll, e.g. either immediately, at the conclusion of the meeting or at a later date. It is usual practice for the poll to be held at the end of the meeting and for it to be kept open for one hour. The meeting then proceeds to its next business until the conclusion of business. At the end of the meeting, the chairman declares the meeting closed and then informs the members of the procedure for the conduct of the poll. The chairman should explain that those who have appointed a proxy need not complete a ballot paper unless they wish to alter their vote.

Stewards then distribute ballot papers to shareholders. Completed papers are handed to the scrutineers. The scrutineers, especially if they are the company's auditors or registrars, will no doubt have their own instructions for checking ballot papers, verifying holdings and preparing a report and final certificate of the result of the poll for the chairman.

Quoted companies must ensure that when a poll vote is taken the following information is made available on a website (CA2006 s.341):

- date of the meeting;
- text or description of the subject matter of the resolution;
- number of votes cast in favour and against.

The information must be made available on the website as soon as reasonably practical and must be retained for a period of at least two years (CA2006 s.353).

Procedural motions

Procedural motions are motions that are used to regulate the conduct of the business of the meeting. For the vast majority of routine meetings, they are never used. However, where contentious resolutions are proposed or where there is a vociferous element present, the use of procedural motions can be used to curtail discussion of a particular resolution.

As with many aspects of the legal system, the terminology of procedural motions has not changed over the years and now sounds arcane and intimidating to those not used to it. There are six common procedural motions:

- the closure ('that the questions be now put');
- next business ('that the meeting proceed to the next business');
- previous question ('that the question be not now put');
- postponement (version 1) ('that the question lie on the table');
- postponement (version 2) ('that the matter be referred back to …');
- adjournment.

Speaking

Shareholders and proxies entitled to attend and vote at a meeting are entitled to speak at the meeting.

Although those attending have the right to speak, they may be prevented from doing so in order to keep the meeting to a reasonable length or to maintain order. The chairman should ensure that all differing opinions on the matter under consideration are expressed and, in doing so, it should not be necessary for every person who wishes to speak to do so.

Adjournment of general meetings

Although the chairman may adjourn the meeting without the consent of the members if there is disorder, the power to adjourn a meeting usually rests with the members attending, who must give their consent. The Model Articles for public companies, art.33(6) and Table A, reg.45 provide that no business at an adjourned meeting shall be transacted other than that which could have been transacted at the original meeting. If the meeting is adjourned for more than 14 days, however, fresh notice of at least seven days, specifying the business to be transacted, must be given. When a resolution is passed at an adjourned meeting, it is deemed to have been passed on the date of the adjourned meeting rather than the date on which the original meeting was adjourned (CA2006 s.332).

If it is necessary to postpone or cancel a meeting after the notice of meeting has been issued, the correct procedure is to hold the meeting at the scheduled time and place and for a resolution to be passed adjourning the meeting to a later date. A circular could be sent to shareholders explaining the reasons for the postponement so that they do not waste their time in attending a purely formal meeting.

Requisitioned meetings

Directors are required to convene a general meeting if requested to do so by any member or members holding between them at least 10 per cent, in nominal value, of the paid-up issued share capital of the company or, if the company does not have share capital, 10 per cent of the voting rights. This percentage is reduced to 5 per cent in the case of a private company if more than 12 months have passed since the previous general meeting was held (CA2006 s.303).

The requisition must state the objects of the meeting, and must be authenticated by all the requisitionists [***see precedent*** *75*]. The requisition may consist of one or more copies signed by one or more requisitionists. If the directors do not issue a notice to convene the meeting within 21 days, the requisitionists may convene the meeting themselves, provided they call it for a date not more than three months later. The directors are deemed not to have convened the meeting if they issue a notice convening a meeting for a date more than 28 days after the date of that notice. Any reasonable expenses incurred by the requisitionists in issuing a notice must be repaid by the company, which can retain the money out of the fees payable to the directors (CA2006 ss.304 and 305).

Class meetings

As the name implies, class meetings are meetings of holders of a certain class of the company's capital and are held in accordance with the Articles of the company or conditions which attach to the securities concerned. Class meetings are required whenever the rights of the holders of the class are to be varied because of some action proposed by the company. Such variations may relate to a change in the voting rights attaching to the class or to changes proposed in a re-organisation of the company's share structure.

Resolutions in writing

With a few exceptions the members of a private company may pass any resolution that could be put to a general meeting by written resolution [***see precedent 4***]. The exceptions are:

- removal of a director under CA2006 s.168;
- removal of an auditor.

Written resolutions may be proposed by the directors or the members (CA2006 s.288).

A copy of the proposed written resolution must be sent by post or electronic means to all members entitled to attend and vote at a general meeting (CA2006 s.289).

A member signifies their agreement to a written resolution by returning to the company a document in hard copy or electronic format identifying the resolution and signifying their consent (CA2006 s.296).

A written resolution is approved when the requisite majority of members have signified their agreement, votes being calculated according to the number of shares held by each member (CA2006 ss.284 and 296).

If agreement has not been given within 28 days from the date the resolution was circulated, it is deemed to have lapsed and any consent given after that date has no effect (CA2006 s.297).

10
Accounts

Introduction

On 6 April 2008 Part 15 of the Companies Act 2006 replaced CA1985 ss.221–262A. Broadly speaking CA2006 does not introduce any new requirements but has re-ordered the sections to make it easier for companies of different sizes to locate the provisions applicable to them. The substantive change relates to the reduction by one month in the filing period allowed for companies to file their accounts at Companies House and in the case of a public company the period for laying the accounts before shareholders in general meeting. The provisions of Part 15 CA2006 apply to accounting periods beginning on or after 6 April 2008.

Accounting records

All companies are required to keep records of their financial transactions. The records must contain sufficient detail to enable the financial position of the company to be determined at any time so that the directors can ensure that any profit and loss account or balance sheet complies with the requirements of the Companies Act 2006 or art.4 of the IAS Regulations if they apply to the company (CA2006 s.386).

The records should contain all details of any income and expenditure and a record of the company's assets and liabilities. If a parent company has a subsidiary undertaking not registered under the Companies Acts, it must ensure that sufficient records are maintained by or for the subsidiary in order to ensure that the profit and loss account and balance sheet of the parent company comply with the provisions of the CA2006.

The accounting records must be kept for a period of three years if the company is a private company and for six years if it is a public company CA2006 s.388(4).

Accounting reference date

A company's first financial year begins on the day of its incorporation and ends on its accounting reference date, the end of the financial year. Each successive financial year begins the day following the date the previous balance sheet is made up to and ends on the next accounting reference date. The accounts may be made up to a date not more than seven days before or after the accounting reference date (CA2006 s.390(3)(b)). This flexibility is allowed to enable a company to arrange a year end stock count at a convenient time.

For a new company, the first accounting period starts on the day of incorporation and ends on the last day of the month in which the anniversary of its incorporation falls. The date on which an accounting period ends is known as the company's 'accounting reference date'. The directors may change the accounting reference date of the company, including its automatically allocated date, provided that the first accounting period is not less than six months and that any period is not longer than 18 months (CA2006 ss.391(5), 392(5)). After the first period a company can fix its accounting reference date to as short a period as it wishes (CA2006 s.392).

If the company becomes a subsidiary undertaking or a parent company, the accounting periods for the two companies must, unless in the directors' opinion there are good reasons against it, coincide (CA2006 s.390(5)). In these circumstances, if necessary, a company may extend its accounting reference period even if it has, in the previous five years, extended its accounting reference date (CA2006 s.392(3)).

The directors will determine any change in the company's accounting reference date [***see precedent** 76*] and must notify the Registrar on the specified Form (Form AA01).

Changing the accounting reference date

A change in accounting reference date is made by notice to the Registrar, also using the specified form (Form AA01). A company can change its accounting reference date at any time, whether or not that period has already expired, provided the time allowed for filing the accounts for that period has not expired. A period cannot be extended beyond 18 months and, except in certain specified circumstances, a company cannot extend its accounting reference date more than once in any five-year period (CA2006 s.392).

Preparation of individual accounts

Pursuant to CA2006 s.395 a company's individual accounts must comply with the provisions of CA2006 or international accounting standards (IAS) with respect to the form and content of the profit and loss account, balance sheet and any additional information that is required to be given. There is an overriding provision that the accounts must give a true and fair view of the state of affairs of the company's financial affairs. In circumstances where it is necessary to depart from the provisions of CA2006 or other provisions, such departure and the reasons for it must be noted in the accounts (CA2006 s.396(5)). In addition to

Companies Act requirements, accounts must be prepared in accordance with accounting standards issued by the Accounting Standards Board (CA2006 s.464). These are stated in Statements of Standard Accounting Practice, issued prior to 1 August 1990, and Financial Reporting Standards, issued after 1 August 1990.

Content

Companies Act individual accounts must comprise (CA2006 s.396):

1 directors' report (CA2006 s.415);
2 applicable to large-sized private companies, public and quoted companies a separate corporate governance statement (CA2006 s.419A);
3 balance sheet made up to the last day of the financial year;
4 profit and loss account covering the period of the accounts;
5 additional information to be provided in the way of notes including:
   - other than companies qualifying as small, employee numbers and costs (CA2006 s.411); and
   - directors' benefits (CA2006 ss.412, 413).

Preparation of group accounts

In addition to the requirement to prepare individual accounts, the directors of a company, if, at the financial year-end, it was a parent company, must prepare group accounts (CA2006 s.399), in accordance with the Companies Act provisions set out in s.404 or IAS accounts (CA2006 s.406). These Companies Act group accounts consist of a consolidated balance sheet and a consolidated profit and loss account. The directors of the holding company can, if they so determine, decide not to consolidate the accounts of a subsidiary if it carries out a substantially different activity to the parent and to consolidate the results would result in the true and fair view being obscured (CA2006 s.405).

Content

Companies Act individual accounts must comprise (CA2006 s.396):

1 group directors' report (CA2006 s.415);
2 applicable to large-sized private companies, public and quoted companies a separate corporate governance statement (CA2006 s.419A);
3 consolidated balance sheet made up to the last day of the financial year;
4 consolidated profit and loss account covering the period of the accounts;
5 additional information to be provided in the way of notes including:
   - related undertakings (CA2006 s.409);
   - other than companies qualifying as small, employee numbers and costs (CA2006 s.411); and
   - directors' benefits (CA2006 ss.412, 413).

Consistency of accounts

The directors of a parent company that prepares group accounts must ensure that the individual accounts of the parent and each subsidiary are prepared using the same financial reporting framework (CA2006 s.407).

Exemptions

There are a limited number of exemptions from the requirement of a parent company to prepare group accounts:

1 The parent company of a group qualifying as small need not prepare group accounts (CA2006 s.398).
2 If the parent is itself a subsidiary and its immediate parent undertaking is incorporated in an EEA State and prepares consolidated accounts including those of the subsidiary in question (CA2006 s.400).
3 If the parent is itself a subsidiary and its immediate parent undertaking is not incorporated in an EEA State and prepares consolidated accounts including those of the subsidiary in question (CA2006 s.401).
4 If all of its subsidiaries meet the conditions for exemption to be included in group accounts (CA2006 s.402).

In each case, although not required to prepare group accounts, the directors may do so if they wish.

Exemption is not available to a company with shares listed on the stock exchange of any EU Member State.

Additional exemptions, set out in CA2006 s.405, apply where:

1 the inclusion of the subsidiary accounts are not material, taken together if there is more than one subsidiary to be excluded from the consolidation, for the purposes of establishing a true and fair view;
2 the exercise of control by the parent company is substantially restricted on a long-term basis;
3 the necessary information to enable the consolidation to take place cannot be obtained without an unreasonable expense; or
4 the parent company holds the shares with a view for re-sale and the company has not previously been included in any consolidated accounts of the parent.

Parent company

A parent company is defined in CA2006 s.1162 as one that:

1 holds the majority of the voting rights in another company;
2 is a member of another company and has the right to remove or appoint a majority of the directors;
3 has the right to exercise dominant control either by a right contained in the Articles of Association or by a contractual arrangement;

4 is a member of the company and controls a majority of the voting rights by agreement with other shareholders;
5 has a participating interest and either exercises dominant control or the affairs of both companies are managed together.

Content of directors' report

The directors of the company must prepare a report containing, as a minimum, the names of those persons who were directors of the company during the financial year and the principal activities of the company in the course of the year (CA2006 s.416).

In addition, other than companies that qualify as small, the following information must be given:

1. the amount, if any, recommended to be paid by way of dividend (CA2006 s.416(3));
2. a **business review** containing (CA2006 s.417):
   - fair review of the company's business comprising a balanced and comprehensive analysis of the development and performance of the company and the position of the company's business at the year end;
   - description of principal risks and uncertainties;
   - the review must contain analysis using financial and, except medium sized companies, non-financial key performance indicators (CA2006 s.417(6) and (7));
   - where the company's accounts are audited the report must contain a statement that so far as each director is aware there is no relevant audit information that the auditor is unaware of and that each director has taken all necessary steps to establish what the relevant audit information is and that the auditor is aware of it (CA2006 s.417);
3. for a quoted company the business review must also include (CA2006 s.417(5)):
   - main trends and factors likely to affect future development, performance or position of the company;
   - information of environmental matters;
   - company employees;
   - social and community interests; and
   - information on those third parties with which the company has contracts or arrangements essential to its business.

Remuneration report

The directors of a quoted company must prepare a remuneration report in respect of each financial year (CA2006 s.420).

Corporate governance statement

Under the Companies Act 2006 (Accounts, Reports and Audit) Regulations 2009 (SI 2009/1581), large-sized private companies, public companies and quoted companies are required to prepare a separate corporate governance statement (i.e. not part of the directors' report) as part of their annual reports and accounts. This requirement applies to accounting periods beginning on or after 29 June 2008, but not ending earlier than 27 June 2009.

The separate corporate governance statement is defined by CA2006 s.472A (as inserted by the Regulations) as a statement required to be given under rules 7.2.1 to 7.2.11 of the Disclosure and Transparency Rules ('DTR').

IAS accounts

The detailed provisions for IAS Individual Accounts or Group Accounts are beyond the scope of this handbook. The following general points should be noted where a company is or is proposing to prepare IAS Accounts.

Once a company has prepared IAS Accounts for the first time it can only revert to preparing Companies Act Accounts if:

- the company becomes a subsidiary of an undertaking that does not prepare IAS Accounts;
- the company ceases to have securities traded on a regulated market; or
- a parent undertaking of the company ceases to have securities traded on a regulated market.

With effect from 1 October 2005 the ability to prepare accounts under IAS was extended to building societies regulated under the Building Societies Act 1986, LLPs, certain banking and insurance undertakings, partnerships and unlimited companies.

Although the bulk of the Companies Act provisions relating to the form and content of accounts do not apply to companies preparing IAS Accounts, those aspects of the Companies Act that deal with accounting provisions outside the scope of IAS will still apply. Accordingly the provisions relating to disclosure requirements relating to staff numbers, directors' emoluments, directors' report and publication of accounts, audit and certain other disclosures remain applicable.

Liability for false or misleading statements

Directors are liable to compensate the company for any loss suffered by it as a consequence of any untrue or misleading statements or omission of any information they knew or should have known were untrue or misleading or where the concealment of information was dishonest (CA2006 s.463).

The directors are liable in respect of the information contained in:

- the directors' report;
- directors' remuneration report (see p. 213); and
- a summary financial statement (see pp. 208–209).

Approval of directors' report

The directors' report must be approved by the board of directors [*see* ***precedent*** 77] and signed on their behalf by a director or the company secretary (CA2006 s.419).

If advantage has been taken of the small companies regime a statement to this effect must be included immediately above the signature.

Approval of corporate governance statement

The separate corporate governance statement must be approved by the board of directors and signed on their behalf by a director or the company secretary (CA2006 s.419A).

Audit

All companies must have their annual accounts audited unless the company is exempt from audit under:

- CA2006 s.477 – small companies;
- CA2006 s.480 – dormant companies;
- CA2006 s.482 – non-profit companies subject to public sector audit.

Small companies audit exemption

A company that meets the following conditions is exempt from audit:

- the company qualifies as small as set out in CA2006 s.382; and
- its turnover for the year is not more than £6.5 million; and
- its balance sheet total for the year does not exceed £3.26 million.

A company qualifies as small if it is not excluded and meets at least two of the following criteria:

- its turnover for the year is not more than £6.5 million;
- its balance sheet total for the year does not exceed £3.26 million;
- average number of employees does not exceed 50.

A company qualifies as small in its first financial year or any subsequent year if it meets the conditions in that year and the year before.

For the purposes of these criteria, balance sheet total is the aggregate value of its assets and excludes liabilities. As a consequence, companies with net assets of less than £3.26m may still be required to have an audit if they have significant liabilities.

Companies that meet any of the following conditions at any time during the financial year are excluded from the small companies regime:

- public companies;
- a company that is an authorised insurance company, banking company, e-money issuer, ISD investment firm or a UCITS management company;
- carries on insurance market activities;
- is a member of an ineligible group.

Small groups consisting only of private companies may still qualify for audit exemption if the following conditions can be satisfied:

1. Aggregate turnover for the year does not exceed £6.5m (net) or £7.8m (gross). For charitable companies, the limits are £350,000 (net) or £420,000 (gross).
2. Aggregate balance sheet total for the year does not exceed £3.26m (net) or £3.9m (gross).
3. The group must qualify as a small group in accordance with CA2006 s.383 and must not be, or have been during the year, an ineligible group as set out in CA2006 s.384.

Details of how the aggregate turnover and balance sheet totals must be calculated are contained in CA2006 ss.382 and 383.

If a group satisfied the conditions in the previous year but not in the current year it will continue to be treated as a small group in the current year. The group will re-qualify as a small group only when the conditions can be met in full once more.

A group is ineligible under CA2006 s.479(2) if any of the group companies is:

1. a public company or a body corporate which is entitled to offer its shares or debentures to the public;
2. a banking or insurance company; or
3. an authorised body under the FSMA2000.

For the above purpose a group company means any company that is either a parent or subsidiary undertaking.

Companies that have adopted Table A of the Companies Act 1948 (or earlier versions) and companies excluding Table A of the Companies Act 1985 may be required by their Articles of Association to appoint auditors. In these circumstances the Articles of Association will need to be amended if the company wishes to take advantage of the audit exemption.

Dormant companies

A dormant company is one which has had no significant accounting transactions as defined in CA2006 s.1169 since the end of its previous financial year or, in the case of a newly incorporated company, since its incorporation. The following transactions can be disregarded for the purposes of assessing the company's dormant status:

1 payment for shares taken by the subscriber(s) to the Memorandum and Articles of Association;
2 fees paid to the Registrar of Companies; and
3 civil penalties imposed by the Registrar of Companies (i.e. late filing penalties).

Any other transactions required to be entered in the company's accounting records will disqualify the company from claiming dormant status (i.e. bank interest/ charges).

A company which would otherwise not be exempt from audit under CA2006 s.480 because it was a subsidiary undertaking, and was a public company or member of an ineligible group for any period in that year may claim the exemption provided it was dormant throughout that period (CA1985 s.480(2)).

The dormant company exemption is not available to any company that is required to prepare group accounts or if it was at any time during the financial year in question:

1 an authorised insurance company, banking company, e-money issuer, ISD investment company or a UCITS management company; or
2 carried on insurance market activities.

Request for audit by shareholders

As the exemption is automatic rather than optional, as in the case of abbreviated accounts, shareholders holding between them 10 per cent of the issued share capital or 10 per cent of any issued class have the right to require that an audit is undertaken. If the company does not have a share capital, 10 per cent of the members may exercise the right to require an audit. To require an audit, notice in writing must be deposited at the company's registered office no later than one month before the end of the financial period for which the audit is requested (CA2006 s.476).

Charities

The rules regulating the preparation of accounts and auditing requirement for a company that is a registered charity are no longer contained in the Companies Act but by regulations issued by the Charity Commission under powers contained in the Charity Act 2006.

Auditor's report

Where a company is required to have its accounts independently audited, the company's auditor is required to report to the members on the accounts (CA2006 s.495(1)).

The auditor's reports must contain:

1 an introduction identifying the accounts that were audited and the financial reporting framework used in their preparation;
2 the scope of the audit work undertaken and auditing standards used;
3 a statement of whether the accounts give a true and fair view:
   - in the case of the balance sheet, of the state of the affairs of the company at the financial year end;
   - in the case of a profit and loss account, of the profit or loss of the company during the period;
   - in the case of group accounts, similar statements in respect of those undertakings whose results have been consolidated;
4 a statement of whether the accounts have been properly prepared in accordance with the stated financial framework;
5 a statement of whether the accounts have been properly prepared in accordance with the provisions of the Companies Act or the IAS Regulations, as appropriate;
6 a statement of whether in their opinion the information in the directors' report is consistent with the accounts;
7 if the company is a quoted company, a statement on the auditable part of the directors' remuneration report and whether that report has been properly prepared in accordance with the Companies Act (CA2006 ss.495–497); and
8 if the company must prepare a separate corporate governance statement, a statement that the company's disclosures made in accordance with DTR rules 7.2.5 and 7.2.6 (information about internal control and risk management systems in relation to financial reporting processes and about share capital structures) are consistent with the accounts.

The auditor's report must be either qualified or unqualified and must include reference to any matter the auditor wishes to draw attention to without qualifying the report (CA2006 s.495(4)).

Every copy of the audit report that is published by the company must state the name of the auditor and, where the auditor is a firm, the name of the individual who signed on behalf of the auditor (CA2006 s.505). There is limited exemption allowing the name of the auditor to be omitted if there are reasonable grounds to believe that the auditor or anyone associated with the auditor is at risk of violence or intimidation. Notification of the information withheld must be given to the Secretary of State (CA2006 s.506).

Publication, laying and delivery of accounts to members

Copies of the full accounts must be sent to all members of the company, all debenture holders and all persons entitled to receive notice of general meetings.

Private companies

Under CA2006 private companies are no longer required to hold annual general meetings, providing there is nothing to the contrary contained in their Articles of Association. However, they are still obliged to circulate the accounts to the members, debenture holders and any other party entitled to receive notice of general meetings. For financial years beginning before 6 April 2008 the accounts must be circulated no later than the end of the period allowed for filing the accounts with the Registrar (usually ten months). For financial years beginning on or after 6 April 2008 the accounts must be sent to members not later than the end of the period allowed for filing the accounts with the Registrar (usually nine months), or if earlier, not later than the date the accounts were actually delivered to the Registrar (CA2006 ss.424, 442).

Public companies

The accounts must be issued to these persons not less than 21 days prior to the general meeting at which they are laid before the members unless all the members agree otherwise (CA1985 s.238, CA2006 s.424(3)).

For financial years beginning before 6 April 2008 the accounts must be laid before the members in general meeting no later than the end of the period allowed for filing the accounts with the Registrar (usually seven months). For financial years beginning on or after 6 April 2006 the period is reduced to six months (CA2006 ss.437, 442).

There is no requirement for the accounts of a public company to be approved by members; they must simply be laid before them in general meeting. Accordingly the resolution put to members should simply be to receive the accounts for the year. [***See precedent 19.***]

Quoted companies

A quoted company must also make its annual reports and accounts available on a website as soon as reasonably practical. The accounts must remain available on the website until the accounts for the following year are made available (CA2006 s.430).

Quoted companies – approval of remuneration report

Quoted companies are required to include within their accounts a remuneration report, and a resolution to approve the remuneration report must be put to the meeting that receives the accounts (CA2006 s.439). [***See precedent 19.***]

Delivery of accounts to Companies House

Companies must deliver a signed copy of their accounts which need not be full accounts, whether audited or not, to the Registrar:

1 Private companies within ten months of the year-end (CA1985 s.244(1)(a)) for financial years beginning before 6 April 2008 and for financial years beginning on or after 6 April 2006 within nine months of the year end (CA2006 s.442).

2 Public companies within seven months of the year-end (CA1985 s.244(1)(b)) for financial years beginning before 6 April 2008 and for financial years beginning on or after 6 April 2006 within six months of the year end (CA2006 s.442).

In the case of a financial year that is not twelve months there are different provisions.

If the company's first accounting period is longer than twelve months the period allowed for filing the accounts ends on the date nine or six months, as appropriate, after the first anniversary of the company's incorporation or, if later, three months after the end of the accounting reference period. For financial years beginning before 6 April 2008 the relevant period is ten or seven months after the anniversary of incorporation.

If the accounting period is shortened the period allowed for filing the accounts is nine or six months, as applicable, or, if later, three months after the date of notice under CA2006 s.392 shortening the accounting period (CA2006 s.442). For financial years beginning before 6 April 2008 the relevant period is ten or seven months after the anniversary of incorporation.

Late delivery of accounts

If accounts are delivered to the Registrar outside the period allowed for delivery in accordance with the provisions of CA2006 s.441 (CA1985 s.244) the company is subject to a late filing penalty calculated as follows under CA2006 s.453 (CA1985 s.242A):

	Private	*Public*
Not more than 1 month late	£150	£750
Between 1 and 3 months late	£375	£1,500
Between 3 and 6 months late	£750	£3,000
More than 6 months late	£1,500	£7,500

Additionally if the previous year's accounts were also late and that financial year had begun on or after 6 April 2008, the penalties in the following year double.

Accounts to be delivered – abbrieviated accounts

Small-sized companies

Companies falling within the definitions of small-sized (see p. 198) may deliver abbreviated accounts to the Registrar under CA2006 s.444 (CA1985 s.246(1)). Full accounts must, however, be prepared and issued to shareholders. As noted above certain companies that qualify as small may be exempt from the requirement to prepare audited accounts.

A company that qualifies as a small company may file abbreviated accounts consisting of:

1. An abbreviated version of the balance sheet together with abbreviated notes, and a statement immediately above the signature(s) of the director(s) that they have relied upon the exemptions available to the company as a small-sized company.
2. A special auditor's report stating that the requirements for qualifying as a small-sized company have been met. A copy of this statement must be included in the full accounts issued to shareholders.

There is no requirement for a profit and loss account or a directors' report to be included in the abbreviated accounts although these may be included if the directors wish to do so.

The balance sheet and auditor's report must have a live signature and state the name of the person who signed them.

Medium-sized companies

A medium-sized company is one that satisfies any two of the following conditions (CA2006 ss.465–467; CA1985 s.247(3)):

- turnover must not exceed £25.9m;
- balance sheet total must not exceed £12.9m;
- average number of employees must not exceed 250.

Companies that meet any of the following conditions at any time during the financial year are excluded from the medium-sized companies regime:

- public companies;
- a company that has permission under Part 4 FSMA2000 to carry out a regulated activity;
- carries on insurance market activities;
- is a member of an ineligible group.

A group is ineligible under CA2006 s.467(2) if any of the group companies is:

1. a public company or a body corporate whose shares are admitted to a regulated market; or
2. a company (other than a small company) that has permission under Part 4 FSMA2000 to carry out a regulated activity;
3. a company that is an authorised insurance company, banking company, e-money issuer, ISD investment firm or a UCITS management company;
4. carries on insurance market activities.

For the above purpose a group company means any company that is either a parent or subsidiary undertaking.

A company qualifies as medium-sized in its first financial year or any subsequent year if it meets the conditions in that year and the year before.

If a company qualifies as medium-sized in one financial year but not in the next, it may still file abbreviated accounts in that second year, unless disqualified under CA1985 s.246. It will not be able to file abbreviated accounts in the third year unless it qualifies in that year as either small- or medium-sized.

A company that qualifies as a medium-sized company may file abbreviated accounts consisting of (CA2006 s.445):

1 the full balance sheet together with notes and a statement immediately above the signature(s) of the director(s) that they have relied upon the exemptions available to the company as a medium-sized company;
2 a profit and loss account which can be abbreviated and does not need to disclose turnover;
3 a special auditor's report stating that the requirements for qualifying as medium-sized have been met. A copy of this statement must be included in the full accounts issued to shareholders'
4 directors' report.

The directors' report, balance sheet and auditor's report must have a live signature and state the name of the person who signed them.

Small- and medium-sized groups

A parent company need not prepare, or deliver, group accounts if the group qualifies as either small- or medium-sized if the aggregate figures for turnover, balance sheet total and average number of employees would, if applied to an individual company, qualify it as either small- or medium-sized.

The qualifying criteria are slightly modified, as shown below, and the group must satisfy any two of the following conditions.

For a small group:

- turnover must not exceed £6.5 (net) or £7.8m (gross);
- balance sheet total must not exceed £3.26m (net) or £3.9m (gross);
- average number of employees must not exceed 50.

For a medium-sized group:

- turnover must not exceed £25.9m (net) or £31.1m (gross);
- balance sheet total must not exceed £12.9m (net); or
- £15.5m (gross);
- average number of employees must not exceed 250.

The reference to 'net' means those aggregate figures for turnover and balance sheet total with the set-offs and other adjustments made in accordance with CA2006 s.404 (CA1985 Sch.4A). The reference to 'gross' turnover or balance sheet total means those aggregate figures prior to any set-off or other adjustment. The group accounts must satisfy the appropriate conditions on either a net or gross basis, but not using one net and the other gross (CA2006 ss.383, 466; CA1985 s.249(4)).

If auditors certify that the parent company is eligible for qualification as either small- or medium-sized, and group accounts are not prepared, the report of the auditor must be attached to the individual accounts of the parent company (CA1985 s.248(3)). If advantage is taken of this exemption by the directors, there is no statutory provision by which the shareholders of the company can require that group accounts be prepared and laid before them.

Unquoted companies

By CA2006 s.446, an unquoted company must file accounts consisting of:

- directors' report;
- separate corporate governance statement;
- profit and loss account;
- balance sheet;
- notes to the accounts;
- audit report, if the accounts are audited.

The directors' report, separate corporate governance statement, balance sheet and auditor's report must have a live signature and state the name of the person who signed them.

The provisions of CA2006 s.446 do not apply to an unquoted company that qualifies as small- or medium-sized (CA2006 s.446(5)).

Quoted companies

A quoted company must file accounts consisting of (CA2006 s.447):

- directors' report;
- separate corporate governance statement;
- directors' remuneration report;
- profit and loss account;
- balance sheet;
- notes to the accounts;
- audit report, if the accounts are audited.

The directors' report, separate corporate governance statement, directors' remuneration report, balance sheet and auditor's report must have a live signature and state the name of the person who signed them.

Unlimited companies

Unlimited companies do not need to file a copy of their accounts with the Registrar (CA2006 s. 448) unless at any time during the period covered by the accounts, the company was:

- a subsidiary or a parent of a limited undertaking; or
- a banking or insurance company (or the parent of such a company); or

- a 'qualifying' company in terms of the Partnerships and Unlimited Companies (Accounts) Regulations 1993; or
- operating a trading stamp scheme.

A company will be a qualifying company if it is a member of a partnership governed by the laws of any part of Great Britain and all the other members of the partnership are either limited companies, Limited Liability Partnerships or unlimited companies or a Scottish firm each of whose members is a limited company.

Unaudited accounts

In addition to filing unaudited accounts at Companies House, whether abbreviated or not, a qualifying company must include a statement immediately above the signature(s) of the director(s) on the balance sheet that:

1. the company is eligible to prepare unaudited accounts and qualifies for audit exemption;
2. no notice from shareholders has been received by the company requesting that an audit be undertaken;
3. the directors acknowledge their responsibilities to maintain proper accounting records and to prepare accounts which give a true and fair view of the company's position and have been prepared in accordance with the provisions of the Companies Acts.

Revised accounts

Directors of a company are permitted to prepare and issue revised accounts to replace accounts they believe are defective. If the original accounts have been circulated to shareholders or filed with the Registrar of Companies then the only modifications required are in respect of those matters within the accounts that do not comply with the requirements of the Companies Act 1985 or IAS Regulations and any consequential amendments CA2006 s 454 (CA1985 s.245).

Where accounts have been circulated to shareholders, or filed at Companies House, and it appears to the Secretary of State that they do not comply with the provisions of the Act, he may issue a notice giving the directors not less than one month in which to give an explanation or to prepare revised accounts CA2006 s.455 (CA1985 s 245A). If the directors do not give a satisfactory explanation or do not prepare revised accounts the Secretary of State may make an application to the Courts for an order directing the preparation of revised accounts (CA2006 s.456; CA1985 s.245B).

Additional reporting requirements for certain companies

The auditors of companies subject to statutory regulation are required to report directly to that company's regulators in certain circumstances. The companies concerned are:

- banks;
- building societies;
- insurance companies;
- friendly societies;
- investment businesses regulated under FSMA 2000.

The duty to report to a company's regulator arises in circumstances where the auditor concludes that a matter is relevant to the regulator's function, having regard to matters specified in statute or any related regulations, including rules of the regulator and where, in the auditor's opinion, there is reasonable cause to believe that a matter may be material to the regulator. Although this additional duty on auditors relates to their role as auditors, if the firm also undertakes non-audit services, those responsible for the audit work should request assurances from their colleagues that they are not aware of any matters that would require disclosure to the regulator.

Summary financial statements

Any company whose accounts have been audited may, subject to any provisions contained in its Articles of Association, issue summary financial statements to its shareholders in place of the full statutory accounts. Any shareholder receiving summary financial statements may require that the full accounts be sent to him (CA2006 s.426).

- The summary financial statement may be made available on a website or sent by electronic communication to members who have supplied an address for that purpose.
- The period allowed for the laying and delivery of the accounts must not have expired.
- The summary financial statement must be approved by the board of directors and the original copy signed on their behalf by a director whose name must be stated on the copies issued to shareholders.

Unquoted companies

The summary financial statement of an unquoted company must (CA2006 s.427):

1. be derived from the full statutory accounts and contain a statement to that effect;
2. state whether it contains additional information from the directors' report and, if so, that it does not contain the full text of that report;
3. contain details of how a member can receive a copy of the full statutory accounts and directors' report;
4. contain a statement from the company's auditor whether the summary financial statement is consistent with the full statutory accounts and complies with CA2006 s.427;

5 state whether the full statutory accounts had a qualified audit report or a statement under CA2006 s.496 or not and, if qualified, the qualified statement must be reproduced in full;
6 state whether the auditor's report to the full statutory accounts contained statements under CA2006 s.498(2) or (3) and if so those statements must be reproduced in full.

Quoted companies

The summary financial statement of a quoted company must (CA2006 s.428):

1 be derived from the full statutory accounts and directors' remuneration report and contain a statement to that effect;
2 state whether it contains additional information from the directors' report and, if so, that it does not contain the full text of that report;
3 contain details of how a member can receive a copy of the full statutory accounts, directors' remuneration report and directors' report;
4 contain a statement from the company's auditor whether the summary financial statement is consistent with the full statutory accounts and directors' remuneration report and complies with CA2006 s.427;
5 state whether the full statutory accounts had a qualified audit report or qualified statement relating to the auditable part of the directors' remuneration report or a statement under CA2006 s.496 or not and, if qualified, the qualified statement must be reproduced in full;
6 state whether the auditor's report to the full statutory accounts contained statements under CA2006 s.498(2) or (3) and if so those statements must be reproduced in full.

Format of summary financial statement

For accounts drawn up under either the Companies Act legislation or under IAS any summary financial statement must be consistent with the format of the full accounts. For IAS Accounts these are based upon the framework for interim statements contained in IAS 34.

Additional disclosure for listed companies

All listed companies must adopt International Financial Reporting Standards (IFRS).

The IASB has issued guidance in the form of IFRS1 to assist companies reporting under IFRS. The main requirements of IFRS1 are:

1 companies must comply with all IASB standards;
2 there are certain exemptions from the standards where the costs of implementation outweigh the benefit;

3 retrospective application is prohibited particularly where the standard requires judgments to be made on circumstances where the outcome is now known;
4 items held as hedged under GAAP may be held as hedged under IFRS provided the various hedge requirements were met from 1 January 2004.

The existing requirements for listed, AIM and PLUS companies require additional disclosure so as to ensure full disclosure of relevant information and to prevent a false market for the shares developing. The full requirements are contained in the *Listing, AIM and PLUS Rules*, and include the following:

1 Two copies of the accounts of a listed company must be submitted to the UK Listing Authority (*LR 9.6.1*).
2 Accounts to be published as soon as possible but not more than six months after the year-end for listed and AIM companies (*LR 9.8.1, AIM rule 19*), PLUS companies must issue their accounts to shareholders within the normal Companies Act periods (six months if a plc or nine months if limited for financial years beginning on or after 6 April 2008).
3 A listed company must make disclosure of the following unless exemption is agreed to by the UK Listing Authority:
   (1) a statement of the amount of interest capitalised by the group during the period under review with an indication of the amount and treatment of any related tax relief;
   (2) any information required by *LR 9.2.18R* (publication of unaudited financial information);
   (3) details of any small related party transaction as required by *LR 11.1.10R(2)(c)*;
   (4) details of any long-term incentive schemes as required by *LR 9.4.3R*;
   (5) details of any arrangements under which a director of the company has waived or agreed to waive any emoluments from the company or any subsidiary undertaking;
   (6) where a director has agreed to waive future emoluments, details of such waiver together with those relating to emoluments which were waived during the period under review;
   (7) in the case of any allotment for cash of equity securities made during the period under review otherwise than to the holders of the company's equity shares in proportion to their holdings of such equity shares and which has not been specifically authorised by the company's shareholders:
      (a) the details relating to the form and content of the accounts;
      (b) the names of the allottees, if less than six in number, and in the case of six or more allottees a brief generic description of each new class of equity holder (e.g. holder of loan stock);
      (c) the market price of the allotted securities on the date on which the terms of the issue were fixed; and

(d) the date on which the terms of the issue were fixed;

(8) the information required by paragraph (7) must be given for any unlisted major subsidiary undertaking of the company;

(9) where a listed company has listed shares in issue and is a subsidiary undertaking of another company, details of the participation by the parent undertaking in any placing made during the period under review;

(10) details of any contract of significance subsisting during the period under review:

   (a) to which the listed company, or one of its subsidiary undertakings, is a party and in which a director of the listed company is or was materially interested; and

   (b) between the listed company, or one of its subsidiary undertakings, and a controlling shareholder;

(11) details of any contract for the provision of services to the listed company or any of its subsidiary undertakings by a controlling shareholder, subsisting during the period under review, unless:

   (a) it is a contract for the provision of services which it is the principal business of the shareholder to provide; and

   (b) it is not a contract of significance;

(12) details of any arrangement under which a shareholder has waived or agreed to waive any dividends; and where a shareholder has agreed to waive future dividends, details of such waiver together with those relating to dividends which are payable during the period under review.

In the case of a listed company incorporated in the United Kingdom, the following additional items must be included in its annual report and accounts:

(1) a statement setting out all the beneficial and non-beneficial interests of each director of the listed company that have been disclosed to the company under DTR 3.1.2 as at the end of the period under review including:

   (a) all changes in the beneficial and non-beneficial interests of each director that have occurred between the end of the period under review and one month prior to the date of the notice of the annual general meeting; or

   (b) if there have been no changes in the period described in paragraph (a), a statement that there have been no changes in the beneficial or non-beneficial interests of each director;

(2) a statement showing, as at a date not more than one month prior to the date of the notice of the annual general meeting:

   (a) all information disclosed to the listed company in accordance with sections 198 to 208 of the Companies Act 1985 (Disclosure of certain major interests in the share capital of a company); or

   (b) that there have been no disclosures, if no disclosures have been made;

(3) a statement made by the directors that the business is a going concern, together with supporting assumptions or qualifications as necessary, that has been prepared in accordance with 'Going Concern and Financial Reporting: Guidance for Directors of listed companies registered in the United Kingdom', published in November 1994;

(4) a statement setting out:

(a) details of any shareholders' authority for the purchase, by the listed company, of its own shares that is still valid at the end of the period under review;

(b) in the case of purchases made otherwise than through the market or by tender to all shareholders, the names of sellers of such shares purchased, or proposed to be purchased, by the listed company during the period under review;

(c) in the case of any purchases made otherwise than through the market or by tender to all shareholders, or options or contracts to make such purchases, entered into since the end of the period covered by the report, information equivalent to that required under Part II of Schedule 7 to the Companies Act 1985 (Disclosure required by company acquiring its own shares, etc.); and

(d) in the case of sales of treasury shares for cash made otherwise than through the market, or in connection with an employees' share scheme, or otherwise than pursuant to an opportunity which (so far as was practicable) was made available to all holders of the listed company's securities (or to all holders of a relevant class of its securities) on the same terms, particulars of the names of purchasers of such shares sold, or proposed to be sold, by the company during the period under review;

(5) a statement of how the listed company has applied the principles set out in Section 1 of the Combined Code, in a manner that would enable shareholders to evaluate how the principles have been applied;

(6) a statement as to whether the listed company has:

(a) complied throughout the accounting period with all relevant provisions set out in Section 1 of the Combined Code; or

(b) not complied throughout the accounting period with all relevant provisions set out in Section 1 of the Combined Code and if so, setting out:

(i) those provisions, if any, that it has not complied with;

(ii) in the case of provisions whose requirements are of a continuing nature, the period within which, if any, it did not comply with some or all of those provisions; and

(iii) the company's reasons for non-compliance; and

(7) a report to the shareholders by the board which contains all the matters set out in *LR 9.8.8R*.

The report to the shareholders by the Board required by *LR 9.8.6R(7)* must contain the following:

(1) a statement of the listed company's policy on executive directors' remuneration;
(2) information presented in tabular form, unless inappropriate, together with explanatory notes as necessary on:
    (a) the amount of each element in the remuneration package for the period under review of each director, by name, including but not restricted to, basic salary and fees, the estimated money value of benefits in kind, annual bonuses, deferred bonuses, compensation for loss of office and payments for breach of contract or other termination payments;
    (b) the total remuneration for each director for the period under review and for the corresponding prior period;
    (c) any significant payments made to former directors during the period under review; and
    (d) any share options, including 'Save-as-you-earn' options, for each director, by name, in accordance with the requirements of the Directors' Remuneration Report Regulations;
(3) details of any long-term incentive schemes, other than share options as required by paragraph (2)(d), including the interests of each director, by name, in the long-term incentive schemes at the start of the period under review;
(4) details of any entitlements or awards granted and commitments made to each director under any long-term incentive schemes during the period, showing which crystallise either in the same year or in subsequent years;
(5) details of the monetary value and number of shares, cash payments or other benefits received by each director under any long-term incentive schemes during the period;
(6) details of the interests of each director in the long-term incentive schemes at the end of the period;
(7) an explanation and justification of any element of a director's remuneration, other than basic salary, which is pensionable;
(8) details of any directors' service contract with a notice period in excess of one year or with provisions for pre-determined compensation on termination which exceeds one year's salary and benefits in kind, giving the reasons for such notice period;
(9) details of the unexpired term of any directors' service contract of a director proposed for election or re-election at the forthcoming annual general meeting, and, if any director proposed for election or re-election does not have a directors' service contract, a statement to that effect;
(10) a statement of the listed company's policy on the granting of options or

awards under its employees' share schemes and other long-term incentive schemes, explaining and justifying any departure from that policy in the period under review and any change in the policy from the preceding year;

(11) for money purchase schemes (as in Part I of Schedule 6 to the Companies Act 1985 (Disclosure of information: emoluments and other benefits of directors and others)) details of the contribution or allowance payable or made by the listed company in respect of each director during the period under review; and

(12) for defined benefit schemes (as in Part I of Schedule 6 to the Companies Act 1985 (Disclosure of information: emoluments and other benefits of directors and others)):

(a) details of the amount of the increase during the period under review (excluding inflation) and of the accumulated total amount at the end of the period in respect of the accrued benefit to which each director would be entitled on leaving service or is entitled having left service during the period under review;

(b) either:

(i) the transfer value (less director's contributions) of the relevant increase in accrued benefit (to be calculated in accordance with Actuarial Guidance Note GN11 but making no deduction for any under-funding) as at the end of the period; or

(ii) so much of the following information as is necessary to make a reasonable assessment of the transfer value in respect of each director:

(A) age;

(B) normal retirement age;

(C) the amount of any contributions paid or payable by the director under the terms of the scheme during the period under review;

(D) details of spouse's and dependants' benefits;

(E) early retirement rights and options;

(F) expectations of pension increases after retirement (whether guaranteed or discretionary); and

(G) discretionary benefits for which allowance is made in transfer values on leaving and any other relevant information which will significantly affect the value of the benefits; and

(c) no disclosure of voluntary contributions and benefits.

11 Auditors

Introduction

Every company that is not exempt, dormant or a non-profit-making company subject to public sector audit must appoint an auditor, whose primary function is to report to the company's members on the statutory accounts prepared in accordance with CA2006 ss.394, 399 for individual company accounts and group accounts respectively (CA2006 s.475).

Where a company is exempt by virtue of being a small company any member or members holding between them at least 10 per cent in nominal value of the company's share capital may require an audit to be carried out (CA2006 s.476).

Eligibility

A person or firm may be appointed as an auditor only if he or it is a member of a recognised supervisory body and is eligible for appointment under the rules of that body (CA2006 s.1212). A firm may be a partnership or a corporate body.

A recognised supervisory body must have rules that prohibit a person from being eligible for appointment as an auditor unless:

1. any individual member holds an appropriate qualification;
2. any firm is controlled by qualified persons and those individuals responsible for corporate audit work hold appropriate qualifications. An appropriate qualification and a qualified person is any person who in accordance with CA2006 Sch.10 s.7:
   - holds a recognised professional qualification obtained in the United Kingdom; or
   - holds an approved overseas qualification and meets any additional criteria that may be required.

All recognised supervisory bodies must maintain a register of individuals and firms eligible for appointment as company auditors and of all individuals holding appropriate qualifications (CA2006 s.1239).

The register must be available for inspection at the principal UK office of the recognised body for at least two hours during normal working hours on every working day. The register must be arranged in alphabetical order and by reference to the appropriate supervisory body. The supervisory bodies are required to keep each other informed of all necessary information to ensure that each recognised body can properly maintain its register.

The recognised supervisory bodies are also required to maintain a register of the names and addresses of the directors or partners and members of each firm. Any amendments to the registers maintained by the supervisory bodies must be made within ten days of the change being notified to them. The five recognised supervisory bodies are:

- the Institute of Chartered Accountants of Scotland;
- the Institute of Chartered Accountants in England and Wales;
- the Institute of Chartered Accountants in Ireland;
- the Association of Chartered Certified Accountants;
- the Association of Authorised Public Accountants.

A person is prohibited by CA2006 s.1214 from acting as auditor to any company of which he:

- is an officer or employee; or
- is a partner or employee of such a person or a member of a partnership of which that person is a partner.

'Officer' includes director, manager or company secretary (CA2006 s.1173(1)). Where an auditor is deemed to be an officer of the company by virtue of any provision of the Companies Acts the auditor is not prohibited from acting as auditor by virtue of CA2006 s.1214(5).

Appointment

Private company

For their first audited financial year auditors must be appointed before the end of the period allowed for sending accounts to members or, if earlier, the date the accounts were sent to members.

For subsequent years the auditors must be appointed or reappointed within the period of 28 days commencing on the deadline for sending accounts to members or, if earlier, the date the accounts were actually sent to members. This period is known as the 'period for appointing auditors' (CA2006 s.485).

The directors may appoint the first auditor to the company. The directors may also appoint an auditor following a period during which the company was exempt from audit or to fill a casual vacancy caused by the resignation or death of the previous auditor (CA2006 s.485(3)). [***See precedent** 78.*]

If a private company fails to appoint an auditor in accordance with CA2006 s.485 the Secretary of State may appoint an auditor to fill the vacancy (CA2006 s.486). In circumstances where auditors have not been appointed the company must give notice to the Secretary of State within seven days of the expiry of the period allowed for appointing auditors.

An auditor can only be appointed pursuant to CA2006 ss.485 and 486 or may be deemed to be reappointed under CA2006 s.487.

Where no auditor has been appointed by the end of the next period allowed for appointing auditors the auditor in office immediately before that time is deemed to have been reappointed unless:

- the appointment was made by the directors;
- the company's Articles of Association require actual reappointment;
- deemed reappointment is prevented by members under CA2006 s.488;
- a resolution to reappoint the auditors is lost; or
- the directors have resolved that no auditor should be appointed for the financial year in question.

Pursuant to CA2006 s.488 members holding between them at least 5 per cent of the total voting rights may prevent the deemed reappointment of an auditor by giving notice in writing to that effect to the company before the end of the accounting reference period immediately prior to the time when the auditor would otherwise be deemed to be reappointed.

Public company

For their first financial year auditors must be appointed before the meeting at which accounts are laid before the members. The auditors would usually be appointed by the directors but can be appointed by the members if the directors fail to do so (CA2006 s.489(3) and (4)).

For subsequent years the auditors must be appointed or reappointed before the conclusion of the meeting at which the accounts for the previous financial year are laid before the members (CA2006 s.489(2)).

The directors may appoint the first auditor to the company. The directors may also appoint an auditor following a period during which the company was exempt from audit or to fill a casual vacancy caused by the resignation or death of the previous auditor (CA2006 s.489(3)) [***See precedent** 78.*]

If a public company fails to appoint an auditor in accordance with the provisions of CA2006 s.489 the company must give notice to the Secretary of State within seven days of the conclusion of the meeting at which the previous accounts were laid before the members (CA2006 s.490).

An auditor to a public company can only be appointed pursuant to CA2006 ss.489 and 490.

The appointment of an auditor to a public company does not automatically renew and their appointment ceases at the conclusion of the meeting at which the accounts are laid before the members, unless they are reappointed (CA2006 s.491).

Appointment of partnership

Unless there is a clear statement to the contrary, the appointment of a partnership as auditor is an appointment of the partnership and not the individual partners (CA2006 s.1216). Where the partnership ceases the appointment is treated as having been extended to:

- any person who succeeds to that partnership having previously carried it on in that partnership and is an eligible person;
- any eligible partnership that succeeds the partnership that has ceased.

A partnership is treated as succeeding another partnership only if the partners are substantially the same or if the new partnership takes over substantially the whole of the business of the previous partnership.

A partnership established under the laws of England and Wales or Northern Ireland or any other country where partnerships do not constitute a legal person ceases whenever there is a change not only on a dissolution, but also a change in partners. Partnerships established under the law in Scotland do constitute legal persons and do not cease on a change of partners.

Many firms of auditors have incorporated as either limited companies or limited liability partnerships. As corporate bodies these firms have legal persona and it is the corporate body that is appointed. Where a partnership ceases, wherever established, and no person or firm succeeds the appointment, the appointment may be extended by ordinary resolution of the members to any person or firm succeeding to the business of the previous firm or such part of the business as comprised the appointment (CA2006 s.1216(5)).

Where a person or firm is to be appointed in place of the previous auditor for whatever reason special notice of that fact must be given to the members and to the previous auditor by the company (CA2006 s.388).

Exempt companies

A company that is exempt from having its accounts audited is also exempt from the obligation to appoint auditors. It should be noted, however, that a private company becoming exempt from the audit requirement does not automatically terminate the appointment of existing auditors and in such circumstances the directors should resolve that no auditors be appointed for the financial year (CA2006 s.487(2)(e)). [***See precedent 79.***]

Remuneration

Remuneration of auditors appointed by the directors must be fixed by the directors. Remuneration of auditors appointed or reappointed by the members must be fixed by the members or in such other manner as the members may decide (CA2006 s.492). In practice it is normal for the members to authorise the directors to fix the remuneration of the auditors. For a public company this resolution is often combined with the resolution reappointing the auditors for the coming year when the current accounts are laid before the members. [***See precedent 19.***]

The amount of the auditors' remuneration in their capacity as auditors including any expenses must be disclosed in the accounts (CA2006 ss.493 and 494). Remuneration includes any cash value of any benefits in kind given to the auditors. In addition to remuneration for audit services, companies are required to disclose amounts paid to auditors and their associates for non-audit services such as financial or taxation services. Companies qualifying as small companies are exempt from the obligation to disclose auditors' remuneration and non-audit remuneration and parent companies qualifying as medium-sized are exempt from the obligation to disclose non-audit remuneration.

Rights and duties of auditors

Auditor's report

The auditor is required to report to the members on all accounts of the company that are, in the case of a private company, sent out to members and, in the case of a public company, laid before the members in general meeting (CA2006 s.495).

The report of the auditor must include an introduction identifying the accounts that have been audited and the financial framework applied together with a description of the scope of the audit work carried out and the accounting standards adopted.

The audit report must state clearly whether, in the auditor's opinion, the accounts (CA2006 s.495):

1 have been properly prepared in accordance with relevant financial reporting framework;
2 have been prepared in accordance with requirements of the Companies Act and, where relevant, the IAS Regulations;
3 whether a true and fair view has been given:
   (a) in respect of the balance sheet the state of affairs of that company at the end of the financial year;
   (b) in respect of the profit and loss account in respect of the financial year;
   (c) in respect of group accounts at the state of affairs of the group at the end of the financial year, the profit and loss account of the company for the year and of any undertakings included in the consolidation as they affect the members of the company.

The auditor's report must be either unqualified or qualified and include a reference to any matters which the auditor wishes to bring to the attention of members without qualifying their report.

The auditor must state in their report whether in their opinion the report of the directors is consistent with the accounts (CA2006 s.496).

Quoted company

If the company is a quoted company the auditor must also report on the auditable parts of the remuneration report and state whether in their opinion the directors' remuneration report has been properly prepared in accordance with the Companies Act 2006 (CA2006 s.497).

Signing of audit report

The auditor's report must state the name of the auditor, and must be signed and dated (CA2006 s.503).

In the case of an auditor who is an individual, the report must be signed by that individual.

In the case of an auditor that is a firm, the report must be signed by the senior statutory auditor in their own name on behalf of the firm.

The senior statutory auditor is the person identified by the audit firm as such in relation to that particular audit and must in their individual capacity be capable of being appointed as auditor of the company (CA2006 s.504).

Except as noted below, every copy of the audit report that is published must state the name of the auditor and where appropriate the name of the senior statutory auditor (CA2006 s.505).

There is limited exemption allowing the name of the auditor to be omitted if there are reasonable grounds to believe that the auditor or anyone associated with the auditor is at risk of violence or intimidation.

Duties of auditor

In carrying out an audit of a company's accounts an auditor must carry out sufficient investigations so that they can form an opinion as to:

- whether adequate accounting records have been maintained; and
- whether the accounts are consistent with the accounting records; and
- in the case of a quoted company whether the auditable part of the directors' remuneration report is consistent with the accounting records.

If in the opinion of the auditor one or more of these statements cannot be made that fact must be stated in their report to members.

If the auditor does not obtain all the information or explanations they require this fact must be stated in their report.

If the accounts do not contain:

- the details of directors' remuneration, pensions and/or compensation for loss of office required by CA2006 s.412; or
- for a quoted company the details required by CA2006 s.421 relating to the auditable part of the directors' remuneration report,

the missing information must be contained within the auditor's report.

If the directors have prepared accounts taking advantage of the regime available to small companies and in the opinion of the auditor the company does not qualify as a small company this fact must be stated in the auditor's report (CA2006 s.498).

Rights to information and access

An auditor of a company enjoys certain statutory rights to information in connection with the exercise of his duties. These rights were extended by the Company (Audit Investigations and Community Enterprise) Act 2004 and have been incorporated within the Companies Act 2006 and they include:

1. A right of access at all times to the company's books, accounts and vouchers and to require from the company's directors and officers such information and explanations as the auditor thinks necessary for the performance of his duties (CA2006 s.499(1)).
2. The auditor is entitled to attend any general meetings of the company and to receive all notices and other communications relating to any general meeting. He may also speak on any business of the meeting that concerns him as auditor (CA2006 s.502).
3. It is the duty of subsidiary undertakings incorporated in the United Kingdom and their auditors to give the auditors of the parent company such information and explanations as those auditors may reasonably require for the purposes of their duties as auditors of the parent company (CA2006 s.499(2)).
4. A parent company, having a subsidiary undertaking which is not a body incorporated in the United Kingdom shall, if its auditors require, take all such steps as are reasonably open to it to obtain from the subsidiary such information and explanations as its auditors may reasonably require (CA2006 s.500).

It is an offence (punishable by fine and/or imprisonment) for an officer of the company, in conveying information and explanations required by the company's auditors, to make a statement which he knows is misleading, false or deceptive in a material particular (CA2006 s.501).

Additional reporting requirements

The auditors of companies subject to statutory regulation are required to report direct to that company's regulators in certain circumstances. The companies concerned are:

- banks;
- building societies;
- insurance companies;
- friendly societies;
- investment businesses regulated under FSMA 2000.

The duty to report to a company's regulator arises in circumstances where the auditor concludes that a matter is relevant to the regulator's function, having regard to matters specified in statute or any related regulations, including rules of the regulator and where, in the auditor's opinion, there is reasonable cause to believe that a matter may be material to the regulator. Although this additional duty on auditors relates to their role as auditors, if the firm also undertakes non-audit services, those responsible for the audit work should request assurances from their colleagues that they are not aware of any matters that would require disclosure to the regulator.

All individuals providing accountancy or legal services as a business are required to make a report to the Serious Organised Crime Agency (SOCA) of any circumstances where they know or suspect that money laundering is or has taken place or that an individual or company is benefiting from the proceeds of a crime (POCA 2002 ss.327–329, TA2000 ss.15–18).

Removal and resignation

Resignation of auditors

Under CA2006 s.516, an auditor may resign his office by giving notice in writing to the company at its registered office. In doing so, he must deposit with the company a statement required by CA2006 s.519. The notice of resignation will not be effective unless it is accompanied by such a statement. [***See precedent 80.***] In practice, where the company's registered office is not also its head office it may be desirable to send a copy of the resignation letter and statement under CA2006 s.519 to both the registered office address and the head office address. Notice of the resignation must be sent to the Registrar of Companies within 14 days by the company (CA2006 s.517).

A resigning auditor whose notice of resignation is accompanied by a statement which he considers should be brought to the attention of members and creditors of the company may lodge with his notice of resignation a requisition calling on the directors to convene a general meeting of the company to consider the explanation of the circumstances connected with his resignation. The directors must convene this meeting within 21 days of the deposit of the requisition, to be held on a date not more than 28 days from the date of the notice convening the meeting (CA2006 s.518). In addition, the auditor's statement must be sent to the members of the company with the notice of the meeting. If the statement is received too late for this to be done, the auditor may require that the statement be read out at the meeting. As noted above the statement need not be sent if, on the application of the company, the Court is of the opinion that the provisions are being used by the auditor to secure needless publicity for defamatory matter.

Notwithstanding his resignation, the auditor is entitled to receive notice and to attend and speak at the meeting convened at his requisition or at any general meeting at which his term of office would otherwise have expired or at which it is proposed to fill the casual vacancy caused by his resignation (CA2006 s.518(10)). Accordingly, where an auditor of a public company resigns during the year, notice of the next general meeting at which accounts are laid before the members must be sent to the previous auditor and the appointment of auditors to fill the casual vacancy will require special notice to be given to the company, usually by a director.

Removal of auditor

The provisions under which members may remove an auditor are almost identical to the provisions under which directors may be removed. As with directors the members have the right to remove an auditor from office at any time by ordinary resolution (CA2006 s.510).

Special notice of the proposed removal must be given to the company and a copy must be forwarded to the auditor. Removal requires an ordinary resolution. The auditor can have a statement circulated or read out at the meeting. If an auditor is removed from office this does not prevent them from seeking compensation or damages as result of the removal from office and termination of the appointment. [***See precedent*** **73.**]

Where a resolution to remove an auditor is approved the company must give notice of this to Companies House within 14 days on Form AA03 (CA2006 s.512).

An auditor removed from office retains the rights to attend and speak at the general meeting at which his term of office would have otherwise expired or at which it is proposed to fill the vacancy caused by his removal (CA2006 s.513).

Non-reappointment of auditors

An auditor can be replaced by a new auditor by written resolution of the members in place of an auditor whose appointment has expired or would expire at the end of the period for appointing auditors.

If the proposed change occurs outside of the period allowed for appointing auditors the company must send a copy of the proposed resolution to both the current and proposed auditors. The current auditor may, within 14 days, make a statement and request its circulation to members. Unless a court order is obtained this statement must be circulated to the members (CA2006 ss.514, 515).

Rights of auditors who are removed or not reappointed

Where a resolution is to be proposed at a general meeting or by written resolution for removing an auditor before the expiration of his term of office or for appointing as auditor a person other than a retiring auditor the following requirements must be adhered to:

1 Special notice must be given to the company of the proposed resolution to be put to a general meeting (CA2006 s.515) [***see precedent** 73*].
2 Copies of the special notice or of the written resolution must be sent as soon as practical by the company to the persons proposed to be removed as auditor, to be appointed as auditor and to the retiring auditor, as appropriate (CA2006 ss.514(3), 515(3)).
3 The auditor proposed to be removed or not reappointed may make representations in writing to the company on the proposed resolution and may ask the company to circulate that representation to the shareholders of the company (CA2006 ss.514(4), 515(4)).
4 The company must comply with that request. If it is too late to include the representation with the notice of the meeting, a note that a representation has been made should be included and a copy of the representations should then be sent to all the shareholders entitled to receive notice of the meeting (CA2006 ss.514(5), 515(5)).
5 If the representation is received too late to be circulated to shareholders, or if the representation is not sent out, the auditor concerned may require the representation to be read out at the meeting (CA2006 s.515(6)).
6 The auditor proposed to be removed or not reappointed is also entitled to receive notice of, and to attend and speak at, the general meeting at which the resolution for his removal or non-reappointment is to be considered.
7 The representations need not be sent out or be read at the meeting if on the application of either the company, or any other person claiming to be aggrieved, the Court is satisfied that the rights conferred on the auditor proposed to be removed or not reappointed are being abused to secure needless publicity of a defamatory nature (CA2006 ss.514(7), 515(7)). In these circumstances the Court may also direct that the company's costs in making the application be met in whole or in part by the auditor.

Auditors ceasing to hold office

Unquoted companies

Where, for any reason, an auditor of an unquoted company ceases to hold office, he must send the company at its registered office a statement of any circumstances connected with his ceasing to hold office which he considers should be brought to the attention of the members or creditors of the company. If there are no circumstances to be reported to them this must be stated (CA2006 s.519(1) and (2)). [***See precedent 80.***]

Quoted company

Where, for any reason, an auditor of a quoted company ceases to hold office, he must send the company at its registered office a statement of the circumstances connected with his ceasing to hold office (CA2006 s.519(3)). [***See precedent 80.***]

Time allowed to provide statement

In the case of a resigning auditor the statement must be deposited with the notice of resignation. If the auditor does not seek reappointment at the next annual general meeting the statement should be delivered not less than 14 days before the end of the period allowed for next appointing auditors. In any other circumstances, the statement should be deposited not later than the end of 14 days beginning with the date on which the auditor ceases to hold office (CA2006 s.519(4)).

Company's obligation on receiving statement

If the statement contains details of circumstances that the auditor considers should be brought to the attention of the members or creditors, the company must within 14 days send copies of the statement to those persons entitled to receive copies of the audited accounts pursuant to CA2006 s.423. The company may, however, apply to the Courts if the directors believe the statement is defamatory or seeking needless publicity (CA2006 s.520).

If application is made to the Court, the company must notify the auditor of the application. The Court may reject the statement made by the auditor and order costs against the auditor in full or in part. Within 14 days of the judgment, the company must send a statement of the Court's decision to those persons entitled to receive copies of the audited accounts. If the Court upholds the auditor's statement, the company must issue the statement to those persons entitled to receive copies of the accounts within 14 days of the Court's decision, including the auditor.

Notification to Companies House

If the auditor is not notified within 21 days that an application is to be made to the Court pursuant to CA2006 s.520(2)(b) he must send a copy of his statement to the Registrar of Companies within seven days. If an application to the Court is made and rejected, the auditor must send a copy of his statement to the Registrar of Companies within seven days of being notified of the Court's decision by the company (CA2006 s.521).

Auditors' liability

Any provision in a contract to exempt the auditors from any liability is void except where such clause is permitted by CA2006 ss.533–536.

Indemnity

CA2006 s.533 permits companies to indemnify an auditor in defending proceedings in which judgment is given in favour of the auditor or relief is granted by the Court.

Limitation of liability

Auditors and companies may agree to limit the liability of the auditor provided:

- the limitation agreement only applies to acts or omissions in respect of the audit of one financial year; and
- the financial year is specified; and
- it is approved by the members.

Any audit liability limitation must be fair and reasonable in all the circumstances and in particular must have regard to the auditors' responsibilities under the Companies Act, the nature and purpose of the agreement to provide audit services and the professional standards expected of the auditor (CA2006 s.537).

Private company

A liability limitation agreement may be approved:

- in advance by waiving the need for approval;
- in advance by approving the agreement's main terms; or
- after the agreement is entered into by agreeing to its terms (CA2006 s.536(2)).

Public company

A liability limitation agreement may be approved:

- in advance by approving the agreement's main terms; or
- after the agreement is entered into by agreeing to its terms (CA2006 s.536(3)).

12 Statutory registers

Introduction

Every company is legally obliged to keep certain specified registers, books and records to reflect the operation of its business. It is the company secretary's primary responsibility to see that they are properly maintained and kept up to date.

Traditionally, companies incorporated by agents were supplied with a bound or loose-leaf book containing pro-forma registers for use by the company in maintaining these registers. As a consequence, the statutory registers of a company are frequently referred to as the statutory records or the **statutory book(s)**.

This chapter looks in detail at the registers, books and records that are legally required by the Companies Act 2006, where they should be kept and also at some of the legal and practical issues concerning the maintenance of each type of register.

Legal requirements

The Companies Act 2006 requires that every company keep the following registers, books and records:

- register of members (CA2006 s.113);
- register of charges (CA2006 s.876);
- books containing minutes of company and directors' meetings (CA2006 ss.248, 355), resolutions in writing of members (CA2006 s.355) and resolutions of a sole member (CA2006 s.357);
- accounting records (CA2006 s.386) (see Chapter 10);
- register of directors (CA2006 s.162);
- register of directors' residential addresses (CA2006 s.165);
- register of secretaries (CA2006 s.275); and
- if the company is a public company, a register of interests in voting shares (CA2006 s.808).

The Act does not require that a company keep registers of individual share allotments or transfers. However, these are often included in bound or loose-leaf statutory books, as this information may be useful if there are future enquiries into movements in shares. If these registers are kept, they must be made available for inspection as set out on pp. 236–237.

Similarly, the Acts do not require that a register of debenture holders is kept and consequently this is not, strictly speaking, a statutory register. Again, however, if such a register is kept, the Act lays down requirements with regard to its maintenance and inspection (CA2006 ss.743, 744).

Specified locations

The statutory registers must be kept at the registered office address of a company or at a single alternative inspection location (SAIL) to its registered office. The alternative location must be in the same part of the UK as the company's registered office and it must be the same location for all the company's registers and records. The company must give notice to Companies House of the location of its SAIL on Form AD02 and which of its records may be inspected there on Form AD03, and any change in location, unless the records have at all times been kept at the registered office address.

Registers held on computer

The statutory books and registers may be kept in the form of a combined register, either a bound book or in loose-leaf form. The statutory registers (including a register of debenture holders, if one is kept) and other records may also be kept on computer or in other non-legible form provided that adequate precautions are taken against falsification and that they are capable of being reproduced in legible form for inspection (CA2006 ss.1134, 1135 and 1138).

Data protection

Registers which have to be made available for public inspection under the requirements of the Companies Act are exempt from the provisions of the Data Protection Act 1998, provided that they include only the information which is required (see below) and no non-statutory information.

Notification under the Data Protection Act is required if the company keeps a list of the non-statutory information and other matters relating to share registration with its statutory records. It is the practice of some companies – particularly private companies – to include the non-statutory information in the register of members rather than go to the expense of maintaining and referring to a separate record, bearing in mind that, in practice, requests for inspection of the register are rare. However, this is not best practice as if a request for inspection is received, the non-statutory information will have to be removed from the copy made available for inspection.

Register of members

The form of the register of members

The statutory information to be kept in the register of members is contained in CA2006 s.113 and is as follows:

- the names and addresses of the members;
- the date on which each person was registered as a member;
- the date on which any person ceased to be a member;
- for a company which has share capital, there should also be included the number of shares held by each member and, if appropriate, the split between different classes and the amounts paid or agreed to be paid on the shares.

Where shares are purchased into treasury and then cancelled the company's details need not be entered in its register of members (CA2006 s.124).

The first entry in an account and the last entry in a closed account are sufficient for the purposes of complying with the legislation.

If the company's capital is in the form of stock, it is usual to show the number of stock units held by each member, e.g. 400 stock units of 25p each, rather than £100 of stock. The accounts in the register would, however, be headed 'Stock units of 25p'.

In the case of private companies with a single member it is necessary to add a note to that person's entry in the register stating that the company has only one member and the date on which the transaction took place (CA2006 s.123). [***See precedent 81***.] If that company subsequently ceases to have only one member, then a further statement must be added to the entry of the former sole shareholder stating that fact and the date on which the transaction took place.

It is good company secretarial practice that the register of members should not include any information not required to be included under the provisions of CA2006 s.113. This will include information such as references to dividend mandates (which will include the name of the member's bank and account number), e-mail addresses supplied for the purposes of electronic communication or powers of attorney. This non-statutory information is consequently suppressed on any copy of the register made available for public inspection and, where copies of the register are supplied, to any member or other person, as required by CA2006 s.116. The non-statutory information may be kept by the company separately.

The entry in a register of members relating to a former member may be removed from the register ten years after the date on which he ceased to be a member (CA2006 ss.121 and 128).

Name of registered holder

Only individuals or corporate bodies should be registered as members. Holders of an office can be registered provided it is a public office such as the Official Receiver.

Names of partnerships, trusts or settlements must not be registered as the holders of shares as they have no legal capacity and accordingly valid instructions cannot be given. If documentation is received to register shares in the name of a trust or partnership, it should be rejected. The shares should be registered in the names of some or all of the partners or trustees. It is usual for the number of joint holders of shares to be restricted to a maximum of four.

Location and inspection of register of members

The register of members must be kept at the registered office address of a company or at a single alternative location to its registered office. The alternative location must be in the same part of the UK as the company's registered office and it must be the same location for all the company's registers and records. The company must give notice to Companies House of the location of its records on Form AD03, and any change in location, unless the records have at all times been kept at the registered office address.

The register of members must be kept at one of three places:

1. The registered office of the company.
2. Some other office of the company at which the work of making up the register is done.
3. At the office of a person employed to make up the register (e.g. a service registrar).

The register of members must be kept in the same part of the UK as the company's registered office.

A separate index of a register of members containing more than 50 accounts must be kept unless the register itself is self-indexing (CA2006 s.115).

The register must be open for inspection during business hours by any member of the company. Under the Companies (Company Records) Regulations 2008, public companies are required to make company records available for inspection for at least two hours between 9.00 am and 5.00 pm on a working day. Private companies must make company records available for inspection for at least two hours between 9.00 am and 5.00 pm on a working day on two working days' notice during the notice period for a general meeting or a class meeting, or, where the company has circulated a written notice, during the period provided in CA2006 s.297(1). Such inspection is free of charge to members and for any other person on payment of the prescribed fee (£3.50 per hour or part thereof) (CA2006 s.116). Although the right of inspection does not include power to take copies of the register, it will probably be convenient for companies to allow those inspecting the register to take notes since, if this is refused, the company may receive a request to supply a copy of all or part of the register (CA2006 s.116(2)). A request from any member or other person obliges companies to send, within five working days of the receipt of the request, a copy of the register or of any part thereof on payment of the prescribed fee (see below) provided the person requesting the information provides their name and address and the purpose for which the information is to be used either by themselves or if acquired for a third party, by that third party. A company is not obliged to make available for inspection or provide copies of any registers or index by reference to geographical location, nationality, size of holding of shares, by person or by corporate body or by gender.

If the company is not satisfied that the request has been made for a proper purpose it must apply to the Court for an order. The Court will then either direct the company not to comply with the request and in the absence of such a direction the company must comply with the request (CA2006 s.117).

The fees that a company may charge for inspection of its registers by non-members or for providing copies of any register to members or non-members are (SI 2007/2612):

The amounts per number of entries copied are:

- £1 for each of the first five entries;
- £30 for the next 95 entries or part thereof;
- £30 for the next 900 entries or part thereof;
- £30 for the next 99,000 entries or part thereof; and
- £30 for the remainder of the entries in the register or part thereof.

Rectification of the register of members

Amendments to the register of members should, strictly speaking, be made only under the sanction of a court order for rectification of a register (CA2006 s.125). However, minor clerical slips in the register may be altered shortly after the entries have been made on the authority of the company secretary or of the company's registrar, subject to confirmation that there has been no sub-sale (i.e. that no change of beneficial ownership has taken place). In the case of a request to register a completely different name, consideration should be given to whether the sanction of the Court is required. Extreme care is required in these cases and such requests should never be accepted if lodged by an individual. In all such cases, full enquiry should be made before accepting the request for rectification as the procedure is open to abuse. In any event, no request for rectification should be accepted if made more than three months from the date of registration or if a dividend has been paid on the shares. Some companies charge a fee for making such corrections.

In any other instance, if the register of members is incorrect it is only possible for it to be amended by order of the Court (CA2006 s.125). An application may be made by the aggrieved person, the company or any other member of the company. Rectification under the Companies Act 2006 is possible in situations where the name of any person is entered or omitted from the register without due cause or where there has been an unnecessary delay in entering the particulars of any transaction. On application, the Court may refuse the application or order rectification of the register, and may order payment by the company for any loss or damage caused.

If the company receives a court order ordering rectification of the register, the appropriate amendments must be made. Any incorrect share certificates must be returned for cancellation and new certificates issued. An order for rectification must be made by a Court in the country of the incorporation of the company; thus, a Scottish Court may not require the rectification of an English company's register. For fuller details on the procedural requirements, see p. 168.

Branch registers

A company may establish an 'overseas branch register' of members resident in territories in which it transacts business (CA2006 s.129). Section 129(2) of CA2006 lists those countries in which overseas branch registers may be kept. Chapter 3 of Part 8 of the Act gives the provisions to be followed with respect to overseas branch registers.

The Registrar of Companies must be informed within 14 days when any overseas branch register is established (on Form AD06 – Notice of opening an overseas branch register) or discontinued (on Form AD07 – Notice of discontinuance of an overseas branch register).

The maintenance of an overseas branch register makes it more convenient to record dealings in the company's shares in the territory concerned, registered in the names of members resident in that country. Such transfers are not, of course, liable to UK *ad valorem* stamp duty, but may be subject to local requirements. A branch register contains only the names and addresses and shareholdings of shareholders with a registered address in the territory in question; the company is not concerned with making enquiries about the residential status of members. A company that keeps an overseas branch register must keep available for inspection the register, or a duplicate of the register at the place in the United Kingdom where the company's main register is kept available for inspection. Any duplicate register is treated as part of the main register.

If a member who is on the main register wishes to have his shares registered in the overseas branch register, he should complete a form of request in duplicate and send it to the company with his share certificate, stating the name of the overseas branch register in which he wishes his holding to be registered. The entry relating to the member will then be deleted in the main register and his share certificate cancelled. The company will prepare a schedule of such requests and send them to the person responsible in the territory concerned for maintaining the overseas branch register. The holding will then be recorded in the overseas branch register and a new certificate prepared which will be clearly marked to indicate that the shares are registered in the overseas branch register. Certificates of companies that have a common seal will be sealed with the company's official seal for use abroad in the relevant territory (CA2006 s49). The reverse procedure will be followed in the case of a member with shares registered in the overseas branch register wishing to have his shares registered in the company's principal register.

Register of bearer shares

It is not possible to maintain a register of members who hold share warrants to bearer since the company will be unaware of the holders from time to time. This is because, as noted above, the warrants can be passed from hand to hand, thereby transferring title to the new holder of the warrant. However, it is usual for a company to maintain the following registers for its information:

1 A warrant register recording the number of warrants printed and issued and the numbers of those surrendered for cancellation, e.g. by a holder wishing to exchange his bearer warrants for registered shares.
2 A coupon register in which the coupons lodged for the payment of dividends are recorded.

It is also desirable for companies to keep a file of applications for share warrants to be issued in exchange for registered shares and vice versa, kept in numerical order and suitably cross-referenced to the warrant register.

Register of charges

The provisions described in this section apply to the registration of company charges with respect to companies registered in Great Britain (CA2006 s.860 (England, Wales and Northern Ireland); CA2006 s.878 (Scotland)). A register of charges should be kept by every company, even if there are no charges to be entered in the register (CA2006 s.876 (England, Wales and Northern Ireland); CA2006 s.891 (Scotland)). Anyone inspecting the register will wish to know whether or not the company has any charges specifically affecting the property of the company or any floating charges on the undertaking or on any of its property. The register must contain particulars of all charges on any property of the company. There is also an obligation on companies to keep copies of instruments creating charges (CA2006 s.877 (England, Wales and Northern Ireland) and CA2006 s.892 (Scotland)).

The register must be open to inspection by any creditor or member of the company without fee and to inspection by any other person on payment of such fee as may be prescribed (CA2006 ss.877 and 892). The register of charges kept by the company should not be confused with the register to be kept by the Registrar of Companies under CA2006 ss.869 and 885 relating to particulars of charges sent to the Registrar of Companies under the provisions of CA2006 ss.860–868 and 878–884 respectively.

Minute books

There are no statutory requirements regarding the location of minute books of directors' meetings, but the records must be kept for at least ten years from the date of the meeting. Every company must keep records comprising copies of all resolutions of members passed otherwise than at general meetings, minutes of all proceedings of general meetings and records of decisions by a sole member. These records must be kept for at least ten years from the date of the resolution, meeting or decision, at the registered office of the company or at a single alternative inspection location at which all the company records and registers are kept.

The type of minute book kept by the company will depend on the size and procedures of the company concerned. For private companies, they may be kept in bound books, either hand-written or with typed sheets of paper pasted into the bound book with the pages serially numbered. It is convenient for the minutes to be numbered consecutively from number 1 upwards throughout the book. Thus in the first minute book, the minutes would be numbered 1.1, 1.2, 1.3, etc., in the second minute book, they would be numbered 2.1, 2.2, 2.3, and so on.

Larger public companies generally use loose-leaf minute books. Again, it is recommended that the pages are numbered serially and the minutes numbered consecutively. Some companies also maintain an index at the back of the minute book giving reference to the items covered by the minutes. The secretary must decide whether the time spent in indexing the minutes will serve any useful purpose.

Minutes of general meetings should be kept separate from board minutes since members have a right to inspect the minutes of general meetings but not of board meetings (CA2006 s.358).

Register of directors and register of secretaries

These registers are now two distinct registers. The register of directors is kept pursuant to CA 2006 s.162 and the register of secretaries is kept pursuant to CA 2006 s.275. If a combined register has been used previously, it is to be treated as two separate registers as from 1 October 2009.

The following points of practice arise in connection with completing the registers:

1 Only former names which a director or secretary used for business purposes have to be recorded. Names not used for more than 20 years, a name used by a peer before adopting or succeeding to the title, and names used before reaching the age of 16 need not be registered (CA 2006 ss.163 and 277).
2 If a person is a director of a number of companies, his occupation may be shown as 'director of companies'. However, if he is a director only of the company to which the register relates, his occupation should be described as 'none', unless he has a business occupation such as 'marketing manager'.
3 The date of birth of every director must be included.
4 Appointments of directors or company secretaries or changes in their particulars must be notified to the Registrar of Companies within 14 days of the appointment or change. The appointment of a new director should be notified

on Form AP01 (or Form AP02 in respect of a corporate director) and the appointment of a company secretary should be notified on Form AP03 (or Form AP04 in respect of a corporate secretary). The form incorporates a form of consent to be signed by a new director or a new company secretary.

5 The register must be open to inspection at reasonable times without charge to any member of the company or subject to payment of the prescribed fee to any other person (CA2006 s.162(5)).

6 A service address must be stated for every director, which may be stated as 'The company's registered office' and can be the same as a director's residential address.

Register of directors' residential addresses

In addition to the register of directors, companies must maintain a separate, but confidential, register of directors' residential addresses, and although kept private, the residential address will also need to be notified to Companies House. The residential address is referred to as 'protected information', and the possible fact that the residential address is the same as the service address is also classified as 'protected information'.

Interests in shares

Directors' interests in shares or debentures

The Companies Act 2006 repealed CA1985 s.324 and as a result companies are no longer required to maintain a register of interests of their directors or connected persons in the company's shares or debentures.

Register of interests in voting shares

Similarly, public companies are no longer required to keep a register of interests in voting shares which exceed 3 per cent of the total voting rights.

Shareholders who hold in excess of 3 per cent of the voting rights of a company whose shares are admitted to trading on a regulated market are still obliged to notify the company in accordance with DTR 5. However where such disclosure is made there is no requirement for the company to maintain a register although it must disclose such notifications. This is dealt with more fully in Chapter 16.

Requisition of information regarding interests in voting shares

A public company has power under CA2006 s.793 to require any person whom it knows or has reason to believe is or was at any time in the previous three years interested in the relevant share capital of the company (i.e. voting shares) to supply information to the company as specified in the section. The information includes the identity of the persons interested in the voting shares in question and information as to whether such persons were parties to an agreement to which CA2006 s.824 relates (i.e. 'concert parties'). [***See precedent 82.***]

Any request for information under CA2006 s.793 may be made in relation to any shareholding; there is no requirement for the shareholding concerned to be a notifiable interest in the company's voting shares under DTR 5.1.2.

The company must maintain a register of interests disclosed to it pursuant to a disclosure request made under CA2006 s.793 (CA2006 s.808). The register must contain details of the date the request for information was made and the information disclosed to the company in pursuance of the notice.

The register kept pursuant to CA2006 s.808 must be kept at the registered office or at a single alternative inspection location at which all the company records and registers are kept. The register must be open for inspection by any person free of charge. Any person may also request a copy of any entry in the register on payment of the prescribed fee. Any person requesting to view or be sent a copy of the register or any entry must provide their name and address and the purpose for which the information is requested. Where the information is requested on behalf of a third party their details and the purpose for which they require that information must also be disclosed (CA2006 s.811).

Where a company receives a request under CA2006 s.811 and it is satisfied that the request is for a proper purpose it must supply the information requested or refuse the request if not satisfied. A person whose request has been refused may apply to the Court. The Court may order the company not to comply and in the absence of such an order the company must provide the requested information. Where an application is made to the Court the applicant must notify the company that the application has been made and the company must use its best endeavors to notify any person whose details would be disclosed if the company was required to comply with the request under CA2006 s.811 (CA2006 s.812).

Entries in the register may only be removed six years after the date the entry was made (CA2006 s.816) or to remove incorrect information (CA2006 s.817).

Where a public company re-registers as a private company it must retain and make any register kept under CA2006 s.808 available for inspection until the end of the period of six years after it ceased to be a public company (CA2006 s.819).

Unless the register has always been kept at the company's registered office, notice of the single alternative inspection location at which the register is located and any change in that place must be given to Companies House on Form AD02 (Notice of single alternative inspection location), Form AD03 (Change of location of the company records to the single alternative inspection location) or Form AD04 (Change of location of the company records to the registered office), as appropriate (CA2006 s.809). Unless the register is kept in a form that is itself an index a separate index must also be maintained (CA2006 s.810).

Members holding not less than one-tenth of the paid-up capital of the company, giving the right to vote at general meetings of the company, may require the company to exercise its powers under the provisions of CA2006 s.793 (CA2006 ss.803 and 804). A report of the information received must be prepared and the members of the company requisitioning the company to make the investigation must be notified that the information is available for inspection at the company's registered office. Copies of the report must also be supplied on request. The report must be made available for inspection within 15 days of the conclusion of the investigation (CA2006 s.805(1)).

Failure to give information to the company under CA2006 s.793 by any persons may result in heavy penalties (CA2006 ss.794 and 797). It is of interest to companies to be aware of the identity of persons who hold significant holdings of voting shares in the company under the cloak of nominee names, not only to improve investor relations but also as this may be the prelude to a takeover bid for the company. If a person on whom a company serves a request for information does not provide the requested information within the time specified the company can apply to the Court for a direction that the shares be subject to restrictions (CA2006 s.794).

The effect of an order under CA2006 s.794 is that:

- any transfer of shares is void unless approved by the Court pursuant to CA2006 s.800(3);
- the voting rights are no longer exercisable;
- no further shares may be issued in right of the holder of the shares or in pursuance of an offer made to the holder;
- other than in liquidation no payment may be made to the holder in respect of the holding whether capital or otherwise.

The Court may make such provisions it deems appropriate to protect the position of third parties (CA2006 s.794(2)).

The restrictions imposed by an order made under CA2006 s.794 may be relaxed by an application under CA2006 ss.799 and 800 made by the company or any aggrieved person.

In addition to an order placing restrictions on the shares, the Court may make an order requiring the shares to be sold and may impose conditions on the sale (CA2006 s.801). The proceeds of any such sale must be paid into Court to be held for the benefit of the beneficial owner(s) who may apply for payment (CA2006 s.802).

Register of debenture holders

It has already been mentioned that keeping a register of debenture holders is not a requirement of the Companies Act 2006, although, if such a register is kept, there are various statutory requirements to be followed (CA2006 ss.743 to 748). The requirements broadly mirror the rights to request a copy of the register of members, the requirement to satisfy the company that the request is for a proper purpose. If there is just one single debenture, an entry could be made in the company's register of charges, which would obviate the need for keeping a separate register of debenture holders. It is, however, convenient to keep a register of debenture holders where a series of debentures is issued.

13

Mortgages and charges

Introduction

Companies sometimes create a mortgage or charge over their assets as security for loans and guarantees provided by a third party. In order to protect potential creditors and others doing business with the company, details of all charges and mortgages must be registered with the Registrar of Companies.

Charges

A charge is security for the payment of a debt or other obligation, such as future rent payments. The charge does not pass title to the assets charged or any right to possession to the person who has been given the charge – the chargee.

Mortgages

A mortgage is security for the payment of a debt or other obligation that does pass title to the assets charged but does not pass the right to possession to the chargee.

Legislation

The provisions for registering mortgages and charges are slightly different for companies registered in England and Wales and those registered in Scotland. In October 2009 provisions contained in the CA2006 came into force which changed the registration procedures and extended the regime to companies registered in Northern Ireland. For the purposes of the legislation references to a charge also includes a mortgage (CA2006 s.861(5)).

English, Welsh and Northern Irish companies

Registration

Where a company creates a registerable charge on any or all of its assets or undertaking, that charge is void against any liquidator, administrator or creditor unless details of the charge have been registered at Companies House within 21 days of the creation of the charge (CA2006 s.874(1) and (2)). As a consequence it is normal for the chargee rather than the company to lodge details of the charge to ensure that their security remains valid.

The types of charges that must be registered are set out in CA1985 s.860(7) and are:

- a charge on land or any interest in land, other than a charge for any rent or other periodical sum issuing out of land;
- a charge created or evidenced by an instrument which, if executed by an individual, would require registration as a bill of sale;
- a charge for the purposes of securing any issue of debentures;
- a charge on uncalled share capital of the company;
- a charge on calls made but not paid;
- a charge of book debts of the company;
- a floating charge on the company's property or undertaking;
- a charge on a ship or aircraft, or any share in a ship;
- a charge on goodwill or on any intellectual property.

Registration is by delivering the original document creating the charge together with the required details on the appropriate form as follows:

- for mortgages and charges, Form MG01;
- for a charge securing a series of debentures, Form MG07;
- particulars of a charge subject to which property has been acquired, Form MG06.

A filing fee of £13 is payable on filing Forms MG01, MG07 and MG06.

It is the responsibility of the company to ensure that details of any charges it creates are registered although, as noted above, in most circumstances it is the chargee that files the form (CA2006 s.860(1)). In such circumstances the chargee is entitled to recover the filing fee from the company.

Where a charge is not registered within the 21-day period set out in CA2006 s.870) the charge is void unless on application to the Court an order is made extending the period allowed for registration or requiring that the omission or mis-statement be rectified (CA2006 s.873(2)).

Companies House register of charges

The Registrar of Companies must maintain a register of all charges registered by a company containing the following particulars (CA2006 s.869):

1. for debentures, the total amount secured by the series of debentures, the dates of the resolutions authorising the issue of the series and the date of the covering deed (if any) by which the series is created or defined, a general description of the property charged and the names of any trustees for the debenture holders;
2. for all other charges, the date of creation of the charge (or acquisition of property subject to an existing charge), amount secured, short details of the charge, details of the chargee.

Once registered, the Registrar of Companies must issue a certificate stating the amount secured by the charge. The certificate is conclusive evidence that the registration requirements have been met (CA2006 s.869(6)(b)).

Enforcement of security

If a chargee appoints or obtains an order for the appointment of a receiver or manager under the power contained in a mortgage or charge document, details of such appointment must be filed with the Registrar of Companies within seven days of such appointment (CA2006 s.871(1)).

A person appointed as a receiver or manager to enforce any security must give notice upon ceasing to act as such receiver or manager.

Company's register of charges

All limited companies must maintain a register of charges, even if there are no details to be entered. Where any charges or mortgages are created details must be entered on its register of charges giving a short description of the property charged, the amount of the charge and the chargee (CA2006 s.876).

A company's register of charges must be available for inspection by any member or creditor without charge. The register may also be inspected by anyone else on payment of a fee (CA2006 s.877(4)).

Satisfaction and release

Although there is no requirement to notify the Registrar of Companies that a charge has been released or satisfied it is in the company's interests to ensure the records are accurate and that potential investors, bankers and creditors are aware that all or part of any previous loans or other obligations have been satisfied.

Any person with an interest in the registration of the charge may give notice of the satisfaction of a charge or mortgage; in practice this is most likely to be the company and signed on its behalf by a director or the company secretary. The company may give notice of the satisfaction of a mortgage in full or in part, by submitting Form MG02 to Companies House. On receipt of a Form MG02 the Registrar of Companies will update the register of charges kept at Companies House (CA2006 s.872).

Overseas companies

Companies registered outside of Great Britain, the Channel Islands and the Isle of Man that have either a place of business or branch in England or Wales must register details of any charges they create on any property in England or Wales or any such property which is already subject to a charge (the Overseas Companies (Execution of Documents and Registration of Charges) Regulations 2009). There is no longer a need for overseas companies that are not registered in Great Britain to register details of charges created, and the 'Slavenburg' register has therefore been abolished.

Scottish companies

Registration

Where a company creates a registerable charge on any or all of its assets or undertaking, that charge is void against any liquidator, administrator or creditor unless details of the charge have been registered at Companies House within 21 days of the creation of the charge (CA2006 s.889(1)). As a consequence it is normal for the chargee rather than the company to lodge details of the charge to ensure that their security remains valid.

The types of charges that must be registered are set out in CA2006 s.878(7) and are:

- a charge on land or any interest in such land, other than a charge for any rent or other periodical sum payable in respect of the land;
- a security over incorporeal moveable property of any of the following categories: goodwill, a patent or a licence under a patent, a trade mark, a copyright or a licence under a copyright, a registered design or a licence in respect of such a design, a design right or a licence under a design right, book debts, uncalled share capital of the company or calls made but not paid;
- a security over a ship or aircraft or any share in a ship;
- a floating charge.

Registration is by delivering the original document creating the charge together with the required details on the appropriate form as follows:

- for mortgages and charges, Form MG01s;
- for a charge securing a series of debentures, Form MG07s;
- where a property is acquired on which an existing charge exists and is to remain, Form MG06s.

A filing fee of £13 is payable on filing these forms.

The filing period for charges created outside of the UK on property located outside of the UK is 21 days from the date when the particulars could have been received in the UK if sent with posted with due diligence rather than 21 days from the creation of the charge itself (CA2006 s.886(1)(b)).

It is the responsibility of the company to ensure that details of any charges it creates are registered although, as noted above, in most circumstances it is the chargee that files the form (CA2006 s.878). In such circumstances the chargee is entitled to recover the filing fee from the company.

Where a charge is not registered within the 21 day period set out in CA2006 s.886 the charge is void unless on application to the Court an order is made extending the period allowed for registration or requiring that the omission or mis-statement be rectified (CA2006 s.888(2)).

Companies House register of charges

The Scottish Registrar of Companies must maintain a register of all charges registered by a company, containing the following particulars (CA2006 s.885):

1. For debentures, the total amount secured by the series of debentures, the dates of the resolutions authorising the issue of the series and the date of the covering deed, a general description of the property charged and the names of any trustees for the debenture holders.
2. For all other charges, the date of creation of the charge (or acquisition of property subject to an existing charge), amount secured, short details of the charge, details of the chargee and for a floating charge details of any restrictions on the company's ability to charge the assets in priority to or *pari passu* with the existing floating charge.

Once registered the Registrar of Companies must issue a certificate stating the amount secured by the charge. The certificate is conclusive evidence that the registration requirements have been met (CA2006 s.885(5)).

Company's register of charges

All limited companies must maintain a register of charges, even if there are no details to be entered. Where any charges or mortgages are created, details must be entered on its register of charges giving a short description of the property charged, the amount of the charge and the chargee (CA2006 s.891).

A company's register of charges must be available for inspection by any member or creditor without charge. The register may also be inspected by anyone else on payment of a fee (CA2006 s.892(4)).

Satisfaction and release

Although there is no requirement to notify the Registrar of Companies that a charge has been released or satisfied it is in the company's interests to ensure the records are accurate and that potential investors, bankers and creditors are aware that all or part of any previous loans or other obligations have been satisfied.

The company may give notice of the satisfaction of a mortgage, in full or in part, by making submitting Form MG02s to Companies House. On receipt of a Form MG02s the Registrar of Companies will update the register of charges kept at Companies House (CA2006 s.887(3)).

Overseas companies

Companies registered outside of Great Britain, the Channel Islands and the Isle of Man that have either a place of business or branch in Scotland must register details of any charges they create on any property in Scotland or any such property which is already subject to a charge. There is no longer a need for overseas companies that are not registered in Great Britain to register details of charges created, and the 'Slavenburg' register has therefore been abolished.

14

Corporate compliance

Introduction

Directors' duties are defined in a number of statutes, and are supplemented by additional common law duties which have evolved over the years and which come under the headings of their **fiduciary** duty to the company and a duty of skill and care. Directors' prime duties are discussed in Chapter 2. This chapter considers compliance duties as well as duties under other legislation. It should be noted, however, that there are many legislative provisions applicable to particular business types and this book can only deal with a general overview of the more common provisions.

In general, as noted in Chapter 2, directors are required to exercise the powers of the company for the benefit of the company and its members as a whole. There are, however, circumstances when this general rule is superseded. For example, under certain circumstances, the directors must take account of the interests of the employees (see, for example, CA2006 s.172(1)(b)). Where a company cannot avoid insolvency, directors are required to take account of the interests of the company's creditors. There will also be occasions when, as agents for individual members, directors have a duty to act in the best interests of those members individually.

The principal compliance issues relating to the accounts and audit, UK Listing Authority (UKLA), London Stock Exchange and PLUS Market and corporate governance are dealt with in detail in Chapters 10, 17 and 18. This chapter discusses compliance issues concerning a company's annual return, its company seal and the authentication and retention of documents. It also looks at other compliance issues including those relating to employees, health and safety, disability discrimination, data and consumer protection, the environment and financial matters.

Compliance and the company secretary

It is the general duty of the company secretary to ensure compliance by the company with the provisions of the Companies Acts and the company's Articles of Association. However, company secretaries of groups and companies engaged in financial services, e.g. banking, insurance, Stock Exchange dealing, investment fund and unit trust management, etc., may also have a specific compliance role to fulfil. They are often required to act as the compliance officer for the group or company in relation to compliance with the provisions of the Financial Services and Markets Act 2000 (FSMA2000), and the rules and regulations of the Financial Services carried on by the group, but the group company secretary usually acts as the coordinator Authority (FSA). In the case of a large financial services group, the day-to-day compliance functions are normally the responsibility of particular managers engaged in the financial businesses of their functions as the group compliance officer.

Companies Act statutory forms

Introduction

Companies are required to ensure that changes to the company's corporate structure are notified to the Registrar of Companies for placing on public record. Additionally, companies must make an annual return each year (CA2006 s.854) (see below).

A list of the forms currently in use, and the period in which they must be filed following the event to which they relate, is shown in Appendix 6. Although the forms are no longer named by reference to the section number in the Act, the forms are named by type and do contain details of the section number on the face of the form for ease of cross-reference.

Copies of all statutory forms are available free of charge from Companies House and may be requested by post, telephone or via the Companies House website (see Directory). Many company incorporation agents and business stationers have their own, approved versions of the most common statutory forms. Approved versions are also available as part of most company secretarial software packages. Companies House has now made a number of forms available for completion directly from their website, enabling users to complete the form, print it out, sign it and then forward it to Companies House for filing.

In the past, Companies House has usually insisted that all forms filed bear an original signature. However, following a review and after seeking counsel's opinion, this policy has changed. Companies House has determined that it is acceptable for a person to authorise others to apply their signature to documents. There is a presumption that the use of an automated signature will be subject to internal controls. Accordingly, forms and documents will not be rejected simply because they do not have, or appear not to have, original signatures. This relaxation does not extend to allowing submission of documents by fax or scanned images, due to issues relating to document quality.

The Companies Act 1989 greatly extended the circumstances under which the Registrar can reject documents if they are incorrectly completed and signed.

For example, Companies House has frequently rejected documents that are illegible in accordance with the strict criteria set out in CA1985.

However, CA2006 has introduced provisions that have relaxed these restrictions, in order to make dealing with the Registrar more practical. For example, under CA2006 s.1073 the Registrar now has the power to accept documents that do not meet the requirements for proper delivery. Furthermore, under CA2006 s.1075 the Registrar has the power to correct a delivered document if it is incomplete or internally inconsistent. This is subject to instructions being given and the company giving its consent to these instructions.

However, under CA2006 s.1068 the Registrar still has the power to impose requirements as to the form, authentication and manner of delivery of documents.

Electronic filing

Companies House has introduced an electronic filing service, not to be confused with the web filing service (see below), which is currently limited to Forms AD01, AP01–AP04, TM01, TM02 and CH01–CH04, annual return Form AR01 and incorporation Form IN01, and the Articles of Association. Electronic filing is available only via appropriate, approved software packages, which must be used to generate the appropriate messages. Companies can develop their own bespoke solutions and initially should contact the Electronic Filing Administration department at Companies House.

Electronic filing is available via the internet. Companies send e-mail messages containing electronic documents, in an approved format, and receive acknowledgements. To use the service, a company must notify Companies House of a code it will use to authenticate documents and of any presenter who will transmit documents on its behalf. The code acts as a replacement for the authenticating signature of the company secretary or a director.

Web filing

Forms AP01–AP04, TM01–TM02 and CH01–CH04 relating to the appointment or resignation of directors and secretaries, changes in their details, Form AD01 changing the location of the registered office, Forms AD02–AD04 for notification of the location of the register of members or register of debenture holders, Form MG01, giving particulars of charges, Form SH01 detailing the issue of shares and Form AR01, the annual return (excluding bulk shareholder listings), may now be completed and filed online via the Companies House website. In order to take advantage of this service, the company secretary or a director must first obtain a company authentication code from Companies House. New directors or company secretaries 'sign' the consent to act part of Forms AP01–AP04, as appropriate, by providing three out of nine items of personal information. This personal information is not made public.

Where advantage is taken of either the electronic or web filing service, groups of companies can choose to have the same authentication code, or presenters can advise companies of the code to be selected. In order to comply with the Companies Act, the authentication code must be delivered to Companies House in writing, signed by a serving officer of the company. This may be done by presenters collating the information from the companies concerned and forwarding it to Companies House with the initial application form, provided that the companies have confirmed that they have authorised the particular presenter to deliver information on their behalf.

Where Forms AP01–AP04 are being delivered, the appointee is required to indicate his consent to act as a director or secretary by providing three pieces of information that other people would not normally be expected to know. This information will not be displayed on the public file, but will be stored and retrieved if any question arises as to the validity of the appointment. If this method is adopted, companies filing Forms AP01–AP04 electronically would be well advised to obtain a separate signed consent to be a director, for internal records, which also authorises the company to use the personal information for electronic filing purposes.

There is no fee for electronic submission of forms; however, the normal document submission or incorporation fees apply. Where the annual return is filed electronically there is a reduced fee of £15. Presenters of fee-bearing documents are invoiced by Companies House.

Information packs on the Electronic Filing Service or Web Filing Service can be obtained from the Companies House help desk or downloaded from the Companies House website.

Annual return

For the vast majority of companies, the annual return will be the only company form with which they have to deal with during the course of the year. This is Form AR01. The obligation on companies to make an annual return is imposed by CA2006 s.854. The return must be made up to a date not more than 12 months after the previous return (or 12 months after incorporation), although a company may choose to make it up to an earlier date. The annual return must be filed with the Registrar of Companies within 28 days of the return date, together with a fee (currently £15 if filed online or £30 if filed in hard copy).

Contents of the annual return

The annual return includes particulars of the members of the company and of their holdings, although there is a concession under CA2006 s.856(5) which allows the filing of changes in membership only, provided that full details have been given for either of the two previous years. The list would thus include only the particulars of persons who have become members, have ceased to be members or whose holdings or stock or shares have changed. In the case of large public companies, however, where the list of members is produced by computer or mechanised means, it is usual to lodge a full list of members with the annual return each year. A full list would certainly be needed if the company has made a rights issue or capitalisation issue within the preceding year, and it is also convenient if there have been a large number of transfers of shares registered during the year.

The principal contents of the annual return are:

1 The name and registered number of the company.
2 The address of the company's registered office.
3 The type of company and its principal business activities.
4 The address (SAIL) where the company keeps certain company records, if these are not kept at the registered office.
5 The prescribed particulars of the company secretary, for all public companies and those private companies with a company secretary.
6 The prescribed particulars of the directors of the company.
7 A marker to show if the company was traded at point during the year.
8 If the company has a share capital, a statement of capital comprising the total number of issued shares of the company of each class at the date to which the return is made and the aggregate nominal value of those shares and amounts paid up or, where the company has converted any of its shares into stock, the aggregate amount of the stock issued.
9 The names of members of the company and the number of shares held by each member (or the amount of stock) of each class held by each member at the date of the return and the names of persons who have ceased to be members since the date of the last return. The return must also give the number of shares transferred by each member or by persons who have ceased to be members; but note the concession under CA2006 s.364A(6) which allows the filing of changes in membership only.

There is authority in CA2006 s.857 for the Secretary of State by regulation to vary the contents of the annual return.

Completing the annual return

The following practical points usually arise in connection with the completion of the annual return:

1 Summary of share capital: the current position must be given with regard to the nominal value and amounts paid, including any premium, of the company's share capital of each class taken up, ignoring cancelled shares. No distinction need be shown between shares taken up by payment wholly in cash, for a consideration other than cash or the extent to partly paid shares are paid up.
2 Past and present members:
   (a) where shares have been converted into stock, the amount of stock held and transferred should be shown;

(b) itemised particulars of transfers of shares transferred need be shown only against the name of the transferor: but see below regarding a customary concession allowed by the Registrar of Companies;

(c) it is not necessary to show separately any shares acquired by members during the period to which the annual return relates under a rights or capitalisation issue: only the total number of shares held by the member at the date of the return need be shown;

(d) it is convenient to arrange issues of shares, e.g. in the case of a rights issue or a capitalisation issue, so that the period of renunciation has expired at the date on which the annual return has to be made. If it is not possible to arrange things in this way, the new shares must be included in the summary of the share capital but the list of members will need to be specially annotated to show, in the case of a rights issue, details of the basis of allotments or provisional allotments and stating the date on which the period of renunciation in respect of the shares allotted or provisionally allotted will expire;

(e) the annual return form may be used to notify amended details, the resignation or ceasing to hold office of a director or company secretary. The appointment of a new director or company secretary may only be made on Forms AP01–AP04.

The Registrar of Companies can accept a return for registration that does not comply with the usual strict requirements. However, if any complaint is made by a person making a search of the company's file at the Companies Registration Office, the Registrar may require an amended return to be submitted. The Registrar may allow the following relaxations of the strict requirements; some could also be altered or varied by regulations:

1. Statement of the number of stock units instead of the total amount of stock. This is, in any event, more appropriate since the stock units may be regarded as being synonymous with shares.
2. Separate alphabetical sections for past and present members without any index.
3. Where shares have been transferred by one person on a number of occasions since the previous annual return, instead of showing the details of each transfer separately, the aggregate may be shown against his name with the word 'various' in the space for date of transfer. This concession is, of course, irrelevant if the company submits a full list of its members each year with the annual return.
4. The omission of past members and the number of shares previously held by them where, since the date of the last annual return, the class of shares concerned has been cancelled under a scheme arrangement, with an appropriate note made on the annual return to this effect.
5. Omission of past members whose shares were acquired under a takeover, with an appropriate note being included.

Accounting reference date – Form AA01

All companies, whether trading or not, must prepare accounts and file a copy with the Registrar of Companies (see Chapter 10). The accounts are prepared for each accounting period. Accounting periods begin at the conclusion of the previous period, or the date of incorporation, and end on the accounting reference date.

Companies may choose another accounting reference date by shortening or extending their accounting year. A change in the accounting year must be authorised by the directors at a board meeting. [***See precedent** 76.*] Form AA01 must be filed at Companies House and the change is not effected until the form has been accepted for filing by Companies House.

A company's first accounting period must be longer than six months and must not exceed 18 months, commencing on the date of incorporation. The first accounting period begins with the date of incorporation, even if the company does not immediately commence trading. The second and subsequent accounting periods may be as short as the directors wish, but may not exceed 18 months.

A company can extend its accounting year only once in any five-year period unless it is being changed to be brought into line with that of its holding company or any subsidiary. The accounting period can be shortened as many times as required.

It is possible to change the length of any accounting period, even one that has ended, provided that the form is received by the registrar before the end of the period in which the accounts for that period must be filed. It is not possible to change the accounting period to a period for which the filing deadline has been reached.

If extending the accounting period, the directors must first check that the accounting year-end has not already been extended in the previous five years.

Appointment of directors – Forms AP01 or AP02

Following incorporation, additional individual or corporate directors may be appointed in accordance with the regulations laid down by the company's Articles of Association.

In the case of individuals, the new director should complete and sign Form AP01, giving details of full name, country/state of residence, nationality, date of birth, business occupation (if any), service address to go on the public record and residential address (which can be the same as the service address but if different will not be put on the public record). The option for a director to provide a service address rather than residential address for the public record is permitted under CA2006. Previously a director had to obtain a confidentiality order (granted by the secretary of state) in order to provide a service address for the public record.

The appointment of a corporate body as a director is made on Form AP02. The details are almost the same with the exception of date of birth, nationality etc.

Form AP01 or AP02 must be countersigned by an existing director or the company secretary and submitted to the Registrar of Companies within 14 days of the appointment.

Directors ceasing to hold office – Forms TM01 or TM02

A director may cease to hold office in a number of ways, including resignation, removal, death, by statute and under the provisions of the Articles of Association (see Chapter 3 for more details).

The company secretary or a director should complete Form TM01 or TM02 (depending on whether an individual or corporate director's appointment is being terminated), notifying the Registrar of Companies of the director's resignation or other reason for vacating office. The form must be submitted to the Registrar within 14 days of the date of vacation.

Registered office – Form AD01

The directors must authorise any change in the registered office address [***see precedent 10***] and, to be effective, notice must be given to Companies House on Form AD01.

Any change does not become effective until the form is received and accepted as valid by the Registrar of Companies. The company's headed stationery must show the new registered office address not later than 14 days after the date that the notice was submitted to the Registrar of Companies.

Documents delivered to the old address within 14 days of the date of change are validly served on the company.

Registration of charges – Forms MG01, MG01s (Scottish companies)

Particulars of every charge to which the Companies Act 2006 applies, created by a company registered in England and Wales, Scotland or Northern Ireland, should, within 21 days of its creation, be delivered for registration to Companies House on Form MG01 or MG01s for Scottish companies, together with any instrument creating or evidencing the charge.

Allotment of shares – Form SH01

Within one month of the date of allotment, a return of allotments (Form SH01) should be filed with the Registrar of Companies.

Additional Companies House requirements

Resolutions

A copy of the following resolutions must be filed with the Registrar of Companies within 15 days of approval (CA2006 s.29):

1 all special resolutions (CA2006 s.29);
2 resolutions or agreements which have been agreed to by all the members of a

company but which, if not so agreed to, would not have been effective for their purpose unless passed as special resolutions (CA2006 s.29);

3 resolutions or agreements which have been agreed to by all the members of some class of shareholders but which, if not so agreed to, would not have been effective for their purpose unless they had been passed by some particular majority or otherwise in some particular manner. All resolutions or agreements which effectively bind all the members of any class of shareholders though not agreed to by all those members (CA2006 s.29);
4 a resolution passed by the directors of a company in compliance with a direction under CA2006 s.64(3) (change of name on Secretary of State's direction);
5 a resolution of a company to give, vary, revoke or renew an authority to the directors for the purposes of CA2006 s.551 [***see precedents 37 and 45***];
6 a resolution conferring, varying, revoking or renewing authority under CA2006 s.701 (market purchase of company's own shares);
7 a resolution for voluntary winding up, passed under IA1986 ss.84(1)(a), (b) or (c);
8 a directors' resolution to amend the Articles of Association of the company to allow title to securities to be transferred through CREST (reg.16(6) of the Uncertificated Securities Regulations 1995, SI 1995/3272) [***see precedent 66***];
9 Forms IC01 and IC02 (notification of intention to carry on business or cease to carry on business as an investment company) (CA2006 s.833).

Name change

Once the resolution has been passed, a copy of the resolution, Form NM01–NM06, as appropriate, together with any justification for the proposed name, must be submitted to the Registrar within 15 days of the date of the meeting or effective date of the resolution in writing, as the case may be, together with the change of name fee (currently £10; same-day fee £50). The change of name is only effective upon the date of the certificate of incorporation upon change of name issued by the Registrar of Companies.

Company accounts

Companies must deliver a signed copy of their **annual accounts** to the Registrar for accounting years beginning on or after 6 April 2008 (CA2006 s.442) as follows:

- for private companies, within nine months of the year-end;
- for public companies, within six months of the year-end.

Listed companies must issue a preliminary announcement of their results within 120 days of the year-end (*LR 9.7.1)* and must publish their audited accounts as soon as possible after the year-end, but in any event not more than six months after the year-end (*LR 9.8.1*). A listed company must announce and publish its interim results within 90 days of the end of the period to which it relates (*LR 9.9.3*).

An AIM company must publish its annual accounts within six months of the end of the financial year and its interim accounts within three months of the end of the period to which it relates (*AIM rules 18 and 19*).

A PLUS quoted company must announce and publish its annual accounts and interim accounts within five months and three months respectively (*PLUS rules 31 and 30*).

Auditors

Resignation

A copy of the notice of the resignation incorporating the CA2006 s.519 statement must be sent to the Registrar of Companies within 14 days by the company (CA2006 s.517).

Removal or non-reappointment

When an ordinary resolution has been passed to remove or not reappoint an auditor, notice must be given to the Registrar of Companies within 14 days (CA2006 s.512).

Overseas companies with branch or place of business in the United Kingdom

The requirements for the publication of information by overseas companies with a branch or place of business in the UK are set out in Chapter 21.

Execution of documents

For companies incorporated in England and Wales or Northern Ireland, a document is executed by:

- the affixing of its common seal; or
- by signature:
  - by two authorised signatories; or
  - by a director in the presence of a witness who attests the signature.

An authorised signatory is any director of the company and for a private company that has a company secretary or a public company the company secretary or any joint secretary.

The above provisions do not apply to Scotland and Scottish companies. Detailed provisions with regard to the execution of documents by Scottish companies, which also need not have a common seal, are contained in CA2006 s.48.

These require that Scottish companies may sign or subscribe to documents in accordance with the provisions of the Requirements of Writing (Scotland) Act

1995 and, if so signed or subscribed, shall have effect as if given under seal or executed.

If a contract is entered into on behalf of a company by a person as agent for a company before the company has been formed, then, subject to any agreement to the contrary, the contract has effect as one entered into by the person purporting to act as agent for the company and he is personally liable on the contract (CA2006 s.51).

The company seal

A company need not have a common seal (CA2006 s.45(1)). Whether or not a company has a seal, however, the following provisions apply with regard to the execution of documents (CA2006 s.44).

It is usual for a common seal – if one exists – to be kept by the company secretary, who will maintain a record of all documents to which the seal has been affixed. In the case of infrequent use of the seal, specific reference to the document sealed may be made in the minutes of the board meeting authorising the sealing. [***See precedent* 83.**] If the seal is used frequently, it will be more convenient for the particulars of the documents sealed to be entered in a seal register and for this to be produced at each board meeting at which an appropriate confirmatory resolution will be passed.

It is common for modern forms of Articles of Association (e.g. Model Articles regs.49 (private), 81 (public) or Table A, reg.101) not to require the physical presence of the director and company secretary or a second director when the seal is affixed to a document. It is also common for large companies to pass a board resolution delegating authority for the use of the seal to various officers of the company. Other persons may be designated 'authorised signatories' to sign documents to which the seal has been affixed. An Article in the form of the Model Articles or Table A would include the necessary authority for the board to do this. If this procedure is followed, there is no need for the sealings to be confirmed by the directors at a board meeting, although a record of all documents sealed should be kept in a seal book.

Securities seal

A company which has a common seal may have a securities seal, which is a copy of the common seal with the addition on its face of the word 'Securities' and which can be used to seal certificates relating to the securities of the company (CA2006 s.50, public company Model Articles reg.47(2)(a)). This is particularly useful where the company has appointed an outside share registrar, the two principal benefits being that the company may keep the use of its common seal, if it has one, under its own control, and secondly that share certificates sealed with a security seal do not also require signature.

The provision allowing companies to have a securities seal came into force on 12 February 1979. Companies incorporated before that date may adopt and use a securities seal notwithstanding the contents of their Articles of Association or of any trust deed securing debenture stock specifying sealing in any other way. Moreover, any provisions in those documents requiring documents relating to the securities to be signed do not apply if the certificates are sealed with the securities seal (CPA1985 s.11).

Companies that intend to use a securities seal upon their share certificates must ensure that they also have a common seal even if they do not intend to use it, as the use of a securities seal is only permitted where the company has a common seal (CA2006 s.50).

Official seal for use abroad

Subject to appropriate authority in the Articles, a company with a common seal which transacts business abroad may have one or more official seals for use in overseas countries (CA2006 s.49). In order for such seals to be validly used, the company must appoint in writing under its common seal the person or persons in the territory concerned who will affix the official seal to documents in that country. [***See precedent 9.***] An official seal for use abroad is a copy of the common seal with the addition on its face of the name of the country in which it is to be used.

Instead of having a seal for use abroad, however, a company may grant a power of attorney to an individual in any place outside the United Kingdom to execute deeds on its behalf in that country. If the company has a common seal, the appointment of the attorney would be made by a document under seal (CA2006 s.47). Articles of Association (e.g. Model Articles reg.5 (private and public), Table A, reg.71) usually provide that the company's powers in this connection may be exercised by the directors.

Authentication of documents

Another duty of the company secretary (or a director or other authorised officer of the company) is to authenticate by signature any document or proceeding which is required to be authenticated by the company (CA2006 s.44). [***See precedent 30.***]

The company secretary is frequently asked to provide certified copies of documents, resolutions, minutes, etc., and will usually do so by signing the document together with the words 'Certified to be a true copy' and the date of signature.

Retention of documents

The company secretary is often responsible for exercising control over the company's policy regarding the filing and retention of documents. The period of time for which documents should be retained depends on the nature of the document. Appendix 7 contains a schedule giving both statutory and suggested retention periods for a large number of documents, including company records and share registration documents.

One area in which the company or its share registrars receive a substantial quantity of documents is in the field of share registration, e.g. instruments of transfer, dividend mandates and change of address notifications. Accordingly, many public companies adopt an Article specifying detailed retention periods for these types of documents.

Microfilming

A considerable amount of storage space can be saved if documents are put on microfilm or microfiche. It is necessary to ensure that the documents filmed are properly authenticated and certified in order to be admissible in evidence. With the advances in electronic storage of documents microfilm and microfiche are becoming less common methods of long-term storage.

Computer records

Information may be retained on a company's computer, but here the situation is more difficult because it is easier to alter records held on computer than a roll of microfilm which has authentication certificates at both the beginning and at the end of the roll. There is the further problem of computer malfunction and breakdowns. Clearly, it is possible to take some precautions to improve the likelihood of information retrieved from the computer being admissible as evidence; it should also be borne in mind that computer-based records will become more usual in future, microfilming now being regarded as somewhat out-of-date. Such precautions might include maintaining audit trails showing details of all changes made and retention of archive copies of the data to show that there have been no changes. Using the services of an external data/image capture company which certifies the accuracy of the data may also be possible.

Compliance and employees

Employment legislation

Directors are required to have regard to their employees' interests when exercising the powers of the company. This is a duty to the company and directors can be held accountable by the company for any breaches.

Broadly speaking, the following matters must be adhered to in connection with employment:

1 Employment contracts or written particulars of employment terms must be issued within two months of the commencement of employment and adhered to.
2 Employees must be paid at a rate not less than the minimum wage.
3 Employers with five or more employees must make a stakeholder pension, or equivalent, available for participation by all employees.

4 There must be systems established to ensure that there is no discrimination by the company or its employees on the grounds of disability, race or sexual orientation.
5 Employees' statutory rights must be observed, including their rights under a transfer of undertaking to a third party.
6 Employees are entitled and must be permitted to work.

It should be noted that if a company employs an illegal immigrant or overstayer, then under s.9 of the Asylum and Immigration Act 1996, the directors can also be found personally guilty of the offence as well (fine of up to £5,000) if it can be shown that the offence was committed with their consent, connivance or was caused by their neglect.

Further information on employment matters may be found on the Department for Business Innovation and Skill's website (see Directory).

Employer's liability insurance

If the company has employees, it must have employer's liability insurance in place, with a minimum cover of £5 million for each claim. It is a criminal offence not to have valid employer's liability insurance or to fail to display the certificate of insurance. Previous insurance certificates should be kept for 40 years. The only exception to this requirement is in circumstances where a company has a sole director who is also the only employee.

Disability discrimination

Directors of companies that provide services should take positive steps to ensure that those services are available to disabled people and prevent discrimination on the grounds of a person's disability (Disability Discrimination Act 2005). A person (including a director) who aids the unlawful discrimination of a disabled customer can face a civil action being brought against them for financial loss and injury to feelings, in addition to any action brought against the company itself. For example, a partially sighted customer of a bank would be entitled to receive statements with extra large print. If the Operations Director of the bank refused to make such statements available, then not only could the bank face action from the customer, but the Operations Director as well.

The Department for Work and Pensions is responsible for the Disability Discrimination Acts and further information may be obtained on the Acts from its website: http://www.dwp.gov.uk.

Health and safety

The Health and Safety Executive recommends that health and safety should be a board matter and recommends a health and safety director is appointed.

What health and safety law requires

The core legislation is the Health and Safety at Work, etc., Act 1974. This Act sets out the general duties which employers have towards employees and members of the public, and employees have to themselves and to each other. An overriding principle of health and safety legislation is 'so far as is reasonably practicable'. In other words, the degree of risk in a particular job or workplace needs to be balanced against the time, trouble, cost and physical difficulty of taking measures to avoid or reduce the risk.

Companies are required to undertake what good management and common sense would require. The Management of Health and Safety at Work Regulations 1999 make specific requirements for employers to manage health and safety under the Health and Safety at Work Act. Employers with five or more employees need to carry out a risk assessment and record the significant findings.

Besides carrying out a risk assessment, employers also need to:

- make arrangements for implementing the health and safety measures identified as necessary by the risk assessment;
- appoint competent people (often themselves or company colleagues) to help them to implement the arrangements;
- set up emergency procedures;
- provide clear information and training to employees; and
- work together with other employers sharing the same workplace.

Other regulations require action in response to particular hazards, or in industries where hazards are particularly high. A list of the main regulations that apply generally is set out below.

Further information on health and safety may be found on the Health and Safety Executive's website (see Directory).

European health and safety legislation

A lot of health and safety legislation has originated in Europe. Modern health and safety law is based on the principle of risk assessment. Where the Health and Safety Executive (HSE) wish to supplement existing arrangements, they have three alternative approaches:

1. guidance;
2. Approved Codes of Practice; and
3. regulations.

Guidance

The HSE publishes a range of guidance which can be specific to the health and safety problems of an industry or of a particular process used in a number of industries.

The main purposes of this guidance are:

- to help people to understand what the legislation says;
- to assist compliance with the regulations;
- technical advice.

Following guidance is not compulsory and employers are free to take other action. But if they do follow guidance they will normally be doing enough to comply with the law.

Approved Codes of Practice

Approved Codes of Practice offer practical examples of good practice on how to comply with the law. Approved Codes of Practice have a special legal status. If employers are prosecuted for a breach of health and safety law, and it is proved that they have not followed the relevant provisions of the Approved Code of Practice, a Court can find them at fault unless they can show that they have complied with the law in some other way.

Health and safety regulations

Regulations are law. These are usually made under the Health and Safety at Work Act, following proposals from HSE.

The Health and Safety at Work Act and general duties in the Management Regulations leave employers flexibility to decide how to control risks they identify. Guidance and Approved Codes of Practice give advice, but employers are free to take other measures provided they do what is reasonably practicable. Some regulations identify more serious risks and set out specific action that must be taken. Often these requirements are absolute.

Some regulations apply across all companies. These include the Manual Handling Regulations, which apply wherever things are moved manually, and the Display Screen Equipment Regulations, which apply wherever VDUs are used. Other regulations apply to hazards unique to specific industries.

As well as the Health and Safety at Work Act itself, the following regulations apply across the full range of workplaces:

1. Management of Health and Safety at Work Regulations 1999: require employers to carry out risk assessments, make arrangements to implement necessary measures, appoint competent people and arrange for appropriate information and training.
2. Workplace (Health, Safety and Welfare) Regulations 1992: cover a wide range of basic health, safety and welfare issues such as ventilation, heating, lighting, workstations, seating and welfare facilities.
3. Health and Safety (Display Screen Equipment) Regulations 1992: set out requirements for work with Visual Display Units (VDUs).
4. Personal Protective Equipment (PPE) Regulations 1992: require employers to provide appropriate protective clothing and equipment for their employees.

5 Provision and Use of Work Equipment Regulations (PUWER) 1998: require that equipment provided for use at work, including machinery, is safe.
6 Manual Handling Operations Regulations 1992: cover the moving of objects by hand or bodily force.
7 Health and Safety (First Aid) Regulations 1981: cover requirements for first aid.
8 The Health and Safety Information for Employees Regulations 1989: require employers to display a poster telling employees what they need to know about health and safety.
9 Employers' Liability (Compulsory Insurance) Regulations 1969: require employers to take out insurance against accidents and ill health to their employees.
10 Reporting of Injuries, Diseases and Dangerous Occurrences Regulations 1995 (RIDDOR): require employers to notify certain occupational injuries, diseases and dangerous events.
11 Control of Noise at Work Regulations 2005: require employers to take action to protect employees from hearing damage.
12 Electricity at Work Regulations 1989: require people in control of electrical systems to ensure they are safe to use and maintained in a safe condition.
13 Control of Substances Hazardous to Health Regulations 2002 (COSHH) require employers to assess the risks from hazardous substances and take appropriate precautions.
14 Control of Asbestos at Work Regulations 2002.
15 Regulatory Reform (Fire Safety) Order 2005.

Directors must ensure that practical provision is made for:

1 supply and maintenance of plant and work systems;
2 establishing systems for the use, handling, storage and transport of materials, substances and articles;
3 informing employees and others using or visiting the company's premises of all necessary instructions, training and supervision to ensure their health and safety at work;
4 maintenance of the workplace environment, including access, in a safe condition;
5 maintenance of a working environment which is safe and free from hazards and health risks.

Any company with five or more employees is required to prepare and review on a regular basis a written statement of its health and safety policy and a written statement of arrangements to facilitate evacuation in the event of fire, fire detection and fire fighting.

In establishing these written statements, formal risk assessments must be undertaken and recorded.

HSE has issued guidance for directors concerning their responsibilities. The guidance, in the form of a code, comprises five action points:

1 Boards of directors should accept joint responsibility and leadership for their organisation's health and safety performance.
2 Individual directors should recognise their liabilities and responsibilities under health, safety and welfare law.
3 Directors should ensure their decisions reflect their health and safety intentions.
4 Directors should recognise their role in engaging the active participation of their staff and improving workplace health and safety.
5 Directors should keep themselves alert to relevant health and safety risk management matters and one director should be appointed as health and safety director.

New arrangements for reporting accidents under the Reporting of Injuries, Diseases and Dangerous Occurrences Regulations 1995 (RIDDOR 1995) were introduced on 1 April 2001. These simplify the reporting procedures and offer a facility to report all cases to a single point: the Incident Contact Centre in Wales (see Directory).

Under RIDDOR 1995 companies are required to report:

- a death or major injury;
- an injury caused at work preventing an employee or self-employed person from working for over three days;
- a work-related disease;
- a dangerous occurrence.

The environment

The principal legislation governing a company's responsibilities in respect of the environment is contained in the Environmental Protection Act 1990 (EPA1990), the Environment Act 1995 and the Pollution Prevention and Control (England and Wales) Regulations 2000 although directors should be aware that there is a great deal of additional legislation relating to specific environmental considerations. The legislation provides that:

1 Companies proposing to operate certain specified procedures or in certain industries which carry inherent risks to the environment must obtain a licence to operate.
2 Regulation of the licences is through either the HM Inspectorate of Pollution or the Local Authority Environmental Health Officer.
3 Breaches of the regulations governing the licence to operate may result in the issue of enforcement notices to require immediate rectification or a prohibition notice requiring cessation of that operation until remedial action has been taken and approved.

4 Certain operations require an environmental risk assessment as part of the planning process.
5 Emissions must be monitored and limits adhered to. Additionally, companies must show that they are using the best practical environmental process in relation to that operation.
6 Adequate arrangements for the safe disposal of waste products must be made.

Although there is no statutory requirement for a company to establish an environmental policy, many regulators, investors and pressure groups are putting increasing pressure on companies to adopt and publish formal environmental policies.

Freedom of Information Act 2000

The Freedom of Information Act 2000 came into force in January 2005 and gives any person the legal right to ask for and be given any information which is held by a public authority. There is no direct impact on those working within the private sector but the provisions are relevant if they wish to obtain information from public bodies. Anyone is able to make a request for information held by public authorities, whether personal or non-personal. In general, public authorities have to respond to requests within 20 working days.

The Freedom of Information Act 2000 is the latest in a series of reforms relating to individual rights including the Human Rights Act 1998 and the Data Protection Act 1998. As part of the process, BIS has published an Information Asset Register which gives details of information or collections of information held electronically or in hard copy and which have not been published or made publicly available. The purpose of the register is to alert the public to the existence of unpublished information and whom to contact.

Trustee Act 2000

The Trustee Act 2000 came into force on 1 February 2001 and makes fundamental changes to the law of trusts and trustees. The main changes are:

1 All trustees have a duty to ensure that they manage and protect the assets that they hold in a diligent and prudent manner. It is now a statutory duty for trustees to exercise the care and skill that is reasonable in all circumstances. Furthermore, trustees with special areas of expertise will owe a higher duty of care in that regard than their fellow trustees. The statutory duty of care is also extended to advisers to trustees.
2 The investment powers in the Act broaden the restrictive powers of investment set out in the Trustee Investment Act 1961.
3 Trustees are obliged to seek proper advice before exercising their powers of investment unless they have reasonably concluded that it is neither appropriate nor necessary to do so.

4 Trustees may now delegate certain functions to an agent including management of the trust. The trustees have a duty to monitor their performance.
5 Trustees are now permitted to acquire freehold or leasehold land in the UK even if the trust deed does not confer such specific power upon them.

The Data Protection Act 1998

The Data Protection Act 1998 (DPA1998) came into force on 1 March 2000. This Act gave effect in the UK to EC Directive 95/46/EC and replaced the Data Protection Act 1984.

DPA 1998 extends the data protection regime to relevant filing systems for the manual handling of data. A relevant filing system is defined as:

> 'any set of information relating to individuals to the extent that, although the information is not processed by means of equipment operating automatically in response to instructions given for that purpose, the set is structured, either by reference to individuals or by reference to criteria relating to individuals, in such a way that specific information relating to a particular individual is readily accessible.'

The Information Commissioner has issued guidance on relevant filing systems as well as other definitions in DPA1998, available online (see Directory).

Anyone processing personal data must comply with the eight principles of data protection. These state that personal data must be:

- fairly and lawfully processed;
- processed for limited purposes;
- adequate, relevant and not excessive;
- accurate;
- not kept longer than necessary;
- processed in accordance with the data subject's rights;
- secure;
- not transferred to countries without adequate protection.

Personal data cover not only facts and opinions about an individual but also information regarding the intentions of the data controller towards that individual.

The Act introduces a new system of notification, which replaces the existing registration scheme. It is an offence to process personal data without notification unless an exemption applies to that data (DPA1998 s.17(1)). It is an offence not to notify the Commissioner of changes to the register entry within 28 days of the change being made (Data Protection (Notification and Notification Fees) Regulations 2000).

The Information Commissioner has published a number of guidance and other publications to assist companies to comply with their obligations as well as informing individuals of their rights. The publications are available on the Information Commission website (see Directory).

Trade descriptions, consumer credit and protection and competition

The Trade Descriptions Act 1968 and Part III of the Consumer Protection Act 1987 impose strict criminal liability for a false description of goods made in the course of a trade or business. The directors, as well as the company, may be personally liable for such an offence where it was committed with their knowledge or consent or was due to their negligence. It is therefore essential to ensure no breaches occur whether in advertising the goods, describing them or packaging them. Directors can also be personally liable in giving a false description or indication of the price of goods or services, if given with their consent, connivance or caused by their neglect.

The Consumer Credit Acts of 1974 and 2006 require companies to obtain a consumer credit licence if they offer goods or services on credit, or lend money to consumers. It is a criminal offence (punishable by imprisonment and/or a fine) to operate without a consumer credit licence, where one is required. Directors, therefore, must ensure that their companies comply with the requirements of the Acts.

The Competition Act 1998 prohibits uncompetitive practices, such as price-fixing, cartels and concerted practices. The Act has brought UK law into line with EU requirements. The Office of Fair Trading polices compliance with the Act and can make referrals to the Competition Commission. It should be noted that directors of companies can be made personally liable under the Act, if with their consent, connivance or caused by their neglect, the company does not co-operate with an investigation, or destroys or falsifies documents, or provides false or misleading information.

Further information for businesses on consumer protection, consumer credit and competing fairly may be found on the Office of Fair Trading's website (see Directory).

Taxation (tax, VAT, NIC and PAYE)

Directors are responsible for ensuring the calculation of taxes due and payable by the company (and in the case of NIC and PAYE, for its employees as well), the filing of returns, making payments to HM Revenue & Customs and the maintenance and retention of tax records. Normally, these tasks would be delegated to a competent person, but this delegation would not relieve the directors of their ultimate responsibility for tax matters.

Further information on taxation may be found on HM Revenue & Customs' website (see Directory).

Money laundering

The Money Laundering Regulations 2007 came into force on 15 December 2007. The regulations require various steps to be taken by credit and financial institutions, auditors, insolvency practitioners, external accountants, tax advisers, legal providers, trust and company service providers, estate agents, high value dealers and casinos to detect and prevent money laundering and terrorist financing. If a company commits an offence under the Regulations, then any officer (including a director) is also personally liable for prosecution alongside the company for any offences committed with their consent or connivance or resulting from their negligence.

Further information on money laundering may be found on the Joint Money Laundering Steering Group's website (see Directory).

15

Flotation, listing and admission to trading

Introduction

Where a company requires significant additional, long-term funding there are four main alternatives available:

- long-term loans from a bank; and/or
- additional funding from existing members; and/or
- funding from a venture capital provider; and /or
- additional funding from new shareholders.

Although one of the duties of company directors is to manage the affairs of a company limited by shares for the benefit of its members they have no obligation to make provision for members to be able to sell their shares.

However, if a company intends to raise additional funding from the public and/or institutional investors, this process will be more likely to succeed if the investors have an 'exit' so that there is a reasonable expectation that the prospective investors will be able to realise their investment at a future date.

This exit can be provided if the company buys back its shares, if it goes into liquidation or if it is sold to another company. However, these routes are not suitable for the majority of public companies, since they would not enable shares to be traded on a regular basis, allowing original investors to realise their investment or new investors to buy shares in the company at a time or times of their own choosing.

For many public companies, therefore, an appropriate exit route is provided by having the shares officially listed and admitted to trading on either the Main Market, operated by the London Stock Exchange plc, or PLUS listed, operated by PLUS Markets Group plc; both of these are Recognised Investment Exchanges (RIE), the highest level of recognition under FSMA2000. As an alternative to listing, companies can have their shares admitted to trading on either AIM or PLUS quoted, which are Exchange Regulated Markets (ERM) operated by the London Stock Exchange plc and Plus Markets Group plc respectively; these have lower levels of regulation than either the Main Market or PLUS listed and are comparatively cheaper to join. For smaller companies requiring an ability for members to buy and sell shares but no need for fundraising, there are other opportunities for trading shares on trading platforms that are neither RIEs or ERMs, such as ShareMark. The process of having shares admitted to trading whether via a listing or otherwise is referred to as having the shares floated.

This chapter looks at the role of the UK Listing Authority (UKLA), the regulatory environment, including the *Listing Rules*, and the process by which companies may be listed and admitted to either the Main Market or PLUS listed or have their shares traded on AIM, PLUS quoted or ShareMark.

There are, of course, both advantages and disadvantages of having a company's shares admitted to a public market, and the directors and existing members need to consider these carefully before embarking on the process to join one of the markets.

Advantages	Disadvantages
Access to the funding	Share price influenced by market conditions over which the company has no control
Providing a market for trading in the shares	Loss of control for existing management
Enables employee participation in ownership via employee share schemes	Continuing obligations and disclosure regimes require significant management time, policing and controls
Ability to acquire other businesses for paper (shares) rather than needing cash	Directors will lose autonomy and become accountable to external investors
Improved perception of financial strength and stability	Professional fees will increase as professional advisers, PR companies, share registrars etc will be required
Corporate governance regimes required of traded companies tend to improve management systems and controls	Increase in director's responsibilities
Raising the profile of the company	

Listing and the UKLA

Prior to May 2000, the London Stock Exchange was the 'competent authority' and exercised its powers under three EU directives regulating the admission of securities to official listing in the UK. Responsibility for these functions, exercised by the LSE under the guise of the UK Listing Authority, was transferred to the Financial Services Authority (FSA) by an order made under the Financial Services Act 1986.

As the competent authority, the UK Listing Authority establishes the listing rules for admission of securities to listing, the continuing obligations of the issuers of those securities and the enforcement of those continuing obligations.

Following the transfer, applications for admission to listing (i.e. for securities to be admitted to the Official List) must be made to the UK Listing Authority, and a separate application must be made to either the London Stock Exchange plc or PLUS Markets Group plc for those securities to be admitted to trading on either the Main Market or PLUS Listed. The procedures for seeking a listing are set out in the listing rules.

These rules and the codes are not technically 'law'. The sanction for their breach is disciplinary action against the company and, ultimately, removal from the Official List so that the company's share price is no longer quoted on an exchange. Following implementation of the Financial Services and Markets Act 2000 (FSMA2000), breaches of the listing rules are now brought within the scope of civil prosecution and the FSA has power to impose unlimited fines on companies, directors or other individuals breaching the rules.

The UK Listing Rules

To be listed on the Official List the company must comply with *Listing Rules* established by the UK Listing Authority and amended from time to time. The *Listing Rules* contain the requirements and procedures for obtaining a listing, the continuing obligations of the company and its officers once the company is admitted to listing and the circumstances giving rise to the suspension and termination of listing.

Objectives and principles

In applying the *Listing Rules*, the UK Listing Authority will have regard to the following objectives and principles:

1. To seek a balance between providing issuers with ready access to the market for their securities and protecting investors.
2. To promote investor confidence in standards of disclosure, in the conduct of listed companies' affairs and in the market as a whole.
3. Securities should be brought to the market in a way that is appropriate to their nature and number and which will facilitate an open and efficient market for trading in those securities.
4. An issuer must make full and timely disclosure about itself and its listed securities, at the time of listing and subsequently.
5. Holders of equity securities should be given adequate opportunity to consider in advance and vote upon major changes in the company's business operations and matters of importance concerning the company's management and constitution.

Recognised Investment Exchanges

Only Recognised Investment Exchanges (RIEs) may lawfully operate in Great Britain. To become an RIE, an investment exchange with its head office in the UK must apply to the FSA. An overseas investment exchange (i.e. an exchange with its head office outside the UK) must apply to the Treasury. There are two RIEs operating in Great Britain. The Main Market is operated by the London Stock Exchange plc which until July 2007 had a monopoly on trading listed shares. Since July 2007 listed shares may be admitted to trading on the PLUS listed market operated by PLUS Markets Group plc.

The regulatory regime

Offers of fully 'listed' securities are governed by FSMA2000 and the *Listing Rules*. These rules and regulations apply to securities that are listed or are the subject of an application for listing or are being offered for sale conditional on their being admitted to listing. Trading on the Stock Exchange is subject to the Stock Exchange Rules, whilst trading on PLUS listed is subject to the PLUS Rules. Members of the Exchanges must also comply with the rules of the self-regulatory organisation to which they belong.

The regime is supervised by the FSA, to which most of the powers of the Secretary of State under the FSMA2000 have been transferred. The main feature of this regime is that, subject to certain exceptions, only authorised or exempt persons may carry on a regulated activity (FSMA2000 s.19).

Regulated activity

Regulated activities are defined in FSMA2000 ss.21 and 22 and Sch.2. In particular it must be noted that financial promotion and investment activity includes giving any form of investment promotion and advice and investment management, as well as undertaking securities transactions as broker-dealer and/or principal within the United Kingdom.

Authorised persons

The status of being an authorised or exempt person is conferred on application to the FSA by an individual or firm. Members of professional bodies such as solicitors and accountants may be authorised by their relevant professional body (FSMA2000, Part XX, ss.325–333).

Unauthorised business

A person carrying on a regulated activity who is not authorised or not exempted commits an offence (FSMA2000 s.20). Agreements made in respect of the regulated activity may be unenforceable by the unauthorised person (FSMA2000 ss.26, 27 and 28) and they may be restrained by injunction or be made subject to a restitution order.

The London Stock Exchange

The London Stock Exchange was for many years the only RIE headquartered in Great Britain.
The Exchange enables companies from global giants to smaller enterprises around the world to raise the capital they need to grow, with a choice of four primary markets:

1. Main Market – regarded by many investors and companies as the world's most prestigious listing and trading environment.
2. AIM – equities market for smaller growing companies.
3. Professional Securities Market – for listed debt and depository receipt securities.
4. Specialist Fund Market – dedicated to specialised investment entities.

The London Stock Exchange provides two forms of market:

1. the primary market gives companies wishing to raise working capital access to investors, who provide working capital in the knowledge that there is also
2. a secondary market enabling investors to trade securities with other investors.

PLUS Markets

PLUS Markets Group plc operates two markets:

1. a primary market for listed securities on listed, on PLUS listed and unlisted securities admitted to trading on PLUS quoted;
2. a secondary market, PLUS traded for trading both listed securities not admitted to trading on PLUS listed and AIM quoted securities.

Types of public issue

There are several methods by which securities may be floated including:

1. *Offers for sale or subscription*. The company issues a prospectus in the form of listing particulars inviting application for its shares from investors. An offer for subscription is in the form of new securities issued directly by the company to the applicants. An offer for sale relates to new or existing securities, which are first acquired by an issuing house, which then offers the securities for sale to the public by issuing listing particulars and inviting applications.
2. *Placings*. As in an offer for sale, securities are subscribed or purchased by the sponsoring firm of stockbrokers or issuing house, but these are then 'placed' with investment clients, a proportion also being sold through the market.
3. *Intermediaries offers*. An intermediaries offer is a marketing of new securities to 'intermediaries' for them to allocate to their own clients, principally private client investors.

4 *Vendor consideration issues.* A company which acquires a business or other assets may issue securities to the vendor instead of, or in addition to, cash.
5 *Introductions.* This is where existing securities are listed for the first time.
6 *Rights issues.* This is where a company offers new shares to its existing shareholders in proportion to the number of shares they already hold. The rights issue may be underwritten so that the company is assured of raising the full amount of the working capital it requires. The right to the new shares can itself be traded.
7 *Open offers.* Essentially this is the same as a rights issue; however, the benefit of the right is not permitted to be traded.
8 *Capitalisation (or bonus) issues.* The directors of a company may arrange for fully paid shares of the same class to be allotted free of charge to existing holders in proportion to their holdings, following the capitalisation of the company's existing reserves. This is usually undertaken where the company's share price has risen to a level that is reducing the liquidity of the shares. The share price will fall approximately in line with ratio of new shares issued.
9 *Exchanges and conversions.* New securities may be listed as the result of existing securities being exchanged for, or converted into, new securities.
10 *Exercise of options or warrants.* Securities may carry rights for the holder to subscribe cash for further securities, which are issued when the rights are exercised.
11 *Other issues.* Securities issued in circumstances other than those described above may be listed, provided the relevant conditions are fulfilled. Shares issued under employees' share schemes are a common example.

Eligibility for listing

There are a number of conditions that must be met before the UKLA will consider an application for listing, the principal ones being:

1 The applicant must be an incorporated entity and operating in accordance with its constitution (the Articles of Association for a UK company) (*LR 2.2.1*).
2 The securities (shares, debt instruments etc.) to be listed must be consistent with the law of the applicant incorporation, and be duly established and authorised by the applicant's constitution *(LR 2.2.2)*.
3 To be listed, the securities must also be admitted to trading on an RIE market (Main Market or PLUS listed) *(LR 2.2.3)*.
4 Securities must be fully paid and freely transferable (*LR 2.2.4*). The exception to transferability is that transfer may be restricted in accordance with CA2006 s.793 where a request for information on the identity of the beneficial owner of shares has not been complied with.
5 For shares, the expected market value of the entire class must be at least £700,000 (*LR 2.2.7*).

6 The application for listing must be in respect of the entire class or additional shares of an existing listed class (*LR 2.2.9*).
7 A prospectus complying with the prospectus rules must be approved (by the FSA for UK companies) and published (*LR 2.2.10*).
8 If applicable, listing particulars must be approved (by the FSA) and published (*LR 2.2.11 and LR 4*).

The listing process

The minimum time between submission of an application for listing, approval and admission to trading on a market is 20 working days. However, in practice the period is usually between 12 and 24 weeks and for many companies the process will have started up to two years prior to admission as it may be necessary to undertake preliminary stages first, including choosing advisers, appointing non-executive directors, establishing appropriate management and corporate governance structures, making changes to the executive board and establishing the correct valuation for the company.

It should be noted that although documents are submitted to the FSA for approval, this approval is only formally given on the last day at the same time as the shares are admitted to trading on a market, as both admission and listing are conditional on each other.

Once the decision to seek a listing has been taken it is usual to convene a meeting at which the various advisers are present to set out the general structure of the application process. This meeting would decide the amount of any working capital required, an approximate issue price, the structure of the issue, advisers' fees, abort costs and commissions payable on applications, the timing of the listing and other general matters.

It is likely that some 'housekeeping' will be required prior to the listing, including appointment of non-executive directors, adoption of new Articles, adoption of employee share option scheme(s) and undertaking a bonus issue or share split to increase the number of shares in issue. If the company has only a few shareholders, it may also be necessary, either before or at the time of the listing, for these original shareholders to dispose of part of their holdings to ensure that there are at least 25 per cent of the issued shares available for trading (*LR 6.1.19*). The following appointments will be required before the listing application is made:

- sponsor and financial adviser;
- brokers to the issue;
- solicitors;
- reporting accountants;
- CREST eligible share registrar (and receiving agent if there is to be a share offer).

Some companies may also need to appoint experts to produce expert technical reports on aspects of the company's trade or proposed trade.

The London Stock Exchange and PLUS normally expect new applicants and their advisers to attend a meeting with them prior to submission of the final application for trading and not later than the time when they first contact the UK Listing Authority regarding their application for admission to the Official List. The meeting is used to discuss matters such as the admission process (including timing) and the issuer's plans to develop the market in its securities after admission.

Drafting the listing particulars

The listing particulars will contain the information by which the investors will judge the issue. The solicitors and/or sponsors will prepare the first draft of the listing particulars, which must comply with the *Listing Rules*. The listing particulars will undergo several drafts and finally detailed verification so that all parties are satisfied that the information is complete, accurate, complies with the *Listing Rules* and gives a complete and accurate report of the company, its history and its future plans. The requirements for the listing application are set out in *LR 3, 4 and 6.*

Professional advisers

It will be necessary to appoint additional advisers including the following parties.

The sponsor to the issue

The sponsor's main duties in the issue are as follows:

1 To obtain approval from the UK Listing Authority for the listing particulars and other documents, which the broker will submit on the company's behalf to the UK Listing Authority in draft and, later, in final form.
2 To apply to the UK Listing Authority for admission to the Official List and to the London Stock Exchange or PLUS for admission to trading, and to ensure the CREST securities application form is submitted (the CREST securities application form is most often submitted by the company's share registrars rather than the broker) and (where a new line of stock is involved) a CREST enablement letter which must be set on the company's headed paper but which will be submitted by the broker or share registrar.
3 To advise on the timing and pricing of the issue.
4 To place a proportion of the sub-underwriting with his clients.
5 To advise on the company's continuing regulatory obligations.

Corporate broker

The broker acts as link between the company and potential investors and following admission to the market in general. Most brokers retain analysts who will issue research notes on companies and it is important to select a broker with appropriate expertise in your company's sector.

Many firms can act as both sponsor and broker and this may be appropriate. However, one firm acting in both capacities can cause difficulties where the sponsoring arm has information which if passed to the broking arm would put them in the position of not being able to trade the company's shares as they would be in possession of price-sensitive information which would give them an unfair advantage when trading shares.

The broker will also actively market the shares to secure the success of the issue. This process is often referred to as book building. During the book building phase non-binding commitments to invest are obtained for an aggregate amount of money as until the last day or so of any offer the actual share price will not be known.

If there is to be a share offer the brokers may well underwrite the offer which means that they will purchase any shares that have not been sold to investors by the closing date. This has obvious advantages for the company as it is guaranteed to raise the funds it requires; the disadvantage is the underwriting fees can be expensive, particularly if the offer is fully subscribed without recourse to the underwriter.

Reporting accountant

Although a separate and distinct function from that of the company auditor, the reporting accountant is often the company auditor, albeit staffed from the corporate finance department rather than the audit department. The reporting accountant's role is to review the company's financial history, accounting systems and internal controls and prepare a report for the benefit of potential investors.

Depending on the nature of the transaction there are three forms of report that might be required.

A long form report is a detailed analysis of past financial performance and management structures, strengths and weaknesses. The long form report is not published but is provided to both directors and the sponsor, and is used to draft the prospectus.

The short form report, as the name implies, is an edited version of the long form report and is reproduced in the prospectus.

The last report that is usually prepared where additional funds are being raised is a working capital report for the sponsor, covering the period 12–24 months following admission. This is to provide comfort to the sponsor that the company will have sufficient working capital for the period covered by the report, assuming any funds to be raised are actually raised. Additionally, although it is preferable to raise slightly more funds than are required, raising surplus capital has a detrimental effect on share price.

Lawyers

Typically there will be two firms appointed: the first advising the company and the second advising the sponsor. The company's lawyers will often lead the process of drafting documents in conjunction with the sponsor and with all other interested parties commenting on those drafts.

The company lawyers will also undertake verification of the documents. This is the process under which factual statements within the documents are verified to prove that they are based on fact. Verification is a painstaking task dreaded by all involved requiring companies to search their archives for old documents, agreements, research notes etc.

PR consultants

Although some companies will already retain a firm of advertising and marketing consultants it is often advisable to retain a firm of specialist financial PR consultants. Financial PR consultants play a crucial role in raising and maintaining a company profile during the book building and fundraising phases leading up to a flotation and after flotation, and maintaining awareness of the company to maintain liquidity once the initial flurry of activity associated with the float has subsided. Financial PR consultants will also ensure, in conjunction with the company lawyers, that statements issued by the company comply with FSMA2000 and UKLA disclosure requirements.

Share registrars

Whether the shares are to be listed and traded on the Main Market or PLUS listed or admitted to trading on AIM or PLUS quoted markets the company will need to retain the services of a CREST compliant share registrar to maintain the share register. CREST compliance is required in order to facilitate electronic share trading and settlement via CREST. Under this system a company's share register is split between the electronic sub-register maintained by CREST and the certificated register maintained by the share registrar. The share registrar will update the full register by a real time link to CREST to ensure that at any particular time they have an accurate and current record of the ownership of the company's shares.

Other advisers

Additional advisers that may be required include surveyors to value properties and other material assets, security printers for the secure and rapid turnaround of the documents, insurance brokers, trade mark and patent attorneys.

Company approval

On the penultimate day, a completion board meeting is held to approve all the documentation (including verification notes), the procedures for listing and any share issue being undertaken. If the issue is being underwritten the underwriting agreement(s) is usually signed at this late stage. The listing particulars are then submitted to the UKLA and application for admission to trading made to the London Stock Exchange or PLUS as appropriate.

Listing timetable

Although each listing is slightly different a typical timetable will be:

Period before admission	Objective
12–24 weeks prior to admission	Appoint advisers Timetable agreed
6–12 weeks prior to admission	Assess problem areas Draft prospectus and other documents Initial pricing review Draft documents submitted to UKLA Initial meeting with LSE/PLUS Draft PR presentations Presentations to analysts
1–6 weeks prior to admission	Due diligence and verification starts PR meetings and roadshow for potential investors Formally submit and agree documents with UKLA (does not constitute approval) Print pathfinder if required
1 week prior to admission	All documents agreed by UKLA Share price agreed Prospectus registered Subscription and underwriting agreements signed
48 hours prior to admission	'48 hour' documents submitted to UKLA Formal applications for listing and admission UKLA and exchange fees paid
Admission date	Shares listed and admitted to trading New shares issued Trading commences

Prospectus Rules

The Prospectus Rules derive from European legislation and implemented the Prospectus Directive on 1 July 2005. The Prospectus Regulations 2005 (SI 2005/1433) require the FSA to draw up rules for the contents, approval and publication of prospectuses.

The FSA's detailed rules came into force on 1 July 2005 and are contained in the Prospectus Rules section of the FSA Handbook. The rules cover the format and detailed content of a prospectus, the period during which a prospectus remains valid and the manner in which a prospectus must be published. They reiterate the general rule that a person may not make an offer of securities to the public, or seek admission to trading on a regulated market, unless a prospectus has been prepared, approved by the UKLA and published. Subject to certain qualifying criteria, a prospectus of a company incorporated in another EU state and approved by the competent authority of that state may be acceptable for circulation in the UK without additional consent. Certain types of offers or specialist securities are exempt from the general rule to prepare a prospectus.

The Prospectus Rules stipulate the criteria by which the FSA will consider a prospectus and, where appropriate, allow the FSA to authorise the omission of information which a prospectus would otherwise have to contain.

What is an offer to the public?

Broadly speaking any offer that is not restricted to a defined, small selection, of potential investors will be a public offer. The definition is very broad and can include offers by private companies. Under the Prospectus Rules there is an offer to the public if there is a communication to any person that presents sufficient information on:

- the transferable securities to be offered; and
- the terms on which they are offered to enable an investor to decide to buy or subscribe for the securities in question.

The communication may be in any form and by any means and includes placing through financial intermediaries.

Exemptions

The key exemptions from the requirement to publish a prospectus under the new regime are:

1. offers addressed to fewer than 100 people (other than qualified investors) in any 12-month period per EEA state;
2. offers to 'qualified investors' i.e. broadly, institutions as at present and companies which are not SMEs; there is to be a self-certification procedure whereby SMEs and certain others can register as qualified investors as well based on certain conditions;
3. offers to persons outside the UK (although local laws would then apply);
4. offers where the total consideration for securities in any period of 12 months is under €2.5 million.

Prospectus approval

If a prospectus is required, the prospectus must be drawn up in accordance with the prospectus rules and submitted to the FSA for approval together with the appropriate fee. The FSA has ten working days to approve the document if the company's shares are already admitted to the Main Market or PLUS listed. If the shares are not listed the FSA are permitted 20 days in which to approve or reject the prospectus.

The prospectus rules include detailed requirements for the contents of a prospectus including:

1 a declaration by those responsible for the prospectus that they have taken all reasonable care to ensure the information to the best of their knowledge is in accordance with the facts and contains no omission likely to affect its import;
2 information about the issuer;
3 financial information;
4 information regarding the investment objective, policy and restrictions;
5 information regarding managers, advisers, other service providers;
6 organisational structure and management details; and
7 risk factors.

Disclosure and Transparency Rules

On 22 December 2006, the FSA published the Transparency Obligations Directive (Disclosure and Transparency Rules) Instrument 2006 (FSA 2006/70) containing the final rules which implement certain provisions of the EU Transparency Directive (2004/109/EC) (the 'Transparency Directive'). The new rules introduce three new chapters into the Disclosure Rules sourcebook, which will be renamed the Disclosure Rules and Transparency Rules sourcebook ('DTR'). The new chapters include DTR 4 ('Periodic financial reporting'), DTR 5 ('Vote holder and issuer notification rules') and DTR 6 ('Continuing obligations and access to information').

Periodic financial reporting

The periodic financial reporting requirements set out in DTR 4 only apply to issuers with shares admitted to trading on a regulated market (i.e. the Main Market or PLUS listed).

Annual Financial Report

The Annual Financial Report must include:

- audited financial statements prepared in accordance with the applicable accounting standards;
- a management report; and
- a statement of assurance from those persons responsible within the issuer (usually the directors).

The annual report and accounts are deemed to be regulated information and accordingly they must be published in the same way as all other regulated information and must be available to the public in all EEA states.

Preliminary Statement of Annual Results ('prelims')

Prelims are optional. Companies that choose to publish prelims must comply with the existing content requirement:

- being published in full text;
- agreed by auditors; and
- if the audit report is likely to be modified, details of the nature of the modification.

Companies that do not to produce prelims are still required to publish inside information as soon as possible in accordance with their obligations under the Market Abuse Directive.

Half-yearly report ('interims')

The half-yearly report must include:

- condensed financial statements;
- interim management report;
- a statement of assurance from those persons responsible within the issuer (usually the directors); and
- if the report has been audited or reviewed by an auditor, a copy of their report.

Interim Management Statements

Issuers must release an Interim Management Statement ('IMS') part-way through each half year, unless it reports quarterly. In the statement issuers should explain the material events and transactions since the start of the relevant period and the issuer's financial position and performance.

The Model Code

The deadlines for producing periodic financial information have required changes to the definition of 'close period' within the Model Code:

1. the close period prior to publishing an annual report will be 60 days before publication or, if shorter, the period from the end of the financial year up to and including publication;
2. the close period prior to publishing a half-yearly report will be from the end of the relevant six-month period until publication; and
3. there will be no close period prior to publishing an IMS. Companies are required to use their discretion as to whether there is any price sensitive information contained within the IMS when making trading decisions.

Major shareholding notification

The major shareholding notification requirements are set out in DTR 5 and apply to issuers with shares admitted to trading on a regulated market (the Main Market or PLUS listed) or an Exchange Regulated Market (such as AIM or PLUS quoted).

1 Disclosure under DTR 5 is required where a person controls the exercise of voting rights rather than where a person acquires an interest in shares. The previous requirements were extended to include those persons who are indirect holders of shares and are entitled to acquire, dispose of or exercise the voting rights in specified cases (for example, where the chairman of a meeting holds discretionary proxies representing more than 3 per cent of the voting rights).
2 The previous 3 per cent and subsequent 1 per cent thresholds for disclosure have been retained. However, the threshold for disclosure of non-material interests has been reduced to 5 per cent (previously 10 per cent).
3 The notification deadline of two business days continues to apply where the shares are held in a UK issuer. For non-UK issuers this has been increased to four business days.
4 Notifications need to be made on the prescribed form available on the FSA website. Shareholders will also need to file a copy electronically (also available on the FSA website).
5 Listed companies must notify via a RIS any notifications which they have received by the end of the following trading day. For other issuers, the deadline is the end of the third business day.
6 Companies are required to keep the market informed of changes in their share capital at the end of every month, as well as transactions in their own shares, within four trading days after the transaction has completed. These requirements are to ensure that shareholders are able to calculate their relative holdings and are therefore better able to meet their own disclosure obligations.
7 While it will no longer be an offence for a shareholder to fail to disclose an interest, if a person breaches the DTR the FSA is able to take enforcement action.

Dissemination of regulated information

DTR 6 only applies to issuers with shares admitted to trading on the Main Market or PLUS listed.

- The requirements of DTR 6 should be applied in a way that is consistent with those of the CA2006. Where a company has already received authority from a shareholder to receiving electronic communications prior to 20 January 2007, companies will be able to rely on such agreements.
- The use of electronic communication must not depend on the location of the shareholder. This means that companies will not be able to use electronic communication for any restricted mailing, e.g. to the US.

The Stock Exchange as a secondary market

Dealings on the London Stock Exchange are conducted in accordance with the rules, regulations and usages of the London Stock Exchange and the conduct of business rules of the Securities and Investments Board (or an SRO, as appropriate), as required by the FSA.

Trading systems

The Stock Exchange operates various trading services to enable trading in constituent company shares.

1 *SEAQ* – the Stock Exchange Automated Quotation system for the trading of SEAQ securities. These are domestic equity securities for which a minimum of two market-makers display two-way prices.
2 *SEAQ International* – the Stock Exchange Automated Quotation system for international equity securities.
3 *SEATS PLUS* – the Stock Exchange Alternative Trading Service for the trading of the SEATS securities (domestic equity securities which are not SEAQ securities) and AIM securities.
4 *SETS* (or the 'Order book') – the Stock Exchange Electronic Trading Service for trading the most liquid domestic equity securities. SETS allows all member firms to enter buy and sell orders, either on their own behalf or for their clients. These orders are automatically matched against corresponding orders from other firms. Any unmatched orders are retained on the order book for future execution, or returned (in full or in part) to the originating member firm.

PLUS as a secondary market

In additional to listed shares admitted to its own market PLUS offers an alternative market for shares listed on the Main Market or traded on AIM as well as European stocks.

The PLUS trading platform was developed in 2005 to offer trading in listed and unlisted UK equity securities. It is a quote-driven trading system, supported by competing market-makers.

The quote-driven system is favoured by many retail brokers as it can facilitate immediate execution and lead to less volatility in share prices. Competing market-makers offer consistent and improved two-way prices in increased sizes for smaller companies, which are typically less liquid, ensuring that there is always the ability to deal in any smaller company share.

Continuing obligations

Listed companies are subject to further regulation and must comply with the continuing obligations contained in the *Listing Rules*, Chapter 9. Additional continuing obligations are set out in Chapters 10–13 of the *Listing Rules*. These continuing obligations are considered necessary to ensure the maintenance of an orderly market in securities and providing all users of the market with access to the same information at the same time.

These continuing obligations are considered in Chapter 16.

London Stock Exchange Admission and Disclosure Standards

A company whose securities are admitted to trading on the London Stock Exchange's main market must also comply with the continuing obligations contained in the Exchange's Admission and Disclosure Standards. For the moment, these replicate the general disclosure obligations contained in Chapter 9 of the *Listing Rules*. Accordingly, compliance with the *Listing Rules* should also ensure compliance with the London Stock Exchange Standards. The Exchange has adopted these Standards to enable it to enforce its market supervision function. The Company Services team at the Exchange processes applications for admission to trading and deals with all other aspects of the Exchange's relationship with companies. The team does not review draft prospectuses, listing particulars or any other circulars. These reviews are carried out by the UK Listing Authority.

Conditions

1 An application for admission to trading of any class of securities must:
   - relate to all securities of that class, issued or proposed to be issued; or
   - relate to further securities of a class that is already admitted, issued or proposed to be issued.
2 The company must be in compliance with the requirements of:
   - any securities regulator by which it is regulated; and/or
   - any stock exchange on which it has securities admitted to trading.
3 In the case of transferable securities, all such securities must be freely negotiable.
4 Securities that are admitted to trading by the Exchange must be capable of being traded in a fair, orderly and efficient manner.
5 The Exchange may refuse an application for the admission if it considers that:
   - the applicant's situation is such that admission of the securities may be detrimental to the orderly operation or integrity of its markets; or
   - the applicant does not or will not comply with the standards or with any special condition imposed by the Exchange.
6 Companies must confirm that they meet the criteria and requirements of the market to which they are applying.

Settlement

To be admitted to trading, securities must be eligible for electronic settlement.

Communication

Companies must provide details of a contact within their organisation who will be responsible for communications between the Exchange and the company. A company may wish to use a nominated representative.

Admission process

1 Companies proposing to admit securities must agree the timetable for the admission to trading of those securities in advance.
2 The company must contact the Exchange no later than ten business days before the application is to be considered.

Provisional application

To ensure the Exchange can properly consider any application for admission to trading, the company must submit the Form 1 to the Exchange's Issuer Implementation team by no later than 12:00 at least ten business days prior to the day on which the issuer is requesting that the Exchange consider the application for admission to trading.

The submission of Form 1 shall be provisional. Formal application will only be deemed to be made when a prospectus relating to the securities to be admitted to trading has been approved.

When further issues of securities are allotted of the same class as securities already admitted, companies must assess whether a prospectus or listing particulars is required. Application for admission of such further securities must be made at the same time as the application for listing, but no later than 48 hours before the application is to be considered.

Documents

Before admission

Except as agreed by the Exchange, the following documents must be submitted by no later than 12:00 at least two business days prior to the day on which the issuer is requesting that the Exchange consider the application for admission to trading:

1 an application for admission to trading on the finalised Form 1 issued by the Exchange signed by a duly authorised officer of the issuer;
2 and an electronic copy of any prospectus;
3 listing particulars, passport, circular, announcement or other document relating to the issue, together with copies of any notice of meeting referred to in such documents; and
4 written confirmation of the number of securities to be allotted or issued pursuant to the board resolution should be provided and must be received by the Exchange no later than 7.30 am on the day that admission is expected to become effective.

After admission

Where relevant, a statement of the number of securities which were, in fact, issued and, where different from the number which were the subject of the application, the aggregate number of securities of that class in issue must be lodged with the Exchange (marked for the attention of Issuer Implementation) as soon as it becomes available.

PLUS listed market admission and disclosure standards

A company whose securities are admitted to trading on a PLUS listed market must also comply with the continuing obligations contained in the PLUS market's admission and disclosure standards. As with the admission and disclosure standards of the London Stock Exchange, these replicate the general disclosure obligations contained in Chapter 9 of the *Listing Rules*. Accordingly, compliance with the *Listing Rules* should also ensure compliance with the PLUS listed market standards.

Eligibility criteria

1. An application for the admission of securities must:
   - relate to securities which are listed or for which an application for listing has been made; and
   - cover all securities, whether issued or proposed to be issued, of the class to which they belong.
2. The company must be in compliance with the law of its place of incorporation and the requirements of any regulatory authority to which it is subject.
3. The securities to which the application relates must be freely transferable and eligible for electronic settlement within a relevant system or other system approved by PLUS allowing for the expeditious settlement of transactions.
4. The applicant must make arrangements with a regulatory information service for the dissemination of regulatory announcements.
5. An applicant must submit the prescribed application fee.

Prospectus requirement

The PLUS listed market is a regulated market. Consequently, the admission of securities requires the publication of an approved prospectus unless the applicant is exempt from such requirement under an applicable provision of FSMA.

An applicant which has produced an approved prospectus within a 12-month period preceding the expected date of admission or whose securities have been admitted to trading on a EU Regulated Market for more than 18 months may qualify for an exemption under FSMA, subject to specific requirements in relation to the production of a supplementary prospectus or summary document in certain circumstances. An applicant must seek appropriate professional advice on its disclosure obligations under FSMA.

Application process

An applicant must submit a provisional application for admission to PLUS at least ten business days prior to the intended date of admission.

An applicant must submit the following additional documents to PLUS at least three business days prior to the intended date of admission:

1 a duly completed and signed final application for admission;
2 an electronic copy of the approved prospectus (or if applicable, the summary document or supplementary prospectus); and
3 an electronic copy of the board resolution allotting the securities which are the subject of the application (or written confirmation of allotment by an authorised representative of the applicant pending such resolution becoming available).

Following admission, an applicant must provide written confirmation to PLUS in the event that the number of securities issued is different from the number of proposed securities stated in its application.

Notwithstanding compliance with the eligibility criteria, PLUS may refuse an application if in its opinion:

1 the admission of the securities to which the application relates would be detrimental to investors' interests or the integrity of the PLUS listed market;
2 the issuer is in breach of, or is likely to breach, the requirements of these standards or a special condition.

An admission of securities is effected via the issue of a market notice by PLUS.

Issues of unlisted securities

Public offers of shares and other company securities that are not listed and admitted to trading on the London Stock Exchange Main Market or PLUS listed are governed by the Prospectus Rules, see pp. 275–276 above.

Alternative Investment Market

As the London Stock Exchange's market for smaller companies, the Alternative Investment Market (AIM) is intended to appeal to a wider range of companies.

Admission requirements

The requirements for admission to AIM set out in the AIM Rules are much less onerous than the requirements for admission to the Exchange's Main Market. In particular, there are no requirements for minimum market capitalisation, the percentage of shares which must be in public hands, or length of trading record.

If the company does not have a two-year trading record, any directors or employees who individually hold one per cent or more of its AIM securities must agree not to dispose of any of their own holdings in the company for at least 12 months from the date of admission (rule 7).

Any type of security of a public company may be admitted to AIM. The securities to be admitted must be freely transferable and all securities of the class must be admitted (rules 32 and 33).

An applicant to AIM must produce an admission document which must be freely available for at least one month prior to admission (rule 3).

A company seeking admission to trading on AIM must make an announcement through a Regulatory Information Service at least ten business days prior to the date on which it wishes its securities to be admitted (rule 2). It must also make a written application to the Exchange at least three business days prior to its proposed admission date (rule 5).

The admission document must include:

1. details of the company's name, place of incorporation, registered and trading address(es) and the website address where details required by rule 26 will be available;
2. a description of its business; the securities for which admission is sought and any capital to be raised on admission;
3. the number of shares not in public hands at admission and details of any other exchange or trading platform the applicant's shares will be admitted to or traded on as a result of an application by the company;
4. the names and functions of the directors (and any proposed directors);
5. any substantial shareholders (3 per cent or more);
6. the company's promoters, nominated advisers and nominated brokers; and state that an AIM admission document will be available at the time of admission;
7. accounting reference date; and
8. anticipated admission date.

The written application to the Exchange is to be accompanied by an electronic copy of the admission document (rule 5) which the company must publish if the application is approved. The admission document must comply with the Prospectus Rules and contain the additional information prescribed by Sch.2 of the AIM Rules.

Application documentation in respect of any further issues of securities must be submitted to the Exchange not less than three business days before the date on which the issuer wishes the securities to be admitted to trading (rule 5).

PLUS quoted

PLUS Markets admit companies to its PLUS quoted market in accordance with the PLUS Rules for Issuers. The PLUS Rules for Issuers contain the application requirements for admission to the PLUS Quoted market and the continuing obligations of PLUS quoted companies once admitted.

Admission requirements

The requirements for admission to PLUS quoted are set out in Part 1 of the Rules for Issuers (RFI).

A company seeking admission to trading on PLUS quoted must appoint and retain a PLUS corporate adviser (RFI 1).

The application for admission is made on the company's behalf by its corporate adviser who is responsible for ensuring that the company and the securities meet the eligibility criteria, satisfactory guidance has been given to the directors to ensure they understand their obligations under the rules and that the information provided to PLUS is accurate and complete (RFI 2).

To be eligible the company must be lawfully incorporated, have securities that are allotted and freely transferable, have arrangements in place for electronic settlement following admission and have sufficient shares in public hands to ensure an orderly market (RFI 3).

If any securities are to be issued to the public a prospectus complying with the prospectus rules must be published, if appropriate. If a prospectus is not required, the company must publish an admission document instead unless the offer is to a restricted number of persons or the amount being raised is less than £250,000 (RFI 4).

PLUS may authorise omissions from the admission document that are minor or relate to matters already in the public domain (RFI 7).

The admission document must include the information set out in schedule 2 to the Rules for Issuers and be submitted at least ten days prior to the expected admission date (RFI 8).

A newly established entity must also submit a three-year business plan and the directors and connected persons must agree not to dispose of any securities during the 12-month period beginning on the date of admission (RFI 9, 10 and 11).

Other securities markets

ShareMark

In 2000 the Share Centre issued free shares to its private clients and at the same time ShareMark was established to provide an internal trading platform, allowing shareholders to quickly and efficiently sell or purchase shares.

The market was opened to other companies for the purposes of share trading in 2002.

ShareMark is a stock market specifically designed to meet the needs of small- and medium-sized companies, either quoted or unquoted. ShareMark is different from other markets because it operates through an electronic auction market, matching buyers and sellers at a single price, thus there is no bid/offer spread on ShareMark stocks. Auctions may occur daily, weekly, monthly or quarterly depending on the needs of the company and the shareholders.

It is particularly suited to companies that:

- are already listed and have a wide bid/offer spread as a result of illiquidity;
- are intending to list but are not ready for the big step onto the main market;
- are looking to provide an exit route for investors;
- operate an employee share plan and want to provide somewhere for employees to trade shares.

To be eligible to join ShareMark a company must:

1. be incorporated in the UK;
2. have at least one year's audited accounts made up to a date not more than six months prior to the date of application which are not qualified or have a statement as to fundamental uncertainty;
3. have arrangements in place to allow electronic settlement from admission;
4. be able to demonstrate that its directors are fit and proper persons with relevant experience to manage the company's affairs and with a suitably qualified person heading its finance function; and
5. have at least one independent non-executive director appointed.

Investbx

Investbx is a similar market to ShareMark also operated by the Share Centre Limited and aimed at smaller companies trading in the West Midlands region seeking to raise up to £2m.

Advertising, marketing and promotion

Regardless of whether or not a public company is proposing to make an offer of listed or unlisted securities, the advertising and marketing of those securities, other than the issue of prospectuses, supplemental prospectuses and announcements concerning their issue, is subject to the provisions of the FSMA2000 s.21 and a number of statutory instruments including: the Financial Services and Markets Act 2000 (Financial Promotion) (Amendment) Order 2001, SI 2001/2633; the Financial Services and Markets Act 2000 (Miscellaneous Provisions) Order 2001, SI 2001/3650; and the Financial Services and Markets Act 2000 (Financial Promotion) (Amendment No. 2) Order 2001, SI 2001/3800.

16
Continuing obligations of listed, AIM and PLUS companies

Introduction

In addition to any legislative duties and responsibilities, directors of companies whose shares are admitted to trading on the London Stock Exchange Main Market or AIM or the PLUS listed or PLUS quoted markets operated by PLUS Markets Group are required to comply with continuing obligations requirements. These are set out in Chapter 9 of the Listing Rules for Main Market and PLUS listed companies, the AIM Rules for AIM companies and the Rules for Issuers for PLUS quoted companies.

Continuing obligations of listed companies

The continuing obligations together with the disclosure and transparency rules require and regulate:

- public announcements of certain matters affecting the company or its securities;
- circulars to be sent to shareholders informing them of imminent substantial transactions;
- the issue of the company's accounts;
- the purchase by the company of its own securities;
- details regarding the directors and in particular their interests in the company's securities.

The obligations set out in the *Listing Rules*, Chapter 9 and the Disclosure and Transparency Rules are:

- general obligations (*Listing Rules 9.2*);
- obligations relating to proxies, sanctions relating to CA2006 s.793, pre-emption rights (*Listing Rules 9.3 and DTR6*);
- documents requiring prior approval (*Listing Rules 9.4*);
- share transactions such as rights issues, open offers and reconstructions (*Listing Rules 9.5 and DTR6*);
- notification of changes (*Listing Rules 9.6*);
- preliminary statement of annual results, dividends and half yearly reports (*Listing Rules 9.7A and DTR4*);

- annual report and account (*Listing Rules 9.8 and DTR4*);
- the Model Code (*Listing Rules annex to Chapter 9*);
- control and notification of inside information (*DTR2*);
- notification of interests in shares (*DTR3*);
- notification of major interests in shares (*DTR5*).

General obligations

A listed company must, at all times, have its shares admitted to trading on an RIE and must notify the FSA that it has requested an RIE to admit or re-admit any shares to trading, requested an RIE to cancel or suspend trading or that its shares have been cancelled or suspended from trading (*LR 2.2.3 and 9.2.2*).

At least 75 per cent of the company's shares business must be independent and controlled by the company (*LR 6.1.4 (2) and (3) and 9.2.2A*).

The shares must be capable of being settled electronically (via CREST) (*LR 6.1.23 and 9.2.3*).

A listed company must comply with the Disclosure and Transparency Rules (*LR 9.2.6 and 9.2.6B*).

Neither a company nor any member of its group may transact any trades in the company's shares at a time when a director is barred under the provisions of the Model Code. All directors and those discharging managerial positions must comply with the Model Code (*LR 9.27 and 9.28*).

At least 25 per cent of the issued shares excluding any shares held in treasury must be held by the public (*LR 6.1.19 and 9.2.15*).

Whenever a company publishes unaudited financial information in a class 1 circular or prospectus it must reproduce that information in its next audited accounts and explain any variance of 10 per cent or more between any profit forecast or estimate and the actual profit. (*LR 9.2 18*).

Obligations relating to shareholders and exercise of rights

A listed company must ensure that a proxy form allows for three-way voting and state that if there is no indication on how the proxy may vote the proxy shall exercise their discretion as to whether and if so how to vote. Where there are five or more directors to retire by rotation the proxy form may give shareholders the opportunity to vote on all elections as a whole in addition to voting on each re-election individually (*LR 9.3.6 and 9.3.7*). Companies must not prevent shareholders from exercising their rights by proxy and must provide all shareholders with either a paper form of proxy or by electronic means. Forms of proxy must be available either with the notice of general meeting or following the announcement of the meeting (*DTR 6.1.5*).

Where a company has power in its Articles of Association to impose sanctions on a shareholder for non-compliance with a request for information under CA2006 s.793, those powers are restricted to:

1 any sanction can only be implemented after 14 days' notice;
2 for shareholdings of less than 0.25 per cent the sanctions are restricted to prohibition on attending meetings and exercise of voting rights;
3 for shareholdings in excess of 0.25 per cent additional permitted sanctions are the withholding of dividend payments and restricting the right of transfer; and
4 any sanctions imposed must cease to apply within seven days of the information requested being supplied or notice of a sale to an unconnected third party has been made through a Regulatory Information Service or overseas exchange or by the acceptance of a takeover offer (*LR 9.3.9*).

A company proposing to issue further equity shares or to sell treasury shares must offer them to existing shareholders in proportion to their holding unless a general disapplication of the statutory pre-emption rights has been given pursuant to CA2006 ss.570 or 571 or a rights issue is proposed and the disapplication relates to fractional entitlements and entitlements that are necessary or expedite (i.e. withholding entitlements from overseas shareholders) or where the sale is to an employee share scheme (*LR 9.3.11 and 12*).

In circumstances where a company is proposing to alter its Articles of Association, notice must be given to the UKLA and the operator of the regulated market on which its shares are traded no later than the date of calling the general meeting of shareholders to consider the proposals (*DTR 6.1.2*). Companies must disclose any changes in the rights attaching to shares (*DTR 6.1.9*).

Companies must ensure equal treatment of shareholders and provide all the facilities and information to enable such holders to exercise their rights (*DTR 6.1.3 and 4*).

Companies must appoint a financial institution through which shareholders may exercise their financial rights (*DTR 6.1.6*).

Companies may take advantage of electronic communications but any decision to do so must be taken in general meting and the use of electronic communication must not be dependent on the location of the shareholder, identification arrangements must be made to ensure shareholders can exercise their rights and are informed, shareholders must be contacted in writing to request their consent to the dissemination of information by electronic means and shareholders must be able to request information in written form (*DTR 6.1.8*).

Companies must provide information to the holders of loan stock or other debt instruments concerning the place, time and agenda of meetings, total number of shares and voting rights and the right of shareholders to participate in meetings (*DTR 6.1.12*).

Documents requiring prior approval of shareholders

Companies must ensure that the terms of any employees' share scheme or long-term incentive scheme are approved by ordinary resolution of shareholders in general meeting before being adopted (*LR 9.4.1*) other than schemes where all or substantially all employees are eligible to participate on similar terms provided that all or substantially all employees are not also directors (*LR 9.4.2*). There is also a limited exemption in circumstances where the only participant is a director and the arrangement is provided in unusual circumstances to facilitate their recruitment or retention as a director (*LR 9.4.2(2)*). In such circumstances full disclosure must be made in the next annual report published after the date on which the individual is eligible to participate in the arrangement.

Companies must not issue options or warrants where the exercise price is less than the market value as determined in accordance with the scheme rules without the prior sanction of shareholders by ordinary resolution in general meeting (*LR 9.4.4*). This rule does not apply where the grant relates to options or warrants being granted in an employees' share scheme and participation is offered on substantially the same terms to all or substantially all employees or in circumstances where the grant of options or warrants is pursuant to the issue of replacement options following a take-over or reconstruction (*LR 9.4.5*).

Share transactions such as rights issues, open offers and reconstructions

Where unsubscribed rights are to be placed prior to the commencement of dealings, a company must ensure that the placing accounts for at least 25 per cent of the total shares issued under the rights issue, that placees are required to purchase any rights placed with them and that the purchase price of those rights does not exceed by more than 50 per cent the difference between the offer price and the theoretical ex-rights price (*LR 9.5.1*).

Where any unsubscribed rights are sold by the company any premium over the offer price less any expenses must be distributed to the holders of the shares to which the rights relate except that amounts of £5.00 or less may be retained by the company (*LR 9.5.4*).

As soon as practical following completion of a rights issue the company must notify a Regulatory Information Service of the issue price and principal terms of the offer, and the results of the issue including the date and price at which any unsubscribed rights were sold, if any. Rights issues must remain open for acceptances for at least ten business days (*LR 9.5.5 and 6*).

The timetable of an open offer of securities must be approved by the RIE on which the shares are traded. The terms of the open offer must contain a note that the terms are subject to shareholder approval if this is the case and the circular relating to the open offer must not imply that the offer gives the same entitlements as a rights issue (*LR 9.5.7 and 8*).

If the company undertakes a vendor placing it must ensure that all vendors have the opportunity to participate equally in the placing (*LR 9.5.9*).

An offer by a listed company by way of open offer, placing, vendor placing, offer for subscription or issues out of treasury must not be at a discount of more than 10 per cent to the mid market price on the day the announcement of the offer or agreeing the placing takes place. The reference to mid market price means the mid market quotation for those shares published by the market on which the company's shares are admitted to trading (*LR 9.5.10*). A discount of more than 10 per cent is permitted if the issue is subject to specific shareholder approval or made pursuant to a pre-existing general disapplication of pre-emption rights.

A company undertaking an offer for sale or offer for subscription must ensure that letters of allotment or acceptance are all issued simultaneously and numbered serially. There must be equality of treatment between certificated and uncertificated holdings. Letters of regret must be issued at the same time or not more than three business days later provided that where letters of regret are not posted at the same time an advertisement is published in a national newspaper to be published on the day following posting of the letters of acceptance or allotment (*LR 9.5.11*).

If a listed company issues a circular in connection with a reconstruction or re-financing, the circular must contain a working capital statement drawn up under the provisions of *LR 13.3* and on the basis that the reconstruction or refinancing is successful (*LR 9.5.12*).

If an issue of shares includes a fractional entitlement the company must ensure that the fractions are sold for the benefit of holders of the shares to which the fractions relate and distribute such amounts to those holders where the net proceeds exceed £5.00 (*LR 9.5.13*).

Where a company issues additional shares of a class already listed, application to have the new shares admitted to listing must be made as soon as possible and in any event within one month of allotment (*LR 9.5.14*).

Temporary documents of title relating to listed shares must be serially numbered and include the following:

1. name and address of first named holder and names of any joint holders;
2. for fixed income shares the amount of the next payment of interest or dividend;
3. pro-rata entitlement;
4. last date, past or future, for registering transfers to be eligible for participation in the issue;
5. how the new shares rank for dividend or interest;
6. nature of the document of title and proposed issue date;
7. how fractions, if any, are to be dealt with; and
8. for a rights issue the period (minimum ten business days) during which the offer can be accepted and details of how any rights not subscribed will be dealt with, if at all.

If the offer is renounceable the documents should also include the following information:

1. state in the heading that the document is of value and negotiable;

2 advise shareholders that if they are in any doubt about what to do to seek advice from an appropriate independent adviser;
3 state that if the securities to which the offer relates have been sold to pass the documents to the person through whom the transfer was made for transmission to the purchaser;
4 have the form of renunciation and registration instructions printed on the reverse or attached to the document;
5 include provision for splitting and for the split form to be certified; and
6 if, at the same time as shares are being offered for cash payment, shares are also being offered credited as fully paid, the offer must provide for the same period of renunciation for both classes. (*LR 9.5.15*)

Definitive certificates of title must include the following details on the front:

1 the authority under which the company is incorporated, the country of incorporation and its registered number, if any;
2 the number of securities represented by the certificate in the top right-hand corner, including if appropriate the number and denomination of those securities;
3 a footnote stating that transfer of all or part of the securities represented by the certificate cannot be registered without production of the certificate;
4 if applicable a note stating the minimum amount or multiples in which the securities may be transferred;
5 the date of issue of the certificate;
6 for a fixed income security the interest payable and payment dates and a summary on the reverse of the redemption, repayment or conversion rights; and
7 if the securities have preferential rights a statement on the front, or if this is not practical, on the reverse of the certificate of the rights to capital, dividends and conversion, if any. (*LR 9.5.16*)

Announcements to UKLA or an RIS

Documents

Companies must forward two copies of all circulars, notices reports or other documents to which the listing rules apply to the UKLA for publishing through the document viewing facility. These copies must be forwarded to the UKLA at the same time they are issued. Other than routine business at its annual general meeting companies must forward two copies of all resolutions passed in general meeting to the ULKA for publication through the document viewing facility as soon as possible after the meeting. Companies must notify a Regulatory Information Service when a document is available for viewing on the document viewing facility unless the full text of the document is also provided to the RIS (*LR 9.6.1–3 and 9.6.18*).

Capital

The UKLA must be informed of the following information in relation to changes in capital:

1 proposed changes to capital structure including any listed debt securities;
2 number of shares redeemed and the number remaining outstanding; and
3 details of any extension to the validity of temporary documents of title.

Details of the results of a share issue must be notified as soon as known except that, subject to DTR2, the announcement may be delayed by up to two business days to enable underwriting commitments to be taken up or lapse (*LR 9.6.4 and 6*).

Directors

A Regulatory Information Service must be notified no later than the end of the business day following the decision or receipt of notice of any change in the board including (*LR 9.6.11*):

1 name, position and function of any new director;
2 resignation, removal or retirement of any director. Notification is not required where a director retires by rotation and is reappointed at a general meeting;
3 significant changes to the role, functions or responsibilities of a director; and
4 the effective date of any changes if not immediate and, if not known, that fact. Additional notification will be required once the date of change is known (*LR 9.6.12*).

In respect of the appointment of a new director the following information must be disclosed within five business days of the decision to appoint them:

1 details of all current directorships of publicly quoted companies held during the preceding five years distinguishing between current and past directorships;
2 any unspent convictions in relation to indictable offences;
3 details of any receiverships, compulsory liquidations, creditors voluntary liquidations, administrations, company voluntary liquidations or compositions or arrangements with creditors or any class of creditors where the director was an executive director at the time or within 12 months preceding those events;
4 details of any compulsory liquidations, administrations or partnership voluntary liquidations or compositions or arrangements with creditors or any class of creditors where the director was a partner at the time or within 12 months preceding those events;
5 details of any receiverships of any asset of such person or partnership in which the director was a partner at the time or within 12 months preceding those events; and
6 details of any public criticisms of the director by statutory or regulatory authorities and whether the director has ever been disqualified by a Court from acting

as a director or from fulfilling management duties or conducting the affairs of a company.

Any changes to these details and any new directorships in a publicly quoted company must be notified to a Regulatory Information Service as soon as possible (*LR 9.6.13 and 14*).

Lock-ups

Companies must notify a Regulatory Information Service as soon as possible of information relating the disposal of shares under an exemption to a lock-up arrangement previously disclosed in accordance with the prospectus regulations. Details of any variation to the terms of any lock-up arrangement must be notified as soon as possible (*LR 9.6.18 and 19*).

Change of name

When a company changes its name it must notify a Regulatory Information Service stating the date on which the change was effective, notify the ULKA in writing and forward to the UKLA a copy of the certificate of incorporation on change of name (*LR 9.6.19*).

Change of accounting date

A company must notify a Regulatory Information Service as soon as possible of any change in its accounting date including the new accounting reference date. Where the effect of the change is to extend an accounting period to more than 14 months the company will be required to issue a second interim report. The second interim report should be made up to either the old accounting reference date or a date not more than six months prior to the new accounting reference date (*LR 9.6.20–22*).

Preliminary statement of annual results, dividends, half-yearly reports and interim management statements

If a company prepares a preliminary statement of its annual results the statement must be published as soon as possible after it has been approved by the board. The statement must be agreed with the company's auditor prior to publication (*LR 9.7A.1*).

The statement must include figures in the form of a table including the items required for its interim report and must be consistent with the presentation to be adopted in the annual report.

The statement must indicate any modification likely to be included in the auditor's report to the annual report together with any significant additional information required to assess the results being announced.

A company must notify a Regulatory Information Service as soon as possible after the board meeting to approve a decision to pay or withhold a dividend or other distribution to shareholders giving details of the net amount per share payable, the payment date, record (if applicable) and any foreign income dividend election together with any income tax treated as payable at the lower rate and not repayable (*LR 9.7A.2)*.

Listed companies are required to issue a half-yearly financial report covering the first six months of the financial year. The half-yearly report must be published as soon as possible and no later than two months after the end of the period to which it relates. Copies of the half-yearly report must be available to the public for at least five years (*DTR 4.2.1 and 2*).

The half-yearly report must contain a condensed set of financial statements, interim management report and a statement of responsibilities (*DTR 4.2.3*).

If the company is required to prepare consolidated accounts the half-yearly report must be prepared in accordance with IAS 34 (*DTR 4.2.4*).

If the company is not required to prepare consolidated accounts the condensed financial statements must contain a condensed balance sheet, condensed profit and loss account and explanatory notes. The half-yearly report must follow the same accounting policies and principles for recognising and measuring used when preparing the annual financial report and for the balance sheet show the same headings and subtotals included in the most recent annual financial statement together with any additional information required to ensure a true and fair view of the assets, liabilities, financial position and profit and loss of the company (*DTR 4.2.5 and 6*).

The interim management report included in the half-yearly report must include details of any important events during the period and their impact on the financial statements and a summary of the principal risks and uncertainties for the remaining six months of the financial year (*DTR 4.2.7*).

The interim management report must also contain details of any related party transactions that have materially affected the financial position or performance of the company and any changes in related party transactions disclosed in the previous financial report that could have a material effect on the financial position or performance of the company during the period covered by the interim management report.

If the half-yearly report has been audited the auditor's report must be reproduced in full. If the half-yearly report has not been audited a statement of this fact must be included in the report (*DTR 4.2.9*).

The half-yearly report must include a responsibility statement made by those responsible confirming that to the best of their knowledge and belief the financial statements have been prepared in accordance with applicable accounting standards and give a true and fair view of the assets, liabilities, financial position and profit or loss of the company and that the interim management report contains a fair review of the information required to be revised by DTR 4.2.7 and 4.2.8. The responsibility statement must disclose the name and functions of those making the responsibility statement (*DTR 4.2.10*).

Subject to the exemption available for specialist issuers set out in DTR 4.4, listed companies must issue interim management statements during the first and second six months of each financial year. The statement must be made during the period beginning ten weeks after commencement and prior to six weeks before the end of the relevant six-month period (*DTR 4.3.2*).

The interim management statement must contain information that covers the period from the beginning of the six-month period up to the date of the statement and must include the following information:

1 details of any material events and transactions and their effect on the company and any controlled undertakings;
2 a general description of the financial position and performance of the company and any controlled undertakings during the period covered by the statement (*DTR 4.3.5*).

Companies that publish quarterly financial reports are deemed to have satisfied the requirement to issue interim financial statements (*DTR 4.3.6*).

Annual report and accounts

A listed company must publish its annual financial report within four months of the end of the financial year and ensure that its annual financial reports are freely available to the public for at least five years after publication (*DTR 4.1.3 and 4*).

The annual financial report of a listed company must include (*DTR 4.1.5*):

- the audited financial statements;
- a management report; and
- responsibility statements.

If the company is required to prepare consolidated accounts the financial statements must comprise consolidated accounts prepared in accordance with IFRS and parent company accounts prepared in accordance with the law of the country of its incorporation.

If the company is not required to prepare consolidated accounts its financial statements must comprise accounts prepared in accordance with the law of the country of its incorporation (*DTR 4.1.6*).

The financial statements must be audited and the full text of the audit report made public (*DTR 4.1.7*).

The management report must contain (*DTR 4.1.8–11*):

1 A fair review of the company's business and a description of the principal risks and uncertainties facing it. The business review must be a balanced and comprehensive analysis if the development and performance of the company during the financial year and the position of the company at the end of the year. The review must also contain sufficient analysis using financial key performance and other key performance indicators including environmental

and employee matters to demonstrate the development, performance and position of the company during the financial year (*DTR 4.1.8 and 9*).

2 Details of any important events since the end of the financial year, likely future development, any activities in research and development, details of any acquisition(s) of own shares and the existence of any overseas branches.
3 In relation to the company's use of financial instruments or where required for the assessment of its assets, liabilities, financial position and profit or loss, details of its financial risk management objectives and policies and the company's exposure to price risk, credit risk, liquidity risk and cash flow risk.

The annual financial report must include a responsibility statement made by those responsible confirming that to best of their knowledge and belief the financial statements have been prepared in accordance with applicable accounting standards and give a true and fair view of the assets, liabilities, financial position and profit or loss of the company and that the management report contains a fair review of the information required to be reviewed. The responsibility statement must disclose the name and functions of those making the responsibility statement (*DTR 4.1.12*).

In addition to the requirements set out in DTR 4.1, listed companies must include in their annual financial report the following (*LR 9.8.4*):

1 a statement of the amount of interest capitalised during the financial year and an indication of the amount and treatment of any related tax relief;
2 if the company has published unaudited financial information in a class 1 circular or prospectus since its previous annual financial report it must reproduce that information and explain any variance of 10 per cent or more between any profit forecast or estimate and the actual profit (*LR 9.2.18*);
3 details of any small related party transaction (*LR 11.1.10*);
4 details of any long-term incentive schemes (*LR 9.4.3*);
5 details of any arrangements under which a director of the company has waived or agreed to waive any emoluments from the company or any **subsidiary** and relating to the period under review or any future year(s);
6 where shares are issued for cash during the period under review otherwise than to shareholders in proportion to their holdings and which has not been specifically authorised by the company in general meeting or where shares are issued in any major subsidiary undertaking the following details must be provided:
   - the classes of shares allotted and for each class of shares, the number allotted, their aggregate nominal value and the consideration paid;
   - the names of the allottees, if there were six or less, and in the case of six or more allottees a brief generic description of each new class of equity holder;
   - the market price of the shares on the date on which the terms of the issue were fixed; and
   - the date on which the terms of the issue were fixed;

7 where the company is a subsidiary undertaking, details of the participation by the parent undertaking in any placing made during the financial year;
8 details of any material contract(s) subsisting during the financial year:
   - in which a director of the company is interested; or
   - between the company, or any subsidiary, and a controlling shareholder;
9 details of any contract for the provision of services to the company or any subsidiary by a controlling shareholder, subsisting during the financial year, unless it is a contract for the provision of services which it is the principal business of the shareholder to provide and it is not a material contract; and
10 details of any arrangement under which a shareholder has waived or agreed to waive future dividends.

In the case of a company incorporated in the United Kingdom, the following additional items must be included in its annual financial report (*LR 9.8.6*):

1 details of all the notifiable interests of each director of the company as at the end of the financial period including:
   - any changes in the interests between the end of the financial period and a date not more than one month prior to the date of the notice of the annual general meeting; or
   - if there have been no changes in a statement to that effect, interests of each director include the interests of connected persons of which the company is, or ought upon reasonable enquiry to become, aware;
2 a statement showing, as at a date not more than one month prior to the date of the notice of the annual general meeting:
   - details of interests in voting shares disclosed to the company in accordance with DTR 5; or
   - if no disclosures have been made, a statement to that effect;
3 a statement made by the directors that the business is a going concern, together with supporting assumptions or qualifications as necessary, that has been prepared in accordance with Going Concern and Financial Reporting: Guidance for directors of listed companies registered in the United Kingdom;
4 a statement setting out:
   - details of any shareholders' authority for the purchase by the company of its own shares that remains valid at the end of the financial period;
   - in the case of purchases made otherwise than through the market or by tender to all shareholders, the names of sellers of any shares purchased, or proposed to be purchased, by the company during the financial period;
   - in the case of any purchases made otherwise than through the market or by tender or partial offer to all shareholders, or options or contracts to make such purchases, entered into since the end of the financial period, information equivalent to that required by Part 2 of Sch.7 to the Large and Medium Sized Companies and Groups (Accounts and Reports) Regulations 2008 (SI 2008/410); and

- in the case of sales of treasury shares for cash made otherwise than through the market, or in connection with an employees' share scheme, or otherwise than pursuant to an opportunity which (so far as was practicable) was made available to all holders of the listed company's securities (or to all holders of a relevant class of its securities) on the same terms, particulars of the names of purchasers of such shares sold, or proposed to be sold;

5 a statement of how the company has applied the principles set out in Section 1 of the **Combined Code**;

6 a statement as to whether the company has:
   - complied throughout the accounting period with all relevant provisions set out in Section 1 of the Combined Code; or
   - not complied throughout the accounting period with all relevant provisions set out in Section 1 of the Combined Code and if not, setting out:
     (a) those provisions it has not complied with;
     (b) in the case of provisions whose requirements are of a continuing nature, the period within which it did not comply with some or all of those provisions; and
     (c) the company's reasons for non-compliance; and
     (d) a report to the shareholders by the Board which contains all the matters set out in LR 9.8.8 (see below).

An overseas company with a primary listing must disclose in its annual report and accounts whether or not it complies with the corporate governance regime of its country of incorporation, the significant ways in which its actual corporate governance practices differ from those set out in the Combined Code; and the unexpired term of the service contract of any director proposed for election or re-election at the forthcoming annual general meeting and, if any director for election or re-election does not have a service contract, a statement to that effect (*LR 9.8.7*).

The board must prepare a report to shareholders containing the following (*LR 9.8.8*):

1 a statement of the company's policy on executive directors' remuneration;

2 information presented in tabular form together with notes as necessary on:
   - the amount of each element in the remuneration package of each director including basic salary and fees, the estimated money value of benefits in kind, annual bonuses, deferred bonuses, compensation for loss of office and payments for breach of contract or other termination payments;
   - the total remuneration for each and for the corresponding prior period;
   - any significant payments made to former directors; and
   - any share options, including save-as-you-earn options, for each director in accordance with the requirements of the Directors' Remuneration Report Regulations;

3 details of any long-term incentive schemes, other than share options,

including the interests of each director in the long-term incentive schemes at the start of the period under review, details of any entitlements or awards granted and commitments made showing which crystallize either in the same year or in subsequent years, details of the monetary value and number of shares, cash payments or other benefits received by each director and details of the interests of each director at the end of the period;

4 an explanation and justification of any element of a director's remuneration, other than basic salary, which is pensionable;

5 details of any directors' service contract with a notice period in excess of one year or with provisions for pre-determined compensation on termination which exceeds one year's salary and benefits in kind, giving the reasons for such notice period;

6 details of the unexpired term of any service contract of a director proposed for election or re-election at the forthcoming annual general meeting, and, if any director proposed for election or re-election does not have a directors' service contract, a statement to that effect;

7 a statement of the company's policy on the granting of options or awards under its employees' share schemes and other long-term incentive schemes, explaining and justifying any departure from that policy and any change in the policy from the preceding year;

8 for money purchase schemes, details of the contribution or allowance payable or made by the company in respect of each director; and

9 for defined benefit schemes:

   (a) details of the amount of the increase during the period under review (excluding inflation) and of the accumulated total amount at the end of the period in respect of the accrued benefit to which each director would be entitled on leaving service or is entitled having left service

   (b) either:

      (i) the transfer value (less director's contributions) of the relevant increase in accrued benefit (to be calculated in accordance with Actuarial Guidance Note GN11 but making no deduction for any under-funding); or

      (ii) so much of the following information as is necessary to make a reasonable assessment of the transfer value in respect of each director:

         (A) age;

         (B) normal retirement age;

         (C) the amount of any contributions paid or payable by the director under the terms of the scheme;

         (D) details of spouses and dependants' benefits;

         (E) early retirement rights and options;

         (F) expectations of pension increases after retirement (whether guaranteed or discretionary); and

         (G) discretionary benefits for which allowance is made in transfer values on leaving and any other relevant information which will significantly affect the value of the benefits; and

(c) no disclosure of voluntary contributions and benefits.

Auditor's report

A listed company must ensure that the auditors review each of the following before the annual report is published (*LR 9.8.10*):

1. the statement by the directors that the business is a going concern; and
2. the parts of the statement relating to corporate governance that relate to the following provisions of the Combined Code:
   (a) C1.1;
   (b) C2.1; and
   (c) C3.1 to C3.7.

A listed company must ensure that the auditors review the following disclosures (*LR 9.8.11*):

1. amount of each element in the remuneration package and information on share options for each director;
2. details of long-term incentive schemes for directors;
3. details of any money purchase schemes; and
4. details of any defined benefit schemes.

If, in the opinion of the auditors the company has not complied with any of the requirements set out in LR 9.8.11 the company must ensure that the auditor's report includes, to the extent possible, a statement giving details of the non-compliance (*LR 9.8.12*).

Any summary financial statement issued by a listed company as permitted under the Companies Act 2006, must disclose (*LR 9.8.13*) earnings per share, and the information required for summary financial statements set out in the Companies Act 2006 (see pp. 208–209).

The Model Code

Listed companies are required to adopt a code on the dealings in company shares by directors and those discharging managerial responsibilities. The code adopted by a company must be no less onerous than the Model Code set out in the Annex to Chapter 9 of the Listing Rules and reproduced in Appendix 5 of this book.

The code imposes restrictions on dealing in shares of a listed company that go beyond those imposed by law. The purpose of the Model Code is to ensure that persons discharging managerial duties do not abuse or put themselves under suspicion of abusing inside information that they may or might be thought to have.

Broadly speaking, those persons subject to the code including any connected persons may not buy or sell shares or options during any close period or while they are in possession of price-sensitive information.

A close period is:

1 the period of 60 days immediately preceding the preliminary announcement of the annual results or, if shorter, the period from the end of the financial year to the date of the announcement; or
2 the period of 60 days immediately preceding the announcement of the annual results or, if shorter, the period from the end of the financial year to the date of the announcement; and
3 if the listed company reports on a half-yearly basis, from the end of the financial period to the date of publication of the half-yearly report; and
4 if the listed company reports on a quarterly basis period of 30 days, immediately preceding the publication of the results or, if shorter, the period from the end of the financial period to the date of the announcement of the quarterly results.

Even when dealing is permitted, clearance to deal must be sought before any transaction is undertaken. Once clearance is given the transaction must be completed as soon as possible and no later than two business days after clearance has been given.

Control and notification of inside information

It is in everyone's best interests that there is a flow of timely and accurate information between listed companies and investors, both actual and prospective. This helps preserve an orderly market in the company's shares and means that investment decisions whether to buy or sell are based on the same information. Timely announcements should minimise potentially volatile share price movements which can result from rumour and speculation.

Companies are required to notify a Regulatory Information Service as soon as possible of any inside price-sensitive information which directly concerns the company (*DTR 2.2.1*). There are a number of exemptions contained in DTR 2.5.1 to prevent disclosure of sensitive information that might prejudice ongoing negotiations.

Many announcements via a Regulatory Information Service relate to routine predictable events such as declaration of financial results, notification of share dealings by directors or declaration of dividends. On other occasions events outside the control of the company may have an impact on the company's prospects, for example flooding following unseasonal heavy rain might impact adversely on some insurance companies and not on others.

It is impossible to set down detailed guidance of what does or does not constitute price-sensitive information as this will vary from company to company. It is for each company to assess the likely price significance of the information to a reasonable investor in assessing the impact of that information on the company's performance, position or profit and loss.

An announcement must also be made if the company has reason to believe that a leak may have occurred about any ongoing negotiations of a price-sensitive nature.

If the company has a website, details of inside information announced via a Regulatory Information Service must also be available on the company's website no later than the close of business on the next business day (*DTR 2.3.2*) and remain available for the following 12 months (*DTR 2.3.5*). Publishing the information on a website is in addition to and not instead of announcing the details via a RIS (*DTR 2.3.3*).

Where a company discloses price-sensitive information to a closed group such as investor presentations or general meetings it must ensure that that information is disclosed no later to a RIS.

Disclosure of price-sensitive inside information via a RIS may be delayed or withheld provided that the omission is not likely to mislead the public, that the person(s) receiving the information owes a duty of confidentiality to the company and the company is able to ensure the confidentiality of that information (*DTR 2.5.1*).

Where inside information is disclosed to a third party in the normal exercise of their duties unless it may be delayed under DTR 2.5.1, an announcement of that information via a Regulatory Information Service should be made simultaneously in the case of intentional disclosure and as soon as possible in the case of non-intentional disclosure (*DTR 2.5.6*).

Companies must ensure that they have systems and controls in place to deny access to inside information other than to those persons who require it for the exercise of their functions (*DTR 2.6.1*). There should also be in place arrangements to disclose information to a Regulatory Information Service in circumstances where there is a breach of confidentiality (*DTR 2.6.2*). In practice this might require the issue of a holding announcement pending the conclusion of investigations to ascertain what information has been leaked.

A disclosure obligation is likely to arise from market or press speculation or rumour where that information is largely true (*DTR 2.7.1*). If the rumours are false, in most cases the knowledge that the rumour is false is unlikely to constitute inside information (*DTR 2.7.3*).

Companies must draw up lists of those persons both in their employment and those working on their behalf who have access to inside information on a regular or occasional basis. The list must contain details of the identity of each person, the reason why they are on the insider list and the date on which the list was created and last updated (*DTR 2.8.1–3*). The FSA may request to be provided with a copy of a company's insider list.

Insider lists must be promptly updated to reflect changes in the reason why any particular person is on the list, when a new person has access to inside information or when a person no longer has such access (*DTR 2.8.4*).

Companies are responsible for ensuring that any of their employees who have access to inside information are aware of their legal and regulatory duties and responsibilities regarding the security of that information and the restrictions imposed on them in dealing in the company's shares (*DTR 2.8.9*).

A company must also ensure that any person acting on its behalf who has drawn up an insider list has taken necessary measures to ensure those persons are aware of their legal and regulatory duties and responsibilities regarding the security of that information and the restrictions imposed on them in dealing in the company's shares (*DTR 2.8.10*).

Notification of transactions in shares

A person discharging managerial responsibilities and any connected persons must notify a company in writing of all transactions on their own account relating to shares in the company within four business days of that transaction taking place (*DTR 3.1.2*).

The notification must contain the following information (*DTR 3.1.3*):

- name of the person or, if applicable, the name of the connected person;
- the reason why notification is required;
- name of the company;
- description of the financial instrument;
- the nature of the transaction;
- date and place of the transaction; and
- price and volume of the transaction.

The company must notify a Regulatory Information Service of any information notified to it pursuant to *DTR 3.1.3* or CA2006 s.793. The notification to a Regulatory Information Service by the company must be made as soon as possible and no later than the end of the business day following receipt of the information by the company (*DTR 3.1.4*).

Notification of major interests in shares (DTR 5)

For the purposes of the rules on notification of transactions a disposal or acquisition of shares is deemed effected on execution unless completion is conditional on an event outside the control of either party, in which case the transaction is deemed effected on settlement.

When calculating whether any percentage threshold has been reached percentages are rounded down to the nearest whole number.

A person must notify a company of shares or other financial instruments they hold, whether directly or indirectly, and whether they carry voting rights which reach or fall below 3 per cent of the total voting rights. Disclosure is also required where the holding reaches or falls below each 1 per cent threshold in excess of 3 per cent up to 100 per cent. If the company is a non-UK incorporated company the thresholds are 5 per cent, 10 per cent, 20 per cent, 25 per cent, 30 per cent, 50 per cent and 75 per cent. Disclosure is required in respect of acquisition and disposal of shares or some other event changing the breakdown of voting rights such as the purchase and cancellation of shares by the company (*DTR 5.1.2*).

Certain transactions or holdings need not be disclosed including (*DTR 5.1.3*):

1 shares acquired for the sole purpose of clearing or settlement provided the transaction is completed by the conclusion of the third business day after the transaction;
2 shares held by a custodian or nominee in their capacity as custodian or nominee provided such custodian or nominee can only exercise the voting rights under instructions given in writing or by electronic means;
3 shares held by a market-maker in that capacity and where the total voting rights are less than 10 per cent;
4 shares held by a credit institution or investment firm on their trading book and the total voting rights do not exceed 5 per cent;
5 shares taken as collateral which involves the transfer of the shares provided the collateral taker does not declare any intention of exercising the voting rights; and
6 shares acquired by a borrower under a stock lending agreement provided the shares are on-lent or otherwise disposed of by the close of the next business day and the borrower does not declare any intention of exercising and does not exercise any of the voting rights.

In determining if a person has a disclosable interest there may be disregarded, other than for disclosure at the 5 per cent and 10 per cent thresholds and above the following holdings (*DTR 5.1.5*):

1 voting rights attaching to shares forming part of property belonging to another which are managed under a written agreement;
2 voting rights attaching to shares exercisable by the person in their capacity as the operator of an authorised unit trust scheme, a recognised scheme or a UCITS scheme;
3 voting rights attached to shares exercisable by an ICVC; and
4 voting rights attaching to shares exercised by investment entities prescribed by the FSA.

Disclosure will also be required where a person acquires or holds financial instruments which entitle that person to acquire shares to which voting rights are attached. Such financial instruments include transferable securities, options, futures, swaps forward rate agreements and other derivative contracts. The agreement must provide for the underlying shares to be acquired either on maturity or at the discretion of the holder of the instrument (*DTR 5.3.2*).

To assist holders of securities in assessing whether they have notifiable interests or not companies are required to announce via a Regulatory Information Service any increase or decrease in the total number of voting rights and capital in respect of each class of shares and any shares held in treasury at the end of each calendar month (*DTR 5.6.1*).

In circumstances where notification is required the notification must include the resulting situation in terms of voting rights, the chain of controlled undertakings through which the voting rights are held, if applicable, the date on which the threshold was reached or crossed and the identity of the shareholder (*DTR 5.8.1*).

If notification relates to a financial instrument the notification must include the resulting situation in terms of voting rights, the chain of controlled undertakings through which the financial instruments are held, if applicable, the date on which the threshold was reached or crossed, an indication of the period during which the shares can or will be acquired, maturity or expiration date of the instrument, the identity of the holder and the name of the underlying company (*DTR 5.8.2*).

Notification is required to be made on Form TR1 (*DTR 5.8.10*) to the issuing company and the FSA (*DTR 5.8.2(2)*). Notification to the issuer is required no later than two business days (four for a non-UK company) after the date on which the person becomes aware of the transaction. Where the person is a party to the transaction they are deemed to know of it no later than two days after the date of the transaction.

A company is required to notify via a Regulatory Information Service any notifications received by it no later than the end of the next business day after receipt (*DTR 5.8.12*).

AIM

Continuing obligations

The continuing obligations imposed on AIM companies include:

1. Appoint and retain at all times a nominated broker and a nominated adviser, although these roles may be combined (Rules 1 and 35). The adviser is responsible for assisting the directors to comply with the rules of AIM (Rule 1).
2. Publish accounts to International Accounting Standards (Rule 19). These accounts must be published within six months of the year-end (Rule 19). Prepare a half-yearly report within three months of the end of the relevant period and send a copy to a Regulatory Information Service (Rule 18).
3. Ensure that appropriate arrangements are in place for electronic settlement of its securities (Rule 36).
4. The board must adopt a code of dealing prohibiting directors and applicable employees from dealing in the company's shares during a close period and take all proper and reasonable steps to ensure compliance by its directors and applicable employees (Rule 21).
5. Documents sent to shareholders must be available to the public on a website

notified to a Regulatory Information Service for a period of not less than one month from the date of the announcement (Rule 26).

6 Forward to a Regulatory Information Service copies of all announcements, circulars, notices, reports or other document at the same time as they are issued to shareholders (Rule 10).

There are no additional requirements for AIM companies with regard to the content of annual accounts, corporate governance, purchase of own shares, etc. The *Listing Rules* do not apply to AIM companies, although some of its provisions are mirrored in the AIM rules.

Announcements

An AIM company must notify a Regulatory Information Service without delay and in writing of the following:

1 Major developments in its sphere of activity and changes in its financial condition which are not public knowledge and may be price-sensitive (Rule 11).
2 Details disclosed by directors in Rule 17 and schedule 5 regarding their interests in the company's securities and the interests of 'connected persons'.
3 Any information disclosed to the company by significant shareholders.
4 Changes of directors or their details.
5 Publication of audited accounts and of any change in its accounting reference date (Rules 17 and 19).
6 The resignation, dismissal or change of any nominated adviser or nominated broker (Rule 17).
7 Any issue of new securities or cancellation of existing securities of a class already admitted to trading on AIM.
8 Details of any decision to pay a dividend or other distribution.
9 Details of substantial transactions (Rule 12).
10 Details of related party transactions where any ratio is 5 per cent or more (Rule 13).
11 Any material change between the issuer's actual trading performance or financial condition and any profit forecast, estimate or projection included in its admission document (Rule 17).

PLUS quoted

Continuing obligations and announcements

The continuing obligations imposed on PLUS quoted companies are set out in schedule 2 of the Rules for Issuers ('RFI') and include:

1 Appoint and retain at all times a PLUS Corporate Adviser (RFI 1 and 19).
2 Announce as soon as possible any price-sensitive information relating to

changes in its sphere of activity, financial position, performance or expected performance. Companies are not required to announce matters under negotiation (RFI 20 and 21).

3 Companies must ensure that any information announced to the market is relevant, accurate and complete and that any information it is required to publish is announced no later than the date of publication (RFI 22 and 23).

4 Electronic copies of documents sent to shareholders must also be forwarded to PLUS as well as publicising the address or internet address where copies of the documents are available for inspection (RFI 25).

5 Companies must disclose any notifiable change in holdings of directors or significant shareholders as soon as possible (RFI 28).

6 Companies must announce their interim results within three months and their final results within five months of the year end. Financial results must be prepared in accordance with UK or US GAAP or International Accounting Standards. If the annual accounts have had a qualified audit opinion in respect of their preparation on an on-going basis the company must publish quarterly accounts in respect of the first and third quarters of each financial year within one month of each period end (RFI 30–33).

7 Companies must announce as soon as possible the terms of any acquisition or disposal or material transaction which is or is likely to be price-sensitive or details of any reverse takeover (RFI 34–38).

8 Companies must announce any changes in their issued share capital as soon as possible except that where a series of issues is made the announcements may be aggregated into monthly amounts. Where the issued share capital changes, the company must announce at the end of that month its issued share capital and that number of shares comprised in that issued share capital (RFI 39).

9 Any additional issues of shares must comply with the prospectus rules and if a prospectus is not required an admission document must be prepared in its place unless an admission document or prospectus has already been issued, the shares are already admitted to PLUS and the company is complying with its continuing obligations or the issue represents 10 per cent or less of the existing shares admitted to PLUS (RFI 40 and 41).

10 Details of any proposed dividend (RFI 43).

11 Any appointment, resignation or removal of directors or change in their executive responsibilities (RFI 45).

12 Companies must have a policy to prohibit directors and their connected persons dealing shares during a close period or on considerations of a short-term nature (RFI 46).

17 Takeovers and mergers

Introduction

The object of a takeover transaction is the acquisition usually by a company (the offeror or acquirer) of the whole or a majority of the issued share capital of another company (the target or offeree). The consideration for the acquisition may be the issue of shares or other securities in the acquiring company, the payment of cash, or a combination of the two.

Types of takeover

The following are the main types of takeover transaction:

1. A formal agreement may be made with the shareholders of the target company. This is practicable only where there is a small number of shareholders. This is the usual type of takeover transaction for private companies.
2. Arrangements may be made to purchase, by private agreement or on a public market, blocks of shares in a company in order to build up a sizeable holding, which could form the basis on which to launch a bid for the remainder of the issued share capital. It is necessary, however, where the target company is a public company to have regard to the provisions of the City Code on Takeovers and Mergers, compliance with both of which is supervised by the Takeover Panel on Takeovers and Mergers.
3. The acquiring company may make a public offer to the shareholders of the company to be acquired by sending documents to its shareholders making an offer to acquire their shares on stated terms.
4. A takeover may be effected under a scheme of arrangement made under the provisions of CA2006 ss.895 to 941, although this is a more complicated procedure. Schemes of arrangement may take the form of a reconstruction, merger or division and in all cases requires the consent of the Courts.

Takeover Panel

The Takeover Panel on Takeovers and Mergers (the 'Takeover Panel') is an independent body, established in 1968, whose main functions are to issue and administer the City Code on Takeovers and Mergers (the 'Code') and to supervise and regulate takeovers and other matters to which the Code applies in accordance with the Rules set out in the Code. It has been designated as the supervisory authority to carry out certain regulatory functions in relation to takeovers pursuant to the Directive on Takeover Bids (2004/25/EC) (the 'Directive'). Its statutory functions are set out in and under Chapter 1 of Part 28 of the Companies Act 2006 (ss.942 to 965).

The Takeover Panel regulates takeover bids and other merger transactions (however effected) for public companies or companies which have been public companies in the previous ten years which have their registered offices in the United Kingdom, the Channel Islands or the Isle of Man if any of their securities are admitted to trading on a regulated market in the United Kingdom or on any stock exchange in the Channel Islands or the Isle of Man. Its remit also extends to unlisted public companies and certain private companies which are resident in the United Kingdom.

In all cases, the Panel's function is to ensure that shareholders are treated fairly and are not denied an opportunity to decide on the merits of a takeover and that shareholders of the same class are afforded equivalent treatment by an offeror. The Code is not concerned with the financial or commercial advantages of a takeover. These are matters for the company and its shareholders.

The Code

The Code has been developed since 1968 to reflect the collective opinion of those professionally involved in the field of takeovers as to appropriate business standards and as to how fairness to shareholders and an orderly framework for takeovers can be achieved. Following the implementation of the Takeovers Directive (2004/25/EC) (the 'directive') by means of Part 28 of the Companies Act 2006 (the 'Act'), the rules set out in the Code have a statutory basis in relation to the United Kingdom and comply with the relevant requirements in the Directive.

The rules set out in the Code will also have a statutory basis in relation to the Channel Islands and the Isle of Man when the provisions of Chapter 1 of Part 28 are extended to them pursuant to the Act or equivalent statutory provision is made in those jurisdictions.

General principles and rules

The Code is based upon a number of General Principles, which are essentially statements of standards of commercial behaviour. These General Principles are the same as the general principles set out in Article 3 of the Directive. They apply to takeovers and other matters to which the Code applies. They are expressed in broad general terms and the Code does not define the precise extent of, or the limitations on, their application. They are applied in accordance with their spirit in order to achieve their underlying purpose.

In addition to the General Principles, the Code contains a series of rules.

Although most of the rules are expressed in less general terms than the General Principles, they are not framed in technical language, and like the General Principles, are to be interpreted to achieve their underlying purpose. Therefore, their spirit must be observed as well as their letter.

The following is a brief summary of some of the most important Rules:

1. When a person or group acquires interests in shares carrying 30 per cent or more of the voting rights of a company, they must make a cash offer to all other shareholders at the highest price paid in the 12 months before the offer was announced (30 per cent of the voting rights of a company is treated by the Code as the level at which effective control is obtained).
2. When interests in shares carrying 10 per cent or more of the voting rights of a class have been acquired by an offeror in the offer period and the previous 12 months, the offer must include a cash alternative for all shareholders of that class at the highest price paid by the offeror in that period. Further, if an offeror acquires for cash any interest in shares during the offer period, a cash alternative must be made available at that price at least.
3. If the offeror acquires an interest in shares in a target company at a price higher than the value of the offer, the offer must be increased accordingly.
4. The target company must appoint a competent independent adviser whose advice on the offer must be made known to all the shareholders, together with the opinion of the board.
5. Favourable deals for selected shareholders are banned.
6. All shareholders must be given the same information.
7. Those issuing takeover circulars must include statements taking responsibility for the contents.
8. Profit forecasts and asset valuations must be made to specified standards and must be reported on by professional advisers.
9. Misleading, inaccurate or unsubstantiated statements made in documents or to the media must be publicly corrected immediately.
10. Actions during the course of an offer by the target company which might frustrate the offer are generally prohibited unless shareholders approve these plans.
11. Stringent requirements are laid down for the disclosure of dealings in relevant securities during an offer.
12. Employees of both the offeror and the offeree must be informed about an offer.

Enterprise Act 2002

Regard should be paid to the provisions of Part 3 of the Enterprise Act 2002 (EA2002) affecting takeovers and mergers and references to the Competition Commission. The EA2002 introduced a new merger regime, with decisions taken in most cases by independent competition authorities against a competition-based test rather than the previous public interest test.

The main provisions of the EA2002 provide for:

1 final decisions on most mergers to be taken by the re-established Office of Fair Trading (OFT) and the Competition Commission (CC) rather than by the Secretary of State;
2 mergers to be considered against a new test of whether they result in a substantial lessening of competition (EA2002 s.35). A number of matters may be potentially relevant to the assessment of whether a merger will result in a substantial lessening of competition. The matters may include, but are not limited to:
   - market shares and concentration;
   - extent of effective competition before and after the merger;
   - efficiency and financial performance of firms in the market;
   - barriers to entry and expansion in the relevant market;
   - availability of substitute products and the scope for supply or demand-side substitution;
   - extent of change and innovation in a market;
   - whether in the absence of the merger one of the firms would fail and, if so, whether its failure would cause the assets of that firm to exit the market;
   - the conduct of customers or of suppliers to those in the market;
3 discretion for the competition authorities to clear a merger or allow it to proceed with less stringent competition remedies in circumstances where it is expected to result in defined types of customer benefit even thought there might be decreased competition (EA2002 s.22);
4 the Secretary of State to continue to decide mergers which raise defined public interest considerations;
5 revisions to the special regime for mergers between water enterprises to align it where possible with the general regime whilst preserving the importance currently attached to the ability of the water regulator to make comparisons between different enterprises;
6 the retention of the existing two-stage approach to merger control. The OFT will carry out the first stage investigation to decide whether a reference to the CC is required. The CC will carry out an in-depth investigation as required;
7 the retention of the system of voluntary rather than compulsory pre-notification of mergers;
8 statutory maximum timetables for competition authorities to reach final decisions (EA2002 ss.24, 25);
9 the replacement of the current worldwide assets-based criteria with a UK-based turnover test for determining whether a merger is subject to merger control (EA2002 s.23) as follows:
   - the value of the turnover in the UK of the enterprise being taken over exceeds £70 million; or
   - the merger would result in the creation or enhancement of at least a 25 per

cent share of supply of goods or services in the UK. This would cover, for example, both a merger between two enterprises each having a 15 per cent share of supply, and between two enterprises where one has a 22 per cent share and the other has a 5 per cent share;

- that between two enterprises where one which already has a 25 per cent share of supply mergers with another having a 5 per cent share.

Substantial acquisitions

A company contemplating the takeover of another company may launch a 'dawn raid' on its target company's shares where a substantial shareholding may be acquired in listed companies at prices not previously publicised.

Substantial acquisitions of shares (SARs)

The SARs which previously restricted the speed by which a person (which would include persons acting together in concert) could increase his holdings or rights in shares amounting to an aggregate between 15 per cent and 30 per cent of a company's voting rights were abolished with effect from 20 May 2006.

The rules relating to the conduct of tender offers previously part of the SARs have been retained and now comprise Appendix 5 of the Code.

Agreements with individual members

A simple way of effecting a transfer of ownership of a company is by making agreements with individual members. It can be effected merely by the exchange of the consideration for duly executed transfers with the share certificates. Usually, however, a formal agreement is entered into between the parties, which should be drawn up with legal advice. The agreement should cover such matters as full details of the shares to be acquired and the consideration to be paid for them with a time for completion, and set out who will be responsible for paying legal costs, duty and any other related expenses. Usually warranties are also required from the directors of the offeree company containing financial information about the offeree company, the title to its property, pending litigation, etc., including any changes affecting the company which may have occurred since the date of the last balance sheet.

The following procedural points arise in connection with the takeover of a company by agreement with individual members:

1. The purchase and sale agreement must be carefully drawn up with legal advice to ensure that the interests of both parties to the agreement are adequately protected.
2. The final agreement is executed and formally exchanged between the parties

and a date set for completion of the exchange of shares for the agreed consideration.

3 At the time of completion the executed transfers, accompanied by the share certificates, are exchanged for the consideration. If any new shares have been issued as part of the consideration, the renounceable certificates for the new shares should be handed over with the forms of renunciation on the renounceable certificates duly signed.
4 The Registrar of Companies should be informed of any changes in director or secretary on Form(s) AP01, AP02, AP03 or AP04 as appropriate and of any change in the registered office address on Form AD01. A return of allotments should also be submitted to the Registrar of Companies on Form SH01 covering the allotments of shares that have been made. If there has been a capitalisation issue, particulars of the contract should also be sent on Form SH01.
5 Entries should then be made in the various statutory registers, e.g. the register of members, reflecting the registration of any share transfers, and the register of directors and secretaries. The share transfers should, of course, be properly stamped or be duly certified as being exempt from stamp duty.
6 Announcements should be made to the UK Listing Authority (for a listed company), the press (if appropriate), the company's customers and its employees. If the offeree company is to become a wholly owned subsidiary of the offeror company, it is necessary to ensure that at least one share in the offeree company is transferred to a nominee of the offeror company in order that the offeree company may have at least two members to ensure compliance with EA2002 s.24.

Purchases in the market

Arrangements may be made whereby a company obtains a significant proportion of the shares in a publicly quoted company by purchases of the company's shares on the market to which the company's shares have been admitted to trading. Fewer formalities are involved with this type of transaction, but care should be taken to ensure compliance with the rules of the City Code on Takeovers and Mergers. It is also important to remember that when the holding reaches 3 per cent or more of nominal value of the company's issued share capital, notice must be given to the company within two days as required by the Disclosure and Transparency Rules (see Chapter 16). The company receiving the notification is required to inform a Regulatory Information Service. In the initial stages, in order to preserve confidentiality, the acquisitions are often made through a nominee or nominees.

However, when calculating the level of holding giving rise to an obligation to notify the company, i.e. 3 per cent, purchases by persons acting in concert with the acquiring company must be included in the total and there is an obligation for such persons to keep each other informed to ensure compliance with the notification requirements. It should also be remembered that the acquisition of certain levels of shareholdings may give rise to an obligation to make a general offer for all the shares of the company which could also affect the price of the shares.

Public offers

A public offer is a takeover offer made to all the shareholders of a company to acquire all or a proportion of their holdings in the offeree company, either for cash or for shares and/or other securities in the offeror company. This is the usual form of takeover and usually receives wide publicity in the press.

Public offers involve many more procedural steps than takeovers by agreement with individual members or by purchases on the Stock Exchange. It is necessary to ensure strict compliance with the City Code, the FSA and, in the case of a listed company, with the requirements of the UK Listing Authority. To comply with the requirements of the FSA, the offer documents will usually be sent direct to the shareholders of the offeree company by a merchant bank or issuing house authorised under that Act. The secretaries and directors of both the offeror and offeree companies will be closely involved in the preparation of the draft documentation, which will require approval by the respective companies' boards.

Offer documentation for a public offer

Although the issuing house and the companies' solicitors will carry out most of the work in preparing the offer documents, the directors of the two companies concerned take legal responsibility for the accuracy of the documents. The company secretary of the offeror company will be particularly concerned with the following matters:

1 If both or either the offeror or offeree company are listed, the documentation must comply with the *Listing Rules* (Chapters 10 and 13). Appropriate documentation will require approval by the UK Listing Authority.
2 If it is considered likely that the matter will be referred to the Competition Commission, the offer document must contain a term that the offer will lapse if the matter is referred to the Commission before the first closing date for the offer or the date upon which the offer is declared unconditional, whichever occurs first. The offeror company will in many instances make the offer conditional on the matter not being referred to the Commission and that any decision not to refer must be on terms acceptable to the offeror. If it is likely that a reference will be made, the offeror should consider the representations to be made to the Commission in support of the merger and whether advance clearance should be sought. Any advance clearance will be the subject of publicity, which may cause the share price of the offeree to rise making the proposed acquisition less likely as the cost of acquisition may rise too high.

3 An increase in the share capital of the offeror company may be required so that the company has sufficient capital for the issue of shares in connection with the offer. Consequently, it may be necessary to call a general meeting of the company to approve the increase in capital, the appropriate documents being submitted to the UK Listing Authority for approval if the company is a listed company. If the shares to be issued in connection with the offer are to be listed on the Official List and admitted to trading on the Main Market or PLUS Listed, the offer documentation should also include the listing particulars contained in the *Listing Rules*.

The following practical matters arise in connection with a takeover by a public offer:

1. The document which the shareholder signs must constitute a transfer of the securities being acquired to the offeror company.
2. Unless contrary instructions are given, any existing dividend mandates applicable to the shares in the offeree company will be applied to the shares in the offeror company being issued in exchange.
3. The form of acceptance and transfer should be designed so that it can be used as a working form, with relevant boxes for various steps in the processing to be filled in as they are completed.
4. Companies whose shares are settled within CREST will need to liaise with their registrars at an early stage to ensure that the appropriate corporate actions procedures are established to enable shareholders to accept the offer within CREST.
5. Envelopes for the offer documents, with reply-paid envelopes for the return of forms of acceptance and transfer with the share certificates, should be prepared to be sent to the shareholders in the offeree company.
6. Envelopes should also be prepared for any circular letter to be sent to the offeror company's own shareholders, either to explain the reasons for the offer or in connection with the convening of an extraordinary general meeting to approve any necessary increase in capital.
7. Since events in takeover battles sometimes move fairly swiftly, it will be prudent to have available further sets of envelope labels, both to the offeror company's shareholders and to the offeree company's shareholders, in case further circulars are to be issued, e.g. perhaps following an improvement in the terms of the offer.

Acceptances of a public offer

Most shareholders, including institutional shareholders, will not accept the offer until the final few days before the closing date. The office of the offeror company, or its registrar's office or the receiving banker's office, should be prepared to deal with the last rush of acceptances. The Takeover Panel requires stringent procedures to be followed to avoid possible double counting of acceptances and purchases of the same shareholding.

The following action should be taken on receipt of the acceptances:

1 Check that the form of acceptance and transfer has been properly completed, with relevant share certificate(s), against the copy of the register of members of the offeree company.
2 Acceptance forms are usually accepted even though not accompanied by the relevant share certificate(s) but such acceptances, although they may be treated as valid, should be set to one side so that they may be completed when the accompanying share certificate(s) is/are sent in.
3 Acceptances may also be certificated if the share certificates for a recent purchase have not yet been prepared.

If a shareholder has lost his certificate(s), it will be necessary to issue an indemnity in order that a duplicate certificate may be prepared to support the acceptance. Also, if forms of acceptance have been signed by a personal representative or a power of attorney, it will be necessary to ensure that the appropriate documents have been duly registered and, if not, to request their submission.

During the period of the offer the offeree company should notify the offeror company of transfers received for registration in order that the offer documents may be sent out to these new shareholders and the copy of the register of members of the offeree company updated. A reminder may be published in the press just before the final date for the acceptance of the offer, sometimes accompanied by a warning that, if there is a cash alternative to the offer in shares, the period for which it remains available for acceptance is subject to the underwriting arrangements. If no underwriting is involved, however, it may be extended indefinitely, subject to the offer being declared unconditional by the 60th day after the posting of the offer.

Action following the first closing date of a public offer

Totals of the complete and incomplete acceptances will be calculated and the board of the offeror company will then consider whether the level of acceptances is such that it may declare the bid to be unconditional or whether it will extend it for a further period. If the level of acceptances is small, the offeror company may decide to extend the period for acceptances and, perhaps, improve the terms of the offer.

The Receiving Agents' Code of Practice issued by the Takeover Panel sets out the procedure which must be closely followed to avoid double counting of acceptances and purchases of the same shareholding. There is thus a need for close cooperation between the receiving agents and the company's registrars.

Once the offer has been declared unconditional, however, it is necessary to prepare the consideration documents, i.e. the definitive certificates for shares and/ or other securities in the offeror company to be issued in exchange for shares in the offeree company, and to draw cheques for those who have accepted a cash alternative. A committee of the board of the offeror company should be established in order to make the allotments of the consideration securities. It would be usual for the consideration to be sent out 21 days after the closing date or 21 days after the date on which valid acceptances are received by the offeror company or its agents. Also, upon an offer becoming unconditional, share options under SAYE and other employee share schemes will often become exercisable.

Arrangements should be made to obtain a listing of the securities issued if the company, being a listed company, has increased its capital in order to implement the offer.

Transfers to offeror company

The transfer which is executed by or on behalf of the offeror company (i.e. the company making the takeover offer) covering the shares in respect of which duly executed forms of acceptance and transfer have been received in order to put these shares into the name of the offeror company is known as a 'bulk transfer'. It is used in conjunction with the individual forms of acceptance and transfer for each separate accepting shareholder. The bulk transfer is obviously more convenient than dealing separately with the many individual forms of acceptance and transfer, each of which has been signed by each accepting shareholder and each of which would have to be duly stamped by HMRC before registration.

The bulk transfer itself must be duly stamped by HMRC in the usual way. In order that this may be assessed, a schedule giving details of the forms of acceptance is attached to the bulk transfer. This is necessary because HMRC calculates the amount of stamp duty separately for each holding transferred and these amounts are then aggregated to ascertain the amount of stamp duty payable on the bulk transfer. The completed forms of acceptance and transfer, together with the covering share certificates and the duly stamped bulk transfer, are lodged with the offeree company.

Compulsory acquisition

Compulsory acquisition is dealt with in CA2006 ss.974–987. These sections are designed to protect the rights of the minority to resist compulsory acquisition if they have reasonable grounds to do so and to ensure that they are treated no less fairly than shareholders who have accepted the offer.

The Companies Act provides a procedure for the offeror company to acquire compulsorily certain non-assented minority shareholdings (squeeze out provisions). If the offeror company has by virtue of acceptances to the offer acquired or contracted to acquire not less than nine-tenths in value of the shares to which the offer relates, it may give notice to the holder of any shares that it has not so acquired, or contracted to acquire, that it desires to acquire his shares (CA2006 s.979).

The notice must be issued during the period of three months after the last date for acceptance of the offer but cannot be given later than six months from the date of commencement of the offer (CA2006 s.980).

Even where the acquiring company, having acquired 90 per cent of the shares does not wish to enforce its right to buy out the minority holders, notice must be given to those holders so that they may exercise their right to be bought out by the acquiring company on the same terms as the offer (sell-out provisions). The notice must be issued within one month of reaching the 90 per cent acceptance level. The non-assenting shareholders can exercise their right to be bought out provided they give notice within three months of the end of the period for acceptance under the offer or, if earlier, within three months of the date of the notice issued by the company pursuant to CA2006 s.984(3) (CA2006 s.984).

Shares already held by the offeror company, i.e. registered in its name at the date the offer was made, including any shares contracted to be acquired but not registered in the offeror company's name at that date, are excluded from calculation of the nine-tenths minimum. However, shares the holders of which are subject to a contract for no consideration to accept the offer after it is made are not excluded. Shares acquired by the offeror company, by market purchases or private agreement subsequent to the date of making the offer, may also count towards the nine-tenths minimum subject to the price paid for the shares not exceeding the value of the offer or revised offer.

The notice that it wishes to acquire shares must be given to a non-assenting shareholder on Form 984. A copy of the notice together with a statutory declaration (Form 980 dec) confirming that the conditions for giving the notice are satisfied must be sent to the offeree company (CA2006 s.980(4)). CA2006 s.981 deals with the effects of giving a notice under CA2006 s.980, the principal ones being:

1 Where the offeror company has given a choice of consideration which may be taken by the offeree company's shareholders for their shares, a non-assenting shareholder must be given the same alternatives as shareholders who have accepted the offer even if some of these may have lapsed. The offeror may stipulate in the s.980 notice the terms which will apply if the non-assenting shareholder does not respond to the notice within six weeks from the date of the notice. This provision prevents those dissenting from blocking the compulsory acquisition.
2 At the end of six weeks from the date of the compulsory acquisition notice, the compulsory acquisition is effected by the offeror company sending the offeree company a copy of the notice together with a form of transfer for each dissenting shareholder covering his shares in the offeree company which have not been assented to the offer. This is accompanied by a share certificate for the total number of consideration shares in the offeror company for the non-assenting shareholders or a cheque for the total cash consideration, as appropriate. Each such transfer is executed by a person appointed by the offeror company on behalf of the shareholders concerned (CA2006 s.981(7)).

3 These transfers will then be registered by the offeree company, thereby putting the dissenting shareholders' shares in the offeree company into the name of the offeror company. The shares in the offeror company received as consideration will be held by the offeree company on trust for the former shareholders. Any cash consideration should be held in a separate interest-bearing bank account.
4 The offeree company is required to hold the consideration for the non-assenting shareholders for a period of 12 years. At the end of this period, providing that it has at intervals during that period made reasonable enquiries to trace the non-assenting shareholders, shares in the offeror company received as consideration may be sold and the proceeds, together with any consideration received in cash being held in the bank account, paid into Court. Similar action would be taken on the winding up of the offeree company. The company's costs in making the enquiries may be recovered from such proceeds or money held in the separate bank account.

The right of a minority (i.e. non-assenting) shareholder to be bought out by the offeror company is provided by CA2006 s.983. When the offeror company has in pursuance of a takeover offer acquired by acceptances not less than nine-tenths in value of all the shares in issue of the offeree company (including any shares which it has otherwise acquired or contracted to acquire since the date of the offer), the holder of any shares who has not accepted the offer may send a written communication to the offeror company requiring it to acquire his shares.

The offeror company must within one month of having acquired nine-tenths of all the shares send a notice to any shareholders who have not assented to the offer informing them of their right to be bought out and they may within three months of the notice or, if later, within three months of the deadline for acceptance of the offer require the offeror company to acquire their shares. The notice is sent on Form 984.

Where the terms of the offer give a choice of consideration which may be taken by the offeree company's shareholders for their shares, the notice under CA2006 s.984 to the non-assenting shareholder must give particulars of the choices available and which option is to apply if the shareholder does not indicate a choice when requiring the offeror company to acquire his shares (CA2006 s.985).

It should be noted that where there is a choice of consideration between shares in the offeror company, or a sum in cash for each share in the offeree company, the underwriting arrangements will usually stipulate that the cash offer is open for a certain period only, at the end of which the consideration may be taken only in shares. However, in the case of compulsory acquisition under CA2006 s.979, and whether or not any time limit was applicable to any of the terms of the offer, e.g. a cash offer, the offeror is bound to pay cash for the non-assenting shareholder's shares or if the choice chosen is shares and the offeror company is no longer able to provide these, the consideration paid to the non-assenting shareholder must consist of an amount of cash which at the date of the compulsory acquisition notice under CA2006 s.979 is equivalent to the chosen consideration (CA2006 s.981(5)). In the case of the exercise of shareholders' rights to be bought out under CA2006 s.983 the same provisions regarding a cash offer apply, but where the offeror company is no longer able to provide the share alternative, the amount of cash payable is equivalent to the chosen consideration as at the date that the non-assenting shareholder requires the offeror company to acquire his shares (CA2006 s.985(5)).

It will be seen, therefore, that the window for the dissenting shareholders to take the cash offer should they so desire is reopened. Care must be taken to ensure that the notices are correctly sent, e.g. by recorded delivery in the United Kingdom or by airmail outside the United Kingdom.

Where the offeror company gives notice of compulsory acquisition under CA2006 s.979, the Court may, on the application of a non-assenting shareholder within six weeks of the date of the CA2006 s.979 notice, order that the offeror not be entitled to acquire his shares or that the shares will be acquired on terms different from those of the offer (CA2006 s.986(1)). In the case of the exercise of the rights of a non-assenting shareholder under s.983, on the application of either the shareholder or the offeror, the Court may order such terms as it thinks fit on which the offeror is entitled and bound to acquire the shares. Compulsory acquisition under s.979 may be impossible where a company has numerous untraceable shareholders. Under subsections (2) or (4) of CA2006 s.979 where a takeover has not been accepted to the extent necessary to effect compulsory acquisition under CA2006 s.979, the Court may, on the application of the offeror company, authorise the company to proceed to give CA2006 s.979 compulsory acquisition notices to shareholders who have not accepted the offer if it is satisfied that the offeror company has taken all reasonable steps to trace the shareholders concerned and if the total of the shares assented to the offer added to the total of the shares held by the untraceable shareholders amounts to not less than the minimum required to implement the CA2006 s.979 compulsory acquisition procedure (CA2006 s.986(9)).

The consideration held by the offeree company on trust for the dissenting shareholders may subsequently be claimed by them on surrender of the documents of title to shares in the offeree company or giving an indemnity if they can no longer be found. Quite often the claim will be made by the executors of a deceased non-assenting shareholder's estate who, in winding up his affairs, find that he held shares in the offeree company and had not accepted the offer.

When a claim is received, any cash will be paid out, or, if the consideration is in the form of shares in the offeror company, the offeree company will execute a transfer in the name of the entitled holder and send this to the offeror company for registration, accompanied by the share certificate for shares in the offeror company being held by the offeree company. The offeror company will prepare a share certificate in the holder's name and send a balance certificate in the name of the offeree company for the shares in the offeror company still to be claimed.

Stamp duty exemptions

Takeovers (and schemes of arrangements) are sometimes arranged in such a way that there is exemption from stamp duty on the transfer of shares to the offeree company. These exemptions are usually only available where the 'takeover' relates to a re-structuring of a company or group of companies and where ultimate ownership does not change as a result of the acquisition. Under FA1986 s.77 exemption from stamp duty may be claimed under circumstances where there has been no change in ownership. The following conditions must be met for a claim for exemption to succeed:

1 The acquiring company must acquire the whole or a part of the target undertaking as part of a scheme of reconstruction.
2 The acquiring company must be a UK registered company.
3 The consideration must consist only of shares to be issued to the shareholders of the target company.
4 There must be no consideration other than the discharge or assumption of any liabilities of the target company by the acquirer.
5 The transaction must be for bona fide commercial reasons and not just a scheme for the avoidance of tax or stamp duty.
6 The shares must be issued to the shareholders of the target company pro rata to their existing holdings so that the shareholders of the acquiring company are in the same proportions after the transaction as their holdings of shares in the target company prior to the transaction.

Reconstruction

Schemes of arrangement

A takeover of one company by another may be effected by a liquidation under the provisions of IA1986 s.110 or a scheme of arrangement under the provisions of CA2006 ss.895–901. These arrangements are, however, more complicated than the forms of takeover described above and involve the incorporation of a new holding company to takeover both the offeree and the offeror companies in order to merge their operations.

Alternatively, the offeror company may acquire the undertaking of the offeree company for cash or the issue of shares in the acquiring company. Schemes of arrangement may be useful where it is desired to acquire 100 per cent of the offeree company but, because of the nature of the business, it would not be possible to obtain the required 90 per cent level of acceptances which would enable the offeror company to effect compulsory acquisition. The approval of the Court is required and consequently the legal advisers of both companies will be involved in settling the necessary documentation.

Reconstruction by liquidation

A takeover by means of a reconstruction is effected by winding up the offeree company. This effects the sale of the company's assets to another company in exchange for shares in that company, which are then distributed to the shareholders of the offeree company in proportion to their holdings. Reconstruction by liquidation and sale of the offeree company's assets is appropriate only in cases where the continued existence of the offeree company is not desired. The liquidation is effected as a members' or creditors' voluntary winding up and the detailed provisions governing procedure are laid down in IA1986 s.110. In view of the many complications that may arise, legal and taxation advice should be taken.

Reconstruction may be suitable where there is to be a reduction of capital combined with the provision of fresh capital for a new company by the members of the reconstructed company. For example, a company with an adverse balance on its profit and loss account but with good prospects could be wound up and its assets sold to a new company (after paying off creditors) in exchange for partly paid shares in the new company allotted to members of the old company in proportion to their existing holdings. The calling up of the unpaid liability on the new shares would provide working capital for the future operations of the business. In the case of a public company it would be usual for the provision of new capital to be underwritten in case there are shareholders who do not assent to the scheme for reconstruction or assenting shareholders who fail to pay up the calls on the partly paid shares. However, the total holdings of the dissenting shareholders should not exceed an agreed percentage because under IA1986 s.111(2) the underwriters would have to buy out the interests of the dissenting shareholders in order that the scheme could be implemented. A dissenting shareholder is a member of the transferor company who does not vote in favour of the special resolution to wind up the company and who notifies the liquidator that he should either abstain from carrying the resolution into effect or purchase his interest at an agreed price.

It is desirable that resolutions for approving a reconstruction under IA1986 s.110 be submitted to two meetings, the first meeting to approve the reconstruction and the second meeting to put the company into liquidation. If both resolutions were passed at the same meeting, the company would still have to be wound up even if the number of dissenting shareholders made the implementation of the scheme of reconstruction impracticable.

The procedural steps for a reconstruction are as follows:

1 A board meeting of the company to be liquidated is convened for the following purposes:
   (a) to make the necessary declaration of solvency;
   (b) to settle the draft agreement to be entered into by the liquidator for the sale of the company to the new company;
   (c) to approve the Articles of the new company;

(d) to approve that the draft underwriting contract be executed by the liquidator or for the company to execute with adoption by the liquidator later;
(e) to approve the circular letter to the shareholders informing them of the reasons for the proposed reconstruction and the terms;
(f) to approve the notice of general meeting and form of proxy (which must be a three-way proxy in the case of listed companies).

2 Special resolutions for reconstruction and liquidation are passed at a general meeting.
3 The business of the offeree company (i.e. the old company) is continued by the liquidator from the date of the resolution to wind up to the date when the business is acquired by the new company.
4 When the sale agreement has been executed, the liquidator transfers the assets to the new company. He must ensure that he retains sufficient assets to pay off the creditors of the old company unless they have agreed that liability for these debts may be transferred to the new company by means of a novation agreement. He must also retain assets to purchase the interests of any dissenting shareholders and to pay the expenses of the liquidation and his own remuneration.
5 A letter is sent to shareholders giving details of their rights to shares in the newly formed company, which will be issued in exchange for their shares in the old company on receipt of their share certificates. As noted above, the shares in the new company would be offered as partly paid shares in proportion to shareholders' existing holdings in the old company; the additional capital would then be called up and thus provide working capital for the future operation of the business by the new company.
6 The liquidator continues to complete the liquidation of the old company in accordance with the usual procedure. On completion of the liquidation, it is usual for the liquidator to execute a conveyance transferring all the residual property of the old company to the new company.

18

Corporate governance

Introduction

Corporate governance is defined in the Cadbury Report as 'the system by which companies are directed and controlled'. Shareholders appoint the directors and the external auditors, and should satisfy themselves that an appropriate governance structure is in place. The board of directors sets the company's aims and has a responsibility to provide the leadership to put these into effect, to supervise the management of the business and to report to shareholders on its stewardship.

The financial aspects of corporate governance are identified as the way in which the board sets financial policy and oversees its implementation (including the use of financial controls) and the process of reporting to the shareholders on the activities and development of the company.

Background

The economic success of the 1980s was followed by a downswing in the economic cycle resulting in large numbers of corporate failures. Additionally, there were several high-profile cases of corporate failure involving fraud and/or spectacular lack of internal controls. In order to restore confidence in financial reporting, strengthening of accounting standards and the position of the external auditor in dealing with boards of directors was called for.

Cadbury

Following the Robert Maxwell/Mirror Group pension scandal and the collapse of BCCI, there was concerted public pressure for reform. Against this background, in May 1992 Sir Adrian Cadbury's Committee issued a consultative document, the *Report of the Committee on the Financial Aspects of Corporate Governance*. The final report was issued in December 1992 and was generally perceived as a major advance.

A core element of the report was the Cadbury Code of Best Practice. Compliance with the code provisions is not mandatory and operates under the so-called comply or explain regime where companies departing from the Code must explain the reasons for non-compliance (*LR 9.8.6(5) and (6)*). Cadbury understood that it was essential to keep the Code up to date and recommended that a new committee be appointed by 30 June 1995 in order to continue the process of review.

Greenbury

Published in July 1995 the report of the new committee, *Directors' Remuneration – Report of a Study Group chaired by Sir Richard Greenbury,* addressed the large salary increases and share option gains enjoyed by directors of the recently privatised utilities, which had led to the popular usage of the title 'fat cat' when describing apparently overpaid directors. The remuneration packages of high-profile directors in other sectors were also attracting attention.

The overriding objective of the Greenbury Committee was to establish a voluntary Code of Best Practice for directors' remuneration, and to impose a more onerous disclosure regime.

Increasing the disclosure requirements would ensure that shareholders were fully informed and able to make informed decisions on the performance of companies and their directors. A central plank of this disclosure regime was the promotion of the remuneration committee. The Report was founded upon three principles:

1 Accountability – directors are accountable to shareholders for the stewardship and performance of their company and responsibility for determining executive remuneration should be delegated to a disinterested body (i.e. the remuneration committee).
2 Transparency – corporate policy on executive remuneration should be reported on annually to shareholders and details of individual directors' packages should be set out in the annual report and accounts.
3 Performance – executive rewards should be linked to the performance of the company and of the individual, and the interests of directors should be aligned with those of shareholders.

Hampel

Following publication of the Greenbury Report, the Committee on Corporate Governance, chaired by Sir Ronald Hampel, was set up in mid-1995 to review progress of the implementation of the findings of the Cadbury and Greenbury Committees. Following wide consultation, the Hampel Committee's final report was issued in January 1998.

The Hampel Committee established a set of broad Principles of Corporate Governance concerning directors, their remuneration, shareholders and accountability and audit, bringing together elements of the earlier codes.

The Committee advocated a flexible approach to compliance, urging shareholders to take note of reasons given by companies for variations from best practice in corporate governance.

The Committee proposed that major changes in corporate governance should be dealt with by the London Stock Exchange and that the Financial Reporting Council should keep a watching brief on the necessity for further studies.

The Hampel Report proposed the consolidation of the Cadbury Code, the Greenbury Code and the Hampel Principles into one consolidated code. The Committee passed its proposals to the Stock Exchange, which published the Combined Code in June 1998.

Turnbull

Following publication of the Cadbury Code, guidance was issued concerning the disclosure required relating to internal controls. The disclosure requirements were restricted to financial controls.

After the Hampel Report, additional guidance on reporting on internal control under the Combined Code was issued in September 1999 by the Institute of Chartered Accountants in England and Wales (ICAEW). *Internal Control: Guidance for Directors on the Combined Code*, known as the Turnbull Report, sets out guidance for directors on:

- maintaining a sound system of internal control to safeguard the shareholders' investment and the company's assets;
- determining the extent of their compliance with Code; and
- periodic consideration of whether an internal audit function should be established.

Higgs and Smith

Since the 1998 Hampel Report, the Financial Reporting Council (FRC) has acted as a focus for considering whether any developments in corporate governance call for further work. After the concerns raised by high-profile failures in the US and UK and the increasing perception of directors receiving rewards for failure, the DTI sponsored a review of the role and effectiveness of non-executive directors. The review chaired by Derek Higgs (the Higgs Review) published its report in January 2003.

On the same day a second review into the role and responsibilities of audit committees under the chairmanship of Sir Robert Smith (the Smith Report) was also published. The two review bodies worked closely together and the Higgs Review included a draft of the Combined Code incorporating both its own and the Smith's Report proposals.

The 2003 Combined Code

On 23 July 2003, the FRC announced that the final text of the amended Combined Code had been agreed and that the changes would be brought into effect for all listed companies for reporting years commencing on or after 1 November 2003. At the same time, the opportunity was taken to take account of the Directors' Remuneration Report Regulations, which came into effect on 1 August 2002. The Regulations made some provisions of the Code redundant.

The revised Code superseded and replaced the code issued by the Hampel Committee 1998. In addition to the Code itself, the 2003 Code included guidance on how to comply with various sections of the Code:

- guidance on Internal Control issued by the Turnbull Committee;
- Audit Committees – Combined Code Guidance issued by the Smith Group. This provides guidance on Code provisions C3;
- suggestions for good practice from the Higgs Report.

Following a review of the Combined Code in 2005, a small number of changes were incorporated in an updated version of the Code published in June 2006. The updated Code applies to reporting years beginning on or after 1 November 2006. A small number of changes were made in 2008 and these apply to accounting periods beginning on or after 29 June 2008. Accordingly, at the time of writing there are two versions of the Code in operation.

The main changes in the 2003 Combined Code were:

1 to enable the company chairman to sit on the remuneration committee where considered independent on appointment as chairman (although it is recommended that he or she should not also chair the committee);
2 to provide a 'vote withheld' option on proxy appointment forms to enable shareholders to indicate if they have reservations on a resolution but do not wish to vote against; and
3 to recommend that companies publish on their website the details of proxies lodged at a general meeting where votes are taken on a show of hands.

The main changes in the 2008 Combined Code are:

1 removal of the restriction on an individual chairing more than one FTSE 100 company; and
2 for listed companies outside the FTSE 350, allowing the company chairman to sit on the audit committee where he or she was considered independent on appointment.

The 2008 Code is reproduced in Appendix 3. The Code, plus additional guidance, is available via the CD-ROM resource bank.

The Code is subject to periodic reviews and changes by the FRC. The next review will take place in 2010. See the FRC website for details (see Directory).

The 2008 Combined Code

Structure

The Combined Code contains main and supporting principles and provisions:

1 Section 1 – Companies:
   (A) Directors;
   (B) Directors' remuneration;
   (C) Accountability and audit;
   (D) Relations with shareholders.
2 Section 2 – Institutional shareholders.
   (E) Institutional shareholders.

There then follow three schedules:

A Provisions on the design of performance related remuneration;
B Guidance on liability of non-executive directors: care, skill and diligence;
C Disclosure of corporate governance arrangements.

Directors

Section 1(A) of the Combined Code identifies six principles in relation to directors.

1 Every company should be headed by an effective board, which is collectively responsible for the success of the company.
2 There should be a clear division of responsibilities at the head of the company between the running of the board and the executive responsibility for the running of the company's business. No one individual should have unfettered powers of decision.
3 The board should include a balance of executive and non-executive directors (and in particular independent non-executive directors) such that no individual or small group of individuals can dominate the board's decision-taking.
4 There should be a formal, rigorous and transparent procedure for the appointment of new directors to the board.
5 The board should be supplied in a timely manner with information in a form and of a quality appropriate to enable it to discharge its duties. All directors should receive induction on joining the board and should regularly update and refresh their skills and knowledge.
6 The board should undertake a formal and rigorous annual evaluation of its own performance and that of its committees and individual directors.
7 All directors should be submitted for re-election at regular intervals, subject to continued satisfactory performance. The board should ensure planned and progressive refreshing of the board.

Directors' remuneration

Section 1(B) of the Combined Code identifies two principles in relation to directors' remuneration.

1 The levels of remuneration should be sufficient to attract, retain and motivate directors of the quality required to run the company successfully, but a company should avoid paying more than is necessary for this purpose. A significant proportion of executive directors' remuneration should be structured so as to link rewards to corporate and individual performance.
2 There should be a formal and transparent procedure for developing policy on executive remuneration and for fixing the remuneration packages of individual directors. No director should be involved in deciding his or her own remuneration.

Accountability and audit

Part 1(C) of the Combined Code identifies three principles on accountability and audit:

1 The board should present a balanced and understandable assessment of the company's position and prospects.
2 The board should maintain a sound system of internal control to safeguard the shareholders' investment and the company's assets.
3 The board should establish formal and transparent arrangements for considering how they should apply the financial reporting and internal control principles and for maintaining an appropriate relationship with the company's auditors.

Relations with shareholders

Part 1(D) of the Combined Code identifies two principles on relations with shareholders:

1 There should be a dialogue with shareholders based on mutual understanding of objectives. The board as a whole has responsibility for ensuring that a satisfactory dialogue with shareholders takes place.
2 The board should use the AGM to communicate with investors and to encourage their participation.

Code provisions

Underlying the main principles in section 1 parts (A)–(D) are a number of detailed Code provisions. These are reproduced in full in Appendix 3.

Compliance statement

The Listing Rules require listed companies to make a disclosure statement in two parts in relation to the Code. In the first part of the statement, the company has to report on how it applies the principles in the Code. In future this will need to cover both main and supporting principles. The form and content of this part of the statement are not prescribed, the intention being that companies should be free to explain their governance policies, including any special circumstances which have led to their approach. In the second part of the statement the company has either to confirm that it complies with the Code's provisions or provide an explanation of why it does not comply. This continues the 'comply or explain' approach and the flexibility it offers has been widely welcomed both by companies and investors.

The requirements in the Code for disclosure in the annual report and accounts are:

1. a statement of how the board operates, including a statement of matters reserved to the board (A.1.1);
2. the names of the chairman, deputy chairman, chief executive, senior independent director and the chairmen and members of the nomination, audit and remuneration committees (A.1.2);
3. individual attendance record for directors at board and committee meetings (A.1.2);
4. the names of the independent non-executive directors, with reasons where necessary to justify independence (A.3.1);
5. any significant external commitments of the chairman and any changes during the year (A.4.3);
6. how performance of the directors both individually and collectively has been conducted (A.6.1);
7. the steps the board has taken to ensure directors develop an understanding of the views of major shareholders (D.1.2);
8. a separate section detailing the work of the nomination committee, including details of the process used in relation to board appointments and in particular in relation to the appointment of a chairman or a non-executive director (A.4.6);
9. a description of the work of the remuneration committee as required under the Directors' Remuneration Reporting Regulations 2002, and including, where an executive director serves as a non-executive director elsewhere, details of any remuneration retained by that director (B.1.4);
10. an explanation from the directors of their responsibility for preparing the accounts and a statement by the auditors about their reporting responsibilities (C.1.1);
11. a statement from the directors that the business is a going concern, with supporting assumptions or qualifications as necessary (C.1.2);
12. a report that the board has conducted a review of the group's internal controls (C.2.1);

13 a section describing the work of the audit committee (C.3.3);
14 if there is no internal audit function, the reasons (C.3.5);
15 where the board overules the audit committee's recommendation on the appointment, reappointment or removal of an external auditor, a statement from the audit committee outlining their recommendation and the reasons for the board not accepting that recommendation (C.3.6);
16 if the auditor provides non-audit services, details of how auditor objectivity and independence is safeguarded (C.3.7).

The following information should be made available (which may be met by making it available on request and making the information available on the company's website):

1 an explanation of the role, authority and terms of reference of the nomination, remuneration and audit committees (A.4.1, B.2.1 and C.3.3);
2 the terms and conditions of appointment of non-executive directors (A.4.4);
3 where remuneration consultants are appointed, a statement of whether they have any other connection with the company (B.2.1). The board should set out to shareholders in the papers accompanying a resolution to elect or re-elect directors sufficient biographical details to enable shareholders to take an informed decision (A.7.1) and why they believe an individual should be elected to a non-executive role (A.7.2); and
4 on re-election of a non-executive director, confirmation that, following a formal evaluation, the individual continues to be effective and to demonstrate commitment to the role (A.7.2).

The board should set out to shareholders in the papers recommending appointment or reappointment of an external auditor, if the board does not accept the audit committee's recommendation, a statement from the audit committee explaining the recommendation and from the board setting out reasons why they have taken a different position (C.3.6).

The Listing Rules require auditors to review certain aspects of the company's compliance statement (see pp. 336–337).

Directors' remuneration report

For listed companies the reporting requirements for directors' remuneration fall into three categories:

- Companies Act requirements;
- Listing Rules requirements; and
- best practice.

The statutory requirements were clarified by the Directors' Remuneration Report Regulations 2002, which came into force for financial years ending on or after 31 December 2002. These were brought in by the Government in the face of growing unease at the perceived rise in so-called rewards for failure where departing directors received large payouts from failing companies.

The Regulations apply to 'quoted' companies, that is only to companies that have equity listed on the UKLA Official List and admitted to trading on the Main Market or PLUS Listed, and not e.g. to AIM companies or companies that have only debt listed.

The rules, however, do apply to companies that have securities listed on an official exchange of an EEA state, the New York Stock Exchange or on NASDAQ.

The board must prepare a directors' remuneration report, which must be approved by the board and signed on its behalf. The report must be circulated in the same manner as the annual report and accounts and laid before the members in general meeting.

Acceptance or rejection of the directors' remuneration report is the subject of a separate resolution at the general meeting.

The report must include:

1 Details of each director who was a member of the remuneration committee during the period under review.
2 Information on the use of any external remuneration consultants including the name of any person providing consultancy services concerning directors' pay, details of any other service provided to the company in that year and whether that person was appointed by the remuneration committee.
3 A forward-looking policy statement on the remuneration of directors, including, for each director:
   (i) a summary of any performance conditions attaching to any share options or long-term incentive scheme;
   (ii) justification for these conditions;
   (iii) a summary and justification of the tests used in determining whether those conditions are met;
   (iv) if any performance condition relates to external factors details about those factors and, if those factors relate to one or more other company or an index, their identity;
   (v) a description of and explanation about any significant amendment proposed to be made for any director's share options or long-term incentive;
   (vi) an explanation of why any share options or long-term incentive schemes are not subject to performance conditions, if that is the case; and
   (vii) an explanation on each remuneration package as to the relative importance of each element that is performance related.

   The policy statement must also disclose details on duration of notice periods in and termination payments under service contracts.
4 A line graph to compare five-year share price performance of the company (by reference to total shareholder return) with that of other shares on a named equity market index.

5 For each director, information on their service contracts including: date, unexpired term and notice periods; provision for compensation payable upon early termination together with other information necessary to calculate an estimate of liability in the event of early termination.
6 Disclosure of each director's remuneration package, split into the component parts: basic salary and fees; bonuses; expenses allowance and benefits in kind; compensation for loss of office and/or other payments connected with early termination or breach of contract; and other non-cash benefits not falling under one of the prescribed heads. The amounts must be totalled and appear in tabular form together with the previous year's comparatives. The nature and the estimated value of 'other non-cash benefits' must be stated.
7 A policy statement on the granting of executive options or awards under any SAYE or other long-term incentive scheme. Any departure from or change to the previous year's policy must be explained and justified.
8 Disclosure of share options and SAYE options for each director, as at the end of the financial year and until a date not more than one month before the circulation of the annual report and accounts. Total interests must be shown and a distinction made between those that are beneficial and those that are non-beneficial. Specific information requiring disclosure includes: share options that were awarded or exercised in the year; options that expired unexercised in the year; and any variation to terms and conditions relating to the award or exercise of share options. For all unexpired share options, disclosure is required of the price paid for its award, if any, the exercise price, the date from which the options may be exercised and date on which the options expire, as well as the market price at the end of the year and the highest and lowest prices during that year. In respect of share options exercised, the disclosures must show market price as at the time when the options were exercised.
9 Details for each director of any long-term incentive schemes (other than share options). Interests in such schemes at both the start and the end of the year under review should be shown. Entitlements and awards granted during the year must also be made public – and the year in which such entitlements and awards can be taken up specified, together with any variations made to any scheme terms.
10 Details of contributions to and entitlements in any defined benefit scheme for each director – the amount of retirement benefits accruing in the year, the accumulated accrued benefits (pension and lump sum) as at the end of the year under review, information on or necessary to determine transfer values, early retirement rights and any discretionary benefits.
11 For money purchase schemes, details of contributions made or payable during the year under review.
12 Aggregate of excess retirement benefits receivable by directors, past directors or their nominees or dependants. Details of the estimated money value and the nature of any non-cash benefits must be given.

13 Disclosure of significant payments made to former directors during the year.
14 Aggregate of consideration payable to third parties for the services of any director.
15 Estimated value and the nature of any non-cash benefits.
16 An explanation and justification for any element of remuneration that is pensionable other than basic salary. A distinction should be made between those amounts paid for services as a director of a company or its subsidiaries, and those paid under a contract of employment either with the company or its subsidiaries. A director of a parent company must also disclose in the parent company's accounts amounts of emoluments paid to him/her by subsidiaries. The 'aggregate amount of directors' emoluments etc.' (CA1985, para.1 of Sch.6) disclosed in the notes to the accounts is still required.

The role of the auditors

The *Listing Rules* require the directors to include a statement on compliance with the Combined Code and a statement on going concern, and stipulate that these statements must be reviewed by the auditors (*LR 9.8.6, LR 9.8.10*). In the case of the compliance statement, the auditors are only required to review compliance with the following seven provisions:

1 [A.1.1] The board should have a formal schedule of matters specifically reserved for its decision.
2 [A.5.2] There should be an agreed procedure for directors especially non-executive directors to have independent professional advice if necessary, at the company's expense.
3 [A.7.2] Non-executive directors should be appointed for specified terms and reappointment should not be automatic.
4 [A.7.1] All directors should be subject to election by the shareholder at the first opportunity after their appointment and to re-election at intervals of no more than three years, and shareholders should be provided with sufficient biographical details of all directors submitted for election or re-election to enable them to take an informed decision.
5 [C.1.1] The directors should explain their responsibility for preparing the accounts and there should be a statement by the auditors about their reporting responsibilities.
6 [C.2.1] The directors should review the effectiveness of the company's system of internal control at least annually, and should report to shareholders that they have done so. The review should cover all controls, including financial, operational and compliance controls, and risk management.
7 [C.3.1–7] The board should establish an audit committee of at least three directors, all non-executive, with written terms of reference dealing clearly with its authority and duties (Smaller companies' audit committees may have two members.) The members of the audit committee, a majority of whom

should be independent non-executive directors, should be named in the annual report and accounts.

Internal control

As outlined above, guidance on reporting on internal control under the Combined Code was originally issued in September 1999 by the Institute of Chartered Accountants in England and Wales as *Internal Control: Guidance for Directors on the Combined Code* (the Turnbull Report). Although not forming part of the Code itself, the Combined Code includes the Turnbull Report (updated in 2005) in its additional guidance section.

The report's preface encourages boards to review application of the guidance on a continuing basis and to use the internal control statement to inform shareholders how the company manages risk and internal control.

The report sets out guidance for directors on:

1 Maintaining a sound system of internal control to safeguard the shareholders' investment and the company's assets.
2 Determining the extent of their compliance with a review of the effectiveness of the system of internal controls and periodic consideration of whether an internal audit function should be established.

The objective of the Internal Control Working Party had been to develop guidance that:

1 Can be tailored to the circumstances of an individual company.
2 Identifies sound business practice, by linking internal control with risk management and placing emphasis on the key controls that a company should maintain.
3 Provides meaningful high-level information and avoids extensive disclosure that does not add to a user's understanding.
4 Will remain relevant and be capable of evolving with the business environment.

The guidance notes that a sound system of internal control plays a key role in the management of risks that could have a significant impact on the fulfilment of business objectives and helps to safeguard both the company's assets and the shareholders' investment.

Significant business risks (e.g. operational, financial and compliance risks) must be identified and assessed on an ongoing basis. Suggested areas for the board to consider include whether the company has clear objectives, whether these have been communicated to employees in a way that provides direction on risk assessment and control issues, and whether objectives and related business plans include measurable performance indicators and targets. Directors are expected to apply the same standard of care when reviewing the effectiveness of internal control as when exercising their general duties.

Financial controls are an important element of internal control, as they help to:

- Avoid exposure to avoidable financial risk.
- Ensure the reliability of financial information for both internal and external use.
- Safeguard assets, including the prevention and detection of fraud.

The risks that any entity faces will inevitably change as the business develops and the environment in which it operates evolves.

Companies must, therefore, regularly review and evaluate the risks to which they are exposed. The aim will usually be to manage and control business risk rather than to attempt to eliminate it completely.

The guidance is based on the principle that companies will adopt a risk-based approach to the establishment of a system of internal control and to the regular review of its effectiveness. The intention is that the review of the effectiveness of the internal control system should be part of the normal process of managing the business rather than a specific exercise carried out only in order to comply with the recommendations of the Combined Code.

Responsibility for maintaining a system of internal control

The detailed work involved in establishing, operating and managing a system of internal control should be carried out by individuals with the necessary skills, technical knowledge, objectivity and understanding of the business, its objectives, the industries and markets in which it operates and the risks that it faces. This detailed work will usually be delegated by the board to management and all employees will have some responsibility for internal control as part of their accountability for achieving objectives. However, the board as a whole retains ultimate responsibility for the company's system of internal control. It must therefore set appropriate policies on internal control and satisfy itself on a regular basis that the system is functioning effectively and that it is effective in managing the risks that the business faces.

Factors to consider

A system of internal control can never provide absolute protection against business failure, material errors, fraud or breaches of law and regulation, but it should be able to provide reasonable assurance against them. The guidance notes that, in determining policies on internal control and assessing what constitutes a sound system of internal control in the particular circumstances of the company, the board should consider:

- the nature and extent of the risks that the company faces;

- the extent and categories of risk that it regards as acceptable for the company to bear;
- the likelihood of the risks materialising;
- the company's ability to reduce the occurrence and impact on the business of risks that do materialise;
- an evaluation of the costs and benefits of any particular action.

Definition of internal control

An internal control system is defined as encompassing the policies, processes, tasks, behaviours and other aspects of the company that, taken together, facilitate its effective and efficient operation by enabling it to respond appropriately to significant risks, help to ensure the quality of internal and external reporting and help to ensure compliance with applicable laws and regulations.

Elements of a sound system of internal control

A system of internal control should reflect the company's control environment and organisational structure and includes:

- control activities;
- information and communication processes; and
- processes for monitoring the continuing effectiveness of the system.

The system of internal control should be embedded in the company's operations and form part of its culture. It must also be capable of responding promptly to new risks as the business evolves and should include procedures for reporting immediately to management when significant control weaknesses or failures are identified.

Control environment

A company's control environment is usually considered to include issues such as:

1. A commitment by directors, management and employees to competence, integrity and a climate of trust (e.g. leadership by example, development of an appropriate culture within the business).
2. The communication to all managers and employees of agreed standards of behaviour and control consciousness, which support the business objectives and risk management and internal control systems (e.g. written codes of conduct, formal disciplinary procedures, formal process of performance appraisal).
3. Clear organisational structures, which help to ensure that authority, responsibility and accountability are clearly defined and that decisions and action are taken by the appropriate people.
4. Clear communication to employees of what is expected of them and their freedom to act (e.g. in relation to customer relations, service levels, health and safety issues, environmental matters, financial and other reporting issues).

5 Allocation of sufficient time and resources to risk management and internal control.
6 The provision of relevant training on risk and control issues, so that management and employees develop the necessary knowledge, skills and tools to support achievement of the company's objectives and the effective management of risk.

Reviewing the effectiveness of internal control

The board may delegate to a committee (usually the audit committee) certain aspects of the review of the effectiveness of the system of internal control, but the board as a whole should form its view on the adequacy of the review. It will not be sufficient for the relevant committee alone to review the effectiveness of the system of internal control.

The precise role of the committee will vary between companies and will depend on factors such as the size, style and composition of the board and the nature of the principal risks that the business faces. The committee will usually consider financial controls, but may also be asked by the board to act as the focal point for reviews of the wider aspects of internal control. Such issues should be considered by the board when the committee's terms of reference are established.

The process of the review

The guidance notes that there should be a defined process for the board's review of the effectiveness of the company's system of internal control, to provide adequate support for the statement in the annual report. Directors are expected to apply the same standard of care when reviewing the effectiveness of internal control as when exercising their general duties. The board should take account of all the information available to it up to the date on which the annual report is approved and signed.

The board should not rely solely on the monitoring processes that form part of the business operations, but should receive and review regular reports on internal control, and also carry out a specific annual assessment to support the statement in the annual report to ensure that all significant aspects of internal control have been covered.

Where significant control weaknesses or failings are identified, the board should determine how these arose and should reassess the effectiveness of management's ongoing processes for designing, operating and monitoring the system of internal control.

The annual statement on internal control

The board's annual statement on internal control should provide users of the annual report and accounts with meaningful, high-level information. Particular care should be taken to ensure that the statement does not give a misleading impression. The board should disclose, where applicable, that:

- there is an ongoing process for identifying, evaluating and managing key risks;
- this process has been in place for the year under review and up to the date of approval of the annual report and accounts;
- this process accords with the relevant guidance on internal control, and that it is regularly reviewed by the board; and
- any necessary action has or is being taken to remedy any significant findings or weaknesses identified in their review of the effectiveness of the internal control system.

It should also summarise the process that it has applied in reviewing the effectiveness of the system of internal control, including, where relevant, the role of the audit committee or other committees. The guidance notes that, in addition, the board may wish to provide additional information to help users of the accounts to understand the company's risk management processes and the system of internal control.

If the board is unable to make any of these disclosures, this fact should be stated and the board should explain what action is being taken to rectify the situation.

The statement should also include an acknowledgement that the board is responsible for the company's system of internal control and for reviewing its effectiveness, together with an explanation that such a system can only provide reasonable and not absolute assurance against material misstatement or loss.

Where relevant, listed companies should disclose the fact that they have failed to conduct a review of the effectiveness of the internal control system.

Review of the need for an internal audit function

C3.5 of the Combined Code requires companies that do not have an internal audit function to review from time to time the need to establish one.

Where there is an internal audit function, the board should review its remit, authority, resources and scope of work, also on an annual basis.

19 Investigations

Introduction

All companies are required to allow access to documents and records on request by individuals and organisations. Certain organisations – principally the Department for Business, Innovation and Skills (BIS) – have power to investigate a company's affairs. Very few individuals have the right of entry to premises. Where a warrant to enter and search premises is given, this is valid only if served by a police officer. Accordingly, entry can be refused to, for example, representatives from HM Revenue & Customs, BIS inspectors and FSA investigators.

Table 19.1 summarises the powers and rights of entry of the various regulatory bodies, directors, members and members of the public covered by this chapter.

Types of access

Directors

All directors, whether executive or non-executive, have the right to review all of the company's records.

Shareholders

Shareholders are entitled to inspect or receive copies of any of the company's statutory registers and minutes of general meetings.

Shareholders are entitled to receive a copy of the company's unabbreviated annual accounts.

Shareholders have no right of access to a company's premises. Shareholders are entitled to attend general meetings of the company. However, as there is no right to enter the premises, unruly shareholders can be excluded or removed from meetings.

Members of the public

Members of the public are entitled to inspect or receive copies of any of the company's statutory registers upon payment of a fee.

Table 19.1: Regulatory bodies – powers and rights of entry

Body/Person	Power to require production of documents or information	Right of entry without warrant	Power of entry and search by warrant (exercised by police)
Directors	Access to all documents	No	No
Company members	Access to statutory records	No	No
Members of the public	Access to statutory registers	No	No
Auditors	Yes	No	No
BIS Inspectors	Yes	No	Yes
HMRC – criminal investigations	Yes	Provided reasonable notice or actual notice (7 days) but not to conduct search	Yes and can be executed by HMRC officer without police
HMRC – civil investigations	Yes	Yes to review records but not conduct search	Yes
FSA	Yes	No	Yes
OFT	Yes	No	Yes
CC	Yes	No	No
Takeover Panel	Yes	No	No

There is no right to receive copies of the company's accounts, although they may obtain a copy of the accounts filed with the Registrar of Companies, which may be abbreviated.

There is no right of access to company premises.

Auditors

As noted in Chapter 11, in preparing their report the auditor must carry out whatever investigations are necessary in order to be able to state whether proper accounting records have been maintained by the company and whether the company's accounts are in agreement with those records. If the auditor is not able to make such a statement, this fact must be stated in his report giving such details of the omissions or inconsistencies as are appropriate in the circumstances (CA2006 s.498(3)).

Access to information

An auditor of a company enjoys certain statutory rights to information in connection with the exercise of his duties. These include:

1. A right of access at all times to the company's books, accounts and vouchers and to require from the company's directors and officers such information and explanations as the auditor thinks necessary for the performance of his duties (CA2006 s.499(1)).
2. The auditor is entitled to attend any general meetings of the company and to receive all notices and other communications relating to any general meeting. He may also speak on any business of the meeting that concerns him as auditor (CA2006 s.502).
3. It is the duty of subsidiary undertakings incorporated in Great Britain and their auditors to give the auditors of the parent company such information and explanations as those auditors may reasonably require for the purposes of their duties as auditors of the parent company (CA2006 s.499(2)).

Right of entry

Auditors have no right of access to company premises.

Investigations, review of records, production of records

A number of regulatory bodies have rights to require production of documents, provision of information and/or power to investigate.

Department for Business, Innovation and Skills (BIS)

All companies are regulated by BIS which has authority, given by the Companies Act 2006 ss.431–453, as amended by CA2006 ss.1035–1039, to investigate companies. These investigations provisions of the Companies Act 1985 are among the few provisions that remain in force and are not being replaced by provisions of the Companies Act 2006. Investigations can be made in a variety of ways and there are levels of investigation common to all investigations. BIS will either appoint inspectors, usually an accountant and a barrister, with power to examine witnesses under caution or require the production of documents and records for examination by BIS officials. Investigations are managed by the Criminal Investigations Branch.

Right of entry

Inspectors or competent persons appointed to enquire into the affairs of a company have no right of entry to or to undertake a search of business or other premises.

A justice of the peace may issue a warrant under CA1985 s.448 for the entry and search of premises if there are reasonable grounds for believing that there are documents in the premises whose production has not been complied with.

A justice of the peace may issue a warrant under CA1985 s.448 for the entry and search of premises if there are reasonable grounds for believing that there are documents in the premises relating to an offence of which the penalty on conviction is not less that two years; that the Secretary of State, or a person appointed by him, has the power to require the production of those documents; and there are grounds for believing that if production were requested the documents would be removed or destroyed.

A warrant issued under CA1985 s.448 authorises a police officer and any named persons with him:

- to enter the specified premises;
- to search and take possession of documents appearing to be relevant;
- to take copies of any such documents; and
- to require explanations concerning the documents from any persons in the premises.

Appointment of inspectors

There are six categories of inspection:

1. appointment of inspectors to investigate the affairs of the company;
2. investigations into ownership of company;
3. investigations of directors' share dealings;
4. production of documents;
5. investigations to assist overseas regulatory authorities;
6. investigations under the Financial Services and Markets Act 2000.

Appointment of inspectors by the Secretary of State can be requested by the company itself, by a minimum of 200 shareholders or, if the company does not have a share capital, by not less than one-fifth of the company's members (CA1985 s.431). Such applications are, however, very rare.

The Secretary of State will appoint inspectors to investigate the affairs of a company, if the Court by order declares the affairs should be investigated, if it appears to him that there are circumstances to indicate that:

1. the company's affairs are or have been undertaken with intent to defraud creditors, or the creditors of another person, for fraudulent or unlawful purpose or in such a way that is unfairly detrimental to some part of its members; or
2. any act or intended act or omission or intended omission whether by or on behalf of the company would be prejudicial to some part of the members, or that the company was formed for any fraudulent or unlawful purpose; or
3. persons forming the company or connected with its management have in that regard been guilty of fraud, misconduct or misfeasance towards the company or its members; or
4. the members have not been given information concerning the affairs of the company which they might reasonably expect.

The terms of appointment will determine the report required and may stipulate that the report will not be made public: CA1985 s.432(2A). Inspectors appointed under CA1985 s.431 or 432 to investigate the affairs of a company have power to extend their investigation to any subsidiary or holding company without the need for any specific appointment by the Secretary of State (CA1985 s.433).

Once inspectors are appointed under CA1985 ss.431 and 432 it is the duty of all officers and agents of the company and of any person who is or may be in possession of information or documents relating to the company under investigation to:

1 produce to the inspectors all documents of or relating to the company in their custody or power;
2 attend before the inspectors when required; inspectors may examine any person on oath and may administer an oath accordingly; and
3 give all assistance in connection with the investigation that they are reasonably able to give (CA1985 s.434, as amended by CA2006 s.1038).

The right to silence has been excluded and the inspectors may compel a witness to answer questions; any answers may be given in evidence against that person. Where a witness refuses to answer any question or refuses to assist in the investigation, the inspectors may certify that fact to the Court. On enquiry, the Court may punish the person as if he or she is guilty of contempt of Court (CA1985 s.436).

The inspectors report to the Secretary of State on the conclusion of their investigation. The publication of the inspectors' report is at the discretion of the Secretary of State and it is the policy of the DTI to only publish a report if it is in the public interest (CA1985 s.437).

If matters have come to light during the course of an investigation which suggest that a criminal offence has been committed, those facts are referred to the appropriate prosecuting authority. Once referred, the inspectors need take no further action (CA1985 s.437(1B)).

If there is evidence to suggest that civil proceedings ought to be brought, in the public interest, by any company, the Secretary of State may bring such proceedings in the name of and on behalf of the company and will indemnify the company for the costs of such action (CA1985 s.438).

The expenses of an investigation under CA1985 s.431 or 432 will be borne by the Secretary of State. The Secretary of State may recover those costs, or part of them, from any person convicted as a result of the investigation. Where the appointment was made at the request of shareholders the company may be liable for some or all of the costs (CA1985 s.439).

Power to investigate ownership

Where it appears to the Secretary of State that there are good reasons for doing so, inspectors or BIS officials may be appointed to investigate the true identity of those financially interested in the success or failure of a company or able to control or materially influence its management (CA1985 ss.442 and 444).

The terms of appointment may limit the investigation to matters connected with specified shares or holdings. Such investigations are usually used to investigate the circumstances where there is potential takeover and there are circumstances to suggest the existence of undisclosed arrangements or undertakings between groups of shareholders (CA1985 s.442(2)).

Inspectors appointed under CA1985 s.442 have the same powers as inspectors appointed under CA1985 ss.431 and 432. As noted above such powers are, however, restricted to those persons who are or have been or appear to be or have been interested in the shares or debentures, together with those other persons it appears to the inspectors possess information relevant to their investigation (CA1985 s.443).

Where the matter to be investigated does not require the appointment of inspectors under CA1985 s.442, the Secretary of State may require the production of documents or information concerning present or past interests in shares or debentures from any person he reasonably believes might have it (CA1985 s.444(1)). Any person failing to provide the information or supplying false information is liable to fine, imprisonment or both (CA1985 s.444(3)).

Production of documents

The majority of investigations initiated by BIS do not require the appointment of inspectors. Instead, the Secretary of State may, if he thinks there are good reasons, give a direction requiring the production of specified documents and records. A competent person may also be authorised to require any company or person to produce specified documents (CA1985 s.447).

The power to require the production of documents extends to the taking of copies and requesting explanation of any matter in those documents from any person. Failure to produce the documents or provide an explanation without good reason is an offence under CA1985 s.447(6). Making false or reckless statements is an offence under CA1985 s.451. Documents can be withheld if they are covered by professional privilege (CA1985 s.452). Some banking records may also be withheld. Information obtained under CA1985 s.447 may not be published or disclosed without the consent of the company and unauthorised publication or disclosure is an offence (CA1985 s.449). Disclosure may, however, be made to a competent authority as set out in CA1985 s.449, including the Secretary of State, the Treasury, the Bank of England, Financial Services Authority and any police officer. HM Revenue & Customs is not a competent authority for the purposes of CA1985 s.449 and Sch.15C.

Overseas regulatory authorities

BIS was given power under CA 1989 ss.82–91 to assist overseas authorities investigating UK companies. The power permits investigation, interviews under oath and seeking documents and records. In deciding whether to provide assistance regard must be given to CA 1989 s.82(4) and, in particular, whether reciprocal assistance would be forthcoming.

HM Revenue & Customs

From 1 April 2009 HMRC powers to obtain information or make inspections are governed by FA2008 Sch.36. This legislation replaces the separate powers that formerly applied to income tax (IT), corporation tax (CT), capital gains tax (CGT), value added tax (VAT) and National Insurance contributions (NIC).

Tax investigations

Generally speaking, HM Revenue & Customs can give notice requiring the production of documents and the provision of information that is reasonably required for the purpose of checking a taxpayer's tax position. This must be complied with within a specified period (frequently 30 days) (FA2008 Part 1 Sch.36).

Under FA2008 Part 2 Sch.36, HM Revenue & Customs officers have the right to enter premises and inspect the premises, goods on the premises and documents on the premises, provided not less than seven days' notice has been provided. Alternatively, an authorised officer of HM Revenue & Customs may enter the premises at any reasonable time. The right of entry to inspect records does not permit a search for records to be undertaken. Visits are usually by appointment, and the HM Revenue & Customs officer has the right to call for any books and records. Where the visit is by appointment and the business owner is therefore on notice of the visit, he is obliged to answer the officer's questions. This is not the case for unannounced visits.

Any documents produced to an officer of HM Revenue & Customs may be copied or removed. If any documents are removed and are reasonably required for any purpose, HMRC, at their own cost, must provided copies.

Additionally the Police and Criminal Evidence Act 1984 (PACE1984) has been amended so that the powers of orders to require production of documents, search warrants, arrest and search following arrest have been made available to authorised HMRC officers. These powers may only be used in relation to HMRC offences and are only used in connection with criminal investigations, not for civil investigations or other activities.

Financial Services Authority

Part XI of the FSMA2000 sets out the powers of the Financial Services Authority (FSA) to gather information and carry out investigations.

Production of documents

The FSA has authority under s.165 of the FSMA2000 to require the production of documents or information from:

- an authorised or formerly authorised person;
- a person connected with an authorised person;
- the operator, trustee or depository of an open-ended investment company;
- a recognised investment exchange;
- a recognised clearing house.

Power to commission reports

The FSA may require an authorised, formerly authorised or connected person to commission and provide a report into any relevant matter (FSMA2000 s.166). A relevant matter is one about which the FSA could require information under FSMA2000 s.165. The person making the report must be nominated by or approved by the FSA. Authorised persons and firms are required to cooperate with any person writing the report. Under FSMA2000 s.167, the FSA may appoint a competent person to conduct a general investigation into the business of an authorised person or appointed representative or into the ownership or control of an authorised person. Written notice of any investigation must be given to the person or firm under investigation in terms of FSMA2000 s.170(2). The competent person appointed to carry out the investigation may be an employee of the FSA or some other person engaged for that purpose.

Under FSMA2000 s.168, the FSA may appoint a competent person to conduct an investigation where it appears there are circumstances to suggest that a specific contravention or offence may have taken place. Such specific investigations would include breaches of the general prohibition to provide investment advice, breaches of any rules or regulations made under the FSMA2000, commission of misleading statements and practices in terms of FSMA2000 s.397, market abuse in terms of FSMA2000 s.188, insider dealing in terms of Part V of the Criminal Justice Act 1993 or suspected breach of the money laundering regulations.

FSMA2000 s.169 gives the FSA power to investigate authorised persons and firms on behalf of an overseas regulator.

Investigators' powers

Investigators appointed under FSMA2000 s.167 have power to require persons to attend before them and answer questions, provide information and to provide documents. This power is restricted to information relevant to the investigation and to the person under investigation or a connected person of that person (FSMA2000 s.171).

Investigators appointed under FSMA2000 s.168 have additional powers set out in FSMA2000 ss.172 and 173. These powers do not apply in all cases and care must be taken to establish the appropriate power in any given case. Generally, the investigators' powers of interview and information gathering are extended to persons not under investigation but who might have relevant information.

FSMA2000 s.175 permits investigators appointed by the FSA or the Secretary of State to compel the production of relevant documents from any person together with any explanation of the document where needed. Banking documents may be withheld without the consent of the person to whom they relate unless their disclosure has been specifically authorised by the FSA or the Secretary of State.

Right of entry

An investigator appointed under the terms of the FSMA2000 has no right of entry or search; accordingly, entry may be refused. The investigator may, however, obtain a warrant to enter and search premises from a justice of the peace or, in Scotland, from a sheriff. A warrant to enter and search must be executed by a police officer. To obtain a warrant the justice of the peace or sheriff must be satisfied that there are grounds for believing that:

1. a request for the production of documents has not been complied with and that the documents are on the premises; or
2. there are grounds to believe that any request to provide documents found on the premises would not be complied with or the documents would be moved, altered or destroyed; or
3. a serious offence has or is being committed and that there is information or documents on the premises relevant to the offence and that a request for their production would not be complied with or might result in the documents being removed, altered or destroyed.

Offences

Where any person fails, without good reason, to comply with a request made under Part XI of the FSMA2000 for information or the production of documents that fact may be certified to the Court. On enquiry, the Court may punish the person as if he were guilty of contempt of Court (FSMA2000 s.177). A person who recklessly provides false or misleading information or who falsifies, withholds or destroys any documents or information is guilty of an offence and on conviction is liable to a fine of up to £5,000, six months' imprisonment, or both.

Office of Fair Trading

Sections 194–201, 224 and 225 of the Enterprise Act 2002 (EA2002) set out the investigation and surveillance powers of the OFT.

Production of documents

EA2002 ss.193 and 224 give the OFT power to require persons to attend interviews to answer questions or to provide documents or other written evidence. The power under EA2002 s.193 relates to the investigation of cartels; EA2002 ss.224 and 225 relate to consumer protection.

Power of entry

EA2002 s.194 allows the OFT to obtain a warrant from the High Court (procurator fiscal in Scotland) to allow a named OFT officer to enter premises and conduct searches for documents or other evidence in connection with investigations into cartels. This power is for use where the OFT believes that:

1 a request for the production of documents has not been complied with and that the documents are on the premises; or
2 there are grounds to believe that any request to provide documents found on the premises would not be complied with or the documents would be moved, altered or destroyed; or
3 a serious offence has or is being committed and that there is information or documents on the premises relevant to the offence and that a request for their production would not be complied with or might result in the documents being removed, altered or destroyed.

Competition Commission

EA2002 ss.31, 109 and 176 give the Competition Commission authority to require the production of specified documents or to require individuals to attend interviews and to give evidence. These powers are in respect of the Competitions Commission's investigations into mergers and abuse of market dominance.

Takeover Panel

CA2006 ss.947–965 set out the investigation and other powers of the Takeover Panel (the Panel).

Production of documents

CA2006 s.947 empowers the Panel to require, by notice in writing, a person to produce specified or described documents and/or to provide in such form or manner as may be specified such information as is specified or described.

The requirement to produce documents or information must be supplied at a specified place and within a reasonable period specified by the Panel and may be required to be authenticated in such manner as the Panel may reasonably require.

The documents or information that the Panel may require are those that they may reasonably require to enable it to exercise its functions (CA2006 s.947(3)).

The Panel may authorise any person to exercise its powers to require the production of documents or information (CA2006 s.947(5)).

The Panel or their authorised representative cannot require the production of documents or information in respect of which a claim for legal professional privilege (confidentiality of communication in Scotland) could be maintained in legal proceedings (CA2006 s.947(10)).

CA2006 s.948 prohibits the Panel from disclosing documents or information, other than those already in the public domain, provided to it in the exercise of its functions that relate to a private individual or a particular business during their lifetime, if an individual, or, if a business, for as long as the business continues in business without their consent. This protection does not apply to any disclosure which is made for the purpose of facilitating the Panel in carrying out its functions, is made to a person, is of a description and is in accordance with CA2006 Schedule 2 (CA2006 s.948(3)).

Right of entry

The Panel and their representatives have no right of entry to premises.

20 Insolvency, liquidation, administration and winding-up

Introduction

The law on corporate insolvency is contained mainly in the Insolvency Act 1986, which came into force with effect from 29 December 1986, as amended by the Insolvency Act 2000 and the Enterprise Act 2002. The insolvency provisions of the Enterprise Act came into force on 15 September 2003. In view of the complexity of the subject, a company secretary faced with a situation in which the company may not be able to pay its debts as they fall due is strongly advised to seek specialist advice. Some special provisions were introduced into the law of insolvency by CA1989 regarding the operations of financial markets.

A company becomes insolvent when it is unable to pay its debts as they fall due. Once this stage has been reached, in order to protect the interest of creditors, employees and shareholders, the directors must take steps for the company's affairs to be wound up. Winding-up involves the realisation of the company's assets. This process is undertaken on behalf of creditors by a licensed insolvency practitioner, who is appointed as the liquidator of the company. As a result, winding-up is frequently referred to as liquidation.

In circumstances where the directors realise that the company will become insolvent, but has not yet reached that point, they might wish to appoint an administrator to manage the company until it is able to continue, to be sold or, if all else fails, to be wound up. Administration is considered on pp. 365–369.

The statute law is principally contained in the Insolvency Act 1986 and the Company Directors Disqualification Act 1986. The Enterprise Act 2002 introduced a number of initiatives in respect of both corporate and individual insolvency. Implementation of the Enterprise Act provisions required a substantial amount of secondary legislation, including the Insolvency (Amendment) Rules 2003, the Insolvency (Scotland) Amendment Rules 2003, a number of orders relating to transitional provisions and consequential amendments and new forms.

Methods of winding-up

There are three methods of winding-up:

- members' voluntary winding-up;
- creditors' voluntary winding-up; and
- winding up by the Court.

Members' voluntary winding-up

A members' voluntary winding-up is a solvent winding-up under which the directors must have prepared a statutory declaration within the five weeks immediately preceding the resolution to wind up. This states that, having made full enquiry, they are of the opinion that the company will be able to pay its debts in full with interest at the official rate within a period not exceeding 12 months from commencement of the winding-up (IA1986 ss.89 and 90). If a director makes such declaration without reasonable grounds and the debts and interest are not paid within the specified period, he is liable to a fine or imprisonment, or both, and the burden of proof of innocence is on the director (IA1986 s.89(4)).

The resolution to wind up is coupled with a resolution to appoint a liquidator. If during the course of the administration the liquidator forms the opinion that the company is unlikely to be able to pay its liabilities in full within the stipulated time, he is required to call a meeting of creditors within 28 days. This converts the administration into a creditors' winding-up.

Creditors' voluntary winding-up

This may be appropriate where a declaration of solvency cannot be made, and the company is wound up as a creditors' voluntary winding-up. A meeting of the creditors must be called and held within 14 days after the meeting of the members of the company at which a resolution to wind up is passed (IA1986 s.98). The liquidation commences at the time of passing the resolution to wind up (IA1986 s.86).

Winding up by the Court

A company may be wound up by the Court if:

1. The company so resolves by special resolution.
2. A **judgment creditor** or a creditor petitions the Court where an amount in excess of £750 has not been paid following written demand for payment (IA1986 s.123).
3. It is just and equitable for the company to be wound up.
4. The company fails to comply with certain statutory requirements, e.g. the minimum number of members (IA1986 ss.122 and 124).

The most usual grounds for a petition to the Court is the inability of the company to pay its debts. A contributory, the Official Receiver, the Secretary of State, the

Bank of England and the Attorney General may present a petition under various statutory provisions even if the company is solvent.

Initial procedures

Members' voluntary winding-up

The procedure for a members' voluntary winding-up is as follows:

1. The company's board resolve to make a declaration of solvency, which must embody a statement of assets and liabilities and be made up to a date within five weeks immediately before the passing of the resolution to wind up. The declaration has to be filed with the Registrar of Companies within 15 days of the passing of the resolution to wind up (IA1986 ss.89 and 90).
2. The board authorises the calling of a general meeting at which a special resolution to wind up will be considered. [***See precedents 2, 4, 5 and 84.***] An ordinary resolution will suffice if the period of life of the company has expired or an event has occurred on the happening of which the Articles provide that the company should be wound up (IA1986 s.84).
3. If the resolution is passed, it will be necessary to appoint a liquidator. This may be done by an ordinary resolution of the company. [***See precedent 84.***]
4. The resolution to wind up, signed by the chairman of the meeting, should be published in the *London Gazette* or the *Edinburgh Gazette,* as appropriate, within 14 days of being passed (IA1986 s.85). The resolution and all documents for publication in each *Gazette* must be authenticated by a solicitor or a member of an established body of accountants or secretaries. The resolution to wind up must also be filed within 15 days with the Registrar of Companies (CA2006 s.30 and IA1986 s.84).
5. The liquidator must, within 14 days of his appointment, advertise his appointment in each *Gazette* and give notice to the Registrar of Companies on *Form LQ01*.
6. The Insolvency Rules 1986 (IR1986) r.4.148A set out provisions for determination of the liquidator's remuneration.

The subsequent procedure is similar to that for a creditors' voluntary winding-up set out below, except that meetings of, and notices to, creditors are not required.

Creditors' voluntary winding-up

The procedure for a creditors' voluntary winding-up is as follows:

1. A meeting of the board authorises the calling of a general meeting to consider a resolution that the company, by reason of its liabilities, cannot continue and that it is advisable to wind up (IA1986 s.84(1)(c)). [***See precedents 2, 4, 5 and 84.***]
2. A meeting of the creditors must be called by the company to be held within 14

days of the members' meeting to consider the resolution to wind up (IA1986 s.98). At least seven days' notice of the meeting must be given to the creditors. Notice of the creditors' meeting should be advertised in the appropriate *Gazette* and two local newspapers (IA1986 s.98(1)(b)(c)).

3 The notice must state either:
   (a) the name and address of the insolvency practitioner who will give such information to the creditors before the meeting takes place as they may reasonably require; or
   (b) a place in the principal area of business of the company where a list of names and addresses of the company's creditors will be available for inspection without charge.
4 The creditors' meeting will be presided over by one of the directors, who should prepare a statement of affairs in the prescribed form, verified by affidavit, to be laid before the creditors' meeting.
5 At the general meeting an extraordinary resolution is passed to wind up and an ordinary resolution is passed to nominate the liquidator.
6 At the creditors' meeting, which must be attended by the liquidator, the directors may answer questions put to them by the creditors concerning the administration of the company, although there is no legal requirement for them to do so.
7 The liquidator is the person nominated by the creditors or, where no other person has been so nominated, the person (if any) nominated by the company. Where a different person is nominated by the creditors, any member or creditor of the company may apply to the Court within seven days for an order that the members' nomination shall remain liquidator instead of, or jointly with, the creditors' nomination, or that some other person be appointed liquidator (IA1986 s.100).
8 On the appointment of a liquidator all the powers of the directors cease.
9 The creditors have the power to appoint a liquidation committee, which may sanction the continuation of some of the directors' powers (IA1986 ss.101 and 103).
10 The remuneration of the liquidator is fixed by the liquidation committee or, if there is no committee, by the creditors, failing which it is based on the scales applicable to the Official Receiver under IR1986 r.19.
11 Upon his appointment, the liquidator should immediately:
   (a) arrange for the redirection of mail, if not already done;
   (b) if thought necessary, change the registered office address;
   (c) take over all books and records of the company;
   (d) make a formal report to each creditor enclosing a copy of the directors' statement of affairs, and a copy of any statement made by the directors at the creditors' meeting. Creditors must be informed of the liquidator's appointment and be invited to forward a statement of their claims;
   (e) advertise for claims at the appropriate time;

(f) inform the appropriate sheriffs and bailiffs of the winding-up resolution and of the appointment of the liquidator;
(g) take into protective custody the company's assets and ensure that there is adequate insurance cover;
(h) open in the name of the liquidator separate bank accounts (any sums not immediately required may and should be transferred into a deposit account in the liquidator's name or in other suitable interest-bearing security);
(i) disclaim onerous property or unprofitable contracts as soon as practicably possible;
(j) consider the position of secured creditors and if necessary discuss and negotiate with them;
(k) consider the position of any landlords, particularly any distress warrants;
(l) consider the most appropriate way of disposing of the company's assets and discuss this with appointed agents;
(m) make a demand for the company's outstanding book debts and consider the position as to work in progress;
(n) consider and discuss any pending or future litigation outstanding against the company with the company's solicitors.

Winding up by the Court

The procedure for winding up by the Court is as follows:

1 When the Court makes a winding-up order, the Official Receiver becomes the liquidator (IA1986 s.136(2)).
2 The Official Receiver may require officers of the company, or other persons as specified, to prepare, swear and submit a statement of affairs within 21 days (IA1986 s.131).
3 Separate meetings of creditors and contributories may be summoned by the Official Receiver at his discretion for the appointment of some other person to be liquidator of the company (IA1986 s.136(4)). Contributions are defined by the IA1986 s.79, but are usually synonymous with the term 'members'. The Official Receiver remains the liquidator if another person is not appointed. The Official Receiver must summon a meeting for the appointment of another liquidator if one-quarter in value of the creditors requisition him to do so on IR1986, Form 4.21 ('Request by creditor(s) for a meeting of the company's creditors and contributories') in accordance with the IA1986 s.136(5) and IR1986 r.4.57.
4 The Court may make any appointment or order to give effect to the wishes of the meetings or make any other order that it may think fit.
5 The creditors and contributories may nominate as liquidator any person who is qualified to act as an insolvency practitioner (IA1986 s.139) and, in the absence of a nomination by the creditors, the contributories' nominee (if any) will be the liquidator.

6 At any time the Official Receiver may apply to the Secretary of State for the appointment of a liquidator in his place. Any such liquidator must send notice of his appointment as the Court may direct (IA1986 s.137(3), (4)).

Liquidator

The liquidator should:

1 Take over responsibility for the assets of the company, together with its books and records.
2 Take other necessary steps to protect and realise the assets, as indicated above in the case of a creditors' voluntary winding-up.
3 Disclaim any onerous property or unprofitable contracts (IA1986 s.178 and IR1986 rr.4.187–4.194).
4 The winding-up order halts any proceedings against the company, except by leave of the Court (IA1986 s.130(2)).
5 Provide the Official Receiver with information, access to books or such other assistance as he may reasonably require.

The liquidator's qualifications

A liquidator must be a person who is qualified to act as an insolvency practitioner (IA1986 s.390). The Secretary of State may give authority for a person to act as an insolvency practitioner or authorise another competent authority to do so (IA1986 s.392). IR1986 r.10 requires every insolvency practitioner who is appointed office-holder in any formal insolvency proceeding to have insurance cover ('bond') for the proper performance of his duties, the value of which may not be less than the value of the relevant assets, subject to a minimum of £5,000 and a maximum of £5,000,000 (IR1986 Sch.2).

Duties and powers of a liquidator

The duties and powers of a liquidator are specified in IA1986 ss.165–170 and IA1986 Sch.4. The principal duties and powers are as follows:

1 To realise the company's assets to the best advantage, determine the claims against the company and distribute the funds realised, to the creditors and contributories, after payment of the costs and expenses in the order of priority laid down under IR1986, r.4.218.
2 The liquidator has considerable powers, although the exercise of some of them requires specific sanctions. No sanction is necessary in respect of the following matters:
   (a) to sell the company's assets and transfer title on behalf of the company;
   (b) to execute deeds, receipts and documents and affix the company's seal, if it has one, where necessary;
   (c) to prove, rank and claim in bankruptcy or insolvency;
   (d) to draw, accept and endorse bills of exchange or promissory notes in the name, and on behalf, of the company;

(e) to raise money on security of the company's assets;
(f) to take out letters of administration to the estate of a deceased contributory;
(g) to appoint agents, although in practice sanction of any liquidation committee is usually sought;
(h) to exercise the Court's power to settle a list of contributories;
(i) to convene general meetings of the company to obtain its sanction by special resolution or for any purpose he may think fit (IA1986 s.65(4)).

3. In the case of a winding-up by the Court, but not in the case of a voluntary winding-up, the liquidator requires sanction of the Court or the liquidation committee to:
(a) bring or defend actions or other legal proceedings;
(b) carry on the business for beneficial winding-up.
4. Sanction is required in all cases to:
(a) pay any class of creditor in full;
(b) make any compromise or arrangement with creditors or contributories;
(c) make any compromise affecting the assets of winding up of the company, take security for the discharge of any debt and give a discharge in respect of it.
5. Sanction for matters in 4 above is usually sought from the liquidation committee in a winding-up by the Court except for matters that are reserved to the Court. If there is no liquidation committee, the Secretary of State may exercise its functions except where they are exercised by the Official Receiver (IA1986 s.141(4), (5) and IR1986 r.4.172).
6. In the case of a creditors' voluntary winding-up, the liquidation committee's sanction for the matters in 4 above is usually sought or, if there is no such committee, it is sought from the creditors.

The acts of a liquidation committee will be valid notwithstanding any defect in the appointment or qualifications of members of the committee (IR1986 r.4.172A as amended by the Insolvency (Amendment) Rules 1987, SI 1987/1919).

Liquidator's records and their audit

The administrative and financial records to be kept by a liquidator are specified in the Insolvency Regulations 1986 (SI 1986/1994) and vary according to whether the winding-up is by the Court or is a voluntary winding-up. These requirements are not dealt with in this book as they are not the responsibility of the company secretary.

Report on conduct of directors

A report must be made immediately to the Secretary of State under s.7(3) of the Company Directors Disqualification Act 1986 (CDDA1986) if, in the winding-up proceedings, it appears to a liquidator or the Official Receiver that the conduct of a director of the company is such as to render him unfit to be concerned in the management of a limited company. Under the provisions of the Insolvent Companies (Reports on Conduct of Directors) No. 2 Rules 1986, SI 1986/2134, a return must be submitted to the Secretary of State within six months of appointment of the liquidator or the Official Receiver, stating whether or not there is any such knowledge of the conduct of director(s) or if the conduct return will be delayed beyond that date. If, subsequent to the conduct return, further information about the conduct of director(s) should come to notice, a further return must be submitted. Appropriate forms for making these returns are annexed to the Rules mentioned above, which also apply to administrative receivers and administrators.

The matters determining the unfitness of directors are set out in CDDA1986 Sch.1. A Court of summary jurisdiction may impose a disqualification order for a maximum of five years, or in the case of superior Courts, 15 years.

Investigations, preferences, fraud and criminal offences

The liquidator must investigate the records of the company to establish whether any of the following have occurred:

1. Transactions at an undervalue and preferences (IA1986 s.238).
2. Floating charges created in favour of a connected person within two years of commencement of the liquidation or within one year if created in favour of any other person or created between the time of presentation of a petition for an administration order and the making of the order (IA1986 s.245).
3. Fraudulent trading (CA2006 s993 and IA1986 ss.213 and 215).
4. Wrongful trading (IA1986 ss.214 and 215).
5. Any misfeasance by any director or manager (IA1986 s.212).
6. Failure to register any charge under CA2006 s.860.

Under IA1986 s.218(4) the liquidator has a statutory duty in a voluntary winding-up to report any fraud or criminal act he discovers to the Director of Public Prosecutions.

The Enterprise Act 2002 introduced new rules under which the liquidator must seek the sanction of the creditors' committee, creditors or the Court before bringing proceedings for wrongful or fraudulent trading, to attack preferential payments or transactions at undervalue. Additionally, the costs of these and any related actions are to be costs of the liquidation.

Employees

The employees' contracts of employment are terminated by the winding-up order of the Court. In a voluntary winding-up the subsequent failure by the liquidator to maintain the terms of the employment terminates the employment. Under the

Employment Rights Act 1996, the liquidator acts as the employer's representative so far as claims are concerned. The employer's representative, with certain limits, is provided with funds from the Department for Work and Pensions to meet the claims of employees, which he then distributes to the employees concerned. The claims of the employees against the insolvent company paid in this way are then assigned to the Department for Work and Pensions, which may claim in the liquidation of the company. The Department for Work and Pensions will also probably claim any sums that have been paid for redundancy.

Tax implication of liquidation

A separate record should be kept of tax liabilities incurred by the liquidator during the course of the liquidation, these being part of the costs of the liquidation as distinct from tax liabilities arising up to the date of commencement of the winding-up, which would be the subject of a claim in the liquidation. Any VAT arising is treated similarly.

Determination of creditors' claims

In a winding-up by the Court, creditors must submit their claims in writing on IR1986 Form 4.25 ('Proof of debt – general form') (IR1986 r.4.73). In the case of voluntary liquidations, the liquidator may require a creditor to submit his claim in writing, but no specific form is provided for this. If the liquidator rejects a claim in whole or in part he must give his reasons in writing to the creditor. A creditor has 21 days to require the matter to be put before the Court if he is dissatisfied with the liquidator's decision (IR1986 r.4.83).

Distributions and release

Voluntary winding-up

After payment of relevant fixed charges, the order of priority for payment is as follows:

1 Costs and expenses of the winding-up in the order of priority laid down under IR1986, r.4.218 (as amended for liquidations commencing after 15 September 2003).
2 Preferential claims as defined in the IA1986 s.386 and Sch.6, although the Enterprise Act 2002 abolished the Crown's preferential status for all companies that went into liquidation, administration or receivership on or after 15 September 2003. The principal categories are therefore:
   (a) employees' unpaid salary or wages for the four months prior to the relevant date limited to the amount fixed by delegated legislation;
   (b) employees' accrued holiday remuneration;

(c) sums paid by third parties on behalf of the company to discharge debts that would have been preferential had the third parties not paid them and which remain outstanding to such third parties (*note*: The 'relevant date' is defined in IA1986 s.387, but it usually means the date of appointment of the liquidator, or if no liquidator has been appointed, the date of the winding-up order.)

3 Creditors who have a floating charge (IA1986 s.175(2)(b)). For floating charges created on or after 15 September 2003 a proportion of floating charge assets is ring-fenced for the benefit of unsecured creditors. This ring-fenced portion is called the 'prescribed part'. The prescribed part of a floating charge is 50 per cent of the net floating charge assets up to £10,000, and 20 per cent over £10,000 subject to an overall maximum prescribed part of £600,000.

4 Admitted ordinary unsecured creditors.

After settlement of all debts and costs any surplus should be paid to contributories (i.e. the members) (IA1986 s.107). Any unclaimed funds should be paid into the Insolvency Services Account at the Bank of England.

Upon completion of a creditors' voluntary winding-up, the liquidator should call a general meeting of the contributories on IR1986 Form 4.23 ('Notice to contributories of meeting of contributories') and of the creditors on IR1986 Form 4.22 ('Notice to creditors of meetings of creditors') to lay an account of his administration before the meetings and to give any explanations which are necessary. At least 28 days' notice of the meetings must be given which must also be published in the appropriate *Gazette* at least one month beforehand (IA1986 s.106(2)). Within one week of the meetings being held, he should file a copy of the accounts and a return of the holding of the meetings with the Registrar of Companies. Three months after the registration of the return with the Registrar the company is deemed to be dissolved (IA1986 s.201(2)).

Similar provisions apply in the case of a members' voluntary winding-up, except that meetings of creditors are not necessary.

Winding up by the court

The order of distribution is generally the same as in the case of a voluntary winding-up. Upon the completion of the winding-up, the liquidator should:

1 Send to all creditors who have proved their debts 28 days' notice on Form 4.22 of a final meeting to receive the liquidator's report and grant his release. Notice must also be gazetted at least one month before the meeting (IA1986 s.146; IR 4.125).

2 File with the Court and the Registrar of Companies notice that the final meeting has been held under the IA1986 s.146, stating whether he has been given his release.

3 If the creditors have not objected to the liquidator's release he vacates office and his release is effective from that time.

4 If the final meeting resolves against the release of the liquidator, he must apply to the Secretary of State to determine the outcome.
5 If there is no quorum at the final meeting, it is deemed to have been held and the creditors not to have resolved against the liquidator's release.

Dissolution without liquidation

See p.22 in Chapter 1.

Winding-up in Scotland

Certain provisions relating to winding up are peculiar to Scottish law and are described in various sections of IA1986. These are ss.120–121, 122(2), 142, 157, 161–162, 169, 185, 193, 198–199, 204 and 243.

Company voluntary arrangements

Until the Insolvency Act 1986 came into force, a company could enter into a binding arrangement with some or all of the creditors to compromise their claims by means of a scheme of arrangement under CA2006 ss.895–901. However, a scheme under this section is extremely complex to put into effect: for example, it is necessary to identify correctly, and call separate meetings of, the various classes of creditors affected by the scheme. The scheme also has to be approved by the Court before it comes into effect. As a result this course has been followed relatively rarely.

The Insolvency Act 1986 Part I ss.1–7 introduced a new procedure enabling the directors of a company, an administrator or a liquidator, as appropriate, to make a proposal to the company's creditors for a composition in satisfaction of its debts or a scheme of arrangement of its affairs, known as a 'voluntary arrangement'.

A proposal containing details outlined in Rule 1.3 must provide for some person ('the nominee'), who is qualified to act as an insolvency practitioner in relation to the company, to act in relation to the voluntary arrangement either as trustee or for the purpose of supervising its implementation.

Procedure

Where the nominee is not the liquidator or administrator of the company, the following procedure must be followed:

1 The directors prepare a document setting out the terms of the proposed voluntary arrangement incorporating a statement of affairs and give formal notice of the same to the nominee. The nominee endorses the notice with his consent to act and submits a report to the Court, within 28 days, stating whether, in his opinion, the meetings of the members and creditors should be summoned

to consider the proposal and, if applicable, the date, time and place at which the meetings should be held. The date on which the meetings are to be held may not be less than 14 or more than 28 days from the date on which the nominee's report is filed in Court. The nominee is required to send notice of the meetings of the members and the creditors, at least 14 days before the day for them to be held, to all creditors of whom he is aware and to all members. Where the nominee is the liquidator or the administrator, he may summon the meetings of the members and creditors, without any application to the Court, by giving at least 14 days' notice. With the notice of the respective meeting, the nominee must send:
(a) a proposal;
(b) a statement of affairs; and
(c) the nominee's comments.

2 At the creditors' meeting a majority in excess of three-quarters in value of those present in person or by proxy is required for approval of the proposal (IR1986 rr.1.19 and 1.20). At the members' meeting a majority in excess of one half of those present in person or by proxy is required for approval of the proposal. Either meeting may propose modifications, which may include another person qualified to act as an insolvency practitioner in relation to the company as nominee. Neither meeting may approve a proposal or any modification under which the rights of preferential creditors are altered without their concurrence.
3 The votes of certain creditors must be left out of account, as specified in IR1986 r.1.19(3), and any resolution is invalid if those voting against it include more than one half in value of qualifying votes (IR1986 r.1.19(4)).
4 Approval of the voluntary arrangement by both meetings binds every person who had notice of, and was entitled to vote at, either of the meetings (IA1986 s.5(2)(b)).
5 If, on the day of the meetings of the creditors and the members, the requisite majority is not obtained, the chairman may, and shall if so resolved, adjourn the meetings for not more than 14 days (IR1986 r.1.21(2)).
6 If the company is being wound up or an administration order is in force, the Court may stay the winding-up proceedings or discharge the administration order so as to facilitate the voluntary arrangement (IA1986 s.5(3)).
7 An application may be made to the Court by a member, a creditor, the nominee, the liquidator or an administrator if the voluntary arrangement is unfairly prejudicial or if there has been material irregularity in relation to either of the meetings (IA1986 s.6).

Remuneration, expenses and completion of the voluntary arrangement

The following fees, costs, charges and expenses may be incurred in connection with the voluntary arrangement:

1 Disbursements by the nominee prior to approval of the arrangement and agreed remuneration for his services.
2 Disbursements, remuneration, expenses and any payments sanctioned by the terms of the arrangement or which would be payable in an administration or winding-up.

The supervisor shall, within 28 days of full implementation of the arrangement, or within such time as may be allowed by Court, send notice to that effect to the Registrar of Companies, the Court, and all creditors and members of the company who were bound by it. With the notice there must be a report by the supervisor summarising all receipts and payments in the arrangement and, if applicable, an explanation of any material disparity between the anticipated and the actual result.

Administration orders

The Enterprise Act 2002 replaced Part II of the Insolvency Act 1986 under which the Court could make an administration order in relation to a company if it is satisfied that the company is or is likely to become unable to pay its debts. Under the new provisions there are three entry routes into administration:

1 application to Court by the company, a majority of the directors of the company, a qualifying floating charge holder or one or more creditors; or
2 out of court appointment by a qualifying floating charge holder; or
3 out of court appointment by the company or a majority of its directors.

An administration order directs that, during the period for which it is in force, the affairs, business and property of the company shall be managed by an administrator. Regardless of which of the three entry routes is used the administrator remains as a Court-appointed officer. According to the definition in IA1986 s.123 a company is deemed to be unable to pay its debts if any of the following holds:

1 It is unable to pay a debt exceeding £750 within a period of 21 days commencing on the date of delivery of a demand for payment made in the prescribed form.
2 In England and Wales, execution issued on a judgment remained unsatisfied in whole or in part.
3 The Court is satisfied that the company is unable to pay its debts as they fall due.
4 The Court is satisfied that the value of the company's assets is less than the amount of its liabilities.
5 In Scotland, a charge for payment on an extract decree, or an extract registered bond, or an extract registered process, has expired without payment.
6 In Northern Ireland, a certificate of unenforceability has been granted in respect of a judgment.

The purpose of the administration has also been amended. In place of the previous four purposes are three objectives:

1. To rescue the company (not necessarily the business) as a going concern.
2. To achieve a better result for creditors than would be likely in a liquidation.
3. To realise property in order to make distributions to secured or preferential creditors.

Appointment of administrator

By Court

Application to the Court is the only way in which creditors (other than the holder of a qualifying floating charge) or the supervisor of a company voluntary arrangement can initiate the appointment of an administrator. Application to Court will also be required where the company is in liquidation or administrative receivership or there is an outstanding winding-up petition.

The application is made on a prescribed form and requires an affidavit setting out details of the company's financial position, any security held by creditors and other matters relevant to the application. The proposed administrator must give written consent to act.

By qualifying floating charge holder

The holder of a qualifying floating charge can effect the appointment of an administrator by giving notice of an intention to appoint an administrator to the relevant Court. Qualifying floating charges are defined in paragraph 14 of Sch.B1 to the Insolvency Act 1986. A qualifying floating charge is one that:

- states that paragraph 14 of Sch.B1 applies to it; or
- purports to empower the holder to appoint an administrator; or
- purports to empower the holder to make an appointment as an administrative receiver.

Where there is more than one holder of qualifying floating charges, each must consent to the appointment of an administrator. A copy of the notice of intention to appoint an administrator must also be given to all other holders of qualifying floating charges.

Provided there are no objections or an application is made for a Court order and all holders of qualifying floating charges have consented, the proposed administrator is appointed five days after the notice of intention to appoint by the filing of a notice of appointment.

By the company or directors

The company itself or its directors can effect the appointment of an administrator by giving notice of an intention to appoint an administrator to the relevant Court.

Where there is one or more qualifying floating charges each charge holder must be sent a copy of the notice of the intention to appoint an administrator.

Provided there are no objections or an application is made for a Court order and all holders of qualifying floating charges have consented, the proposed administrator is appointed ten days after the notice of intention to appoint by the filing of a notice of appointment. If there are no qualifying floating charges there is no need to file a notice of intention to appoint and the appointment can be made by filing the notice of appointment alone.

Administration process

Once a company is in administration all business documents issued by it must state the name of the administrator and contain a statement to the effect that the affairs and the business of the company are being managed by the administrator.

As soon as practical, the administrator must obtain details of the company's financial position and details of all creditors. Creditors must be informed of the administrator's appointment and notice advertised in the *Gazette* and a relevant newspaper.

The administrator will require one of or more of the company's directors to assist in the preparation of a statement of the company's affairs.

Within eight weeks of appointment the administrator must circulate to all creditors and members of the company a statement of proposals setting out details of their appointment, the circumstances leading up to their appointment and how they intend to achieve the purposes of the administration. A copy of the statement must be filed with the Registrar of Companies. The statement issued to creditors and members must have attached to it the statement of affairs. An extension to this eight-week period can be sanctioned by the creditors and/or Court.

The first creditors' meeting must be convened, upon at least two weeks' notice, for a date not more than ten weeks after the administrator was appointed, subject to any extension permitted by the creditors and/or the Court. The purpose of the meeting is to consider the administrator's proposals, which can be accepted, modified or rejected by the creditors. Voting of creditors is by simple majority by value of their claim.

Where the administrator's proposals indicate that all creditors will be paid in full or that there will be no distribution to unsecured creditors other than out of the prescribed part of any assets secured by a floating charge, no meeting need be held unless requested by the creditors, and the proposals will be deemed to have been approved. Creditors can request a meeting within 12 days of issue of the administrator's proposals.

Following any creditors' meeting the administrator must circulate a report on the meeting to each creditor, the Court and the Registrar of Companies.

The administrator must manage the affairs and business of the company in accordance with the proposals agreed or deemed agreed by creditors. Reports on the progress of the administration covering each successive period of six months must be issued to each creditor, the Court and the Registrar of Companies. Any changes to the original proposal agreed or deemed agreed by creditors must be approved by the creditors, either in a meeting or by correspondence. Where any proposal is rejected the administrator will seek directions from the Court.

During the course of the administration, the administrator can remove and appoint directors, call meetings of the members and cooperate with the creditors' committee. The administrator must consider the actions of the directors as required by the Company Directors Disqualification Act 1986 and submit a report on their conduct to the Secretary of State for Trade within six months from commencement of the administration.

The administrator may make distributions to secured and preferential creditors without any further authority. Distributions to unsecured creditors, whether out of the prescribed part of any floating charges or from the realisation of assets, may be made only with the sanction of the Court. Where there are sufficient assets to enable a distribution to unsecured creditors, it is expected that the company will move from administration into a creditors' voluntary liquidation to enable the liquidator to make the distributions.

Ending administration

Administration is no longer an open-ended process and the administration will end 12 months after its commencement, subject to any extension sanctioned by the creditors and/or the Court. On cessation of the administration the administrator must circulate a copy of their final report and the notice of cessation to each person who received a copy of the original proposal, to the Court and to the Registrar of Companies.

There are nine possible exits for a company in administration:

1. Automatic termination 12 months after commencement.
2. By Court order on application of the administrator in circumstances where it is concluded that the company should not have been put into administration or the proposals cannot be achieved. Additional for a Court-appointed administration this process is required where the purposes of the administration have been achieved.
3. An out of court appointed administrator can terminate the administration where its purpose is achieved by filing notice of termination.
4. The administrator can apply for the company to be dissolved if there is nothing to distribute to creditors.
5. Where secured creditors have been paid or amounts set aside for their payment and a distribution can be made to unsecured creditors, the administrator can put the company into company voluntary liquidation.
6. If the creditors reject the administrator's proposals the administration will cease, subject to any direction of the Court.
7. Disgruntled creditors or members can seek to have the administration closed

or a new administrator appointed in circumstances where they think the administration is being run too slowly or inefficiently.

8 Creditors can apply for the administration to end on the grounds of 'improper motive' on the part of the applicant for the administration or appointer.
9 Administrations can cease on application to the Court on the grounds of public interest.

Administrator

An administrator must be a person authorised to act as an insolvency practitioner as defined under IA1986 Part XIII. Any person acting as an administrator who is not so qualified is liable to imprisonment or to a fine, or both (IA1986 s.389). An administrator's remuneration may be determined by a creditors' committee or, if there is no creditors' committee, or the committee does not make the requisite determination, the administrator's remuneration may be fixed by a resolution of a meeting of creditors or, ultimately, by the Court.

Powers of an administrator

In general, an administrator of a company has power to do all things necessary for the management of the affairs, business and property of the company. The powers are specified in IA1986 ss.14 and 15 and Sch.1 and include the following:

1 Removal and appointment of directors and holding meetings of the members or creditors of the company.
2 Dealing with the property of the company subject to a floating charge, as if it were not charged, without the leave of the Court. However, the property directly or indirectly representing property so disposed shall be subject to the security in the same priority as the disposed property.
3 Dealing with any other charged property or goods subject to a hire purchase agreement, with the consent of the Court, subject to a condition that the net proceeds of the disposal are applied towards discharging the sums secured by the security or payable under the hire purchase agreement.

Receiverships

The law governing receiverships is considerable and in this book only general matters affecting the appointment and procedures to be followed when a receiver is appointed are considered. Consequently, further reference should be made to appropriate books on the subject and expert advice sought, if necessary.

Definition of an administrative receiver

An administrative receiver is a receiver or manager of the whole or substantially the whole of a company's property and business, appointed by or on behalf of the holders of debentures of the company secured by a floating charge (IA1986 s.29(2)(a)). An appointee under a fixed charge will normally have no power to manage the business and is, as such, known as a 'receiver'.

The legislation relating to receivers in England and Wales is contained in CA1985 s.196 (as substituted by IA1986 s.439(1) Sch.13 Part I), ss.403 and 405, IA1986 ss.29–49 and s.72 and in IR1986 rr.3.1–3.38. The law relating to receivers in Scotland is different and is found in the Bankruptcy and Diligence etc (Scotland) Act 2007.

The Enterprise Act 2002 restricts the use of administrative receivership. Holders of floating charges created on or after 15 September 2003 will no longer be able to appoint an administrative receiver unless they fall within a limited number of exemptions. These are: capital market arrangements, public–private partnerships, utility projects, project finance and financial market contracts and registered social landlords.

Qualification and remuneration of an administrative receiver

Under IA1986 s.390, only a qualified practitioner may act as an administrative receiver of a floating charge and any person acting as such who is not so qualified is liable to imprisonment or a fine, or both (IA1986 s.389). There are detailed provisions in IA1986 ss.396–398 as to who may be regarded as a fit and proper person and as to the education, practical training and experience required for the appointment as a licensed insolvency practitioner. A person who is adjudged bankrupt or who is subject to a disqualification order under the CDDA1986 is not qualified to act as an insolvency practitioner. In the case of receivers appointed under a fixed charge, it is desirable to appoint a professionally competent person as receiver because of the administrative and legal tasks involved. It should be noted that a corporate body may not be appointed as a receiver (IA1986 s.30). It is usual for debentures to specify the maximum rate of remuneration for the receiver or that it shall be agreed between the receiver and the debenture holder. If the receiver is appointed by the Court, the receiver's remuneration will be determined by the Court. In addition, a liquidator of a company may apply to the Court to determine the receiver's remuneration (IA1986 s.36).

Appointment by the Court

A Court may appoint a receiver on the application of a mortgagee or a debenture holder in the following circumstances:

- Where repayment of principal and/or interest is in arrears.
- When the security has become crystallised into a specific charge by the making of a winding-up order or passing of a resolution to wind up.
- Where the security of the mortgagee or the debenture holder is in jeopardy.

A receiver may also be appointed by the Court on the application either of a contributory (i.e. a person liable to contribute to the assets of the company in the event of its being wound up) or of the company. The Court will sometimes appoint a receiver and a manager on a short-term basis if the directors are not fulfilling their functions, for instance because of a dispute between them, and pending a general meeting where there has been no governing body.

A Court will not appoint a receiver if winding up would be more appropriate.

Appointment by debenture holders

The appointment is made under a deed executed by the debenture holder and is, together with the debenture, evidence of his capacity.

The appointment of a receiver usually arises in the following circumstances:

1 Failure to pay the principal and/or interest in accordance with the terms of the debenture.
2 Where a borrowing limit has been exceeded and has not been reduced within a specified period.
3 A breach of some other provisions in the debenture or trust deed.

The debenture usually confers fixed and floating charges on the assets of a company. It is possible, however, for the security to be simply a fixed or a floating charge. It is therefore important to consider the following at the commencement of a receivership:

1 Under a fixed charge a receiver will not normally have power to manage the business and may call in and realise the relevant assets only for the purpose of redeeming the debt due to the debenture holder.
2 An appointment under a floating charge may be made as 'receiver' or 'administrative receiver'. The former cannot be appointed with the powers of the latter unless the deed contains such provision.
3 A 'receiver' will have power to manage if such right is given to him by the debenture deed containing a charge on the goodwill of business of the company.

The appointment as receiver or manager must be accepted before the end of the next business day following receipt of the instrument of appointment and shall be deemed to be effective from the time and date the instrument of appointment was received (IR1986 r.3.1, as amended by the Insolvency (Amendment) Rules 1987).

The receiver must advertise notice of his appointment in the *London Gazette* and an appropriate newspaper (IR1986 r.3.2, as amended by the Insolvency (Amendment) Rules 1987). Following appointment, the receiver or manager should:

1 Examine the deed of appointment and a copy of the debenture (or trust deed) in order to consider the validity of the debenture and his appointment.
2 Ensure that his appointment has been registered with the Registrar of Companies by the debenture holder within seven days on *Form LQ01* ('Notice of appointment of receiver or manager') (CA2006 s.871(1)).

3. Advise the directors of his appointment and take possession of the appropriate assets.
4. Ensure that adequate insurance is in force.
5. Notify the appointment to the company's bankers and open an account in the name of the receiver or manager, as appropriate.
6. Consider the position of employees, in particular whether they should be dismissed or retained.
7. Check arrangements for the receipt and dispatch of goods and collect the book debts.
8. Ensure that all documents bearing the company's name leaving the company's premises contain a statement that a receiver has been appointed (IA1986 s.39(1)).
9. Consider the position of current contracts, whether they should be completed or whether the business should be disposed of in whole or in part and, if applicable, the mode of disposal.
10. Ensure that the company's books are written up to the date of his appointment, if appropriate.
11. Inform all creditors within 28 days (IA1986 s.46) of his appointment and, in particular, notify judgment creditors, persons who have issued writs against the company, and their solicitors, if known. The position of other secured creditors, hire purchase agreements and claims by landlords should also be considered.
12. Maintain proper records and books of account of the receivership.
13. Require officers of the company and/or other relevant persons to prepare and submit to the receiver within 21 days a statement of affairs verified by affidavit on IR1986 Form 3.2 (IR1986 r.3.4).
14. An administrative receiver must, within three months of his appointment (or such longer period as the Court may allow), send to the Registrar of Companies, to any trustees for secured creditors and to all such creditors (so far as he is aware of their addresses) a report giving details of the following matters (IA1986 s.48(1)):
    (a) the events leading to his appointment;
    (b) disposal or proposed disposal of any property and the continuation or proposed continuation of the business;
    (c) the amounts of principal and interest payable to the debenture holders who appointed him and the amounts due to preferential creditors; the amount likely to be available for payment to other creditors.

The administrative receiver must also, within the same time limit send a copy of the report to all unsecured creditors (or publish a notice of availability) and, unless the Court directs otherwise, summon a meeting on not less than 14 days' notice to receive the same (IA1986 s.48(2)). An administrative receiver is not required to comply with sub-section (2) if the company is or goes into liquidation, provided a copy of the report is sent to the liquidator within the time limit in reference (IA1986 s.48(4)).

The employees' legal position

The appointment of a receiver does not automatically terminate the employment of the company's employees and, unless the receiver negotiates new terms, he will be taken to have adopted any contract of employment not terminated within 14 days after his appointment (IA1986 s.44).

It should be noted, however, that the Insolvency Act 1994 provides that in respect of adoptions of contracts of employment on or after 15 March 1994, the receiver must discharge certain 'qualifying liabilities'. These liabilities are wages, salaries and contributions to an occupational pension scheme 'in respect of services rendered'. Sick pay and holiday pay arising during a period in respect of which services would, apart from absence for illness or while on holiday, have been rendered to the receiver, also constitute qualifying liabilities. Services rendered by employees before 'adoption' of the service contract are not 'qualifying liabilities'. Thus, the general principle is that in respect of contracts adopted on or after 15 March 1994, receivers need now only 'pay for what they use'.

Powers, liabilities and responsibilities

An administrative receiver has the powers which the debenture holders have conferred on him which are deemed to include the powers listed in IA1986 Sch.A (IA1986 s.42). On application to the Court, a receiver may seek authority to dispose of any of the company's properties as if it were not subject to the security (IA1986 s.43(l)).

An administrative receiver is deemed to be the company's agent until the commencement of liquidation and, unless the contract provides otherwise, is personally liable on any contract entered into by him in carrying out his functions albeit that he is normally entitled to indemnity out of the assets of the company (IA1986 s.43(5)). If the administrative receiver enters into contracts without authority, his liability is unlimited and he has no right of indemnity.

Taxation

Tax on any income arising during the receivership, for instance from trading profits, deposit interest and capital gains, is usually considered to be assessable on the company and is not a liability of the receiver. If the assessment relates to a period after liquidation, it is an expense in the liquidation, but otherwise it is merely a claim against the company.

Priority in distribution of funds

1 The proceeds realised from specific assets charged under a fixed charge must be used first to meet the costs of realisation, then the receiver's remuneration

and then the claims of the debenture holders. If there is any surplus, it is to be distributed in accordance with the priorities for floating charges.

2 The order of priority for distribution of funds arising from a floating charge is as follows:
   (a) costs of realisations;
   (b) other outgoings and costs of the receivership;
   (c) the receiver's remuneration;
   (d) preferential debts listed in IA1986 Sch.6; for example, money owed to HM Revenue & Customs for income tax and National Insurance contributions deducted at source, VAT, remuneration, etc. of employees are all subject to limits specified in the Schedule. As noted on p. 361, the Crown's preferential status was abolished by the Enterprise Act 2002 for all liquidations, administrations and receiverships commencing on or after 15 September 2003.
   (e) interest due under the debenture subject to the debenture's terms;
   (f) principal sum secured by the debenture.

Phoenix companies

Directors of an insolvent company cannot be appointed as directors of a company with a prohibited name. A prohibited name is one that is the same as that of the insolvent company or so similar as to suggest an association with that company.

21

Overseas and non-CA companies

Introduction

Any overseas company which opens a UK establishment must register with the Registrar of Companies within one month (SI 2009/1801). The regime which existed under CA1985, enabling a foreign company wishing to register a presence in the UK in two ways, either as a 'place of business' or as a 'branch', no longer exists. Under CA2006 and the Overseas Companies Regulations 2009 (SI 2009/1801) ('the Regulations'), a foreign company may register a 'UK establishment'. The requirements and obligations relating to a UK establishment are similar to those which were in existence for 'a branch'.

From 1 October 2009, 'places of business' registered under CA 1985 will incur more onerous obligations. Those with registered places of business will need to ensure they are aware of their new obligations.

The concept of a 'branch' was introduced by an EC Directive, but there was no statutory definition. Under the new legislation an 'establishment' is defined as being a branch within the meaning of the Eleventh Company Law Directive or a place of business that is not such a branch. A 'UK establishment' is defined as being an establishment in the UK. From the legislation, it is clear that a UK establishment is a permanent place of business and part of the structure of the overseas company. A UK establishment may well have its own management and have delegated responsibility for its actions.

Registration of a UK establishment

Every overseas company which is incorporated outside the United Kingdom (England and Wales, Scotland and Northern Ireland) and Gibraltar and which wishes to open a UK establishment within the UK is required to register with the Registrar of Companies.

An overseas company may have more than one UK establishment within the UK. If they each have management independence, each UK establishment will require to be registered. If there is a main office to which the other offices report, it is only necessary for the main UK establishment to register. If two UK establishments both report direct to the overseas parent, both must register.

An overseas company which opens a UK establishment or new UK establishment must register the necessary details with the Registrar by submitting Form OS IN01 ('Registration of an overseas company opening a UK establishment application') containing the following details in respect of the overseas company:

1. the company's registered name;
2. details of an alternative name, if the company wishes to carry on business under an alternative name;
3. its registered number and the identity of the country of incorporation;
4. its legal form (public, private, etc.);
5. address of principal place of business or registered office in the country of incorporation, if not included in the constitutional documents;
6. details of directors and secretary or equivalent;
7. the authority of the directors to represent the company and their capacity to bind the company in dealings with third parties together with a statement of whether this authority may be exercised solely or jointly with other directors;
8. whether the company is a credit or financial institution;
9. if the overseas company is not incorporated in a Member State of the EU, additional information is required: namely, the legislation under which the company was incorporated, confirmation that any sensitive words within the corporate name have been authorised, and a copy of that authorisation and accounting period together with time period for public disclosure.

In respect of the UK establishment itself, the following information should be registered:

1. The address of the UK establishment.
2. The date on which it was established.
3. The business carried on by the UK establishment.
4. The trading name if different from the parent's registered name.
5. The name and address of all persons resident in the UK authorised to accept service on behalf of the parent company in respect of that branch.
6. The name and address of all persons authorised to represent the company as permanent representatives for the business of that UK establishment.
7. The authority of the permanent representatives to contract on behalf of the UK establishment and whether they may exercise such authority solely or if jointly the name of the joint authorised representatives (reg.7(1)).

If an overseas company has more than one establishment in the UK, there is no need to repeat all the information on each Form OS IN01, as reference may be made to a Form OS IN01 previously filed. Only information exclusive to the particular UK establishment need be disclosed.

In addition to Form OS IN01, a certified copy of the constitutional document of the overseas company and, if not in English, a certified translation must be submitted. This document need only be submitted once and must be referred to for other UK establishment registrations. Any alterations to the constitutional documents must be notified on Form OS CC01 ('Return by an overseas company of an alteration to constitutional documents').

If the UK establishment for which full registration was made is subsequently closed, the constitutional documents may be 'transferred' to another UK establishment using Form OS AD01 ('Return by an overseas company of change of UK establishment relating to constitutional documents'). A UK establishment registration fee of £20 (in 2009) is payable. Any change in the details of the UK establishment must be notified within 21 days, or if they are changes to the details of the overseas company within 21 days of the date on which notice could have been made in the normal course of post from the overseas country, using the applicable form available at Companies House (www.companieshouse.gov.uk). Each overseas company with registered UK establishments must register its annual report and accounts. The full accounts of the overseas company are required and not just accounts relating to the UK establishment(s). The form of accounts required will depend on the requirements in the overseas company's country of incorporation. If the overseas company is required to publish audited accounts, those accounts and any other accounting information published must be filed with the Registrar within three months of their publication in their home country. If the accounts are not in English, a certified translation must also be filed. If, however, the overseas company is not required in its own country to publish audited accounts then it must publish accounts as if it were incorporated under the Companies Acts, as amended by Part 5 of the Regulations.

The effect of this legislation is to allow any overseas company registered in a Member State of the EU to file the accounts prepared for its host country, with a certified translation if necessary. The relevant CA2006 provisions concerning overseas companies which are not required by the laws of their country of incorporation to publish audited accounts have been amended. A filing fee of £15 (in 2009) is payable on submission of the accounts.

A UK establishment which owns property over which charges have been given is required to register details with the Registrar.

Every UK establishment of an overseas company must state the following information on all business letters, order forms and websites that are used in carrying on business in the UK:

- country of incorporation;
- identity of the registry (if applicable);
- the company number;
- location of its head office;
- legal form of the company;
- whether the liability of the members is limited and whether the company is limited;
- where applicable, whether the company is being wound up or subject to insolvency proceedings; and

- if there is a reference to share capital, the reference must be to paid-up share capital.

Where an overseas company has more than one registered UK establishment and is being wound up, it must, within 14 days of the commencement of the winding-up, give details of its name, particulars of the winding-up and the date on which the winding-up is or will be effective (Form OS LQ03 or OS LQ02). Within 14 days of appointment, the liquidator must notify his name and address, the date of his appointment and a description of his powers (Form OS LQ01). Following the termination of the winding-up, for whatever reason, the liquidator must file details of the termination within 14 days (Form OS DS02 or OS LQ04). Details must be given for each UK establishment, although one return may be made provided the registered UK establishment numbers of each UK establishment are stated on the return. These provisions do not apply to any winding-up under the provisions of Part V of IA1986.

Filing requirements

An overseas company with registered UK establishments must register its annual report and accounts. The full accounts of the overseas company are required, not the accounts relating to the UK establishment(s). The form of accounts required will depend on the requirements in the overseas company's country of incorporation. If the overseas company is required to publish audited accounts those accounts and any other accounting information published must be filed with the Registrar within three months of their publication in their home country. If the accounts are not in English, a certified translation must also be filed.

If the overseas company is not required in its own country to publish audited accounts then it must prepare and file accounts in respect of each financial period as if it were a company formed under the Companies Acts. The accounts of the overseas company as a whole entity are required, not simply accounts relating to trade within the UK. Again, if the accounts are not in English, a certified translation is also required to be filed.

There is a currently a filing fee of £15 for the submission of UK establishment accounts.

European Economic Interest Groupings (EEIGs)

EEIGs were established by Council Regulation (EEC) No. 2137/85. The appropriate legislation was brought into effect in England and Wales and Scotland by the European Economic Interest Grouping Regulations 1989, SI 1989/638.

EEIGs are designed to help businesses in different Member States establish and maintain links. The EEIG provides an alternative to takeover, merger or joint venture where the costs involved usually preclude smaller companies from participating. An EEIG enables such links to be established without losing the identity and independence of the members.

Additional advice is available in the Companies House guidance booklet GPO4, *European Economic Interest Groupings*.

What is an EEIG?

The EEIG is an association between corporate bodies, firms or individuals from different Member States so as to operate together across national borders. Its aim is to facilitate or develop the commercial activities of its members. Although an EEIG carries out activities on behalf of its members, its activities are separate from those of its members.

An EEIG may be registered in any Member State, can operate in any Member State and can contract with people outside the EU. Only corporate bodies, firms or individuals resident in the EU can become members of an EEIG. An EEIG registered in the UK is a corporate body.

An EEIG cannot:

- be formed with the object of making a profit (an EEIG can make a profit, however, as a consequence of its operations);
- exercise control over any other undertaking and/or its members;
- hold shares or own part or all of any of its members;
- issue shares or receive investment from the public;
- be a member of another EEIG;
- employ more than 500 people;
- be used for the transfer of any property between a company and a director, or a connected person, other than allowed by national law.

Advantages of an EEIG

An EEIG has the following advantages:

- legal capacity;
- tax transparency;
- flexibility regarding financing;
- no capital requirement; and
- no requirement to prepare or file accounts.

Disadvantages of an EEIG

An EEIG has the following disadvantages:

- unlimited joint and several liability of the members;
- an EEIG cannot seek funds from the public; and
- an EEIG cannot buy a share in another EEIG.

Registration

An EEIG must be registered in the Member State where its official address is situated. The official address must be either:

- where its central administration is carried out; or
- where one of its members has its central administration.

If an EEIG opens an establishment in another Member State, that establishment must be registered in that other State.

The official address may be transferred within the EU. If the transfer is to another Member State a transfer proposal must be drawn up and filed with Companies House. The transfer may not take place until two months after publication of the proposal.

The formation and termination of an EEIG must be published in the *London, Edinburgh* or *Belfast Gazette* (as appropriate) and in the *Official Journal of the European Union* within one month of formation or termination as appropriate.

There are three different types of registration:

1. A new EEIG which is to have its official address in the UK must register:
   (a) Form EE FM01;
   (b) the contract of formation with a certified translation if not in English.
2. An existing EEIG that is moving its official address to the UK must register:
   (a) Form EE FM01, formation contract and certified translation (if appropriate);
   (b) evidence of the publication of the transfer proposal; and
   (c) a statement that no competent authority has opposed the transfer.
3. An EEIG setting up an establishment in the UK but which will continue to have its official address outside the UK must register:
   (a) Form EE FM02;
   (b) certified copies of all documents registered in the Member State where the EEIG has its official address together with certified translations, if appropriate.

Regardless of which type of registration is being effected there is a filing fee (currently £20).

Formation contract

The contract of formation of an EEIG must include the following information:

- its registered name;
- its official address;
- the objects for which it was formed;
- the names, business names, legal form and address or registered office of its members;
- the number and place of registration (if any) of its members;
- if formed for a specific event or period, the length of that period.

Name of an EEIG

The name of an EEIG must include the words 'European Economic Interest Grouping' or 'EEIG'. With this exception, the rules and restrictions on names for EEIGs are substantially the same as those for companies formed and registered under the Companies Act 2006.

Changes in registered information

Notice of changes to the registered details of an EEIG must be registered as follows:

1 Notice of the appointment and removal of managers on Forms EE AP01, EE AP02 or EE TM01 where the official address is in Great Britain, and Form EE MP01 where it is elsewhere.
2 Form EE MP01 must also be used to file the following documents and particulars:
   (a) amendment to the formation contract;
   (b) any judicial or members' decision ordering or establishing the winding-up of the EEIG;
   (c) any judicial decision nullifying the EEIG;
   (d) notice of a member's assignment of all or part of its participation in the EEIG;
   (e) notice of the appointment or termination of appointment of a liquidator of the EEIG;
   (f) notice of the conclusion of liquidation of the EEIG;
   (g) a proposal to transfer the official address to another Member State; and
   (h) notice of any proposal exempting new member(s) from liabilities incurred prior to their admission.
3 Form EE MP02 must be used to register the setting up or closing of any establishment other than where registration on Form EE FM01 is required.

Structure of an EEIG

An EEIG must be formed by at least two members from different Member States, and a manager or managers must be appointed to manage the day-to-day affairs of the EEIG.

Membership of an EEIG is intended to be open to as many people and organisations as possible within the EU. The main requirement is that each member should have been engaged in an economic activity in the EU before becoming a member of the EEIG.

To be eligible for membership, companies, firms and other legal bodies must:

- have been formed according to the law of one of the Member States and have their registered or statutory office (if applicable) within the EU; and
- have their central administration and control within the EU.

Individuals may become members if they carry on any industrial, commercial, craft or agricultural activity or provide professional or other services within the EU.

The members decide how the EEIG will be run and this provision will normally be set out in the formation contract. There is no requirement for regular meetings of the members.

Each member has at least one vote and no one member can hold a majority of the votes.

The members are free to decide the voting procedures to be set down in the contract of formation. Certain decisions require a unanimous decision of the members, as follows:

- alteration of the objects of the EEIG;
- changes to the votes allotted to members;
- extension to the duration of the EEIG;
- changes to members' financing of the EEIG;
- changes to members' obligations;
- changes to the formation contract; and
- transfer of the official address to another Member State.

Management of an EEIG

The members appoint managers who run the EEIG and make normal daily decisions. At least one manager must be appointed. EEIGs registered in the UK may appoint a corporate as manager, provided that an individual is then registered as the manager's representative. The actions of the managers are binding on the EEIG and the members are jointly liable for those actions. The only limitation that can be applied to the managers by the members is a requirement for dual signatories, provided that this requirement is published in the appropriate *Gazette*.

Funding

Members of an EEIG are not required to subscribe any capital. EEIGs can be financed by capital invested, by loans or donations from members or others. The contribution may be in the form of the services and skills. EEIGs may not seek investment from the public.

Accounts

The EEIG is not subject to any accounting requirements and does not have to file an annual return with Companies House. A return to HM Revenue & Customs, however, is required.

Taxation

Taxation operates under a system of fiscal transparency with any profits, losses or gains shared between the members according to their capital share. These profits, losses or gains are then taxed in the hands of the members according to the relevant taxation treatment in their own Member State. In the UK these provisions are set out in the Finance Act 1990 Sch.11.

This tax transparency does not extend to taxes such as VAT and stamp duty. An EEIG will have to register for VAT purposes if it makes taxable supplies in the same way as any other company, firm or person.

Societas Europaea

The European Company Statute Regulation (Council Regulation (EC) No. 2157/2001) was adopted on 8 October 2001 and came into force with effect from 8 October 2004. The statute created a new type of company that can operate on a Europe-wide basis and be governed by Community law directly applicable in Member States, rather than by national law. The European company or 'Societas Europaea' is available to businesses operating in more than one Member State and can be formed in a number of ways:

1. by the merger of two or more existing public limited companies from at least two different EU Member States;
2. by the formation of a holding company promoted by public or private limited companies from at least two EU Member States;
3. by the formation of the subsidiary of companies from at least two different Member States;
4. by the transformation of an existing public limited company with an EU registered office and head office and which has for at least two years had a subsidiary in another Member State; or
5. as a subsidiary of an existing Societas Europaea.

There is no central European registry and registration will be published in the *Official Journal*. Registration must be made in one of the Member States and will need to comply with national registration requirements of the country in which the administrative office is located. For a Societas Europaea with a registered office in England or Wales, this would require filing and registering at Companies House in Cardiff.

Companies House has issued a series of statutory forms for SE companies; these are listed in Appendix 6. Additional advice is available in the Companies House guidance booklet GPO6, *The European Company: Societas Europaea (SE)*.

Precedents

Introduction

This section contains suggested wording for minutes, letters, notices and other documents required from time to time. Whilst in many cases the wording is standard in all circumstances there will be instances where the wording will need to be amended to reflect the particular situation. Every company and indeed every company secretary will have their own style when preparing minutes, notices etc. There are, however, a number of common features that should be included:

1. Name of the company.
2. Type of meeting together with the place, date and time of the meeting.
3. List of those present.
4. Apologies for absence.
5. Minutes of the proceedings. These should not be an transcript of exactly what was said but a formal record of the discussions leading to a particular decision, the decision itself, any action points arising and, where appropriate, details of any disagreement with that decision.
6. Signature of chairman. Although there is no statutory requirement for minutes to be signed it does facilitate the identification of the final version of a particular minute and exactly what has been agreed. Additional signed minutes are prima facie evidence in court proceedings.

The notice and return of proxy periods noted in these precedents are based upon the Model Articles and the Companies Act 2006. When preparing documents based on these precedents you must check the articles of association of the company concerned to ensure the correct notice or return of proxy deadlines are used.

Precedent 1 Pro forma directors' minute

ANY COMPANY LIMITED
("the Company")
Company Number: 987654321

Minutes of a Meeting of the Board of Directors of the Company held at Company Office, 1 The Street, Any Town, This County on 1st January 2010 at 10.00 am

Present: J Smith
T Jones

Attending: J Doe – company secretary

Chairman
It was noted that John Smith was chairman of the meeting.

Notice and Quorum
The chairman reported that notice of the meeting had been given to all of the directors and noted that the quorum necessary for a meeting of the board of directors was present.

Topic heading
Brief introduction of matter being discussed, synopsis of discussion and decision reached.

Close of Meeting
There being no further business the chairman declared the meeting closed.

____

CHAIRMAN

Notes:
Section 172 of the Companies Act 2006

(1) A director of a company must act in the way he considers, in good faith, would be most likely to promote the success of the company for the benefit of its members as a whole, and in doing so have regard (amongst other matters) to -
  (a) the likely consequences of any decision in the long term,
  (b) the interests of the company's employees,
  (c) the need to foster the company's business relationships with suppliers, customers and others,
  (d) the impact of the company's operations on the community and the environment,
  (e) the desirability of the company maintaining a reputation for high standards of business conduct, and
  (f) the need to act fairly as between members of the company.
(2) Where or to the extent that the purposes of the company consist of or include purposes other than the benefit of its members, subsection (1) has effect as if the reference to promoting the success of the company for the benefit of its members were to achieving those purposes.
(3) The duty imposed by this section has effect subject to any enactment or rule of law requiring directors, in certain circumstances, to consider or act in the interests of creditors of the company.

Precedent 2 Pro forma directors' resolution to convene general meeting

General Meeting

The meeting considered the matter and **IT WAS RESOLVED THAT** a general meeting of the Company be convened and held on [•] 20 [•] at [•][on short notice immediately following this meeting] to consider and if deemed fit approve a [special/ordinary] resolution to [•] **AND THAT** the company secretary be and is hereby authorised to sign and issue to the shareholders a notice convening the said meeting.

Precedent 3 Pro forma general meeting minute

[•] LIMITED
("the Company")
Company Number: [•]

Minutes of a General Meeting of the Company
held at [•]
on [•] 20[•] at [•] am/pm

Present:

Attending:

Chairman

It was noted that [•] was chairman of the meeting.

Notice and Quorum

[The chairman reported that all the Company's shareholders had consented to the meeting being held on short notice.] The notice convening the meeting was taken as read.

Business of the Meeting

The Chairman proposed resolution 1 as set out in the notice of the meeting and enquired if any members present had any questions.

There being no questions the resolution was put to the meeting, as an ordinary resolution, and passed unanimously on a show of hands.

Close of Meeting

There being no further business the chairman declared the meeting closed.

____

CHAIRMAN

Precedent 4 Pro forma members' written resolution

Company Number: [•]

The Companies Acts 1985 and 2006
PRIVATE COMPANY LIMITED BY SHARES
WRITTEN RESOLUTION[S]

[•] **LIMITED**
("the Company")

We, the undersigned, being members of the Company eligible to attend and vote at general meetings of the Company, hereby pass the following resolution[s] designated as [an ordinary] [a special] resolution[s] and agree that the said resolution[s] shall be as valid and effective as if it [they] had been passed at a general meeting the Company duly convened and held.

IT IS RESOLVED:

[•]

Signed:

.... Date: ....20[•]
[Name]

.... Date: ....20[•]
[Name]

Notes:

1. These written resolutions have been proposed by the directors of the Company. The purpose of these resolutions is [ ].
2. The circulation date of these written resolutions is [•] 20[•].
3. Please signify your agreement to those resolutions which you do agree to by signing against your name where indicated, enter the date on which you signed the document and initial those boxes relating to the corresponding resolutions to which you agree. Please then return the document to the Company.
4. If you sign the document and return it to the Company without indicating whether you agree to all the resolutions or any particular resolution being passed, it will be assumed by the Company that you agree to all of the resolutions being passed.
5. If you return the document signed, but un-dated, it will be assumed by the Company that you signed the document on the day immediately preceding the day on which it was received by the Company.
6. If not passed by the requisite majority of the total voting rights of eligible members, these written resolutions shall lapse on the [•] 20[•].
7. As the resolution is [an ordinary] [a special] resolution, the requisite majority

needed to pass the resolution is a [simple majority] [three-fourths] of the total voting rights of eligible members.

8. Once these resolutions have been signed and returned to the Company, your agreement to them may not be revoked.

Precedent 5 Pro forma general meeting notice

[•] LIMITED
("the Company")
Company Number: [•]

Notice of General Meeting

NOTICE IS HEREBY GIVEN THAT a General Meeting of the Company will be held at [•] on [•] 20[•] at [•] am/pm to consider and if deemed fit to approve the following resolutions, resolution [•] being proposed as an ordinary resolution and resolution [•] being proposed as a special resolution:

Resolutions

1.
2.

Date: [•] 20[•] **BY ORDER OF THE BOARD**

Registered Office:

____
COMPANY SECRETARY

Notes:

1. A member entitled to attend and vote at the meeting is entitled to appoint more than one proxy, to exercise all or any of his rights to attend, speak and vote in his place on a show of hands or on a poll provided that each proxy is appointed to a different share or shares, or to a different £10.00 or multiple of £10.00 of stock. Such proxy need not be a member of the Company.
2. To be valid, the completed and signed form of proxy must be returned to [•] not less than 48 hours (excluding weekends, Christmas Day, Good Friday or recognised public and bank holidays) before the time fixed for the meeting. Lodging a form of proxy does not preclude a member from attending and voting at the meeting.

Precedent 6 Members' resolution to change company name

Special Resolution

THAT the name of the Company be changed to:

[•]

Precedent 7 Three-way form of proxy

[Company Name]

Company No. [ ]

FORM OF PROXY

Please use a black pen. Mark with an X inside the box as shown in the example. [X]

I/We hereby appoint the Chairman of the meeting OR the following person

[ ]

Please leave this box blank if you have selected the chairman. Do not insert your own name.

as my/our proxy to exercise all or any of my/our rights to attend, speak and vote in respect of my/our voting entitlement* on my/our behalf at the general meeting of [Company Name] to be held at [Address] on [Date] at [Time] a.m./p.m. and at any adjourned meeting.

Please tick here if this proxy appointment is one of multiple appointments being made* [ ]

* For the appointment of more than one proxy please refer to note 2 below.

Ordinary Resolutions:

	For	**Against**	**Vote Withheld**
1. To [ ]	[ ]	[ ]	[ ]
2. To [ ]	[ ]	[ ]	[ ]

Special Resolution:

	For	**Against**	**Vote Withheld**
3. To [ ]	[ ]	[ ]	[ ]

I/We would like my/our proxy to vote on the resolution proposed at the meeting as indicated on this form.

Signature	**Date**

Explanatory Notes:

1. You may appoint a proxy or proxies to exercise all or any of your rights to attend, speak and vote on your behalf at the meeting. If you wish to appoint a person other than the chairman, please insert the name of your chosen proxy holder in the space provided.

2. To appoint more than one proxy you may photocopy this form. Please indicate in the box next to the proxy holder's name the number of shares in relation to which they are authorised to act as your proxy. Please also indicate by ticking the box provided if the proxy instruction is one of multiple instructions being given. All forms must be signed and should be returned together in the same envelope.
3. Unless otherwise indicated the proxy may vote as he or she sees fit or abstain in relation to any business of the meeting.
4. The 'Vote Withheld' option is provided to enable you to abstain on a resolution. Please note that a 'Vote Withheld' is not a vote in law and will not be counted in the votes 'For' and 'Against' a resolution.
5. If the appointor is a corporation, this form must be under its common seal or under the hand of some officer or attorney duly authorised in that behalf.
6. In the case of joint holders, the signature of any one holder will be sufficient, but the names of all the joint holders should be stated.
7. If this form is returned without indication as to how the person appointed proxy shall vote, he will exercise his discretion as to how he votes or whether he abstains from voting.
8. To be valid, this form must be completed and deposited at the Company's registered office not less than 48 hours (excluding any day that is not a working day) before the time fixed for holding the meeting.

Precedent 8 Copy of resolution for Companies House

Company Number: [•]

THE COMPANIES ACTS 1985 TO 2006

SPECIAL RESOLUTION

OF

[•] LIMITED

COMPANY LIMITED BY SHARES

At a general meeting of the above-named Company, duly convened and held at [•] on the [•] day of 200[•], the following **SPECIAL RESOLUTION** was duly passed:

THAT the name of the Company be changed to:

[•]

____

DIRECTOR/COMPANY SECRETARY

Precedent 9 Directors' resolution to adopt company seal, overseas seal or security seal

[Company/Securities/Overseas] Seal

IT WAS RESOLVED THAT the seal, an impression of which is made in the margin of these minutes be adopted as the [company/security/overseas] seal of the company. In respect of the use of the overseas seal its use is authorised under the hand of Mr James Smith.

Precedent 10 Directors' resolution to change location of registered office.

Registered Office

IT WAS RESOLVED THAT the registered office of the Company be changed to [•] and that the company secretary be instructed to file form AD01 with the Registrar of Companies.

Precedent 11 Members' resolution to amend/adopt new articles of association

Special Resolution

THAT the articles of association of the Company be amended in the manner following, that is to say, by the deletion of the present clause [•] and the adoption of a new clause [•] namely:-

(see attached sheet)

OR

THAT the regulation attached hereto and initialled by the chairman for the purposes of identification be adopted as the articles of association of the company in substitution for and to the exclusion of the existing articles.

Precedent 12 Members' resolution to re-register Ltd company as a Plc

Special Resolutions

(1) **THAT:**
  (a) the Company be re-registered as a public company limited by shares within the meaning of the Companies Act 2006;
  (b) the name of the Company be changed to [•] Plc; and
  (c) with the exception of the subscriber clause the memorandum of association of the Company be deleted.

(2) **THAT** the regulations produced to the meeting and signed by the Chairman for the purposes of identification be adopted as the articles of association of the Company in substitution for and to the exclusion of the existing articles of association.

(see attached copy)

Precedent 13 Members' resolution to re-register a Plc company as Ltd

Special Resolutions

(1) **THAT:**

(a) the Company be re-registered as a private company limited by shares within the meaning of the Companies Act 2006;

(b) the name of the Company be changed to **[•]** Limited; and

(c) with the exception of the subscriber clause the memorandum of association of the Company be deleted.

(2) **THAT** the regulations produced to the meeting and signed by the Chairman for the purposes of identification be adopted as the articles of association of the Company in substitution for and to the exclusion of the existing articles of association.

(*see attached copy*)

Precedent 14 Directors' resolution to appoint additional director

Appointment of Director

IT WAS RESOLVED THAT [•] having consented to act, be appointed as a director of the Company with [immediate effect][effect from [•] 20[•]] and that the company secretary be instructed to file form [AP1/AP02] with the Registrar of Companies.

Precedent 15 Director's general notice of interests

General notice of interests by a director

Director's Name
Director's Address

The Directors
[ ] [Limited][Plc]

Pursuant to section 185 of the Companies Act 2006, I give notice that I have the interest in each of the companies or firms listed below which is shown against its name below and that I am to be regarded as interested in any transaction or arrangement which may, after the date hereof, be made with any of those companies or firms.

Name of company or firm	Nature and extent of interest
[ ]	[ ]
[ ]	[ ]

I also give notice that under that section I am connected with [each of] the person[s] listed below and am to be regarded as interested in any transaction or arrangement which may, after the date hereof, be made with [any of] the undermentioned person[s].

Name of person	Nature and connection with that person
[ ]	[ ]
[ ]	[ ]

[date]
Signed:

____
[name of director]

Precedent 16 Directors' resolution to approve appointment of alternate director

Alternate Director
There was produced to the meeting a letter from [•] appointing [•] as their alternate director with effect from [•] 20[•]. It was noted that in accordance with article [•] of the Company's articles of association it was necessary for the directors to approve the appointment.

After due consideration **IT WAS RESOLVED THAT** the appointment of [•] as alternate director to [•] be approved and that the company secretary be instructed to file form [AP01/AP02] with the Registrar of Companies and make an appropriate entry in the Register of Directors.

Precedent 17 Members' resolution to approve director service contract where more than two years' notice of termination required

Ordinary resolution
THAT the service contract proposed to be entered into between the company and Mr Smith, a director, as set out in the memorandum of terms attached to the notice convening this meeting be approved in terms of s.188 Companies Act 2006.

Precedent 18 Directors' resolution to approve another director's conflict of interest

At this point Mr Smith formally declared his interest in the matter. It was noted that, in accordance with article [•] of the Company's articles of association, having declared his interest Mr Smith was entitled to consider and vote upon the matter.

In reaching their decision, the Directors considered the need to promote the success of the Company for the benefit of its members as a whole and, in doing so, had regard to the specific requirements of s.172 of the Companies Act 2006.

Precedent 19 Pro forma AGM notice for a Plc

[•] PLC
("the Company")
Company Number: [•]

Notice of Annual General Meeting

NOTICE IS HEREBY GIVEN THAT the 20[•] Annual General Meeting of the Company will be held at [•] on [•] 20[•] at [•]am/pm to consider and, if deemed fit, to approve the following resolutions, all of which are being proposed as ordinary resolutions:

Ordinary Resolution

1. To receive [and adopt] the accounts of the Company for the year ended/period to [•] 20[•] together with the reports thereon of the directors and the auditors of the Company.
2. To [receive the statement of the auditors made pursuant to Section 837(4) of the Companies Act 2006 ("the 2006 Act") and to] approve the recommendation of the directors that a final dividend of [ ]p per ordinary share be declared in respect of the year ended/period to [•] 20[•].
3. To reappoint [•] retiring as a director in accordance with the Company's articles of association and, being eligible, offering [himself/herself] for reappointment as a director of the Company.
4. To reappoint [•] retiring as a director due to [his/her] appointment having been made since the last annual general meeting of the Company in accordance with the Company's articles of association and, being eligible, offering [himself/herself] for reappointment as a director of the Company.
5. To [re]appoint [•] as auditors of the Company in accordance with Section 489 of the 2006 Act, until the conclusion of the next general meeting of the Company at which audited accounts are laid before members and to authorise the Directors to determine their remuneration.
6. That the Directors of the Company be and they are hereby authorised generally and unconditionally pursuant to and in accordance with section 551 of the Companies Act 2006 ("the 2006 Act") to exercise all the powers of the Company to allot relevant securities (within the meaning of section 560 of the 2006 Act up to an aggregate nominal amount of £[•] [(representing [•] per cent of the Company's issued ordinary share capital on [•] 20[•]) [specify applicable reference date] provided that this authority shall expire [on [•] 20[•]]/[on whichever is earlier of the date of the Company's next Annual General Meeting (and at the conclusion thereof) or 15 months from the date on which this resolution is passed] save that the Company may, pursuant to this authority, make offers or agreements before the expiry of this authority which would or might require relevant securities to be allotted after such expiry and the Directors may allot relevant securities in pursuance of such offers or agreements as if the authority conferred by this resolution had not expired *[and all authorities previously conferred upon the Directors pursuant to section 80 of the 1985 Act shall be revoked but without prejudice to*

any exercise of such other authorities prior to the date on which this resolution is passed].

7. That:
   (a) [subject to the passing of resolution [6] above,] the Directors be and they are hereby empowered pursuant to section 570 of the 2006 Act to allot equity securities (within the meaning of section 560 of the 2006 Act) for cash pursuant to the authority conferred by [resolution [6] above] as if section 561 of the 2006 Act did not apply to such allotment, provided that this power shall be limited to the allotment of equity securities:
      (i) in connection with an offer of equity securities by way of rights to the holders of ordinary shares [and/or any other persons entitled to participate therein] [(other than the Company itself in respect of any shares held by it as treasury shares within the meaning of section 573 of the 2006 Act)] in proportion (as nearly as may be) to their respective holdings of ordinary shares [(or, as appropriate, the number of ordinary shares which such other persons are, for the purposes of such offer, deemed to hold)] on a record date fixed by the Directors but subject to such exclusions or other arrangements as the Directors may consider necessary or expedient to deal with [any legal or practical] problems under the laws of any territory or the requirements of any regulatory body or any stock exchange in any territory or in connection with fractional entitlements or otherwise howsoever; or
      (ii) [pursuant to the terms of any share scheme for directors and employees of the Company and/or its subsidiaries approved by the shareholders of the Company in general meeting; or]
      (iii) (other than pursuant to paragraph[s] (i) [or (ii)] above) having (in the case of relevant shares (as defined in section 560 of the 2006 Act)) a nominal amount or (in the case of any other equity securities) giving the right to subscribe for or convert into relevant shares having a nominal amount, not exceeding in aggregate £[•] [(the "Relevant Amount")] [(representing [•] per cent of the Company's issued ordinary share capital on [•] 20[•], being *[specify applicable reference date]*;
   (b) [the Directors be and they are hereby empowered pursuant to section 573 of the 2006 Act to effect a sale of relevant shares held by the Company as treasury shares for cash as if section 561 of the 2006 Act did not apply to such sale[, provided that this power shall be limited to the sale of relevant shares held by the Company as treasury shares having a nominal amount which, when aggregated with the nominal amount of any relevant shares allotted or the subject of rights of subscription or conversion pursuant to paragraph (a) (iii) above, does not exceed the Relevant Amount].]

   [Each of] the power[s] conferred by paragraph[s (a) [and (b)]] above shall expire [on [•] 20[•]]/[on whichever is earlier of the date of the Company's next Annual General Meeting (and at the conclusion thereof) or 15 months from the date on which this resolution is passed] save that the Company may, before the expiry of such power[s], make offers or agreements which would or might require equity securities to be allotted [and/or relevant shares held as treasury shares to be sold] after such expiry and the Directors may allot equity securities [and/or sell relevant shares held as treasury shares] in pursuance of such offers or agreements as if the power[s] conferred hereby had not expired [and all powers previously conferred upon the Directors pursuant to section 570 [and section 573] of the 2006 Act shall be revoked but without prejudice to any exercise of such other powers prior to the date on which this resolution is passed].

8. That, pursuant to section 366 of the 2006 Act, the Company and all companies that are subsidiaries of the Company [at the time this resolution is passed at any time during the period for which this resolution has effect] be and are hereby authorised to make/incur (in aggregate):
   (a) political donations to political parties or independent election candidates not exceeding in total the amount of £[•];
   (b) political donations to political organisations other than political parties not exceeding in total the amount of £[•];
   (c) political expenditure not exceeding in total the amount of £[•], during the period beginning with the date of this resolution and ending [on [•] 20[•]]/[on whichever is the earlier of the date of the Company's next Annual General Meeting (and at the conclusion thereof) or [12 months] from the date on which this resolution is passed].

For the purposes of this resolution, the terms "political donations", "political parties", "independent election candidates", "political organisation" and "political expenditure" have the meanings set out in Part 14 of the 2006 Act.]

Date: [•] 20[•] **BY ORDER OF THE BOARD**

Registered Office:

____

SECRETARY

[insert notice notes here]

Precedent 20 Members' resolution to remove a director

Ordinary Resolution

THAT [•] be removed as a director of the company with immediate effect.

Precedent 21 Special notice of proposed removal of director

[Proposer's name and address]

The Directors
[Company Name]

[Company Registered Office Address]

Date: [•] 20[•]

Dear Sirs

I hereby give notice pursuant to section 168(2) of the Companies Act 2006 of my intention to propose the following resolution as an ordinary resolution at the next annual general meeting of the company.

Ordinary Resolution

THAT [•] be removed as a director of the company with immediate effect.

Yours faithfully

____

[Name]
[Address]

Precedent 22 Draft article where all directors have died

In the event of the Company having no members and no directors as the result of the death or deaths of the members and/or directors, the personal representative of the last member or director to die has the right by notice in writing to appoint a director of the Company and this appointment shall have the same effect as if made in a general meeting. Where due to circumstances resulting in the death of two or more members or directors it is uncertain which of them survived the longest it shall be assumed that death occurred in the order of seniority, thus the younger will be assumed to have outlived the elder.

Precedent 23 Directors' resolution to note director resignation

Resignation of Director
It was noted that a letter of resignation had been received from [•] resigning as a director with [immediate effect][effect from [•] 20[•]].

Precedent 24 Directors' resolution to establish board committee

Board committee
IT WAS RESOLVED THAT [•] and [•] be appointed as a board committee to consider [•] and that the committee shall have all the powers of the board [subject to any regulations or resolutions or restrictions that may be imposed upon them by the board from time to time/subject to the terms of reference produced to the meeting and forming part of these minutes].

Precedent 25 Pro forma notice of directors' meeting and agenda

[•] LIMITED
("the Company")
Company Number: [•]

Notice is given that a Meeting of the Board of Directors of the Company will be held at [•] on [•] 20[•] at [•] am/pm

AGENDA

1. Minutes of the meeting held on [•] 20[•]
2. Matters arising
3. Operations report
4. Finance report
5. Project overview
6. AOB
    Change of registered office
    Meeting dates for 2010

Precedent 26 Directors' resolution to appoint chairman, vice chairman or deputy chairman

Chairman/Deputy chairman/Vice chairman
IT WAS RESOLVED THAT [•] be and is hereby appointed as [chairman/deputy chairman/vice chairman] of the board of directors until [further notice/for a period of 3 years].

Precedent 27 Sole director's resolution to appoint additional director(s)

Director
It was resolved that in accordance with regulation 1(3) of the Model Articles and forming part of the articles of association of the company that **[•]** be and is hereby appointed as an additional director with immediate effect.

Precedent 28 Draft article to vest all powers in a sole director

A sole Director shall have authority to exercise all the powers and discretions by Table A or these articles expressed to be vested in the directors generally and the quorum for the transaction of the business of the directors shall be one and the provisions of regulation 89 in Table A shall be modified accordingly. Regulation 64 in Table A shall not apply to the Company.

OR

A sole Director shall have authority to exercise all the powers and discretions by the Model Articles for Private Companies (the Model Articles) or these articles expressed to be vested in the directors generally and the quorum for the transaction of the business of the directors shall be one and the provisions of regulation 11 in the Model Articles shall be modified accordingly. Regulation 11(3) of the Model Articles shall not apply to the Company.

Precedent 29 Pro forma directors' resolution in writing

[•] LIMITED
("the Company")
Company Number: [•]

Resolution in writing of the sole director of the Company in accordance with [regulation 93 of Table A of the Companies Act 1985/regulation 8 of the Model Articles for private companies OR regulation 7 of the Model Articles for public companies] that forms part of the Articles of Association of the Company.

20[•]

[subject heading]

IT WAS RESOLVED THAT [•].

In reaching their decision, the Directors considered the need to promote the success of the Company for the benefit of its members as a whole and, in doing so, had regard to the specific requirements of s. 172 of the Companies Act 2006.

____

(Director's Name)

Notes:
Section 172 of the Companies Act 2006

(1) A director of a company must act in the way he considers, in good faith, would be most likely to promote the success of the company for the benefit of its members as a whole, and in doing so have regard (amongst other matters) to:
  (a) the likely consequences of any decision in the long term,
  (b) the interests of the company's employees,
  (c) the need to foster the company's business relationships with suppliers, customers and others,
  (d) the impact of the company's operations on the community and the environment,
  (e) the desirability of the company maintaining a reputation for high standards of business conduct, and
  (f) the need to act fairly as between members of the company.

(2) Where or to the extent that the purposes of the company consist of or include purposes other than the benefit of its members, subsection (1) has effect as if the reference to promoting the success of the company for the benefit of its members were to achieving those purposes.
(3) The duty imposed by this section has effect subject to any enactment or rule of law requiring directors, in certain circumstances, to consider or act in the interests of creditors of the company.

Precedent 30 Company secretary's certification of minutes

I hereby certify that the following is an extract of the minutes of the board of directors of the Company held on [•] 20[•].

____
Company secretary

Precedent 31 Members' resolution to approve substantial property transaction

Ordinary Resolution
THAT in accordance with ss.190(1) and (2) of the Companies Act 2006 the sale by the Company to [•] Limited, a company in which Mr [•], Director of the company is interested by virtue of being a director and shareholder, of the freehold property situated at [•] for the sum of [•] be approved.

Precedent 32 Members' resolution to approve political donation by Company

THAT, pursuant to section 366 of the 2006 Act, the Company and all companies that are subsidiaries of the Company [at the time this resolution is passed at any time during the period for which this resolution has effect] be and are hereby authorised to make/incur (in aggregate):

(a) political donations to political parties or independent election candidates not exceeding in total the amount of £[•];
(b) political donations to political organisations other than political parties not exceeding in total the amount of £[•];
(c) political expenditure not exceeding in total the amount of £[•], during the period beginning with the date of this resolution and ending [on [•] 20[•]]/[on whichever is the earlier of the date of the Company's next Annual General Meeting (and at the conclusion thereof) or [12 months] from the date on which this resolution is passed].

For the purposes of this resolution, the terms "political donations", "political parties", "independent election candidates", "political organisation" and "political expenditure" have the meanings set out in Part 14 of the 2006 Act.]

Precedent 33 Directors' resolution to appoint company secretary or joint company secretary

Appointment of Company Secretary
IT WAS RESOLVED THAT [•] having consented to act, be appointed as the [joint] company secretary of the Company with [immediate effect][effect from [•] 20[•]]. And that [•] be instructed to file form [AP03/AP04] with the Registrar of Companies.

Precedent 34 Directors' resolution to note resignation of company secretary

Resignation of Company Secretary
It was noted that a letter of resignation had been received from [•] resigning as the company secretary with [immediate effect][effect from [•] 20[•]] and that a form TM02 be filed with the Registrar of Companies.

Precedent 35 Directors' resolution to remove company secretary and appoint replacement

Removal and Appointment of Company Secretary
IT WAS RESOLVED THAT [•] be removed as company secretary with immediate effect and that [•] having consented to act, be appointed as the company secretary of the Company with [immediate effect][effect from [•] 20[•]] and that the new company secretary be instructed to file forms [AP03/AP04] and TM02 with the Registrar of Companies.

Precedent 36 Members' resolution to remove restriction of issuing shares by virtue of legacy authorised share capital statement

THAT clause [•] formerly contained in the company's memorandum of association and now forming part of the articles of association be deleted and that subject to section [550 [and 551]] of the Companies Act 2006 there be no restriction on the number of shares that the Company can issue.

Precedent 37 Draft article to restrict issue of share over specified amount

THAT the articles of association be amended by the adoption of a new clause [•] as set out below:

The Directors shall have power to issue or allot shares up to a maximum issued and allotted share capital of £[•].

Precedent 38 Members' resolution to consolidate shares

Ordinary Resolution

THAT the 5,000 ordinary shares of £10 each in the capital of the Company[, both issued and unissued,] be consolidated into 2,500 ordinary shares of £20 each on the basis that no member shall be entitled to a fraction of a share and fractional entitlements shall be aggregated and sold and purchased by the Company in accordance with resolution [•] the proceeds of sale, exceeding £3.00 will be distributed to the members concerned.

Precedent 39 Members' resolution to subdivide shares

Ordinary Resolution

THAT the 50 ordinary shares of £100 each in the capital of the Company [, both issued and unissued,] be subdivided into 5,000 ordinary shares of £1.00 each on the basis of 100 new shares for each share currently held.

Precedent 40 Members' resolution to reconvert stock into shares

Ordinary Resolution

THAT £[•] of the principal amount outstanding on the 20[•] loan stock be converted into fully paid ordinary shares on the basis of 10 ordinary shares of £1.00 for each £10 unit of loan stock converted.

Precedent 41 Directors' resolution to cancel shares forfeited/ purchased

IT WAS RESOLVED THAT [•] ordinary shares of 50 pence each in the capital of the company, unpaid, and registered in the name of [•] be forfeited for non-payment of the call of 50 pence per share payable on or before [•] due notice of which was given to the said member on [•] in accordance with the resolution of the board dated [•] and that the said shares be sold, disposed of, reissued or cancelled in such manner as the directors may determine.

Precedent 42 Members' resolutions to authorise reduction of capital

Ordinary Resolution

THAT the issued capital of the company comprising 25,000 ordinary shares of £1.00 each be reduced to 5,000 ordinary shares of £1.00 each by the cancellation of 20,000 shares and the return of £20,000 to the members.

OR

THAT the issued capital of the company comprising 25,000 ordinary shares of £1.00 each be reduced to 25,000 ordinary shares of £0.10 each by the cancellation of £22,500 from the share premium account.

Precedent 43 Draft notice to convene class meeting to vary class rights

[•] LIMITED
("the Company")
Company Number: [•]

Notice of Class Meeting

NOTICE IS HEREBY GIVEN THAT a Class Meeting of the holders of Preference shares of the Company will be held at [•] on [•] 20[•] at [•]am/pm to consider and, if deemed fit, to approve the following resolution being proposed as a special resolution:

Special Resolution
THAT [•]

Date: [•] 20[•] **BY ORDER OF THE BOARD**

Registered Office:

____
COMPANY SECRETARY

Notes:

1. A holder of preference shares entitled to attend and vote at the meeting is entitled to appoint more than one proxy, to exercise all or any of his rights to attend, speak and vote in his place on a show of hands or on a poll provided that each proxy is appointed to a different share or shares, or to a different £10.00 or multiple of £10.00 of stock. Such proxy need not be a member of the Company.
2. To be valid, the completed and signed form of proxy must be returned to **[•]** not less than 48 hours (excluding weekends, Christmas Day, Good Friday or recognised public and bank holidays) before the time fixed for the meeting. Lodging a form of proxy does not preclude a member from attending and voting at the meeting.

Explanatory notes on the resolution
Resolution 1
[•]

Precedent 44 Draft notice to consider serious loss of capital

[•] LIMITED
("the Company")
Company Number: [•]

Notice of General Meeting

NOTICE IS HEREBY GIVEN THAT a General Meeting of the Company will be held at [•] on [•] 20[•] at [•]am/pm pursuant to s. 656 of the Companies Act 2006, to consider whether any, and if so what steps should be taken to deal with the situation arising by virtue of the fact that the net assets of the Company are half or less that half of its called-up share capital.

Date: [•] 20[•] **BY ORDER OF THE BOARD**

Registered Office:

____

COMPANY SECRETARY

Notes:

1. A member entitled to attend and vote at the meeting is entitled to appoint more than one proxy, to exercise all or any of his rights to attend, speak and vote in his place on a show of hands or on a poll provided that each proxy is appointed to a different share or shares, or to a different £10.00 or multiple of £10.00 of stock. Such proxy need not be a member of the Company.

Explanatory notes on the resolution

Resolution 1

The directors are required to convene a general meeting to consider what action to take, if any, if the company's net assets are half or less than half of its called up share capital. There is no resolution to be put to the meeting.

Precedent 45 Members' resolution to give directors authority to issue shares

Ordinary Resolution

THAT with effect from the time of the passing of this resolution the directors are unconditionally authorised, pursuant to Section 551 of the Companies Act 1985, to allot shares at any time or times during the period of five years from the date hereof.

Precedent 46 Members' resolution to waive pre-emption provisions on issue of new shares

Ordinary Resolution

THAT the provisions of s. 561 of the Companies Act 2006 shall not apply to the issue of up to 25,000 ordinary shares of £1.00 each provided such allotment shall take place within 12 months of the date of this resolution.

OR

THAT pursuant to the provisions of s. 570 of the Companies Act 2006 (the Act) the provisions of s. 561 of the Act shall not apply to the allotment of any shares where the directors have general authority in terms of s. 551 of the Act to allot shares.

Precedent 47 Application for new shares

[Applicant's address]

The Directors
[Company Name Limited
Company Number
Company Address]

Dear Sirs
I/We hereby apply for the issue of [•] ordinary shares of £[•] each in the capital of [•] Limited (the Company) to be issued at £[•] per share fully paid and hereby request you to allot such shares to me/us. I/We enclose herewith a cheque in the sum of £[•] in full payment for the said shares.

I/We agree to take the said shares subject to the articles of association of the Company and authorise you to enter my/our name in the register of members as the holder of the said shares.

Dated this [•] day of [•] 20[•]

Yours faithfully

____

[Print Name]

Precedent 48 Directors' resolution to issue new shares

Application for Shares
The chairman reported that the following application[s] had been received for the allotment of [a] share[s] in the capital of the Company:

[•] ordinary shares of £1.00 each from [•].
[•] ordinary shares of £1.00 each from [•].

Declaration of Interest
At this point [•] formally declared [his/her] interest in the matter as one of the applicants for the issue of shares. It was noted that having declared [his/her] interest [•] was permitted by article [•] of the articles of association of the Company to consider and vote upon the matter.

Waiver of Pre-emption Rights
The chairman reported that the rights of pre-emption on allotment of these new shares, set out in the Company's articles of association, had been waived by the existing shareholders.

Allotment of Shares
After due consideration **IT WAS RESOLVED THAT** pursuant to the authority conferred upon the directors by the articles of association, the said applications be and are hereby approved and that the said shares be allotted to the applicants fully paid at [par value/a price of £[•] per share] for cash.

In reaching their decisions, the Directors considered the need to promote the success of the Company for the benefit of its members as a whole and, in doing so, had regard to the specific requirements of s. 172 of the Companies Act 2006.

Share Certificates
IT WAS RESOLVED THAT any two directors or one director and the company secretary be and are hereby authorised to issue appropriate share certificates to the allottees signed on behalf of the Company.

Filing of Forms
IT WAS RESOLVED THAT the company secretary be instructed to file a form SH01 with the Registrar of Companies.

Precedent 49 Declaration of trust by nominee for shares

To: [•]
[•]

[•] Limited

I, the undersigned [•] hereby acknowledge that I am a nominee and trustee for you in respect of [•] ordinary shares of £[•] each fully paid and held by me in the capital of [•] Limited (hereinafter called "the Company").

I hand you herewith the share certificate for the said shares together with a transfer duly executed by me and I hereby irrevocably authorise you to complete such transfer by filling in the date and the name and address of the transferee and the amount of the consideration for the transfer and to pass the duly completed document to the Company for registration.

I will pay all dividends, bonuses and other payments received by me in respect of the said shares to you and I will, so long as I remain as registered holder of the said shares, vote in respect thereof as you may from time to time direct and not otherwise.

Dated this [•] day of [•] 20[•]

Signed as a Deed and delivered
by the above named

____

[•]

Witnessed by:

Witness Signature	]	________________
Witness Name	]	________________
Witness Address	]	________________
		________________
Witness Occupation	]	________________
Date	]	________________

Precedent 50 Members' resolution to approve acquisition of non-cash asset from subscribers

Ordinary Resolution

THAT in accordance with the provisions of s.601 of the Companies Act 2006 the terms of the proposed acquisition of [•] from [•], a subscriber to the company's memorandum, be approved.

Precedent 51 Directors' resolution to call unpaid amounts on shares

IT WAS RESOLVED THAT a call of [•] pence per share be made on the [•] issued ordinary shares of £1.00 of the company, such call to be paid on or before [•] and that the company secretary be instructed to issue call letters on [•] 20[•].

Precedent 52 Call letter and reminder

[Company Name Limited
Company Number
Company Address]

[Member's name and address]

Dear Sir

Call letter for a call of [•] pence per ordinary share

I am instructed to inform you that pursuant to a resolution of the Board of Directors made on [•] 20[•], a call of [•] p per ordinary share in the capital of the Company has been made, such call to be paid on or before [•] 20[•].

Accordingly you are requested to pay the total amount of the call, shown above, in respect of the shares registered in your name(s) at this date to [•] by the due date.

Upon payment of the call you should lodge this call letter and the relevant share certificate(s) with the Company to allow the certificates to be endorsed and returned. Interest may be charged on the call at the rate of [•] % per annum if payment is not made by the due date. Failure to pay the call by such date will render the shares liable to forfeiture. You will remain liable for this call notwithstanding any subsequent transfer of the shares hereafter.

Yours faithfully

Company Secretary

Company Name Limited
Company Number
Company Address]

[Member's name and address]

Dear Sir

Call Letter Ref:

I am instructed to bring to your attention your failure to comply with the notice sent to you on [•] 20[•] requiring payment of the call upon your partly-paid shares amounting to £[•].
The call was due on [•] 20[•]. You are required to pay to the company the amount of your call, together with interest at the rate of [•] per cent per annum from [•] 20[•] up to and including the date of payment, on or before [•] 20[•]. Payment, accompanied by the original call notice, must be sent to the company. Should you fail to pay the call (together with the interest on it) within this time, the shares are, under the articles of association, liable to be forfeited. I must remind you, however, that forfeiture of the shares in no way releases you from liability for the call and the interest, and that, under its articles of association, the company is entitled to enforce its claims without any deduction or allowance for the value of the shares at the time of forfeiture.
The company also holds a first and paramount lien over the [•] fully paid shares of the company of which you are the registered holder, for all monies due to the company. No transfer of any shares of which you are the registered holder can be accepted by the company until the call and interest have been paid.

By order of the Board

Company Secretary

Precedent 53 Letter to confirm forfeiture of shares by directors

Dear Sir or Madam

I am directed to inform you that the [•] ordinary shares of £[•] each in the above company, of which you were the registered holder, have, by a resolution of the directors passed at a board meeting held on [•] 20[•] been duly forfeited in consequence of your having failed to pay the call due on them on[•] 20[•].

[I am also to request you to pay such call amounting to £[•] with interest at [•] per cent from [•] 20[•] up to the day of actual payment, and to inform you that in default of your complying with this request before [•] 20[•] proceedings will be taken against you to enforce such payment without further notice.]

By order of the Board

Company Secretary

Precedent 54 Directors' resolution to recommend bonus issue

The Chairman reported the proposal to undertake a capitalisation issue to increase the Company's issued share capital from [•] to [•] Ordinary Shares of £1.00 each. It was noted that the increase would be effected by capitalising £[•] from revenue reserves.

It was further noted that a General Meeting of the shareholders of the Company would need to be convened and held to approve resolutions authorising the Directors to allot additional shares and declaring a capitalisation issue. There was produced to the meeting a Notice convening a General Meeting of the Shareholders to be held immediately upon short notice and IT WAS RESOLVED THAT:

1. The Directors do recommend to the shareholders that the sum of £[•] be capitalised and appropriated to the holders of the Ordinary Shares in the Capital of the Company pro rata to their existing holdings.
2. The Secretary be and is hereby instructed to sign and issue to the shareholders a Notice convening a General Meeting of the members.

At this point, the meeting was adjourned to enable the General Meeting of the shareholders to be held upon short notice. Upon resumption of the meeting the Chairman reported that the General Meeting of the shareholders had been duly held and that the resolutions set out in the notice of the meeting had been approved unanimously.
The meeting now considered the proposed capitalisation issue and IT WAS RESOLVED THAT:

1. Pursuant to the authority given by and the directions contained in the resolution of the Company passed at the General Meeting held this day, the sum of £[•] therein referred to, be capitalised and appropriated as therein set out.
2. [•] Ordinary Shares of £1.00 each credited as fully paid be and are hereby provisionally allotted to the persons and in the numbers set out in the respective renounceable entitlement forms now produced to the meeting, such allotments being as follows: a. [•] Ordinary Shares of £1.00 each fully paid to [•]. b. [•] Ordinary Shares of £1.00 each fully paid to [•].
3. The secretary be and is hereby authorised to issue renounceable letters of allotment to the provisional allottees, renunciations to be made within 14 days of the date hereof.

Precedent 55 Letter of provisional allotment for bonus issue

Dear Sir/Madam

I am instructed to inform you that you have been allotted [•] ordinary shares of £[•] each in the capital of the Company, credited as fully paid, subject to the Articles of Association of the Company. The shares will rank for all dividends declared and paid after the date hereof.

If you wish to have all the shares comprised herein registered in your name, you need do nothing with this letter until [•] 20[•] when it should be exchanged for a definitive share certificate at the registered office of the Company. If you wish to dispose of the shares comprised in this letter, you should complete and sign the form of renunciation and hand this letter to the renouncee on or before [•] 20[•].

(*Note:* If you are the person in whose favour this letter has been renounced you must complete the registration application form and lodge this allotment letter at the registered office of the Company not later than [•] to be exchanged for a definitive share certificate.)

BY ORDER OF THE BOARD

Company Secretary

Precedent 56 Notice to members of redemption of shares

Formal notice of shares to be redeemed

Dear

Redemption [•] [Preference] Shares

In accordance with the terms of issue and the Company's articles of association, there have been drawn for redemption and the Company will redeem at [•] pence per share on [•] 20[•],[•] of the preference shares held by you.

A payment authority and discharge form will be sent to you in due course.

Yours faithfully

Company Secretary

Letter detailing procedure and payment and discharge forms

Dear

Redemption [•] Shares

Further to the notice sent to you on [•] 20[•] advising that the above [Preference] Shares held by you will be redeemed on [•] 20[•], I enclose payment authority and discharge form for your signature and return.

Please complete the form and return it together with appropriate share certificate(s) not later than [•] 20[•]. Subject to receipt of the form and appropriate share certificate(s) a cheque for the value of the preference shares will be posted on [•] 20[•].

In accordance with the terms of issue of the shares the value has been calculated as follows:

If the preference shares now being redeemed are only part of your holding, and you do not have a certificate for the exact number a balance certificate will be issued.

There will be no further dividend payments in respect of the preference shares being redeemed.

Yours faithfully,

Company Secretary

Payment authority and discharge form

To the Directors
[•] Limited
I hereby authorise and request you to send a cheque for the sum of pounds) being the amount due to me/us on redemption of [•] preference shares to:

and I confirm that your compliance with this request shall discharge the company's liability for such payment.

I enclose .... preference share certificate(s) for cancellation.

Signed:

Shareholder's name

Precedent 57 Members' resolution to approve share purchase contract

Ordinary Resolution
THAT the contract proposed to be made between the Company and [•] for the purchase by the Company of [•] Ordinary Shares of £1.00 each fully paid in the capital of the Company upon the terms of the draft attached hereto and initialled by the Chairman for the purposes of identification be and is hereby approved.

Precedent 58 Simple share purchase contract – by company

THIS AGREEMENT is made the [•] day [•] 20[•] BETWEEN [•] of [•] (hereinafter called 'the Vendor') and [•] Limited whose registered office is at [•] (hereinafter called 'the Company').

WHEREAS:

(a) The Company was incorporated in England and Wales on with a registered number of and has an issued share capital of £ [•] divided into [•] ordinary shares of £[•] each all of which are fully paid.
(b) The Vendor is the beneficial owner of [•] ordinary shares of £ [•] each ('the shares') in the capital of the Company.
(c) The parties have proposed that the Vendor shall sell and the Company shall purchase the shares on the terms set out in this agreement and in accordance with all applicable laws.

NOW IT IS HEREBY AGREED THAT:
1 The Vendor shall sell and the Company shall purchase the shares beneficially held by the Vendor, free of all liens, charges and encumbrances.
2 The consideration for the shares shall be £ [•] payable in full upon completion.
3 Completion of the sale and purchase of the shares hereby agreed shall take place at [•] on [•] 20[•] at [•] am/pm when:
   (a) the Vendor shall deliver to the Company the share certificate(s) in respect of the shares to be sold by him pursuant to this agreement;
   (b) the Company shall deliver to the Vendor a draft for the purchase monies due.
4 This agreement shall be governed by the laws of England.

AS WITNESS the hands of the parties hereto the day and year first before written.

Precedent 59 Members' resolution to approve market purchase of shares

Ordinary Resolution

THAT the company be authorised to make market purchases (as defined by Section 163(3) of the Companies Act 1985 as amended) of ordinary shares of 25p each in its capital be renewed provided that:
(a) the maximum aggregate number of ordinary shares hereby authorised to be purchased is 5,000,000;
(b) the minimum price which may be paid for each such ordinary share is the nominal value of such share and the maximum price which may be paid for such ordinary shares is not more than 5 per cent. above the average of the middle market quotations for such shares taken from the Daily Official List of London Stock Exchange plc for the five business days in respect of which such Daily Official List is published immediately preceding the date of purchase (in each case excluding expenses);
(c) unless previously revoked or varied the authority hereby conferred is to expire at the conclusion of the annual general meeting of the Company to be held in 20[•] or on 31 March 20[•], whichever is the earlier; and
(d) the Company may make a contract to purchase ordinary shares under the authority hereby conferred prior to the expiry of such authority which may be or will be executed wholly or partly after the expiry of such authority, and may make a purchase of ordinary shares in pursuance of any such contract notwithstanding such expiry.

Precedent 60 Directors' statement under s. 714

[•] Limited (the Company)
Directors' Statement under Section 714 of the Companies Act 2006 (the Act)
The amount of the permissible capital payment for the shares to be purchased by the Company in accordance with the share buyback agreement proposed to be entered into between the Company and [•] whose shares are to be purchased [wholly/partly] out of capital] as set out in the [notice of general meeting/draft written resolution] circulated on [•] is £[•].
We, the undersigned being all the directors of the Company as at the date of this statement, having made full inquiry into the affairs and prospects of the company and having taken account of all of the Company's liabilities (including any contingent or prospective liabilities), have formed the opinion that:
(a) As regards the Company's initial situation immediately following the date on which the payment out of capital is proposed to be made, there will be no grounds on which the Company could be found to be unable to pay its debts; and
(b) As regards the Company's prospects for the year immediately following the date on which the payment out of capital is proposed to be made that:
   (i) taking into account our current intentions with respect to the management of the Company business during this year; and
   (ii) the amount and character of the financial resources that will, in our view, be available to the Company during this year,

   the Company will be able to continue to carry on business as a going concern (and will accordingly be able to pay its debts as they fall due) throughout this year.

An auditor's report from [•] dated [•] in accordance with s.714(6) of the Act is attached to this statement.
The Company's business does not include that of a banking company or an insurance company.

Signed by:
[all directors must sign the statement]

Precedent 61 Members' resolution to approve purchase of shares out of capital

Ordinary Resolution
THAT the payment of £[•] out of the capital of the Company as defined in Sections 710 to 712 of the Companies Act 2006 in respect of the purchase of [•] Ordinary Shares of £1.00 each under Section 709 of the said Act from [•] be and is hereby approved.

Precedent 62 London Gazette notice re purchase out of capital

[•] Limited

NOTICE IS HEREBY GIVEN THAT:
1 By a special resolution of the shareholders of the above-named Company approved at a general meeting of the shareholders held on [•] 20[•] the payment out of

capital of £[•] for the purpose of the Company acquiring [•] ordinary shares of £1.00 each from [•] was authorised.

2 The amount of the permissible capital repayment as defined by Sections 711 and 772 of the Companies Act 2006 was £[•].

3 The directors' statement and the auditors' report required by Section 714 of the said Act are available for inspection at the registered office of the Company situated at [•].

4 Any creditor of the Company may at any time within the period of five weeks immediately following [•] 20[•] (being the date of the above mentioned special resolution) apply to the High Court under Section 721 of the said Act for an order prohibiting the payment.

Precedent 63 Letter re conversion of loan stock

Notice of conversion of loan stock

Dear Sir

Conversion of [•] Loan Stock of the Company

In accordance with the terms of issue of the convertible loan stock created by a resolution of the Board of Directors approved on [•] 20[•] you are entitled to convert all or part of your holding of convertible loan notes during the period [•] to [•] by giving notice to the company. According to our records you are the registered holder of 100,000 such convertible loan notes.

The convertible loan notes are convertible into [•] ordinary shares for each £100 of loan stock held.

If you want to convert any of your loan stock please complete the attached form of conversion and return it together with your loan stock certificate no later than[•].

By order of the Board

Company Secretary

Notice to company by loan stock holder requiring conversion

Dear Sirs

Take notice that in exercise of the power conferred upon me by the terms of issue of the [•] Convertible Loan Stock I require £[•] of the convertible loan stock held by me to be converted on [•] on the terms fixed for their conversion, for which purpose I enclose a loan stock certificate comprising such loan stock. Kindly acknowledge receipt and forward to me a certificate for any unconverted balance of such loan stock and a share certificate for the new shares allotted to me as a result of this conversion.

[signature
full name and address of loan stock holder]

Precedent 64 Directors' resolution to approve transfer of shares

Transfer of shares

There was produced to the meeting [a] stock transfer form[s] transferring shares in the capital of the Company as follows:

[•] ordinary shares of £[•] each fully paid from [•] to [•].

[•] ordinary shares of £[•] each fully paid from [•] to [•].

The meeting considered the matter and **IT WAS RESOLVED THAT** the said transfer[s] be and [is/are] hereby approved and, subject to stamping by HM Revenue & Customs, registered in the books of the Company and that any two directors or one director and the company secretary be and are hereby authorised to issue the share certificate[s] to the transferee[s] signed on behalf of the Company.

In reaching their decision, the Directors considered the need to promote the success of the Company for the benefit of its members as a whole and, in doing so, had regard to the specific requirements of s. 172 of the Companies Act 2006.

Precedent 65 Members' waiver of pre-emption rights on transfer

I/We, [name[•]] of [address[•]] being the registered holder of [•] ordinary shares of £[•] each in the capital of [•] (the "Company") do hereby waive all rights of pre-emption on the transfer of shares conferred upon [me/us] by article [•] of the articles of association of the Company so as to permit the transfer and registration of [•] ordinary shares of £[•] each in the capital of the Company from [•] to [•].

EXECUTED AS A DEED this [•] day of [•] by the said

Precedent 66 Directors' resolution to amend articles to enable electronic settlement of shares

IT WAS RESOLVED THAT pursuant to Regulation 16(2) of the Uncertified Securities Regulations 2001 ('the Regulations'):

(a) title to the ordinary shares of £1.00 each in the capital of the Company ('the Shares'), in issue or to be issued, may be transferred by means of a relevant system (as defined in the Regulations);

(b) such relevant system shall include the relevant system of which Euroclear UK & Ireland Limited is to be the Operator (as defined in the Regulations);

(c) the Shares shall not include any shares referred to in Regulation 18; and

(d) this resolution ('the Resolution') shall become effective immediately prior to Euroclear UK & Ireland Limited granting permission for the Shares to be transferred by means of the CREST system.

It was noted that, upon the Resolution becoming effective in accordance with its terms, and for as long as it is in force, the Articles of Association of the Company in relation to the Shares will not apply to any uncertificated shares to the extent that they are inconsistent with:
(a) the holding of any Shares in uncertificated form;
(b) the transfer of title to any Shares by means of the CREST system; and
(c) any provision of the Regulations.
There was produced to the meeting a notice of the passing of the resolution ('the Notice').

IT WAS RESOLVED THAT the Notice, as set out below, be approved and sent to every member of the Company in accordance with the Company's Articles of Association within 60 days of the passing of the Resolution as required by Regulation 16(4).

TO: ALL THE MEMBERS OF THE COMPANY

Notification of directors' resolution relating to
the CREST system.

This is to give you notice, in accordance with the Uncertificated Securities Regulations 2001 ('the Regulations'), that on [date], the Company resolved by a resolution of its directors that title to the ordinary shares of £1.00 each in the capital of the Company, in issue or to be issued, may be transferred by means of a relevant system. The resolution of the directors will become effective immediately prior to Euroclear UK & Ireland Limited granting permission for the shares concerned to be transferred by means of the CREST system.

Precedent 67 Directors' resolution to approve bank mandate

Bank Account
IT WAS RESOLVED THAT a bank account in the Company's name be opened with [•] ("the bank") and that the bank be instructed to operate the said account according to the instructions set down in the bank's standard form of mandate, a copy of which is attached to and forms part of these minutes.

[Two directors]/[a] [the sole] director [and the company secretary] were instructed and authorised to complete and sign all appropriate application documentation and a bank mandate as required.

In reaching their decision, the Directors considered the need to promote the success of the Company for the benefit of its members as a whole and, in doing so, had regard to the specific requirements of s. 172 of the Companies Act 2006

Precedent 68 Pro forma dividend tax voucher

PAYMENT No: [•]

TAX VOUCHER

Limited

Ordinary shares all fully paid

Date:

	Total Holding of Shares	Tax Credit	Dividend Payable
	[•]	£ [•]	£[•]

This voucher should be kept. It will be accepted by the HM Revenue & Customs as evidence of a tax credit.

Correspondence regarding this holding should be addressed to:

interim dividend on ordinary shares
rate: [] pence per share
year to [•]
to holders registered on [•]

Precedent 69 Members' resolution to authorise scrip dividend

Special Resolution

THAT the articles of association of the company be amended in the following manner that is to say by the adoption of a new clause [•], as set out below, and by the renumbering of the existing clauses [•] to [•] (inclusive) as clauses [•] to [•] (inclusive).

"[•] The issued share capital of the Company at the date of adoption of this article is £30,000 divided into 300,000 ordinary shares of £0.05 each and 300,000 "B" ordinary shares of £0.05 each.

(a) The ordinary shares and "B" ordinary shares shall rank *pari passu* in all respects save that: as regards income:

(b) (1)

(a) The holders of the ordinary shares shall be entitled as a class to 15.222% of the profits of the Company and as between holders of the ordinary shares any distribution shall be calculated pro rata to the amounts paid up or credited as paid up thereon.

(b) The holders of the "B" ordinary shares shall be entitled as a class to 84.778% of the profits of the Company and as between holders of the "B" ordinary shares any distribution shall be calculated pro rata to the amounts paid up or credited as paid up thereon.

(2) Subject to the limits imposed by sub-clause (b)(1) above the directors shall be entitled in their absolute discretion to declare dividends on both classes or on one class and not on the other classes as they see fit.

(3) With the prior approval of an Ordinary Resolution of the Company the Directors may, in respect of any dividend proposed to be paid or declared thereafter on any particular class or classes offer the shareholders the right to elect to receive in lieu of such dividend (or part thereof) an allotment of additional shares of the same class credited as fully paid. In any such case the following provisions shall apply:

(a) the basis of allotment shall be determined by the Directors, in their absolute discretion;

(b) no fraction of any share shall be allotted. The Directors may make such provisions as they think fit for any fractional entitlements including provisions whereby, in whole or in part, the benefit thereof accrues to the Company and/or under which fractional entitlements are accrued and/or retained and in each case accumulated on behalf of any shareholder and such accruals or retentions are applied to the allotment by way of bonus to or cash subscription on behalf of such shareholder of fully paid shares and/or under which fractional entitlements and/or accruals or retentions are paid as cash dividends;

(c) if the Directors determine to allow such right of election on any occasion they shall give notice in writing to the shareholders of the right of election offered to them and shall issue forms of election and shall specify the procedure to be followed and the place at which, and the latest date and time by which, duly completed forms of election must be lodged in order to be effective; the Directors may also issue forms under which shareholders may elect to receive shares instead of cash both in respect of the relevant dividend and in respect of future dividends not yet declared or resolved (and accordingly in respect of which the basis of allotment shall not have been determined);

(d) the dividend (or that part of the dividend in respect of which a right of election has been accorded) shall not be payable on shares in respect whereof the share election has been duly exercised ("the Elected Shares"), and in lieu thereof additional shares (but not any fraction of a share) shall be allotted to the holders of the Elected Shares on the basis of allotment determined as aforesaid. For such purpose the Directors shall capitalise, out of such of the sums standing to the credit of reserves (including any share premium account or capital redemption reserve fund) or profit and loss account as the Directors may determine, a sum equal to the aggregate nominal amount of additional shares to be allotted on such basis and shall apply the same in paying up in full the appropriate number of unissued shares for allotment and distribution to and amongst the holders of the Elected Shares on such basis;

(e) the additional shares so allotted shall rank *pari passu* in all respects with the fully paid shares of the same class then in issue save only as regards participation in the relevant dividend;

(f) the provisions of regulation 36 of the Model Articles for private companies shall apply (*mutatis mutandis*) to any capitalisation made pursuant to this [Article [•]];

(g) the Directors may on any occasion determine that rights of election shall not be made available to any shareholders with registered addresses in any territory where in the absence of a registration statement or other special formalities the circulation of an offer of rights of election would or might be unlawful, and in such event the provisions aforesaid shall be read and construed subject to such determination; and

(h) in relation to any particular proposed dividend the Directors may in their absolute discretion withdraw the offer previously made to shareholders to elect to receive additional Shares in lieu of the cash dividend (or part thereof) at any time prior to the allotment of the additional Shares."

Ordinary Resolution

THAT pursuant to Clause [•] of the Articles of Association of the Company adopted by resolution [•] above the Directors be authorised to offer the holders of "B" ordinary shares the right to elect to receive an allotment of "B" ordinary shares credited as fully paid in lieu of any dividend proposed to be paid or declared hereafter.

Precedent 70 Indemnity for lost share certificate

INDEMNITY FOR LOST CERTIFICATE

(above this line for Registrar's use only)

To the Directors of [•] Limited (Company Number [•])

The original certificate of title relating to the under-mentioned securities of the above-named Company has been lost or destroyed.

Neither the securities nor the certificate of title thereto have been transferred, charged, lent or deposited or dealt with in any manner affecting the absolute title thereto and the person named in the said certificate is the person entitled to be on the register in respect of such securities.

I request you to issue a duplicate certificate of title for such securities and in consideration of your doing so, undertake (jointly and severally) to indemnify you and the Company against all claims and demands (and any expenses thereof) which may be made against you or the Company in consequence of your complying with this request and of the Company permitting at any time hereafter a transfer of the said securities, or any part thereof, without the production of the said original certificate.

I undertake to deliver to the Company for cancellation the said original certificate should the same ever be recovered.

PARTICULARS OF CERTIFICATE LOST OR DESTROYED

Particulars of Certificate	Amount and Class of Securities	In Favour of
Share Certificate No. [•]	[•] ordinary shares of £1.00 each	

Dated this [•] day of [•] 20[•].

Signature ____

Precedent 71 Letter of request by executor

<table>
<tr><td>LETTER OF REQUEST</td><td colspan="2">Above this line for Registrar's use only</td></tr>
<tr><td colspan="3">REQUEST BY EXECUTORS OR ADMINISTRATORS OF A DECEASED HOLDER TO BE PLACED ON THE REGISTER AS HOLDERS IN THEIR OWN RIGHT</td></tr>
<tr><td>Full name and address of Undertaking</td><td colspan="2">TO THE DIRECTORS OF</td></tr>
<tr><td>*Full description of security</td><td colspan="2"></td></tr>
<tr><td>Name or amount of Shares, Stock or other Security and, in figures column only, number and denomination of units if any.</td><td>WORDS
________________________</td><td>FIGURES
(____________
units of ______)</td></tr>
<tr><td></td><td colspan="2"></td></tr>
</table>

Full name of deceased	______________________________ Deceased
	late of______________________________
I/We, the undersigned, being the personal representative(s) of the above named deceased, hereby request you to register me/us in the books of the Company as the holder(s) of the above mentioned Stock/Shares now registered in the name of the said deceased.	
	Dated this............day of...20
	Signature(s) of Personal Representative(s)
	....
	....
Full name(s) and address(es) of the Personal Representative(s) (IN THE ORDER IN WHICH THEY ARE TO BE REGISTERED) (TYPEWRITTEN OR IN BLOCK CAPITALS)	
IF AN ACCOUNT ALREADY EXISTS IN THE ABOVE NAME(S) THE ABOVE-MENTIONED HOLDING WILL BE ADDED TO THAT ACCOUNT, UNLESS INSTRUCTIONS ARE GIVEN TO THE CONTRARY.	
The Certificate(s) in the name of the deceased if not already with the Company's Registrars must accompany this form *A separate Letter of Request should be used for each class of Security.	Stamp or name and address of person lodging this form

Precedent 72 Members' consent to short notice

[•] LIMITED
("the Company")
Company Number: [•]

Agreement to Short Notice

We, the undersigned, [all the members for the time being of the Company /representing not less than 90% of the Company's members] having a right to attend and vote at general meetings of the Company hereby agree, in respect of the general meeting to be held on [•] 20[•] at [•] am/pm:

(a) to accept shorter notice of the said meeting than the period of notice prescribed by Section 307(1) of the Companies Act 2006; and
(b) to accept service of the documents specified in Section 424(3) of the Companies Act 2006, less than twenty-one days before the date of the said meeting.

Signed:

______________________________ ______________________________

Dated this [•] day of [•] 20[•].

Precedent 73 Members' resolutions to approve change in auditors

THAT [•] be [re]appointed as auditors of the Company in accordance with Section 485(4) of the Companies Act 2006, until such time that they resign from office or are removed by the members in accordance with the provisions of that Act or are deemed not reappointed in accordance with Section 488 of that Act, and to authorise the directors to fix the auditors' remuneration.

OR

THAT [•] be appointed auditors of the company in accordance with the provisions of s. 485(4) of the Companies Act 2006 in place of [•], the retiring auditors, until such time that they resign from office or are removed by the members in accordance with the provisions of that Act or are deemed not reappointed in accordance with Section 488 of that Act, and to authorise the directors to fix the auditors' remuneration.

OR

THAT [•] be appointed auditors of the company in accordance with the provisions of s. 485(4) of the Companies Act 2006 in the place of [•], who have resigned, until such time that they resign from office or are removed by the members in accordance with the provisions of that Act or are deemed not reappointed in accordance with Section 488 of that Act, and to authorise the directors to fix the auditors' remuneration.

OR

THAT [•] appointed during the year to fill the casual vacancy caused by the resignation of [•], be reappointed auditors of the company in accordance with the provisions of s. 485(4) of the Companies Act 2006 until such time that they resign from office or are removed by the members in accordance with the provisions of that Act or are deemed not reappointed in accordance with Section 488 of that Act, and to authorise the directors to fix the auditors' remuneration.

Precedent 74 Members' resolution to appoint third party in place of retiring director

Ordinary Resolution

THAT [•] be appointed as a director of the Company in place of [•] the retiring director who has indicated his unwillingness to continue as a director.

Precedent 75 Members' notice of requisition of members' meeting

To: ***The Board of Directors***

[•] Limited
Date:
WE, the undersigned, being holders of more than one-tenth of the paid up capital of the Company, as at the date of this notice, and representing at least 10% of the right of voting at general meetings of the Company require you forthwith to proceed to convene a General Meeting of the Company for the purpose of considering and if thought fit approving the following resolution which will be proposed as an Ordinary Resolution namely:

ORDINARY RESOLUTION THAT [•]

Dated this [•] day of [•] 20[•]

Precedent 76 Directors' resolution to change accounting reference date

Accounting Reference Date

IT WAS RESOLVED THAT the accounting reference date of the Company be [shortened/extended] from [•] 20[•] to [•] 20[•] with the next set of Accounts to be finalised and filed at Companies House being drawn up for the period from [•] 20[•] to [•] 20[•]. The company secretary was instructed to file form AA01 with the Registrar of Companies.

Precedent 77 Directors' resolution to approve accounts and circulation to members

Annual Accounts

The directors' report and the audited accounts for the year ended/period to [•] 20[•] produced to the meeting were signed and approved for submission to the Company's members.

Dividend

IT WAS RESOLVED THAT no dividend be declared in respect of the year ended/period to [•] 20[•].

OR

It was noted that an interim dividend of [•]p per ordinary share had been declared in respect of the year ending/period to [•] 20[•].

OR

The chairman reported the proposal to declare a final dividend of [•]p per ordinary share in respect of the year ended/period to [•] 20[•].

[There was produced to the meeting a letter from the Company's auditors confirming that the qualification to their report to the accounts for the year ended/period to [•]20[•] was not material in determining whether the proposed dividend should be paid.]

IT WAS RESOLVED THAT the payment of a final dividend of [•]p per ordinary share be and is hereby recommended and that a resolution to this effect be put to the [sole] member[s] at the forthcoming annual general meeting.

Precedent 78 Directors' resolution to appoint auditors

Auditors

It was noted that [•] had indicated their willingness to continue as auditors of the Company and that a resolution for their reappointment would be proposed at the forthcoming [annual] general meeting in respect of the accounting period of the Company ending [•] 20[•].

OR

In accordance with s.485(3)(a) of the Companies Act 2006 **IT WAS RESOLVED THAT** [•] be hereby appointed as auditors of the Company for the first accounting period of the Company ending [•] 20[•].

OR

As the Company was no longer exempt from appointing auditors in respect of the accounting period ending [•], in accordance with s.485(3)(b) of the Companies Act 2006 **IT WAS RESOLVED THAT** [•] be and are hereby appointed as auditors of the Company.

OR

In accordance with s.485(3)(c) of the Companies Act 2006 **IT WAS RESOLVED THAT** [•] be and are hereby appointed as auditors of the Company to fill a casual vacancy in respect of the first accounting period of the Company ending [•] 20[•].

Precedent 79 Directors' resolution not to appoint auditors where company exempt

It was noted that the Company was exempt from audit in respect of its accounts for the year ended [•]. The meeting considered the matter and **IT WAS RESOLVED THAT** pursuant to s.487(1)(e) no auditors be appointed in respect of the year ended [•].

Precedent 80 Auditors' letter of resignation

Dear Sirs

We hereby resign as auditors of the Company with effect from the date hereof.

In accordance with Section 519(1) of the Companies Act 2006, we wish the following circumstances connected with our ceasing to hold office as auditors to be brought to the attention of the members and creditors of the company.
[statement of circumstances]

OR

In accordance with Section 519(2) of the Companies Act 2006, we hereby state that there are no circumstances connected with our resignation which we consider should be brought to the attention of the members or creditors of the Company.

Yours faithfully
(signature of auditors)

OR

Dear Sirs
We write to inform you that we are not willing to be reappointed as auditors of the company as from the conclusion of the next general meeting of the company at which the requirements of the Companies Act 2006 Section 437 are complied with.
There are no circumstances connected with our ceasing to hold office as auditors which should be brought to the attention of the members or creditors of the company.

OR

We wish the following circumstances connected with our ceasing to hold office as auditors to be brought to the attention of the members and creditors of the company.
[statement of circumstances]

Yours faithfully
(signature of auditors)

Precedent 81 Statement in register of members where company has or ceases to have only one member

On [•] 20[•] [•] became the sole member of the Company.

OR

On [•] 20[•] [•] ceased to be the sole member of the Company.

Precedent 82 Company enquiry into interests in shares (s.793 request)

Dear [•],

Interests in Ordinary Shares of £[•] each (the "Shares") of [•] (the "Company")

Pursuant to section 793 of the Companies Act 2006 (the "Act") we require you to provide us in writing, by no later than 5pm (London, UK time) on [•] the [•] day of [•] 20[•], the following information concerning your interest (within the meaning of sections 820 – 825 of the Act) in the Shares:

1. The number of Shares in which you have an interest as at the date of your reply to this letter ("Current Interest") and the number of Shares in which you have had an interest at any time since the incorporation of the Company on [•] 20[•] but which no longer form part of your Current Interest ("Past Interest").
2. Confirmation as to the nature of your Current Interest or your Past Interest in the Shares including whether such interests are or were held legally and/or beneficially.
3. The dates upon which you acquired an interest in any Shares forming part of your Current Interest and your Past Interest.
4. If it is a Past Interest, please specify the dates on which an interest in any Shares forming part of your Past Interest was disposed of and, as far as lies within your knowledge, the complete details of the identity of the person who held that interest immediately after your interest in the Shares ceased.
5. In relation to your Current Interest, as far as lies within your knowledge, the full name and address of each person (including but not limited to nominees and investment managers) who also has an interest in such Shares, together with particulars of the nature of each interest and the number of Shares in which each person had an interest.
6. Full details of any agreement to which section 824 of the Act applies (agreements or arrangements between persons to acquire interests in the Company) or any other agreement or arrangement known to you relating to the exercise of any rights conferred by the holding of the Shares.

Your response to this letter should be posted, faxed or e-mailed to the address set out below, marked for the attention of [•].

Yours faithfully

Company Secretary
[response address]

Precedent 83 Directors' resolution to approve use of company seal

IT WAS RESOLVED THAT [•] be and is hereby approved and that any two directors or any one director and the company secretary be and are hereby authorised to sign and seal the said document on behalf of the Company.

Precedent 84 Members' resolution to approve winding-up of company

Special resolution
THAT the company be wound up voluntarily, and that [•] of [•] be appointed liquidator for the purposes of such winding-up.

OR

Special resolution
THAT it has been proved to the satisfaction of this meeting that the company cannot, by reason of its liabilities, continue its business and that it is advisable to wind up the company and accordingly that the company be wound up voluntarily and that [•] of the firm of [•], Chartered Accountants of [•] be nominated liquidator for the purpose of such winding-up.

Appendix 1

Model articles for private companies limited by shares

Model Articles under CA2006

The Companies (Model Articles) Regulations 2008

PART 1 INTERPRETATION AND LIMITATION OF LIABILITY

Defined terms

1. In the articles, unless the context requires otherwise—

'articles' means the company's articles of association;

'bankruptcy' includes individual insolvency proceedings in a jurisdiction other than England and Wales or Northern Ireland which have an effect similar to that of bankruptcy;

'chairman' has the meaning given in article 12;

'chairman of the meeting' has the meaning given in article 39;

'Companies Acts' means the Companies Acts (as defined in section 2 of the Companies Act 2006), in so far as they apply to the company;

'director' means a director of the company, and includes any person occupying the position of director, by whatever name called;

'distribution recipient' has the meaning given in article 31;

'document' includes, unless otherwise specified, any document sent or supplied in electronic form;

'electronic form' has the meaning given in section 1168 of the Companies Act 2006;

'fully paid' in relation to a share, means that the nominal value and any premium to be paid to the company in respect of that share have been paid to the company;

'hard copy form' has the meaning given in section 1168 of the Companies Act 2006;

'holder' in relation to shares means the person whose name is entered in the register of members as the holder of the shares;

'instrument' means a document in hard copy form;

'ordinary resolution' has the meaning given in section 282 of the Companies Act 2006;

'paid' means paid or credited as paid;

'participate', in relation to a directors' meeting, has the meaning given in article 10;

'proxy notice' has the meaning given in article 45;

'shareholder' means a person who is the holder of a share;

'shares' means shares in the company;

'special resolution' has the meaning given in section 283 of the Companies Act 2006;

'subsidiary' has the meaning given in section 1159 of the Companies Act 2006;

'transmittee' means a person entitled to a share by reason of the death or bankruptcy of a shareholder or otherwise by operation of law; and

'writing' means the representation or reproduction of words, symbols or other information in a visible form by any method or combination of methods, whether sent or supplied in electronic form or otherwise.

Unless the context otherwise requires, other words or expressions contained in these articles bear the same meaning as in the Companies Act 2006 as in force on the date when these articles become binding on the company.

Liability of members

2. The liability of the members is limited to the amount, if any, unpaid on the shares held by them.

PART 2 DIRECTORS

DIRECTORS' POWERS AND RESPONSIBILITIES

Directors' general authority

3. Subject to the articles, the directors are responsible for the management of the company's business, for which purpose they may exercise all the powers of the company.

Shareholders' reserve power

4.—(1) The shareholders may, by special resolution, direct the directors to take, or refrain from taking, specified action.

(2) No such special resolution invalidates anything which the directors have done before the passing of the resolution.

Directors may delegate

5.—(1) Subject to the articles, the directors may delegate any of the powers which are conferred on them under the articles—

(a) to such person or committee;

(b) by such means (including by power of attorney);

(c) to such an extent;

(d) in relation to such matters or territories; and
(e) on such terms and conditions;
as they think fit.
(2) If the directors so specify, any such delegation may authorise further delegation of the directors' powers by any person to whom they are delegated.
(3) The directors may revoke any delegation in whole or part, or alter its terms and conditions.

Committees

6.—(1) Committees to which the directors delegate any of their powers must follow procedures which are based as far as they are applicable on those provisions of the articles which govern the taking of decisions by directors.
(2) The directors may make rules of procedure for all or any committees, which prevail over rules derived from the articles if they are not consistent with them.

DECISION-MAKING BY DIRECTORS

Directors to take decisions collectively

7.—(1) The general rule about decision-making by directors is that any decision of the directors must be either a majority decision at a meeting or a decision taken in accordance with article 8.
(2) If—
(a) the company only has one director, and
(b) no provision of the articles requires it to have more than one director, the general rule does not apply, and the director may take decisions without regard to any of the provisions of the articles relating to directors' decision-making.

Unanimous decisions

8.—(1) A decision of the directors is taken in accordance with this article when all eligible directors indicate to each other by any means that they share a common view on a matter.
(2) Such a decision may take the form of a resolution in writing, copies of which have been signed by each eligible director or to which each eligible director has otherwise indicated agreement in writing.
(3) References in this article to eligible directors are to directors who would have been entitled to vote on the matter had it been proposed as a resolution at a directors' meeting.
(4) A decision may not be taken in accordance with this article if the eligible directors would not have formed a quorum at such a meeting.

Calling a directors' meeting

9.—(1) Any director may call a directors' meeting by giving notice of the meeting to the directors or by authorising the company secretary (if any) to give such notice.

(2) Notice of any directors' meeting must indicate—
(a) its proposed date and time;
(b) where it is to take place; and
(c) if it is anticipated that directors participating in the meeting will not be in the same place, how it is proposed that they should communicate with each other during the meeting.
(3) Notice of a directors' meeting must be given to each director, but need not be in writing.
(4) Notice of a directors' meeting need not be given to directors who waive their entitlement to notice of that meeting, by giving notice to that effect to the company not more than 7 days after the date on which the meeting is held. Where such notice is given after the meeting has been held, that does not affect the validity of the meeting, or of any business conducted at it.

Participation in directors' meetings

10.—(1) Subject to the articles, directors participate in a directors' meeting, or part of a directors' meeting, when—
(a) the meeting has been called and takes place in accordance with the articles, and
(b) they can each communicate to the others any information or opinions they have on any particular item of the business of the meeting.
(2) In determining whether directors are participating in a directors' meeting, it is irrelevant where any director is or how they communicate with each other.
(3) If all the directors participating in a meeting are not in the same place, they may decide that the meeting is to be treated as taking place wherever any of them is.

Quorum for directors' meetings

11.—(1) At a directors' meeting, unless a quorum is participating, no proposal is to be voted on, except a proposal to call another meeting.
(2) The quorum for directors' meetings may be fixed from time to time by a decision of the directors, but it must never be less than two, and unless otherwise fixed it is two.
(3) If the total number of directors for the time being is less than the quorum required, the directors must not take any decision other than a decision—
(a) to appoint further directors, or
(b) to call a general meeting so as to enable the shareholders to appoint further directors.

Chairing of directors' meetings

12.—(1) The directors may appoint a director to chair their meetings.
(2) The person so appointed for the time being is known as the chairman.
(3) The directors may terminate the chairman's appointment at any time.
(4) If the chairman is not participating in a directors' meeting within ten minutes of the time at which it was to start, the participating directors must appoint one of themselves to chair it.

Casting vote

13.—(1) If the numbers of votes for and against a proposal are equal, the chairman or other director chairing the meeting has a casting vote.

(2) But this does not apply if, in accordance with the articles, the chairman or other director is not to be counted as participating in the decision-making process for quorum or voting purposes.

Conflicts of interest

14.—(1) If a proposed decision of the directors is concerned with an actual or proposed transaction or arrangement with the company in which a director is interested, that director is not to be counted as participating in the decision-making process for quorum or voting purposes.

(2) But if paragraph (3) applies, a director who is interested in an actual or proposed transaction or arrangement with the company is to be counted as participating in the decision-making process for quorum and voting purposes.

(3) This paragraph applies when—

(a) the company by ordinary resolution disapplies the provision of the articles which would otherwise prevent a director from being counted as participating in the decision-making process;

(b) the director's interest cannot reasonably be regarded as likely to give rise to a conflict of interest; or

(c) the director's conflict of interest arises from a permitted cause.

(4) For the purposes of this article, the following are permitted causes—

(a) a guarantee given, or to be given, by or to a director in respect of an obligation incurred by or on behalf of the company or any of its subsidiaries;

(b) subscription, or an agreement to subscribe, for shares or other securities of the company or any of its subsidiaries, or to underwrite, sub-underwrite, or guarantee subscription for any such shares or securities; and

(c) arrangements pursuant to which benefits are made available to employees and directors or former employees and directors of the company or any of its subsidiaries which do not provide special benefits for directors or former directors.

(5) For the purposes of this article, references to proposed decisions and decision-making processes include any directors' meeting or part of a directors' meeting.

(6) Subject to paragraph (7), if a question arises at a meeting of directors or of a committee of directors as to the right of a director to participate in the meeting (or part of the meeting) for voting or quorum purposes, the question may, before the conclusion of the meeting, be referred to the chairman whose ruling in relation to any director other than the chairman is to be final and conclusive.

(7) If any question as to the right to participate in the meeting (or part of the meeting) should arise in respect of the chairman, the question is to be decided by a decision of the directors at that meeting, for which purpose the chairman is not to be counted as participating in the meeting (or that part of the meeting) for voting or quorum purposes.

Records of decisions to be kept

15. The directors must ensure that the company keeps a record, in writing, for at least 10 years from the date of the decision recorded, of every unanimous or majority decision taken by the directors.

Directors' discretion to make further rules

16. Subject to the articles, the directors may make any rule which they think fit about how they take decisions, and about how such rules are to be recorded or communicated to directors.

APPOINTMENT OF DIRECTORS

Methods of appointing directors

17.—(1) Any person who is willing to act as a director, and is permitted by law to do so, may be appointed to be a director—

(a) by ordinary resolution, or

(b) by a decision of the directors.

(2) In any case where, as a result of death, the company has no shareholders and no directors, the personal representatives of the last shareholder to have died have the right, by notice in writing, to appoint a person to be a director.

(3) For the purposes of paragraph (2), where two or more shareholders die in circumstances rendering it uncertain who was the last to die, a younger shareholder is deemed to have survived an older shareholder.

Termination of director's appointment

18. A person ceases to be a director as soon as—

(a) that person ceases to be a director by virtue of any provision of the Companies Act 2006 or is prohibited from being a director by law;

(b) a bankruptcy order is made against that person;

(c) a composition is made with that person's creditors generally in satisfaction of that person's debts;

(d) a registered medical practitioner who is treating that person gives a written opinion to the company stating that that person has become physically or mentally incapable of acting as a director and may remain so for more than three months;

(e) by reason of that person's mental health, a court makes an order which wholly or partly prevents that person from personally exercising any powers or rights which that person would otherwise have;

(f) notification is received by the company from the director that the director is resigning from office, and such resignation has taken effect in accordance with its terms.

Directors' remuneration

19.—(1) Directors may undertake any services for the company that the directors decide.

(2) Directors are entitled to such remuneration as the directors determine—
(a) for their services to the company as directors, and
(b) for any other service which they undertake for the company.
(3) Subject to the articles, a director's remuneration may—
(a) take any form, and
(b) include any arrangements in connection with the payment of a pension, allowance or gratuity, or any death, sickness or disability benefits, to or in respect of that director.
(4) Unless the directors decide otherwise, directors' remuneration accrues from day to day.
(5) Unless the directors decide otherwise, directors are not accountable to the company for any remuneration which they receive as directors or other officers or employees of the company's subsidiaries or of any other body corporate in which the company is interested.

Directors' expenses

20. The company may pay any reasonable expenses which the directors properly incur in connection with their attendance at—
(a) meetings of directors or committees of directors,
(b) general meetings, or
(c) separate meetings of the holders of any class of shares or of debentures of the company,
or otherwise in connection with the exercise of their powers and the discharge of their responsibilities in relation to the company.

PART 3 SHARES AND DISTRIBUTIONS

SHARES

All shares to be fully paid up

21.—(1) No share is to be issued for less than the aggregate of its nominal value and any premium to be paid to the company in consideration for its issue.
(2) This does not apply to shares taken on the formation of the company by the subscribers to the company's memorandum.

Powers to issue different classes of share

22.—(1) Subject to the articles, but without prejudice to the rights attached to any existing share, the company may issue shares with such rights or restrictions as may be determined by ordinary resolution.
(2) The company may issue shares which are to be redeemed, or are liable to be redeemed at the option of the company or the holder, and the directors may determine the terms, conditions and manner of redemption of any such shares.

Company not bound by less than absolute interests

23. Except as required by law, no person is to be recognised by the company as holding any share upon any trust, and except as otherwise required by law or the articles, the company is not in any way to be bound by or recognise any interest in a share other than the holder's absolute ownership of it and all the rights attaching to it.

Share certificates

24.—(1) The company must issue each shareholder, free of charge, with one or more certificates in respect of the shares which that shareholder holds.
(2) Every certificate must specify—
(a) in respect of how many shares, of what class, it is issued;
(b) the nominal value of those shares;
(c) that the shares are fully paid; and
(d) any distinguishing numbers assigned to them.
(3) No certificate may be issued in respect of shares of more than one class.
(4) If more than one person holds a share, only one certificate may be issued in respect of it.
(5) Certificates must—
(a) have affixed to them the company's common seal, or
(b) be otherwise executed in accordance with the Companies Acts.

Replacement share certificates

25.—(1) If a certificate issued in respect of a shareholder's shares is—
(a) damaged or defaced, or
(b) said to be lost, stolen or destroyed,
that shareholder is entitled to be issued with a replacement certificate in respect of the same shares.
(2) A shareholder exercising the right to be issued with such a replacement certificate—
(a) may at the same time exercise the right to be issued with a single certificate or separate certificates;
(b) must return the certificate which is to be replaced to the company if it is damaged or defaced; and
(c) must comply with such conditions as to evidence, indemnity and the payment of a reasonable fee as the directors decide.

Share transfers

26.—(1) Shares may be transferred by means of an instrument of transfer in any usual form or any other form approved by the directors, which is executed by or on behalf of the transferor.
(2) No fee may be charged for registering any instrument of transfer or other document relating to or affecting the title to any share.
(3) The company may retain any instrument of transfer which is registered.
(4) The transferor remains the holder of a share until the transferee's name is entered in the register of members as holder of it.

(5) The directors may refuse to register the transfer of a share, and if they do so, the instrument of transfer must be returned to the transferee with the notice of refusal unless they suspect that the proposed transfer may be fraudulent.

Transmission of shares

27.—(1) If title to a share passes to a transmittee, the company may only recognise the transmittee as having any title to that share.
(2) A transmittee who produces such evidence of entitlement to shares as the directors may properly require—
(a) may, subject to the articles, choose either to become the holder of those shares or to have them transferred to another person, and
(b) subject to the articles, and pending any transfer of the shares to another person, has the same rights as the holder had.
(3) But transmittees do not have the right to attend or vote at a general meeting, or agree to a proposed written resolution, in respect of shares to which they are entitled, by reason of the holder's death or bankruptcy or otherwise, unless they become the holders of those shares.

Exercise of transmittees' rights

28.—(1) Transmittees who wish to become the holders of shares to which they have become entitled must notify the company in writing of that wish.
(2) If the transmittee wishes to have a share transferred to another person, the transmittee must execute an instrument of transfer in respect of it.
(3) Any transfer made or executed under this article is to be treated as if it were made or executed by the person from whom the transmittee has derived rights in respect of the share, and as if the event which gave rise to the transmission had not occurred.

Transmittees bound by prior notices

29. If a notice is given to a shareholder in respect of shares and a transmittee is entitled to those shares, the transmittee is bound by the notice if it was given to the shareholder before the transmittee's name has been entered in the register of members.

DIVIDENDS AND OTHER DISTRIBUTIONS

Procedure for declaring dividends

30.—(1) The company may by ordinary resolution declare dividends, and the directors may decide to pay interim dividends.
(2) A dividend must not be declared unless the directors have made a recommendation as to its amount. Such a dividend must not exceed the amount recommended by the directors.
(3) No dividend may be declared or paid unless it is in accordance with shareholders' respective rights.

(4) Unless the shareholders' resolution to declare or directors' decision to pay a dividend, or the terms on which shares are issued, specify otherwise, it must be paid by reference to each shareholder's holding of shares on the date of the resolution or decision to declare or pay it.
(5) If the company's share capital is divided into different classes, no interim dividend may be paid on shares carrying deferred or non-preferred rights if, at the time of payment, any preferential dividend is in arrear.
(6) The directors may pay at intervals any dividend payable at a fixed rate if it appears to them that the profits available for distribution justify the payment.
(7) If the directors act in good faith, they do not incur any liability to the holders of shares conferring preferred rights for any loss they may suffer by the lawful payment of an interim dividend on shares with deferred or non-preferred rights.

Payment of dividends and other distributions

31.—(1) Where a dividend or other sum which is a distribution is payable in respect of a share, it must be paid by one or more of the following means—
(a) transfer to a bank or building society account specified by the distribution recipient either in writing or as the directors may otherwise decide;
(b) sending a cheque made payable to the distribution recipient by post to the distribution recipient at the distribution recipient's registered address (if the distribution recipient is a holder of the share), or (in any other case) to an address specified by the distribution recipient either in writing or as the directors may otherwise decide;
(c) sending a cheque made payable to such person by post to such person at such address as the distribution recipient has specified either in writing or as the directors may otherwise decide; or
(d) any other means of payment as the directors agree with the distribution recipient either in writing or by such other means as the directors decide.
(2) In the articles, 'the distribution recipient' means, in respect of a share in respect of which a dividend or other sum is payable—
(a) the holder of the share; or
(b) if the share has two or more joint holders, whichever of them is named first in the register of members; or
(c) if the holder is no longer entitled to the share by reason of death or bankruptcy, or otherwise by operation of law, the transmittee.

No interest on distributions

32. The company may not pay interest on any dividend or other sum payable in respect of a share unless otherwise provided by—
(a) the terms on which the share was issued, or
(b) the provisions of another agreement between the holder of that share and the company.

Unclaimed distributions

33.—(1) All dividends or other sums which are—

(a) payable in respect of shares, and
(b) unclaimed after having been declared or become payable,
may be invested or otherwise made use of by the directors for the benefit of the company until claimed.
(2) The payment of any such dividend or other sum into a separate account does not make the company a trustee in respect of it.
(3) If—
(a) twelve years have passed from the date on which a dividend or other sum became due for payment, and
(b) the distribution recipient has not claimed it,
the distribution recipient is no longer entitled to that dividend or other sum and it ceases to remain owing by the company.

Non-cash distributions

34.—(1) Subject to the terms of issue of the share in question, the company may, by ordinary resolution on the recommendation of the directors, decide to pay all or part of a dividend or other distribution payable in respect of a share by transferring non-cash assets of equivalent value (including, without limitation, shares or other securities in any company).
(2) For the purposes of paying a non-cash distribution, the directors may make whatever arrangements they think fit, including, where any difficulty arises regarding the distribution—
(a) fixing the value of any assets;
(b) paying cash to any distribution recipient on the basis of that value in order to adjust the rights of recipients; and
(c) vesting any assets in trustees.

Waiver of distributions

35. Distribution recipients may waive their entitlement to a dividend or other distribution payable in respect of a share by giving the company notice in writing to that effect, but if—
(a) the share has more than one holder, or
(b) more than one person is entitled to the share, whether by reason of the death or bankruptcy of one or more joint holders, or otherwise,
the notice is not effective unless it is expressed to be given, and signed, by all the holders or persons otherwise entitled to the share.

CAPITALISATION OF PROFITS

Authority to capitalise and appropriation of capitalised sums

36.—(1) Subject to the articles, the directors may, if they are so authorised by an ordinary resolution—
(a) decide to capitalise any profits of the company (whether or not they are available for distribution) which are not required for paying a preferential dividend, or any sum

standing to the credit of the company's share premium account or capital redemption reserve; and

(b) appropriate any sum which they so decide to capitalise (a 'capitalised sum') to the persons who would have been entitled to it if it were distributed by way of dividend (the 'persons entitled') and in the same proportions.

(2) Capitalised sums must be applied—

(a) on behalf of the persons entitled, and

(b) in the same proportions as a dividend would have been distributed to them.

(3) Any capitalised sum may be applied in paying up new shares of a nominal amount equal to the capitalised sum which are then allotted credited as fully paid to the persons entitled or as they may direct.

(4) A capitalised sum which was appropriated from profits available for distribution may be applied in paying up new debentures of the company which are then allotted credited as fully paid to the persons entitled or as they may direct.

(5) Subject to the articles the directors may—

(a) apply capitalised sums in accordance with paragraphs (3) and (4) partly in one way and partly in another;

(b) make such arrangements as they think fit to deal with shares or debentures becoming distributable in fractions under this article (including the issuing of fractional certificates or the making of cash payments); and

(c) authorise any person to enter into an agreement with the company on behalf of all the persons entitled which is binding on them in respect of the allotment of shares and debentures to them under this article.

PART 4 DECISION-MAKING BY SHAREHOLDERS

ORGANISATION OF GENERAL MEETINGS

Attendance and speaking at general meetings

37.—(1) A person is able to exercise the right to speak at a general meeting when that person is in a position to communicate to all those attending the meeting, during the meeting, any information or opinions which that person has on the business of the meeting.

(2) A person is able to exercise the right to vote at a general meeting when—

(a) that person is able to vote, during the meeting, on resolutions put to the vote at the meeting, and

(b) that person's vote can be taken into account in determining whether or not such resolutions are passed at the same time as the votes of all the other persons attending the meeting.

(3) The directors may make whatever arrangements they consider appropriate to enable those attending a general meeting to exercise their rights to speak or vote at it.

(4) In determining attendance at a general meeting, it is immaterial whether any two or more members attending it are in the same place as each other.

(5) Two or more persons who are not in the same place as each other attend a general meeting if their circumstances are such that if they have (or were to have) rights to speak and vote at that meeting, they are (or would be) able to exercise them.

Quorum for general meetings

38. No business other than the appointment of the chairman of the meeting is to be transacted at a general meeting if the persons attending it do not constitute a quorum.

Chairing general meetings

39.—(1) If the directors have appointed a chairman, the chairman shall chair general meetings if present and willing to do so.
(2) If the directors have not appointed a chairman, or if the chairman is unwilling to chair the meeting or is not present within ten minutes of the time at which a meeting was due to start—
(a) the directors present, or
(b) (if no directors are present), the meeting,
must appoint a director or shareholder to chair the meeting, and the appointment of the chairman of the meeting must be the first business of the meeting.
(3) The person chairing a meeting in accordance with this article is referred to as 'the chairman of the meeting'.

Attendance and speaking by directors and non-shareholders

40.—(1) Directors may attend and speak at general meetings, whether or not they are shareholders.
(2) The chairman of the meeting may permit other persons who are not—
(a) shareholders of the company, or
(b) otherwise entitled to exercise the rights of shareholders in relation to general meetings,
to attend and speak at a general meeting.

Adjournment

41.—(1) If the persons attending a general meeting within half an hour of the time at which the meeting was due to start do not constitute a quorum, or if during a meeting a quorum ceases to be present, the chairman of the meeting must adjourn it.
(2) The chairman of the meeting may adjourn a general meeting at which a quorum is present if—
(a) the meeting consents to an adjournment, or
(b) it appears to the chairman of the meeting that an adjournment is necessary to protect the safety of any person attending the meeting or ensure that the business of the meeting is conducted in an orderly manner.
(3) The chairman of the meeting must adjourn a general meeting if directed to do so by the meeting.
(4) When adjourning a general meeting, the chairman of the meeting must—
(a) either specify the time and place to which it is adjourned or state that it is to continue at a time and place to be fixed by the directors, and
(b) have regard to any directions as to the time and place of any adjournment which have been given by the meeting.
(5) If the continuation of an adjourned meeting is to take place more than 14 days after

it was adjourned, the company must give at least 7 clear days' notice of it (that is, excluding the day of the adjourned meeting and the day on which the notice is given)—
(a) to the same persons to whom notice of the company's general meetings is required to be given, and
(b) containing the same information which such notice is required to contain.
(6) No business may be transacted at an adjourned general meeting which could not properly have been transacted at the meeting if the adjournment had not taken place.

VOTING AT GENERAL MEETINGS

Voting: general

42. A resolution put to the vote of a general meeting must be decided on a show of hands unless a poll is duly demanded in accordance with the articles.

Errors and disputes

43.—(1) No objection may be raised to the qualification of any person voting at a general meeting except at the meeting or adjourned meeting at which the vote objected to is tendered, and every vote not disallowed at the meeting is valid.
(2) Any such objection must be referred to the chairman of the meeting, whose decision is final.

Poll votes

44.—(1) A poll on a resolution may be demanded—
(a) in advance of the general meeting where it is to be put to the vote, or
(b) at a general meeting, either before a show of hands on that resolution or immediately after the result of a show of hands on that resolution is declared.
(2) A poll may be demanded by—
(a) the chairman of the meeting;
(b) the directors;
(c) two or more persons having the right to vote on the resolution; or
(d) a person or persons representing not less than one tenth of the total voting rights of all the shareholders having the right to vote on the resolution.
(3) A demand for a poll may be withdrawn if—
(a) the poll has not yet been taken, and
(b) the chairman of the meeting consents to the withdrawal.
(4) Polls must be taken immediately and in such manner as the chairman of the meeting directs.

Content of proxy notices

45.—(1) Proxies may only validly be appointed by a notice in writing (a 'proxy notice') which—
(a) states the name and address of the shareholder appointing the proxy;
(b) identifies the person appointed to be that shareholder's proxy and the general meeting in relation to which that person is appointed;

(c) is signed by or on behalf of the shareholder appointing the proxy, or is authenticated in such manner as the directors may determine; and
(d) is delivered to the company in accordance with the articles and any instructions contained in the notice of the general meeting to which they relate.
(2) The company may require proxy notices to be delivered in a particular form, and may specify different forms for different purposes.
(3) Proxy notices may specify how the proxy appointed under them is to vote (or that the proxy is to abstain from voting) on one or more resolutions.
(4) Unless a proxy notice indicates otherwise, it must be treated as—
(a) allowing the person appointed under it as a proxy discretion as to how to vote on any ancillary or procedural resolutions put to the meeting, and
(b) appointing that person as a proxy in relation to any adjournment of the general meeting to which it relates as well as the meeting itself.

Delivery of proxy notices

46.—(1) A person who is entitled to attend, speak or vote (either on a show of hands or on a poll) at a general meeting remains so entitled in respect of that meeting or any adjournment of it, even though a valid proxy notice has been delivered to the company by or on behalf of that person.
(2) An appointment under a proxy notice may be revoked by delivering to the company a notice in writing given by or on behalf of the person by whom or on whose behalf the proxy notice was given.
(3) A notice revoking a proxy appointment only takes effect if it is delivered before the start of the meeting or adjourned meeting to which it relates.
(4) If a proxy notice is not executed by the person appointing the proxy, it must be accompanied by written evidence of the authority of the person who executed it to execute it on the appointor's behalf.

Amendments to resolutions

47.—(1) An ordinary resolution to be proposed at a general meeting may be amended by ordinary resolution if—
(a) notice of the proposed amendment is given to the company in writing by a person entitled to vote at the general meeting at which it is to be proposed not less than 48 hours before the meeting is to take place (or such later time as the chairman of the meeting may determine), and
(b) the proposed amendment does not, in the reasonable opinion of the chairman of the meeting, materially alter the scope of the resolution.
(2) A special resolution to be proposed at a general meeting may be amended by ordinary resolution, if—
(a) the chairman of the meeting proposes the amendment at the general meeting at which the resolution is to be proposed, and
(b) the amendment does not go beyond what is necessary to correct a grammatical or other non-substantive error in the resolution.
(3) If the chairman of the meeting, acting in good faith, wrongly decides that an

amendment to a resolution is out of order, the chairman's error does not invalidate the vote on that resolution.

PART 5 ADMINISTRATIVE ARRANGEMENTS

Means of communication to be used

48.—(1) Subject to the articles, anything sent or supplied by or to the company under the articles may be sent or supplied in any way in which the Companies Act 2006 provides for documents or information which are authorised or required by any provision of that Act to be sent or supplied by or to the company.

(2) Subject to the articles, any notice or document to be sent or supplied to a director in connection with the taking of decisions by directors may also be sent or supplied by the means by which that director has asked to be sent or supplied with such notices or documents for the time being.

(3) A director may agree with the company that notices or documents sent to that director in a particular way are to be deemed to have been received within a specified time of their being sent, and for the specified time to be less than 48 hours.

Company seals

49.—(1) Any common seal may only be used by the authority of the directors.

(2) The directors may decide by what means and in what form any common seal is to be used.

(3) Unless otherwise decided by the directors, if the company has a common seal and it is affixed to a document, the document must also be signed by at least one authorised person in the presence of a witness who attests the signature.

(4) For the purposes of this article, an authorised person is—

(a) any director of the company;

(b) the company secretary (if any); or

(c) any person authorised by the directors for the purpose of signing documents to which the common seal is applied.

No right to inspect accounts and other records

50. Except as provided by law or authorised by the directors or an ordinary resolution of the company, no person is entitled to inspect any of the company's accounting or other records or documents merely by virtue of being a shareholder.

Provision for employees on cessation of business

51. The directors may decide to make provision for the benefit of persons employed or formerly employed by the company or any of its subsidiaries (other than a director or former director or shadow director) in connection with the cessation or transfer to any person of the whole or part of the undertaking of the company or that subsidiary.

DIRECTORS' INDEMNITY AND INSURANCE

Indemnity

52.—(1) Subject to paragraph (2), a relevant director of the company or an associated company may be indemnified out of the company's assets against—
(a) any liability incurred by that director in connection with any negligence, default, breach of duty or breach of trust in relation to the company or an associated company,
(b) any liability incurred by that director in connection with the activities of the company or an associated company in its capacity as a trustee of an occupational pension scheme (as defined in section 235(6) of the Companies Act 2006),
(c) any other liability incurred by that director as an officer of the company or an associated company.
(2) This article does not authorise any indemnity which would be prohibited or rendered void by any provision of the Companies Acts or by any other provision of law.
(3) In this article—
(a) companies are associated if one is a subsidiary of the other or both are subsidiaries of the same body corporate, and
(b) a 'relevant director' means any director or former director of the company or an associated company.

Insurance

53.—(1) The directors may decide to purchase and maintain insurance, at the expense of the company, for the benefit of any relevant director in respect of any relevant loss.
(2) In this article—
(a) a 'relevant director' means any director or former director of the company or an associated company,
(b) a 'relevant loss' means any loss or liability which has been or may be incurred by a relevant director in connection with that director's duties or powers in relation to the company, any associated company or any pension fund or employees' share scheme of the company or associated company, and
(c) companies are associated if one is a subsidiary of the other or both are subsidiaries of the same body corporate.

Appendix 2

Companies Act 1985 Table A (as amended)

The 1985 Table A is contained in the Companies (Tables A to F) Regulations 1985. These Regulations were amended on 22 December 2000 by the Companies Act 1985 (Electronic Communications) Order 2000. The amendments made by the Order have been incorporated in the following text and are highlighted in italics. Where necessary, the text of the unamended version of the 1985 Table A is given by way of notes.

Companies which adopted the 1985 Table A prior to 22 December 2000 will need to refer to these notes. However, if a company with Articles which make no provision for electronic communications takes advantage of the new statutory procedures, it must in certain circumstances comply with the relevant provisions of the amended Table A, even though they do not form part of its Articles.

In relation to companies incorporated on or after 1 October 2007, Table A has been further amended by the Companies (Tables A to F) (Amendment) Regulations 2007 (SI 2007/2541) and the Companies (Tables A to F) (Amendment) (No.2) Regulations 2007 (SI 2007/2826). The revised text of Table A incorporating these amendments (as they apply to private and public companies respectively) is available via the Companies House website (see Directory).

TABLE A
REGULATIONS FOR MANAGEMENT OF A COMPANY LIMITED BY SHARES

Interpretation

1. In these regulations –

'the Act' means the Companies Act 1985 including any statutory modification or re-enactment thereof for the time being in force.

'the articles' means the articles of the company.

'clear days' in relation to the period of notice means that period excluding the day when the notice is given or deemed to be given and the day for which it is given or on which it is to take effect.

'communication' means the same as in the Electronic Communications Act 2000.

'electronic communication' means the same as in the Electronic Communications Act 2000.[1]

'executed' includes any mode of execution.

'office' means the registered office of the company.

'the holder' in relation to shares means the member whose name is entered in the register of members as the holder of the shares.

'the seal' means the common seal of the company.

'secretary' means the secretary of the company or any person appointed to perform the duties of the secretary of the company, including a joint, assistant or deputy secretary.

'the United Kingdom' means Great Britain and Northern Ireland.

Unless the context otherwise requires, words or expressions contained in these regulations bear the same meaning as in the Act but excluding any statutory modification thereof not in force when these regulations become binding on the company.

Share capital

2. Subject to the provisions of the Act and without prejudice to the rights attached to any existing shares, any share may be issued with such rights or restrictions as the company may by ordinary resolution determine.

3. Subject to the provisions of the Act, shares may be issued which are to be redeemed or are to be held liable to be redeemed at the option of the company or the holder on such terms and in such manner as may be provided by the articles.

4. The company may exercise the powers of paying commissions conferred by the Act. Subject to the provisions of the Act, any such commissions may be satisfied by the payment of cash or by the allotment of fully or partly paid shares or partly in one way and partly in the other.

5. Except as required by law, no person shall be recognised by the company as holding a share upon any trust and (except as otherwise provided by the articles or by law) the company shall not be bound by or recognise any interest in any share except an absolute right to the entirety thereof in the holder.

Share certificates

6. Every member, upon becoming the holder of any shares, shall be entitled without payment to one certificate for all the shares of each class held by him (and, upon transferring part of his holding of shares of any class, to a certificate for the balance of such holding) or several certificates each for one or more of his shares upon payment for every certificate after the first of such reasonable sum as the directors may determine. Every certificate shall be sealed with the seal and shall specify the number, class and respective amounts paid thereon. The company shall not be bound to issue more than one certificate for shares held jointly by several persons and delivery of a certificate to one joint holder shall be sufficient delivery to all of them.

7. If a share certificate is defaced, worn-out, lost or destroyed, it may be renewed on such terms (if any) as to evidence and indemnity and payment of the expenses reasonably incurred by the company in investigating evidence as the directors may determine but otherwise free of charge, and (in the case of defacement or wearing-out) on delivery up of the old certificate.

Lien

8. The company shall have a first and paramount lien on every share (not being a fully paid share) for all moneys (whether presently payable or not) payable at a fixed time or called in respect of that share. The directors may at any time declare any share to be wholly or in part exempt from the provisions of this regulation. The company's lien on a share shall extend to any amount payable in respect of it.
9. The company may sell in such manner as the directors determine any shares on which the company has a lien if a sum in respect of which the lien exists is presently payable and is not paid within fourteen clear days after notice has been given to the holder of the share or to the person entitled to it in consequence of the death or bankruptcy of the holder, demanding payment and stating that if the notice is not complied with the shares may be sold.
10. To give effect to a sale the directors may authorise some person to execute an instrument of transfer of the shares sold to, or in accordance with the directions of, the purchaser. The title of the transferee to the shares shall not be affected by any irregularity in or invalidity of the proceedings in reference to the sale.
11. The net proceeds of the sale, after payment of the costs, shall be applied in payment of so much of the sum for which the lien exists as is presently payable, and any residue shall (upon surrender to the company for cancellation of the certificate for the shares sold and subject to a like lien for any moneys not presently payable as existed upon the shares before the sale) be paid to the person entitled to the shares at the date of the sale.

Calls on shares and forfeiture

12. Subject to the terms of allotment, the directors may make calls upon the members in respect of any moneys unpaid on their shares (whether in respect of nominal value or premium) and each member shall (subject to receiving at least fourteen clear days' notice specifying when and where payment is to be made) pay to the company as required by the notice the amount called on his shares. A call may be required to be paid by instalments. A call may, before receipt by the company of any sum due thereunder, be revoked in whole or part and payment of a call may be postponed in whole or part. A person upon whom a call is made shall remain liable for calls made upon him notwithstanding the subsequent transfer of the shares in respect whereof the call was made.
13. A call shall be deemed to have been made at the time when the resolution of the directors authorising the call was passed.
14. The joint holders of a share shall be jointly and severally liable to pay all calls in respect thereof.
15. If a call remains unpaid after it has become due and payable the person from whom it is due and payable shall pay interest on the amount unpaid from the day it became due and payable until it is paid at the rate fixed by the terms of allotment of the share or in the notice of the call or, if no rate is fixed, at the appropriate rate (as defined by the Act) but the directors may waive payment of the interest wholly or in part.
16. An amount payable in respect of a share on allotment or at any fixed date, whether in respect of nominal value or premium or as an instalment of a call, shall be deemed to be a call and if it is not paid the provisions of the articles shall apply as if the amount had become due and payable by virtue of a call.

17. Subject to the terms of allotment, the directors may make arrangements on the issue of shares for a difference between the holders in the amounts and times of payment of calls on their shares.
18. If a call remains unpaid after it has become due and payable the directors may give to the person from whom it is due not less than fourteen clear days' notice requiring payment of the amount unpaid together with any interest which may have accrued. The notice shall name the place where payment is to be made and shall state that if the notice is not complied with the shares in respect of which the call was made will be liable to be forfeited.
19. If the notice is not complied with any share in respect of which it was given may, before the payment required by the notice has been made, be forfeited by a resolution of the directors and the forfeiture shall include all dividends or other moneys payable in respect of the forfeited shares and not paid before the forfeiture.
20. Subject to the provisions of the Act, a forfeited share may be sold, re-allotted or otherwise disposed of on such terms and in such manner as the directors determine either to the person who was before the forfeiture the holder or to any other person and at any time before sale, re-allotment or other disposition, the forfeiture may be cancelled on such terms as the directors think fit. Where for the purposes of its disposal a forfeited share is to be transferred to any person the directors may authorise some person to execute an instrument of transfer of the shares to that person.
21. A person any of whose shares have been forfeited shall cease to be a member in respect of them and shall surrender to the company for cancellation the certificate for the shares forfeited but shall remain liable to the company for all moneys which at the date of forfeiture were presently payable by him to the company in respect of those shares with interest at the rate at which interest was payable on those moneys before the forfeiture or, if no interest was so payable, at the appropriate rate (as defined by the Act) from the date of forfeiture until payment but the directors may waive payment wholly or in part or enforce payment without any allowance for the value of the shares at the time of forfeiture or for any consideration received on their disposal.
22. A statutory declaration by a director or the secretary that a share has been forfeited on a specified date shall be conclusive evidence of the facts stated in it as against all persons claiming to be entitled to the share and the declaration shall (subject to the execution of an instrument of transfer if necessary) constitute a good title to the share and the person to whom the share is disposed of shall not be bound to see to the application of the consideration, if any, nor shall his title to the share be affected by any irregularity in or invalidity of the proceedings in reference to the forfeiture or disposal of the share.

Transfer of shares

23. The instrument of transfer of a share may be in any usual form or in any other form which the directors may approve and shall be executed by or on behalf of the transferor and, unless the share is fully paid, by or on behalf of the transferee.
24. The directors may refuse to register the transfer of a share which is not fully paid to a person of whom they do not approve and they may refuse to register the transfer of a share on which the company has a lien. They may also refuse to register a transfer unless –

(a) it is lodged at the office or at such other place as the directors may appoint and is accompanied by the certificate for the shares to which it relates and such other evidence as the directors may reasonably require to show the right of the transferor to make the transfer;
(b) it is in respect of only one class of shares; and
(c) it is in favour of not more than four transferees.

25. If the directors refuse to register a transfer of a share, they shall within two months after the date on which the transfer was lodged with the company send to the transferee notice of the refusal.

26. The registration of transfers of shares or of transfers of any class of shares may be suspended at such times and for such periods (not exceeding thirty days in any year) as the directors may determine.

27. No fee shall be charged for the registration of any instrument of transfer or other document relating to or affecting the title to any share.

28. The company shall be entitled to retain any instrument of transfer which is registered, but any instrument of transfer which the directors refuse to register shall be returned to the person lodging it when notice of the refusal is given.

Transmission of shares

29. If a member dies the survivor or survivors where he was a joint holder, and his personal representatives where he was a sole holder or the only survivor of joint holders, shall be the persons recognised by the company as having any title to his interest; but nothing herein contained shall release the estate of a deceased member from any liability in respect of any share which had been jointly held by him.

30. A person becoming entitled to a share in consequence of the death or bankruptcy of a member may, upon such evidence being produced as the directors may properly require, elect either to become the holder of the share or to have some other person nominated by him registered as the transferee. If he elects to become the holder he shall give notice to the company to that effect. If he elects to have another person registered he shall execute an instrument of transfer of the share to that person. All the articles relating o the transfer of shares shall apply to the notice or instrument of transfer as if it were an instrument of transfer executed by the member and the death or bankruptcy of the member had not occurred.

31. A person becoming entitled to a share in consequence of the death or bankruptcy of a member shall have the rights to which he would be entitled if he were the holder of the share, except that he shall not, before being registered as the holder of the share, be entitled in respect of it to attend or vote at any meeting of the company or at any separate meeting of the holders of any class of shares in the company.

Alteration of share capital

32. The company may by ordinary resolution –
(a) increase its share capital by new shares of such amount as the resolution prescribes;
(b) consolidate and divide all or any of its share capital into shares of larger amount than its existing shares;

(c) subject to the provisions of the Act, sub-divide its shares, or any of them, into shares of smaller amount and the resolution may determine that, as between the shares resulting from the subdivision, any of them may have any preference or advantage as compared with the others; and
(d) cancel shares which, at the date of the passing of the resolution, have not been taken or agreed to be taken by any person and diminish the amount of its share capital by the amount of the shares so cancelled.

33. Whenever as a result of a consolidation of shares any members would become entitled to fractions of a share, the directors may, on behalf of those members, sell the shares representing the fractions for the best price reasonably obtainable to any person (including, subject to the provisions of the Act, the company) and distribute the net proceeds of sale in due proportion among those members, and the directors may authorise some person to execute an instrument of transfer of the shares to, or in accordance with the directions of, the purchaser. The transferee shall not be bound to see to the application of the purchase money nor shall his title to the shares be affected by any irregularity in or invalidity of the proceedings in reference to the sale.

34. Subject to the provisions of the Act, the company may by special resolution reduce its share capital, any capital redemption reserve and any share premium account in any way.

Purchase of own shares

35. Subject to the provisions of the Act, the company may purchase its own shares (including any redeemable shares) and, if it is a private company, make a payment in respect of the redemption or purchase of its own shares otherwise than out of distributable profits of the company or the proceeds of a fresh issue of shares.

General meetings

36. All general meetings other than annual general meetings shall be called extraordinary general meetings.

37. The directors may call general meetings and, on the requisition of members pursuant to the provisions of the Act, shall forthwith proceed to convene an extraordinary general meeting for a date not later than eight weeks after receipt of the requisition. If there are not within the United Kingdom sufficient directors to call a general meeting, any director or any member of the company may call a general meeting.

Notice of general meetings

38. An annual general meeting and an extraordinary general meeting called for the passing of a special resolution or a resolution appointing a person as a director shall be called by at least twenty-one clear days' notice. All other extraordinary general meetings shall be called by at least fourteen clear days' notice but a general meeting may be called by shorter notice if it is so agreed –
(a) in the case of an annual general meeting, by all the members entitled to attend and vote thereat; and
(b) in the case of any other meeting by a majority in number of the members having a right to attend and vote being a majority together holding not less than ninety-five per cent in the nominal value of the shares giving that right.

The notice shall specify the time and place of the meeting and the general nature of the business to be transacted and, in the case of an annual general meeting, shall specify the meeting as such.

Subject to the provisions of the articles and to any restriction imposed on any shares, the notice shall be given to all members, to all person entitled to a share in consequence of the death or bankruptcy of a member and to the directors and auditors.

39. The accidental omission to give notice of a meeting to, or the non-receipt of notice of a meeting by, any person entitled to receive notice shall not invalidate the proceedings at that meeting.

Proceedings at general meetings

40. No business shall be transacted at any meeting unless a quorum is present. Two persons entitled to vote upon the business to be transacted, each being a member or a proxy for a member or a duly authorised representative of a corporation, shall be a quorum.

41. If such a quorum is not present within half an hour from the time appointed for the meeting, or if during a meeting such a quorum ceases to be present, the meeting shall stand adjourned to the same day in the next week at the same time and place or to such time and place as the directors may determine.

42. The chairman, if any, of the board of directors or in his absence some other director nominated by the directors shall preside as chairman of the meeting, but if neither the chairman nor any such other director (if any) be present within fifteen minutes after the time appointed for holding the meeting and willing to act, the directors present shall elect one of their number to be chairman and, if there is only one director present and willing to act, he shall be chairman.

43. If no director is willing to act as chairman, or if no director is present within fifteen minutes after the time appointed for holding the meeting, the members present and entitled to vote shall choose one of their number to be chairman.

44. A director shall, notwithstanding that he is not a member, be entitled to attend and speak at any general meeting and at any separate meeting of the holders of any class of shares in the company.

45. The chairman may, with the consent of a meeting at which a quorum is present (and shall if so directed by the meeting), adjourn the meeting from time to time and from place to place, but no business shall be transacted at an adjourned meeting other than that business which might properly have been transacted at the meeting had the adjournment not taken place. When a meeting is adjourned for fourteen days or more, at least seven days' notice shall be given specifying the time and place of the adjourned meeting and the general nature of the business to be transacted. Otherwise it shall not be necessary to give any such notice.

46. A resolution put to the vote of a meeting shall be decided on a show of hands unless before, or on the declaration of the result of, the show of hands a poll is duly demanded. Subject to the provisions of the Act, a poll may be demanded –

(a) by the chairman; or

(b) by at least two members having the right to vote at the meeting; or

(c) by a member or members representing not less than one-tenth of the total voting rights of all the members having the right to vote at the meeting; or

(d) by a member or members holding shares conferring a right to vote at the meeting being shares on which an aggregate sum has been paid up equal to not less than one-tenth of the total sum paid up on all the shares conferring that right;

and a demand by a person as proxy for a member shall be the same as a demand by the member.

47. Unless a poll is duly demanded a declaration by the chairman that a resolution has been carried unanimously, or by a particular majority, or lost, or not carried by a particular majority and an entry to that effect in the minutes of the meeting shall be conclusive evidence of the fact without proof of the number or proportion of the votes recorded in favour or against the resolution.

48. The demand for a poll may, before the poll is taken, be withdrawn but only with the consent of the chairman and a demand so withdrawn shall not be taken to have invalidated the result of a show of hands declared before the demand was made.

49. A poll shall be taken as the chairman directs and he may appoint scrutineers (who need not be members) and fix a time and place for declaring the result of the poll. The result of the poll shall be deemed to be the resolution of the meeting at which the poll was demanded.

50. In the case of an equality of votes, whether on a show of hands or on a poll, the chairman shall be entitled to a casting vote in addition to any other vote he may have.

51. A poll demanded on the election of a chairman or on a question of adjournment shall be taken forthwith. A poll demanded on any other question shall be taken either forthwith or at such time and place as the chairman directs not being more than thirty days after the poll is demanded. The demand for a poll shall not prevent the continuance of a meeting for the transaction of any business other than the question on which the poll was demanded. If a poll is demanded before the declaration of the result of a show of hands and the demand is duly withdrawn, the meeting shall continue as if the demand had not been made.

52. No notice need be given of a poll not taken forthwith if the time and place at which it is to be taken are announced at the meeting at which it is demanded. In any other case at least seven clear days' notice shall be given specifying the time and place at which the poll is to be taken.

53. A resolution in writing executed by or on behalf of each member who would have been entitled to vote upon it if it had been proposed at a general meeting at which he was present shall be as effectual as if it had been passed at a general meeting duly convened and held and may consist of several instruments in the like form executed by or on behalf of one or more members.

Votes of members

54. Subject to any rights or restrictions attached to any shares, on a show of hands every member who (being an individual) is present in person or (being a corporation) present by a duly authorised representative, not being himself a member entitled to vote, shall have one vote and on a poll every member shall have one vote for every share of which he is the holder.

55. In the case of joint holders the vote of the senior who tenders a vote, whether in person or by proxy, shall be accepted to the exclusion of the votes of the other joint holders; and seniority shall be determined by the order in which the names of the holders stand in the register of members.

56. A member in respect of whom an order has been made by any court having jurisdiction (whether in the UK or elsewhere) in matters concerning mental disorder may vote, whether on a show of hands or on a poll, by his receiver, curator bonis or other person authorised in that behalf appointed by that court, and any such receiver, curator bonis or other person may, on a poll, vote by proxy. Evidence to the satisfaction of the directors of the authority of the person claiming to exercise the right to vote shall be deposited at the office, or at such other place as is specified in accordance with the articles for the deposit of instruments of proxy, not less than 48 hours before the time appointed for holding the meeting or adjourned meeting at which the right to vote is to be exercised and in default the right to vote shall not be exercisable.

57. No member shall vote at any general meeting or at any separate meeting of the holders of any class of shares in the company, either in person or by proxy, in respect of any share held by him unless all moneys presently payable by him in respect of that share have been paid.

58. No objection shall be raised to the qualification of any voter except at the meeting or adjourned meeting at which the vote objected to is tendered, and every vote not disallowed at the meeting shall be valid. Any objection made in due time shall be referred to the chairman whose decision shall be final and conclusive.

59. On a poll votes may be given either personally or by proxy. A member may appoint more than one proxy to attend on the same occasion.

60. *The appointment of a proxy shall be executed by or on behalf of the appointor and shall be in the following form (or in a form as near thereto as circumstances allow or in any other form which is usual or which the directors may approve) –*[2]

' PLC/Limited
I/We, , of , being a member/members of the above-named company, hereby appoint of , or failing him, of , as my/our proxy to vote in my/our name[s] and on my/our behalf at the annual/extraordinary general meeting of the company to be held on 19 , and at any adjournment thereof.
Signed on 19 .'

61. Where it is desired to afford members an opportunity of instructing the proxy how he shall act the *appointment of*[3] a proxy shall be in the following form (or in a form as near thereto as circumstances allow or in any other form which is usual or which the directors may approve) –

' PLC/Limited
I/We, , of , being a member/members of the above-named company, hereby appoint of , or failing him, of , as my/our proxy to vote in my/our name[s] and on my/our behalf at the annual/extraordinary general meeting of the company to be held on 19 , and at any adjournment thereof.
This form is to be used in respect of the resolutions mentioned below as follows:
Resolution No 1 *for *against
Resolution No 2 *for *against.
*Strike out whichever is not desired.
Unless otherwise instructed, the proxy may vote as he thinks fit or abstain from voting.
Signed this day of 19 .'

62. *The appointment of a proxy and any authority under which it is executed or a copy of such authority certified notarially or in some other way approved by the directors may –*

(a) in the case of an instrument in writing, be deposited at the office or such other place within the United Kingdom as is specified in the notice convening the meeting or in any instrument of proxy sent out by the company in relation to the meeting not less than 48 hours before the time for holding the meeting or adjourned meeting at which the person named in the instrument proposes to vote; or (aa) in the case of an appointment contained in an electronic communication, where an address has been specified for the purpose of receiving electronic communications –

(i) in the notice convening the meeting, or

(ii) in any instrument of proxy sent out by the company in relation to the meeting, or

(iii) in any invitation contained in an electronic communication to appoint a proxy issued by the company in relation to the meeting, be received at such address not less than 48 hours before the time for holding the meeting or adjourned meeting at which the person named in the appointment proposes to vote;

(b) in the case of a poll taken more than 48 hours after it is demanded, be deposited or received as aforesaid after the poll has been demanded and not less than 24 hours before the time appointed for the taking of the poll; or

(c) where the poll is not taken forthwith but is taken not more than 48 hours after it was demanded, be delivered at the meeting at which the poll was demanded to the chairman or to the secretary or to any director;

and an appointment of proxy which is not deposited, delivered or received in a manner so permitted shall be invalid.

In this regulation and the next, 'address', in relation to electronic communications, includes any number or address used for the purposes of such communications.[4]

63. A vote given or poll demanded by proxy or by the duly authorised representative of a corporation shall be valid notwithstanding the previous determination of the authority of the person voting or demanding a poll unless notice of the determination was received by the company at the office or at such other place at which the instrument of proxy was duly deposited or, where the appointment of the proxy was *contained in an electronic communication, at the address at which the appointment was duly received*[5] before the commencement of the meeting or adjourned meeting at which the vote is given or the poll demanded or (in the case of a poll taken otherwise than on the same day as the meeting or adjourned meeting) the time appointed for taking the poll.

Number of directors

64. Unless otherwise determined by ordinary resolution, the number of directors (other than alternate directors) shall not be subject to any maximum but shall be not less than two.

Alternate directors

65. Any director (other than an alternate director) may appoint any other director, or any other person approved by resolution of the directors and willing to act, to be an alternate director and may remove from office an alternate director so appointed by him.

66. An alternate director shall be entitled to receive notice of all meetings of directors and of all meetings of committees of directors of which his appointor is a member, to attend and vote at any such meeting at which the director appointing him is not personally present, and generally to perform all the functions of his appointor as a director in his absence but shall not be entitled to receive any remuneration from the company for his services as an alternate director. But it shall not be necessary to give notice of such a meeting to an alternate director who is absent from the United Kingdom.

67. An alternate director shall cease to be an alternate director if his appointor ceases to be a director; but if a director retires by rotation or otherwise but is reappointed or deemed to have been reappointed at the meeting at which he retires, any appointment of an alternate director made by him which was in force immediately prior to his retirement shall continue after his reappointment.

68. Any appointment or removal of an alternate director shall be by notice to the company signed by the director making or revoking the appointment or in any other manner approved by the directors.

69. Save as otherwise provided in the articles, an alternate director shall be deemed for all purposes to be a director and shall alone be responsible for his own acts and defaults and he shall not be deemed to be the agent of the director appointing him.

Powers of directors

70. Subject to the provisions of the Act, the memorandum and the articles and to any directions given by special resolution, the business of the company shall be managed by the directors who may exercise all the powers of the company. No alteration of the memorandum or articles and no such direction shall invalidate any prior act of the directors which would have been valid if that alteration had not been made or that direction had not been given. The powers given by this regulation shall not be limited by any special power given to the directors by the articles and a meeting of directors at which a quorum is present may exercise all powers exercisable by the directors.

71. The directors may, by power of attorney or otherwise, appoint any person to be the agent of the company for such purposes and on such conditions as they determine, including authority for the agent to delegate all or any of his powers.

Delegation of directors' powers

72. The directors may delegate any of their powers to any committee consisting of one or more directors. They may also delegate to any managing director or any director holding any other executive office such of their powers as they consider desirable to be exercised by him. Any such delegation may be made subject to any conditions the directors may impose, and either collaterally with or to the exclusion of their own powers and may be revoked or altered. Subject to any such conditions, the proceedings of a committee with two or more members shall be governed by the articles regulating the proceedings of directors so far as they are capable of applying.

Appointment and retirement of directors

73. At the first annual general meeting all the directors shall retire from office, and at every subsequent annual general meeting one-third of the directors who are subject to retirement by rotation or, if their number is not three or a multiple of three, the number nearest to one third shall retire from office; but, if there is only one director who is subject to retirement by rotation, he shall retire.

74. Subject to the provisions of the Act, the directors to retire by rotation shall be those who have served longest in office since their last appointment or reappointment, but as between persons who became or were last reappointed directors on the same day those to retire shall (unless they otherwise agree among themselves) be determined by lot.

75. If the company, at the meeting at which a director retires by rotation, does not fill the vacancy the retiring director shall, if willing to act, be deemed to have been reappointed unless at the meeting it is resolved not to fill the vacancy or unless a resolution for the reappointment of the director is put to the meeting and lost.

76. No person other than a director retiring by rotation shall be appointed or reappointed a director at any general meeting unless –

(a) he is recommended by the directors; or

(b) not less than fourteen nor more than thirty-five clear days before the date appointed for the meeting, notice executed by a member qualified to vote at the meeting has been given to the company of the intention to propose that person for appointment or reappointment stating the particulars which would, if he were so appointed or reappointed, be required to be included in the company's register of directors together with notice executed by that person of his willingness to be appointed or reappointed.

77. Not less than seven nor more than twenty-eight clear days before the date appointed for holding a general meeting notice shall be given to all who are entitled to receive notice of the meeting of any person (other than a director retiring by rotation at the meeting) who is recommended by the directors for appointment or reappointment as a director at the meeting or in respect of whom notice has been duly given to the company of the intention to propose him at the meeting for appointment or reappointment as a director. The notice shall give particulars of that person which would, if he were so appointed or reappointed, be required to be included in the company's register of directors.

78. Subject as aforesaid, the company may by ordinary resolution appoint a person who is willing to act to be a director either to fill a vacancy or as an additional director and may also determine the rotation in which any additional directors are to retire.

79. The directors may appoint a person who is willing to act to be director, either to fill a vacancy or as an additional director, provided that the appointment does not cause the number of directors to exceed the number fixed by or in accordance with the articles as the maximum number of directors. A director so appointed shall hold office only until the next following annual general meeting and shall not be taken into account in determining the directors who are to retire by rotation at the meeting. If not reappointed at such annual general meeting, he shall vacate office at the conclusion thereof.

80. Subject as aforesaid, a director who retires at an annual general meeting may, if willing to act, be reappointed. If he is not reappointed, he shall retain office until the meeting appoints someone in his place, or if it does not do so, until the end of the meeting.

Disqualification and removal of directors

81. The office of director shall be vacated if –

(a) he ceases to be a director by virtue of any provision of the Act or becomes prohibited by law from being a director; or

(b) he becomes bankrupt or makes any arrangement or composition with his creditors generally; or

(c) he is, or may be, suffering from mental disorder and either –

(i) he is admitted to hospital in pursuance of an application for treatment under the Mental Health Act 1983 or, in Scotland, an application for admission under the Mental Health (Scotland) Act 1960, or

(ii) an order is made by a court having jurisdiction (whether in the United Kingdom or elsewhere) in matters concerning mental disorder for his detention or for the appointment of a receiver, curator bonis or other person to exercise powers with respect to his property or affairs; or

(d) he resigns his office by notice to the company; or

(e) he shall for more than six consecutive months have been absent without permission of the directors from meetings of the directors held during that period and the directors resolve that his office be vacated.

Remuneration of directors

82. The directors shall be entitled to such remuneration as the company may by ordinary resolution determine and, unless the resolution provides otherwise, the remuneration shall be deemed to accrue from day to day.

Directors' expenses

83. The directors may be paid all travelling, hotel, and other expenses properly incurred by them in connection with their attendance at meetings of directors or committees of directors or general meetings or separate meetings of the holders of any class of shares or of debentures of the company or otherwise connection with the discharge of their duties.

Directors' appointments and interests

84. Subject to the provisions of the Act, the directors may appoint one or more of their number to the office of managing director or to any other executive office under the company and may enter into an agreement or arrangement with any director for his employment by the company or for the provision by him of any services outside the scope of the ordinary duties of a director. Any such appointment, agreement or arrangement may be made on such terms as the directors determine and they may remunerate any such director for his services as they think fit. Any appointment of a director to an executive office shall terminate if he ceases to be a director but without prejudice to any claim for damages for breach of the contract of service between the director and the company. A managing director and a director holding any other executive office shall not be subject to retirement by rotation.

85. Subject to the provisions of the Act, and provided that he has disclosed to the directors the nature and extent of any material interest of his, a director notwithstanding his office –

(a) may be a party to, or otherwise interested in, any transaction or arrangement with the company or in which the company is otherwise interested;

(b) may be a director or other officer of, or employed by, or party to any transaction or arrangement with, or otherwise interested in, any body corporate promoted by the company or in which the company is otherwise interested; and

(c) shall not, by reason of his office, be accountable to the company for any benefit which he derives from any such office or employment or from any such transaction or arrangement or from any interest in any such body corporate and no such transaction or arrangement shall be liable to be avoided on the ground of any such interest or benefit.

86. For the purposes of regulation 85 –

(a) a general notice given to the directors that a director is to be regarded as having an interest of the nature and extent specified in the notice in any transactions or arrangement in which a specified person or class of persons is interested shall be deemed to be a disclosure that the director has an interest in any such transaction of the nature and extent so specified; and

(b) an interest of which a director has no knowledge and of which it is unreasonable to expect him to have knowledge shall not be treated as an interest of his.

Director's gratuities and pensions

87. The directors may provide benefits, whether by payment of gratuities or pensions or by insurance or otherwise, for any director who has held but no longer holds any executive office or employment with the company or with any body corporate which is or has been a subsidiary of the company or a predecessor in business of the company or of any such subsidiary, and for any member of his family (including a spouse and a former spouse) or any person who is or was dependent upon him, and may (as well before as after he ceases to hold such office or employment) contribute to any fund and pay premiums for the purchase of any such benefit.

Proceedings of directors

88. Subject to the provisions of the articles, the directors may regulate their proceedings as they think fit. A director may, and the secretary at the request of a director shall, call a meeting of the directors. It shall not be necessary to give notice of a meeting to a director who is absent from the United Kingdom. Questions arising at a meeting shall be decided by a majority of votes. In the case of an equality of votes, the chairman shall have a second or casting vote. A director who is also an alternate director shall be entitled in the absence of his appointor to a separate vote on behalf of his appointor in addition to his own vote.

89. The quorum for the transaction of business of the directors may be fixed by the directors and unless so fixed at any other number shall be two. A person who holds office only as an alternate director shall, if his appointor is not present, be counted in the quorum.

90. The continuing directors or a sole continuing director may act notwithstanding any vacancies in their number, but, if the number of directors is less than the number fixed as the quorum, the continuing directors or director may act only for the purpose of filling vacancies or of calling a general meeting.

91. The directors may appoint one of their number to be the chairman of the board of directors and may at any time remove him from that office. Unless he is unwilling to do so, the director so appointed shall preside at every meeting of directors at which he is present. But if there is no director holding that office, or if the director holding it is unwilling to preside or is nor present within five minutes after the time appointed for the meeting, the directors present may appoint one of their number to be chairman of the meeting.

92. All acts done by a meeting of directors, or of a committee of directors, or by a person acting as a director shall, notwithstanding that it be afterwards discovered that there was a defect in the appointment of any director or that any of them were disqualified from holding office, or had vacated office, or were not entitled to vote, be as valid as if every such person had been duly appointed and was qualified and had continued to be a director and had been entitled to vote.

93. A resolution signed in writing by all the directors entitled to receive notice of a meeting of directors or of a committee of directors shall be as valid and effectual as if it had been passed at a meeting of directors or (as the case may be) a committee of directors duly convened and held and may consist of several documents in the like form each signed by one or more directors; but a resolution signed by an alternate director need not also be signed by his appointor and, if it is signed by a director who has appointed an alternate director, it need not be signed by the alternate in that capacity.

94. Save as otherwise provided by the articles, a director shall not vote at a meeting of directors or a committee of directors on any resolution concerning a matter in which he has, directly or indirectly, an interest or duty which is material and which conflicts or may conflict with the interests of the company unless his interest or duty arises only because the case falls within one or more of the following paragraphs –

(a) the resolution relates to the giving to him of a guarantee, security, or indemnity in respect of money lent to, or an obligation incurred by him for the benefit of, the company or any of its subsidiaries;

(b) the resolution relates to the giving to a third party of a guarantee, security, or indemnity in respect of an obligation of the company or any of its subsidiaries for which the director has assumed responsibility in whole or in part and whether alone or jointly with others under a guarantee or indemnity or by the giving of security;

(c) his interest arises by virtue of his subscribing or agreeing to subscribe for any shares, debentures or other securities of the company or any of its subsidiaries, or by virtue of his being, or intending to become, a participant in the underwriting or sub-underwriting of an offer of any such shares, debentures or other securities by the company or any of its subsidiaries for subscription, purchase or exchange;

(d) the resolution relates in any way to a retirement benefits scheme which has been approved, or is conditional upon approval, by the Board of Inland Revenue for taxation purposes.

For the purposes of this regulation, an interest of a person who is, for any purpose of the Act (excluding any statutory modification thereof not in force when this regulation becomes binding on the company), connected with a director shall be treated as an interest of the director and, in relation to an alternate director, an interest of his appointor shall be treated as an interest of the alternate director without prejudice to any interest which the alternate director has otherwise.

95. A director shall not be counted in the quorum present at a meeting in relation to a resolution on which he is not entitled to vote.

96. The company may by ordinary resolution suspend or relax to any extent, either generally or in respect of any particular matter, any provision of the articles prohibiting a director from voting at a meeting of directors or of a committee of directors.

97. Where proposals are under consideration concerning the appointment of two or more directors to offices or employments with the company or any body corporate in which the company is interested the proposals may be divided and considered in relation to each director separately and (provided he is not for another reason precluded from voting) each of the directors concerned shall be entitled to vote and be counted in the quorum in respect of each resolution except that concerning his own appointment.

98. If a question arises at a meeting of directors or of a committee of directors as to the right of a director to vote, the question may, before the conclusion of the meeting, be referred to the chairman of the meeting and his ruling in relation to any director other than himself shall be final and conclusive.

Secretary

99. Subject to the provisions of the Act, the secretary shall be appointed by the directors for such term, at such remuneration and upon such conditions as they may think fit; and any secretary so appointed may be removed by them.

Minutes

100. The directors shall cause minutes to be made in books kept for the purpose –

(a) of all appointments of officers made by the directors; and

(b) of all proceedings at meetings of the company, of the holders of any class of shares in the company, and of the directors, and of committees of directors, including the names of the directors present at each such meeting.

The seal

101. The seal shall only be used by the authority of the directors or of a committee of directors authorised by the directors. The directors may determine who shall sign any instrument to which the seal is affixed and unless otherwise so determined it shall be signed by a director and by the secretary or by a second director.

Dividends

102. Subject to the provisions of the Act, the company may by ordinary resolution declare dividends in accordance with the respective rights of members, but no dividend shall exceed the amount recommended by the directors.

103. Subject to the provisions of the Act, the directors may pay interim dividends if it appears to them that they are justified by the profits of the company available for distribution. If the share capital is divided into different classes, the directors may pay interim dividends on shares which confer deferred or non-preferred rights with regard to dividend as well as on shares which confer preferential rights with regard to dividend, but no interim dividend shall be paid on shares carrying deferred or non-preferred rights if, at the time of payment, any preferential dividend is in arrear. The directors may also pay at intervals settled by them any dividend payable at a fixed rate if it appears to them that the profits available for distribution justify the payment. Provided the directors act in good faith they shall not incur any liability to the holders of shares conferring preferred rights for any loss they may suffer by the lawful payment of an interim dividend on any shares having deferred or non-preferred rights.

104. Except as otherwise provided by the rights attached to shares, all dividends shall be declared and paid according to the amounts paid up on the shares on which the dividend is paid. All dividends shall be apportioned and paid proportionately to the amounts paid up on the shares during any portion or portions of the period in respect of which the dividend is paid; but, if any share is issued on terms providing that it shall rank for dividend from a particular date, that share shall rank for dividend accordingly.

105. A general meeting declaring a dividend may, upon the recommendation of the directors, direct that it shall be satisfied wholly or partly by the distribution of assets and, where any difficulty arises in regard to the distribution, the directors may settle the same and in particular may issue fractional certificates and fix the value for distribution of any assets and may determine that cash shall be paid to any member upon the footing of the value so fixed in order to adjust the rights of members and may vest assets in trustees.

106. Any dividend or other moneys payable in respect of a share may be paid by cheque sent by post to the registered address of the person entitled or, if two or more persons are the holders of the share or are jointly entitled to it by reason of the death or bankruptcy of the holder, to the registered address of that one of those persons who is first named on the register of members or to such person and to such address as the person or person entitled may in writing direct. Every cheque shall be made payable to the order of the person or persons entitled or to such other person as the person or persons entitled may in writing direct and payment of the cheque shall be a good discharge to the company. Any joint holder or other person jointly entitled to a share as aforesaid may give receipts for any dividend or other moneys payable in respect of the share.

107. No dividend or other moneys payable in respect of a share shall bear interest against the company unless otherwise provided by the rights attached to the share.

108. Any dividend which has remained unclaimed for twelve years from the date when it became due for payment shall, if the directors so resolve, be forfeited and cease to remain owing by the company.

Accounts

109. No member shall (as such) have any right of inspecting any accounting records or other book or document of the company except as conferred by statute or authorised by the directors or by ordinary resolution of the company.

Capitalisation of profits

110. The directors may with the authority of an ordinary resolution of the company –

(a) subject as hereinafter provided, resolve to capitalise any undivided profits of the company not required for paying any preferential dividend (whether or not they are available for distribution) or any sum standing to the credit of the company's share premium account or capital redemption reserve;

(b) appropriate the sum resolved to be capitalised to the members who would have been entitled to it if it were distributed by way of dividend and in the same proportion and apply such sum on their behalf either in or towards paying up the amounts, if any, for the time being unpaid on any shares held by them respectively, or in paying up in full unissued shares or debentures of the company of a nominal amount equal to that sum, and allot the shares or debentures credited as fully paid to those members, or as they may direct, in those proportions, or partly in one way and partly in the other: but the share premium account, the capital redemption reserve, and any profits which are not available for distribution may, for the purposes of this regulation, only be applied in paying up unissued shares to be allotted members credited as fully paid;

(c) make such provision by the issue of fractional certificates or by payment in cash or otherwise as they determine in the case of shares or debentures becoming distributable under this regulation in fractions; and

(d) authorise any person to enter on behalf of all members concerned into an agreement with the company providing for the allotment to them respectively, credited as fully paid, of any shares or debentures to which they are entitled upon such capitalisation, any agreement made under such authority being binding on all such members.

Notices

111. *Any notice to be given to or by any person pursuant to the articles (other than a notice calling a meeting of the directors) shall be in writing or shall be given using electronic communications to an address for the time being notified for that purpose to the person giving the notice.*

In this regulation, 'address', in relation to electronic communications, includes any number or address used for the purposes of such communications.[6]

112. The company may give any notice to a member either personally or by sending it by post in a prepaid envelope addressed to the member at his registered address or by leaving it at that address or by giving it using *electronic communications to an address for the time being notified to the company by the member.* In the case of joint holders of a share, all notices shall be given to the joint holder whose name stands first in the register of members in respect of the joint holding and notice so given shall be sufficient notice to all the joint holders. A member whose registered address is not within the United Kingdom and who gives to the company an address within the United Kingdom at which notices may be given to him, or an address to which notices may be sent by electronic communications, shall be entitled to have notices given to him at that address, but otherwise no such member shall be entitled to receive any notice from *the company. In this regulation and the next, 'address', in relation to electronic communications, includes any number or address used for the purposes of such communications.*[7]

113. A member present, either in person or by proxy, at any meeting of the company or of holders of any class of shares in the company shall be deemed to have received notice of the meeting and, where requisite, of the purposes for which it was called.

114. Every person who becomes entitled to a share shall be bound by any notice in respect of that share which, before his name is entered in the register of members, has been duly given to a person from whom he derives his title.

115. Proof that an envelope containing a notice was properly addressed, prepaid and posted shall be conclusive evidence that the notice was given. Proof that notice contained in an electronic communication *was sent in accordance with guidance issued by the Institute of Chartered Secretaries and Administrators shall be conclusive evidence that the notice was given.* A notice shall be deemed to be given at the expiration of 48 hours after the envelope containing it was posted *or, in the case of a notice contained in an electronic communication, at the expiration of 48 hours after the time it was sent.8*

116. A notice may be given by the company to the persons entitled to a share in consequence of death or bankruptcy of a member by sending or delivering it, in any manner authorised by the articles for the giving of notice to a member, addressed to them by name, or by the title of representatives of the deceased, or trustee of the bankrupt or by any description at the address, if any, within the United Kingdom supplied for that purpose by the persons claiming to be so entitled. Until such an address has been supplied, a notice may be given in any manner in which it might have been given if the death or bankruptcy had not occurred.

Winding up

117. If the company is wound up, the liquidator may, with the sanction of an extraordinary resolution of the company and any other sanction required by the Act, divide among the members in specie the whole or any part of the assets of the company and may, for that purpose, value any assets and determine how the division shall be carried out as between members or different classes of members. The liquidator may, with the like sanction, vest the whole or any part of the assets in trustees upon such trusts for the benefit of the members as he with the like sanction determines, but no member shall be compelled to accept any assets upon which there is a liability.

Indemnity

118. Subject to the provisions of the Act, but without prejudice to any indemnity to which a director may otherwise be entitled, every director or other officer or auditor of the company shall be indemnified out of the assets of the company against any liability incurred by him in defending any proceedings, whether civil or criminal, in which judgment is given in his favour or in which he is acquitted or in connection with any application in which relief is granted to him by the court from liability for negligence, default, breach of duty or breach of trust in relation to the affairs of the company.

FOOTNOTES

1 The italicised words were inserted by Sch.1 to the Companies Act 1985 (Electronic Communications) Order 2000 on 22 December 2000. Prior to that date Table A did not include a definition of an 'electronic communication' or a 'communication'.

2 Regulation 60 was amended by Sch.1 to the Companies Act 1985 (Electronic Communications) Order 2000 on 22 December 2000. Prior to that date it read as follows: 'An instrument appointing a proxy shall be in writing, executed by or on behalf of the appointor and shall be in the following form . . .'.

3 The words 'appointment of ' were inserted in reg.61 by Sch.1 to the Companies Act 1985 (Electronic Communications) Order 2000 on 22 December 2000. Prior to that date it read as follows: 'Where it is desired to afford members an opportunity of instructing the proxy how he shall act the instrument appointing a proxy . . .'.

4 Regulation 62 was amended by Sch.1 to the Companies Act 1985 (Electronic Communications) Order 2000 on 22 December 2000. Prior to that date it read as follows: 'The instrument appointing a proxy and any authority under which it is executed or a copy of such authority certified notarially or in some other way approved by the directors may –

(a) be deposited at the office or such other place within the United Kingdom as is specified in the notice convening the meeting or in any instrument of proxy sent out by the company in relation to the meeting not less than 48 hours before the time for holding the meeting or adjourned meeting at which the person named in the instrument proposes to vote; or

(b) in the case of a poll taken more than 48 hours after it is demanded, be deposited as aforesaid after the poll has been demanded and not less than 24 hours before the time appointed for the taking of the poll; or

(c) where the poll is not taken forthwith but is taken not more than 48 hours after it was demanded, be delivered at the meeting at which the poll was demanded to the chairman or to the secretary or to any director; and an instrument of proxy which is not deposited or delivered in a manner so permitted shall be invalid'.

5 The words in italics in reg.63 were inserted by Sch.1 to the Companies Act 1985 (Electronic Communications) Order 2000 on 22 December 2000.

6 Regulation 111 was amended by Sch.1 to the Companies Act 1985 (Electronic Communications) Order 2000 on 22 December 2000. Prior to that date it read as follows: 'Any notice to be given to or by any person pursuant to the articles shall be in writing except that notice calling a meeting of directors need not be in writing'.

7 The words in italics in reg.112 were inserted by Sch.1 to the Companies Act 1985 (Electronic Communications) Order 2000 on 22 December 2000.

8 The words in italics in reg.115 were inserted by Sch.1 to the Companies Act 1985 (Electronic Communications) Order 2000 on 22 December 2000.

Appendix 3

The Combined Code on Corporate Governance – June 2008

CODE ON CORPORATE GOVERNANCE

Preamble

1. Good corporate governance should contribute to better company performance by helping a board discharge its duties in the best interests of shareholders; if it is ignored, the consequence may well be vulnerability or poor performance. Good governance should facilitate efficient, effective and entrepreneurial management that can deliver shareholder value over the longer term. The Combined Code on Corporate Governance ('the Code') is published by the FRC to support these outcomes and promote confidence in corporate reporting and governance.
2. The Code is not a rigid set of rules. Rather, it is a guide to the components of good board practice distilled from consultation and widespread experience over many years. While it is expected that companies will comply wholly or substantially with its provisions, it is recognised that non-compliance may be justified in particular circumstances if good governance can be achieved by other means. A condition of non-compliance is that the reasons for it should be explained to shareholders, who may wish to discuss the position with the company and whose voting intentions may be influenced as a result. This 'comply or explain' approach has been in operation since the Code's beginnings in 1992 and the flexibility it offers is valued by company boards and by investors in pursuing better corporate governance.
3. The Listing Rules require UK companies listed on the Main Market of the London Stock Exchange to describe in the annual report and accounts their corporate governance from two points of view, the first dealing generally with their adherence to the Code's main principles, and the second dealing specifically with non-compliance with any of the Code's provisions. The descriptions together should give shareholders a clear and comprehensive picture of a company's governance arrangements in relation to the Code as a criterion of good practice.
4. In relation to the requirement to state how it has applied the Code's main principles, where a company has done so by complying with the associated provisions it should be sufficient simply to report that this is the case; copying out the principles in the annual report adds to its length without adding to its value. But where a company has taken additional actions to apply the principles or otherwise improve its governance, it would be helpful to shareholders to describe these in the annual report.

5. If a company chooses not to comply with one or more provisions of the Code, it must give shareholders a careful and clear explanation which shareholders should evaluate on its merits. In providing an explanation, the company should aim to illustrate how its actual practices are consistent with the principle to which the particular provision relates and contribute to good governance.
6. Smaller listed companies, in particular those new to listing, may judge that some of the provisions are disproportionate or less relevant in their case. Some of the provisions do not apply to companies below the FTSE 350. Such companies may nonetheless consider that it would be appropriate to adopt the approach in the Code and they are encouraged to do so. Externally managed investment companies typically have a different board structure, which may affect the relevance of particular provisions; the Association of Investment Companies's Corporate Governance Code and Guide can assist them in meeting their obligations under the Code.
7. In their turn, shareholders should pay due regard to companies' individual circumstances and bear in mind in particular the size and complexity of the company and the nature of the risks and challenges it faces. Whilst shareholders have every right to challenge companies' explanations if they are unconvincing, they should not be evaluated in a mechanistic way and departures from the Code should not be automatically treated as breaches. Institutional shareholders should be careful to respond to the statements from companies in a manner that supports the 'comply or explain' principle and bearing in mind the purpose of good corporate governance. They should put their views to the company and be prepared to enter a dialogue if they do not accept the company's position. Institutional shareholders should be prepared to put such views in writing where appropriate.
8. Companies and shareholders have a shared responsibility for ensuring that 'comply or explain' remains an effective alternative to a rules-based system. Satisfactory engagement between company boards and investors is therefore crucial to the health of the UK's corporate governance regime. Although engagement has been improving slowly but steadily for many years, practical obstacles necessitate a constant effort to keep the improvement going.
9. Companies can make a major contribution by spreading governance discussion with shareholders outside the two peak annual reporting periods around 31st December and 31st March and by raising further the general standard of their explanations justifying non-compliance. Shareholders for their part can still do more to satisfy companies that they devote adequate resources and scrutiny to engagement.
10. References to shareholders in this Preamble also apply to intermediaries and agents employed to assist shareholders in scrutinising governance arrangements.
11. This edition of the Code applies to accounting periods beginning on or after 29 June 2008, and takes effect at the same time as new FSA Corporate Governance Rules implementing European requirements relating to audit committees and corporate governance statements. The relevant sections of these Rules are summarised in Schedule C. There is some overlap between the content of the Code and the Rules, and the Rules state that in these areas compliance with the Code will be deemed sufficient also to comply with the Rules. However, where a company chooses to explain rather than comply with the Code it will need to

demonstrate that it nonetheless meets the minimum requirements set out in the Rules.

12. The Code itself is subject to periodic reviews by the FRC, the latest of which was conducted in 2007 and was generally reassuring about the Code's content and impact. In the normal course of events the next review will take place in 2010.

Financial Reporting Council
June 2008

CODE OF BEST PRACTICE

SECTION 1 COMPANIES

A. DIRECTORS

A.1 The Board

Main Principle

Every company should be headed by an effective board, which is collectively responsible for the success of the company.

Supporting Principles

The board's role is to provide entrepreneurial leadership of the company within a framework of prudent and effective controls which enables risk to be assessed and managed. The board should set the company's strategic aims, ensure that the necessary financial and human resources are in place for the company to meet its objectives and review management performance. The board should set the company's values and standards and ensure that its obligations to its shareholders and others are understood and met.

All directors must take decisions objectively in the interests of the company.

As part of their role as members of a unitary board, non-executive directors should constructively challenge and help develop proposals on strategy. Non-executive directors should scrutinise the performance of management in meeting agreed goals and objectives and monitor the reporting of performance. They should satisfy themselves on the integrity of financial information and that financial controls and systems of risk management are robust and defensible. They are responsible for determining appropriate levels of remuneration of executive directors and have a prime role in appointing, and where necessary removing, executive directors, and in succession planning.

Code Provisions

A.1.1 The board should meet sufficiently regularly to discharge its duties effectively. There should be a formal schedule of matters specifically reserved for its decision. The annual report should include a statement of how the board operates, including a high level statement of which types of decisions are to be taken by the board and which are to be delegated to management.

A.1.2 The annual report should identify the chairman, the deputy chairman (where there is one), the chief executive, the senior independent director and the chairmen and members of the nomination, audit and remuneration committees. It should also set out the number of meetings of the board and those committees and individual attendance by directors[1].

A.1.3 The chairman should hold meetings with the non-executive directors without the executives present. Led by the senior independent director, the non-executive directors should meet without the chairman present at least annually to appraise the chairman's performance (as described in A.6.1) and on such other occasions as are deemed appropriate.

A.1.4 Where directors have concerns which cannot be resolved about the running of the company or a proposed action, they should ensure that their concerns are recorded in the board minutes. On resignation, a non-executive director should provide a written statement to the chairman, for circulation to the board, if they have any such concerns.

A.1.5 The company should arrange appropriate insurance cover in respect of legal action against its directors.

A.2 Chairman and chief executive

Main Principle

There should be a clear division of responsibilities at the head of the company between the running of the board and the executive responsibility for the running of the company's business. No one individual should have unfettered powers of decision.

Supporting Principles

The chairman is responsible for leadership of the board, ensuring its effectiveness on all aspects of its role and setting its agenda. The chairman is also responsible for ensuring that the directors receive accurate, timely and clear information. The chairman should ensure effective communication with shareholders. The chairman should also facilitate the effective contribution of non-executive directors in particular and ensure constructive relations between executive and non-executive directors.

Code Provisions

A.2.1 The roles of chairman and chief executive should not be exercised by the same individual. The division of responsibilities between the chairman and chief executive should be clearly established, set out in writing and agreed by the board.

A.2.2 The chairman should on appointment meet the independence criteria set out in A.3.1 below. A chief executive should not go on to be chairman of the same company. If exceptionally a board decides that a chief executive should become chairman, the board should consult major shareholders in advance and should set out its reasons to shareholders at the time of the appointment and in the next annual report[2].

A.3 Board balance and independence

Main Principle

The board should include a balance of executive and non-executive directors (and in particular independent non-executive directors) such that no individual or small group of individuals can dominate the board's decision taking.

Supporting Principles

The board should not be so large as to be unwieldy. The board should be of sufficient size that the balance of skills and experience is appropriate for the requirements of the business and that changes to the board's composition can be managed without undue disruption.

To ensure that power and information are not concentrated in one or two individuals, there should be a strong presence on the board of both executive and non-executive directors.

The value of ensuring that committee membership is refreshed and that undue reliance is not placed on particular individuals should be taken into account in deciding chairmanship and membership of committees.

No one other than the committee chairman and members is entitled to be present at a meeting of the nomination, audit or remuneration committee, but others may attend at the invitation of the committee.

Code Provisions

A.3.1 The board should identify in the annual report each non-executive director it considers to be independent[3]. The board should determine whether the director is independent in character and judgement and whether there are relationships or circumstances which are likely to affect, or could appear to affect, the director's judgement. The board should state its reasons if it determines that a director is independent notwithstanding the existence of relationships or circumstances which may appear relevant to its determination, including if the director:

- has been an employee of the company or group within the last five years;
- has, or has had within the last three years, a material business relationship with the company either directly, or as a partner, shareholder, director or senior employee of a body that has such a relationship with the company;
- has received or receives additional remuneration from the company apart from a director's fee, participates in the company's share option or a performance-related pay scheme, or is a member of the company's pension scheme;
- has close family ties with any of the company's advisers, directors or senior employees;

- holds cross-directorships or has significant links with other directors through involvement in other companies or bodies;
- represents a significant shareholder; or
- has served on the board for more than nine years from the date of their first election.

A.3.2 Except for smaller companies[4], at least half the board, excluding the chairman, should comprise non-executive directors determined by the board to be independent. A smaller company should have at least two independent non-executive directors.

A.3.3 The board should appoint one of the independent non-executive directors to be the senior independent director. The senior independent director should be available to shareholders if they have concerns which contact through the normal channels of chairman, chief executive or finance director has failed to resolve or for which such contact is inappropriate.

A.4 Appointments to the Board

Main Principle

There should be a formal, rigorous and transparent procedure for the appointment of new directors to the board.

Supporting Principles

Appointments to the board should be made on merit and against objective criteria. Care should be taken to ensure that appointees have enough time available to devote to the job. This is particularly important in the case of chairmanships.

The board should satisfy itself that plans are in place for orderly succession for appointments to the board and to senior management, so as to maintain an appropriate balance of skills and experience within the company and on the board.

Code Provisions

A.4.1 There should be a nomination committee which should lead the process for board appointments and make recommendations to the board. A majority of members of the nomination committee should be independent non-executive directors. The chairman or an independent non-executive director should chair the committee, but the chairman should not chair the nomination committee when it is dealing with the appointment of a successor to the chairmanship. The nomination committee should make available[5] its terms of reference, explaining its role and the authority delegated to it by the board.

A.4.2 The nomination committee should evaluate the balance of skills, knowledge and experience on the board and, in the light of this evaluation, prepare a description of the role and capabilities required for a particular appointment.

A.4.3 For the appointment of a chairman, the nomination committee should prepare a job specification, including an assessment of the time commitment expected, recognising the need for availability in the event of crises. A chairman's other significant commitments should be disclosed to the board before appointment and included in the annual report. Changes to such commitments should be reported to the board as they arise, and their impact explained in the next annual report.

A.4.4 The terms and conditions of appointment of non-executive directors should be made available for inspection[6]. The letter of appointment should set out the expected time commitment. Non-executive directors should undertake that they will have sufficient time to meet what is expected of them. Their other significant commitments should be disclosed to the board before appointment, with a broad indication of the time involved and the board should be informed of subsequent changes.

A.4.5 The board should not agree to a full time executive director taking on more than one non-executive directorship in a FTSE 100 company nor the chairmanship of such a company.

A.4.6 A separate section of the annual report should describe the work of the nomination committee, including the process it has used in relation to board appointments[7]. An explanation should be given if neither an external search consultancy nor open advertising has been used in the appointment of a chairman or a non-executive director.

A.5 Information and professional development

Main Principle

The board should be supplied in a timely manner with information in a form and of a quality appropriate to enable it to discharge its duties. All directors should receive induction on joining the board and should regularly update and refresh their skills and knowledge.

Supporting Principles

The chairman is responsible for ensuring that the directors receive accurate, timely and clear information. Management has an obligation to provide such information but directors should seek clarification or amplification where necessary.

The chairman should ensure that the directors continually update their skills and the knowledge and familiarity with the company required to fulfil their role both on the board and on board committees. The company should provide the necessary resources for developing and updating its directors' knowledge and capabilities.

Under the direction of the chairman, the company secretary's responsibilities include ensuring good information flows within the board and its committees and between senior management and non-executive directors, as well as facilitating induction and assisting with professional development as required.

The company secretary should be responsible for advising the board through the chairman on all governance matters.

Code Provisions

A.5.1 The chairman should ensure that new directors receive a full, formal and tailored induction on joining the board. As part of this, the company should offer to major shareholders the opportunity to meet a new non-executive director.

A.5.2 The board should ensure that directors, especially non-executive directors, have access to independent professional advice at the company's expense where they judge it necessary to discharge their responsibilities as directors. Committees should be provided with sufficient resources to undertake their duties.

A.5.3 All directors should have access to the advice and services of the company secretary, who is responsible to the board for ensuring that board procedures are complied with. Both the appointment and removal of the company secretary should be a matter for the board as a whole.

A.6 Performance evaluation

Main Principle

The board should undertake a formal and rigorous annual evaluation of its own performance and that of its committees and individual directors.

Supporting Principle

Individual evaluation should aim to show whether each director continues to contribute effectively and to demonstrate commitment to the role (including commitment of time for board and committee meetings and any other duties). The chairman should act on the results of the performance evaluation by recognising the strengths and addressing the weaknesses of the board and, where appropriate, proposing new members be appointed to the board or seeking the resignation of directors.

Code Provision

A.6.1 The board should state in the annual report how performance evaluation of the board, its committees and its individual directors has been conducted. The non-executive directors, led by the senior independent director, should be responsible for performance evaluation of the chairman, taking into account the views of executive directors.

A.7 Re-election

Main Principle

All directors should be submitted for re-election at regular intervals, subject to continued satisfactory performance. The board should ensure planned and progressive refreshing of the board.

Code Provisions

A.7.1 All directors should be subject to election by shareholders at the first annual general meeting after their appointment, and to re-election thereafter at intervals of no more than three years. The names of directors submitted for election or re-election should be accompanied by sufficient biographical details and any other relevant information to enable shareholders to take an informed decision on their election.

A.7.2 Non-executive directors should be appointed for specified terms subject to re-election and to Companies Acts provisions relating to the removal of a director. The board should set out to shareholders in the papers accompanying a resolution to elect a non-executive director why they believe an individual should be elected. The chairman should confirm to shareholders when proposing re-election that, following formal performance evaluation, the individual's performance continues to be effective and to demonstrate commitment to the role. Any term beyond six years (e.g. two three-year terms) for a non-executive director should be subject to particularly rigorous review, and should take into account the need for progressive refreshing of the board. Non-executive directors may serve longer than nine years (e.g. three three-year terms), subject to annual re-election. Serving more than nine years could be relevant to the determination of a non-executive director's independence (as set out in provision A.3.1).

B. REMUNERATION

B.1 The Level and Make-up of Remuneration

Main Principles

Levels of remuneration should be sufficient to attract, retain and motivate directors of the quality required to run the company successfully, but a company should avoid paying more than is necessary for this purpose. A significant proportion of executive directors' remuneration should be structured so as to link rewards to corporate and individual performance.

Supporting Principle

The remuneration committee should judge where to position their company relative to other companies. But they should use such comparisons with caution, in view of the risk of an upward ratchet of remuneration levels with no corresponding improvement in performance. They should also be sensitive to pay and employment conditions elsewhere in the group, especially when determining annual salary increases.

Code Provisions

Remuneration policy

B.1.1 The performance-related elements of remuneration should form a significant proportion of the total remuneration package of executive directors and should be designed to align their interests with those of shareholders and to give these directors keen incentives to perform at the highest levels. In designing schemes of performance-related remuneration, the remuneration committee should follow the provisions in Schedule A to this Code.

B.1.2 Executive share options should not be offered at a discount save as permitted by the relevant provisions of the Listing Rules.

B.1.3 Levels of remuneration for non-executive directors should reflect the time commitment and responsibilities of the role. Remuneration for non-executive directors should not include share options. If, exceptionally, options are granted, shareholder approval should be sought in advance and any shares acquired by exercise of the options should be held until at least one year after the non-executive director leaves the board. Holding of share options could be relevant to the determination of a non-executive director's independence (as set out in provision A.3.1).

B.1.4 Where a company releases an executive director to serve as a non-executive director elsewhere, the remuneration report[8] should include a statement as to whether or not the director will retain such earnings and, if so, what the remuneration is.

Service Contracts and Compensation

B.1.5 The remuneration committee should carefully consider what compensation commitments (including pension contributions and all other elements) their directors' terms of appointment would entail in the event of early termination. The aim should be to avoid rewarding poor performance. They should take a robust line on reducing compensation to reflect departing directors' obligations to mitigate loss.

B.1.6 Notice or contract periods should be set at one year or less. If it is necessary to offer longer notice or contract periods to new directors recruited from outside, such periods should reduce to one year or less after the initial period.

B.2 Procedure

Main Principle

There should be a formal and transparent procedure for developing policy on executive remuneration and for fixing the remuneration packages of individual directors. No director should be involved in deciding his or her own remuneration.

Supporting Principles

The remuneration committee should consult the chairman and/or chief executive about their proposals relating to the remuneration of other executive directors. The remuneration committee should also be responsible for appointing any consultants in respect of executive director remuneration. Where executive directors or senior management are involved in advising or supporting the remuneration committee, care should be taken to recognise and avoid conflicts of interest.

The chairman of the board should ensure that the company maintains contact as required with its principal shareholders about remuneration in the same way as for other matters.

Code Provisions

B.2.1 The board should establish a remuneration committee of at least three, or in the case of smaller companies[9] two, independent non-executive directors. In addition the company chairman may also be a member of, but not chair, the committee if he or she was considered independent on appointment as chairman. The remuneration committee should make available[10] its terms of reference, explaining its role and the authority delegated to it by the board. Where remuneration consultants are appointed, a statement should be made available[11] of whether they have any other connection with the company.

B.2.2 The remuneration committee should have delegated responsibility for setting remuneration for all executive directors and the chairman, including pension rights and any compensation payments. The committee should also recommend and monitor the level and structure of remuneration for senior management. The definition of 'senior management' for this purpose should be determined by the board but should normally include the first layer of management below board level.

B.2.3 The board itself or, where required by the Articles of Association, the shareholders should determine the remuneration of the non-executive directors within the limits set in the Articles of Association. Where permitted by the Articles, the board may however delegate this responsibility to a committee, which might include the chief executive.

B.2.4 Shareholders should be invited specifically to approve all new long-term incentive schemes (as defined in the Listing Rules) and significant changes to existing schemes, save in the circumstances permitted by the Listing Rules.

C. ACCOUNTABILITY AND AUDIT

C.1 Financial Reporting

Main Principle

The board should present a balanced and understandable assessment of the company's position and prospects.

Supporting Principles

The board's responsibility to present a balanced and understandable assessment extends to interim and other price-sensitive public reports and reports to regulators as well as to information required to be presented by statutory requirements.

Code Provisions

C.1.1 The directors should explain in the annual report their responsibility for preparing the accounts and there should be a statement by the auditors about their reporting responsibilities.

C.1.2 The directors should report that the business is a going concern, with supporting assumptions or qualifications as necessary.

C.2 Internal Control[12]

Main Principle

The board should maintain a sound system of internal control to safeguard shareholders' investment and the company's assets.

Code Provision

C.2.1 The board should, at least annually, conduct a review of the effectiveness of the group's system of internal controls and should report to shareholders that they have done so[13]. The review should cover all material controls, including financial, operational and compliance controls and risk management systems.

C.3 Audit Committee and Auditors[14]

Main Principle

The board should establish formal and transparent arrangements for considering how they should apply the financial reporting and internal control principles and for maintaining an appropriate relationship with the company's auditors.

Code Provisions

C.3.1 The board should establish an audit committee of at least three, or in the case of smaller companies[15] two, independent non-executive directors. In smaller companies the company chairman may be a member of, but not chair, the committee in addition to the independent non-executive directors, provided he or she was considered independent on appointment as chairman. The board should satisfy itself that at least one member of the audit committee has recent and relevant financial experience[16].

C.3.2 The main role and responsibilities of the audit committee should be set out in written terms of reference and should include[17]:

- to monitor the integrity of the financial statements of the company, and any formal announcements relating to the company's financial performance, reviewing significant financial reporting judgements contained in them;
- to review the company's internal financial controls and, unless expressly addressed by a separate board risk committee composed of independent directors, or by the board itself, to review the company's internal control and risk management systems;
- to monitor and review the effectiveness of the company's internal audit function;
- to make recommendations to the board, for it to put to the shareholders for their approval in general meeting, in relation to the appointment, reappointment and removal of the external auditor and to approve the remuneration and terms of engagement of the external auditor;
- to review and monitor the external auditor's independence and objectivity

and the effectiveness of the audit process, taking into consideration relevant UK professional and regulatory requirements;

- to develop and implement policy on the engagement of the external auditor to supply non-audit services, taking into account relevant ethical guidance regarding the provision of non-audit services by the external audit firm; and to report to the board, identifying any matters in respect of which it considers that action or improvement is needed and making recommendations as to the steps to be taken.

C.3.3 The terms of reference of the audit committee, including its role and the authority delegated to it by the board, should be made available[18]. A separate section of the annual report should describe the work of the committee in discharging those responsibilities[19].

C.3.4 The audit committee should review arrangements by which staff of the company may, in confidence, raise concerns about possible improprieties in matters of financial reporting or other matters. The audit committee's objective should be to ensure that arrangements are in place for the proportionate and independent investigation of such matters and for appropriate follow-up action.

C.3.5 The audit committee should monitor and review the effectiveness of the internal audit activities. Where there is no internal audit function, the audit committee should consider annually whether there is a need for an internal audit function and make a recommendation to the board, and the reasons for the absence of such a function should be explained in the relevant section of the annual report.

C.3.6 The audit committee should have primary responsibility for making a recommendation on the appointment, reappointment and removal of the external auditors. If the board does not accept the audit committee's recommendation, it should include in the annual report, and in any papers recommending appointment or reappointment, a statement from the audit committee explaining the recommendation and should set out reasons why the board has taken a different position.

C.3.7 The annual report should explain to shareholders how, if the auditor provides non-audit services, auditor objectivity and independence is safeguarded.

D. RELATIONS WITH SHAREHOLDERS

D.1 Dialogue with Institutional Shareholders

Main Principle

There should be a dialogue with shareholders based on the mutual understanding of objectives. The board as a whole has responsibility for ensuring that a satisfactory dialogue with shareholders takes place[20].

Supporting Principles

Whilst recognising that most shareholder contact is with the chief executive and finance director, the chairman (and the senior independent director and other directors as appropriate) should maintain sufficient contact with major shareholders to understand their issues and concerns.

The board should keep in touch with shareholder opinion in whatever ways are most practical and efficient.

Code Provisions

D.1.1 The chairman should ensure that the views of shareholders are communicated to the board as a whole. The chairman should discuss governance and strategy with major shareholders. Non-executive directors should be offered the opportunity to attend meetings with major shareholders and should expect to attend them if requested by major shareholders. The senior independent director should attend sufficient meetings with a range of major shareholders to listen to their views in order to help develop a balanced understanding of the issues and concerns of major shareholders.

D.1.2 The board should state in the annual report the steps they have taken to ensure that the members of the board, and in particular the non-executive directors, develop an understanding of the views of major shareholders about their company, for example through direct face-to-face contact, analysts' or brokers' briefings and surveys of shareholder opinion.

D.2 Constructive Use of the AGM

Main Principle

The board should use the AGM to communicate with investors and to encourage their participation.

Code Provisions

D.2.1 At any general meeting, the company should propose a separate resolution on each substantially separate issue, and should in particular propose a resolution at the AGM relating to the report and accounts. For each resolution, proxy appointment forms should provide shareholders with the option to direct their proxy to vote either for or against the resolution or to withhold their vote. The proxy form and any announcement of the results of a vote should make it clear that a 'vote withheld' is not a vote in law and will not be counted in the calculation of the proportion of the votes for and against the resolution.

D.2.2 The company should ensure that all valid proxy appointments received for general meetings are properly recorded and counted. For each resolution, after a vote has been taken, except where taken on a poll, the company should ensure that the following information is given at the meeting and made available as soon as reasonably practicable on a website which is maintained by or on behalf of the company:

- the number of shares in respect of which proxy appointments have been validly made;
- the number of votes for the resolution;
- the number of votes against the resolution; and

- the number of shares in respect of which the vote was directed to be withheld.

D.2.3 The chairman should arrange for the chairmen of the audit, remuneration and nomination committees to be available to answer questions at the AGM and for all directors to attend.

D.2.4 The company should arrange for the Notice of the AGM and related papers to be sent to shareholders at least 20 working days before the meeting.

SECTION 2 INSTITUTIONAL SHAREHOLDERS

E. INSTITUTIONAL SHAREHOLDERS[21]

E.1 Dialogue with companies

Main Principle

Institutional shareholders should enter into a dialogue with companies based on the mutual understanding of objectives.

Supporting Principles

Institutional shareholders should apply the principles set out in the Institutional Shareholders' Committee's "The Responsibilities of Institutional Shareholders and Agents – Statement of Principles"[22], which should be reflected in fund manager contracts.

E.2 Evaluation of Governance Disclosures

Main Principle

When evaluating companies' governance arrangements, particularly those relating to board structure and composition, institutional shareholders should give due weight to all relevant factors drawn to their attention.

Supporting Principle

Institutional shareholders should consider carefully explanations given for departure from this Code and make reasoned judgements in each case. They should give an explanation to the company, in writing where appropriate, and be prepared to enter a dialogue if they do not accept the company's position. They should avoid a box-ticking approach to assessing a company's corporate governance. They should bear in mind in particular the size and complexity of the company and the nature of the risks and challenges it faces.

E.3 Shareholder voting

Main Principle

Institutional shareholders have a responsibility to make considered use of their votes.

Supporting Principles

Institutional shareholders should take steps to ensure their voting intentions are being translated into practice.

Institutional shareholders should, on request, make available to their clients information on the proportion of resolutions on which votes were cast and non-discretionary proxies lodged.

Major shareholders should attend AGMs where appropriate and practicable. Companies and registrars should facilitate this.

Schedule A: Provisions on the design of performance related remuneration

1. The remuneration committee should consider whether the directors should be eligible for annual bonuses. If so, performance conditions should be relevant, stretching and designed to enhance shareholder value. Upper limits should be set and disclosed. There may be a case for part payment in shares to be held for a significant period.
2. The remuneration committee should consider whether the directors should be eligible for benefits under long-term incentive schemes. Traditional share option schemes should be weighed against other kinds of long-term incentive scheme. In normal circumstances, shares granted or other forms of deferred remuneration should not vest, and options should not be exercisable, in less than three years. Directors should be encouraged to hold their shares for a further period after vesting or exercise, subject to the need to finance any costs of acquisition and associated tax liabilities.
3. Any new long-term incentive schemes which are proposed should be approved by shareholders and should preferably replace any existing schemes or at least form part of a well considered overall plan, incorporating existing schemes. The total rewards potentially available should not be excessive.
4. Payouts or grants under all incentive schemes, including new grants under existing share option schemes, should be subject to challenging performance criteria reflecting the company's objectives. Consideration should be given to criteria which reflect the company's performance relative to a group of comparator companies in some key variables such as total shareholder return.
5. Grants under executive share option and other long-term incentive schemes should normally be phased rather than awarded in one large block.
6. In general, only basic salary should be pensionable.
7. The remuneration committee should consider the pension consequences and associated costs to the company of basic salary increases and any other changes in pensionable remuneration, especially for directors close to retirement.

Schedule B: Guidance on liability of non-executive directors: care, skill and diligence

1. Although non-executive directors and executive directors have as board members the same legal duties and objectives, the time devoted to the company's affairs is likely to be significantly less for a non-executive director than for an executive director and the detailed knowledge and experience of a company's affairs that

could reasonably be expected of a non-executive director will generally be less than for an executive director. These matters may be relevant in assessing the knowledge, skill and experience which may reasonably be expected of a non-executive director and therefore the care, skill and diligence that a non-executive director may be expected to exercise.

2. In this context, the following elements of the Code may also be particularly relevant.
   (i) In order to enable directors to fulfil their duties, the Code states that:
   - The letter of appointment of the director should set out the expected time commitment (*Code provision A.4.4*); and
   - The board should be supplied in a timely manner with information in a form and of a quality appropriate to enable it to discharge its duties. The chairman is responsible for ensuring that the directors are provided by management with accurate, timely and clear information. (*Code principle A.5*).

   (ii) Non-executive directors should themselves:
   - Undertake appropriate induction and regularly update and refresh their skills, knowledge and familiarity with the company (*Code principle A.5 and provision A.5.1*)
   - Seek appropriate clarification or amplification of information and, where necessary, take and follow appropriate professional advice. (*Code principle A.5 and provision A.5.2*)
   - Where they have concerns about the running of the company or a proposed action, ensure that these are addressed by the board and, to the extent that they are not resolved, ensure that they are recorded in the board minutes (*Code provision A.1.4*).
   - Give a statement to the board if they have such unresolved concerns on resignation (*Code provision A.1.4*)

3. It is up to each non-executive director to reach a view as to what is necessary in particular circumstances to comply with the duty of care, skill and diligence they owe as a director to the company. In considering whether or not a person is in breach of that duty, a court would take into account all relevant circumstances. These may include having regard to the above where relevant to the issue of liability of a non-executive director.

Schedule C: Disclosure of Corporate Governance Arrangements

Corporate governance disclosure requirements are set out in three places:

- FSA Listing Rule 9.8.6 (which includes the 'comply or explain' requirement);
- FSA Disclosure and Transparency Rules Sections 7.1 and 7.2 (which set out certain mandatory disclosures); and
- The Combined Code (in addition to providing an explanation where they choose not to comply with a provision, companies must disclose specified information in order to comply with certain provisions).

These requirements are summarised below. The full text of Listing Rule 9.8.6 and Disclosure and Transparency Rules 7.1 and 7.2 are contained in the Listing,

Prospectus and Disclosure section of the FSA Handbook, which can be found at http://fsahandbook.info/FSA/html/handbook/.

There is some overlap between the mandatory disclosures required under the Disclosure and Transparency Rules and those expected under the Combined Code. Areas of overlap are summarised in the Appendix to this Schedule. In respect of disclosures relating to the audit committee and the composition and operation of the board and its committees, compliance with the relevant provisions of the Code will result in compliance with the relevant Rules.

Listing Rules
Paragraph 9.8.6 R of the Listing Rules states that in the case of a listed company incorporated in the United Kingdom, the following items must be included in its annual report and accounts:

- a statement of how the listed company has applied the Main Principles set out in Section 1 of the Combined Code, in a manner that would enable shareholders to evaluate how the principles have been applied;
- a statement as to whether the listed company has:
  - complied throughout the accounting period with all relevant provisions set out in Section 1 of the Combined Code; or
  - not complied throughout the accounting period with all relevant provisions set out in Section 1 of the Combined Code and if so, setting out:
    (i) those provisions, if any, it has not complied with;
    (ii) in the case of provisions whose requirements are of a continuing nature, the period within which, if any, it did not comply with some or all of those provisions; and
    (iii) the company's reasons for non-compliance.

Disclosure and Transparency Rules
Section 7.1 of the Disclosure and Transparency Rules concerns *audit committees or bodies carrying out equivalent functions*.

- DTR 7.1.1 R to 7.1.3 R sets out requirements relating to the composition and functions of the committee or equivalent body:
- DTR 7.1.1 R states that an issuer must have a body which is responsible for performing the functions set out in DTR 7.1.3 R, and that at least one member of that body must be independent and at least one member must have competence in accounting and/or auditing.
- DTR 7.1.2 G states that the requirements for independence and competence in accounting and/or auditing may be satisfied by the same member or by different members of the relevant body.
- DTR 7.1.3 R states that an issuer must ensure that, as a minimum, the relevant body must:
  (1) monitor the financial reporting process;
  (2) monitor the effectiveness of the issuer's internal control, internal audit where applicable, and risk management systems;
  (3) monitor the statutory audit of the annual and consolidated accounts;
  (4) review and monitor the independence of the statutory auditor, and in particular the provision of additional services to the issuer.

DTR 7.1.5 R to 7.1.7 R explain what disclosure is required:

- DTR 7.1.5 R states that the issuer must make a statement available to the public disclosing which body carries out the functions required by DTR 7.1.3 R and how it is composed.
- DTR 7.1.6 G states that this can be included in the corporate governance statement required under DTR 7.2 (see below).
- DTR 7.1.7 R states that compliance with the relevant provisions of the Combined Code (as set out in the Appendix to this Schedule) will result in compliance with DTR 7.1.1 R to 7.1.5 R.

Section 7.2 concerns *corporate governance statements*. Issuers are required to produce a corporate governance statement that must be either included in the directors' report (DTR 7.2.1 R); or in a separate report published together with the annual report; or on the issuer's website, in which case there must be a cross-reference in the directors' report (DTR 7.2.9 R).

DTR 7.2.2 R requires that the corporate governance statements must contain a reference to the corporate governance code to which the company is subject (for listed companies incorporated in the UK this is the Combined Code). DTR 7.2.3 R requires that, to the extent that it departs from that code, the company must explain which parts of the code it departs from and the reasons for doing so. DTR 7.2.4 G states that compliance with LR 9.8.6R (6) (the 'comply or explain' rule in relation to the Combined Code) will also satisfy these requirements.

DTR 7.2.5 R to 7.2.7 R and DTR 7.2.10 R set out certain information that must be disclosed in the corporate governance statement:

- DTR 7.2.5 R states that the corporate governance statement must contain a description of the main features of the company's internal control and risk management systems in relation to the financial reporting process. DTR 7.2.10 R states that an issuer which is required to prepare a group directors' report within the meaning of Section 415(2) of the Companies Act 2006 must include in that report a description of the main features of the group's internal control and risk management systems in relation to the process for preparing consolidated accounts.
- DTR 7.2.6 R states that the corporate governance statement must contain the information required by paragraph 13(2)(c), (d), (f), (h) and (i) of Schedule 7 to the Large and Medium-sized Companies and Groups (Accounts and Reports) Regulations 2008 (SI 2008/410) where the issuer is subject to the requirements of that paragraph.
- DTR 7.2.7 R states that the corporate governance statement must contain a description of the composition and operation of the issuer's administrative, management and supervisory bodies and their committees. DTR 7.2.8 G states that compliance with the relevant provisions of the Combined Code (as set out in the Appendix to this Schedule) will satisfy the requirements of DTR 7.2.7 R.

The Combined Code
In addition the Code includes specific requirements for disclosure which are set out below:

The annual report should record:

- a statement of how the board operates, including a high level statement of which types of decisions are to be taken by the board and which are to be delegated to management (A.1.1);
- the names of the chairman, the deputy chairman (where there is one), the chief executive, the senior independent director and the chairmen and members of the nomination, audit and remuneration committees (A.1.2);
- the number of meetings of the board and those committees and individual attendance by directors (A.1.2);
- the names of the non-executive directors whom the board determines to be independent, with reasons where necessary (A.3.1);
- the other significant commitments of the chairman and any changes to them during the year (A.4.3);
- how performance evaluation of the board, its committees and its directors has been conducted (A.6.1);
- the steps the board has taken to ensure that members of the board, and in particular the non-executive directors, develop an understanding of the views of major shareholders about their company (D.1.2).

The annual report should also include:

- a separate section describing the work of the nomination committee, including the process it has used in relation to board appointments and an explanation if neither external search consultancy nor open advertising has been used in the appointment of a chairman or a non-executive director (A.4.6);
- a description of the work of the remuneration committee as required under the Directors' Remuneration Report Regulations 2002, and including, where an executive director serves as a non-executive director elsewhere, whether or not the director will retain such earnings and, if so, what the remuneration is (B.1.4);
- an explanation from the directors of their responsibility for preparing the accounts and a statement by the auditors about their reporting responsibilities (C.1.1);
- a statement from the directors that the business is a going concern, with supporting assumptions or qualifications as necessary (C.1.2);
- a report that the board has conducted a review of the effectiveness of the group's system of internal controls (C.2.1);
- a separate section describing the work of the audit committee in discharging its responsibilities (C.3.3);
- where there is no internal audit function, the reasons for the absence of such a function (C.3.5);
- where the board does not accept the audit committee's recommendation on the appointment, reappointment or removal of an external auditor, a statement from the audit committee explaining the recommendation and the reasons why the board has taken a different position (C.3.6); and

- an explanation of how, if the auditor provides non-audit services, auditor objectivity and independence is safeguarded (C.3.7).

The following information should be made available (which may be met by placing the information on a website that is maintained by or on behalf of the company):
- the terms of reference of the nomination, remuneration and audit committees, explaining their role and the authority delegated to them by the board (A.4.1, B.2.1 and C.3.3);
- the terms and conditions of appointment of non-executive directors (A.4.4) (see footnote 8 on page 10); and
- where remuneration consultants are appointed, a statement of whether they have any other connection with the company (B.2.1).

The board should set out to shareholders in the papers accompanying a resolution to elect or re-elect directors:
- sufficient biographical details to enable shareholders to take an informed decision on their election or re-election (A.7.1);
- why they believe an individual should be elected to a non-executive role (A.7.2); and
- on re-election of a non-executive director, confirmation from the chairman that, following formal performance evaluation, the individual's performance continues to be effective and to demonstrate commitment to the role, including commitment of time for board and committee meetings and any other duties (A.7.2).

The board should set out to shareholders in the papers recommending appointment or reappointment of an external auditor:
- if the board does not accept the audit committee's recommendation, a statement from the audit committee explaining the recommendation and from the board setting out reasons why they have taken a different position (C.3.6).

Additional guidance
The Turnbull Guidance and Smith Guidance contain further suggestions as to information that might usefully be disclosed in the internal control statement and the report of the audit committee respectively. Both sets of guidance are available on the FRC website at http://www.frc.org.uk/corporate/.

Overlap between the Disclosure and Transparency Rules and the Combined Code

Disclosure and Transparency Rules	*Combined Code*
D.T.R 7.1.1 R Sets out minimum requirements on composition of the audit committee or equivalent body.	**Provision C.3.1** Sets out recommended composition of the audit committee.
D.T.R 7.1.3 R Sets out minimum functions of the audit committee or equivalent body.	**Provision C.3.2** Sets out the recommended minimum terms of reference for the committee.

Overlap between the Disclosure and Transparency Rules and the Combined Code *continued*

Disclosure and Transparency Rules	*Combined Code*
D.T.R 7.1.5 R The composition and function of the audit committee or equivalent body must be disclosed in the annual report. *DTR 7.1.7 R states that compliance with Code provisions A.1.2, C.3.1, C.3.2 and C.3.3 will result in compliance with DTR 7.1.1 R to DTR 7.1.5 R.*	**Provision A.1.2** The annual report should identify members of the board committees. **Provision C.3.3** The annual report should describe the work of the audit committee. Further recommendations on the content of the audit committee report are set out in the Smith Guidance.
D.T.R 7.2.5 R The corporate governance statement must include a description of the main features of the company's internal control and risk management systems in relation to the financial reporting process. *While this requirement differs from the requirement in the Combined Code, it is envisaged that both could be met by a single internal control statement.*	**Provision C.2.1** The Board must report that a review of the effectiveness of the internal control system has been carried out. Further recommendations on the content of the internal control statement are set out in the Turnbull Guidance.
DTR 7.2.7 R The corporate governance statement must include a description of the composition and operation of the administrative, management and supervisory bodies and their committees. *DTR 7.2.8 R states that compliance with Code provisions A.1.1, A.1.2, A.4.6, B.2.1 and C.3.3 with result in compliance with DTR 7.2.7 R.*	This requirement overlaps with a number of different provisions of the Code: **A.1.1**: the annual report should include a statement of how the board operates. **A.1.2**: the annual report should identify members of the board and board committees. **A.4.6**: the annual report should describe the work of the nomination committee. **B.2.1**: a description of the work of the remuneration committee should be made available. [Note: in order to comply with DTR 7.2.7 R this information will need to be included in the corporate governance statement]. **C.3.3**: the annual report should describe the work of the audit committee.

NOTES

1 Provisions A.1.1 and A.1.2 overlap with FSA Rule DTR 7.2.7 R; Provision A.1.2 also overlaps with DTR 7.1.5 R (see Schedule C).
2 Compliance or otherwise with this provision need only be reported for the year in which the appointment is made.
3 A.2.2 states that the chairman should, on appointment, meet the independence criteria set out in this provision, but thereafter the test of independence is not appropriate in relation to the chairman.
4 A smaller company is one that is below the FTSE 350 throughout the year immediately prior to the reporting year.
5 The requirement to make the information available would be met by including the information on a website that is maintained by or on behalf of the company.
6 The terms and conditions of appointment of non-executive directors should be made available for inspection by any person at the company's registered office during normal business hours and at the AGM (for 15 minutes prior to the meeting and during the meeting).
7 This provision overlaps with FSA Rule DTR 7.2.7 R (see Schedule C).
8 As required under the Directors' Remuneration Report Regulations 2002.
9 See footnote 4.
10 This provision overlaps with FSA Rule DTR 7.2.7 R (see Schedule C).
11 See footnote 5.
12 The Turnbull guidance suggests means of applying this part of the Code. Copies are available at www.frc.org.uk/corporate/internalcontrol.cfm
13 In addition FSA Rule DTR 7.2.5 R requires companies to describe the main features of the internal control and risk management systems in relation to the financial reporting process (see Schedule C).
14 The Smith guidance suggests means of applying this part of the Code. Copies are available at www.frc.org.uk/corporate/auditcommittees.cfm
15 See footnote 4.
16 This provision overlaps with FSA Rule DTR 7.1.1 R (see Schedule C).
17 This provision overlaps with FSA Rules DTR 7.1.3 R (see Schedule C).
18 See footnote 5.
19 This provision overlaps with FSA Rules DTR 7.1.5 R and 7.2.7 R (see Schedule C).
20 Nothing in these principles or provisions should be taken to override the general requirements of law to treat shareholders equally in access to information.
21 Agents such as investment managers, or voting services, are frequently appointed by institutional shareholders to act on their behalf and these principles should accordingly be read as applying where appropriate to the agents of institutional shareholders.
22 Available at www.institutionalshareholderscommittee.co.uk.

Appendix 4

ICSA Guide to Good Boardroom Practice

The Institute of Chartered Secretaries and Administrators (ICSA) believes that reliance on unwritten boardroom procedures and practices is no longer acceptable in the modern business environment. Whilst it is acknowledged that company law should not attempt to prescribe any particular style of boardroom management, ICSA believes that certain basic principles of good boardroom practice can be considered to be universally applicable.

Accordingly, ICSA has formulated this Code for directors and company secretaries as a guide to the matters which it believes should be addressed and, wherever applicable, accepted formally by boards of directors in recognition of a commitment to adhere to an overall concept of best practice.

ICSA also recommends that boardroom procedures should be periodically reviewed to ensure both the satisfactory operation of the Code and the identification of matters which individual companies could advantageously bring within its scope.

The Code

1 The board should establish written procedures for the conduct of its business which should include the matters covered in this Code. A copy of these written procedures should be given to each director. Compliance should be monitored, preferably by an audit committee of the board, and breaches of the procedures should be reported to the board.

2 The board should ensure that each director is given on appointment sufficient information to enable him/her to perform his/her duties. In particular, guidance for non-executive directors should cover the procedures: for obtaining information concerning the company; and for requisitioning a meeting of the board.

3 In the conduct of board business, two fundamental concepts should be observed: each director should receive the same information at the same time, and each director should be given sufficient time in which to consider any such information.

4 The board should identify matters which require the prior approval of the board and lay down procedures[1] to be followed when, exceptionally, a decision is required before its next meeting on any matter not required by law to be considered at board level.

5 As a basic principle, all material contracts, and especially those not in the ordinary course of business, should be referred to the board for decision prior to the commitment of the company.

6 The board should approve definitions of the terms 'material'[2] and 'not in the ordinary course of business' and these definitions should be brought to the attention of all relevant persons.

7 Where there is any uncertainty regarding the materiality or nature of a contract, it should normally be assumed that the contract should be brought before the board.

8 Decisions regarding the content of the agenda for individual meetings of the board and concerning the presentation of agenda items should be taken by the chairman in consultation with the company secretary.

9 The company secretary should be responsible to the chairman for the proper administration of the meetings of the company, the board and any committees thereof. To carry out this responsibility the company secretary should be entitled to be present at (or represented at) and prepare (or arrange for the preparation of) minutes of the proceedings of all such meetings.

10 The minutes of meetings should record the decisions taken and provide sufficient background to those decisions. All papers presented at the meeting should be clearly identified in the minutes and retained for reference. Procedures for the approval and circulation of minutes should be established.

11 Where the articles of association allow the board to delegate any of its powers to a committee, the board should give its prior approval to: the membership and quorum of any such committee; its term of reference; and the extent of any powers delegated to it.

12 The minutes of all meetings of committees of the board (or a written summary thereof) should be circulated to the board prior to its next meeting and the opportunity should be given at that meeting for any member of the board to ask questions thereon.

13 Notwithstanding the absence of a formal agenda item, the chairman should permit any director or the company secretary to raise at any board meeting any matter concerning the company's compliance with this Code of Practice, with the company's memorandum and articles of association and with any other legal or regulatory requirement.

NOTES

1 If it is practicable, the approval of all the directors should be obtained by means of a written resolution. In all cases, however, the procedures should balance the need for urgency with the overriding principle that each director should be given as much information as possible and have an opportunity to requisition an emergency meeting of the board to discuss the matter prior to the commitment of the company.

2 Different definitions of the term 'material' should be established for 'contracts not in the ordinary course of business' and 'contracts in the ordinary course of business'. Financial limits should be set where appropriate.

Appendix 5

The Model Code

Introduction

This code imposes restrictions on dealing in the *securities* of a *listed company* beyond those imposed by law. Its purpose is to ensure that *persons discharging managerial responsibilities* do not abuse, and do not place themselves under suspicion of abusing, *inside information* that they may be thought to have, especially in periods leading up to an announcement of the *company's* results.

Nothing in this code sanctions a breach of section 118 of the *Act* (Market abuse), the insider dealing provisions of the Criminal Justice Act or any other relevant legal or regulatory requirements.

Definitions

1. In this code the following definitions, in addition to those contained in the *Listing Rules*, apply unless the context requires otherwise:

(a) 'close period' means:

(i) the period of 60 days immediately preceding a preliminary announcement of the listed company's annual results or, if shorter, the period from the end of the relevant financial year up to and including the time of announcement; or

(ii) the period of 60 days immediately preceding the publication of its annual financial report or if shorter the period from the end of the relevant financial year up to and including the time of such publication; and

(iii) if the listed company reports on a half yearly basis the period from the end of the relevant financial period up to and including the time of such publication; and

(iv) if the listed company reports on a quarterly basis the period of 30 days immediately preceding the announcement of the quarterly results or, if shorter, the period from the end of the relevant financial period up to and including the time of the announcement;

(b) 'connected person' has the meaning given in section 96B (2) of the Act (Persons discharging managerial responsibilities and connected persons);

(c) 'dealing' includes:

(i) any acquisition or disposal of, or agreement to acquire or dispose of any of the *securities* of the *company*;

(ii) entering into a contract (including a contract for difference) the purpose of which is to secure a profit or avoid a loss by reference to fluctuations in the price of any of the *securities* of the *company*;

(iii) the grant, acceptance, acquisition, disposal, exercise or discharge of any option (whether for the call, or put or both) to acquire or dispose of any of the *securities* of the *company*;

(iv) entering into, or terminating, assigning or novating any stock lending agreement in respect of the *securities* of the *company*;

(v) using as security, or otherwise granting a charge, lien or other encumbrance over the *securities* of the *company*;

(vi) any transaction, including a transfer for nil consideration, or the exercise of any power or discretion effecting a change of ownership of a beneficial interest in the *securities* of the *company*; or

(vii) any other right or obligation, present or future, conditional or unconditional, to acquire or dispose of any *securities* of the *company*;

(d) [deleted]

(e) 'prohibited period' means:

(i) any close period; or

(ii) any period when there exists any matter which constitutes *inside information* in relation to the *company*;

(f) '*restricted person*' means a person discharging managerial responsibilities; and

(g) '*securities* of the *company*' means any publicly traded or quoted *securities* of the *company* or any member of its *group* or any securities that are convertible into such *securities*.

Dealings not subject to the provisions of this code

2. The following dealings are not subject to the provisions of this code:

(a) undertakings or elections to take up entitlements under a rights issue or other offer (including an offer of *securities* of the *company* in lieu of a cash dividend);

(b) the take up of entitlements under a rights issue or other offer (including an offer of *securities* of the *company* in lieu of a cash dividend);

(c) allowing entitlements to lapse under a rights issue or other offer (including an offer of *securities* of the *company* in lieu of a cash dividend);

(d) the sale of sufficient entitlements nil-paid to take up the balance of the entitlements under a rights issue;

(e) undertakings to accept, or the acceptance of, a takeover offer;

(f) dealing where the beneficial interest in the relevant *security* of the *company* does not change;

(g) transactions conducted between a *person discharging managerial responsibilities* and their spouse, civil partner, child or step-child (within the meaning of section 96B(2) of the *Act*);

(h) transfers of *shares* arising out of the operation of an *employees' share scheme* into a savings scheme investing in *securities* of the *company* following:

(i) exercise of an option under an approved SAYE option scheme; or

(ii) release of *shares* from a HM Revenue and Customs approved share incentive plan;

(i) with the exception of a disposal of *securities* of the *company* received by a restricted person as a participant, dealings in connection with the following *employees' share schemes*;
   (i) an HM Revenue and Customs approved SAYE option scheme or share incentive plan, under which participation is extended on similar terms to all or most employees of the participating *companies* in that scheme; or
   (ii) a scheme on similar terms to a HM Revenue and Customs approved SAYE option scheme or share incentive plan, under which participation is extended on similar terms to all or most employees of the participating *companies* in that scheme; or

(j) the cancellation or surrender of an option under an *employees' share scheme*;

(k) transfers of the *securities* of the *company* by an independent trustee of an *employees' share scheme* to a beneficiary who is not a restricted person;

(l) transfers of *securities* of the *company* already held by means of a matched sale and purchase into a saving scheme or into a pension scheme in which the restricted person is a participant or beneficiary;

(m) an investment by a restricted person in a scheme or arrangement where the assets of the scheme (other than a scheme investing only in the *securities* of the *company*) or arrangement are invested at the discretion of a third party;

(n) a dealing by a restricted person in the units of an authorised unit trust or in *shares* in an *open-ended investment company*; and

(o) bona fide gifts to a restricted person by a third party.

Dealing by restricted persons

3. A restricted person must not deal in any *securities* of the *company* without obtaining clearance to deal in advance in accordance with paragraph 4 of this code.

Clearance to deal

4. (a) A *director* (other than the chairman or chief executive) or company secretary must not deal in any *securities* of the *company* without first notifying the chairman (or a *director* designated by the board for this purpose) and receiving clearance to deal from him.

(b) The chairman must not deal in any *securities* of the *company* without first notifying the chief executive and receiving clearance to deal from him or, if the chief executive is not present, without first notifying the senior independent director, or a committee of the board or other officer of the *company* nominated for that purpose by the chief executive, and receiving clearance to deal from that director, committee or officer.

(c) The chief executive must not deal in any *securities* of the *company* without first notifying the chairman and receiving clearance to deal from him or, if the chairman is not present, without first notifying the senior independent director, or a committee of the board or other officer of the *company* nominated for that purpose by the chairman, and receiving clearance to deal from that director, committee or officer.

(d) If the role of chairman and chief executive are combined, that *person* must not deal in any *securities* of the *company* without first notifying the board and receiving clearance to deal from the board.
(e) *Persons discharging managerial responsibilities* (who are not *directors*) must not deal in any *securities* of the *company* without first notifying the company secretary or a designated *director* and receiving clearance to deal from him.

5. A response to a request for clearance to deal must be given to the relevant restricted person within five *business days* of the request being made.
6. The *company* must maintain a record of the response to any dealing request made by a restricted person and of any clearance given. A copy of the response and clearance (if any) must be given to the restricted person concerned.
7. A restricted person who is given clearance to deal in accordance with paragraph 4 must deal as soon as possible and in any event within two *business days* of clearance being received.

Circumstances for refusal

8. A restricted person must not be given clearance to deal in any *securities* of the *company*:
   (a) during a prohibited period; or
   (b) on considerations of a short term nature. An investment with a maturity of one year or less will always be considered to be of a short term nature.

Dealings permitted during a prohibited period

Dealing in exceptional circumstances

9. A restricted person, who is not in possession of *inside information* in relation to the *company*, may be given clearance to deal if he is in severe financial difficulty or there are other exceptional circumstances. Clearance may be given for such a *person* to sell (but not purchase) *securities* of the *company* when he would otherwise be prohibited by this code from doing so. The determination of whether the *person* in question is in severe financial difficulty or whether there are other exceptional circumstances can only be made by the *director* designated for this purpose.
10. A *person* may be in severe financial difficulty if he has a pressing financial commitment that cannot be satisfied otherwise than by selling the relevant *securities* of the *company*. A liability of such a *person* to pay tax would not normally constitute severe financial difficulty unless the *person* has no other means of satisfying the liability. A circumstance will be considered exceptional if the *person* in question is required by a court order to transfer or sell the *securities* of the *company* or there is some other overriding legal requirement for him to do so.
11. The *FSA* should be consulted at an early stage regarding any application by a restricted person to deal in exceptional circumstances.

Awards of securities and options

12. The grant of options by the board of *directors* under an *employees' share scheme* to individuals who are not restricted persons may be permitted during a prohibited period if such grant could not reasonably be made at another time and failure to make the grant would be likely to indicate that the *company* was in a prohibited period.
13. The award by the *company* of *securities*, the grant of options and the grant of rights (or other interests) to acquire *securities* of the *company* to restricted persons is permitted in a prohibited period if:
    (a) the award or grant is made under the terms of an *employees' share scheme* and the scheme was not introduced or amended during the relevant prohibited period; and
    (b) either:
        (i) the terms of such *employees' share scheme* set out the timing of the award or grant and such terms have either previously been approved by shareholders or summarised or described in a document sent to shareholders, or
        (ii) the timing of the award or grant is in accordance with the timing of previous awards or grants under the scheme; and
    (c) the terms of the *employees' share scheme* set out the amount or value of the award or grant or the basis on which the amount or value of the award or grant is calculated and do not allow the exercise of discretion; and
    (d) the failure to make the award or grant would be likely to indicate that the *company* is in a prohibited period.

Exercise of options

14. Where a *company* has been in an exceptionally long prohibited period or the *company* has had a number of consecutive prohibited periods, clearance may be given to allow the exercise of an option or right under an *employees' share scheme*, or the conversion of a convertible security, where the final date for the exercise of such option or right, or conversion of such security, falls during a prohibited period and the restricted person could not reasonably have been expected to exercise it at a time when he was free to deal.

15. Where the exercise or conversion is permitted pursuant to paragraph 14, clearance may not be given for the sale of the *securities* of the *company* acquired pursuant to such exercise or conversion including the sale of sufficient *securities* of the *company* to fund the costs of the exercise or conversion and/or any tax liability arising from the exercise or conversion unless a binding undertaking to do so was entered into when the *company* was not in a prohibited period.

Qualification shares

16. Clearance may be given to allow a *director* to acquire qualification *shares* where, under the *company's constitution*, the final date for acquiring such *shares* falls during a prohibited period and the *director* could not reasonably have been expected to acquire those shares at another time.

Saving schemes

17. A restricted person may enter into a scheme under which only the *securities* of the *company* are purchased pursuant to a regular standing order or direct debit or by regular deduction from the *person*'s salary, or where such *securities* are acquired by way of a standing election to re-invest dividends or other distributions received, or are acquired as part payment of the *person*'s remuneration without regard to the provisions of this code, if the following provisions are complied with:

(a) the restricted person does not enter into the scheme during a prohibited period, unless the scheme involves the part payment of remuneration in the form of *securities* of the *company* and is entered into upon the commencement of the *person*'s employment or in the case of a non-executive *director* his appointment to the board;

(b) the restricted person does not carry out the purchase of the *securities* of the *company* under the scheme during a prohibited period, unless the restricted person entered into the scheme at a time when the *company* was not in a prohibited period and that person is irrevocably bound under the terms of the scheme to carry out a purchase of *securities* of the *company* (which may include the first purchase under the scheme) at a fixed point in time which falls in a prohibited period;

(c) the restricted person does not cancel or vary the terms of his participation, or carry out sales of *securities* of the *company* within the scheme during a prohibited period; and

(d) before entering into the scheme, cancelling the scheme or varying the terms of his participation or carrying out sales of the *securities* of the *company* within the scheme, the restricted person obtains clearance in accordance with paragraph 4.

Acting as a trustee

18. Where a restricted person is acting as a trustee, dealing in the *securities* of the *company* by that trust is permitted during a prohibited period where:

(a) the restricted person is not a beneficiary of the trust; and

(b) the decision to deal is taken by the other trustees or by investment managers on behalf of the trustees independently of the restricted person.

19. The other trustees or investment managers acting on behalf of the trustees can be assumed to have acted independently where the decision to deal:

(a) was taken without consultation with, or other involvement of, the restricted person; or

(b) was delegated to a committee of which the restricted person is not a member.

Dealing by connected persons and investment managers

20. A *person discharging managerial responsibilities* must take reasonable steps to prevent any dealings by or on behalf of any *connected person* of his in any *securities* of the *company* on considerations of a short term nature.

21. A *person discharging managerial responsibilities* must seek to prohibit any dealings in the *securities* of the *company* during a close period:

(a) by or on behalf of any *connected person* of his; or
(b) by an investment manager on his behalf or on behalf of any *person* connected with him where either he or any *person* connected has funds under management with that investment fund manager, whether or not discretionary (save as provided by paragraphs 17 and 18).

22. A *person discharging managerial responsibilities* must advise all of his *connected persons* and investment managers acting on his behalf:
(a) of the name of the listed company within which he is a person discharging managerial responsibilities;
(b) of the *close periods* during which they cannot deal in the *securities* of the *company*; and
(c) that they must advise the *listed company* immediately after they have dealt in *securities* of the *company*.

Appendix 6

Companies House forms – filing periods and fees

Company Forms

Functional Area	Form	Name of Form	Filing fee * £	CA2006 Section Number	Filing Period
Accounts	**AA01**	Change of accounting reference date		392	Effective on registration
Accounts	**AA02**	Dormant Company Accounts (DCA)		480	9 months
Accounts	**AA03**	Notice of resolution removing auditors from office		512	14 days
Administration Restoration	**RT01**	Application for administrative restoration to the Register	**£100**	1024	On application
Annual Return	**AR01**	Annual Return	**£30**	854	28 days of made up date
Annual Return	**AD02**	Notification of single alternative inspection location (SAIL)		114. 162, 228, 237, 275, 358, 702, 720, 743, 805, 809, 877& 892	Effective on registration
Annual Return	**AD03**	Change of location of the company records to the single alternative inspection location (SAIL)		114. 162, 228, 237, 275, 358, 702, 720, 743, 805, 809, 877& 892	Effective on registration

Functional Area	Form	Name of Form	Filing fee * £	CA2006 Section Number	Filing Period
Annual Return	**AD04**	Change of location of the company records to the registered office		114. 162, 228, 237, 275, 358, 702, 720, 743, 805, 809, 877& 892	Effective on registration
Change of Constitution	**CC01**	Notice of restriction on the company's articles		23	Effective on registration
Change of Constitution	**CC02**	Notice of removal of restriction on the company's articles		23	Effective on registration
Change of Constitution	**CC03**	Statement of compliance where amendment of articles restricted		24	Effective on registration
Change of Constitution	**CC04**	Statement of company's objects		31	Effective on registration
Change of Constitution	**CC05**	Change of constitution by enactment		34	Effective on registration
Change of Constitution	**CC06**	Change of constitution by order of court or other authority		35	Effective on registration
Change of Name	**NE01**	Exemption from requirement as to use of "limited" or "cyfyngedig" on change of name		60	On application
Change of Name	**NM01**	Notice of change of name by resolution	**£10**	78	On application
Change of Name	**NM02**	Notice of change of name by conditional resolution	**£10**	78	On application
Change of Name	**NM03**	Notice confirming satisfaction of the conditional resolution for change of name	**£10**	78	On application
Change of Name	**NM04**	Notice of change of name by means provided for in the articles	**£10**	79	On application
Change of Name	**NM05**	Notice of change of name by resolution of directors	**£10**	64 or 1033	On application
Change of Name	**NM06**	Request to seek comments of government department or other specified body on change of name		56	On application

Functional Area	Form	Name of Form	Filing fee * £	CA2006 Section Number	Filing Period
Change of Registered Office	**AD01**	Change of registered office address		87	Effective on registration
Change of Registered Office	**AD05**	Notice to change the situation of an England and Wales company or a Welsh company		88	Effective on registration
Directors & Secretaries	**AP01**	Appointment of director		167	14 days
Directors & Secretaries	**AP02**	Appointment of corporate director		167	14 days
Directors & Secretaries	**AP03**	Appointment of secretary		276	14 days
Directors & Secretaries	**AP04**	Appointment of corporate secretary		276	14 days
Directors & Secretaries	**TM01**	Termination of appointment of director		167	14 days
Directors & Secretaries	**TM02**	Termination of appointment of secretary		276	14 days
Directors & Secretaries	**CH01**	Change of director's details		167	14 days
Directors & Secretaries	**CH02**	Change of corporate director's details		167	14 days
Directors & Secretaries	**CH03**	Change of secretary's details		276	14 days
Directors & Secretaries	**CH04**	Change of corporate secretary's details		276	14 days
Dissolution	**DS01**	Striking off application by a company	**£10**	1003	On application
Dissolution	**DS02**	Withdrawal of striking off application by a company		1010	On application
Incorporation	**IN01**	Application to register a company	**£20**	9	On application
Investment Companies	**IC01**	Notice of intention to carry on business as an investment company		833(1)	Effective on registration
Investment Companies	**IC02**	Notice that a company no longer wishes to be an investment company		833(4)	Effective on registration
Liquidation	**LQ01**	Notice of appointment of an administrative receiver, receiver or manager		871(1)	7 days

Functional Area	Form	Name of Form	Filing fee * £	CA2006 Section Number	Filing Period
Liquidation	**LQ02**	Notice of ceasing to act as an administrative receiver, receiver or manager		871(2)	Effective on registration
Mortgage	**MG01**	Particulars of a mortgage or charge	**£13**	860	21 days
Mortgage	**MG02**	Statement of satisfaction in full or in part of mortgage or charge		872(1)(a)	Effective on registration
Mortgage	**MG04**	Application for registration of a memorandum of satisfaction that part (or the whole) of the property charged (a) has been released from the charge; (b) no longer forms part of the company's property		872(1)(b)	Effective on registration
Mortgage	**MG06**	Particulars of a charge subject to which property has been acquired	**£13**	862	21 days
Mortgage	**MG07**	Particulars for the registration of a charge to secure a series of debentures	**£13**	863(1)	21 days
Mortgage	**MG08**	Particulars of an issue of secured debentures in a series		863(3)	
Mortgage	**MG09**	Certificate of registration of a charge comprising property situated in another UK jurisdiction		867(2)	Effective on registration
Opening of Overseas Branch Register	**AD06**	Notice of opening of overseas branch register		130	14 days
Opening of Overseas Branch Register	**AD07**	Notice of discontinuance of overseas branch register		135	14 days
Other Appointments	**AP05**	Appointment of a manager under Section 47 of the Companies (Audit, Investigations and Community Enterprise) Act 2004 or receiver and manager under Section 18 of the Charities Act 1993 or judicial factor (Scotland)		1154	14 days

Functional Area	Form	Name of Form	Filing fee * £	CA2006 Section Number	Filing Period
Other Appointments	**TM03**	Termination of appointment of manager under Section 47 of the Companies (Audit, Investigations and Community Enterprise) Act 2004 or receiver and manager under Section 18 of the Charities Act 1993 or judicial factor (Scotland)		1154	14 days
Other Appointments	**CH05**	Change of service address for manager appointed under Section 47 of the Companies (Audit, Investigations and Community Enterprise) Act 2004 or receiver and manager under Section 18 of the Charities Act 1993 or judicial factor (Scotland)		1154	14 days
Registrar's Powers	**RP01**	Replacement of document not meeting requirements for proper delivery		1076	As specified in request from Companies House
Registrar's Powers	**RP02A**	Application for rectification by the Registrar of Companies		1095	On application
Registrar's Powers	**RP02B**	Application for rectification of a registered office or a UK establishment address by the Registrar of Companies		1095	On application
Registrar's Powers	**RP03**	Notice of an objection to a request for the Registrar of Companies to rectify the Register		1095	Within 28 days of application
Registrar's Powers	**VT01**	Certified voluntary translation of an original document that is or has been delivered to the Registrar of Companies		1106	Effective on registration
Re-Registration	**RR01**	Application by a private company for re-registration as a public company	**£20**	94 & 765(4)	15 days

Functional Area	Form	Name of Form	Filing fee * £	CA2006 Section Number	Filing Period
Re-Registration	**RR02**	Application by a public company for re-registration as a private limited company	**£20**	100	15 days
Re-Registration	**RR03**	Notice by the company of application to the court for cancellation of resolution for re-registration		99(2)	15 days
Re-Registration	**RR04**	Notice by the applicants of application to the court for cancellation of resolution for re-registration		99(1)	On application to the Court
Re-Registration	**RR05**	Application by a private limited company for re-registration as an unlimited company	**£20**	103	15 days
Re-Registration	**RR06**	Application by an unlimited company for re-registration as a private limited company	**£20**	106	15 days
Re-Registration	**RR07**	Application by a public company for re-registration as a private unlimited company	**£20**	110	15 days
Re-Registration	**RR08**	Application by a public company for re-registration as a private limited company following a court order reducing capital	**£20**	651	15 days
Re-Registration	**RR09**	Application by a public company for re-registration as a private company following a cancellation of shares	**£20**	654	15 days
Re-Registration	**RR10**	Application by a public company for re-registration as a private company following a reduction of capital due to redenomination	**£20**	766	15 days
Resolutions	**Res CA2006**	Special resolution on change of name			15 days
Resolutions	**Written Res CA2006**	Written special resolution on change of name			15 days

Functional Area	Form	Name of Form	Filing fee * £	CA2006 Section Number	Filing Period
Share Capital	**980(1)**	Notice of non-assenting shareholders			3 months after offer lapses
Share Capital	**980(dec)**	Statutory Declaration relating to a Notice to non-assenting shares			3 months after offer lapses
Share Capital	**984**	Notice to non-assenting shares			Within 1 month of date of 980(1) notice
Share Capital	**SH01**	Return of allotment of shares		555	1 month
Share Capital	**SH02**	Notice of consolidation, sub-division, redemption of shares or re-conversion of stock into shares		619, 621 & 689	1 month
Share Capital	**SH03**	Return of purchase of own shares		707	28 days
Share Capital	**SH04**	Notice of sale or transfer of treasury shares by a public limited company (PLC)		728	28 days
Share Capital	**SH05**	Notice of cancellation of treasury shares by a public limited company (PLC)		730	28 days
Share Capital	**SH06**	Notice of cancellation of shares		708	28 days
Share Capital	**SH07**	Notice of cancellation of shares held by or for a public company		663	1 month
Share Capital	**SH08**	Notice of name or other designation of class of shares		636	1 month
Share Capital	**SH09**	Return of allotment by an unlimited company allotting new class of shares		556	1 month
Share Capital	**SH10**	Notice of particulars of variation of rights attached to shares		637	1 month
Share Capital	**SH11**	Notice of new class of members		638	1 month
Share Capital	**SH12**	Notice of particulars of variation of class rights		640	1 month

Functional Area	Form	Name of Form	Filing fee * £	CA2006 Section Number	Filing Period
Share Capital	**SH13**	Notice of name or other designation of class of members		639	1 month
Share Capital	**SH14**	Notice of redenomination		625	1 month
Share Capital	**SH15**	Notice of reduction of capital following redenomination		627	15 days
Share Capital	**SH16**	Notice by the applicants of application to court for cancellation of the special resolution approving a redemption or purchase of shares out of capital		722(1)	On application to Court
Share Capital	**SH17**	Notice by the company of application to court for cancellation of the special resolution approving a redemption or purchase of shares out of capital		722(1)	15 days of Court order
Share Capital	**SH19 (644 &649)**	Statement of capital (Section 644 & 649)		644 & 649	15 days
Share Capital	**SH19 (108)**	Statement of capital (Section 108)		108	15 days
Share Capital	**SH50**	Application for trading certificate for a public company		761 & 762	On application
Scottish Mortgage	**466**	Particulars of an instrument of alteration to a floating charge created by a company registered in Scotland			21 days
Scottish Mortgage	**MG01s**	Particulars of a charge created by a company registered in Scotland	**£13**	878	21 days
Scottish Mortgage	**MG02s**	Statement of satisfaction in full or in part of a fixed charge for a company registered in Scotland		887(1)(a)	Effective on registration
Scottish Mortgage	**MG03s**	Statement of satisfaction in full or in part of a floating charge for a company registered in Scotland		887(1)(a) & 887(2) (a) or (b)	Effective on registration

Functional Area	Form	Name of Form	Filing fee * £	CA2006 Section Number	Filing Period
Scottish Mortgage	**MG04s**	Application for registration of a memorandum of satisfaction that part (or the whole) of the property charged (a) has been released from the fixed charge; (b) no longer forms part of the company's property for a company registered in Scotland.		887(1)(b)	Effective on registration
Scottish Mortgage	**MG05s**	Application for registration of a memorandum of satisfaction that part (or the whole) of the property charged (a) has been released from the floating charge; (b) no longer forms part of the company's property for a company registered in Scotland.		887(1)(b) & 887(2) (a) or (b)	Effective on registration
Scottish Mortgage	**MG06s**	Particulars of a charge subject to which property has been acquired by a company registered in Scotland	**£13**	880	21 days
Scottish Mortgage	**MG07s**	Particulars for the registration of a charge to secure a series of debentures by a company registered in Scotland	**£13**	882(1)	21 days
Scottish Mortgage	**MG08s**	Particulars of an issue of secured debentures in a series by a company registered in Scotland		882(3)	21 days

*Fees quoted are for paper-based submissions. Where documents are filed online lower fees may be available.

Appendix 7

Recommended retention periods

Type of document	Period of retention
Certificate of Incorporation	Original to be kept permanently
Certificate to Commence Business (public company)	Original to be kept permanently
Board minutes	Originals to be kept permanently
Minutes of general and class meetings, directors' minutes, written resolutions	Originals to be kept permanently
Directors' service contracts	Copy to be kept available for inspection at registered office or SAIL for one year following termination, thereafter as per employment contracts
Annual Report and Accounts	Signed copy to be kept permanently (A stock of spare copies should be maintained for up to three years to meet casual requests)
Trust Deeds	Originals to be kept for 12 years after stock has been redeemed
Circulars to shareholders including notices of meetings	Master copy to be kept permanently
Memorandum and Articles of Association	Original copy to be kept permanently
Seal Book/Register	Original to be kept permanently
Proxy forms/Polling cards	One month if no poll demanded; one year if poll demanded
Minutes of meetings	Copies must be available for inspection for at least ten years from the date of the meeting, thereafter original minutes should be kept permanently
Register of Directors and Secretaries, Register of Interests in Voting Shares, Register of Charges, Register of Members	Originals to be kept permanently

Type of document	Period of retention
Register of Debenture or Loan Stock Holders	A minimum of six years, although ten is recommended
Forms for application of shares, debentures, etc., forms of acceptance and transfer, Renouncable Letters of Acceptance and Allotment, Renouncable Share Certificates	A minimum of six years or, if longer, six years after shares are fully paid
Request for designation or redesignation of accounts, letters of request, allotment sheets	20 years if the request was made before 6 April 2008, ten years if after
Letters of Indemnity for lost Share Certificates	All originals to be kept permanently
Stop Notices and other Court Orders	Until the notice or order is no longer valid. However, if the notice or order evidences action taken, then 20 years for actions prior to 6 April 2008 and ten years if after
Powers of Attorney	12 years after they cease to be valid
Dividend and interest bank Mandate forms	Six years after they cease to be valid
Cancelled Share or Stock Certificates	One year from date of registration of transfer
Notification of change of address	Two years
Any contract or memorandum to purchase the company's own shares	Ten years
Report of an interest in voting shares for investigations requisitioned by members	Six years
Register of Interest in Shares when company ceases to be a public company	Six years
Contracts with customers, suppliers or agents	Six years after expiry, 12 if executed as a deed
Licensing agreements	15 years after expiry
Rental and hire purchase agreements	Six years after expiry
Indemnities and guarantees	Six years after expiry
Deeds of Title	Until sold or transferred
Leases	15 years after lease has terminated
Agreements with architects, builders, etc.	15 years after contract completion

Type of document	Period of retention
Patent and trade mark records	Permanently
Accounting records required by the Companies Acts	Six years
Taxation Returns and records	Seven years
Internal Financial Reports	Signed copy to be kept permanently
Statements and instructions to banks	Six years
Staff personnel records	Six years after employment ceases
Patent agreements with staff	20 years after employment ceases
Applications for jobs	Three months after notifying successful candidate
Payroll records	Six years
Salary registers	Six years
Tax Returns	Permanently
Expense accounts	Six years
Employment agreements	Six years after termination of employment
Time cards and piece-work records	Two years
Wages records	Six years
Medical records	12 years
Industrial training records	Six years after termination of employment
Accident books	Three years from date of entry
Trustees and rules (pension schemes)	Permanently
Trustees' Minute Book	Permanently
Pension fund annual accounts and HMRC approvals	Permanently
Investment records	Permanently
Actuarial valuation records	Six years after scheme year
Contribution records	Six years after scheme year
Records of ex-pensioners	Six years after cessation of benefit
Pension scheme investment policies	12 years after cessation
Group health policies	12 years after final cessation of benefit

Type of document	Period of retention
Group personal accident policies	12 years after cessation of benefit
Public liability policies	Permanently
Product liability policies	Permanently
Employers' liability policies	Permanently
Certificate of employers' liability insurance	40 years
Directors' and officers' insurance	Copy to be kept available for inspection at registered office ot SAIL for one year after expiry thereafter copy to be retained for three years after lapses
Sundry insurance policies	Three years after lapse
Claims correspondence	Three years after settlement
Accident reports and relevant correspondence	Three years after settlement
Insurance schedules	Ten years
HMRC VAT Returns	Six years
Vehicle registration records, MOT Certificates and vehicle maintenance records	Two years after disposal of vehicle
Certificates and other documents of title	Permanently or until investment disposed of

Glossary of key terms

The following definitions are not intended to be legal definitions.

Abbreviated accounts A condensed version of the annual accounts which small and medium-sized companies (according to the specified size criteria) are allowed to file with the register of companies. They may not be used as a substitute for the full annual accounts for the circulation to members.

Administration order Court order to appoint an administrator to manage the affairs of a company in financial difficulty.

Administrator A person appointed by the court to manage a company in financial difficulties in order to protect creditors and, if possible, avoid liquidation. The administrator has the power to remove and appoint directors. Also a person who administers the estate of a deceased person in the absence of any executors.

Agent Someone who is authorised to carry out business transactions on behalf of another (the principal), who is thereby bound by such actions.

Allotment The issue of shares.

Allottee A person or company to whom shares have been allotted.

Alternate director A person appointed by a director to represent them, usually at board meetings, and who assumes the responsibilities and duties of their appointor when acting in their place.

Annual accounts The accounts which are prepared to fulfil the directors' duty to present audited accounts to members in respect of each financial year. Annual accounts of limited companies must be filed with the Registrar of Companies.

Annual general meeting A general meeting of the company's members, which must be held in each calendar year within 15 months of the previous AGM. Under Companies Act 2006, private companies are (generally) no longer required to hold AGMs, although the requirement remains for public companies.

Annual return A form filed each year with the Registrar of Companies, containing specified information about the company's directors, secretary, registered office, shareholders, share capital, etc. The majority of the information is preprinted by the Registrar of Companies.

Articles of Association The constitutional document setting out the internal regulations of the company. Unless modified or excluded, the specimen Articles in the relevant version of Table A/Model Articles have effect.

Audit The independent examination of, and expression of opinion on, the company's accounts. All persons or firms offering audit services must be registered auditors and belong to one of the recognised accountancy bodies.

Authorised share capital Capital. *See* share capital.

Bearer shares Shares that can be transferred simply by passing the certificate from one person to the next. The 'bearer' of the certificate having title to the shares represented by it.

Bonus issue Issue of additional shares to existing shareholders, in proportion to their current holding, already paid up in full out of the distributable reserves of the company.

Book debts Amounts owed to a company resulting from its trading activities, usually in the form of unpaid invoices rendered to customers.

Business review The statutory format for the annual publication of non-financial company information as part of the directors' report (see below).

Capital The money or money's worth used by a company to finance its business. *See also* working capital.

Certificate of incorporation A certificate issued by the Registrar of Companies on receipt of specified constitutional and other documents of the company. The company assumes its identity as a legal person on the date of incorporation shown on the certificate.

Charge A means by which a company offers its assets as security for a debt. A charge is a general term that includes, but is not limited to, a mortgage. A fixed charge relates to a specific asset or assets. A floating charge relates to whatever assets of a specified class are in the company's possession at the time the charge crystallises (if it does so).

Class rights Where a company has more than one class of shares, the rights attached to those different classes of shares.

The Combined Code The code on corporate governance that applies to UK listed companies. It is a voluntary code rather than a legal requirement. The UK Listing Rules require listed companies to disclose in their annual report the extent of their compliance and to explain any non-compliance. This will become the *UK Corporate Governance Code* from 29 June 2010.

Common law The body of law based on custom and usage and decision reached in previous cases. The principles and rules of common law derive but from judgments and judicial opinions and not legislation introduced by parliament.

Common seal A seal bearing a company's name for affixing to legal documents.

Company An association of persons which, on incorporation, becomes a legal entity entirely separate from the individuals comprising its membership. In the Companies Act 2006, 'company' is restricted to companies registered under that Act or previous Companies Acts.

Company secretary An officer of the company with a number of statutory duties, such as to sign the annual return and accompanying documents, and usually charged with a range of duties relating to the company's statutory books and records, filing requirements, etc. Under the Companies Act 2006, private companies are no longer required to appoint a company secretary.

Company voluntary arrangement An arrangement under the Insolvency Act 1986 between the company and its members.

Compulsory Winding-up of a company by order of the winding-up court.

Contract An agreement between two or more persons creating a legally enforceable obligation between them.

Creditor A person or company owed money.

Creditors' voluntary winding-up Insolvent winding-up of a company by resolution of its members.

Debenture A written acknowledgement of a debt owed by a company, often – but not necessarily – secured. It is common practice for a debenture to be created by a trust deed by which company property is mortgaged to trustees for the debenture holders, as security for the payment of interest and capital.

De facto In reality.

Debt An amount of money owed by one person, the debtor, to another, the creditor.

Debtor A person or company that owes money.

Department for Business, Innovation and Skills (BIS) The government department responsible for the administration of company law. The Companies Act confers certain powers of the Secretary of State. (Formerly the DTI and BERR).

Director An officer of the company responsible for determining policy, supervising the management of the company's business and exercising the powers of the company. Directors must generally carry out these functions collectively as a board.

Directors' report A statement attached to the annual accounts containing certain information laid down in the Act.

Distributable reserves Profit retained by a company which may be distributed to its members.

Distribution The transfer of some or all of a company's assets (usually cash) to its members, generally by way of dividend or on a winding up.

Dividends The distribution of a portion of the company's assets (usually cash) to its members, generally by way of dividend or on a winding up.

Dormant company A company which has not traded or has ceased trading.

Fiduciary Having a position of trust, such that the power and authority conferred by the position must be exercised solely in the interest of the person with whom the fiduciary relationship exists. Trustees are in a fiduciary position, as are solicitors in relation to their clients. Directors have a fiduciary duty to the company, obliging them to act always in good faith and not to derive a personal profit from their position.

Financial statements The term adopted by the joint accountancy bodies to signify 'balance sheet, profit and loss accounts, statements of source and application of funds, notes and other statements which collectively are intended to give a true and fair view of financial position and profit or loss'.

Financial year The period in respect of which the company's profit and loss accounts are drawn up; it need not coincide with the fiscal or calendar year and need not be a period of twelve months.

Fixed charge Security, usually for a loan, over a specific asset such as a building or equipment.

Floating charge Security, usually for a loan, over a class of assets the individual components of which vary over time, such as stock or book debts.

Flotation *See* IPO.

Formation *See* registration.

Gazette Official BIS publication for formal announcements. Published daily.

General meeting Any general meeting of the company's members that is not an annual general meeting.

Guarantee A formal agreement under which a guarantor undertakes to meet the contractual obligations of one person to another in the event of default. A company limited by guarantee is one in which the liability of the members is limited to a specified amount in a winding-up.

Holding company A company which has subsidiaries.

Incorporation *See* registration.

Insider dealing Buying or selling shares on the basis of an unfair advantage derived form access to price-sensitive information not generally available. Insider dealing is a criminal offence.

IPO/Initial Public Offering The raising of finance from the public when a public company first has its shares traded on the Stock Exchange, AIM or PLUS.

Issued capital *See* share capital.

Judgment creditor A creditor who has obtained a court order in their favour.

Limited company The commonest form of company, in which the liability of members for the debts of the company is limited – either to the amount of share capital for which they have applied (a company limited by shares) or to a specific amount guaranteed in the event of a winding-up (a company limited by guarantee).

Limited liability partnership/LLP A corporate body where the members have limited liability but undertake the management themselves rather than appointing directors to manage the company on their behalf.

Liquidation The process under which a company ceases to trade and realises its assets for distribution to creditors and then shareholders. The term 'winding-up' is synonymous.

Listed company A company whose shares are listed by the Financial Services Authority on the Official List of the UK and admitted for trading on the Main Market operated by the London Stock Exchange or admitted to trading on the PLUS Listed market operated by PLUS Markets Group.

Members The company's shareholders, of which there must be at least two in a public company. A private company can have a single shareholder.

Members' voluntary liquidation Solvent winding-up of a company by resolution of its members.

Memorandum of Association A constitutional document now comprising only the subscriber clauses required for the incorporation od a company. Any other clauses are deemed to form part of the Articles of Association of the company.

Model Articles Model, default, Articles of Association for companies incorporated on or after 1 October 2009. There are three sets of Model Articles suitable for private companies limited by shares, private companies limited by guarantee and public companies.

Nominal capital *See* share capital.

Objects The purpose for which the company was incorporated, as set out in the object clause of its Memorandum of Association. Prior to 1 October 2009 most companies were formed with general trading objects rather than specific objects. Companies registered under the Companies Act 2006 from 1 October 2009 will no longer be required to specify an object clause and are deemed to have full power to undertake any trade unless restricted by their Articles.

Officer Includes a director, manager or (where appointed) the secretary of a company. Not everyone with the title of manager is sufficiently senior to be regarded as an officer, who must have a level of supervisory control which reflects the general policy of the company. Also includes the company's auditor.

Ordinary resolution A resolution at a general meeting carried by a simple majority of votes actually cast.

Ordinary shares The most common form of share in a company, giving holders the right to share in the company's profits in proportion to their holdings and the right to vote at general meetings (although non-voting ordinary shares are occasionally encountered).

Paid-up capital Refers to the amounts actually paid up on any issued shares.

Partnership A business run by two or more persons where the owners share ownership (partners) and have unlimited liability for the businesses debts.

PLUS The trading facility operated by PLUS Markets Group plc to facilitate trading in securities not on the Stock Exchange.

Pre-emption rights Preferential right of existing members to purchase new shares to be issued or existing shares being offered for sale by way of transfer by an existing member.

Preference shares Shares carrying the right to payment of a fixed dividend out of profits before the payment of an ordinary dividend or the preferential return of capital or both.

Prima facie On the face of it, at first sight.

Private company A company that is not a public company.

Pro rata In proportion, rateably.

Promoter A person engaged in setting up a company or in raising capital for a newly formed company. A person who acts merely as a professional adviser is not usually a promoter.

Prospectus Any prospectus, notice, circular, advertisement or other invitation to the public to subscribe for purchase of a company's shares or debentures.

Proxy A person authorised by a member to vote on his behalf at a general meeting.

Public company (plc) A company which meets specified requirements as to its minimum share capital and which is registered as a public company. Only public companies are allowed to offer shares and debentures to the public.

Quasi-loan A loan where a company reimburses the director's creditor.

Redeemable shares Shares which are issued as redeemable may be bought back by the company at a future date.

Registrar of companies The official responsible for maintaining the company records filed under the requirements of the Companies Act.

Registration Process by which companies are created by filing (or registering) a number of specified documents at Companies House.

Regulatory Information Service (RIS) An information provider approved by the FSA to disseminate information to the market.

Resolution A decision at a meeting reached by a majority of member actually voting.

Retirement by rotation The annual standing down of directors (usually one third) for re-election by members at the company's annual general meeting.

Service contract A director's contract of employment.

Shadow director A person, not appointed as a director, managing or directing the affairs of a company or who directs the actions of the directors.

Share A unit of ownership of the company, representing a fraction of the share capital and usually conferring rights to participate in distributions. There may be several kinds of shares each carrying different rights. Shares are issued at a fixed nominal value, although the company may actually receive a larger amount, the excess representing share premium. Members may not be required to subscribe the full amount immediately, in which case the shares are partly paid. The members then await calls, which require them to pay further amounts until the shares are fully paid.

Share capital The capital of a company contributed or to be contributed by members. Issued, or allotted, share capital represents the amount actually contributed. Nominal capital represents the nominal value of the shares issued and excludes any premium paid. The concept of authorised share capital, being the pool of shares available for issue, was abolished by the Companies Act 2006 with effect from 1 October 2009.

Share premium The excess of the price at which shares are issued above their nominal value.

Special resolution A resolution required either by the Companies Act or a company's Articles which must be carried by at least 75 per cent of the members voting at a general meeting. Such resolutions tend to be required where the proposal would change the nature of the relationship between a company and its members, such as an amendment to the Articles.

Statute law The body of law represented by legislation, and thus occurring in authoritative written form. Statue law contrasts with common law, over which it takes precedence.

Statutory books A general term applied to the registers and minute books, etc. that a company is required by the Companies Act to maintain.

Stock transfer form Document used to transfer ownership of shares from one person (transferor) to another (transferee).

Subscriber A person who subscribes to the Memorandum of Association and agrees to take up shares in the company on incorporation.

Subsidiary A company controlled by another which usually holds a majority of the issued shares.

Table A The specimen Articles of Association for a company limited by shares set out in the relevant Companies Act for companies incorporated prior to 1 October 2009. Unless specifically modified or excluded, the version of Table A/Model Articles in force at the time of a company's incorporation automatically applies to the company.

Takeover The process under which one company acquires control of another usually by acquiring all the shares.

Three-way proxy A proxy form, which must be used by a listed company, which allows a member to instruct his proxy how to vote or to abstain on each resolution.

Transfer Process where ownership of shares passes from one person to another usually by way of a sale.

Transferee A person acquiring shares by way of transfer.

Transferor A person disposing of shares by way of transfer.

Ultra vires Beyond its powers. Usually refers to transaction entered into by a company or director which they do not have authority to do.

Unlimited company A company in which the members have unlimited liability for the company's debts in the event of a winding-up.

Uncalled capital Partly paid shares where the amount unpaid has not been requested (called) by the company.

Voluntary winding-up Winding-up of a company at the instigation of its members.

Working capital The capital required by a company on a day-to-day basis to meet its operating costs.

Written resolution Allows private companies to conduct – with some exceptions – business that requires member approval without having to convene a general meeting.

Directory

Useful addresses and web resources

AIM Rules
www.londonstockexchange.com/companies-and-advisors/aim/documents/aim-rules-for-companies.pdf

The Association of Authorised Public Accountants
29 Lincoln's Inn Fields
London WC2A 3EE
Tel: 020 7059 5000
www.acca.co.uk/aapa

The Association of Chartered Certified Accountants (ACCA)
29 Lincoln's Inn Fields
London WC2A 3EE
Tel: 020 7059 5000
email: info@accaglobal.com
www.acca.co.uk

BACS Payment Systems Limited
BACS Payment Schemes Limited
3rd Floor, Livingstone House
12 Finsbury Square
London EC2A 1AS
Tel: 020 7711 6370
www.bacs.co.uk

Companies House
England and Wales
Companies House
Crown Way
Cardiff CF14 3UZ
Tel: 0303 1234 500
email: enquiries@companies-house.gov.uk
www.companieshouse.gov.uk

London Office
Companies House Executive Agency
21 Bloomsbury Street
London WC1B 3XD
Tel: 0303 1234 500

Scotland
Companies House
37 Castle Terrace
Edinburgh EH1 2EB
Tel: 0303 1234 500

Northern Ireland
Companies Registry
1st Floor, Waterfront Plaza
8 Laganbank Road
Belfast BT1 3BS
Tel: 0845 604 8888

Competition Commission
Victoria House
Southampton Row
London WC1B 4AD
Tel: 020 7271 0100
email: info@competitioncommission.gsi.gov.uk
www.competition-commission.org.uk

Department for Business, Innovation and Skills (formerly the DTI and BERR)
1 Victoria Street
London SW1H 0ET
Tel: 020 7215 5000
email: enquiries@bis.gsi.gov.uk
www.bis.gov.uk

Euroclear UK and Ireland Ltd (formerly CRESTCo)
33 Cannon Street
London EC4M 5SB
Tel: 020 7849 0000
email: uk-info@euroclear.com
www.euroclear.com/site/public/EUI

Data protection – see Information Commissioner

Financial Reporting Council (FRC)
5th Floor, Aldwych House
71–91 Aldwych
London WC2B 4HN
Tel: 020 7492 2300
www.frc.org.uk

Financial Services Authority
25 The North Colonnade
Canary Wharf
London E14 5HS
Tel: 020 7066 1000
www.fsa.gov.uk

Health and Safety Executive (HSE)
Caerphilly Business Park,
Caerphilly CF83 3GG
Tel: 0845 345 0055
www.hse.gov.uk

HSE Incident Centre (RIDDOR reporting)
Contact Centre Address as above
Tel: 0845 300 9923
www.riddor.gov.uk

HM Revenue & Customs
www.hmrc.gov.uk
HMRC Birmingham Stamp Office
9th Floor, City Centre House
30 Union Street
Birmingham B2 4AR
Tel: 0845 603 0135
Postal applications only

ICSA Information & Training Ltd
16 Park Crescent
London W1B 1AH
Tel: 020 7612 7020
email: publishing@icsa.co.uk
www.icsainformationandtraining.co.uk

Information Asset Register
www.opsi.gov.uk/iar/index.htm

Information Commissioner (data protection)
Wycliffe House
Water Lane
Wilmslow
Cheshire SK9 5AF
Tel: 01625 545 745
email: mail@ico.gsi.gov.uk
www.ico.gov.uk

The Institute of Chartered Accountants in England and Wales
Chartered Accountants' Hall
PO Box 433
London EC2P 2BJ
Tel: 020 7920 8100
www.icaew.co.uk

The Institute of Chartered Accountants in Ireland
Chartered Accountants House
47–49 Pearse St
Dublin 2
Tel: +353 1 637 7200
www.charteredaccountants.ie
email: ca@icai.ie

The Institute of Chartered Accountants of Scotland
CA House
21 Haymarket Yards
Edinburgh EH12 5BH
Tel: 0131 347 0100
email: enquiries@icas.org.uk
www.icas.org.uk

The Institute of Chartered Secretaries and Administrators (ICSA)
16 Park Crescent
London W1B 1AH
Tel: 020 7580 4741
e-mail: info@icsa.co.uk
www.icsa.org.uk

Joint Money Laundering Steering Group
www.jmlsg.org.uk

The London Stock Exchange
10 Paternoster Square
London EC4M 7LS
Tel: 020 7797 1000
www.londonstockexchange.com

National Association of Pension Funds (NAPF)
NIOC House
4 Victoria Street
London SW1H 0NE
Tel: 020 7808 1300
Fax: 020 7222 7585
www.napf.co.uk

Office of Fair Trading (OFT)
Fleetbank House
2–6 Salisbury Square
London EC4Y 8JX
Tel: 020 7211 8000
E-mail: enquiries@oft.gsi.gov.uk
www.oft.gov.uk

Office of Public Sector Information
www.opsi.gov.uk

The Panel on Takeovers and Mergers
10 Paternoster Square
London EC4M 7DY
Tel: 020 7382 9026
www.thetakeoverpanel.org.uk

PLUS Markets Group Plc
5th Floor
Standon House
21 Mansell Street
London E1 8AA
Tel: 020 7553 2000
www.plusmarketsgroup.com

The Stationery Office
See Office of Public Sector Information

The Treasury Solicitor's Department
One Kemble Street
London WC2B 4TS
Tel: 020 7210 3000
E-mail: thetreasurysolicitor@tsol.gsi.gov.uk
www.tsol.gov.uk

UK Listing Authority
The Financial Services Authority
25 The North Colonnade
Canary Wharf
London E14 5HS
Tel: 020 7066 1000
www.fsa.gov.uk

Further reading

Company law

Butterworths Company Law Handbook (Butterworths, annual editions). Sets out the relevant texts of the most important statutes, statutory instruments and European legislation, as well as certain FSA legislation.

The ICSA Companies Act 2006 Handbook, 2nd edition (ICSA Information & Training, 2009). The full text of the fully implemented 2006 Act, together with commentary, indexes and tables of destination and derivation.

Company secretarial practice

Armour, Douglas, *The ICSA Company Secretary's Checklists*, 6th edition (ICSA Information & Training, 2009). Procedural checklists, timetables and other quick reference material associated with the statutory functions and responsibilities of company secretaries, presented in A–Z format.

Bruce, Martha and Hollowell, Sara, *A Practical Guide to the Memorandum and Articles of Association*, 2nd edition (ICSA Information & Training, 2009). Full guidance on the new Model Articles and how they relate to Table A, including full destination/derivation and comparison tables.

Hamer, Andrew C., *The ICSA Guide to Document Retention*, 2nd edition (ICSA Information & Training, 2008).

Lai, Jerry and Martin, Stephen, *Tolley's Company Secretary's Handbook* (Tolley, annual editions).

Leighton, Gerald, Van Duzer, Peter and Gillard, Cecile, *Jordans Company Secretarial Precedents* (Jordans, 2008). A comprehensive selection of precedents aimed primarily at private companies.

Martin, David, *One Stop Company Secretary*, 6th edition (ICSA Information & Training, 2009). Short 'nuts and bolts' overview of core company secretarial functions.

Wallace, Susan, *The ICSA Company Secretary's Troubleshooter*, 2nd edition (ICSA Information & Training, 2010). Q&As for company secretaries.

Walmsley, Keith and Hamer, Andrew, *Company Secretarial Practice* (ICSA Information & Training). Official ICSA information service available in loose-leaf and on CD-ROM and with comprehensive update service. Also available online as part of Corporate Compliance Online (see www.icsabookshop.co.uk).

Corporate governance

Cassley, Vivienne and Mensley, David, *The ICSA Corporate Governance Planner* (ICSA Information & Training, 2007).

The Combined Code on Corporate Governance (Financial Reporting Council, 2008) – see Appendix 2, the full text on the CD, or download from www.frc.co.uk.

Cooper, Barbara, *The ICSA Handbook to Good Boardroom Practice*, 2nd edition (ICSA Information & Training, 2006).

Corporate Governance Handbook (Gee Publishing). A single-volume loose-leaf publication dealing primarily with the application of UK corporate governance codes.

Directors

Bruce, Martha, *The ICSA Director's Guide*, 4th edition (ICSA Information & Training, 2010). Short guide to directors' duties, responsibilities and liabilities.

Bruce, Martha, *Rights and Duties of Directors*, 9th edition (Tottel Publishing, 2008).

Dattani, Rita (ed), *The ICSA Directors Handbook* (ICSA Information & Training, 2009).

Loose, Peter, Griffiths, Michael and Impey, David, *The Company Director*, 10th edition (Jordans, 2008).

Markets

Keepin, Alexander, *A Practical Guide to the AIM* (ICSA Information & Training, 2008).

Herbert Smith LLP, *A Practical Guide to the UK Listing Regime*, 2nd edition (ICSA Information & Training, 2010).

Meetings

The ICSA Meetings and Minutes Handbook, 2nd edition (ICSA Information & Training, 2009). A practical guide to running company meetings.

Reporting

Hoskins, Tony, *The ICSA Company Reporting Handbook* (ICSA Information & Training, 2007).

Magazines and newsletters

Boardroom Update. Bi-monthly newsletter published by ICSA Information & Training Ltd.

The Company Secretary. The monthly newsletter for company secretaries covering both plc and private company issues. Available from ICSA Information & Training as part of a subscription to *The Company Secretarial Practice* (see www.icsabookshop.co.uk).

Chartered Secretary Magazine. Monthly ICSA magazine, available in print and online at www.charteredsecretary.net. Subscribe online at www.icsabookshop.co.uk.

Company Secretary's Review (Butterworths Tolley). The long-established fortnightly journal.

PLC (Practical Law Co.). A monthly magazine focusing on technical legal issues for in-house lawyers and company secretaries.

The Register (Companies House). A free quarterly magazine on Companies House and other company law developments.

Other Information Sources

Companies House guidance booklets

Company Guidance

GP1 Incorporation and Names

GP2 Life of a Company – Part 1 Annual Requirements

GP3	Life of a Company – Part 2 Event driven filings
GP4	Strike Off, Dissolution & Restoration
GP5	Late Filing Penalties
GP6	Registrar's Rules and Powers
GP7	Restricting Disclosure of your Address

Limited Liability Partnerships

GPLLP1	Limited Liability Partnership Incorporation and Names
GPLLP2	Life of a Limited Liability Partnership
GPLLP3	Limited Liability Partnership Strike Off, Dissolution & Restoration
GPLLP4	Limited Liability Partnership Late Filing Penalties
GPLLP5	Limited Liability Partnership Liquidation and Insolvency
GPLLP5s	Limited Liability Partnership Liquidation and Insolvency (Scotland)

Other legislation

GPO1	Oversea Companies Registered in the UK
GPO2	Limited Partnership Act
GPO3	Newspaper Libel and Registration Act
GPO4	European Economic Interest Groupings
GPO5	Conducting Business in Welsh
GPO6	The European Company: Societas Europaea (SE)
GPO7	Cross Border Mergers
GPO8	Liquidation and Insolvency
GPO8s	Liquidation and Insolvency (Scotland)

The text of all Guidance Booklets is available in downloadable form on www.companieshouse.gov.uk.

ICSA Guidance Notes

Available free for download from **www.icsa.org.uk/knowledge**. Recent titles include a range of guidance on the implementation of the Companies Act 2006, including: *Statements of Capital*; *Access to the Register of Members: the Proper Purpose Test* and *Proxies and Implementation of the Shareholder Rights Directive*.

ICSA Best Practice Guides

More information about this series is available via **www.icsa.org.uk**. Titles include: Duties of the Company Secretary; A Guide to Best Practice for Annual General Meetings; Establishing a Whistleblowing Procedure.

Index

Page numbers in *italics* refer to precedents.
Page numbers in **bold** refer to appendices.